HIGH TIDE AT GETTYSBURG

HIGH TIDE
AT GETTYSBURG

The Campaign in Pennsylvania

by Glenn Tucker

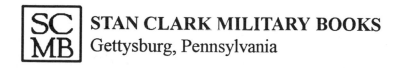

STAN CLARK MILITARY BOOKS
Gettysburg, Pennsylvania

Reprinted in 1995 in accordance with the copyright laws
of the United States by:
STAN CLARK MILITARY BOOKS
915 Fairview Avenue
Gettysburg, Pennsylvania 17325
(717) 337-1728

Cover artwork from the original oil painting: "The Angle"
by Mort Kunstler. Copyright © 1988

ISBN: 1-879664-25-9 (Clothbound)
ISBN: 1-879664-26-7 (Softcover)

Printed and bound in the United States of America

INTRODUCTION

Following its publication in 1958, **High Tide at Gettysburg** remained the standard study of the Gettysburg Campaign and Battle of Gettysburg for ten years, until Edwin Coddington's, *The Gettysburg Campaign* was published. Although Coddington's scholarly, richly researched work eclipsed Tucker's earlier study in many respects, neophytes to the Gettysburg story found it a bit overwhelming. **High Tide at Gettysburg**, with its highly readable text, was not as daunting. Tucker, with his interesting writing style, brought Gettysburg to life. He wrote in his forward that he felt the soldiers of the battle were too often presented merely as names to identify units, not as people. He corrected this by sketching the career and character of dozens of these men, such as Stephen Ramseur, Henry Morrow, and many others. Some of these are well known, others more obscure but all played a pivotal role in the battle, and whose stories make Gettysburg so interesting and appealing. Tucker also presented the battle in a fair, even-handed manner, applying praise and criticism judiciously. He addressed famous controversies, such as Lee and Longstreet, with an open mind and resisted the temptation to take sides and attempt to sway the reader to his point of view.

High Tide at Gettysburg is approaching its fortieth anniversary, yet, it remains the most readable text on the entire Battle of Gettysburg. Subsequent scholarship, most notably by Coddington, may have challenged Tucker's interpretation on various points, but for those seeking a good first book to read on Gettysburg, **High Tide at Gettysburg** is a fine place to start.

D. Scott Hartwig
Historian, GNMP
Gettysburg, Pennsylvania
January, 1995

Foreword

ALL OF MY ADULT LIFE I have wanted to write a book about Gettysburg—since the time when, as a young captain in World War I, I studied the contour map of the Gettysburg terrain almost nightly in problems involving minor tactics.

While in Washington newspaper work I made frequent visits to Gettysburg as a hobby and on bonus occasions covered news stories on the field. Thereafter I had a recurring interest in this exciting battle, the most gripping three days of American history. What person who reads history has not?

In 1930 the Reverend Dr. William E. Barton, of Oak Park, Illinois, a great Lincoln scholar, in inscribing to me his *Life of Abraham Lincoln,* wrote: "Dear Mr. Tucker—I have told the story of Lincoln's speech at Gettysburg in a book to appear in February. Now you please tell the story of the battle." I made a resolution and a beginning. Less interesting writing work intruded, but the ambition lingered.

Then D. Laurance Chambers, chairman of the board of The Bobbs-Merrill Company, one who is rich with the experience of fifty-five years in book publishing, and has contributed immeasurably to the present generation's reading of American history, suggested out of a clear sky about three years ago that I write this book. His gently phrased but unsparing criticism had guided me through other efforts. Though he is now retired from active publishing work, I am indebted to him for proposing the book, patiently reading it in manuscript, and making numerous recommendations, usually involving less content and more clarity.

My original draft greatly exceeded book length. Necessity arose to eliminate incidents and personality sketches and condense preliminary details—treasured episodes to me which the reader will not miss.

To say that the literature on this battle is extensive is an inordinate understatement. Perhaps more has been written about Gettysburg than Waterloo or any other battle. Many studies concentrate on certain limited aspects; relatively few take up the whole battle with approximately equal attention to both sides. To cover all sources carefully would require decades, possibly a lifetime, and the story would not then be complete. Many stirring incidents were unrecorded; many others cannot be included in a book of normal length.

Still, I felt there was occasion for this and for other studies that may be undertaken, because of the tremendous impact of this battle on our present-day life and customs. Gettysburg is much more deeply imbedded in American institutions than is implied by the mere preservation of the union of thirty-three states, now grown to forty-nine.

The weakening of the doctrine of States' rights on the battlefield reduced the restraints on a fuller expression of the opposing concept. Centralized government then strengthened has asserted its supremacy more strongly with the years. A government which in 1861 was ordinarily remote now touches the life of the citizen many times daily.

The war, fought for national solidarity, became a fierce, relentless war of subjugation. Never did a nation struggle against stupendous odds with greater devotion to its cause than did the new Confederacy. Because it was burdened with the repelling incubus of slavery, it had to fight unaided.

The South came near to victory—how near may be judged by these pages. After a series of triumphs, Lee's army reached the field of greatest opportunity at Gettysburg. Had Lee destroyed Meade's forces there and captured Washington, Baltimore, or other seaboard cities, of what possible consequence would have been the loss of Vicksburg or the threat of other Northern armies? This was indeed the moment when the Confederate cause was at high tide.

Gettysburg is a fascinating battle from the standpoint of maneuver. Fortunes rose and waned; victory seemed to flutter back and forth between the two armies. A frequent explanation is that destiny shaped the result. If God had grown weary of Napoleon at Waterloo, did He in like manner at Gettysburg withdraw His hand from the cause He had seemed to prosper?

More clearly than by destiny or chance, it seems to this writer that the result was governed at various stages by the steadfastness and initiative of a particular group or officer. Character played a more decisive role than caprice. Leadership, often of smaller units, was the vital quality in the outcome of this battle. Decisions by brigadier generals and colonels were of paramount significance.

In reading about the battle I have felt often that these commanders of divisions, brigades, and regiments appeared only as names in the books, not as persons at the head of their troops. Because I have always wanted to know more about them, I have given, where space and the sequence of the story permit, personality sketches of those who had forward positions in the fighting, from Meade and Lee down to the grown-up Senate page boy, Colonel Henry A. Morrow, and tough old Central American filibusterer, Colonel Birkett D. Fry, who headed the Confederate advance as the battle opened.

The task of dealing dispassionately with General James Longstreet is quite obviously difficult for the historian. This book does not follow him beyond the battle, though in order to understand his personality as fully as possible, I made two visits to Gainesville, Georgia, to talk with any who might remember him from personal contact or observation. These—boys who had picked his muscadine grapes—recalled him both as a compassionate old soldier, gentle to the lads who came to his vineyards, and also as a man apart in the community, almost a pariah, unyielding, stern, aloof.

Sitting erect in his saddle, a black patch over his blind eye, his right arm grown almost useless from the wound he had taken in the Wilderness, he rode alone through the streets, where he had the tolerance but never the friendship of his home people. He was looked on as a religious and political apostate, and was, in turn, bitter and defiant against his detractors to the very end.

The attitude was different among the old soldiers, who respected or admired him. The survivors of the war invariably tipped their hats to the white-haired, white-whiskered veteran about whose character so much of the battle of Gettysburg and destiny of the Southern republic had turned.

Perhaps it is too often forgotten that the conflicts of Longstreet's later years have no place in a strict appraisal of his work at Gettysburg. I have tried to deal with him impartially, and to set forth objectively the sequence of the events he influenced.

The intimate accounts of the men and lower-grade officers, and the regimental and brigade histories, etc., have been carefully considered along with the more studied reports of the generals. The action exceeds in importance the explanation. An attempt has been

made to clear up some misunderstandings. The splendid role of Pettigrew's and Trimble's men on the third day has often been obscured.
Actually some of Pettigrew's men made the deepest penetration of the
Federal position. None could have struck harder than the North Carolina, Tennessee, Alabama, and Mississippi units that accompanied
Pettigrew, yet they are usually neglected in accounts of what history
has come to know as Pickett's charge.

While I do not presume to disclose many new facts at this late date,
those presented probably have not been assembled before in the same
volume. From them I have made my own, at times perhaps uncon-
ventional, evaluations. I have attempted to show dispassionately how
the battle was won and lost, and why the Gettysburg campaign remains such an appealing study to large numbers even after the passing
of nearly a century.

GLENN TUCKER

Contents

Maps

HIGH TIDE AT GETTYSBURG

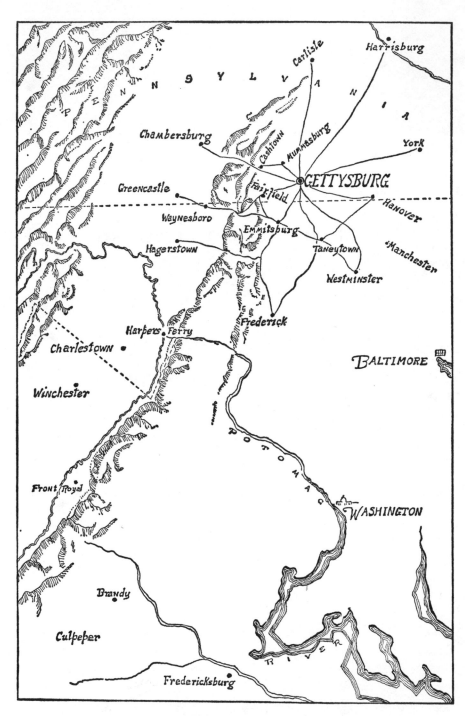

Theater of Lee's Gettysburg Campaign

CHAPTER ONE

Substitutes for Genius

1. Summertime in Southern Hearts

Judge James F. Crocker, of Isle of Wight County, Virginia, reflecting on the Confederate War a quarter of a century after Lee's surrender at Appomattox, declared that the phase of his personal history which he recalled with the greatest satisfaction and delight was the ardor and unquestioning devotion with which he took up arms for the independence of the South.

This was no mere matter of pride, he explained, nor passionate excitement nor ebullition, but a sheer joy of conviction "akin to what we feel for our religion and our God in our most devout moments."[1] Twelve years before his enlistment, young Crocker had journeyed to the drowsy little town of Gettysburg, Pennsylvania, in the beautifully rolling country of the Catoctin and South Mountain foothills, to attend the small school then known as Pennsylvania College. He had applied himself, led his class, and been valedictorian at the commencement exercises in 1850. Then he had returned to his Virginia home to practice law, serve in the House of Delegates, and, when Virginia reasserted her state sovereignty, step forward with "the glow that burned in every true heart of the South."[2]

More than two years afterward, in mid-1863, the ardor of his enlistment had not abated, but had been warmed by the high fervor of apparent triumph, as had that of most of his comrades of the Virginia regiments. It remained a glorious exaltation, a cause far greater than himself. A member of Armistead's brigade of Pickett's division, Long-

3

street's corps, he had been reunited with Lee's army after the march
back from Suffolk, where the spring calm and ample rations drawn
from the fertile valleys of the Roanoke and Chowan rivers had given
rest and robustness to Longstreet's men. And now he was moving out
on a campaign which virtually every soldier in the Army of Northern
Virginia believed would determine the destiny of the Southern republic. By one of those caprices of chance which often stand out boldly in
the unfolding record of events, this destiny was to be decided while he
was battling in front of a low stone fence near a little clump of trees he
had often looked out on from his remote and secluded college halls.

The Confederate march began on June 3, 1863. As the freshness
of early summer touched the tent-covered hills along the Rappahannock, and tinted the fields of wheat with the amber promise of the
approaching harvest, General Lee put his magnificent army into motion for the invasion of the North.

It was summer, too, in the heart of the Confederacy. The superiority of Southern arms appeared to have been fully established on many
fields. Lee had just won at Chancellorsville, in early May, another and
perhaps the greatest of his splendid triumphs. He had enmeshed Hooker
in the thickets along the Rapidan River, by skillful maneuvers had
nullified his vast numerical superiority, and for a time had threatened
him with destruction or capture.

Hooker had scarcely regained the north bank of the river before
Lee began his preparations to move to Northern soil. The death of
Jackson necessitated a reorganization. Rarely had the loss of one
man compelled such extensive readjustments. The infantry of the
Army of Northern Virginia had been divided into two corps, commanded by Lieutenant Generals Longstreet and Jackson. In the interests of greater flexibility, and because there was no other Jackson,
Lee now adopted a three-corps arrangement, and shifted and added
to his units so that each corps had three divisions of approximately
equal strength.

2. *Old Peter Has Lee's Confidence*

Longstreet, taciturn, thorough, and blunt almost to arrogance, retained
the command of the First Corps. Between him and Lee there appeared
to be an extraordinary affection, baffling at times in the light of Longstreet's stubborn self-assertion. But almost from the day he assumed
command of the army in front of Richmond, Lee had pitched his headquarters tent near that of the great hulk of vibrant manhood to whom

the other officers applied the West Point nickname of "Old Peter." Anyone supposing that Lee rode and tented with Longstreet because he believed "Old Peter" needed prodding where Jackson required neither spur nor restraint, found this reasoning unsupported after Jackson's passing. Manifestly Jackson's untried successors as corps commanders would need even closer scrutiny, for a period at least. But Lee continued to move with Old Peter—Peter the deliberate, the hard hitter, and on occasion in the Richmond gossip, "Peter the Slow."[3]

There had been little companionship between the cultured, stimulating General Lee, accustomed to the society of the leading intellects in both South and North, and the peculiar, uncommunicative genius, Jackson, who had proved as much of an enigma to the army as he had as "Tom Fool" Jackson to the Virginia Military Institute cadets.[4]

Close as the professional ties may have been between Lee and Jackson, the commander-in-chief's association with Longstreet was of a more personal and also of a somewhat challenging nature. Longstreet was not a fluent conversationalist nor an engaging speaker. He was more dogged than dynamic. But there was something so robust, dominating and unyielding about him—in character as well as physique—that he enjoyed a store of affection from his troops ample enough for them to pass it on to their sons, grandsons and great-grandsons in the South, despite the fact that Longstreet's personality and generalship were to be subjected to the hammerings of unsympathetic historians over the greater part of three generations.

Brigadier General G. Moxley Sorrel, the Savannah bank clerk who rose to be Longstreet's chief of staff and by almost a consensus to be regarded as the best staff officer in the army, gives a picture of Longstreet as he appeared when he first became conspicuous, at Blackburn's Ford in the first Manassas campaign. He was then "a most striking figure, about forty years of age, a soldier every inch, and very handsome, tall and well proportioned, strong and active, a superb horseman, and with . . . expression and features fairly matched." His eyes were "glint steel-blue, deep and piercing." He wore a full, brown beard and his head was "well shaped and poised."[5]

Major General Fitzhugh Lee saw him likewise for the first time at Blackburn's Ford and his initial impression was of Longstreet's insensibility to danger. "I recollect well my thinking, there is a man that cannot be stampeded."[6] Fitz Lee then gave a view of him at the time the curtain descended: ". . . the night before the surrender at

Appomattox Court House, . . . there was still the bull dog tenacity, the old genuine sang froid about him which made all feel he could be depended on to hold fast to his position as long as there was ground to stand on." These were the solid characteristics that "gained for him the sobriquet of 'General Lee's old war-horse.' "[7]

The Indiana-born author, George Cary Eggleston, who as a Confederate soldier had opportunities to observe General Lee closely at different occasions, felt that common impressions about high-ranking Confederate officers were at times woefully inaccurate. Jackson, he pointed out, though he was a military genius second only to Lee, had a reputation as a superb marcher who was always on time. Yet he quoted Lee as saying that "Jackson was by no means as rapid a marcher as Longstreet," and that "he had an unfortunate habit of *never being on time*."[8] But Longstreet's main trait was his care for his soldiers, extending to a parsimonious husbanding of them out of a concern that they were not expendable. This more than any other quality won and held their affection. At Fredericksburg he said, "if we only save the finger of a man, that's enough."[9] Sorrel noticed that he never failed to encourage and praise good work. "There was no illiberality about him, and the officers knew it and tried for his notice."[10] An example was the report of Colonel John R. Cooke at Sharpsburg, when Longstreet dispatched Sorrel to commend the colonel and tell him to hold firm. Cooke sent back thanks, and: "But say, by God almighty, he needn't doubt me. We'll stay here, by Jesus Christ, if we must all go to hell together."[11]

Stonewall Jackson's chaplain and biographer, Robert Lewis Dabney, specified three varieties of courage: that of the man insensible to danger; that of one who conquers his fears with pride, and that of one who keenly appreciates danger but rises above it out of a high sense of duty.[12] It is clear that Longstreet's bravery was of the rare, first sort. Someone has called him "Bull" Longstreet and the name is apt. It implies his power in combat and his blind charging when tormented by the red flag of verbal attack. This insensibility to danger shone clearly at Monterey and when he was shot down while carrying the flag at Chapultepec. He was fearless.

Longstreet had experienced a spiritual regeneration in the early days of the war, caused by the loss in a single week of three of his children from scarlet fever.[13] The change in him was pronounced when he returned from the funeral to the army at Centerville. Along with Earl Van Dorn, Gustavus W. Smith and Burnett Rhett, he had been one of the gay coterie of officers who drank and stayed up most of the night playing poker.[14] But after his family tragedy Longstreet quit his cards, drank so sparingly as to be almost abstemious, became a devout member of the Episcopal Church, and grew reserved in his attitude and conduct.[15]

Longstreet's poker playing helps to explain his military thinking. He was rated a good player—"very skillful," according to Sorrel. A good poker player is rarely a gambler at heart. Not addicted to playing against odds, he is, instead, a student of averages who calculates his chances carefully. He is not emotional and regards that trait in others a weakness. He does not try to force the cards when they are running against him.

Longstreet liked to win. He was not a man to gamble much in battle. He would rather wait for a situation like the one at Fredericksburg, where he could sit behind his defenses and let Burnside shatter the Federal army against his well-protected ranks. If the odds were not in his favor, he would wait for a fresh deal. Eventually he would hold the aces.

What Longstreet possessed, the faculty of stirring his soldiers to unusual responsiveness, he had no doubt acquired from his remarkable uncle, Augustus Baldwin Longstreet, one of the outstanding writers and educators of the pre-war South. James Longstreet as a youth, after the death of his father when he was twelve years old, lived for a time with this uncle, then president of Emory University, which he built up from an obscure neighborhood school to an institution of standing. Known widely for his extraordinary ability to inspire young people to their supreme effort, he was the undoubted source of the same power in Longstreet the general.

Longstreet radiated ideas. Sometimes they were bold notions dealing with the grand strategy of the war, in which he, with an ambition commendable in a new nation that had appalling casualty lists and was always requiring fresh army leaders, would play a heroic role. At times they were minor tactical recommendations. Often they had to be discarded. But Longstreet did not take unsolved problems to his chief. The trait must have proved a relief to Lee in an army where subordinates, due to his own able leadership and Jackson's, had often been more disposed to await instructions than generate suggestions.

Lee possessed a staff grievously small even by nineteenth-century standards. In 1863 it was composed of officers of relatively modest rank, whose main functions were reconnaissance, the writing and transmittal of orders, and the preparation of reports. It had no plans board, no intelligence branch, no propaganda corps—none of the numerous other requirements of a modern high command. To European observers it appeared puny.

Lee did not resort to the custom frequent in the Northern army of holding councils of war. Very apparently Longstreet's concepts, at times presumptuously advanced and irritatingly adhered to, served to test and sharpen his own conclusions. Lee's keen perceptive powers would not allow him to fall into a failing fairly common among lesser commanders, of desiring the attendance of sycophants.[16] He could have freed himself at any moment from Longstreet's presence, and that he did not do so is testament of his respect and fondness.

So Old Peter retained command of the First Corps of the Army of Northern Virginia. There was never a doubt about it in the mind of either Lee or President Jefferson Davis. He was the general on whom the fortunes of the Confederacy would depend should Lee be incapacitated in battle. Much of the striking power of the army was in Longstreet's three divisions, commanded by Lafayette McLaws, George E. Pickett and John B. Hood.

3. *The Dragoon Rides in a Buggy*

The dead hand of Jackson influenced the appointment of the commander of the Second Corps, composed of Jackson's old foot cavalry. But the Richard S. Ewell who became a lieutenant general and the army's third-ranking officer, was not the hard-riding, hard-swearing, quick-tempered old trooper Jackson had known in the Shenandoah Valley. Marriage and the wound he received at the Second Manassas had bridled and subdued his fierce spirit, while conversion to the life of a devout Christian had softened his temper and curbed his profane tongue.

Richard Taylor, son of President Zachary Taylor, who commanded one of his brigades in Jackson's Valley campaign, has given a description of Ewell's peculiarities, which were excessive. "He fancied he had some mysterious internal malady, and would eat nothing but frumentary, a preparation of wheat; and his plaintive way of talking of his disease, as if he were someone else, was droll in the extreme."[17] Ewell, however, suspected not his own, but Jackson's rationality. He overheard Stonewall remark that he never seasoned his food with pepper because it weakened his left leg. That was enough for Ewell to judge him crazy, although, of course, a sheer genius.

Ewell was so nervous and fidgety he could not sleep regularly. He had "bright, prominent eyes, a bomb-shaped, bald head, and a nose like that of Francis of Valois" which "gave him a striking resemblance to a woodcock." This his subordinate found to be emphasized by "his bird-like habit of putting his head to one side to utter his quaint speeches."[18] Sorrel found him "a perfect horseman" and "without a superior as a cavalry captain." Ewell talked much about a horse named "Tangent" he had owned in Texas. The name was apparently well chosen, for the horse went off in all directions and never won a race. Ewell always lost money backing him, but his confidence never weakened. His boasts about "Tangent" gave the officers secret amusement.

In excitement Ewell tended to lisp. This became so pronounced at times as to be an affliction. Sorrel said he called him "Mather Torrel."

Perhaps the summit of Ewell's genius may be found in his instructions to Brigadier General L. O'Brien Branch to travel lightly when he advanced from Gordonsville to the Valley. They ended with the injunction: "The road to glory cannot be followed with much baggage."[19] The words were Ewell's closest approach to the Napoleonic. In the Valley fighting he could be seen at times, when Jackson was not at hand, stealing forward to the skirmish line and dodging about so as not to be detected by "Old Jackson." In all of the Valley campaign there was only one note that might have sounded caution about entrusting a corps to Ewell's leadership: he always wanted the confirmation of another officer's judgment before putting his own ideas into operation.[20] That did not promise the resolution called for from the leader of a corps, who would often be on independent missions.

One moment of initiative the army told of with relish—the night at Fairfax Court House when Ewell was still a colonel. The Federal cavalry stormed into town and drove back the Confederate horse. An apparent stranger rushed from a house to rally the men. The Richmond *Whig* told the story.[21] Though unarmed and directly from his bed, he stood in the middle of the street, "defied the Yankees, and rained down upon them a torrent of imprecations such as were never heard before." His fury was more effective than bullets. When the atmosphere cleared someone thought to look at the man who could master the enemy with the violence of his oaths, and discovered it was Richard S. Ewell. And they noticed he had rallied the defenders and routed the Yankees while wearing merely his nightshirt.

Sometimes even the champion, knocked senseless to the canvas, is never the same fighter again. That appears to have been the case with

Ewell. After he lost his leg at Groveton, he was no longer, even in spirit, the tough old hussar who liked to crash pell mell into the timber and plunge through water, but a sedate, bald-headed old man who campaigned in a buggy. The junior officers were the first to detect the change.[22] Ewell reached camp from his long convalescence on May 20, 1863, accompanied by his new wife, the widow Lizinka Campbell Brown. Even after the marriage the lovesick general, a trifle muddled, continued to introduce his wife as "Mrs. Brown."[23] Ewell had courted her in his early life but she had jilted him and he had remained a bachelor.

The impact of the new situation appears to have been overwhelming. Observed the clear-speaking Lieutenant Randolph H. McKim, a staff officer of the Stonewall Brigade: "From a military point of view, the addition of the wife did not compensate for the loss of the leg. We were of the opinion that Ewell was not the same soldier he had been when he was a whole man—and a single man."[24]

Mrs. Ewell, who had nursed the general back to health after his wound, was definitely the dominant force in the family, even to the supervision of the headquarters couriers. The result was much talk about petticoat control over the army.

Longstreet worked well with Ewell and rated him "a safe, reliable corps commander, always zealously seeking to do his duty." But he, too, found that Ewell "lost much of his efficiency with his leg at the Second Manassas."[25] In Longstreet's eyes, Ewell's tremendous handicap was Jubal Early, "who, as a division commander, was a marplot and a disturber."[26] Early, of course, disliked Longstreet as cordially.

Jackson was quoted as saying on his deathbed that Ewell should succeed him as a protection to his men.[27] His statement apparently impressed Lee, for the commanding general, who had seen little of Ewell, could not have known at firsthand much about his capabilities, or his lack of them.

But the new Richard S. Ewell filled the boots and saddle that had once been Stonewall's and commanded three hard-fighting, veteran divisions, led by Jubal A. Early, Robert Emmett Rodes and Edward Johnson, all major generals and all, like the corps commander, Virginians.

4. The Punctilious Mr. Hill

Lee created a Third Corps by taking one division away from what had been Jackson's corps and one from Longstreet. Jackson's lost A. P.

Hill's division and Longstreet lost that of Richard H. Anderson of South Carolina. A third division was built up and assigned to Major General Henry Heth, a Virginian who had been a rifle expert in the old Federal army. These three divisions comprised the Third Corps. Command was given to Ambrose Powell Hill, called A. P. Hill in the army records and Powell Hill by his friends. Hill's old division was then assigned to the newly commissioned major general, the twenty-nine-year-old North Carolinian W. Dorsey Pender.

Hill is a nebulous, inconsistent figure, the most difficult to characterize of Lee's generals. He had not been distinguished in the old army, from which he had resigned prior to secession. The West Point accolade, the most persuasive recommendation to President Davis, gave him the command of a regiment at the start. He performed well but not conspicuously under Johnston in northern Virginia, and had little opportunity to distinguish himself at the First Manassas. At Williamsburg he appeared strong as a brigadier and soon thereafter was a major general.

A comparison might be made between Powell Hill and Timothy Pickering, in that it was said of Pickering, when he was elevated in the President's Cabinet, that Washington had "spoiled a good Postmaster General in order to make a bad Secretary of State."[28] Hill had developed into an able combat leader with a division but never rose to any heights with a corps. The son of a Culpeper County, Virginia, merchant, Hill had stretched his stay at West Point to five years, owing to frail health. He had commanded his division at times under both Longstreet and Jackson and had been placed under arrest for petty rebelliousness by both generals. Perhaps the fact that he was not of the landed aristocracy of the South made him more than ordinarily punctilious about matters of right and honor. The "social noodles of Richmond"[29] were surprised when Powell Hill became a lieutenant general. Somewhere along the line he had come by money, and he complained that the Federal general Ambrose E. Burnside, a West Point classmate, owed him a personal debt of $8,000, which he had never made an effort to repay.[30] There was a suggestion of swagger in the fact that he put on a flaming red shirt when he went into battle, at a time when officers were learning that they and their cause had better protection from sharpshooters if they wore a private's blouse.

The controversy with Longstreet arose when Hill was the object of a puff story in a Richmond newspaper, the *Examiner,* written by Editor John M. Daniel, who had served in his command on the Peninsula, and

who gained reflected glory out of exalting Hill.[31] Hill made no effort
to set the facts in their proper light, although he was erroneously
credited with the genius that hurled back the invaders and with commanding Longstreet's division as well as his own, when the opposite
was the case. Hill had not inserted the stories, and Lee had ignored
them, but Longstreet fretted about them and sent Major Sorrel with a
correction to be inserted in an opposing paper.[32] This so incensed
Hill that he wrote to Lee asking to be transferred out of Longstreet's
command. He then went on a sort of sit-down strike, refusing to hold
conversation with Major Sorrel or to pay any further attention to Longstreet's communications.

Finally Longstreet, who had handled the matter smoothly and without passion, sent Sorrel with notice to Hill that he was under arrest.
The situation degenerated to apprehension of a duel between Hill and
Longstreet, which according to Sorrel was averted only by Lee's intercession.[33] The commanding general a short time later transferred
Hill's division to Jackson, then on his way to confront the Federal general John Pope. The disagreeable affair could not have left a com-
radely feeling for Powell Hill with Longstreet or his subordinates.[34]

Again, Hill's controversy with Jackson revealed his sulky nature.
Jackson, apparently on one of his bad mornings, became irritated when
Hill was half an hour late in marching his division and Jackson directed
that he turn the command over to his subordinate, General Branch.
This Hill, with flashing anger, deeply resented. He unbuckled his sword
and handed it to Jackson with the remark that his own services apparently were not needed, and, according to one version, with the scathing
addition that Jackson wasn't "fit to be a general."[35] The pressure from
the martinet Jackson had finally made him explode, but it was childish
in a major general nearly forty years old. Jackson "stopped him with
stern abruptness," in the words of observer Kyd Douglas,[36] and placed
him under arrest, but released him temporarily for the battle of
Sharpsburg.

Back in Virginia after the Maryland campaign, Hill demanded a
hearing on Jackson's charges. Now he exchanged bitter recriminations
with Jackson just as he had done with Longstreet. His fuming was a
trifle ludicrous. Lee in the end managed to pigeonhole the compen-
dious record but never was able to allay the bad feeling.

Lee meantime wrote to President Davis that Hill "fights his troops
well and takes good care of them."[37] There was much high spirit and
bursts of hotheadedness were not infrequent in the Southern army, but

Lee recognized that docile men did not make the good officers. Personalities were clashing and Hill was forgiven. He was intrepid and seemed to have quick perceptions. His expression was "grave but gentle" and "his manner so courteous as almost to lack decision," but those who knew him still found firmness in his mouth and chin and his "bright, flashing eyes."[38]

Longstreet in later years of reflection thought there was "a good deal of 'curled darling' about Hill."[39] Though gallant, he was uncertain. He could perform what Longstreet called prodigies, but at other times he would fall below expectations. Old Pete judged that Hill's capacity was about equal to the command of a division. Ewell was "greatly Hill's superior in every respect"[40] as a corps commander.

At the time of the reorganization Longstreet recommended Major General Lafayette McLaws, a Georgian who commanded the first division of the First Corps.[41] There was nothing Jacksonian about McLaws but Sorrel thought he "could always be counted on,"[42] was exceedingly careful and fond of detail, and kept his command in excellent condition. He was as hard a fighter as Powell Hill and had carried one of the heavy loads at Chancellorsville, as he had earlier at Fredericksburg.

5. *Another Hill Is Absent*

Lee completed his reorganization plans May 20 and President Davis approved them. They left the high command topheavy with Virginians.

Of the fifteen ranking positions in the army, Virginia officers held ten: Lee, Ewell, A. P. Hill, Jeb Stuart, Early, Edward Johnson, Pickett, Rodes, Heth and the chief of artillery, William N. Pendleton. There were forty-three Virginia infantry regiments, thirty-seven Georgia, twenty-nine North Carolina, and smaller numbers from the other Confederate states and Maryland. North Carolina, with many regiments well recruited, probably supplied as many soldiers as any other state, yet was represented by a single new division commander, the youthful Dorsey Pender. Georgia had Longstreet and McLaws, Texas John B. Hood[43] and South Carolina Richard H. Anderson.

Davis and the War Department had insisted that in so far as was practical the brigades should be organized out of regiments from the same state, which was undoubtedly one of the reasons for the superb fighting power of the Southern army. But if the army was to be organized thus, then leadership might have been distributed more generously

among the states. No possible affront to Lee as a general was involved
in this system, as none had been to Washington by the prudent continental policy of sharing the general officers among the different colo-
nies. The Confederacy was a new nation in which fragmentation was
always a danger. Davis leaned heavily on the archaic system of giving
top consideration to seniority, even seniority in the old Federal service.

No army ever had more latent talent than the Army of Northern
Virginia. Its main strength, aside from its commanding general and
the fighting quality of its foot soldiers, was in its brigadiers. Some of
them were to show later that they could accomplish as much with
meager resources as their superiors had with much greater advantages
in and before the Gettysburg campaign. But if it was too early in the
war to detect the high capacity of these brigadier generals, there were
still other possibilities. At Gettysburg some of the North Carolinians
clearly believed they did not have close at hand anyone of high rank
to whom they might confide their wishes, and who would protect the
record of their performance.[44] They felt forced to rely on correspondence with their Governor, Zebulon Vance.

One of the best fighting records in the army—perhaps the best after
Jackson's—was that of the North Carolinian Daniel Harvey Hill, Jackson's brother-in-law. He had won the first brush of the war at Bethel
and had been one of the main strengths on the Peninsula and at Sharpsburg. Governor Vance had him back in North Carolina in the spring
of 1863 and presumably the Governor would not again surrender him
to the Army of Northern Virginia. But no individual in the South was
more imbued with the spirit of Confederate victory than Vance. Most
of North Carolina's young manhood was with Lee. An explanation of
the need undoubtedly would have taken Harvey Hill back to Virginia
to command the Third Corps, and possibly to change the fate of the
Confederacy at a critical moment at Gettysburg.[45] A void in the army
as it moved north was the absence of the other Hill.

CHAPTER TWO

The Gray Host Unleashed

1. "...No Beggars, No Complaints"

As the war for Southern independence moved into its third year, the Confederate capital was buoyant with verve and confidence but was beginning to show ragged at the elbows. Inflation was daily gaining ground: gold in mid-March was worth five dollars in Confederate paper. Much of the financial difficulty was attributed to "the stupidity of our Dutch Secretary of the Treasury, Mr. Memminger."[1]

In the sure light of hindsight, the complaint recorded was that he lacked prescience: obviously he should have bought up cotton when it was selling at seven cents a pound. Profits that would have been realizable by early 1863 would have "defrayed the greater portion of the cost of the war," besides "affording immense diplomatic advantages." The presumption was that the cotton could have been slipped past the lurking Federal blockaders.

Money in early 1863 was merely sliding on to the first gentle slopes of the toboggan ride on which it would plunge later in the year. "There are some pale faces seen in the streets from deficiency of food; but no beggars, no complaints. We are all in rags, especially our underclothes."[2] The South was long on cotton at the gins, short on garments in the homes.

On April 2 Richmond women rioted for food. They met on Capitol Square, two or three hundred at the beginning. Soon there were a thousand women and boys milling about the streets. They marched in Ninth, Main and Clay streets, ransacking the stores and emptying them of merchandise. They seized all the drays and carts in the streets and loaded them with food, mainly flour and meal. They stripped the shoe stores, which had stocks on hand though General Lee had been writing that many of his men were barefoot.

The mob grew as pillaging continued. A boy was seen rushing from a store with his hat full of money.[3] Brigadier General Josiah Gorgas, Confederate chief of ordnance, noted in his diary that "the pretense was bread, but their motive really was license."[4] He pointed out that laborers were earning $2.50 to $3.00 a day and women and children from $1.50 to $2.50, and that they would not starve even with "flour at thirty dollars." These were the statistics, but the women no doubt were hungry. They had been whipped into riotous indignation by charges of rampant profiteering. Most merchants, however innocent, were grouped as "extortionists," but War Clerk Jones put the blame for the mob scenes on "foreigners and Marylanders."[5] Many thought the looting was incited by Northern agents.

President Davis was a distressful figure, with frail constitution and recurring illness. Momentarily he was disturbed by the theft of his favorite mount on the night before the riot. He was feeble, nervous, and easily agitated; one eye was blind and the sight of the other was seriously weakened. "But he works on and no visitors are admitted."[6] He was occasionally forced to remain away from his office for ten days at a time.

Like the President, the Secretary of War was emaciated and unhealthy. James Alexander Seddon, a former Virginia Congressman, was so sallow that many thought he would break down quickly. But he went about his work briskly, to the surprise of the War Department, where he was declared to "resemble an exhumed corpse after a month's interment."[7]

By mid-April garden planting was in progress. The city brightened with the knowledge that in a month the Alabama wheat would be harvested. Of the happy events the most inspiring was the passage and return through Richmond of two divisions of Longstreet's corps, on the trip to the south side of the James River to be boarded out in fresh country. Hood's division, containing the tough, rollicking Texas brigade, had been the center of attention when it marched along Main Street during a heavy snow. The Texans, unfamiliar with snow of such depth, fought snowball battles, to the delight of the city crowds. That night they slept in the snow without tents. "Can such soldiers be vanquished?"[8] asked the busy War Department scribe.

Finally on May 8 Longstreet's troops were a heartening sight as they marched north to rejoin Lee—"perhaps 15,000 of the best fighting men of the South."[9] This time the attention of Richmond was fastened on the Virginia regiments. "General Pickett himself, with his long, black ringlets, accompanied his division, his troops looking like fighting veterans. . . ."

2. Lee Makes the Decision

Against a background of hunger, sacrifice and assiduous effort, Lee planned his invasion of the Northern states. The gloom of the early spring had been largely dispelled and the army had slowly recovered from the anguish that attended Stonewall Jackson's passing. Lee was in Richmond May 15 for conferences, appearing a little pale after the exactions of Chancellorsville. The city buzzed with gossip: First, Pickett would be sent to Mississippi[10] to help Pemberton: then all was to be changed and he would go with Lee to raid the North, capture Philadelphia, march on to New York.

Lee's eagerness to invade the North sprang from the simple reasoning that since he had gained no major advantages from defeating four Federal armies in succession in Virginia, he would have to alter his strategy. The sands of the Confederacy were running out in triumphs. McClellan, Pope, Burnside and Hooker had been hurled back bloody and staggering. The victories had been impressive but in the end almost futile. After each stunning defeat the Army of the Potomac and its appendages had been able to re-form behind its entrenchments north of the Rappahannock or in the Washington defenses. It had bandaged its wounds, filled in the gaps with recruits, and resumed its merciless pressure against the diminishing resources of the South.

The apparent remedy was for Lee to advance boldly northward and draw the Army of the Potomac away from the Washington forts and the Virginia tidewater where it had been so easily provisioned by the Federal fleet. Then he might overwhelm it and operate against its communications. He could follow his victory with a series of hammer-like blows that would possibly open the way to seizure of Washington or other Northern cities.

Colonel Armistead L. Long, Lee's military secretary, said Lee went so far, in considering the place where the Federal army might be defeated remote from its capital city, as to mention Gettysburg and York, Pennsylvania, as suitable points for a battle.[11] Later, in reviewing his thinking, Lee told General Heth: "An invasion of the enemy's country breaks up all his preconceived plans, relieves our country of his presence, and we subsist while there on his resources. The question of food for this army gives me more trouble than everything else combined. . . ."[12]

Of equal urgency was the way in which Confederate territory was being sliced off by Federal armies in the West. The head and shoulders of the Confederacy along the Atlantic seaboard were safe enough at the moment, but the vitals were being hacked at and lacerated up and down the Mississippi. Chattanooga was menaced. Assistance was imperatively demanded by the Western armies. President Davis was gravely concerned over the Federal drive deep into his home state of Mississippi and talked about little else.[13] The Confederacy occupied the interior lines and might shift troops more readily than the Federals. But they were long, long lines, connected by slow, overtaxed transportation systems.

Lee's army was woefully inferior in numbers to what Hooker might momentarily throw against it. Certainly Lee could not at this stage detach any worth-while force for the journey to faraway Mississippi. Too much time would be required to draw the force back if some supreme emergency arose in Virginia.

Nevertheless, the plan of sending troops to Mississippi was under contemplation at the time Longstreet passed through Richmond. He found Secretary of War Seddon engaged in seeking to create a succoring force for Pemberton, around whom Grant was then tightening the noose at Vicksburg. No doubt the plan was an example of what military men have liked to call the "crude strategical conceptions of the Confederate President,"[14] but in any event Seddon said Longstreet's corps might be required to make the journey if the succoring army was to be strong enough to be effective. He asked Longstreet's opinion. The Georgian, thus invited, advanced the more realistic counterproposal—a plan which worked admirably during the Chickamauga campaign a few months later—of transferring two of his divisions to reinforce General Braxton Bragg, who was being pressed back step by step by the Federal general Rosecrans. Bragg was at Tullahoma, about midway between Murfreesboro and Chattanooga. The army forming under General Joseph E. Johnston at Jackson, Mississippi, for the relief of Pemberton, would move simultaneously to join Bragg. This grand combined force could brush Rosecrans aside, march through Tennessee and Kentucky and threaten the invasion of Ohio. The plan, in Longstreet's opinion, would compel the Washington government to recall Grant from Vicksburg.[15]

Seddon hummed over it for a time but expressed opposition because it involved the detachment of such a large force from Lee's army, though his own strategy would have required the same or a larger detachment of troops to be sent about twice the distance. But Longstreet had the bit in his teeth and was unwilling to be hauled up so briskly. Although he had not been the author of the proposal to transfer his divisions to the relief of the Western armies, his own adaptation of the idea grew on him as he rode back to army headquarters at Hamilton's Crossing on the Rappahannock. He immediately sought out Lee and outlined to him "with the freedom justified by our close personal and official relations"[16] his proposition to take two of his divisions to help Bragg drive Rosecrans into the Ohio River. By that time the plan had become the most certain method of freeing the Deep South from invading armies and winning the war.

Lee analyzed Longstreet's proposal carefully. Doubtless it had already passed through his alert mind along with other projects he had been contemplating since the victory at Chancellorsville. But Lee was understandably opposed to a prolonged division of his army. He was thinking in aggressive terms, but of an invasion of Maryland and Pennsylvania rather than of Tennessee and Kentucky. He tested the Pennsylvania plan with Longstreet, who opposed it as being too hazardous. It would take the army into states thoroughly Federal in sentiment, and so would call for much greater preparation than a movement into states like Tennessee and Kentucky, where a friendly population would more gladly assist with food and provisions. It is difficult to read any inordinate lust for personal glory in Longstreet's advocacy of the Kentucky movement. Certainly the chances for distinction would seem greater under Lee in Pennsylvania than under the somewhat phlegmatic Bragg in the Western theater. Either plan might well prove successful if properly carried out. As is generally true, execution was the question.

But the invasion of Pennsylvania appeared to Lee and eventually to Davis to offer greater promise than an advance toward Ohio. The war might be lost in the West but it had to be won in the East. What benefit could the North gain from Grant's siege of Vicksburg or Rosecrans' capture of Chattanooga if Lee could deliver a crushing defeat to the Army of the Potomac in Pennsylvania? The tail might wiggle but the snake would be dead. Success of the Confederacy in the West would only prolong the defensive; a march into Pennsylvania offered the opportunity to win the war with a single stroke. Of the South's many requirements, food remained the number-one priority. The South needed wheat and the season of the Pennsylvania harvest was approaching. Said Brigadier General John B. Gordon: "The hungry hosts of Israel did not look across Jordan to the vine-clad hills of Canaan with more longing eyes than did Lee's braves contemplate the yellow grainfields of Pennsylvania beyond the Potomac."[17]

Also, an invasion threatening Philadelphia and New York might create a panic in the financial centers, put gold at a high premium and cause the great business interests of the North to demand peace. That, at least, was the hope of many, the expectation of some. Jubal Early held that a victory north of the Potomac would do "more to produce a financial crisis in the North and secure our independence than a succession of victories on the soil of Virginia."[18]

Greater reliance was placed in the old trust that the Confederacy would be recognized ultimately by friendly European powers. Some additional stimulus to bring recognition was now imperiously required. The demand for cotton in England had not been a sufficient cause to give the Confederacy relief. The cotton statesmen at the beginning of the war had calculated that England would be depleted of stocks by the summer of 1862,[19] and hence would be compelled to liberate Southern ports from the Federal blockade.

But cotton had not proved to be that kind of king. Another year was almost past and England did not appear perturbed. Bales were piled high on Nassau docks. Recognition by Great Britain or France, or both, might come with Southern victory—victory that would be clear and compelling. The ghastly incubus of slavery was a check on the conscience of the scrupulous British queen. She was not persuaded there was need for haste. It was apparent that recognition of Southern independence would come only as a *fait accompli*. It would spring not from British economic conditions but from Southern triumph on the field of battle.

3. Lee Looks Across the River

Lieutenant Randolph H. McKim, who had been sojourning in Staunton, received a letter from Brigadier General George H. Steuart, a fellow Marylander whom he served as a staff officer, directing him to "come to Fredericksburg immediately by the shortest route."[20] Complying, he arrived at Lee's headquarters at 1:45 P.M. May 28, and although only a first lieutenant, paid his respects to the commanding general. Lee, even amid preparations for a momentous and complicated movement, had time for the military and social amenities. He and young McKim were distantly akin, both being descended from the Virginia landowner Robert Carter, commonly called "King" Carter, a colonial governor, legislator and patron of William and Mary College. Lee, when he was building Fort Sellars in Baltimore Harbor, had been a guest at the McKim house, "Belvidere." The lieutenant was not overwhelmed by the commanding general's presence, although he explained that "the simple courtesy and genial hospitality of General Lee would have put me at ease, if I had been a stranger."[21] A gracious host, General Lee conversed during the meal about the young man's family, then looked across the shallow Rappahannock at the point where it deepened into tidewater, and fixed his attention on the scattered tents of the Federal infantrymen on the hills. "I wish I could get at those people over there," he said ruefully.[22]

The words summed up the purpose for the march northward—to find a place where he could come to grips again with the Federal army. In Longstreet's conversations with Lee about the invasion, he had urged—and later claimed he had exacted from the commanding general a promise—that although the army would move north on an offensive campaign, when it fought it would stand on the defensive. Lee did not so understand it nor did he feel committed: he intended to give battle when conditions were inviting.

Lee issued his marching orders. McLaws would break camp first, to be followed a day later by Rodes and then by Early and Edward Johnson. In the predawn blackness of the third of June he commenced the unobtrusive movement, westward and northward, of his three great corps, each with its three divisions—Old Peter Longstreet, ruffled, tough and innately pugnacious; maimed Richard Ewell, the buggy-riding dragoon; and sickly, headstrong Powell Hill.

Anxious for new adventures, the army was at its peak in zest and confidence. Colonel Risden T. Bennett of the 14th North Carolina looked on it and judged it "as tough and efficient as any army of the same number ever marshaled on this planet."[23] Randolph McKim was impressed with its devoutness. When he could look back after four years of soldiering and forty-five years in the ministry, he declared that "in my whole experience I have never found men so open to the frank discussion of the subject of personal religion."[24]

The British lieutenant colonel, Arthur J. L. Fremantle, was "tre-

mendously impressed with the *élan*," as well as with the manner in
which "they wore their tooth brushes like roses in their button-holes."[25]
General Harry Heth summed it up: ". . . there was not an officer or
soldier in the Army of Northern Virginia, from General Lee to the
drummer boy, who did not believe . . . that it was able to drive the
Federal army into the Atlantic Ocean."[26]

The press was confident. "It is said," chirped the Richmond *Whig,*
"that an artificial leg ordered some months ago awaits General Ewell's
arrival in the city of Philadelphia."[27]

Over the hills moved the long lines of gray and drab-brown soldiers,
the dust from their feet rolling off toward the more distant haze of
the Blue Ridge, and behind lumbered the guns and caissons and the
forty-two miles of wagon trains. The Southern host was at last unleashed for its march through the North, few indeed believing they
would halt before they planted their cannon on the banks of the
Schuylkill, perhaps even of the Hudson.

4. *"Without Offending . . . a High Civilization"*

Twice the army was delayed by business in Virginia. Hooker, growing
curious, threw his cavalry with infantry supports across the Rappahannock River and fought at Fleetwood with Jeb Stuart on June 8. The
Northern horse under Pleasanton showed a new audacity and forced
Lee to call up infantry from Culpeper, which disclosed to Hooker that
the Southern army was moving westward.

The second pause came after Ewell had pressed across the Blue
Ridge and reached Winchester, where the Federal commander, Major
General Robert H. Milroy, inadvertently remained in his path. Edward
Johnson skillfully closed the gap behind the Federals at Stephenson's
Depot and captured 2,300 of Milroy's army, though the general per-
sonally wiggled through the cordon and escaped.

As Lee marched, the stifling heat of the Virginia summer demanded
its toll as surely as ever had Northern bullets. On June 15, one of the
hottest days of the summer, five hundred of Hood's soldiers fell out
exhausted and a number died by the roadside. Some attributed the
deaths to drinking cold water and wading creeks and rivers without
the men taking off their shoes.[28] That night the division "slept gloriously" on a cushion of blue grass and clover. It reached Upperville on
June 17. The country was "perfectly charming." "I cannot see why
any Virginian ever leaves Virginia," a Texan reflected.[29] On June 18
they waded the yellow, swollen Shenandoah River, the water coming

up to their armpits. They crossed in column, the four men of each rank holding hands as a life line against the current and slippery boulders.

They camped a mile west of the river, where a driving rainstorm soaked their uniforms again and drenched the blankets and cartridge boxes they had held so carefully above their heads as they crossed the river. The discomfort was duplicated on the following day. Word that the Federal cavalry was in their rear caused Longstreet to order Hood's and McLaws' divisions to recross the Shenandoah and march through Snicker's Gap to the eastern side of the mountains, there to maintain a screen shielding the northern movement of the balance of Lee's army, aiding Stuart's cavalry.

Rain continued in torrents. Each morning the Texans awoke cold, wet and stiff. The mails did not come up as expected, although there were rumors that stacks of letters from home had accumulated at the Texas depot in Richmond.[30] On the night of June 19 the command "experienced the hardest storm of rain and wind I ever saw,"[31] a superlative statement for a Texan accustomed to northers blowing across the plains.

And so the gray host pressed on, like a great tide inundating the roadways, advancing and receding, marching and countermarching, but relentless in its progress northward. When finally released from Fredericksburg, Hill's corps made a rapid passage to the Shenandoah Valley. The South Carolinians of McGowan's brigade, among them cotton and rice men from lowlands and swamps, were delighted with the rolling cattle and grain farms of northern Virginia and even more elated by the friendliness of the people. Spencer Glasgow Welch, surgeon of the 13th South Carolina, noted that "the ladies waved their handkerchiefs from every little farm house."[32] Bands played sprightly music as the Palmetto boys made their Sunday march through Front Royal. "The people were in ecstacies." Surgeon Welch attributed the excellent health of his men to the abundance of meat, bread and milk. "I have never before seen them get along half so well on a march," he observed. "Not a man has given out since the rain."

Major General Isaac Ridgeway Trimble wrote Lee on June 18, stating that he was again fit for service. He was one of the elders of the army, reaching toward sixty years. A Virginian whose family had moved to Kentucky, he had been appointed to West Point from that border state, had served in the artillery ten years after his graduation in 1822, and had resigned to build and operate railroads, live in Baltimore, and become in most respects a Marylander. But when Maryland

remained with the Union he had gone to Virginia and by persistence
had won the command of a brigade in Joseph E. Johnston's and later
Stonewall Jackson's army. Scoffed at as "Old Trimble," he finally
found opportunity calling to him at Cross Keys, where he became the
deciding factor in Ewell's victory over Frémont. The success added
glory to the closing phases of Jackson's Valley campaign.

Trimble had been wounded by an explosive bullet at Groveton, of a
type later outlawed as inhumane in warfare. Although his leg was
injured, he recovered partially, returned to duty and before Sharpsburg
told Jackson, "By God, I intend to be a major general or a corpse!"[33]
Jackson looked dour and unimpressed, though he must have seen
Trimble's fire, for a little later he recommended the Marylander for
promotion, explaining that it was largely because of Trimble's distinguished service at Manassas Junction in the campaign against Pope.
Undoubtedly the elevation had been well earned by fighting and night
marching that would have done credit to a man half Trimble's age.

Trimble had been recuperating from trouble with his old wound
and from erysipelas at Shocco Springs, North Carolina.[34] None knew
better than he did the Maryland and southern Pennsylvania country
over which he had supervised much railroad construction. Lee told
him to come on and suggested that he raise a division of Maryland
troops—there being no vacancy for a major general. Otherwise he could
have command of the troops left behind in the Shenandoah Valley.

Trimble reached Berryville just as Lee was completing a lunch of
mutton. Lee told him to eat also and then come to the headquarters
tent. There the commanding general explained that the army had been
compelled to push on without him and added, "But you must go with
us and help to conquer Pennsylvania." Before Trimble could reply,
Lee continued with enthusiasm:

"We have again outmaneuvered the enemy, who even now does not
know where we are or what our designs are. Our whole army will be
in Pennsylvania day after tomorrow, leaving the enemy far behind and
obliged to follow us by forced marches. I hope with these advantages
to accomplish some signal result and to end the war, if Providence
favors us."[35]

Lee then alluded to a decision that was to make his Gettysburg campaign outstanding for its humaneness. He told Trimble he had received
letters from many prominent men in the South pointing to the ravages
committed by Northern armies and urging a campaign of retaliation
against Northern property.

"What do you think should be our treatment of the people in Pennsylvania?" he asked Trimble.

"General," said Trimble, "I have never thought that a wanton destruction of property of noncombatants in an enemy's country advanced any cause. Our aims are higher than to make war on defenseless citizens or women and children."

Trimble observed that when Lee replied it was "with that solemnity and grandeur so characteristic of the man." He told Trimble:

"These are my own views. I cannot hope that heaven will prosper our cause when we are violating its laws. I shall, therefore, carry on the war in Pennsylvania without offending the sanction of a high civilization and of Christianity."

In Trimble's description of the meeting, he said he was never so much impressed with the exalted moral worth and true greatness of Lee than when he perceived the "serene earnestness" of his words and saw "the noble expression of magnanimity and justice which beamed from his countenance."[36]

5. Lee Gives Davis His Peace and War Views

Lee was indeed subjected to strong pressure to carry ruthless warfare into the North. But he had his own positive views on the philosophy of warfare, quite as much as on the strategy of a campaign or the tactics on the field of action. He had, on June 10, just after the battle of Fleetwood, written a letter to President Davis which disclosed the breadth of his generalship. The purport was to admonish Southern firebrands gently and to substitute a policy of restraint for one of vehemence. Lee obviously recalled the inflammatory statements of the Richmond press when nine months earlier he had set out on his Maryland campaign. "The fate of Carthage must be that of Washington" breathed the fiery Richmond *Whig*.

Now, in June 1863, the South appeared to hold the position of near victor. The odds against her in a long and bitterly contested war remained stupendous. But a quick peace might be attainable after another successful battle. Lee could appreciate the value of what has since become known as psychological warfare. He wanted to reflect a soft rather than vengeful attitude. Peace should be made attractive, not humiliating. He asked that the government and press "abstain from measures or expressions that tend to discourage any [Northern] party whose purpose is peace." He pointed out that Southern journalists and others had in the past responded to Northern peace advocates in a manner to weaken them and to encourage those who wanted to pursue the war to the bitter end.[37] Manifestly his thinking was that a campaign for "unconditional surrender" might be showy for history but costly in battle casualties. It could have no other result than to make the enemy more resolute. Lee felt that peace should be held out as an inviting lure and not a bitter dreg that had to be swallowed at the point of a pistol:

Should the belief that peace will bring back the Union become general, the war would no longer be supported, and that, after all, is what we are interested in bringing about. When peace is proposed to us, it will be time enough to discuss its terms, and it is not a part of prudence to spurn the proposition in advance, merely because those who wish to make it believe, or affect to believe, that it will result in bringing us back into the Union. . . .[38]

Lee's desire to encourage the Northern peace party by restraint came at a time when the peace advocates appeared to be gaining ground. The Richmond press gave play to all stories of Northern discord. It carried on June 11 an account of the great peace rally held in New York under the aegis of Horatio Seymour and Fernando Wood, attended by thirty thousand. The meeting adopted resolutions denouncing the war and calling for immediate peace, and declaring the Federal government had no constitutional power to coerce a state. The Southern capital was stirred by the news.

It was by all odds the hour to strike. The peace hope was high in the South. President Davis entrusted a carefully prepared letter to Vice President Alexander Hamilton Stephens, who had been a friend and close political ally of Lincoln in the Thirtieth Congress.[39] The diminutive but resolute Georgian would carry it toward Norfolk, where he would be prepared at the proper moment to ask for passage into the Federal lines, and proceed to Fortress Monroe and Washington if possible. This letter was the peace offer. It would be laid on the White House table when Lee had shattered the Northern army somewhere beyond the Potomac.

CHAPTER THREE

The Army Crosses

1. The Horses Are Hid in the Houses

Jenkins was over the river with his 2,000 troopers, riding beyond the Mason-Dixon line on June 15, the day that Rodes, opposite Williamsport, threw over Ramseur, Iverson and Doles—three brigades and three batteries. They were followed shortly by Daniel and O'Neal and four days later, when Longstreet was approaching, by Ewell in person with the rest of the corps.

The 14th North Carolina infantry waded the Potomac to spearhead the invasion. The "Rough and Ready Guards" of Asheville encountered at once the divided sentiments of Maryland. A beautiful young lady seized the reins of Colonel Risden T. Bennett's horse and tried to tell about the "oppression" the citizens had been suffering under Northern rule.[1] Equally emphatic was an old Dutch woman who brandished a paddling stick and shouted: "You eats up everything. The Union soldiers fetch in something and you scoundrels waste it." She threatened to hit the officers until one, pretending severity, told her to be quiet or he would "pull every hair out of her head."[2] Understanding direct action, she desisted. As the balance of Ramseur's brigade came up, the advance guard of Lee's army marched to Hagerstown.

Wild excitement already prevailed in Pennsylvania. Highways leading north were choked with caravans of wagons and carts, former slaves fleeing in fear of impressed servitude, men and women carrying on their shoulders their most valued household effects, great droves of cattle and horses being driven to security north of the Susquehanna

27

River. Dashing through Chambersburg went forty wagons of McReynold's train, a portion of Milroy's scattered command from Winchester, the teamsters lashing at the mules and glancing back over their shoulders, fearful that the Southern cavalry was close behind.[3]

Both North and South appeared amused over the stark terror of the civilians in the face of what from the very outset promised to be a merciful invasion. A published letter from Baltimore described how "in many instances the refugees saw no rebels and were pursued only by their fears."[4] They crowded the Baltimore & Ohio railroad station and slept on the benches. Continually they asked the station master if he had any reports of depredations.[5]

The mountainous section of Pennsylvania offered many hiding places, and numerous citizens took to the hills. The mails were suspended. Stores and schools were closed.[6] Work was stopped. Citizens who in the past had been critical of the Northern army's movements were suspected as spies. Homes were deserted. It was something of a relief to the distressed territory when Ewell finally arrived to restore order, even that of an unwelcomed invader.[7]

Six cavalrymen rode into Chambersburg on the night of June 15, the advance element of Lee's army, followed shortly by two hundred others and later in the night by Jenkins and the balance of the brigade.[8] They camped on the ground of Alexander K. McClure (later editor of the Philadelphia *Times*), where Mrs. McClure cooked up a propitiatory supper for the officers.[9] Jenkins' main purpose was to collect provisions for the infantry, which he did with an efficiency that appalled the Pennsylvania Dutch farmers. He paid for everything in Confederate script, and was diligent to prevent looting. When he saw a soldier in Chambersburg stealing some women's apparel, he jerked the man back into the store, brandished his sword, and declared that he had a mind to cut off the miscreant's head.

"Sell my men all the goods they want," he told the merchant, "but if anyone attempts to take anything without paying for it, report to me at my headquarters. We are not thieves."[10]

When the Richmond *Examiner* learned that Jenkins was paying Confederate money at Chambersburg, it could scarcely credit the information. On June 22 its readers were told:

This sounds strange. If our army has invaded the enemy's soil merely to respect private property, and pay out their money to the Yankees, they had better never have gone. We had hoped that if our army had ever have put its foot on Northern soil, it would have been to bring the horrors of war to the homes of the Yankees—burn, destroy, devastate, and make them feel the ravages of war—in a word, treat them as enemies who have never spared us.

Some of the farmers hid their horses in their own homes, but Artilleryman Stiles bore witness that however ingenious the tricks, the sharp Confederate commissary and impressment squads became even more adept in searching. He and others saw that the great Percherons, Conestogas and other draught breeds common on the Pennsylvania farms were of little value to the Southern army. They consumed twice the feed "our compact, hard-muscled little horses required" yet could perform only half the service and stand about half the hardship. "It was pitiful later," he said, "to see these great brutes suffer when compelled to dash off at full gallop with a gun, after pasturing on dry broom sedge and eating a quarter of feed of weevil-eaten corn."[11]

Lee kept close check on the cost of commodities. He wrote Davis on June 23, as he was about to cross the Potomac, that he was purchasing flour in Maryland at $6.50 a barrel, beef at $5.00 a hundred gross, and salt at 75 cents a bushel. "We use Confederate money for all payments," he said.[12] Its value was of course dependent on the outcome of the campaign. The invasion was already boosting the purchasing power of Confederate script in the South. At a Richmond auction on July 2, lawns which only a week before sold at from $2.50 to $2.75 a yard went for 75 cents. The *Examiner* reported that other staple dry goods showed a decline because of ample stocks and "an increased confidence in Confederate money."[13]

The *Examiner* on June 16 had attributed the depreciation of the currency to a wait-and-see attitude about the invasion, with investments going into real estate or gold. "If our champion rises victor from the death struggle of this month, Confederate notes will recover their value as suddenly as they did after the second battle of Manassas last year," the paper explained.

The route of the Confederate army could be marked through the towns by the old boots, shoes and hats thrown into the gutters as better ones were purchased.[14] Two of the main requirements of the quartermasters were onions and sauerkraut, both antiscorbutics, and they were in more than ample supply in this Dutch country.

Jenkins' cavalry brigade, after delivering provisions to Lee, returned to Chambersburg on June 23. On the following morning the citizens heard the distant strains of "The Bonnie Blue Flag" and a little later witnessed the approach of Rodes's division, the first Confederate infantry to march north of the Mason-Dixon line. The soldiers, mostly North Carolinians, passed directly through the town and north on the Harrisburg road, then halted at Shirk's Hill, where Jenkins already was in position. All day long the march of Rodes's strung-out division continued, first the infantry and the rolling guns and caissons, then immense wagon trains, and finally great droves of cattle that had been rounded up by Jenkins from the lush Pennsylvania farms. The alert Chambersburg citizens kept count; that day 10,300 men marched through the town.[15]

Half an hour after the head of Rodes's division passed the square a two-horse carriage stopped in front of the Franklin Hotel, followed by a group of horsemen. A "thin, sallow-faced man, with strongly marked Southern features"[16] emerged slowly, assisted by some of his escort. The crowd that had gathered saw that he had a wooden leg and walked with a crutch. He entered the hotel aided by the other officers, took over the large front parlor, ran up the Confederate flag and established the headquarters of the Second Corps of Lee's army.

Richard S. Ewell's first order prohibited the sale of intoxicants and required all who possessed whisky to report it so that a guard might be placed over the stock. Said the observant Jacob Hoke: "If there were any cases of drunkenness among the soldiers, I did not see [them]."[17] Ewell did convene a court-martial which cashiered one lieutenant for drunkenness on duty. He issued a series of requisitions to which the community responded with varying degrees of reluctance, but some of Ewell's officers who had been merchants made an inventory of what the town possessed and commandeered what they wanted. The presses were set to rolling and a great deal of army printing work was completed, including many thousands of parole papers, few of which were ever used since they were for the parole of the Army of the Potomac.

One of the Confederate officers engaged in procuring supplies was identified by Hoke as Major Todd, brother of President Lincoln's wife. Hoke was a careful reporter but this statement has not been verified. Mrs. Lincoln had one full brother and three half brothers in the Confederate army. Three served in the west and the fourth is not known to have accompanied Lee into Pennsylvania, though the possibility cannot be eliminated. Dr. George Todd, Mrs. Lincoln's full brother, was a medical officer who ordinarily had charge of a Confederate hospital at Rickersville, South Carolina, four miles from Charleston. All of her

half brothers were killed in the Confederate service: Samuel Todd at
Shiloh, Alexander Todd at Baton Rouge, and David Todd, mortally
wounded at Vicksburg.[18]

2. Lee Has His Letter Repeated

Before crossing into Maryland Lee was confronted with one of the
misunderstandings that contributed heavily to his drama of shattered
hopes. His cavalry was severed from the main army. When Longstreet
left Stuart in Virginia, the cavalry commander had a loose authority
directly from Lee allowing his discretionary action, which by his interpretation authorized him to ride around the rear of the Federal army
and join Ewell on the Susquehanna.

The story of the missing cavalry began on June 21, when Lee was
camped in tents in a stubble field near Millwood. Strong wind and rain
lashed at the canvas. Lee adhered in spite of the weather to his custom
of tenting, although a large white house where he was well acquainted
was close at hand—a house built in the Revolutionary War by British
prisoners whom General Daniel Morgan had sent to Winchester.[19]
While the storm blew, Lee learned that Stuart, watching the Blue Ridge
passes to prevent penetration of the Valley by Federal cavalry, had
been engaged in a whirl of cavalry clashes and was being pressed
severely by the aggressive Federal horse, emboldened by the showing
they had made at Fleetwood. Sharp encounters—little Fleetwoods—had
been fought at Aldie, Middleburg, and Upperville. Being typical cavalry
affrays, none was decisive.

The New York *World* took a realistic view of these cavalry clashes,
which at times have been given places of undue importance in the
history of the Gettysburg campaign. The *World* quoted reports that
the cavalry was "fighting like fiends," then noted that the battles lasted
only about twenty minutes and that the Federal loss would be about
ten killed and a hundred wounded. Take four New York fire companies
in a "muss," the *World* contended, give them no arms except fists,
wrenches and the megaphones of the foremen, and "we will engage
that the number killed and wounded will equal that of Pleasanton and
Stuart's cavalry 'fighting like fiends.' "[20] Somewhere, the *World* felt,
something must be wrong with the accounts. The battles were, indeed,
inconclusive and neither hastened nor impeded Lee's movement
northward.

When Lee, as a precaution, ordered Longstreet to recross the Shenandoah River, move along the east side of the Blue Ridge, and remain

in supporting distance of Stuart until Hill's corps had cleared the Valley behind him, Longstreet was thereby put in command east of the mountains, and consequently of Stuart's movements.

On the next day, at Berryville, Lee instructed his aide, Colonel Charles Marshall, to write a series of orders; these were destined to have vital bearing on the campaign. The army was beginning to clear the Valley. Hill had crossed the Shenandoah at Front Royal and was approaching Berryville. Lee decided to cross the Potomac with Hill the next day, so as to close on Ewell, who was still waiting around Chambersburg. Marshall wrote the first of the orders, a letter to Ewell which suggested that his best course toward the Susquehanna River was on a front reaching from Emmitsburg through Chambersburg to McConnellsburg. Especially, he emphasized, success in gathering supplies would control whether or not the balance of the army could follow. Then came the heart of the order: "If Harrisburg comes within your means, capture it."[21]

Before Colonel Marshall wrote his next letter, Lee told him of a conversation he had held with Jeb Stuart at headquarters near Paris a day or so earlier. Lee had advised Stuart that cavalry details should be left in Snicker's and Ashby's gaps—the two passes of the Blue Ridge by which the Federals might menace the army's rear—and the remainder of the cavalry should go with the main army directly into Pennsylvania. Stuart, according to Lee, countered with the suggestion that he should move close to Hooker and impede his crossing of the Potomac, then, when Hooker crossed, "rejoin the army in good time."[22] Stuart "ardently favored" this plan.[23] Longstreet had agreed to it and Lee then consented, at least tacitly, but insisted that when Stuart learned of Hooker's actual crossing, he himself must cross immediately and take his proper position on the right flank of the army.

On later reflection Lee was disturbed about the arrangements with Stuart, who had been persuasive in his presentation. He told Marshall he wanted to make certain that Stuart and the cavalry should join the main army immediately after Hooker crossed. That was the paramount consideration. Perhaps, he said, Stuart could cross east of the Blue Ridge, thus avoiding the long march through Snicker's or Ashby's Gap, but he foresaw that circumstances might work against such a route and he wanted to be sure that Stuart understood the urgency of rejoining the main army with speed.[24] He therefore directed Marshall to write Stuart a letter containing more explicit directions.

Marshall wrote the letter, showed it to Lee and sent it by messenger.

It expressed concern that Hooker might cross undetected. The heart of the letter said: "If you find he is moving northward, and that two brigades can guard the Blue Ridge and take care of your rear, you can move with the other three into Maryland, and take position on General Ewell's right, place yourself in communication with him, guard his flank, keep him informed of the enemy's movements, and collect all the supplies you can for the use of the army."[25] It went on to explain that one of Ewell's columns was probably moving by Emmitsburg and the other by Chambersburg and that there were no Federals west of Frederick.

The letter did not specify routes nor annul any oral orders Stuart had received, but it pointed up the main task of the cavalry: to patrol Ewell's right flank. Marshall forwarded the letter through Longstreet, who sent it on and then wrote Lee, explaining that he had suggested at the same time that Stuart "pass to the enemy's rear, if he thinks he can get through."[26] Here again everything was reverting to the understanding reached at the conferences among Lee, Longstreet and Stuart, during which Stuart's route into Pennsylvania was left strictly to the cavalryman's own judgment.

What Lee said in his letter to Longstreet, with which he conveyed his written instructions to Stuart, probably never will be known, for the text is missing. This lost letter may have supplied additional incentive to Stuart in a correspondence marked by much vagueness.

Longstreet referred to it in writing to Stuart: "He [Lee] speaks of your leaving via Hopewell Gap and passing by the rear of the enemy. If you can get through by that route, I think you will be less likely to indicate what our plans are than if you should cross by passing in our rear."[27] Passing in the rear would be through Snicker's or Ashby's Gap and crossing above Harpers Ferry. Hopewell is a gap in the Bull Run Mountains which would lead to a crossing of the Potomac between Washington and Harpers Ferry, east of the Blue Ridge.

Later in the afternoon of June 22 Lee again wrote Ewell, telling him that he had directed Stuart, in case the enemy had left his front, to move three brigades across the Potomac and place them on Ewell's right. Imboden had been directed to cross with his brigade and place himself on Ewell's left.

Recognizing that now more than ever before he needed full information, Lee was still dissatisfied with the situation and directed Colonel Marshall to repeat his last letter to Stuart. Marshall demurred; Stuart had been instructed orally and then had received a "very full and explicit" explanation in the letter already written.[28] But Lee insisted that, to guard against error, the instructions should be repeated. Marshall therefore wrote again, using different wording. The heart of this letter, written on the afternoon of June 23, was:

If General Hooker's army remains inactive, you can leave two brigades to watch him, and withdraw with the three others, but should he not appear to be moving northward, I think you had better withdraw this side of the mountains tomorrow night, cross at Shepherdstown next day, and move to Frederickstown.

You will, however, be able to judge whether you can pass around their army without hindrance, doing them all the damage you can, and cross the river east of the mountains. In either case, after crossing the river, you must move on and feel the right of Ewell's troops, collecting information, provisions, etc.[29]

It is not clear from Marshall's comments whether or not Lee read this letter, as he had the first, before it was dispatched. Marshall stated that Lee read the first, but made no reference to submitting the second for approval. But again, Marshall, the composer of it, left conditions as they had been when the earlier letter was sent, or as they had been at the time of the conferences among Lee, Stuart and Longstreet.

Colonel Charles Marshall usually wrote Lee's orders. His legal training might have tended to make his sentences guarded and involved, and ambiguities did creep in. Marshall was of a family that had produced both good soldiers and good lawyers. His grandfather, Thomas Marshall, had commanded one of the Virginia infantry regiments in the Revolutionary War, and his distinguished uncle, John Marshall, had been Chief Justice. Charles Marshall, after graduation from the University of Virginia, had been a professor at Indiana University, in Bloomington, Indiana. He had left teaching to study law, had established his practice in Baltimore, and had returned to Virginia after that state seceded. Bad health kept him out of the early engagements but in March 1862 he joined Lee as an aide, beginning an association that was to endure until the final hours at Appomattox.

Marshall's letter to Stuart was not a model of conciseness or clarity. Had Lee been disturbed before, he had no reason to feel assured after it was sent. The specific instructions it contained were those to be followed if Hooker's army *remained inactive,* which it was not likely to do: Stuart was to leave two brigades on watch, retire with three others west of the mountains, and cross at Shepherdstown.

The orders to be followed in case Hooker moved northward were stated merely by implication, and they left matters to Stuart's judgment. Virtually all that had happened since Lee's conference with Stuart and Longstreet had pointed to the likelihood that the cavalry commander would ride around Hooker's rear unless restrained by a firm negative, which had not been forthcoming. Blackford noted that Stuart had presented two plans to Lee—one for the cavalry to follow the army down the Valley, and the other for it to ride around Hooker's rear. Stuart himself eagerly favored the second, which would allow him to get between the enemy and Washington, "cutting his communications, breaking up the railroads, doing all the damage possible."[30] Both letters written by Marshall for Lee, as well as Longstreet's suggestions, appeared to court a ride around Hooker if Stuart felt it compatible with the rest of his instructions. Nothing in either of the letters covered what should be done if he judged he could get around Hooker and then found himself blocked.

3. The Wanderers Reach the Maryland Shore

Lee's last letter reached Stuart's camp near Middleburg by courier before midnight on June 23, the day it was written, but Stuart was asleep. He was rolled in oilcloth and blankets beneath a tree while the rain fell in torrents—a "pitiless rain," Adjutant McClellan called it—unwilling to go into a near-by house while his men were exposed. He had ordered McClellan to sleep on the front porch, where he might light a candle if dispatches came.

McClellan risked Stuart's displeasure by breaking the confidential seal of Lee's letter, then woke Stuart, who reproved him "mildly" for the technical violation of orders. They managed to keep a light burning under the dripping tree long enough for Stuart to read the message. The words that leaped out boldly were: "You will . . . be able to judge whether you can pass around their army without hindrance . . . and cross the river east of the mountains."[31]

Clearly this was assent and assent was all that Stuart required. As McClellan put it: "The whole tenor of the letter gave evidence that the commanding general approved of the proposed movement, and thought that it might be productive of the best results." He nevertheless left the responsibility of the decision with Stuart.

Stuart went back to sleep and McClellan prepared the orders for the movement east of the mountains, then slept himself, and woke Stuart again at daybreak.

The restriction imposed on Stuart was that he be able to ride around Hooker's army "without hindrance," a condition about which he could not be certain until he explored the possibility. Major John Mosby advised him that the Federal army was scattered but immobile, with gaps between the different corps ample to let the Southern cavalry pass. Complying with Lee's stipulation that two brigades be left to protect the rear, Stuart detached those of Robertson and William E. (Grumble) Jones, a force of three thousand men, with Robertson in command. This force dallied behind in Virginia and did not reach Lee's army until the closing phases of the Gettysburg campaign.

After waiting another day for Longstreet to follow Hill, Stuart assembled at Salem his remaining three brigades—those of Munford, Chambliss and Hampton—and on June 25, just after midnight, set out on his adventure, carrying three days' rations for the men and a day's forage for the horses. "No one could ride along the lines of this splendid body of men," said Blackford, "and not be struck with the spirit which animated them."[32]

Passing through the Bull Run Mountains at Glascock's Gap, Stuart was moving toward Haymarket when the big Second Corps of the Army of the Potomac loomed immediately in his path, marching from Thoroughfare Gap to Gum Springs. Manifestly the thought of turning back never entered seriously into his calculations. He paid the Federals the courtesy of a few rounds from his artillery, then detoured to the south, using up his forage, so that he was compelled to wait half a day while his horses grazed. On June 26 he crossed the Occoquan at Wolf Run Shoals and passed through Fairfax Court House, thus making a wide circuit to the east and entering into the environs of Washington.

Instead of riding around Hooker, he was in the rear of the Federals as they moved north on a broad front. Danger was ever present. Each stop showed the recent presence of Federal infantry. He entered Dranesville a few hours after the Federal Sixth Corps had left, then came up to the Potomac at Great Falls, the spectacular cataract about twelve miles above Washington. Rowser's Ford, a short distance upstream, was deep and difficult and would have been judged impassable for artillery by a less enterprising general. But he took all the ammunition from the caissons and distributed it among the men, who kept it above water as they rode through the flooded stream. The cannon and wagons disappeared from sight entirely as they were drawn through the current by the mules. It required four hours to make the crossing in the darkness, but at three o'clock on the morning of June 28 they "stood wet and dripping on the Maryland shore."[33]

Two mountain ranges divided Stuart from Lee's infantry. The Army of Northern Virginia was moving into the Free States in two separate invasions.

4. Lee Recommends an "Army in Effigy"

On June 25, when Lee was on the Potomac opposite Williamsport, he wrote a letter to President Davis that was destined to have profound bearing on the outcome of the campaign. He acknowledged the President's answer to his "psychological warfare" letter and emphasized again his belief that nothing should be done to discourage the peace feeling in the North.

He then called attention to a proposal he had made on earlier occasions, that the Confederate government organize an "army in effigy"[34] under General Beauregard, and concentrate it at Culpeper, where it would not only defend Richmond but also impose a threat against Washington. He suggested the concentration of such brigades from North and South Carolina as Generals D. H. Hill and Arnold Elzey, commanding those two departments, could spare. He particularly wanted Beauregard, even if that general should be lent only temporarily by South Carolina. Beauregard had commanded high respect in the North ever since the first battle at Manassas and, Lee felt, his presence at Culpeper would have a cautioning effect on Washington, highly beneficial during the invasion of Pennsylvania.[35]

The road from Culpeper to Washington could not be left wide open to one of Beauregard's reputed resourcefulness. Part of the Army of the Potomac, surely a minimum of one corps, would have to be added to the normal Washington garrison. In the Confederate Department of North Carolina on June 30, 1863, were the brigades of Cooke, Colquitt, Ransom, Clingman, Martin and Micah Jenkins, together with a body of troops under Major General W. H. C. Whiting at Cape Fear and scatterings of unattached infantry and three unattached cavalry regiments.[36] From what might have been spared from these brigades and brought up from South Carolina, a presentable Fourth Corps could be created. Corse's brigade and the 44th North Carolina regiment of Pettigrew's brigade were in or near Richmond and available as impressive additions. But Lee wanted Corse and Micah Jenkins to join him in Pennsylvania. Both brigades belonged to Pickett's division.

Lee dispatched his recommendations, then continued his march with hope and apparently some confidence that a distraction by Beauregard at Culpeper would slow the Federal pursuit and give him time for leisurely operations.

Lee was exposed to some warnings from subordinates as he rode northward. Hood was uncertain. Colonel Eppa Hunton of the 8th Virginia was far from sanguine.

Dick Garnett, who commanded the first of Pickett's three brigades, was ill, and suffering also from a foot injury. He had to be carried in an ambulance, so Hunton led the brigade. As he was riding up the Shenandoah Valley a party of horsemen came up from the rear and General Lee fell in beside him. They talked for half an hour as they rode. Hunton boldly advanced objections to the movement into Pennsylvania. His main fear was that if the army encountered disaster, Lee would have great difficulty in getting it back to Virginia.

Lee explained the necessity. He said provisions of every variety were nearly exhausted and that the army had to go to Pennsylvania for supplies. He did not know in 1863 just how tight the Confederacy would be able to draw in its belt before the end of the trail at Appomattox. Lee radiated confidence. He forecast that the invasion would be a great success. If so, he said, it would mean an end to the war and everyone could then rest. Hunton found the commander's ardor contagious. "I threw away my doubts and became as enthusiastic as he was."[37]

On June 24, while Ewell waited in Chambersburg, A. P. Hill's corps crossed the Potomac at Williamsport and Longstreet crossed at Shepherdstown. Both concentrated that night in Hagerstown.

As Longstreet's men marched through Martinsburg, Virginia, they were greeted by a native daughter, Belle Boyd, who was home briefly between spells in Northern prisons. This "most sensational of Southern spies," called also "the Secesh Cleopatra," who had won Stonewall Jackson's unstinted praise by her daring exploits,[38] was an admiring, blue-eyed girl, twenty years old, when the soldiers of her beloved Confederacy passed by. An unappreciative New Orleans artilleryman complained that as usual she wanted buttons, but "we cut and ran."[39] He thought she had "no soul above buttons." Jackson, Turner Ashby and many others would have disputed that if they could.

For all of the brigades the invasion was proving fascinating and eventful. Perrin's South Carolinians, unaccustomed to such profligate abundance, found the country glorious, despite the continued rainfall.

"In every direction yellow fields of grain extended themselves; in every farm were droves of the largest, fattest cattle; gardens thronged with inviting vegetables; orchards gave promise of a bounteous fruit yield."[40] Nor were the residents disagreeable: "The citizens were amazed at our moderation. Many of them bade us help ourselves to poultry, milk, vegetables, fruit, honey, bread, whatever we wanted to eat, provided we spared more valuable property."[41]

Physician Welch was still impressed with both the beauties of the land and the health of the troops: "Such wheat I never dreamed of, and so much of it! . . . The free Negroes are all gone, as well as thousands of white people. My servant, Wilson, says 'he don't like Pennsylvania at all,' because he 'sees no black folks.' "[42]

Fitzgerald Ross, British magazine writer, trudged along with the Southern infantry and left one of the best descriptions of Lee's army as it moved northward. The hotels were so jammed at Martinsburg that he stayed at the home of Colonel Charles J. Faulkner, Ewell's chief of staff, a Virginia Congressman whom President Buchanan had appointed Minister to France. The town was filled with cavalry and infantry hurrying to the front. "The men's shoes are good, and so are their clothes, though they look very coarse."[43] Ross noticed that many of the blankets were made from carpets of bright colors. Southern families in 1863 were living on bare floors. Invariably the soldier had cut a hole in the center through which he could put his head in cold or rainy weather. With the gay carpet tones, "the effect is marvelously picturesque."[44] That was especially the case when the men were squatting in groups about a fire, cooking their meals.

The roads were loaded far beyond capacity, with men and trains going forward, droves of cattle and sheep "the spoils of Pennsylvania," being sent to the rear. The army was already living off the bounty of the enemy. Ross compared some of the Confederate wagons to Noah's ark—they were "of extraordinary size, being drawn by six or eight horses." Perhaps the thing that most impressed the British observer was the army's temperance. He offered a drink to a soldier, who refused and said he would not drink again until the end of the war. "Teetotallers will rejoice to hear," said Ross, "that none of the Confederate soldiers ever touch spirits, and they get on very well without."[45] The statement was extravagant, of course, and Ross no doubt would have corrected it with longer observation, for the army had plenty of drinkers. But it was correct in substance to say that Lee's was not a drinking army.

CHAPTER FOUR

Feasting on Northern Plenty

1. The Texans Have Food by the Acre

Benjamin Russell Hanby, of Westerville, Ohio, a sophomore in Otterbein College, read a story in the Cincinnati *Gazette* in 1856 about a beautiful mulatto slave girl who had been torn away from her Negro lover in Kentucky and sold to a planter who had taken her to Georgia. Although he had never written a song before, that night he composed "My Darling Nellie Gray," which the *Gazette* published. Soon it was being hummed and whistled on nearly every street corner of the country.

The era was one of Negro tunes and minstrel shows. Daniel Decatur Emmett, a more experienced song writer of Mt. Vernon, Ohio, whose compositions already included "Old Dan Tucker" and "Jordan Is a Hard Road to Travel," in 1859 composed a song for the Bryant Minstrels, of 470 Broadway, New York, entitling it, "I Wish I was in Dixie Land." The Bryant Brothers used it without creating much commotion and in 1860 it was copyrighted by another firm farther up Broadway.[1]

In the spring of 1861 Mrs. John Wood was playing *Pocahontas,* by John Brougham, in the Varieties Theater in New Orleans. Any slight inconsistency with the Pocahontas title did not prevent Carlo Patti, the orchestra leader, from introducing in the last scene a march of the Zouaves, for which many tunes had been tried out in the rehearsals. Then Patti ran across the Emmett minstrel air of "Dixie" and adapted it for the jaunty Zouaves.

In New Orleans Miss Susan Denin led the singing as the brightly garbed Zouaves marched. The audience went wild with excitement. It was a season of high emotions, with states seceding and war imminent. Encore after encore was demanded. On the next day "Dixie" rang out in the parlors and music rooms of stately homes, in water-front saloons, in army barracks and on every New Orleans street.

The Washington Artillery, oldest military organization of Louisiana, was preparing to depart for Virginia. When it took the cars for the front, to become a celebrated unit of Longstreet's corps, it carried with its baggage and caissons something of greater worth even than its ammunition—the refrain that would inspire Lee's army, sweep through the Confederacy as a martial air comparable to the "Marseillaise," and in time come to be surrounded with all the romance and nostalgia of the old South, to which it would give its name.[2] Back in Ohio the innocent Emmett, who was merely trying to entertain, was abused and threatened and some suggested that he would look good on a gallows.

Next most popular among the Southern soldiers was the plaintive refrain about the slave girl snatched from the old Kentucky shore. And now as Longstreet's troops approached the Potomac and the guns of the Washington Artillery rolled out of the Virginia mountains and the soldiers looked across to the green Maryland hills, the bands struck up "Dixie" and "Nellie Gray." Regiment after regiment took up the chorus as the men moved down the bank to ford the swollen river. John Hood had never before witnessed such enthusiasm in the Southern army as when his troops touched Maryland, or when, a little later, "amid extravagant cheers," and with bands blaring "Dixie," they passed the Mason-Dixon line.[3]

Drink followed song. Hood, shortly after the men waded the Potomac, issued a ration of whisky from captured supplies. Colonel William C. Oates, commanding the 15th Alabama Infantry of Law's brigade, said the result was "quite a number of drunken officers and men.[4] Although there were ample rations in camp, the men preferred to forage off the country and care had to be taken to enforce Lee's orders. Adjutant Wadell encountered some of the Alabamians committing "depredations" on Dutch farmers. These were venial offenses—pilfering food and using fence rails for fuel—but he reprimanded them and ordered them back to camp. Some were milking cows and catching the milk in canteens, which required accurate aim and showed they were in no manner inebriated.[5]

Oates and Wadell ate with a family where one of the young women, while expressing her loyalty to the Union, thought that the best way to stop the war would be for the armies to hang both President Lincoln and President Davis. According to the Alabama colonel, the people were "remarkably ignorant" of the causes of the war and thought it a quarrel between "two ambitious men."[6]

Private West, fresh from Texas, summed up the march, his first: "We have crossed and recrossed streams, waist deep, with water cold and chilling. We have passed four or five nights and days without changing clothes, which were soaking wet the entire time. . . . A soldier's motto is to sleep at all hazards whenever he has a chance." The country was the most beautiful he had ever beheld. The barns were "positively more tastily built than two-thirds of the houses in Waco." The cherries were delicious. He wrote to his wife, "I enclose two varieties of cherry seed and will endeavor to bring some if I ever get back." That question of returning to Texas was on his mind. As he passed a woman who was inducing some small girls to sing the "Red, White and Blue," she remarked, "Thank God, you will never come back alive." The private had a quick response: "No, we intend to go to Cincinnati by way of New York." Still, thoughts of the future could not be shaken off: "My impression is that we will have a desperate battle in a few days." Then reassuringly: "I would not have missed this campaign for $500."[7]

West was elated with "breakfast in Virginia, whisky in Maryland and supper in Pennsylvania." It was, he said, "a brilliant and eventful day."

Robertson's brigade of Texas and Arkansas troops found the whisky ration ample because many nondrinkers passed their doles to the imbibers. In the 3rd Arkansas those who walked tortuously were doused in the cold streams.[8] By June 27 the Texas brigade was camped in a beautiful grove of great trees near Chambersburg. When the men went out to buy fresh supplies, much was given to them and they returned loaded with delicacies. At the mess call "every square foot of an acre . . . was covered with choice food."[9] The Texans remembered the menu. They had turkeys, chickens, ducks, geese, corned beef, hams, sides of bacon, cheeses, loaves of bread, crocks of apple butter, jelly, jam, pickles, preserves, bowls of yellow butter and demijohns of buttermilk. They feasted until three o'clock in the afternoon. When the march call sounded they "moved lazily and plethorically"[10] into line.

Pennsylvania was fairly stripped of cherries. Even Sorrel, Longstreet's chief of staff, was tempted. From the saddle he pulled the fruit down, "branch after branch," and remembered the pleasure of it through later decades.[11] He remembered also the bolt of velveteen he procured in Chambersburg. Well he might, for the suit he made from it was what he wore for the remainder of the war.[12] Like other Confederates, Sorrel was quite surprised that so many Pennsylvania citizens could speak no English. To him they were "a hard-working, thrifty class, with, it seems, no thought but for their big horses and barns, huge road-wagons like ships at sea, and the weekly baking, and apple butter. This last appeared to be their staple food."[13]

Randolph A. Shotwell of the 8th Virginia mimicked what he termed the propitiating "Deutchers," saying they talked about "Dose nice Rebel gentlemens from de Souf."[14]

Marching toward the Potomac, Kershaw's South Carolinians heard reports that Washington had been thrown into confusion by the invasion and that "Lincoln was the only one who seemingly had not lost his head."[15] Reaching the Pennsylvania line, they were met by a delegation of "rigorously righteous old Quakers," who stood in the roadway and commanded, as though speaking the word of God, "So far thou can go, but no farther." The Confederates moved on; obviously they doubted the authority of the Quakers, but they were certain of Lee's orders. The Quakers went home, "perfectly satisfied," according to Dickert, with their passive resistance.[16] To a woman who displayed a large flag across her bosom, a Texan cautioned: "Take care, Madam, for Hood's boys are great at storming the breastworks when the Yankee colors is on them."

The British correspondent Ross noticed that groups of curious civilians gathered about the wells where Confederate soldiers drank. The conversation was friendly. At one halt a man who "seemed half crazy" was preaching in "very abusive style." He "used Bible language, but words of wrath."[17] The soldiers laughed and joshed at him in good humor. At Greencastle Ross fell in with a train and tramped through the dark beside the wagons. "Innumerable fires" burned along the side of the road, each surrounded by soldiers, "a strange and picturesque sight."[18] Great swarms of men were scattered over the countryside. They bivouacked in the fields, slept in hay in the barns, often marched through the night. Ross got milk for breakfast from a farmer's wife. He found that the population was called Dutch, "though neither they nor their ancestors ever had anything to do with Holland." When he asked a farmwife and her daughters what part of Germany they were from, they replied merely, "Pennsylvania Dutch." He found the mother's accent decidedly Swabian.[19]

2. Pickett Salutes the Little Flag Waver

Pickett's progress was marked by letters to his sweetheart. Because the ardors of middle age are warmer, or less easily dissembled, the commanding general of Longstreet's second division wrote passionate missives at every halt, blatantly indiscreet—at least by modern army standards—in their coverage of army movements. The indiscretion was the more pronounced because the young lady to whom he was affianced was attending a girls' school at Lynchburg, and at such a college conversation is free and letters home frequent.

En route to Pennsylvania, it was: "Each day, my darling, takes me farther and farther away from you, from all I love and hold dear. . . . Today, under orders from Marse Robert, we cross the Potomac." Then, as he reflected on the coming battle: "Oh, the desolate homes, the widows, the orphans, and the heart-broken mothers, that this campaign will make!"[20]

Possibly it was because of his sentimentality that when his men entered Greencastle the band played "Her Bright Smile Haunts Me Still."[21] In any event, from this town he indited a prose poem to his fair lady which suggests he was not much of a killer at heart, although destined to have one of the bloodiest assignments in history. "I want to lie down in the grass, away off in the woods somewhere or in some lone valley on the hillside far from all human sound, and rest my soul and put my heart to sleep and get back something—I know not what—but something I had that is gone from me—something subtle and unexplainable—something I never knew I possessed till I had lost it—till it was gone—gone."[22] What Stonewall Jackson would have thought of such feverish ebullience may readily be judged, although that hard-headed realist was not without sentiment.

Pickett had a chance for a bit of knight-errantry at Greencastle, where a young girl rushed out on a porch and waved the United States flag while the band was playing "Dixie." She fastened the flag around her waist like an apron. Holding each side, she waved it defiantly and shouted, "Traitors—traitors—traitors. Come and take this flag, the man of you who dares." Pickett, fearful that some of the soldiers "might forget their manhood," took his hat off, bowed to the girl, saluted the flag, and had the men present arms. "They were all Virginians," he wrote. "Almost every man lifted his cap and cheered the little maiden." The result was that she stopped calling them traitors, let her flag fall and, according to Pickett, finally said, "Oh, I wish I had a rebel flag. I'd wave that, too."[23] But she was last seen clutching the Union flag to her bosom.

In Chambersburg Pickett found groups of "uncheerful Boers of Deutschland descent" talking, "more sylvan shadows than smiles wreathing their faces."[24] The general had silenced the bands for this march-through but young ladies on a veranda requested music. So the bands resumed and they serenaded with the old songs, among them "Home, Sweet Home," "Annie Laurie," "Nellie Gray," "Hazel Del," "The Old Oaken Bucket," "Swanee River," "The Old Arm Chair," "The Lone Rock by the Sea," and finally, "Auld Lang Syne." There could have been few dry eyes in the town, with a battle looming. Pickett marched out on the Cashtown road four miles and camped. From there he wrote that Lee's order was a sermon on the text of "Vengeance is Mine, saith the Lord." He thought "the mourner's bench was not overcrowded with seekers for conversion" and said the soldiers were thinking of "their own despoiled homes, looted of everything, and were not wildly enthusiastic as they obediently acquiesced to our beloved Commander's order."[25]

Pickett's letters from Pennsylvania to his fiancée, LaSalle Corbell, suggested one thing very definitely: that it was not because he lacked power of expression that he was last in his class at West Point.

Another view of the Southern army's advance was provided by Thomas McCammon, a Hagerstown blacksmith, "a good man" to the Federals, who rode through Armistead's brigade on July 28 to give Federal officers a fuller picture of the invasion.[26] Jenkins' cavalry had arrived on June 15, begun the herding of cattle for the infantry, and sent back large quantities of beef. Ewell had come on June 20 and on the day following, Sunday June 21, had attended services at the Catholic Church with Rodes and two other generals. Confederate soldiers had continued through the town every day that week, and finally Lee and Longstreet had made their headquarters on the James H. Groves place just north of town. The leading Confederate sympathizer of Hagerstown, James D. Roman, a lawyer, had announced on June 27 that the entire Confederate army, 100,000 strong, was in Maryland or Pennsylvania, with the exception of the cavalry.

William H. Protzman had checked the infantry as it passed and "could not make the total over 80,000." Union men assembled each night to compare figures. Their count of the artillery showed 275 guns.

Many regiments were woefully reduced, having only 175 men, while two had only 150. The largest Protzman counted was a Maryland regiment of about 700, apparently in Steuart's brigade. He estimated the average regiment at 400 men. The army had good and ample transportation, many of the wagons having been captured from the Federals, and well-cared-for horses. Officers and men, who appeared in good condition, said they were going to Philadelphia. They carried their paper money in flour barrels and used it freely. The blacksmith reported that they paid five dollars for two horseshoes, the ordinary charge being fifty cents in United States money.

Pleased with the invasion was an old Dutchman with whom a member of the Washington Artillery ate and spent the night. The German couple were paid $100 a year for tending a large farm. The artillery-man gave them two silver half dollars, which Hans looked at with delight. "Johanna," he said, "put dis silber mit der du-bit piece dat you got last Christmas. Py jimminy, dis war is big luck for some peebles."[27]

Gordon told a story of a Pennsylvanian who found his stall empty and would not be solaced with Confederate money. "I've been married, sir, t'ree times," he said, "and I vood not geef dot mare for all dose voomans."[28]

A sincere admirer of women, Gordon was not impressed by the words, but because of the man's acute anguish he had the mare returned.

While Ewell's corps tarried in Chambersburg, its assistant quarter-master, Captain Sandy Garber, learned how poignantly the memory of Jackson lingered with his old foot cavalry. Garber came into camp late and did not know the countersign. At the outpost he was halted by a diligent sentry. Groping about for something that might serve the purpose, he drew from his blouse an old pass which had been signed by Stonewall. The sentry lighted a match and read the pass carefully. His eyes lingered fondly over the signature. He handed it back, looked up at the stars and said sadly, "Captain, you can go to Heaven on that pass, but you can't get by this post."[29]

Jackson was remembered also in unexpected quarters. Seeing an elderly woman on a porch, Major Stiles requested water for his horse. She gave permission and invited him to rest, and consented to mail a letter for him to a sister living in New Haven, Connecticut. She asked if he had ever seen Stonewall Jackson and when he answered yes, she said she expected to see Jackson soon. It startled Stiles, but she explained, "If any one ever left this earth who went straight to Heaven, it was he."[30] Born in Virginia, she had been taken to Pennsylvania when a girl, but home was still across the river.

When Correspondent Ross reached Chambersburg, McLaws' division was marching through "in high spirits." That day he heard the Rebel yell, a "very peculiar sound," which could be heard a mile off. "They learned it from the Indians I believe."[31] He noticed that most of the Confederate bands were composed of Germans, and explained that the Southerners are "extremely fond of music" but had never taken the trouble to learn to play, as this had always been done for them by slaves.

3. Lee Touches the Map at Gettysburg

While waiting near Hagerstown on June 26, Lee held another meeting with Old Trimble, who suggested that a brigade be sent to capture Baltimore and stir Maryland into action. The state had responded indifferently to Lee on his first invasion, but Trimble was hopeful Maryland could be shaken out of her lethargy by vigorous measures. Lee thought well of the plan and wrote to A. P. Hill, whose corps was then closest at hand, asking if he could spare a brigade for a descent on Baltimore. It would have been a bold move to sever Washington from the North, but the detachment of a brigade for operations that far from the main army would have been hazardous indeed, as Lee must have recognized. In any event, when Hill said it would weaken his corps too severely, Lee did not pursue the matter.

That afternoon he called Trimble to his tent again,[32] unfolded a map of Pennsylvania, and began to inquire about the topography of the country east of the South Mountain range, the continuation of the Blue Ridge north of the Potomac. He was interested in Adams County and the terrain around Gettysburg.

"As a civil engineer," he said to Trimble, "you may know more about it than any of us." Trimble described the area and explained that every square mile contained good battle positions or ground for maneuvering.

"Our army is in good spirits," Lee continued, "not overfatigued, and can be concentrated at any one point in twenty-four hours or less. I have not yet heard that the enemy have crossed the Potomac and am waiting to hear from General Stuart. When they hear where we are, they will make forced marches to interpose their forces between us and Baltimore and Philadelphia. They will come up, probably through Frederick, broken down with hunger and hard marching, strung out on a long line, and much demoralized when they come into Pennsylvania. I shall throw an overwhelming force on their advance, crush it, follow up the success, drive one corps back on another, and by successive repulses and surprises before they can concentrate create a panic and virtually destroy the army."

Trimble said he recalled and recorded the words "nearly verbatim." They give the clearest view available of what was in Lee's mind when the campaign began to take focus. Lee then asked Trimble's opinion and Trimble said the plan should prove successful.

"I never knew the men in finer spirits," he added.

"That is, I hear, the general impression," Lee responded. As he brought the interview to a close, he put his hand to the map and touched Gettysburg.

"Hereabout we shall probably meet the enemy and fight a great battle, and if God gives us the victory, the war will be over and we shall achieve the recognition of our independence." Then he instructed Trimble: "General Ewell's forces are by this time in Harrisburg; if not, go and join him and help him take the place."

The astute Jacob Hoke busily conversed with the Confederates and kept a record of everything that happened in Chambersburg. While Washington groped to know whether the blow would fall against Harrisburg and Philadelphia, or whether Lee would turn back toward the capital and Baltimore, Hoke thought of a ready means of answering the question, to his own satisfaction at least.

Chambersburg was at an important crossroads. As the Southern troops passed through, some of them turned—at the diamond, or public square—onto the road from Pittsburgh to Baltimore which ran toward Cashtown and Gettysburg; others continued straight ahead, toward Harrisburg, thus giving no clew to the real direction of the army. But Hoke decided that he would watch the direction Lee himself selected, and thus would know the Southern commander's true aims.

At length, there was a break in the long line of infantry and General A. P. Hill stopped in front of a grocery store. Townsmen crowded about and someone asked when Lee would come.

"I expect him at any minute," Hill replied. He glanced down the main street and added, "There he comes now."[33]

The crowd stirred and all heads turned instantly. Riding along the shaded street beneath the arching trees, mounted on a tall, gray, slim-ankled horse and followed by a small staff, came the awesome figure of Southern victory.

Lee paused at the grocery store to converse privately with Hill. They talked briefly, then Lee remounted, took up the reins, and moved to the divergence of the highways. A tingle must have passed through Hoke as he witnessed this drama of his own deduction.

The cavalryman's pressure of the left rein fell gently across the horse's neck. The ears of the spirited steed pointed upward, and Lee turned sharply to the right. It must be Baltimore and Washington and battle with the Army of the Potomac.[34]

The deduction was judged valid enough for Hoke and other Union sympathizers in Chambersburg to rush off a messenger to Governor Curtin in Harrisburg, who relayed it to Halleck in Washington. It was the first information reaching the War Department that Lee might be turning toward the South Mountain passes.

Lee stopped on the Cashtown Pike on the eastern outskirts of Chambersburg and set up his headquarters at Shetter's Woods, a place where Fourth of July picnics were held. Farmers who at first had fled now crowded into Chambersburg for a closer look at the Confederates. The town was packed with Northern civilians and Southern soldiers. The headquarters grove was soon as busy as any Pennsylvania public square on Saturday morning. One of Lee's early acts was to issue an order for flour to be distributed to the needy of the town.[35]

Lee was joined on June 27 by Longstreet, who set up his headquarters near by. Sorrel saw the many visitors who went to Lee's headquarters, usually with trumped-up complaints, and judged that they merely wanted to see the two celebrated soldiers.[36]

At Chambersburg Hood paid his respects to Lee, whom he found in "the same buoyant spirits which pervaded his magnificent army." Lee greeted him and exclaimed, "Ah, General, the enemy is a long time finding us. If he does not succeed soon, we must go in search of him."[37] There was no hint of defensive tactics here.

In Maryland and Pennsylvania Lee apparently made the mistake of eating an abundance of fresh fruit. The entire army indulged in the cherries. On his earlier invasion of Maryland a lad named Leighton Parks had met him and now Parks returned with a quantity of raspberries for the general. Fresh raw fruit undoubtedly was the cause of Lee's partial indisposition on the second day of the battle of Gettysburg.

4. The General Has a Well-Worn Coat

Most of those who encountered Lee at this period commented on his handsome strength. Age had given serenity to what had always been a reserved bearing. He was then in his fifty-seventh year. His hair, black at the outbreak of the war, was grizzled after little more than two years of conflict. In place of the black mustache he wore a full gray beard. The alertness of his posture and graveness of his countenance were softened by gentle brown eyes. "Sad eyes!" wrote Sorrel.[38] "The saddest it seems to me of all men's—beaming the highest intelligence and with unvarying kindliness. . . ."

George Cary Eggleston felt that the war years altered Lee's appearance so sharply that a picture of the middle-aged man of the spring of 1861 would scarcely have been recognized as that of the general with furrowed face and whitened hair and beard. But the furrows added intensity to his commanding appearance. He was a large man with a big head and a countenance which told instantly of his high character and "perfect balance of faculties, mental, moral and physical."[39] A Northerner who saw him commented on his large neck. "Yes" was the ready reply of a Confederate soldier. "It takes a damn big neck to hold his head."[40]

Although Eggleston spoke of Lee's grace of movement, the quality that he found most emphasized was Lee's "robustness," a term applicable both physically and mentally. "If his shapely person suggested a remarkable capacity for endurance, his manner, his countenance and his voice quite as strongly hinted at [his] great soul."[41]

Sorrel was impressed with "the perfect poise of head and shoulders," and said, "his white teeth and winning smile were irresistible." True to the pattern of the southern planter, he liked the company of ladies and "had a good memory for pretty girls."[42] The sophisticated Mrs. Chesnut said she "blushed like a schoolgirl" when Lee smiled at her in recognition as they were leaving church.[43]

Lee possessed a trait of continuous activity suggesting strong extroversion. When not otherwise engaged he took rambles of inspection about post or camp. Eggleston saw him in South Carolina in the winter of 1861-1862 when he was on detached service strengthening the coastal defenses. He would wander unescorted through the stables and gun park almost every afternoon. As he wore no insignia of rank, he excited curiosity. "I say, sergeant," exclaimed a teamster, "who is that darned old fool? He's always pokin' round my horses just as if he meant to steal one of 'em."[44]

Eggleston became an established author after the war and eventually a trenchant editorial writer of the rejuvenated New York *World,* where one of Joseph Pulitzer's main requirements was terseness. During the war he was attentive to Lee's concise language. A competent judge, he found the words chosen happily. "A single sentence from his lips left nothing more to be said." Many of Lee's remarks were recorded by his auditors in the stilted rhetoric of the day and must lack the crispness of their original form, but they still suggest that he usually thought and spoke with compactness.

Lieutenant Colonel Fremantle, introduced to Lee by Longstreet, judged him "the handsomest man of his age I ever saw." Lee was "tall, broadshouldered, very well made, well set up, a thorough soldier in appearance."[45] During this campaign he wore a long gray jacket that showed age, and hence seemed in keeping with an army dressed largely in homespun. His hat on this campaign was a high black felt. His blue trousers were tucked into Wellington boots. These were high leather boots covering the knee in front but cut low behind. The only evidence of rank were the three stars on his collar. Despite his worn coat Fremantle found his appearance "smart and clean." He never carried firearms but always had his binoculars handy, carried in a strap around his neck in battle.

Other qualities which impressed this British observer were the courteous dignity of his manner and his complete freedom from small vices. "His bitterest enemies never accused him of any of the greater ones." Fremantle also was impressed by the fact that Lee was a campaigner and camper in the fullest sense. The general had not slept in a house since assuming command of the Army of Northern Virginia more than a year before.

At Chambersburg British correspondent Ross called at headquarters. After Lee's council with Longstreet and A. P. Hill, Ross was presented to him, and Lee invited him to a modest dinner. "The general has little of the glorious pomp and circumstance of war about his person," the writer said. At the headquarters were tents, baggage wagons, ambulances, and a private carriage, or ambulance, for the personal service of the commanding general. It had been captured from the Federal general John Pope, but Lee preferred his mount, Traveler, and never used it.

5. "Washington . . . There Was None Like Him"

Perhaps none had a closer grasp of Lee's character and habits than his military secretary, Colonel Long, who was by his side at Gettysburg. Lee, he said, was not only abstemious but was "pained" by intemperance in subordinates. "I cannot consent to place in the control of others one who cannot control himself."[46] Lee, according to Long, never used tobacco in his life. On rare occasions he took a glass of wine but not whisky or brandy.

Lee had a nice conception of the limits of the military authority. Benjamin Harvey Hill, who served as chairman of the Judiciary Committee of the Confederate Senate, declared the commanding general had contempt for "military statesmen and political generals," and never expressed his views to the Congress, the President or even friends, on public questions not strictly military.

Hill once met him on a Richmond street.[47] "General," he said, "I wish you would give me your opinion as to the propriety of changing the seat of government, and going further South."

"That is a political question, Mr. Hill, and you politicians must determine it," Lee replied. "I shall endeavor to take care of the army and you must make the laws and control the government."

"Ah, General," Hill continued, "you will have to change that rule, and form and express political opinions; for, if we establish our independence, the people will make you Mr. Davis' successor."

"Never, sir," Lee asserted firmly. "That I will never permit. Whatever talents I may possess, and they are but limited, are military talents. My education and training are military. I think the military and civil talents are distinct, if not different, and full duty in either sphere is about as much as one man can qualify himself to perform. I shall not do the people the injustice to accept high civil office, with whose questions it has not been my business to become familiar."

Hill was insistent. "Well, General," he countered; "history does not sustain your view. Caesar and Frederick of Prussia and Bonaparte were all great statesmen as well as great generals."

"And all great tyrants," Lee replied quickly. "I speak of the proper rule in republics, where, I think, we should have neither military statesmen nor political generals."

"But Washington was both, and yet not a tyrant."

At that General Lee's face took on a beautiful smile and he spoke with finality: "Washington was an exception to all rule, and there was none like him."[48]

Hood, who had a strong affection for his chief, found greatness in Lee's willingness to perform humble tasks. Hood had served under Lee in the 2nd Cavalry in Texas. Upon reaching Richmond after the outbreak of war he naturally reported to his old superior. Lee had an office on the fourth floor of the Mechanics Institute. Gathered around him was every cobbler in Richmond. Lee was showing them how to make cartridge boxes, haversacks, bayonets and scabbards, of which the Confederacy was destitute. "He was studiously employing his great mind to this apparently trivial but most important work."[49]

This care about details had to be sacrificed at times in the interest of allowing others to discharge their responsibilities but it was deep in Lee's character. One of his near relatives emphasized the quality, describing it as a "beautiful neatness and love of order."[50] Mrs. Lee told how he returned from the Mexican war "with every article of clothing he had taken with him, and a bottle of brandy which he had taken in case of sickness, *unopened*."[51] Some have questioned Lee's scholarship, saying he was not a careful student of military history like Jackson, or even a habitual reader. But his attentiveness to details and mental orderliness implies capacity as a student, and such Lee showed not only at West Point, where he was second in his class, but also in the school of Benjamin Hallowell at Alexandria, Virginia, where he studied mathematics in the winter of 1824-1825. Hallowell said Lee was never behind in his studies and observed all the rules perfectly, but his specialty was finishing with a neatness and completeness everything he undertook. In making complicated diagrams for a course in conic sections, he used a slate for his drawings which obviously had no permanency. But according to the school principal he drew each one of them "with as much accuracy and finish, lettering and all, as if it were to be engraved and printed."[52]

Nevertheless, he shunned army paper work and simplified it as much as possible. "I never presented a paper . . . unless it was of decided importance," said his chief of staff, Colonel Charles Marshall.[53] One of his rules was that petitioners for clemency should not be admitted. He asked to be spared the anguish of meeting relatives of condemned men whose cases had been decided by court-martial. He favored conciliation in personal grievances. When he received a written complaint from an officer, he usually passed it over to Marshall with the instructions, " 'Suage him, Colonel, 'suage him."[54]

A revealing incident is cited by Marshall. A caller having a complaint against the Confederate government gained access to the headquarters tent and punished Lee with a long rant. When he finally departed Lee came out "flushed in anger" and delivered a severe rebuke. "Why did you permit that man to come to my tent and make me show my anger?"[55] If necessary, he could be patient during the strain of unnecessary talk. Marshall said he had never heard Lee speak of

President Davis in any except terms of kindly respect, but he did comment once, after being closeted with Davis for several hours, that "he had lost a good deal of time in fruitless talk."[56]

The soldiers knew how compassionate he could be in a reprimand. After Chancellorsville he stopped in front of a Mississippi boy who had been wounded in the hand. The lad said, "By God, General, the Yankees have done me up, but we have given them hell."

"Well, you are a brave soldier but you must not swear," Lee replied. Then he jumped from his horse, took out a white linen handkerchief, bandaged the wound, made a sling from another silk handkerchief, and sent the lad to the hospital to get a better dressing.[57]

A Missive Among the Roses

1. *"Extra Billy" Parades into York*

In response to Lee's orders, Ewell began a wide movement toward Harrisburg, intending to employ Early and Rodes as his attacking force and use Johnson in reserve to maintain contact with the balance of the army. Rodes moved through Greencastle and Chambersburg to Carlisle. Early marched by Waynesboro and halted on June 25 on the Chambersburg-Gettysburg pike at Greenwood. At daybreak June 26 he moved toward Gettysburg.

Early was accompanied by a battalion of cavalry under Colonel Elijah V. White, a scant complement for work of the magnitude cut out for him. As the eastern wing of Lee's army, he was, in fact, serving the role of Stuart's absent squadrons. Preceded by the meager cavalry detail, he took three of his brigades over the wet dirt roads through Hilltown to Mummasburg, while he detached Gordon's brigade to march on the macadam through Cashtown to Gettysburg.

En route he had the pleasure of burning the Caledonia Iron Works owned by the vociferous anti-Southern Congressman, Thaddeus Stevens. John Sweeney, the manager, argued that the only persons Early would hurt were poor people who would be thrown out of employment and said the industry was unprofitable.

"That's not the way Yankees do business," Early answered sourly as he ordered up the torches.[1]

On learning that Gettysburg was occupied by a Federal force of unknown strength, he directed Gordon to amuse it in front while he endeavored to gain its rear. But before reaching Gettysburg he learned that White's cavalry had already encountered the Federals, who proved to be the 26th Pennsylvania Militia, containing a company of Gettysburg townsmen. They had formed an irresolute line on the heights west of Gettysburg but fled across the fields toward Mummasburg when the Southern troopers, followed by Gordon's infantry, appeared. Hays sent two regiments to help White pursue them and 175 were captured and paroled.[2]

Early and Gordon entered Gettysburg in a downpour on the evening of June 26. The town was placid and unresisting and had little the Confederates might want. Early seized 2,000 rations found on some railroad cars, issued them to Gordon's brigade, and then burned the cars.[3] He requisitioned clothing, provisions and $10,000 in currency. Mayor Kendlehart representing the town authorities answered that it was impossible to comply because the quantities requested were far beyond what Gettysburg possessed.

Early had to move to York at daybreak the next morning and did not have time to investigate the town's resources, which he judged to be limited. It seemed a trivial matter, but had he done so the conditions of the campaign probably would have been greatly altered. He sent back word to Hill's men, who were soon on the road from Chambersburg to Cashtown, that the town had been touched lightly and possessed a supply of shoes.

White's cavalry destroyed the railroad bridges toward Hanover Junction while the infantry was again put on the road eastward. Gordon still moved on the macadam, the other brigades in the mud. Ahead was York, once the capital of the American continental government,[4] but in 1863 only the trade center of one of the richest farming communities of the Northern states.

On the following morning, with the division near the town, it was Smith's turn to head the column.

Brigadier General William ("Extra Billy") Smith, commanding the third brigade of Jubal Early's division, was a Virginian who symbolically tied the secession era to the days of Monroe and Andrew Jackson. He had served as Governor of Virginia during the War with Mexico, and now, just prior to Lee's march to Pennsylvania, he had been elected to the same office for the term beginning January 1, 1864. None in the South surpassed him as a politician of personal magnetism and instinctive leadership. His generalship, however, was proving deficient, and Early judged it advisable at times to keep his brigade in the close proximity of that of Gordon so that the Georgian could exercise what amounted to a joint command. Smith had not had a happy introduction to the military, for at the beginning of his career he had read law in the Baltimore office of William Henry Winder, the Maryland attorney who commanded the American army at the battle of Bladensburg, where his ludicrous tactics exposed Washington to capture by the British invading army in the War of 1812.

The name "Extra Billy," by which Smith was known to both North and South, had been the inspiration of Senator Benjamin W. Leigh of Virginia. As a mail contractor in Jackson's administration, Smith had once handled a daily postal service between Washington, D.C., and Milledgeville, Georgia, and had extended it to numerous spur routes, for which he received extra payments. When Postmaster General William T. Barry came under political attack for increasing payments to contractors, Smith's "extras" were disclosed. Hence the sobriquet. He served a number of terms in the Federal Congress prior to the war.

Major Robert Stiles, of the Confederate artillery, who was riding with Extra Billy across southern Pennsylvania, had been reared from early boyhood in New York City, and had been graduated from Yale in 1859, but having been Georgia-born, he had elected to fight for the South. He had first seen Smith when he had sat in the House galleries to hear the prolonged speakership debate of 1859-1860, in which the Virginian had been active. Now he was about to witness the high point of the old politician's career, his entry of York, Pennsylvania, amid antics that delighted both friend and enemy.

York, in the path of the invasion, had built no defenses, although redoubts were being thrown up at Philadelphia and even New York was sending valuables to Poughkeepsie for storage. As Early's division approached, the mayor came out to surrender,[5] followed by a deputation of citizens with notice that the populace would not resist. Stiles, being certain that "there would be a breeze blowing at the head of the column,"[6] as he put it, rode up to where he could observe Extra Billy.

Smith was instructing his son and aide, Fred, to hurry up the music. "Go back and look up those tooting fellows and tell them to come up here and march into town tooting 'Yankee Doodle' in their best style."[7]

Quickly the band appeared, the June sun glinting off their polished brass, but the refrain they were playing was "Dixie." As they reached the head of the column, however, they struck up the Northern song as a compliment to the good citizens of the old continental capital. Smith might have been leading any Virginia torchlight political procession.

His hat off, he rode into town bowing to crowds, first on one side then the other, saluting especially every pretty girl "with that manly, hearty smile which no man or woman ever doubted or resisted."[8] Stiles noticed that the attitude of the York residents changed from astonishment to pleasure, until finally, when the head of the column reached the town square, they broke out into a hearty cheer for Extra Billy. Most of the citizens were on the street. Bells were ringing and the crowds were going to church. Now they congregated at the square. The pack became so dense that the gray column which the Northern army often had been unable to slow in battle, was surrounded and finally halted by the crowd of curious, milling, peacefully disposed citizens. Smith cleared enough room for his men to stack arms. He did not dismount, but from his saddle he launched into "a rattling, humorous speech," which both the Pennsylvanians and his own brigade applauded.[9]

"My friends," he said, "how do you like this way of coming back into the Union? I hope you like it; I have been in favor of it for a good while. . . . We are not burning your houses or butchering your children. On the contrary, we are behaving ourselves like Christian gentlemen, which we are."

He rambled on, explaining the reason for the invasion. "We needed a summer outing and thought we would take it in the North, instead of patronizing the Virginia springs, as we generally do. We regret to say our trunks haven't gotten up yet; we were in such a hurry to see you that we could not wait for them." Then he gave a brief picture of his brigade. "They are such a hospitable, wholehearted, fascinating lot of gentlemen. . . ." He invited the Yorkers to remain. "You are quite welcome to stay here and make yourselves at home, so long as you behave yourselves pleasantly and agreeably as you are doing now."

The speech might have continued during the sermon hours but Stiles heard a commotion back in the crowd, then a stream of oaths emitted in the "piping, querulous treble" that belonged to the irascible commander of Ewell's first division. Jubal Early, riding with Gordon's brigade, had found the street obstructed by Extra Billy's rally. Early had difficulty in elbowing his way through.

Smith, amid his exhortations, was not aware of his superior's approach until Early caught his blouse, jerked him around rudely and half-screamed, "General Smith, what in the devil are you about, stopping the head of this column in this cursed town!"

"Having a little fun, General," Smith replied good-naturedly, "which is good for all of us."[10]

Stiles observed that "even Jube did not dare curse the old general in an offensive way." Smith ordered his troops to fall in and he then marched to Laucks Mills, near the railroad two miles north of York. There he was joined by Hays's brigade and the road was cleared for the passage of Gordon toward the Susquehanna River.

2. Prompted by a Potential Catherine

General Gordon had breakfasted with a Pennsylvanian whose peculiar dining room was built directly over a spring, so that half of the room was floored with smooth limestone while the other half was a bubbling fountain of clear, fresh water. After the dusty marches, the cool room plus a meal of hot biscuits and milk and cream fresh from the rippling water were novelties the Georgian remembered into late life.[11]

Gordon entered York while the bells were still pealing and the sidewalks were filled with churchgoers. Amid the finery he felt apologetic about the slovenly appearance of his marching column, begrimed from the fine white dust of the macadamized pike. The grotesque nature of his column was accentuated by the barefoot men riding double on huge shaggy horses.

Hoke's brigade followed those of Smith and Gordon and entered York to the cadence of church bells. Colonel Hamilton C. Jones of the 57th North Carolina had been impressed with the calmness of the country through which they had marched and attributed it as much to the phlegmatic disposition of the population as to the restraint of the troops. Barns were filled and the fields were dotted with cattle; the quartermaster provided for the army's food "in an orderly way." There was virtually no straggling. He found that in York the crowds gazed at the Confederate troops "with something like stupefaction. . . ."[12] They gave up thought of church, the ladies went home and the men hobnobbed with the Confederates with little evidence of bitterness." Civilians and officers "drank together and discussed the war."[13] The ardent Union men expressed their sentiments freely but Colonel Jones thought a majority "were bitterly hostile to Mr. Lincoln's administration and condemned the war."[14] Hoke's brigade was quartered in York in a large building erected as a hospital.

Gordon halted his troops on the main street and rode forward, reassuring a group of ladies by saying that "York could have the head of any soldier who destroyed private property or insulted a woman."[15]

As he rode a girl about twelve years old rushed up to his horse and handed him a bunch of roses. He noticed a note in the center of the bouquet and found it was written in a delicate, feminine hand. It gave the number and description of Federal forces at Wrightsville, the Susquehanna River town twenty miles ahead that was his immediate objective.

"I carefully read and reread this strange note," he said. "It bore no signature and contained no assurance of sympathy for the Southern cause, but it was so terse and explicit in its terms as to compel my confidence."[16]

Gordon marched rapidly through the hot June day to gain the Susquehanna River bridge that was the key to Ewell's plan for the capture of Harrisburg. Early planned to cross with his full division, capture Lancaster, sever the main railroad connecting Philadelphia with the west, then move up the Susquehanna and approach Harrisburg from the rear while Rodes, moving from Carlisle, would invest it in front. If Harrisburg fell, Early would mount his division on Pennsylvania horses and raid westward, destroying railroads and canals.[17]

Wrightsville, a small town sleeping on the river opposite the larger community of Columbia, had not changed greatly since Revolutionary War days, when the Continental Congress had fled through it seeking a place to hold sessions during the British occupation of Philadelphia. But while Wrightsville slept, greatness had hovered over it, then passed it by. After the British burned Washington in 1814 sentiment developed in Congress for a removal of the seat of government farther west.[18] Wrightsville was mentioned and soon appeared to be highly favored. But opinion congealed to retain Washington as the capital city and Wrightsville was forgotten. Now the town on the Susquehanna was to have the simple distinction of marking the northeastern march of the Confederate army.

The note the little girl had handed Gordon suggested that he halt when he arrived at the ridge overlooking Wrightsville and examine the position of the Federal troops. From the ridge Gordon looked out over the beautiful Pennsylvania country, green and golden with corn and wheat. Immediately below him, in full view, nestled the town on one of the most beautiful of American rivers. Beyond it was the low, wide bridge he was to capture. It was a mile and a quarter long, a wooden superstructure set on stone pillars.

On its single span was a railroad, a roadway for vehicles and a towpath for the canal which here crossed the Susquehanna. In front of it was the blue line of soldiers precisely as they had been described by the missive among the roses. Their front ran along a lower ridge between Gordon and the river, and to the right was the gorge, just as described, which permitted an approach around the left flank of the Federal defending force.

Finding the note completely accurate, Gordon did not fear to follow its suggestion and move down the gorge toward the rear of the Federals, hoping to surround and capture them. The general was amazed at the military perspicacity of his correspondent, whose handwriting was clearly that of a woman, and "whose evident genius for war . . . might have made her a captain equal to Catherine."[19] Who was she? Gordon never knew.

Confronting Gordon were sensitive Pennsylvania militiamen who had no intention of being trapped. Already combustibles had been placed on the bridge preparatory to the flight of its guards. On the bursting of the third Confederate shell the militia retired hurriedly across the span, lighting the fire at the center as they passed.[20] The flames had made good headway before Gordon and his men reached the structure. The general tried to push on but was beaten back by the flames. The soldiers fought the fire as best they could while Gordon called on Wrightsville citizens for buckets. Blandly the townspeople reported that none could be found.

Flames ate at the wooden structure in both directions. At the southern bank a Wrightsville lumber yard caught fire and from it the flames soon leaped to the town. Now the buckets, pails, tubs and cans which Gordon had called for in vain suddenly appeared in abundance, and soldiers and citizens together labored to save the houses. A bucket brigade reached up from the river, and through the afternoon and night they worked until, late at night, the flames were extinguished.

The fire was arrested just before it reached the home of a kindly lady, Mrs. L. L. Rewalt, who insisted on entertaining Gordon and his officers at breakfast. Gordon found her gracious and self-possessed and wondered about her sympathies. It developed that she was staunchly Unionist and had a husband serving in the Federal army. But the Confederate general and his officers felt great respect for her, willing as she was to recognize a kindly deed from an enemy.[21]

While in York Early requisitioned 2,000 pairs of shoes, 1,000 hats, 1,000 pairs of socks, three days' rations and $100,000 in money. He received the hats and socks, about 1,200 pairs of shoes and 1,500 pairs of boots, but only $28,600.[22] The mayor seemed unable to raise more

and Early felt he had made an honest effort. Early rode to Wrightsville to inspect the ruined bridge—and his thwarted hopes—then ordered
Gordon to return on the next day to York.

3. Serenades and a New Banner

Rodes reached Carlisle on June 27 and remained three days. The rest
was luxurious but temptation was present. The town was loaded with
United States government whisky. Private Joe Duncan, in his foraging,
kicked a haystack and uncovered a full barrel.[23] He took a pail of
whisky back to the North Carolina boys. Plenty of ice was found in
icehouses for those who wanted it. More whisky was discovered. "Mint
juleps in tin cans were plentiful." That night the gay party decided to
serenade the officers. Accompanied by the bands of the 14th and 23rd
North Carolina regiments, they visited the quarters, sang, and called
for speeches.[24] The officers declined in good humor.

In the plain words of Captain Vines E. Turner of the 23rd North
Carolina, "Many of our jaded, weary boys" drank too much.[25] For a
time open hostilities appeared likely with some members of a Georgia
regiment, camped on the campus of Dickinson College, who were likewise "drowning their weariness."[26] Brigadier General Alfred Iverson,
the Georgian commanding a North Carolina brigade, had been stationed
in Carlisle as a lieutenant and now met old friends. One of Ramseur's
men ascribed the loss of Gettysburg two days later to the liquor found
in Carlisle and did not hesitate to name Iverson as showing the effects
on the battlefield.[27]

At Carlisle the mail came up from Richmond and Brigadier General Dod Ramseur got a backlog of letters. His practice when he received no letters was to make "spirit visits" to his fiancée, Miss Ellen
Richmond of Milton, North Carolina, whom he addressed as "My
Heart's Precious Darling." He wrote her ardent, graceful letters, and—
unlike Pickett—was discreet about military matters.

"Our advance has been wonderfully rapid and gloriously successful,"
he had said from Greencastle. "Our troops are in the finest spirits and
when we meet the enemy's horde we will give a good account of
ourselves."

He answered at once the letters reaching him at Carlisle: "Are you
surprised to find that we are so far advanced into the Enemy's territory? We are; or rather we are surprised that we have met with so
feeble resistance so far." He mentioned that the Federal barracks had
been well stocked. "This morning I breakfasted on salmon left in ice."

Saying it would not be prudent to detail the army's plans, he commented, "Let this suffice, they are bold and well conceived."[28]

The troops that were shooting off and receiving sparks from the North Carolinians were Doles's Georgia brigade which had forded the Potomac at sunset on the first day of the crossing and bivouacked on the edge of Williamsport. Here the men were given time to rest feet that were bruised and swollen by the rapid marching. On June 19 they broke camp, halted again for two days beyond Hagerstown and on June 22 entered Pennsylvania. They marched through Chambersburg on June 24 with bands blaring "Dixie" and arms at the right shoulder shift, exchanging banter with civilians they described as "gloomy-faced." "Here's your played-out rebellion,"[29] some of them shouted to an assembled group. When finally bivouacked on the Dickinson College campus in Carlisle, twenty miles from Harrisburg, they were "elated with the hope that we would have that city before the setting of another sun."[30]

At Carlisle the 32nd North Carolina regiment was signally honored. The official flag of the Confederate States, red with its cross of blue, which was to become so familiar to the South, was first unfurled by this regiment. The design of the flag had been adopted shortly before by the Confederate Congress[31] and was the last of the several flags flown by the Southern armies. Richmond ladies immediately made a banner of the new design and sent it to General Lee for his approval and for presentation to the regiment he judged most worthy to carry it. Lee did not make that decision but in honor of the departed Jackson sent it to Ewell, commanding Jackson's corps. Ewell passed it on to "his favorite division commander,"[32] Robert Rodes, who in turn sent it to the officer described as "his most favored brigadier," General Junius Daniel. Daniel's brigade had just come up from North Carolina and had not served under Rodes earlier. Its selection could be explained only as a compromise or on personal grounds. Neither Rodes nor Daniel survived the war to explain. Daniel designated the 32nd North Carolina as entitled to the honor.

On June 29 all of the Confederate troops in Carlisle, the major part of Rodes's division, were paraded on the spacious grounds of the United States army barracks which later became the Carlisle Indian School. Ewell and many of his officers had been stationed here before the war. "Oh! it was a grand occasion," said Private Henry A. London, of Company I of the favored regiment. He found it in "striking contrast with the sad scenes witnessed by the same soldiers, two days thereafter, on the blood-stained heights at Gettysburg." The proud flag of the Confederacy, crimson as the blood shed so freely beneath it, was hoisted on the flagpole above the barracks, to meet the Northern breeze. "And thus it was," recorded the historian of the 32nd, "that North Carolinians can boast that it was the flag of one of their regiments that defiantly waved on the enemy's soil at a point farther north than any other Confederate flag during the whole war." Carlisle is farther north than Wrightsville.

Ewell's remaining division, that of Major General Edward Johnson, patrolled the left as the corps spread fanlike over this southern Pennsylvania section. The division crossed the Potomac at Shepherdstown, Steuart's brigade making the passage in midafternoon of June 18. Steuart rode with his aide and fellow Baltimorian, Lieutenant Randolph H. McKim. As their horses' feet touched Maryland sod, the fervid and emotional Steuart sprang from the saddle, dropped to his hands and knees and kissed the beloved soil of his own state. "We loved Maryland," explained McKim, who followed Steuart's action. "We felt that she was in bondage against her will, and we burned with desire to have a part in liberating her."[33]

Steuart commanded one Maryland, two North Carolina and three Virginia regiments, along with a battery and glamorous Major Harry Gilmore's cavalry detachment. The Marylanders received a tremendous ovation from the ladies as they passed through Hagerstown, to camp at midafternoon near the Pennsylvania line. On the next day they marched through Greencastle, Upton and Mercersburg, then Cove Gap and up over the Tuscarora Mountain to McConnellsburg. Ewell's left wing was thus roughly one hundred miles from his right, on the Susquehanna at Wrightsville. Johnson's other brigades marched to Greenwood, a good concentration point for Rodes and Early.

Johnson's men responded with pleasant laughter to ladies who sat at the upstairs windows and waved Union flags. When the men received more scornful looks, they asked the names of the maidens and said they wanted to make vinegar by writing them on pieces of paper and putting them in bottles of water. A red-haired girl who became insulting was mildly called "Brick-top" and told to put on men's clothing and join the army.[34] To a group who scoffed at the frayed garments of some of Johnson's soldiers, a southern Irishman shouted, "Bejabbers, we always put on our dirty clothes when we go hog killing."[35]

McKim rode with Gilmore, one of the several giants among Steuart's officers, and as powerful with his profanity as with his muscles. The devout McKim, who aspired to the ministry, was amused to hear Gilmore tell a Pennsylvania farmer, amid bursts of oaths, that the Confederates were certain of victory because the army from Lee down was "composed of Christian gentlemen." Apparently observing the questioning glint in the sharp farmer's eye, Gilmore explained that he was the exception.[36]

From McConnellsburg, which was soon occupied by Imboden's cavalry coming up from Hancock, Steuart marched toward Harrisburg, by way of Green Village and Shippensburg, and camped at Big Spring. The rapid nature of his movement may be seen from the note in McKim's diary, that he slept only twelve hours in five days. At Springfield, near Big Spring, he bought seven copies of the New Testament for use among the troops. "The surprise of the storekeeper when an officer of the terrible Rebel army desired to purchase copies of the New Testament may be imagined," he wrote that night.[37] Through June 28 Steuart's men pressed toward Harrisburg, many of them marching barefoot. The shoes with which even the better-clad men had left the Rappahannock were beginning to give way and replacements had been scant.

The loose, almost trusting nature of the Confederates can be understood from the ease with which an adventurous correspondent of the New York *Herald* walked through Lee's army and casually interviewed privates and generals. Wanting to see the Confederates firsthand, he rode west from Gettysburg to find them. Soon he came to a tall, "well looking personage, very dignified and gentlemanly in manner" with a full beard and a major general's uniform. It was Early en route to York. He wore "a capacious brown hat, looped up on the right side, resting easily on his head." The journalist caught Early at a favorable moment, one of the rare times when the general was not doubled up with arthritis.

The newsman told Early that he wanted a pass to go home to the Cumberland valley. The general answered in "a sharp and decisive manner but still without being tinged with anything like discourtesy."

"I have no time to attend to you just now," Early said, "but if it is proper for you to go, there will be no obstructions offered to your departure."

The New Yorker mingled with the soldiers and noticed that private property was respected rigidly by both soldiers and officers. Those staying in the hotels paid with Confederate script. Behind Early's lines he met three Irishmen from New Orleans with a canteen of whisky.

They had been in all of Stonewall Jackson's campaigns, declared they had never been whipped, and said the Yankees couldn't raise enough men to do it.

"By my sowl," one was quoted, "we'll fight till the last man ov us is kilt, and thin, be jabers, the women will take a hand in it. You may fight us for all eternity, and then we won't be whipped afther all!"

He found that Early's men had no love for the general and the Irish stragglers said they knew several men who would shoot him "just as quick as they would a 'damned Yankee.' " But they all appeared to be fond of Ewell.

He drove past the smoldering ruins of the Stevens iron works and ran into A. P. Hill's corps, which had advanced fifteen miles on that day and was bivouacked along the roadside from Greenwood to Fayetteville. Foragers were coming in loaded with chickens, butter, eggs, and all kinds of vegetables. "I passed through the entire corps of A. P. Hill without difficulty or having any questions asked me. I pushed boldly ahead, as if I had a perfect right to do so," he said. Was Lee's army naïve? Or was it so self-confident as to be indifferent about espionage?

Finally he came to Stouffertown, where he heard that Lee was camped in a near-by woods. When he asked where Lee might be found, one soldier pointed to "a tall, fine looking officer, sitting in front of a spacious tent, with one leg crossed over the other." Lee's head was depressed and his eyes were resting "evidently vacantly" on the ground. "He appeared to be in deep thought, and seemingly did not notice what was occurring around him." Undoubtedly he was still pondering over what to do without Stuart.

The correspondent came at last to the Texans in Longstreet's corps. One was demonstrating his dexterity with a lasso by throwing it over the head of a mounted officer. As the Texans marched, a "Union dog" came out and barked at the column and the cowhand roped him neatly. Almost every regiment had either a fife and drum corps or a brass band and all were playing "Dixie," the "Bonnie Blue Flag," or "Massa's in the Cold, Cold Ground." The correspondent was able to get through and file his story, which must have given the North a clear impression of the carefree spirit of the Southern host.[38]

Hooker and Meade Pursue

1. Hooker Would Trust the Yeomanry

To "Old Joe Hooker," butt of the chant the Confederates sang around the Chancellorsville wilderness, fell the task of replying to Lee's maneuver, either by following him into the Shenandoah, moving hot on his flank and crowding and harassing him into engagements that would halt his progress, or devising better measures to thwart his invasion plans.

Hooker, as much of an enigma to the Army of the Potomac as to history, was unhurried about any sort of response. After he learned at the battle of Fleetwood that Lee was moving his infantry, he devoted three days to reflecting and writing letters. Although the Federal cavalry was alert and combative, he was informed by a friendly Negro, not by his scouts, that on June 12 Ewell had passed through Sperryville on the eastern slope of the Blue Ridge.

That night Hooker decided to break up his Falmouth encampment on the familiar heights above the Rappahannock, which the Federal army had come to regard almost as home. Scarcely were his leading units on the march before he was rudely awakened by the disaster to Milroy at Winchester.

Hooker's correspondence with Lincoln after June 5, the day on which he reported that Lee was north of the Rappahannock, was anything but satisfactory and consisted largely of Lincoln's denial of his recommendations. On that date Hooker suggested that in case Lee went north, he might go south. He would cross the Rappahannock and attack Hill's force left to defend the old lines. This provoked from Lincoln the homely warning not to be entangled with the river, "like an ox jumped half over the fence and liable to be torn by dogs front and rear, without a fair chance to gore one way or kick the other."[1]

He wrote to Lincoln again on June 10 that if Lee's infantry were moving north, there could be nothing to interpose "any serious obstacle to my rapid advance on Richmond."[2] This plan became known as "swapping Queens," Washington for Richmond. Lincoln replied four hours later that he would not go south of the Rappahannock if Lee were north of it.

The President disclosed a heavy memory of McClellan's operations when he patiently explained:

If you had Richmond invested today, you would not be able to take it in twenty days; meanwhile your communications, and with them your army, would be ruined. I think Lee's army, and not Richmond, is your sure objective point. If he comes toward the Upper Potomac, follow on his flank and on his inside track, shortening your lines while he lengthens his. Fight him, too, when opportunity offers. If he stays where he is, fret him and fret him.[3]

Disgust over the management of the Army of the Potomac was being expressed sharply in a quarter sensitive for President Lincoln. The Chicago *Tribune,* which had been as responsible as any one factor for his elevation to the Presidency, denounced the miserably lax conditions at the front, and the article, timed just before the invasion, was republished in Richmond on June 12. "Higher and higher mounts the summer sun," the Tribune began; "week succeeds week in the rapidly advancing season; time glides rapidly yet stealthily along, and still the great Army of the Potomac rests as quietly and with as much ease on the north bank of the Rappahannock as though it had no great mission to perform." Great pains, the correspondent said, were being taken to fit up Hooker's headquarters "and thus everything conspires to indicate another long reign of inactivity."

Continued lethargy for the army was suggested also by "the prodigality with which leaves of absence are bestowed" on both officers and men. Even the corps commanders were taking vacations. Stoneman was away for honors after his cavalry raid; Howard was "leaving his 'flying Dutchmen' to look after themselves"; Sickles "goes off in a day or two to aid in a little political pipe laying in New York." Others were

departing whose presence perhaps would be required if any army movement were meditated.

The *Tribune* summed it up: "Under the leadership of 'fighting Joe
Hooker' the glorious Army of the Potomac is becoming more slow in
its movements, more unwieldy, less confident in itself, more of a football to the enemy, and less an honor to the country than any army we
have yet raised."

On June 15, the day Hill broke camp around Fredericksburg and
Ewell crossed the Potomac, the Southern army extended ninety-five air
miles from the heights above the Rappahannock to the Maryland shore
at Williamsport. Lincoln, observing its length and agitated by the
catastrophe at Winchester, told Hooker, "the animal must be pretty slim
somewhere in the middle," and wondered if he could not cut it.[4]

Lincoln did not altogether despair of Hooker despite the Chancellorsville fiasco. Hooker, to avoid the unpleasantness of contact with those
who distrusted him, had come to ignore Stanton and Halleck as much
as possible and corresponded over their heads directly with Lincoln.
Lincoln was obviously willing to have Hooker engage the army again,
while Stanton and Halleck were emphatically opposed.[5] Sometimes
Stanton's fixed notions and schemes stood the Federal government in
good stead. He felt strongly that Hooker should be ousted before he
had further opportunity to abuse the army and perhaps wreck the
Northern cause.[6] The plain fact was, to Stanton, that Hooker had been
a bombastic failure.

After Hooker had left the Rappahannock, the Richmond *Examiner*
sent a correspondent to Stafford Heights to study the Federal army by
what it had left behind.[7] The heights above the Rappahannock were a
desolation, stripped of trees and fuel, littered with "innumerable dead
horses and men" and camp debris. Huge piles of manure extended in
ridges half a mile long where the artillery and cavalry horses had been
stabled and cattle penned. Barrels of flour, meats, bags of salt and
coffee, boxes of lemons and oranges, and crates of cheese had been
burst open and scattered over the countryside in the hasty withdrawal.
Much of this food was in good condition, the cases being intact, while
fancy articles and luxuries could be found among abandoned suttlers'
supplies.

The Richmond scribe had a pleasant time scanning the reading
material. He discovered in the officers' quarters occasional copies of
the *Atlantic* and *Harper's* but found that "their literature for the most
part is of the lowest and most depraved character." More specifically,

"the works of licentious French authors, and the blood and thunder productions of Ned Buntline and Sylvanus Cobb, Jr., were strewed about as thick as autumnal leaves in Vallambrose." This literature, he told Southern readers, showed "the most dissolute and abandoned" characteristics of the Army of the Potomac. He threw in the statement that "throughout the winter the camps swarmed with women from the North." The encampments themselves stirred his admiration. They exhibited a "high degree of cleanliness, convenience, and in some instances even elegance."

Firm was the insistence in the North that Hooker should resign. It was not difficult for artful and able operators like Stanton and Halleck, who, distrusting each other in most things, could move in close harmony on matters of mutual interest, to bring that about. Halleck's dislike of Hooker dated back to their California days; Stanton's was based on discernment. The method of obtaining his resignation would have to be by fretting and fretting him, as Lincoln had recommended that Hooker fret Lee.

As the Federal army moved north, Hooker's messages were filled with considerable nonsense. Writing on June 24 that Ewell "is over the river, and is now up the country, I suppose," he hearkened back to the days of King Henry and said that "the yeomanry of that district should be able to check any extended advance of that column, and protect themselves from their aggression."[8] The yeomanry was indeed aroused. Home guards were assembling throughout Pennsylvania, New Jersey and New York—callow youths and portly men to whom a day's marching would be as devastating as a round of Southern bullets.

Hooker's task at the outset was relatively simple—to swing on the inside arc and keep his army interposed between Lee and Washington. Held beneath the restraining hand of Stanton and Lincoln's injunction to guard the capital, he had little discretion and commanded his army merely in semblance. From Falmouth he had moved his headquarters to Dumfries, then Fairfax Court House, while the corps were pushing north by well-planned marches. Hancock's Second Corps was the last to leave the old Falmouth lines, on June 15, the day Ewell's first brigades crossed the Potomac.

Upon withdrawing from Falmouth Hooker divided his army into two wings. The left wing, consisting of the First, Third, and Eleventh corps, he put under Major General John Reynolds, commander of the First Corps. Hooker retained personal command of the left wing, consisting of the Second, Fifth, Sixth, and Twelfth corps.

Brigadier General Gouverneur K. Warren made an investigation at Hooker's request and on June 24 wrote a memorandum recommending an immediate crossing of the Potomac in the neighborhood of Harpers Ferry. While Hooker was preparing to comply, he sent his chief of staff, Major General Daniel Butterfield, to Washington to request that all the troops which could be spared from the Washington and Baltimore garrisons be sent to the main army. The request was altogether reasonable in view of the certainty that the army must soon fight a major battle, but Halleck saw in it an opportunity for fretting tactics.

When Butterfield called at the War Department, Halleck could give him no encouragement. Then he went to the White House. Lincoln was disturbed by the failure of his request and summoned Halleck, who came and reported that there were no troops in Washington that might be spared to reinforce Hooker. "You hear Halleck's answer" was Lincoln's summation of the matter.

The Washington garrison was commanded by Major General Samuel P. Heintzelman, who had been the object of Hooker's barbs and could not be expected to go out of his way to co-operate. He denied Hooker the use of 2,000 men at Poolesville, where he claimed they were needed. Butterfield went on to Baltimore, where he met the department commander, Major General Robert C. Schenck. The department embraced the Federal garrison of approximately 10,000 men at Harpers Ferry, to which Major General William H. French was assigned as commander on June 26. Schenck was more accommodating than the military authorities in the capital and sent Hooker the brigade of Brigadier General Harry H. Lockwood, composed of New York and Maryland troops.

Harpers Ferry was indeed of little value, having been bypassed by Lee. It had proved no more than a trap for about 10,000 men under Colonel Dixon S. Miles when Lee invaded Maryland in 1862. Hooker meantime told General French to issue three days' rations and stand ready to co-operate with the Army of the Potomac. He ordered Slocum with the Twelfth Corps to move to the mouth of the Monocacy River and be prepared to pick up French, enter the Cumberland Valley in Lee's rear, and operate against the Southern army's communications with Virginia. On Saturday June 27 he inquired of the War Department if there was any reason why Maryland Heights, which overlooked Harpers Ferry and was the key to that position, might not be abandoned. Halleck replied promptly that the heights had always been thought an important point, fortified at much expense, and he would not approve abandonment except as an absolute necessity. Clearly he would yield nothing.

That brought another telegram from Hooker, who said he had found 10,000 men at Harpers Ferry in condition to take the field but "of no earthly account" in a garrison. Somewhere else they might be of some service, but "now, they are but bait for the rebels, should they return."[9]

As the day wore on Halleck's rebuff must have rankled. Finally, just after noon, before Hooker had received an answer, he dashed off another telegram pointing out that his original instructions required him to cover Harpers Ferry and Washington, but that he had in his front an enemy of more than his own numbers. That was a miscalculation, but made in good faith no doubt; the size of Lee's army was being exaggerated by civilians who were sending in reports. He told Halleck he could not comply with the conditions imposed on him with the means at his disposal and therefore requested to be relieved of the command.

At eight o'clock that evening Halleck sent another telegram: since Hooker had been appointed by the President, the request that he be relieved would have to be referred to the executive for action.

2. The War Department Messenger Startles Meade

James A. Hardie, assistant adjutant general of the Federal army, left Washington by special train on the night of June 27 for army headquarters in Frederick. Butterfield rode with him, returning from his largely unsuccessful quest for reinforcements. They chatted pleasantly, but Hardie did not disclose that he carried orders relieving Butterfield's chief from the command of the army.[10] Sickles also was on the train, returning to the Third Corps after a jaunt to the capital. At the Frederick station Hardie took a carriage alone.[11] It was two o'clock on the morning of Sunday June 28 when he reached the tent of General Meade, whom he awoke from a heavy sleep. Meade thought he was being put under arrest, and wondered about his misdeeds.

Meade's reaction to his promotion must have been one of inner exultation, yet he kept it carefully concealed and protested to Hardie, probably with sincerity, that the order was unfair to Reynolds. The two attitudes were not inconsistent, for Meade admired and respected his senior major general and had served under him long enough to appreciate his merits. Meade did not know then that he had been recommended for the top by Reynolds himself, who had been summoned to the White House by the President after the battle of Chancellorsville, where they talked late into the night of June 2.[12] Lincoln had felt him out about assuming the command if another change were necessary, and Reynolds had stipulated that he would accept only if allowed untrammeled authority to direct the army's movements, i.e., if he were free of orders from Halleck. Reynolds had mentioned Meade at that conference and said he would support him to the best of his ability.[13]

McClellan, who was one of the few earlier army commanders competent to reach solid judgments, rated Meade "an excellent officer; cool, brave and intelligent" and said he was "an honest man."[14] Lincoln's determination to go along with Hooker during the early part of the Gettysburg campaign cannot be explained by any chagrin that he had already made so many unsatisfactory changes in the last year and hated to face another.[15] But the resignation had altered the situation. For reasons never fully explained—though no doubt because he was not prepared to accept the condition imposed by Reynolds and supersede Halleck—Lincoln passed over Reynolds and selected Meade.

Meade and Hardie went together to the headquarters tent, which they reached at dawn. Butterfield, who had by this time arrived, was with Hooker when Meade conveyed the news, and Hooker suavely prevented any embarrassment by his courtesy and expressions of gratitude that Meade,[16] whose division had been in his corps at Sharpsburg, had been the choice.

Meade was deferential and polite in return, explained that the appointment came as a surprise to him and added the peculiar remark—to cover his own conscience?—that it was against his personal inclinations though as a soldier he was subject to orders. The meeting lasted half an hour. The only moment of tension came at Meade's indiscreet remark that the army, as located for him on the map by Hooker, was too widely scattered. Both Hooker and Butterfield immediately challenged him and Meade desisted, but his point was well taken; the army had been advancing on an unusually wide front, as Stuart had learned when he attempted to ride around it.

Hooker thought that since Lee had not taken pontoons with him into Pennsylvania, he could not be thinking seriously of crossing the Susquehanna River and capturing Harrisburg, but was planning instead to move down the south bank of the Susquehanna and isolate Baltimore and Washington from the northern and western states. This deduction did not take into consideration that the Susquehanna was wide and shallow near Harrisburg and that Lee always had with him his "Confederate pontoons," which meant wading.

Hooker was in jauntier spirits at this closing scene than when, less than two months before, he and Meade had faced each other after the battle of Chancellorsville. Despondently Hooker had told Meade then, as Meade described the interview to his wife, that "he was ready to turn over to me the Army of the Potomac; that he had enough of it, and almost wished he had never been born."[17]

3. "I Ventured to Tell the President . . . Stories"

Meade is a rather pathetic figure in American history, his career being marked more by somber frustration than gaiety and triumph. In his tendency to self-pity, the cards usually seemed stacked against him. Six weeks before achieving the top command he was writing his wife that "a poor devil like myself, with little merit and no friends, has to stand aside and see others go ahead. . . ."[18] Only three days before his elevation he told her again, in analyzing his prospects, that he had no chance because he was without friends while others had influential politicians working in their interests. Then came the customary self-depreciating note: "Besides, I have not the vanity to think my capacity so pre-eminent. . . ."

Analyzing a man on the basis of his private letters to his wife is like prying into the dressing room before the curtain is lifted. Meade's published letters suggest, however, that he was a bit of a dissembler. He was trying to ingratiate himself into the good opinion of the White House and working anxiously for promotion, and at the same time proclaiming so insistently that he did not want the high command that that has become the common impression. Mr. and Mrs. Lincoln had attended the military reviews on the Rappahannock in early April prior to the opening of the spring campaign. On April 9 Meade recorded how he had been endeavoring to make himself "agreeable to Mrs. Lincoln, who seems an amiable sort of personage. In view also of the vacant brigadier-ship in the regular army, I have ventured to tell the President one or two stories, and I think I have made decided progress in his affections. . . ."[19]

Mrs. Lincoln sent him a bouquet. "My vanity insinuated," he wrote, "that my *fine appearance* had taken Mrs. Lincoln's eye and that my fortune was made." But he soon learned from the orderly that all of the principal generals had been similarly remembered after the reviews.[20]

The letters, like Pickett's to his sweetheart, are filled with indiscreet disclosures of military matters. Jackson would have been delighted to intercept Meade's letter of April 18, saying that the Federal army would lose nearly 25,000 men in the next twenty days, and that "I see no indication of their being replaced. Over eight thousand go out of my corps alone."[21] It would have suggested that the Southerners should wait before undertaking any contemplated movement, or else should be on the lookout for Federal activity before the enlistments expired. There was also a vein of cynicism in the correspondence, as, for example, on April 17 from Falmouth: "I see some of the papers are disposed to criticise and find fault with du Pont, but I have just read a vigorous defense of him in the New York *Tribune,* so he is all right. . . ."[22]

Meade's caution and ultra-conservatism appear to have been a reaction from his father's business enterprise, which involved taking long chances. The family was of Irish descent. Robert Meade, the general's great-grandfather, immigrated to Philadelphia before 1732 and set himself up as a commission merchant in the Barbados trade. One of a small group of Catholics in the Quaker city, he was a leading factor in building the first Catholic chapel. His son, the general's grandfather, was "Honest George" Meade, a devout Catholic and an organizer, just before the Revolutionary War, of the Friendly Sons of St. Patrick.

The general's father, Richard Worsham Meade, was a big earner and a big loser.[23] He first entered his father's countinghouse, visited Europe before he was seventeen, and journeyed as a supercargo to the West Indies, where by the time he was twenty-five he had acquired wealth. Eventually, after "Honest George" had gone bankrupt in 1801, Richard settled in Cadiz, Spain, where he lived for seventeen years. During the Peninsular War he helped provision Wellington's army and sold merchandise and supplies to Spain in the uncertain Napoleonic days of shifting sovereigns. Bills accumulated. An assignee for a bankrupt British firm, he became the object of lawsuits by creditors, and although he appears to have been guilty of no moral turpitude, was arrested and held for two years in the Santa Catalina prison in Cadiz, being released finally through the intercession of the United States minister. During this imprisonment his son, George Gordon Meade, the eighth of ten children, was born, on the last day of 1815.

The Meade family thereafter tried futilely to collect the money owed them by Spain. In 1817 the father sent the family back to Philadelphia while he remained in Madrid to prosecute his claim. When the United States purchased Florida in 1819 it assumed the debts owed by Spain to American citizens. So the elder Meade returned to the United States and joined that group eternally present in Washington, of petitioners for redress or payment of moneys due or alleged to be due. After he died in 1828, his widow took permanent residence in the capital to work for the appropriation that would re-establish the family. But the Meades, rebuffed at the Spanish court, were to learn to put their trust no more in republics than in princes. President Jackson at that time was making a cipher out of the national debt, and the Meade item went unrecognized. Where the earlier Meades had lived in affluence, George was reared frugally. Enough money was raked together to place him at the age of eight in a Washington school conducted by Salmon P. Chase. Meade's reticence in maturity was shown by a letter to his wife in 1862. General McDowell had invited him to meet some cabinet members, including Secretary of the Treasury Chase. "I did not recall to Mr. Chase's recollection that I was a ci-devant pupil of his, not knowing how such reminiscences might be taken. . . ."[24] West Point provided an economical education; in manhood he was to confess, "I like fighting as little as any man."[25] President Jackson had appointed him to fill a vacancy from Pennsylvania. He was slender and frail and fourth from the youngest in a class of ninety-four, but at graduation he stood nineteenth among the fifty-six commissioned.

At no point in these early years were there signs of warmth in Meade's character; yet he was capable of the deepest affection, as was shown clearly after his marriage in 1840 to Margaretta Sergeant. Her father, John Sergeant, a leader of the Philadelphia bar, had been a representative in Congress and candidate for Vice President on the Henry Clay National Republican ticket in 1832.

Their companionship and devotion form a bright spot in Meade's rather somber personality. During his absences he wrote her daily letters expressing his intimate impressions, his hopes and confidences, words that suggest a deep spiritual faith as well as a sense of personal frustration, and small pleasantries that show a side the army never perceived of the irascible, high-tempered general. Even during active campaigning, Meade found time to write frequently—if not daily—and without haste or brevity. His marriage brought him into contact with Henry A. Wise, congressman for many terms and Governor of Virginia before the war, who married another of Sergeant's daughters. A close and lasting friendship sprang up between the brothers-in-law, which endured after Wise's wife died and he married again and after the two became generals in opposing armies.

Meade owed his army career to Wise's intercession. He had resigned a year after his graduation from West Point, to become a civil engineer and railroad builder, but found the going rough. Through the influence of his brother-in-law he was enabled to re-enter the service in 1842 as a second lieutenant of topographical engineers.[26] After his return from the Mexican War, Wise helped him to gain a transfer to the Army Engineer Corps. He was assigned to the Great Lakes area with headquarters in Detroit, where he was stationed, a captain, at the outbreak of the war.

Meade was intensely Unionist, was unalterably opposed to slavery, and looked on the war as one of subjugation, a term he used in letters to his wife. He told her the task was to overpower the South completely; "to do this we must have immense armies to outnumber them everywhere."[27] His irritability was well known to an army in which he had served successively as brigade, division, and corps commander. When he was aroused, according to Brigadier General Joseph W. Keifer, he "showed a fierce temper, yet was, in general, just."[28] He let his responsibilities weigh heavily and always seemed careworn. The worry trait was emphasized by bagginess under his eyes and a tendency to frown. His nearsightedness may have contributed to his nervousness and impatience. But above all else he was solid and reliable and these were the qualities most needed after the erratic Hooker.

Meade was confronted with difficult and shifty leadership in the War Department. Stanton, at heart a tyrant, was driving, ruthless, quarrelsome, but altogether patriotic; he was boisterous at his desk, contemptuous of opposition, unconcerned about niceties. He was amenable only to Lincoln, whose capacity he had eventually come to acknowledge. The conditions under which Lincoln and in turn Meade had to work were suggested by McClellan, who declared it "eminently characteristic" of Stanton to "say one thing to a man's face and just the reverse behind his back."[29]

How Stanton and Halleck pulled in harness is told, probably without much reportorial overstatement, by McClellan:

Speaking of Halleck, a day or two before he arrived in Washington Stanton came to caution me against trusting Halleck, who was, he said, probably the greatest scoundrel and most barefaced villain in America; he said that he was totally destitute of principle, and that in the Almaden Quicksilver case he had convicted Halleck of perjury in open court.[30] When Halleck arrived he came to caution me against Stanton, repeating almost precisely the same words that Stanton had employed. . . .

Of all the men whom I have encountered in high position Halleck was the most hopelessly stupid. It was more difficult to get an idea through his head than can be conceived by any one who never made the attempt. I do not think he ever had a correct military idea from beginning to end.[31]

4. The Riffraff Follows the Army

Conditions behind the Federal army at the time Meade took command were nothing short of frightful. Whitelaw Reid, one of the best of the Northern correspondents, had come from Washington to Frederick. His dispatch of June 29, the day after Meade took command, said the town was pandemonium, full of stragglers, with the liquor shops doing a land-office business; "just under my window scores of drunken soldiers are making the night hideous."[32] Meade had ordered the army to move north at four o'clock that morning and after it was on the roads he established his headquarters at Taneytown.

What Reid saw was the backwash. All over Frederick soldiers were trying to steal horses, sneak into unwatched private residences, or "are filling the air with the blasphemy of their drunken brawls." The loose nature of Hooker's generalship had invited rowdy elements to express themselves.

Reid gives a picture of Meade's headquarters near Taneytown, the Maryland hamlet named after Chief Justice Roger B. Taney, who lived near by. The town, like its distinguished resident, was "somewhat fallen into the sere and yellow leaf,"[33] blighted by the sudden descent of war. The vast trains of the Army of the Potomac blocked the streets; quartermasters were hurriedly searching for provisions, already grown scant; along the roads and across the rolling hills "far as the eye could reach, rose the glitter from the swaying points of bayonets." This mighty armed host was composed of the Second and Third corps of the Federal army, veterans as sturdy as ever marched on the continent, and worthy of better army commanders than Pope, Burnside and Hooker. The Second was Couch's old corps, from which Couch had resigned despairingly, having too weak a stomach for any more of Hooker.

Here at Taneytown was the nerve center of the army that must determine whether the United States would be one nation or two. Here were the hard-fighting men, quite a different crowd from the drunks and tramps Reid had passed on the road from Frederick. Half a mile east of Taneytown he reached a large camp which he compared to that of a battalion of cavalry. Couriers were coming and departing, engineers were scanning maps, baggage train was packed for moving at an instant's notice, horses remained saddled. Reid turned into the field, found a plain little tent, walked in, and saw the serious, thin-faced general seated on a campstool, bending over a map, a pen in his hand— Meade, the new commander of the army, a man to "impress you as a thoughtful student more than a dashing soldier."[34]

He considered Meade neither ungainly nor graceful. Although he was two years short of fifty his beard was grizzled and his hair, slightly curly, receded on a retreating forehead and gave an impression of baldness. Reid had overheard Lincoln say after the battle of Chancellorsville, "I tell you, I think a great deal of that fine fellow Meade,"[35] and now the fine fellow was issuing orders in the headquarters tent.

Perhaps Meade's first caller after his elevation was Reynolds, who said the command had "fallen where it belongs."[36] Next came Howard, the Eleventh Corps commander, nineteen years Meade's junior at West Point. He had traveled with Meade on the Great Lakes before the war and had served alongside him, but thought he looked different now. "He was excited," Howard recorded. "His coat was off. . . . As I entered his tent, he extended his hand and said, 'How are you, Howard?' He demurred at my congratulation. He looked tall and spare, weary, and a little flushed. . . ."[37]

Meade took over the Harpers Ferry garrison, with authority to shift it as he saw fit, but he did not pursue the plan of moving it and the Twelfth Corps into the Cumberland Valley to sever Lee's communications. Slocum brought up the Twelfth Corps to the main army while French was ordered to march the Harpers Ferry garrison to Frederick to protect the rear. These matters and a few promotions were Meade's first business, together with a long conference with trusted John Reynolds, whom he confirmed in command of the left wing. He also retained Butterfield as his chief of staff, recognizing the disadvantages of a change when a battle was momentarily expected. Like most new commanders, he wanted to hold a grand review. He quickly abandoned all thought of it when events showed that any day might bring a battle.[38]

Concentration

1. *A Grimy Spy Finds Longstreet*

Late on the night of June 28 at Longstreet's headquarters Colonel Sorrel was awakened by the provost guard, who had captured a suspicious character trying to make his way into camp. He was ragged and dirty—Sorrel's word was "filthy"—and he appeared to be suffering from exposure.[1] But Sorrel recognized him readily behind the grime and mud; he was Harrison, a shadowy character who flitted into and out of the story of the Confederacy and was last heard of after the war living in want in Baltimore. And not in many places, if any, did he leave any record of a home or first name.

Harrison had been sent by Secretary of War Seddon to Longstreet when he was besieging Suffolk; Sorrel had put him on the payroll at $150 a month, payable in United States currency. Sorrel watched him closely, aware that through the history of warfare, spies not uncommonly give as much information as they receive and thrive on more than one payroll. Eventually he concluded that of Harrison's leading passions, his love of greenbacks was equaled only by his hatred of Yankees. He was a man of medium height, stooped and bearded although only thirty, with unobtrusive manner and soft hazel eyes, and possessed such an ability to get around unnoticed that Sorrel soon found he could cover Washington and even comb through Secretary Stanton's office in the War Department.[2] Checking on him, Sorrel found that he did come from Mississippi and was fond of danger. The information he brought

80

proved accurate and no one could discover that he ever sold anything to the Federals. Thus a happy relationship was established between the spy—more gently termed a scout at Longstreet's headquarters—and the First Corps commander.

Before Longstreet left Culpeper for Pennsylvania he had summoned Harrison, loaded him with gold, and told him to go to the Federal camp and to Washington and bring back all the information he could garner. Asked where he could be found for a report, the general, always guarded, replied, "With the army. I shall be sure to be with it." Any man with gumption, he added, ought to be able to locate the headquarters of the First Corps of the Army of Northern Virginia.[3]

Harrison vanished, reappeared chatting in the Washington saloons, joined the Army of the Potomac as it entered Maryland, talked with the soldiers, traveled over the roads by night. When Longstreet learned later that Harrison drank and gambled, habits he judged incompatible with good intelligence work, he had Sorrel quit honoring his vouchers and turn him back to the War Department; but at the moment Harrison's methods were yielding beneficial results. When he appeared at Chambersburg he was loaded, not with liquor but with facts. He had procured a horse in Frederick and ridden the fifty miles through the rainy darkness.

Sorrel got a summary of what Harrison had and took him at once to Longstreet, whom he awoke. When Longstreet heard the report, he was "immediately on fire."[4] He had Major John W. Fairfax of his staff conduct the scout to General Lee. Lee questioned Harrison and listened with "great composure and minuteness."[5]

Harrison's first piece of news was that the entire Federal army was north of the Potomac, with headquarters at Frederick. To that moment Lee had not known of the crossing and judged it had not taken place because of his confidence in Stuart, who was expected to report any such move with all possible speed. Harrison stated also that Hooker had been relieved and Meade placed in command of the Federal army, which was all-important news to Lee, who respected Meade's ability whereas he had had little esteem for Hooker. Two corps were at Frederick and a third was near by.

Lee was disturbed and uncertain, but manifestly impressed. He had no corroborating intelligence from Stuart and did not know how much reliance he could place on Harrison. But he made quick decisions and almost at once he decided to accept the report and act on it. The word of a lone scout, about whom nobody knew a great deal, had to be relied on in place of information that should have been forthcoming from a cavalry division that was missing when most needed.[6]

Harrison brought another report which seemed vital. Federal troops, he said, were close to South Mountain. Colonel Marshall had been directed by Lee earlier that night to order Longstreet to move on the morning of the twenty-ninth to support Ewell in the attack on Harrisburg. Hill had been directed to cross the Susquehanna below Harrisburg, seize the railroad, and co-operate. Now Marshall was again summoned. With Lee sat a man in civilian dress who, Lee told him, was Longstreet's scout, who had brought them the first information about the enemy's movements north of the Potomac.[7]

According to Marshall, Lee inferred from Harrison's report that the main body of the Federals was turning west from Frederick to Middletown, which lay in the valley between the Catoctin and South Mountain ranges. Lee thought the enemy's purpose was to cross South Mountain and enter the Cumberland Valley, thus severing the communications between the Confederate army and Virginia. After Harrison had been dismissed, Lee pointed out that while his communications were by no means complete, they nevertheless were all he required as long as the Federals did not occupy the Cumberland Valley. What he needed chiefly was a line to replenish his ammunition. If the Federals occupied the valley, munitions convoys would be out of the question. Therefore, Lee explained, he would move his army east of the South Mountain range and threaten Baltimore and Washington, which would hold the Federal army east of South Mountain so as to protect those cities.[8]

Lee's decision was made within an hour or so after he heard Harrisons' report. Marshall was asked to countermand the marching orders of Ewell and Hill and to tell Longstreet to follow Hill eastward across South Mountain.

An element of irony here was that the Federal army was not moving toward the Cumberland Valley. Buford's cavalry was en route to Middletown that day and this apparently is what attracted the scout Harrison and bothered Lee. The three corps that had been there, the First, the Third, and the Eleventh, moved from Middletown to Frederick on June 28.[9] But, as has been noted, Meade had abandoned Hooker's plan of operating against Lee's communications. Halleck, the fretful guardian of Washington, felt that the Federal army was too far west already. He wanted it kept in a direct line between Lee and the capital. In response to his suggestion, Meade was inclining the army to the east to guard Baltimore and Washington, and not to the west to menace Lee's life line with Virginia.

Longstreet rose early and went directly to Lee's headquarters. General Lee already had issued his orders. The army would concentrate at Cashtown, where the Chambersburg-Baltimore turnpike debouched from South Mountain, or at Gettysburg, the first main road center east of the mountain.

Because the army was scattered over five southern Pennsylvania counties, most of June 29 had to be devoted to dispatching messengers and receiving the responses of the corps commanders. Dr. J. S. D. Cullen, medical director of Longstreet's corps, saw the excitement at headquarters "among couriers, quartermasters, commissaires, etc., all betokening some early movement." That afternoon Lee talked with a group in front of headquarters, Dr. Cullen among them. "Tomorrow, gentlemen," he said, "we will not move to Harrisburg as we expected, but will go over to Gettysburg and see what General Meade is after."[10]

2. Wagons, Bacon, Oats and Trouble

On the morning of June 28, when General Meade was beginning the first day of his new command, while the 32nd North Carolina Infantry was running up the official flag of the Confederacy in Carlisle and Extra Billy Smith was haranguing the York churchgoers, Jeb Stuart's wet and bedraggled troopers lay along the canal towpath near the Great Falls of the Potomac, resting and sleeping while their horses grazed on the fresh Maryland pastures.[11] The artillery horses were in the worst condition after their night's work of drawing the guns through the river. Whatever the urgency, the horses must be fed and rested or the world-famous Confederate cavalry would be rendered impotent.

When the animals had knocked the sharp edge from their hunger, Stuart ordered his men to start the search for the will-o-the-wisp right flank of Lee's army. Shortly before noon they reached the village of Rockville, nine miles from the District of Columbia line, astride the main highway linking Washington and Meade's army at Frederick. People were just leaving church. Girls attending a large female academy gathered in front of the school to watch the celebrated Confederate horsemen, who had appeared in a great gray cloud out of nowhere, riding unchallenged almost on the outskirts of fort-rimmed Washington. They greeted the gray-clad soldiers with outbursts of applause, partly no doubt because of the novelty of the spectacle and partly through sympathy with the Southern cause. Lieutenant Colonel Blackford judged it was a show of sympathy when the men stopped and the girls rushed up and cut souvenir buttons from their uniforms.[12]

Stuart was scarcely in the town when he saw a long creeping train of 150 Federal wagons winding in on the main road from Washington. Here was a luscious prize for the grasping. Hampton and a detail charged into the head of the train, surprised the unsuspecting wagoneers, and captured the guard and more than half the wagons. They were brand-new, were drawn by splendid mule teams, with fresh harness and gleaming trappings, and were loaded with provisions for Meade's army. These included hams, bacon, sugar, bread and crackers, and a goodly quantity of whisky in bottles, along with the main load of feed for stock.

While the head of the convoy was being attacked the teamsters in the rear turned around, lashed their mules, and sped back toward Washington. Hampton's men were quick to pursue. At a sharp turn a wagon overturned and something between twelve and twenty-four piled up behind it, an easy prey for the pursuers. On rushed the others, followed by Confederates, until Blackford of Stuart's staff found himself on a hill looking down on the city of Washington. There he had recall sounded and turned back. This was too big a morsel to be gobbled by a single squadron.[13]

When the total was counted Stuart found that he had captured 125 wagons, 900 mules and 400 men. Twenty-five wagons had escaped into Washington, where the teamsters spread the tidings of the Confederate Cavalry. Stuart toyed with the idea of a quick dash into Washington—how the enemy would talk about the boldness of such a stroke! —but he was already straining his orders to the limit, and such a gamble was not to be considered, although the thought of it was judged worthy of a place in his report.

As he rode out of Rockville the long train of wagons followed. Usually his failure to reach Ewell on time has been attributed to the necessity of adjusting his march to the pace of this creeping convoy. But the capture undoubtedly saved his command and was worth all the time expended. The main load was oats intended for Meade's horses.[14] The worn mounts of the Confederate cavalry, and especially the artillery horses, seemed to take on new life from one feeding after days of nothing but hasty pasturage.[15] For the time being Stuart's worry about feed could be dismissed.

Stuart's close approach threw terror into Washington. It became "a city beseiged, as after Bull Run," wrote Reid, the Cinncinnati *Gazette* correspondent. "All night long, troops were marching; orderlies with clanking sabres clattering along the streets; trains of wagons grinding over the bouldering avenues. . . . The quartermaster's department was like a bee-hive; everything was motion and hurry."[16] Stuart might have made a *coup de main* on the White House, but he could not have held the Federal capital more than half an hour.

A clear view of the enlistment difficulties in the Northern army was provided by an incident reported by Reid in Washington on the very day Stuart threatened the city. The term of enlistment of a New England regiment of more than 900 men had just expired. They marched sprucely down the street with "brilliant uniforms and unstained arms; faultless appearing officers and gorgeous drum major; clanging band; banners waving and bayonets gleaming in the morning sunlight." These men were marching home at a moment when a battle was about to decide the fate of the nation, although implored to stay two weeks, or even a week longer. "Would that Stuart could capture the train that bears them!" Reid wrote.[17]

Baltimore likewise was thrown into a near panic. Alarm bells were rung, home guards assembled.

Soon more apprehension was felt in Washington and the North. From Frederick, Meade, on his first day as commander, had sent in a list of promotions, and his recommendations had been approved by telegraph. Then the wire went dead and all communication between the army and the capital was severed. Rumors spread and Stanton feared Meade's army had encountered disaster. Halleck telegraphed Couch in Harrisburg that he had no contact with the army; Secretary of State Seward notified New York that the government was in extreme peril. Stuart had merely cut the telegraph lines as well as the railroad, and demonstrated again that fear feeds on the unknown.

Moving north to Cooksville, from which he drove a minor Federal force on the morning of the twenty-ninth, Stuart struck the Baltimore & Ohio Railroad at Hood's Mill, about midway between Baltimore and Harpers Ferry. He demolished it even though he had to work slowly with ill-suited tools, burned the bridge at Sykesville, and disrupted the flow of supplies to Meade's army; the trains which came up while the troopers hacked at the rails were able to stop at a safe distance and back away.

Meanwhile, Stuart was running short on time and information. He combed the surrounding country for intelligence from friendly Marylanders and read the newspapers eagerly. One account, "with great particularity," said that Early had reached Wrightsville; consequently, he continued his northward movement and entered Westminster, on the Baltimore-Gettysburg pike, in the late afternoon. There the Confederates were startled by a sudden gallant charge of a Federal squadron which dashed impetuously against their vastly superior force. The attackers proved to be the 1st Delaware Cavalry, who were dispersed toward Baltimore, where they carried new alarms.

Stuart's captured wagon train now became an impediment, as his sleepless and haggard men rode gropingly[18] forward. The oats that had saved the horses were exhausted. Fortunately they found at Westminster ample forage for one feeding.

At Westminster Stuart was twenty-four miles from Gettysburg, which he could readily have reached on the morning of June 30, perhaps to have formed a juncture with Johnston Pettigrew's North Carolina brigade, moving toward Gettysburg from the opposite direction.[19] But as Blackford pointed out, he knew nothing on June 29—nor did anyone else at that time—of the concentration that would occur two days later at Gettysburg. If Stuart could but have obtained an inkling of Lee's orders for concentration at Cashtown or Gettysburg, to which the other Confederate commands were responding at that very moment, his course would have been clear. As it was he guessed wrong and moved north to Hanover, instead of northwest to Gettysburg.

3. A Five Mile Gap Rules a Nation's Fate

Jeb Stuart selected the route by Hanover, still moving north, in order to avoid the Federal cavalry commanded by Judson Kilpatrick, which he heard was in the vicinity of Littlestown, fourteen miles from Westminster. But Kilpatrick outguessed him and instead of waiting at Littlestown, moved to Hanover, where Stuart ran head on into him. From the hills south of the town Stuart saw the blue column of horsemen and while he would have preferred not to fight, he had no alternative.

Before noon on June 30 the 2nd North Carolina entered Hanover, charged the Federal troopers, and drove them beyond the town limits. [20] Kilpatrick, coming up with Farnsworth's brigade, in turn struck the North Carolinians and hurled them back in confusion. Stuart and Blackford were approaching and witnessed the clash. They tried to rally the regiment but it had been scattered and had no formation.

Stuart's command had been strung out along the roadway, with Hampton two miles in the rear behind the wagon train. Fitzhugh Lee's brigade came up first and launched itself against Kilpatrick's rear at the moment when Custer was coming to the aid of Farnsworth. Thereafter the battle was a desultory charge and countercharge, then long-range firing.[21] The opposing commanders appeared to have the same desire. Kilpatrick wanted to prevent Stuart from taking the Gettysburg road, and Stuart in turn wanted to move away from the Gettysburg road and take the York road north and east, continuing his search for Early. To protect his wagons Stuart could not unite his entire command for a mass attack, nor could Kilpatrick make headway against the guns that protected the Confederate position south of the town. After fighting for four hours, both let the engagement lull, and when darkness came, both drew off. Stuart made a detour around Hanover and rode through the night toward York with his 125 wagons and the 400 prisoners he had captured since paroling the 400 teamsters he had taken at Rockville.

The engagement at Hanover, while minor, is of interest to those who believe that either destiny or chance control great events. While Stuart was trying to free himself and find the right flank of Lee's army, Early's division was passing across his front on the roads leading from York to Gettysburg and from York to Heidlersburg. Gordon's brigade and White's cavalry battalion were on the York-Gettysburg pike, which at Abbottstown is six miles north of Hanover and at the crossing of the Yellow Springs road five miles from New Oxford. As the Confederate infantry passed along the road they heard the firing five and six miles to the south, but did not suspect it was Stuart. Here Lee's staff had been at fault. After having written Stuart orders—lacking in sharpness—telling him to get in touch with Ewell's right, Colonel Marshall did not emphasize to Early the need of keeping a sharp lookout for the cavalry. In complete ignorance that he might be approaching, Early moved across Stuart's front.[22]

Possibly the fate of the Confederacy rested on a gap of five or six miles.

At York Stuart found that time had run out. Early had gone. The York residents who had fraternized with Extra Billy Smith were chary with their information about the direction Early had taken. Stuart was still gambling on the whereabouts of Lee's army. He guessed Carlisle, and again guessed wrong. On the verge of exhaustion he moved northwest through the night, his mounts jaded and mules famished and some of his men asleep in their saddles.

As he started toward Carlisle Stuart sent two staff officers, Major Andrew W. Venable and Captain Henry Lee, to look for army headquarters somewhere to the west, the direction in which Early had vanished.[23] When he approached Carlisle on the evening of July 1, he found it occupied not by Lee, but by Major General William F. ("Baldy") Smith with Federal militia forces. He had ridden 125 miles since the previous morning and was not in good spirits. When his demand for surrender was rejected, he dropped some shells into the Carlisle barracks and set them on fire. At last, after a long, difficult and almost futile ride—which had given the enemy only minor inconveniences and had severely impeded the movements of his own army—Stuart learned, from one of Lee's messengers instead of his own, the whereabouts of the Confederate army. In place of bringing intelligence, it was he who received it.

Colonel Marshall later tried to have Stuart court-martialed; he even declared, at a small dinner party, that Stuart should have been shot. He did not recognize that the lack of positive statement in his own composition of orders was perhaps more responsible for the absence of the cavalry than any other factor.[24]

4. The Wagons Roll Toward Gettysburg

Through June 27 to the night of June 28, while Lee waited in Messersmith's woods, his distress over his missing cavalry became obvious to almost the entire army. "He repeatedly observed," said Chief of Staff Marshall, "that the enemy's army must still be in Virginia as he had heard nothing from Stuart."[25] The distraught general asked virtually all comers if they had heard anything of Stuart. Marshall and others had been struck by the unusual lethargy of the army, slowed near to paralysis by lack of information. It could easily have been in Gettysburg on the morning of July 1, occupying the heights south of the town, had it known the locations of the Federal corps—the information Stuart was supposed to provide.[26]

Lee's apprehension, extending almost to physical agony, impressed itself forcibly on Dr. J. L. Suesserott, one of Chambersburg's leading physicians, although the doctor did not understand its cause. He went to Lee on Monday, June 29, to obtain an exemption of his neighbor's blind mare from seizure. While Lee had the paper prepared, the doctor studied the features and movements of the noted commander. He said he had never seen so much emotion depicted on a human countenance as on Lee's. "With his hands at times clutching his hair, and with contracted brow, he would walk with rapid strides for a few rods and then, as if he bethought himself of his actions, he would with a sudden jerk produce an entire change in his features and demeanor and cast an inquiring gaze on me, only to be followed in a moment by the same contortions of face and agitation of person."[27] Even if allowance is made for some exaggeration, it is clear that Lee was deeply disturbed or physically unwell.

Major General Henry Heth, who saw him from time to time, said he discussed the absence of Stuart with every officer who visited him. "Can you tell me where General Stuart is?" he would say, or, "Where on earth is my cavalry?" or "Have you any news of the enemy's movements? What is the enemy going to do?" And again: "If the enemy does not find us, we must try to find him, in the absence of the cavalry, as best we can."

Mrs. Ellen McClellan visited Lee mainly to get his autograph but ostensibly to request help for the town's needy, which Lee supplied. She was impressed with his sadness. He told her war was a cruel thing: all he desired was that "they" would let him go home and eat his bread in peace. Mrs. McClellan particularly noticed that Lee had the headquarters horses carefully picketed so that they could not injure the trees in the grove where he camped.[28]

On one of his last days in Messersmith's woods, a caller was heard to congratulate him on having a mediocre opponent in the new Federal commander. Lee corrected him quickly; Meade, he said, was a soldier of ability and intelligence, conscientious and painstaking. He would make no mistake in front of the Confederate army, as some of his predecessors had done, and if Lee made a mistake, Meade would be certain to take advantage of it.[29]

Quite as much as the cavalry, Lee missed Stuart himself, on whom he had come to rely for inspiration almost as much as for information. As Sorrel pointed out, the cavalry which Stuart had left with Lee amounted to nothing. "It was the great body of that splendid horse under the leader Stuart that Lee wanted. He was the eyes and ears and strong right arm of the commander. . . ."

Stuart's delay possibly cost Lee also the Wrightsville bridge, which the cavalry might have taken and held until Early could bring up his infantry. That would have allowed Early to operate on the north side of the Susquehanna against Lancaster and Harrisburg. The odds were great that both would have fallen.

Lee's concentration toward Cashtown and Gettysburg was in full progress on June 30. Longstreet arrived in the early morning; after a brief discussion Lee broke up his headquarters in Messersmith's woods and the two rode together to Greenwood, a hamlet in the South Mountain pass between Chambersburg and Cashtown.

The concentration had begun in the early morning hours. Sometime after midnight in Chambersburg, Jacob Hoke, who had been sending all important information to Governor Curtin, awakened his wife with news of activity in the Confederate army. The roll of a drum was heard from Pickett's camp. Lights shown for miles along South Mountain and up the valley toward Shippensburg. The Hokes peered through half-closed shutters at the long line of heavily loaded wagons groaning on their axles as they passed through Chambersburg. Some were being driven at a trot. They were coming from the direction of Carlisle, turning at the diamond and heading toward Gettysburg.[30] Next morning Hoke dispatched a messenger to Governor Curtin, telling of Lee's concentration. Apparently the intelligence got through to Washington by telegraph and on to Meade's headquarters in Taneytown that night.[31] Confirmatory information that Lee was falling back from the Susquehanna was sent by Brigadier General Hermann Haupt from Harrisburg at 11:30 P.M., June 30. York and Carlisle had been evacuated and Lee's aim, Haupt suggested, apparently was to move suddenly against Meade. His concentration was expected near Chambersburg instead of at Gettysburg.

5. *Meade's Object Is to Fight*

Meade's plan, as he drove northward, was to find the enemy and fight him: "My object being, at all hazards, to compel the enemy to loose his hold on the Susquehanna, and meet me in battle at some point." He was not thinking then in terms of a defensive action, of holding Lee, but of expelling him.

When it became clear on June 30 that the Southern army was concentrating, Meade began to study the terrain. He directed Reynolds to proceed to Gettysburg and examine the ground there. He told the accomplished engineer, Brigadier General Andrew A. Humphreys, commanding a division of Sickles' corps, to determine the nature of the positions around Emmitsburg. He ordered his engineers to examine the topography in his immediate section of northern Maryland and draw up a defensive line along which the army could concentrate if Lee crossed South Mountain.

They laid out a line along Pipe Creek, reaching from Manchester, on the right, to Middleburg on the left. The right was on high ground and the left near the confluence of Pipe Creek with the Monocacy River. This line would be of particular value in guarding the approaches to both Baltimore and Washington. It was a strong line, with the meandering stream immediately in its front. The two eminences in its rear,

Paris Ridge and Dug Hill Ridge, would be suitable for the location of reserves and for a secondary defense in case of trouble. It had a good base at Westminster, a road center to which Meade ordered the army trains retired.

Late on June 30 Meade issued his Pipe Creek Circular, assigning to the corps commanders their positions in the Pipe Creek line. The orders were tentative. The line would be adopted if developments did not dictate his fighting elsewhere. Employment of this line would involve a withdrawal, to which some of the Federal generals took exception, but its preparation was a wise precaution even though the chance encounter of the armies elsewhere meant that it was never used.

Meade's instructions to Reynolds at noon on June 30 gave a clear, concise picture of his situation: "We are as concentrated as my present information of the position of the enemy justifies. I have pushed out the cavalry in all directions to feel for them, and as soon as I have made up any positive opinion of their position I will move again. In the meantime, if they advance against me I must concentrate at that point where they show the strongest force."[32]

Those instructions, rather than the Pipe Creek Circular, guided Reynolds as he went to Gettysburg.

On the night of June 30 Lee's infantry was well up, extending from Heidlersburg to Chambersburg, a distance of about twenty-eight miles. The Federal army was extended about the same distance but had greater depth. Hancock at Uniontown was twenty miles south of Gettysburg and Sedgwick at Manchester was thirty-five miles southeast. In a concentration at Gettysburg Lee would have the advantage of bringing his army together near its center, while Meade would have to close on the corps farthest to his left. Meade's concentration consequently would require more time.

Of Lee's army, Ewell's corps had been most dispersed. After Lee had told Trimble to join Ewell and help capture Harrisburg, Trimble began to apply pressure. He reached Ewell in Carlisle on Sunday, June 28, told him the city could be captured easily, emphasized that Lee expected it, and volunteered to take it with one brigade. Ewell fell in with the idea. They arranged their plans on the twenty-ninth and Trimble made ready to march on Harrisburg before daybreak on the thirtieth.

Jenkins had taken his cavalry brigade into Mechanicsburg, eight miles from Harrisburg, on the night of the twenty-eighth and had bivouacked his men two miles nearer the city. His patrols reached almost within sight of the Pennsylvania capital. It is likely Trimble could have carried the town, defended only by militia, although he might have required more than a brigade. But on the night of June 29 Ewell received Lee's concentration orders, notifying him to march to Cashtown or Gettysburg "according to circumstances."

Lee's attitude, leisurely for several days, now called for celerity. Ewell at once dispatched Captain Elliott Johnston with a copy of the orders for Early at York, together with oral instructions for Early to return speedily to the foot of South Mountain. At daylight on June 30 Early's troops were moving toward Heidlersburg and Gettysburg. Ewell left Carlisle with Rodes and Trimble on the same morning and stopped at Heidlersburg. Johnson kept his division in the vicinity of Fayetteville guarding the corps trains that had passed during the night of the twenty-ninth through Chambersburg.

After dark on June 30 Early, on whom Ewell had come to rely so heavily as to be almost dominated by him, joined the corps commander at Heidlersburg, his division having been left in bivouac three miles east. The four generals—Ewell, Trimble, Early and Rodes—met in conference and studied Lee's dispatch.[33] Ewell was a general devoted to the letter of his orders. He had received some false information that the Eleventh Federal Corps was in Gettysburg and was baffled about how to comply with Lee's wishes. The dispatch from Lee was read and reread and commented on repeatedly. Early in particular let fly a stream of oaths about an order written with such ambiguity as to name both Cashtown and Gettysburg, seven miles apart, as concentration points. Which one, the generals debated, did Lee prefer? Ewell asked Trimble's opinion. He had been with Lee more recently than the others and had seen Lee touch the map at Gettysburg. He said he could interpret the order in only one way, which was that they should advance on Gettysburg and notify Lee at once of their movement.[34] But talk continued and nothing was determined that night.

Next morning Ewell decided on what was, in effect, a straddle. They would march toward Middletown, Pennsylvania, the town being about what its name implied—a midway place from which either Cashtown or Gettysburg might be reached conveniently. As they began their march a messenger was sent to Lee for more positive orders. Ewell reached Middletown at ten o'clock on the morning of July 1. Fifteen minutes later a message came from A. P. Hill requesting Ewell to come to Gettysburg with all possible speed.

CHAPTER EIGHT

Pettigrew's Encounter

1. A Rifleman, a Nephew and a Scholar

Heth, commanding Hill's advance division, was at Cashtown on the night of June 29, Pettigrew's brigade holding the forward position. As a precaution Pettigrew sent Company B of the 52nd North Carolina Infantry, under Lieutenant W. E. Kyle, to Millerstown, a village five miles to the south and a short distance north of Fairfield, which was on the main road from Hagerstown to Gettysburg.[1]

Buford's Federal cavalry division, which had been at Middletown, Maryland, had crossed South Mountain into the Cumberland Valley early on the morning of June 29, moved up the western side of the range from Boonsboro, Maryland, to Waynesboro, Pennsylvania, and again crossed the mountain, moving to the east side by way of Monterey Pass.

As Buford left the mountains one of his brigades, under Colonel William Gamble, passed near Fairfield and saw the bivouac fires of Lieutenant Kyle's outpost on Newpilman's farm north of the town. Later in the evening Gamble drew nearer to drive off the Confederates if possible, and some shots were exchanged—a skirmish, both Gamble and Kyle termed it.[2] Gamble did not want to bring down additional Confederates by heavy artillery firing. Buford seemed confused about this force, saying it was two Mississippi regiments which he could have destroyed had he been given timely information and a guide. He declared the inhabitants knew of his arrival and the enemy's whereabouts but appeared to be afraid to tell, saying, "the rebels will destroy our houses if we tell anything."[3]

Buford withdrew southward to Emmitsburg on the morning of the thirtieth and reported the incident to his chief, Pleasanton, who passed on to Reynolds news of Gamble's brush with Southern infantry, the first encountered in the Gettysburg area. Kyle continued his outpost at Millerstown until that night, then rejoined Pettigrew on Marsh Creek, three and a half miles west of Gettysburg.

Heth's division, which was becoming the spearhead as Lee approached Gettysburg, had been the last organized of the Army of Northern Virginia, having been brought together from scattered brigades and regiments to fill out the new corps created for A. P. Hill.

Henry Heth, usually called Harry, had fallen instinctively into a military career, being the grandson of an officer in Washington's army and son of an officer in the War of 1812. He was cousin of George Pickett and had been at West Point at the same time, though he had been appointed from Virginia a year later than Pickett, appointed from Illinois. Like Pickett, he had remained in the regular army until Virginia, their native state, seceded.

Heth had the distinction of being the foremost authority on the rifle in the old army, a recognition he had won by much study, practice and writing as a lieutenant and captain after the Mexican War. When the 9th and 10th Regular Army infantry regiments were organized in 1855, they were designated rifle regiments and given special drill and equipment. For field music they had bugles in place of the customary fife and drum corps. They wore distinctive uniforms with green facings. They held regular rifle practice under the direction of Captain Heth. Heth's book, *A System of Target Practice,* was the official range guide used in the service.

At the age of thirty-seven, when he was given a division in the Confederate army, he was looked on as a capable officer despite his failure to halt the enemy in West Virginia, a theater that had proved unfortunate for Confederates and propitious for Federals in earlier stages of the war. He was an intelligent conversationalist whose company Lee enjoyed, yet he lacked Hood's verve or Early's brusqueness and does not stand out among the sharp, vital personalities of this spirited army. Some of his associates came to regard him as impetuous in decisions and rash in combat, but there was no tendency as yet to distrust him.

Heth's division included two brigades that had served in A. P. Hill's old division, the Virginians now under Colonel John M. Brockenbrough and the Alabama and Tennessee regiments of Brigadier General James

J. Archer. The others were Pettigrew's North Carolinians and a brigade thrown together from the Richmond defenses, consisting of Mississippi and North Carolina troops, commanded by Brigadier General Joseph R. Davis, nephew of the Confederate President.

The President's nephew had been commissioned in the autumn of 1862, a bit of nepotism that provoked grumblings in the Confederate War Department. Favorites were advanced, ran the complaint, while "men of mind, men who wrought up the Southern people . . . are hurled into the background."[4] The promotion was also noted as an event that helped bring on the resignation of George Wythe Randolph, grandson of Thomas Jefferson, as the Confederate Secretary of War, possibly having "operated on him as an emetic."[5] Davis was a pleasant and unpretending man; he would have been more discreet, considering his lack of military experience and his kinship to the President, to take a lower grade.

Of the four brigade commanders in the new division the most arresting was Pettigrew. In the brief term of life that remained for him before a Federal bullet found his vitals, he was to bring on the battle and end the campaign, and command nearly half the troops in the most spectacular assault of that epochal combat.

Brigadier General James Johnston Pettigrew—he dropped the James for most purposes—was regarded in North Carolina as versatile almost to the point of genius. A superior officer judged him capable of assuming the responsibilities even of Lee himself,[6] should events make it necessary, although he had never attended a class in professional military tactics. His early education by private tutors at the spacious family estate of Bonvara, in coastal Tyrrell County, North Carolina, was aimed at a professional, not a military career. But his comprehension was keen and his capacity for acquiring new information apparently inexhaustible. The peaceful homestead where he spent his early years overlooked the blue waters of Lake Scuppernong, and the plantation extended along the Scuppernong River, from which the luscious Southern grapes, with their rare bouquet, take their name.

Pettigrew was a slender, handsome man of quick gestures and prompt decisions, with shining black hair and mustache and a dark complexion denoting the strong Latin strain of his French ancestry. His black eyes were sharp and penetrating. Now a soldier at the age of thirty-five, he had already achieved recognition as author, diplomat, lawyer, linguist, and legislator.

His marks were the highest that had ever been made at the University of North Carolina,[7] which had graduated many eminent scholars and men distinguished in national and state affairs. A graceful, athletic youth, he had led his class at Chapel Hill in fencing, boxing and the singlestick, as well as in mathematics, the classical languages, and all the other liberal arts courses.

Pettigrew had received distinction from the start. When he delivered the valedictory address at the graduation exercises in 1847, the silver-haired President of the United States, James Knox Polk, had by chance returned to visit his alma mater, where he, too, had won high scholastic honors. Polk was accompanied by a fellow alumnus, Secretary of the Navy John Young Mason, and by Captain Matthew F. Maury, the distinguished naval hydrographer and meteorologist, who was then engaged in establishing the National Observatory and Hydrographic Office, and was launching into his career of oceanography and the preparation of his great work, *The Physical Geography of the Sea.* Before the commencement events, these three looked in on the final examinations in mathematics and astronomy, and were so impressed with young Pettigrew's proficiency that they invited him to return with them and become an instructor in the Naval Observatory. There he also worked as a teacher in the Nautical Almanac Office.

The ardor of his devotion to the cause of the Southern people was a revolt, no doubt, from association with his cantankerous uncle, James Louis Petigru, dean of the Charleston, South Carolina, bar. When Johnston Pettigrew decided to take up law, he studied for a time in Baltimore and then entered his uncle's office, where the shingle was confusing because the contentious senior preferred the shorter version of the family's Huguenot surname.

Petigru the elder had been combating public opinion in South Carolina ever since the nullification days of John C. Calhoun, standing always for the Federal Union. By 1863, when he was seventy-one years old, he was looked on as the only man in the state who had not seceded. This distinction he prankishly sought to emphasize in church each Sunday morning by rising from his knees when the rector in his prayer reached the regular request for divine assistance for the President of the Confederate States.[8] Petigru appeared to delight in the consternation his intransigence provoked. The eminent old man left behind the monumental work of the codification of South Carolina laws, for which he is still respected. But long after he is forgotten his trenchant irony will be remembered in a wartime witticism often repeated in periods of inflation that "you take your money to the market in your market basket and bring home your groceries in your pocketbook."[9]

After obtaining his license to practice in South Carolina young Pettigrew departed to study civil law in Germany. He traveled extensively, became proficient in French, German, Italian and Spanish, with a reading knowledge of Hebrew and Arabic, and spent seven years abroad writing and in diplomatic service.

Pettigrew sensed the approach of hostilities between the states. Late in 1859, as a lawyer in Charleston, he entered a rifle company and soon became its colonel. His command of a North Carolina brigade resulted from the fortuitous circumstance that he was recognized on the Raleigh railroad station platform as he traveled to Richmond with South Carolina troops. Delay in mustering his Charleston regiment into the Confederate service caused it to disband, so that the men might enlist with other units. The impatient Pettigrew enlisted as a private in Hampton's Legion, which was heading for the front. Word passed among his North Carolina friends that he had been seen going to battle without even a corporal's stripes. Almost in a twinkling he was elected colonel of the 22nd North Carolina Regiment, then stationed at Camp Ellis near Raleigh.

An officer who tented near him for several months described him: "He was quick in his movements and quick in his perception and in his decision. . . . His habit was to pace restlessly up and down in front of his tent with a cigar in his mouth which he never lighted. . . . As gentle and modest as a woman, there was [about him] an undoubted capacity to command, which obtained for Pettigrew instant obedience." He was "courteous, kindly and chivalric," and "unfailingly a gentlemen."[10]

When he was offered a brigadier generalship he declined it. But both President Davis and General Joseph E. Johnston had noticed Pettigrew and the offer was renewed with more emphasis in the spring of 1862. Pettigrew commanded a brigade in the early part of the campaign at Yorktown. He was left for dead on the Fair Oaks battlefield and his loss was mourned in Richmond and Raleigh. But he recovered consciousness in a Federal prison camp and was exchanged, to find that his brigade had been assigned to his fellow Carolinian, Brigadier General Dorsey Pender. A new brigade was formed for Pettigrew, which he led on the North Carolina coast and at Gettysburg.

2. Pettigrew's Quest for Shoes

In Cashtown on the night of June 29 Heth recalled Jubal Early's report of a quantity of boots and shoes in Gettysburg. The need for shoes in both armies was already refuting the oracular Napoleon's dictum that "an army marches on its stomach"; Heth directed Pettigrew to take his brigade and probe Early's statement.[11]

Pettigrew mustered his brigade for pay at Cashtown in the early morning of June 30, then marched down the Gettysburg road, the 11th North Carolina Regiment in front, preceded by skirmishers.

The 11th was one of the most highly regarded regiments in the service. At the time it was incorporated, the inspector general stated to General Lee that "the Eleventh Regiment of North Carolina troops is the best drilled, the best equipped and the best armed regiment in the Army of Northern Virginia."[12] It contained the survivors of the old 1st North Carolina Volunteers, called the "Bethel Regiment," that at Bethel had fought the first engagement of the war and suffered the first loss of life in battle in the cause of Southern freedom. Its colonel, Collett Leventhorpe, was looked on as "probably the best finished and equipped field officer in the Confederate service."[13]

About two miles from Gettysburg the advance party arrested a well-mounted civilian who said he was a physician making a visit to a patient. Though not suspecting that any enemy was near, Colonel Leventhorpe questioned the doctor closely. To his surprise the man said there were between four and five thousand Federal troops in the vicinity and a much larger Federal force a few miles distant.[14]

Whether the doctor knew or was trying to frighten the Confederate regiment is not clear, but his statement caused Leventhorpe to halt until he could consult Pettigrew, farther back in the column. The doctor's account—whether he spoke from knowledge or guile—and Leventhorpe's halt probably served to prevent a clash between elements of the two armies in Gettysburg until the day following.

Another of Pettigrew's regiments had a delaying encounter. The 47th North Carolina was marching eagerly from Cashtown, supposedly on an expedition for shoes—many of the soldiers were barefoot—when a civilian on a farm horse rode leisurely out of a near-by woods and asked where he could find the commanding officer. Some of the men thought he was a spy, but he was sent to the head of the column. Almost at once the regiment was halted and the men were directed to take cover. A minute later several shots were fired at long range from woods on both sides of the road. The farmer had come not to spy, but to warn. The regiment was quite certain it escaped an ambuscade.[15] He was probably the member of the Knights of the Golden Circle whom Pettigrew's assistant adjutant general, Captain Louis G. Young, said rode out to tell the general that Federal cavalry was close at hand.

While Petttigrew was marching toward Gettysburg, Harrison, Longstreet's spy, rode past into the town. Before the troops approached the outskirts, Harrison rode back and confirmed for Pettigrew the information he already had from two other sources that elements of the Army of the Potomac were not far distant.[16] These warnings made the general still more circumspect. An officer reported he heard a drum roll on the other side of the town. Pettigrew had been told that he would likely encounter home guards but orders to him were "prc-cmptory," that if he found any portion of the Army of the Potomac, he was not to attack it.[17]

Pettigrew rode abreast Leventhorpe at the head of the column and halted the brigade near the Willoughby Run crossing a mile outside the town. He went forward with an advance party to the ridge crossed by the Cashtown pike northwest of Gettysburg, from which he could view the surrounding country. Gettysburg with its ten roads, a town of about three thousand people, lay drousing in a peaceful valley, with golden wheat fields stretching north and south and the glory of early summer spread about; beyond the town broken, wooded hills were capped by a jutting promontory at the southern end. Southern eyes swept the country cursorily, their interest fastened on the village, about which hurried numerous civilians gathering at the public square. It was near noon. The appearance of Southern infantry again had caused the town to seethe with excitement.

Observing that Gettysburg was unoccupied by Federal troops, Pettigrew sent skirmishers ahead and was preparing to move the entire brigade forward when his attention was arrested by a movement far to the south. There on the road from Emmitsburg was a long dark column. Through his glasses he was able to identify it as Northern cavalry.

Buford's two brigades had come through Emmitsburg after encountering Pettigrew's picket near Fairfield on the preceding evening. Dashing ahead of Buford's division was a detachment of Company C, 3rd Indiana Cavalry, commanded by Captain Henry B. Sparks. They entered Gettysburg at a gallop and picked up three or four Confederate prisoners.[18] These may have been some of Pettigrew's skirmishers, but in view of the Indianian's account that they "seemed to be straggling through the streets and mingling with the citizens,"[19] more likely they remained from Early's passage four days before.

Gamble, commanding the first of Buford's brigades, took credit for driving Pettigrew out of Gettysburg, but there was no exchange of fire and Pettigrew retired slowly, reluctant to abandon the needed shoes.

Pettigrew's orders were not sufficiently flexible to allow him to hazard his brigade in a chance encounter with a large force that might have infantry support. He halted three and a half miles out on the Cashtown road, just west of the stone bridge over Marsh Creek, where the brigade bivouacked in a beautiful grove south of the roadway.

Guard duty falling on the 26th North Carolina, Lieutenant Colonel John R. Lane established a picket line that included a segment of the roadway. Later two distressed women conducted by a sentry told him they had been cut off from their houses, which were close at hand. Lane promptly reassured them that the regiment did not make war on women, ordered the picket line re-established so that it would embrace their houses, and let them pass.[20]

Pettigrew rode into Cashtown in the late afternoon and was telling Heth of his encounter when A. P. Hill came up and received the report in person.

"The only force at Gettysburg is cavalry, probably a detachment of observation," said Hill. "I am just from General Lee and the information he has from his scouts corroborates what I have received from mine—that is, the enemy are still at Middleburg, and have not yet struck their tents."

"If there is no objection, General," interjected Heth, "I will take my division tomorrow and go to Gettysburg and get those shoes."

"None in the world," Hill replied.[21]

Both Hill and Heth discredited Pettigrew's information. He had served under neither and they appeared more impressed with his civilian background than his extraordinary capacity. As he moved away from Gettysburg Pettigrew had left two mounted staff officers, Captain Young and Lieutenant Walter H. Robertson, to watch Buford. They found the assignment easy because the rolling country offered ridges behind which they could hide.[22]

The Federal troopers came out of Gettysburg and moved northwest on the Cashtown road. Whenever their advance party came within three or four hundred yards, the two Confederates showed themselves atop a ridge and the Federals halted. This process was repeated several times, each side being more intent on observation than on molesting the other.

As Pettigrew talked with Hill and Heth he saw that neither believed that units of the main Federal army were anywhere near Gettysburg. Pettigrew was insistent that where cavalry was clearing the way, infantry would not be far behind. Hill and Heth apparently became a bit impatient. In the words of Captain Young, they "expressed their doubts so positively"[23] that Pettigrew called Young over and asked him to tell the corps commander exactly what he had seen while reconnoitering the force that had followed them out of Gettysburg. Since Young had served under Hill during the Seven Days' Battles around Richmond, Pettigrew thought his words might have weight where those of a brigadier general did not.

Hill asked Young to describe the character of the troops he had seen and Young said their movements were unquestionably those of trained soldiers, not home guards. But it was difficult to dislodge fixed notions. Hill had prejudged the case and would not correct his conclusions. He still did not think any portion of the Army of the Potomac was in their front. Then, in "emphatic words," he asserted that he indeed hoped it was true, as that was exactly the place where he wanted the Army of the Potomac to be.[24] It was clear from his attitude, however, that he did not accept the intelligence at full value even after talking with Young.

"This spirit of unbelief had taken such hold," Young wrote, "that I doubt if any of the commanders of brigades, except General Pettigrew, believed that we were marching to battle, a weakness on their part which rendered them unprepared for what was about to happen."

Pettigrew then sought General Archer, whose brigade by the normal process of rotation would head the march on the next day. Pettigrew described in minute detail the topography between Cashtown and Gettysburg. He called attention to a road leading in at right angles from the south which the enemy might employ to disrupt his line of march. He cautioned about the right flank. He reviewed also the configuration of the ground around Gettysburg and mentioned in particular a ridge west of the town which would be suitable for defensive purposes, and where, he emphasized, Archer "would probably find the enemy."

Captain Young commented: "Archer listened, but believed not [and] marched on unprepared."[25]

Buford's long column of blue-clad hussars quieted and inspired the Gettysburg citizenry. As the column passed out the Cashtown road Buford galloped ahead to the crest of the western hill to witness the retirement of the brigade of hostile infantry. He sent the information to Reynolds at once. Back from Reynolds to Meade, then on to Halleck and Stanton in Washington, went the word that large infantry detachments of Lee's army were emerging east of the South Mountain passes. This gave the most positive notice yet received that Lee was abandoning his efforts against Harrisburg and Philadelphia and was concentrating toward Baltimore and Washington to shake off the Federal army that had followed him across the Potomac.

Buford established pickets west and north of the town. He deduced that the Confederates would return in greater strength in the morning, and wholly on his own responsibility he determined to hold the ground until Reynolds could bring up infantry assistance. He spent the evening inspecting the terrain and outlining his plan to his two brigade commanders, Gamble and Colonel Thomas C. Devin. He gently rebuked Devin when that confident officer assured him he could look after everything in his front for the next twenty-four hours.

Buford selected for his main line the ridge on which stood the McPherson house and farm buildings a scant mile northwest of the Gettysburg town square, overlooking the long sweep of the road toward Cashtown.

Preparations were being made as well in the Confederate camp. On the night of June 30 Hill sent couriers informing Lee of Pettigrew's encounter with Buford and advising Ewell that he intended to advance the next morning. At five o'clock on the morning of July 1 Heth took up his line of march, accompanied by Pegram's battalion of artillery, and Hill ordered Pender to fall in behind with his division and McIntosh's battalion of artillery. The quest for shoes and Federal soldiers would be undertaken in force. At Marsh Creek Heth picked up Pettigrew and in the hot mist of the July morning approached Gettysburg, concealed behind its hills.

CHAPTER NINE

McPherson's Heights

1. Reynolds Decides on a Battlefield

As Heth moved toward Gettysburg with Archer's veteran Alabama brigade in the lead, first place in the march went to the 13th Alabama regiment commanded by Colonel Birkett Davenport Fry.

Fry, a subtle old soldier whom General Braxton Bragg called "a man with a gunpowder reputation,"[1] had been a top lieutenant of the Tennessee adventurer William Walker in the conquest of Nicaragua. He had fought at Rivas, commanded a brigade at Granada, quieted the Metagalpa Indians, and no doubt ultimately would have been noosed with his chief had he not been sent on a recruiting expedition to San Francisco. He obtained the men but not return transportation, and Walker's cause meantime spiraled downward.

A Virginian by birth, a wanderer by instinct, he studied at Washington College, Pennsylvania, at Virginia Military Institute, and at West Point, though he did not graduate; gained distinction under Joseph E. Johnston in the Mexican War; became a Sacramento, California, lawyer, then a Tallassee, Alabama, cotton ginner, and when the war broke, leader of an Alabama infantry regiment.

And thus the Confederate army set out for Gettysburg with a toughened Central American filibusterer heading the front rank, while in the procession of command behind him were Brigadier General Archer, who might be counted on to swagger in without much caution, impulsive Harry Heth, and quick-tempered A. P. Hill. It should have been obvious that the forward elements of Lee's army would find on that humid

Wednesday morning some more entertaining employment than seeking shoes.

Half a mile beyond the village of Seven Stars and about three and a half miles from Gettysburg the regiment entered the woods and swamplands of Marsh Creek, where Fry halted to reconnoiter. A light, misty rain began to fall, a threatening carry-over from the intermittent mountain showers of June 30.[2] Fry rode to the rear of the regiment and told the color-bearer to uncase the colors. That, done in the drizzle, was notice to the men that they were about to meet the enemy and would fight.

The Federals soon showed themselves, a dismounted cavalry patrol in a field to the right. They dashed off, three to the rear and a fourth to the bridge where the Cashtown road crossed Marsh Creek. Fry ordered his men to load at will. Archer then came up and directed them to file to the right through an old apple orchard. He had Fry throw out three companies of the 13th and all of the 5th Alabama battalion as skirmishers; when the balance of the brigade was up, he moved it through the orchard on the south side of the turnpike, formed it in battle line, and resumed the advance.[3]

Davis' brigade, the second in Heth's column, took a corresponding position on the north side of the pike. The brigades of Pettigrew and Brockenbrough followed in support. As Archer's skirmish line approached the Marsh Creek bridge a shot rang out, the first of the battle. It was fired by one of the four men who had been in Gamble's forward picket. The other three rushed off to tell Buford that the Confederate infantry was in sight. The first shot of the battle is credited to both Corporal Alpheus Hodges, Company F, 9th New York Cavalry, and Lieutenant Marcellus E. Jones of Du Page County, Illinois, 8th Illinois Cavalry. Probably the distinction belongs to Jones, who seized the carbine of Sergeant Leir S. Shafer and fired.[4]

Moving abreast, Archer and Davis easily drove in the Federal skirmishers until they approached Willoughby Run a mile west of Gettysburg.

Heth's troops had been delighted to see Major William J. Pegram, who had been ill since Chancellorsville, suddenly appear to take command of his artillery battalion. He immediately moved it from the reserve, with Pender, to the front with Heth. A gunner wrote to his father: "Now what was the astonishment that morning when the skirmishing began, to see our 'fighting Major' galloping up to our camp crying out, 'harness and hitch,' which being quickly done, off he took us . . . in advance of the whole army."[5]

Others also were pleased to welcome Pegram. Lee had seen him farther back and told Hill, "I have good news for you. Major Pegram is up."[6] The artilleryman, one of the best in the service, was still feverish when he reported but after hearing of the invasion he would not be left behind. Of his battalion, Captain Mayre's Fredericksburg battery moved first and opened the battle, followed by the Purcell and Crenshaw batteries.

The dominating feature of the terrain toward Gettysburg was a double ridge merging together to the north into a larger, timbered elevation called Oak Hill. Between the two ridges at the place where the Cashtown road crosses is a gentle dip of 400 yards, with a little ripple of a ridge about the center. These can best be identified as McPherson's Ridge to the west; the Ripple; and Seminary Ridge to the east. The first was named after the farmhouse and barn of Edward McPherson south of the pike. McPherson, a former editor of the Pittsburgh *Daily Times,* was a lame-duck Congressman from the Gettysburg district. The district had gone Democratic in November 1862, showing the existence of a strong peace party. He had much later prominence, including that of presiding over the Republican National Convention at which Robert G. Ingersoll delivered his famous "Plumed Knight" oration, but none so noteworthy as having the battle of Gettysburg begin on his farm, though he was not present to witness it. The Ripple has never been so named, but the designation is appropriate.

An apple orchard stood west and north of the McPherson house while to the south was a wood lot of about five acres. Elsewhere the hill was cleared and cultivated. The eastern ridge, which is little more than the eastern face of the small plateau, was known as Seminary Ridge because a Lutheran seminary was situated on it in a grove of great trees 100 yards south of the Cashtown road. The road as it crosses Seminary Ridge is 1,400 yards from the Gettysburg town square.

Unlike McPherson's, Seminary Ridge was little cultivated, but was crowned with timber north toward Oak Hill and south to where it petered off toward the Emmitsburg road.

Soon after dawn Buford learned from his pickets of the stirring among Confederates beyond Marsh Creek and hurried word to General Reynolds, commanding the left wing of Meade's army, that Southern infantry was moving toward Gettysburg. Reynolds had bivouacked on Marsh Creek, downstream from Pettigrew's camp, at a point four and a half miles south of Gettysburg on the Emmitsburg pike. Buford was confident he could rely on Reynolds for speedy relief and told his troopers to hold. He had John Calef's six guns of the regular artillery to assist. The early morning hours wore on without either vigorous pressure from the Confederates in front or the arrival of Northern reinforcements. While waiting for Pender's division, Heth was engaged mainly in what he termed a feeling process, which satisfied him that he faced nothing but dismounted cavalry. Shortly after eight o'clock the Confederate general decided to brush the cavalrymen off McPherson's Heights and move into the town. One of his shells hit Trooper John E. Weaver of the 3rd Indiana Cavalry, the first man killed in the battle.[7]

Heth seems to have retained an aberration that he began the battle on some sort of time schedule. Thirty years later, when he was going over the field in a carriage with Chief Justice Walter Clark of North Carolina, pointing out the position of Confederate troops, he drew a large silver watch from his pocket and said, "By that watch the battle of Gettysburg opened." Clark recorded his statement without explanation.[8] Heth must have been thinking of the moment when he ordered Archer and Davis forward.

At 8:30 A.M. Buford was feeling the new pressure. He made a final survey of his situation, recognizing that he could not sustain a contest long. The sun was burning through the clouds and a hot mist was rising over the countryside, promising a sultry day. Buford retired to the seminary, a three-story brick building crowned with a cupola, and mounted the high ladder to the top.[9] Through the lifting haze, he viewed the long stretch of the pike toward Cashtown, now filled in the distance with the gray of Pender's advancing division.

Buford glanced south toward Emmitsburg. His pulse tingled and his heart jumped, for there on the roadway was a long, dark column. Faintly discernible at the front, alongside the Stars and Stripes, was the First Corps emblem. Reynolds had kept his word. The infantry was coming.

Elated, Buford rushed down the ladder to carry the news to his hard-pressed cavalry. A familiar voice sounded beside him, asking calmly, "What is the matter, John?"

Turning, he looked into the composed face of General Reynolds. "Hell's to pay," he answered quickly.

G. B. Garrison, one of Buford's scouts, who had a feeling for history's details, jotted down the time in his notebook—Reynolds reached the field at twenty-five minutes before nine.[10] The general's aide-de-camp, Captain Stephen M. Weld, Jr., noted, in his diary, the events that followed in rapid succession.

Reynolds had seen the approach of Confederate soldiers. He decided instantly that Gettysburg was the place for a major battle.

To Weld he said: "Ride at once with your utmost speed to General Meade. Tell him the enemy are advancing in strong force, and that I fear they will get to the heights beyond the town before I can. I will fight them inch by inch, and if driven into the town, I will barricade the streets and hold them as long as possible."[11]

Then Reynolds galloped back to the Emmitsburg road to show the approaching column the shortest route to its combat position. Meade had told him he meant to strike at the point where the enemy showed the greatest strength. On the mucky morning of July 1 Reynolds had found it. He sat on the west side of the Emmitsburg pike inspecting the head of the corps as it passed. "We had a fair view of his features," wrote Captain Robert K. Beecham. "The general looked careworn, and we thought, very sad. . . . It was the last time we ever saw him."[12]

2. A Quaker with an Iron Brigade

The 1st Division of the First Corps of the Army of the Potomac reached McPherson's Heights quickly, led across the fields by Reynolds and its commander, Brigadier General James S. Wadsworth, breaking down fences, throwing aside haversacks and blankets, stripping for action.

Wadsworth, the squire of Geneseo, New York, wealthy planter and upstate philanthropist and politician, was as ardently devoted to the cause of the Federal union as any man in Meade's army. To it he gave much of his fortune and eventually his life. His uncle, William Wadsworth, had commanded the New York militia in the unfortunate affair at Queenston Heights in the War of 1812. The general had declined to leave the army to campaign when nominated by the Republicans as candidate for governor of New York in 1862. He had been defeated by Horatio Seymour, apparently much to his satisfaction, because he enjoyed the excitement of service with the troops. At fifty-six he was one of the oldest of Meade's generals.

Cutler's brigade of Wadsworth's division was in the lead, carrying at its head the blue banner of the Empire State. Reynolds directed the brigade to the ground north of the Cashtown pike, the 76th New York on the right, the 56th Pennsylvania in the center and the 147th New York on the left. This last regiment commanded the unfinished railroad

grading that ran parallel to and 150 yards north of the Cashtown road
and had sharp cuttings through Seminary and McPherson's ridges and
the Ripple. The right of way had been prepared but the ties and iron
tracks had not been laid.

Colonel John W. Hofmann had just brought the 56th Pennsylvania
into line when the Southern infantry showed in his front. A crash re-
sounded over the field as the 56th let loose a volley, the first Northern
infantry fire of the battle. Two members of the color guard of the 55th
North Carolina dropped. The Confederates replied; their first fire un-
horsed General Cutler and two of his staff. The exchange continued
for fifteen minutes, while the balance of the Federal division was coming up.

Reynolds, returning from his quest of Wadsworth, rode with Captain James A. Hall of the 2nd Maine Battery, which was composed of
six three-inch guns and men from Knox, Lincoln, Cumberland, and
other rugged seacoast counties, augmented by infantrymen detailed
from the 16th Maine Regiment. Reynolds showed Hall where to put
his pieces to sweep the Cashtown road, replacing Calef's horse artillery.
He pointed to the locations from which about twenty Confederate cannon were shelling the ground over which Wadsworth's soldiers were
deploying and told Hall, "Pay your attention to those guns and draw
their fire from our infantry while it is forming."[13]

Wadsworth's other brigade, celebrated in Northern song and story,
came up, the men wearing their familiar black sombreros,[14] rolled
and looped up on the right side and adorned with a plume and the light-
blue infantry ribbon which gave Archer's Alabamians the certain
knowledge that they were no longer fighting merely cavalry. This was
the 1st Brigade, 1st Division, of the First Army Corps—the "Iron Brigade." Heth's men had suspected that infantry was near when they
had heard a band playing the strains of "The Girl I Left Behind Me."

Tradition and romance already clustered about the Iron Brigade's
achievements. The tenacity and hardihood of these men from the
Northwest had won them their celebrated name—bestowed on them by
McClellan. Solomon Meredith, a giant North Carolina Quaker, six feet
six, who had moved to Cambridge City, Indiana, and with his three sons
cast lots with the Union, led the brigade into action. His love for the
Federal cause deepened as succeeding sons fell from Southern bullets.
Of peaceful faith, he commanded one of the most audacious of combat
units.[15]

Meredith, reared in poverty, had known the hardships of being a poor white laborer in the South. He was uneducated and without a trade. He worked at day jobs and at the age of thirty went North and got work cutting cord wood at six dollars a month. Out of this he reared his family, saved, paid for schooling, and developed into a man of commanding presence and great personal force. He was elected sheriff and appointed United States Marshal for Indiana by President Tyler. His natural leadership caused the men to elect him colonel of the 19th Indiana, which regiment became the darling of the tough-fibered Indiana governor, Oliver P. Morton. Meredith had but one military defect: his great body made him an easy target. When he went down it was in a hot corner where his men were going with him.

Reynolds directed the Iron Brigade into line *en échelon,* the 2nd Wisconsin in front on the right, nearest the Cashtown road, followed by the 7th Wisconsin, 19th Indiana, and 24th Michigan, while the closing regiment, the 6th Wisconsin, had been halted and held in reserve on Seminary Ridge. Mindful that west of Gettysburg his right flank was exposed to an enemy approaching from the north, he sent orders to Major General Abner Doubleday, commanding the First Corps division next in line: "I will hold on to this road [Cashtown] and you hold on to the other [Mummasburg]." This would bring Doubleday's division into line north of the Cashtown pike and on Wadsworth's right.

The 6th Wisconsin, last in line of the Iron Brigade regiments, was commanded by Lieutenant Colonel Rufus R. Dawes. It had a lusty-lunged sergeant, John Ticknor, whose voice could usually be heard on the march above the scuff of leather and rattle of canteens and scabbards. Ticknor already had been a part of one of the great American episodes. In late 1861, returning from McClellan's review at Bailey's Cross Roads, the regiment had been accompanied back to Arlington by Julia Ward Howe. She heard Sergeant Ticknor's clear tenor lead the regiment in "We'll Hang Jeff Davis to a Sour Apple Tree," set to the tune of "John Brown's Body," which in turn was that of the old spiritual, "Say Brothers, Will You Meet Us, on Canaan's Happy Shore." The regiment's bayonets glistened in "burnished rows of steel" and about it spread "the watchfires of a hundred circling camps." All this had inspired Mrs. Howe that night to write the "Battle Hymn of the Republic," the treasured song of the Northern armies.[16]

But as the 6th Wisconsin came up the Emmitsburg road Colonel Dawes told Drum Major R. N. Smith to play, not this hymn, but the equally stirring notes of "The Campbells Are Coming." The regimental band struck up the old Scottish battle song just as the firing opened in front of Cutler's brigade. General Meredith's aide, Lieutenant Gilbert M. Woodward, came dashing up with orders, more stirring than the music: "Colonel, form your line and prepare for action." The men loaded their muskets as they advanced on the run but they were disappointed to learn that for the moment they would have to wait in reserve.

3. Meade Loses His "Noblest and Bravest"

At mid-morning, before McPherson's Heights, two Confederate brigades, Archer's and Davis', faced the two Federal brigades of Meredith and Cutler. The alignment was far from exact. On the Confederate left, Davis overlapped Cutler, while on the Confederate right, Archer was overlapped by Meredith. The result was that in the opening phase of the battle, the right regiments of Archer, the Confederate, and Cutler, the Federal, were pressed back.

As the other Iron Brigade regiments followed the 2nd Wisconsin into McPherson's Woods, the 19th Indiana and 24th Michigan at the left of the Federal line worked down the incline on the edge of the timber and felt for Archer's flank at the very moment when he was embarrassed by having half his command on the west and half on the east bank of Willoughby Run. Near the summit of McPherson's Ridge, Reynolds was directing the two regiments in the enveloping movement. He was mounted on his black horse and wore the major general's shoulder straps. Carelessly exposing himself and obviously an officer of high rank, he at once drew the fire of Archer's skirmishers, who had crossed Willoughby Run and worked their way up the wooded hillside.

Reynolds, expecting support, had turned in the saddle to look toward the crest of the ridge behind him. It was 10:15 A.M. He was struck in the back of the neck by a Minié ball fired by a marksman from a tree on the bank of the stream. The ball passed through his head and came out the other side at the eye.

The Minié ball, used freely in the War between the States, had been invented by Captain C. E. Minié of Vincennes, France, during the Crimean War. It was a long, hollow bullet into which an iron cup was inserted in its base. Upon firing, this cup pushed the bullet into the rifling of the barrel.

Reynolds fell forward without speaking a word. His frightened horse was dashing toward the open fields when his aides caught it. The body dropped lifeless from the saddle. They wrapped him in an army blanket, and a detail from the 76th New York carried him to the seminary and on to the little stone house of George George on the Emmitsburg road. While the fateful battle he had elected to begin still roared west of Gettysburg, his body was put in an ambulance for Baltimore and Lancaster, Pennsylvania. The Confederates learned of his death quickly but thought it resulted from one of Pegram's shells.[17]

Reynolds was perhaps the most universally admired among the generals of the Army of the Potomac. Meade called him the "noblest" and "bravest,"[18] and even his opponent Heth, when informed of his death, said the country "well might mourn, and in doing so honor herself."[19] Reynolds was a handsome man, six feet tall, narrow-waisted, with black hair and a deep tan gained from years of exposure. He was rated almost by concensus the army's best horseman. He was forty-two years old when he fell.

Had Archer entrusted the command of the front line to the wily filibusterer Fry, or had he heeded the warning given him on the previous evening by Pettigrew, all might have gone well for his brigade. Pettigrew had studied the approaches to Gettysburg carefully and had cautioned Archer to guard against his right flank being turned. Pettigrew described McPherson's Ridge and suggested that this would probably be the line the Northern army would defend.

Here it was that Meredith, undeterred by the death of Reynolds, pressed the action against Archer. While the 2nd and 7th Wisconsin engaged him in front, the 19th Indiana and 24th Michigan appeared almost at right angles to his disconcerted line caught halfway across the stream. The 19th Indiana was able to work undetected around the shoulder of the heavily wooded bluff above the creek and confront Archer unexpectedly. This regiment had been on picket duty the night before and the men's guns were already loaded, which gave them a time advantage over the Confederates, cramped up along the two banks.

The color-bearer of the 19th, whose name was Cunningham, was about to uncase the colors for the charge when a staff officer rode up and shouted, "Do not unfurl that flag."[20] Near by was Cunningham's companion, A. J. Buckles. Cunningham, seeing the battle line moving, defied the adjutant and said to Buckles, "Abe, pull the shuck." Off came the casing, and the Stars and Stripes flew in the breeze. It brought a shower of bullets and Flag-Bearer Cunningham fell. Buckles dropped his gun, caught up the flag, and kept it so far in advance of the line that Lieutenant Colonel W. W. Dudley rebuked him for his daring. Before the first day's battle ended eight color-bearers of the 19th Indiana had been shot down.

Dudley, a well-known Indiana political figure—who came to be called "Blocks of Four" Dudley because of his custom of bringing in his henchmen on election day in more than single units—led the firing line. A Confederate ball that day took off his foot.

The quick fire of the Hoosiers sprayed the Confederates who had gained the east bank. On the west bank Colonel Fry with the right regiment fought a gallant battle. The old filibusterer was not to be trapped. Lieutenant Colonel G. H. Stevens of the 2nd Wisconsin was killed. A few minutes later the regiment's colonel, Lucius Fairchild, had his arm shot off. Major John Mansfield took command.

But the impetuous Alabamians found themselves hopelessly out-flanked. They faced not the right, but almost the center of the Federal line.[21] The situation was what Pettigrew had feared. Archer had been heedless. Here, where Pettigrew said he would find the Federal army, he had allowed himself to be surprised and outmaneuvered because, as predicted, they were there. "All we could do," wrote Private E. T. Boland, of Brewton, Alabama, "was to wind them around ourselves." The fight was sharp but short. Archer, in the front line, had dismounted to lead his brigade. He and two companies of the 13th Alabama, re-cruited in Greenville and Camden, tried to put up a resistance in a clump of willows on the west bank of Willoughby Run.[22] But the Wis-consin men came crashing in on them while the Hoosier regiment held them in front. Fry was able to extricate most of them, but Archer and seventy-five others were taken prisoner.

The capture of Archer sent a stir of elation through the Iron Brigade. The details were related with relish. Private Patrick Maloney, an Irish-man of Company G, rushed after Archer as he was trying to escape, caught him and marched him to Captain Charles C. Dow, who greeted him courteously. Archer offered to surrender his sword.

"Keep your sword, General, and go to the rear," said Dow. "One sword is all I need on this line."[23]

Archer crossed Willoughby Run and walked toward the Federal rear. He had covered about forty yards when he met Lieutenant D. B. Dailey of Meredith's staff, who demanded his sword. Archer explained that he had retained it by the indulgence of Captain Dow, but the lieutenant, who had taken no part in the capture, insisted on the trophy. Another Iron Brigade captain, Robert K. Beecham, observed that "it is not al-ways that the man on the outmost line receives the reward which is his due."[24] The incident must have nettled Archer and with the humiliation of his capture, left him in ill humor. When General Doubleday, an

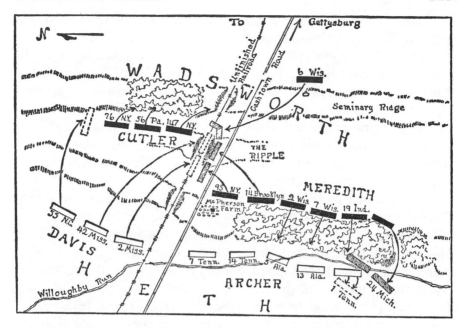

Heth's attack on Wadsworth. July 1, 1863, 10:00 to 11:30 A.M.

acquaintance in the old army, rode up with the greeting, "General Archer, I am glad to meet you," Archer refused his hand.

"I am not glad to meet you, sir," he replied coldly.[25]

The story of the capture came to have embellishments. Pat Maloney —who was killed later in the day and could have had no part in the elaborations—was said to have seized the general by the throat, and commanded: "Roight about face, Gineral. March." At the seminary, Maloney saluted and said, "Gineral Wadsworth, I make you acquainted with Gineral Archer."[26] But in truth Archer never got beyond the lieutenant and that officer was the one who retained Archer's sword. No other general officer of the Army of Northern Virginia had been captured since Lee took command. Fry now took over the brigade.

4. Davis Is Tricked by a Railroad Cut

The misfortunes which befell Davis were more severe even than those encountered by Archer. Triumph was suddenly turned into disaster.

The 11th Mississippi was on detached service and only three of Davis' regiments were present, the 2nd and 42nd Mississippi, and the 55th North Carolina. The last was distinctly a young man's regiment, not a member of it having attained the age of thirty.

"Old Graybeard" Cutler's brigade was divided and part of it was isolated as it went into action.[27] Three of the regiments—the 56th Pennsylvania and the 76th and 147th New York—were north of the railroad cut. Two others, the 84th New York (14th Brooklyn) and 95th New York, connected with the Iron Brigade south of the railroad right of way and the Cashtown road. The 7th Indiana was behind the lines, bringing up the division trains. Hall's guns occupied the position between the road and the right of way. Thus a distance of a hundred yards separated Cutler's three right regiments from the balance of the Federal infantry.

Davis advanced against Cutler with the 55th North Carolina on the Confederate left, the 42nd Mississippi in the center and the 2nd Mississippi nearest the Cashtown road and the railroad cut. As the North Carolinians reached Cutler's flank, they wheeled to the right with a rush. Colonel John Kerr Connally seized the battle flag, jumped to the front and aligned the regiment on the colors. The gesture was foolhardy. Instantly he drew Federal fire and fell with his leg wounded and his arm so shattered that it had to be amputated. Major A. H. Belo ran to inquire if he were badly hurt. "Yes," said Connally, "but pay no attention to me. Take the colors and keep ahead of the Mississippians."[28]

Captain J. V. Pierce of the 147th New York heard the cry that ran down the Federal lines, "They are flanking us on the right."[29] He described the movement: the Confederate regiment was "pressing far to our right and rear and came over to the south side of the rail fence, their colors dropped to the front. An officer in front of the center corrected the alignment as if passing in review. It was the finest exhibition of discipline and drill I ever saw before or since on a battlefield."

The flank attack broke Cutler's regiments, which retired at a run across the fields 400 yards to the northern extension of Seminary Ridge. Here they paused briefly, then continued their retrograde movement to the outskirts of Gettysburg. Hall meantime found his battery exposed and its infantry supports vanished. He had opened on the enemy at 10:45 and had been firing for twenty-five minutes when Davis' men showed within sixty yards of his right gun. Hall fired with canister, which broke their advance, but when the infantry fled he had to withdraw the battery hastily by sections, and abandon one gun.

In response to Doubleday's messengers, Lieutenant Colonel Dawes, guided by a staff captain, brought the 6th Wisconsin forward at the double quick. He saw the flight of Cutler's men "in disorder" and the withdrawal of Hall's battery. A group of officers passed in front of the regiment carrying something in a blanket, but no one knew it was the body of General Reynolds. They plunged ahead to the fence along the Cashtown road, where they faced north. Their volley struck the flank of the Confederates who were in a headlong pursuit north of the railroad right of way. The gray line swayed and buckled. Cutler's two regiments south of the road, the 14th Brooklyn and 95th New York, now faced north on the left of the 6th Wisconsin, and fired obliquely almost into the rear of the Mississippians.

Then the two Mississippi regiments, surprised by the enfilade attack, made a fatal mistake. Partly because Davis had allowed them to get out of hand, and partly because of their instinctive search for cover under flank fire, they crowded into the railroad cut. The 2nd Mississippi on the right and a part of the 42nd Mississippi in the center quickly gained the security of the steep bank at the cut in the Ripple, midway between the two ridges. It was too deep to serve as an entrenchment. In it the men lost command of the approaches and to all effective purposes, they were out of action. Davis ordered their further retirement and directed the 55th North Carolina to cover it.

But it was too late. Dawes, seeing the Confederates huddled in the cut, rushed to Major Edward Pye, commanding the 95th New York, and said, "We must charge." "Charge it is," replied the major, and together they gave the command, "Forward, charge!"[30]

Across the field from the road to the cut streamed the two regiments, followed by the 14th Brooklyn under Colonel E. B. Fowler. The Confederate fire proved much more destructive than Dawes could have anticipated, coming chiefly from the North Carolinians on the other side of the cut. Of the 420 Wisconsin soldiers who left the roadside fence, only 240 reached the railroad right of way, but there they were complete masters of the Mississippians gathered helplessly beneath them.

In this internecine conflict there were chivalric episodes of courtesy and indulgence not so often encountered in later-day wars, where the propaganda machines take over to coarsen the conflict and make all allies virtuous and all enemies brutes. Here the first instinct of the Wisconsin soldiers was not to kill, but to save the lives of the men at their mercy. Lieutenant Colonel Dawes, advancing on foot, heard his men shouting, "Throw down your muskets! Down with your muskets!" Forcing his way through the line he reached the edge of the cut and, as he described it, "found myself face to face with hundreds of rebels." In later years, when he thought of this moment, he was always thankful for his presence of mind. "Surrender or I fire," he shouted. An officer in gray uniform silently handed over his sword. He was Major John A. Blair, commanding the 2nd Mississippi. At his word about 250 men threw down their guns.

Said Dawes, in reflecting on the restraint of his soldiers: "The coolness, self-possession, and discipline which held back our men from pouring in a general volley saved a hundred lives of the enemy, and as my mind goes back to the fearful excitement of the moment, I marvel at it."[31]

Dawes took Blair's sword and those of six other officers and turned them over to Adjutant E. P. Brooks; to Major John F. Hauser he assigned the task of taking the prisoners—7 officers and 225 enlisted men, mainly of the 2nd Mississippi—to the provost guard. Other prisoners were captured by the two New York regiments, which brought Davis' loss to about half his force. The balance of the brigade withdrew to the west side of Willoughby Run. The Federals re-established their old line facing west along McPherson's Ridge, and Cutler again advanced his regiments.

Meredith in a companion realignment brought the victorious Iron Brigade back to the east side of the run, on the line it had occupied before Reynolds sent it against Archer. The 19th Indiana changed places with the 24th Michigan and took the left of the line, while the 7th Wisconsin held the right. Buford meantime had been ordered to the far left as a flank guard. The five companies of the 3rd Indiana Cavalry declined to hear the order and remained to fight with the Iron Brigade.[32]

Heth, too, reorganized his division by moving Archer's remnants to the right and bringing Pettigrew forward to the center. He pulled Davis out of the line to allow him to collect his stragglers, judging him almost useless for the rest of the day. He sent Brockenbrough to Pettigrew's left. It was 11:30. Two Confederate brigades had been deplorably led and badly worsted. Instead of taking advantage of his numerical superiority over Wadsworth—a Confederate division had greater strength than a Federal—Heth had attacked timidly with half his force and had seen it defeated and scattered without making an effort to support it. That he had expected to encounter nothing but cavalry was not a sufficient explanation. Pathetically droll was his report that "the enemy had now been felt, and found to be in heavy force. . . ." To that some hundreds of dead Confederates might have liked to testify.

On the Federal side, the two remaining First Corps divisions were coming into line. While Doubleday was commanding the corps, his own division was led by Brigadier General Thomas A. Rowley, a West Point graduate from Pennsylvania, who had two small brigades, one his own, mainly Pennsylvanians, now commanded by Colonel Chapman Biddle, and the other consisting of three Pennsylvania mountain regiments commanded by Colonel Roy Stone.

The other First Corps division was that of Brigadier General John C. Robinson, a bushy-whiskered West Point graduate from New York, with two brigades, commanded by West Point graduates, Brigadier Generals Gabriel R. Paul and Henry Baxter. At Reynolds' order they had marched behind Wadsworth. On separate roads they arrived almost simultaneously on the battlefield.

Doubleday used Rowley's men to strengthen the line held by the Iron Brigade. He put the two brigades on the two extremes of Mc-Pherson's Woods, Biddle on the left and Stone on the right. Stone's right rested on the Cashtown road. Robinson's division was held in reserve at the Seminary.

5. A Shot Is Fired from the Rear

At the outbreak of the war a young West Point graduate, Lieutenant Colonel Thomas Leiper Kane, began to drill a rifle regiment from the Pennsylvania mountain country. Their distinctive garb was a cap adorned with the tail of a buck deer. The regiment had the successive official names of the 1st Rifles, the 13th Reserves and the 42nd Pennsylvania Infantry, but to the Federal army it was known as the "Bucktails."[33]

Kane, ahead of his time, realized that the rifle had ended the close-order infantry attack and had drilled his men in infiltration tactics, instructing them to scatter under heavy fire, to make full use of whatever cover the ground offered, to press continually forward where the ground gave an advantage, and to fire only when they had a target in their sights. He placed emphasis on the individual soldier's responsibility. He conducted regular target practice among men already skilled as squirrel and deer hunters, and specialized in long-range firing, from 200 to 1,000 yards.

Such was the success of the Bucktails as sharpshooters and skirmishers in the early fighting that the War Department wanted more of them. In July 1862 it detached Major Roy Stone from the 1st Rifles, sent him into the Pennsylvania mountains, and told him to bring out an entire new brigade of riflemen with bucktail caps. The 149th and 150th Regiments were the result. They were assembled from fourteen counties, from Potter, McKean, and Tioga bordering on New York, through Lycoming, Mifflin, Clarion, Clearfield, and Huntingdon, and from Crawford on the Ohio line to a scattering from Philadelphia at the east. Sergeant William R. Ramsey gave their qualifications: ". . . well formed, of hardy habits, skilled in the use of the rifle. . . ." To these two Bucktail regiments was joined the 143rd Pennsylvania Infantry, recruited in the Wyoming Valley.

The original Bucktails were incensed. They claimed the Secretary of War had authorized them to wear the bucktail as a distinctive badge to which green recruits were not entitled. They summed up their attitude: "There was but one Bucktail regiment, viz., the First Rifles, Pennsylvania Reserves." Public opinion rallied to the side of the 1st Rifles. Stone's men were scorned and dubbed contemptuously the "Bogus Bucktails."

But now the Bogus Bucktails were to have an opportunity such as had never come to those mountaineers who had pre-empted the bucktail name. Doubleday came out to meet them on the field east of the seminary, accompanied by Rowley and their staffs. The artillery bombardment had opened in more deadly earnest across Willoughby Run, and, scarcely heard above the exploding shells, Doubleday addressed the three regiments, emphasizing the importance of victory. As Pennsylvanians, he reminded them, they were defending their own soil. Major Thomas Chamberlain of the 150th noted that it was 11:30 when the regiment, aggregating 397 officers and men, took position on the north end of the woods that concealed the Iron Brigade. To the right of the 150th, extending past the McPherson farm buildings to the Cashtown pike, were the 149th and 143rd.

When Stone's men reached this position, littered with the debris of the battle between Cutler and Davis and manifestly the center of the Federal line, the Bogus Bucktails let out a shout, "We have come to stay, boys!"[34] They could not then know how prophetic was their cry.

Colonel Langhorne Wister of the 150th now sent out his Company B as skirmishers, telling them to work ahead until they felt the enemy. They moved down the western slope of McPherson's Ridge to Wil-

loughby Run, where they encountered Heth's skirmishers on the opposite bank. The rivulet along which the fighting had begun was still
the dividing line between the armies.

The action lulled. From the ridge Stone's men could look across
and see Pender's division in Heth's rear. "The enemy seemed to be
formed in continuous double lines of battle," said Major Chamberlain; "as a spectacle it was striking."[35] Although Heth's bombardment
continued, the Confederates made no effort to renew the infantry
battle.

At noon a fleshy little man, old and peculiar, dragging an antiquated
Enfield rifle and wearing a blue swallow-tailed coat with burnished
brass buttons—of a style not commonly seen for forty years—a buff
vest, and a high silk hat, appeared on the left of the 150th and asked,
"Can I fight with your regiment?" He was referred to Colonel Wister,
who was coming up. The peculiar intruder was a resident of Gettysburg, John Burns, more than seventy years old.

"Well, old man, what do you want?" the colonel asked bluntly.

"I want a chance to fight with your regiment."

"Can you shoot?"

"Oh, yes," said the old man, a smile stealing over his face. "If you
knew you had before you a soldier of the War of 1812, who had
fought at Lundy's Lane, you would not ask such a question."

The colonel inquired about his ammunition and Burns slapped his
pockets. "Certainly you can fight with us," Wister said. "I wish
there were many more like you."[36] But he told him to go into the
woods and fight with the Iron Brigade, where he would have better
shelter.

The old man obeyed reluctantly. In the woods he encountered the
7th Wisconsin, where Colonel Callis discouraged him: "Old man,
you had better go to the rear or you'll get hurt."

Just then a shell burst near by. "Tut! tut! tut! I've heard that
sort of thing before," said Burns.[37]

When Callis again ordered him to the rear, he took out an old-
fashioned powder horn and a cartridge box of bullets, and said if he
could not fight with the regiment, he would have to fight alone. "There
are three hundred cowards back in that town," he said, "who ought
to come out of their cellars and fight. I will show you that there is
one man in Gettysburg who is not afraid."

Someone handed him a better gun, captured from Archer. His
condemnation of his home town was scarcely appropriate. Company

K of the 1st Pennsylvania Reserves, 5th Corps, part of McCandless' brigade, was composed of veteran soldiers from Gettysburg. A company of students from Pennsylvania College and the Theological Seminary had skirmished with Early's division and then marched off to Harrisburg under the command of a theological student, Captain F. Klinefelter. Some in Gettysburg were in hiding, to be sure. But the Burns "bushwhacker" warfare, celebrated in poetry by Bret Harte and monumented on the Gettysburg battlefield, was of the exact type the Federal General John Pope had threatened to suppress in Virginia with retaliatory shootings.

Lee had not been oppressive in Pennsylvania. He made no war on civilians and there was no just occasion for them to rise in a partisan outbreak. Lee, in fact, had spared civilians, even when they fired on his men at Chambersburg. He had merely confiscated their guns.

Fighting with the 7th Wisconsin, Burns dropped a Confederate officer from a white horse.[38] When the Federal line later was dislodged, he crawled away from his gun and buried his ammunition. When he was found wounded, he denied to the Confederates that he had been a combatant and said he was hit while seeking help for his invalid wife. The truth and heroics had gone out of him. A pitying Southern officer had his four wounds dressed by a Confederate surgeon. Then several Confederates loaded him carefully into a wagon, to be taken home for acclaim and renown as "the hero of Gettysburg," a title neither discerning nor deserved.

John Burns had scarcely departed when a shot was heard from the rear and a shell burst behind the Bogus Bucktails. Colonel Edmund L. Dana of the 143rd thought it was from a Federal battery. When a second shell followed he sent word to Colonel Charles S. Wainwright, commanding the First Corps artillery, demanding that the reckless firing be stopped.[39]

Another shell, and the truth broke on Stone's men. Rodes's division, heading Ewell's corps, had pushed down from the north and seized Oak Hill, the eminence on the flank of the Federal line. The entire First Corps, facing west and suddenly menaced from the north, was in a most critical situation.

Fortunately Robinson's division was still in reserve at the seminary. Doubleday hurriedly formed a new line north of the railroad, prolonging that of the balance of the corps. Stone's brigade was shifted to secure protection where possible from the enfilade artillery fire. Stone kept the 150th Pennsylvania facing west and changed front with the 143rd and 149th regiments. The 143rd faced north along the edge of the Cashtown road, forming a salient where it joined with the 150th.

Anticipating an assault on the salient, Stone advanced his other regiment, the 149th, to the line of the railroad right of way that had proved a trap for the Mississippians. The regiment was in position when Daniel's brigade of Rodes's division—the 32nd North Carolina flying the new Confederate banner—approached across the northern field.

But Doubleday was fortunate. Along with the arrival of Ewell's 1st division under Rodes, Howard's Eleventh Corps of the Federal army was sighted by the seminary lookout, marching up the Emmitsburg road at top speed for Gettysburg.[40]

Oak Hill

1. Schurz Is Greeted with a Salvo

Major General Oliver O. Howard, young, nervous, and a question mark in the army since Chancellorsville, reached Gettysburg about mid-morning, riding ahead of his men and escorted by two companies of the 1st Indiana Cavalry. Reynolds had sent him an urgent message to bring on the Eleventh Corps, which had camped near Emmitsburg and was already on the road when the courier met it.

Howard had been under marching orders for the morning of July 1 and had anticipated the need for speed. Dividing his corps, he had put Brigadier General Francis C. Barlow on the direct road from Emmitsburg to Gettysburg and had shifted his other two divisions, those of Major General Carl Schurz and Brigadier General Adolph von Steinwehr, to the Taneytown Road. Due to obstructions on the main road caused by the passage of the First Corps artillery and wagons, he expected the two detachments to reach Gettysburg at about the same time.

Howard's arrival was timed by witnesses all the way from 9:45 to 11:30 A.M. and he was uncertain about his own watch, but the hour was probably about ten-thirty. He witnessed the retreat of Cutler's regiments under pressure from Davis in the opening phase of the battle. That was the cause of his doleful and premature report to Meade that the First Corps had fled on its initial contact with the enemy.[1] The oral message was the first of his criticisms of the First Corps which disturbed Meade and caused him to send Major General John Newton, commander of a division of the Sixth Corps, to supersede Doubleday, who had been guilty of nothing more than leading one of the best day's fighting in the whole history of the Army of the Potomac. Newton did not arrive until after the conclusion of the first day.

Howard was in the cupola of Pennsylvania College[2] at 11:30 A.M. surveying the country when he received intelligence that Reynolds, for whom his couriers had been searching, but whom he had not sought himself, was lying dead at the seminary; thus, by virtue of his seniority Howard commanded all the left-wing forces present on the battlefield.

Howard had not seen Buford or Doubleday and knew nothing of the conditions of the conflict. But he learned quickly from Devin's cavalrymen that fresh Confederate columns were expected at any instant along the roads leading into Gettysburg from Carlisle and Harrisburg. His view of the action west of the town, which had lapsed into exchanges between the artillery and skirmishers of the two armies, reassured him that there was no emergency in that quarter. Gray-coated prisoners, those captured from Archer and Davis, were being herded into the town and it appeared that Doubleday had turned an initial defeat into a Federal victory. Howard was forced to postpone a visit to the seminary to inspect the lines west of the town, but he left Doubleday in charge there, while he returned—"slowly" he said—to the Emmitsburg road. At the foot of Cemetery Hill he met Schurz, who likewise had ridden ahead of his men. Howard turned over to Schurz the command of the Eleventh Corps and gave him directions about posting his own division, now under Brigadier General Alexander Schimmelfennig, and that of Barlow, north of Gettysburg.

Howard directed his remaining division, Steinwehr's, to remain in reserve on Cemetery Hill south of the town. One of the minor but prolonged controversies after the battle concerned whether Howard did this of his own inspiration or in compliance with orders received from Reynolds. The selection of the position was presumed by most of Washington officialdom, grown accustomed to defeat, to be the main reason for Northern victory. Cemetery Ridge provided a strong rallying point with many tactical advantages, and consequently the selection of the ground, more than the army or its commander, was held to be the essential thing, and the most important of all the decisions at Gettysburg. But the ridge was so conspicuous that none could miss it, and whether Buford, Reynolds, Howard, or—more certainly in the final decision—Hancock selected it, the army was fairly sure to gravitate to it when a rallying point was needed. A general was not called for—any private could have picked it out readily and made his way there without orders.

Howard received the thanks of Congress for selecting the position. Congress is not infallible in such matters, nor was the Congress in question particularly studiously inclined, and certainly all the evidence was not in. At this later day it seems clear that Reynolds fought a delaying action west of Gettysburg for no other purpose than to secure Cemetery Ridge as a concentration point for the other Federal columns coming up. Both direct and circumstantial evidence support this view. Reynolds had told Meade his purpose was to save this high ground: such was the implication of his statement that he feared the enemy "will get to the heights beyond the town before I can." He had said he would fight "inch by inch" through the streets. This could mean only that, in his mind, he was falling back all the while to Cemetery Ridge.

More direct testimony was supplied by Doubleday, who said that one of Howard's aides arrived soon after Reynolds descended from the seminary cupola after an inspection with Buford. The aide requested instructions regarding the Eleventh Corps, and Reynolds "directed that General Howard bring his corps forward at once and *form them on Cemetery Hill* as a reserve."[3]

Lieutenant Joseph G. Rosengarten of Reynolds' staff said this order was given in his presence. Howard held Rosengarten in error.

Even more persuasive is a consideration of the dangerous nature of Reynolds' position on McPherson's Ridge. It was exposed to flank attack by the enterprising enemy known to be approaching. Reynolds' keen military perception would have rejected it for anything more than a holding engagement which he would try to sustain until other Federal corps came up to his relief.

The Eleventh Corps had an unenviable reputation in both armies. It was preponderantly German, made up mainly of immigrants who had fled their mother country during the uprisings of 1848, and who were drawn to the Federal cause by their leaders, notably Blenker, Schurz, and Franz Sigel. Being chiefly artisans, most of them had settled in the North. Their ardor for the cause could not be expected to equal that of soldiers possessing an American heritage. Their inability to speak English caused Confederates to believe they were mercenaries like the Hessians of the Revolutionary War. Antiforeign sentiment was still rampant at the outbreak of the war because the heavy immigration had depressed wages in the 1850s and crowded the slum areas of the Northern cities. The antipathy had its expression in a wave of nativism and, politically, in the Know-Nothing Party, which had made substantial headway for a time in the decade before the war.

Oliver Howard was thirty-two years old, a native of Leeds, Maine, and a graduate of Bowdoin and West Point. He took command of a Maine regiment when war broke out and led a brigade at First Manassas, but at the battle of Fair Oaks he lost his right arm. The question might have been raised with him as with Ewell, whether one maimed in battle retained the same zest for combat. Howard was a man of deeply religious sentiments who prayed in his tent each night. He won respect, but, because of a testiness, little affection. This was his last battle with the Army of the Potomac. Later he served congenially in Sherman's "scorched earth" campaigns in Georgia and the Carolinas.

The positions Howard designated for Schimmelfennig and Barlow were north of Gettysburg, in open, cultivated country, running at a right angle with Doubleday's line west of the town. Howard, since he commanded troops that had shown uncertain qualities at Chancellorsville, might have reflected on the disadvantage of fighting a battle in the clearings. The information he already possessed, forecasting the approach of heavy Confederate columns from the north, might have suggested that he station his corps at the outset on Cemetery and Culp's hills, to which Doubleday could then have retired in orderly fashion, although losses in any withdrawal would have been inevitable.

But time was short and decisions had to be made in haste. Doubtless Howard considered a withdrawal of the entire army to Cemetery Hill premature. Slocum had reached Two Taverns, only five miles distant, with the Twelfth Corps, and might reasonably be counted on for support. Sickles was eleven miles away with the Third Corps at Emmitsburg, and Howard now sent urgent messages for assistance to both Sickles and Slocum.

Sickles received Howard's summons at two o'clock in the afternoon; though he was under orders to maintain his position at Emmitsburg and watch the South Mountain pass, the fighting spirit was strong in his heart. Whatever the orders, a part of the army was in danger. He required only a moment for reflection. Leaving two of his brigades to watch the pass, he put the balance of his corps on the road for rapid marching to Gettysburg.

Slocum, believing that an army could respond to but one commander, declined to budge without direct orders from Meade, maintaining that the commanding general's Pipe Creek Circular—which Sickles considered no obstacle to succoring a force under attack—fixed a battle position farther back. It would be unwise, he thought, to bring on a general engagement elsewhere without Meade's positive instructions. Howard repeated his entreaties to Slocum and finally sent his aide and brother, Major Charles Howard, to request Slocum to come to the field in person, even with no troops. The Twelfth Corps commander declined "to go to the front or take any responsibility."[4]

Slocum's attitude amazed his soldiers, who had been forewarned of the proximity of the enemy when skirmishers were thrown out well to the front and flanks, though they were marching through an open country where visibility was good in all directions. Puzzled that the pace was not increased with an enemy near, they filed leisurely into a field at Two Taverns and went into bivouac, still perplexed, because the firing ahead indicated the battle had grown more intense. Three couriers dashed up to Slocum in rapid succession, their horses lathered and jaded. The men looked on curiously; a knot of officers and orderlies would form around the commanding general with each arrival, then would break up and scatter. Through the grapevine the private soldiers finally heard that Slocum was being summoned by Howard but since he was acting under Meade's orders, he would not join the fighting yet. Late in the day the corps resumed its march toward Gettysburg.[5]

Schimmelfennig's troops, with their blaring German bands, marched into Gettysburg at twelve-thirty. Schimmelfennig was a Prussian officer who had served in the Schleswig-Holstein revolution of 1848-1850, and with the Prussian force that invaded Baden to quell insurgents in 1849. He became colonel of the 74th Pennsylvania Infantry, a Germant regiment recruited largely in Pittsburgh, which he was reputed to have made into "a model regiment in drill and discipline."[6]

After halts and conferences, Schurz directed Schimmelfennig to march out the Mummasburg road and occupy Oak Hill, on the right of Doubleday. The division commander threw out skirmishers and began his advance, but even as he left the town he was arrested by a salvo from Rodes's batteries proclaiming that the Confederates were ahead of him and had occupied the hill.

Instead of falling back to a new position where he might fight in conjunction with Doubleday, Howard chose to defend the line in the fields which Schimmelfennig had reached when he came under fire. Its left ran partly along a small stream that had its source at the base of Oak Hill and flowed eastward into Rock Creek, crossing the Carlisle road less than half a mile north of Gettysburg. Howard and Schurz placed Barlow on the right of Schimmelfennig, his right resting on a wooded hump on the bank of Rock Creek, which came to be known as Barlow's Knoll.

Rock Creek gave some protection on the right and the open fields gave security against surprise attack from any direction, but the position was untenable because the Heidlersburg road, along which Devin had reported the enemy's approach, led directly to Barlow's right rear and allowed the position to be easily turned.[7]

On the opposite flank, Schimmelfennig had halted before he made a juncture with Doubleday's line. A fatal gap of a quarter of a mile remained between the two corps. After the line was formed Howard came out from Gettysburg and approved it, then rode to Doubleday's position and gave orders that if retreat became necessary, the First Corps commander should retire to Cemetery Hill.

At this moment Doles's brigade of Rodes's division moved along the eastern slope of Oak Hill and advanced toward the gap that separated Howard from Doubleday. But Doles's mission for the moment was only to hold the Eleventh Federal Corps in check until Rodes could strike Doubleday's right with his other brigades, mainly those of O'Neal and Iverson.

2. The Slaughter of the Carolinians

Iverson's brigade, which at the June 30 muster numbered 114 officers and 1,356 enlisted men, a total of 1,470 present for duty, had headed the march of Rodes's division and Ewell's corps on the morning of July 1, and was the first to turn south at Hill's summons.

As they approached Gettysburg from the northeast, along the Heidlersburg road, they heard heavy firing. Two miles from the town Rodes marched them by the right flank under cover of the woods toward the Mummasburg road, which runs southeast into Gettysburg. When they reached Oak Hill, the importance of which Rodes intuitively recognized, he had Lieutenant Colonel Thomas H. Carter, commanding the division's artillery, put sixteen guns in position on the promontory and open on the flank of Doubleday to the south. It was 1:30 P.M.

As the first shells exploded amid the gnarled cherry trees of the McPherson farm, Rodes could see the quick movements among the startled Federals and the deployment of fresh troops coming from Gettysburg. These were the first of Robinson's two brigades hurrying into line, Baxter in front, to be followed shortly by Paul. The new line was recessed from Stone's salient, a broken extension of the line of Wadsworth and Rowley. Baxter was on the right but Paul sent two regiments in rear of the extreme right of Doubleday's line, and bent them around to reach toward Howard. Paul placed the rest of his brigade in line, prolonging Baxter's left, reaching toward Cutler on Seminary Ridge north of the railroad. Rodes could see also units of the Eleventh Federal Corps marching rapidly out of Gettysburg.

Rodes formed his division for attack, Iverson on the right, O'Neal in the center, and Doles on the left, while Daniel and Ramseur were held in support. Daniel was to assist Iverson and if not needed was to attack on his right.

Iverson is entitled to attention because he was perhaps the most conspicuous Confederate failure at Gettysburg. His father, Alfred Iverson, Sr., former United States Representative and Senator from Georgia, whom Robert Toombs had defeated for the Confederate Senate, was one of the earliest and most fiery advocates of secession. He was scholarly, a Princeton graduate, an orator of great power, and a close friend of President Davis, with whom he had served in the United States Senate.

Iverson, Jr., was reared in Columbus, Georgia; he was seventeen and a student at the military institute at Tuskegee, Alabama, when war began with Mexico. The father raised and equipped a regiment which the son entered as a soldier. In 1855, when Jefferson Davis was Secretary of War and Iverson, Sr., was a Senator, he was appointed by Davis a first lieutenant in the 1st United States Cavalry. The regular army commission of that grade was a distinction for a young man fresh from civilian life. He served during the Kansas statehood troubles and when the Southern states seceded he resigned to obtain a commission from his old patron, Davis. Stationed with the 20th North Carolina Regiment, he was elected camp commander and in consequence colonel.

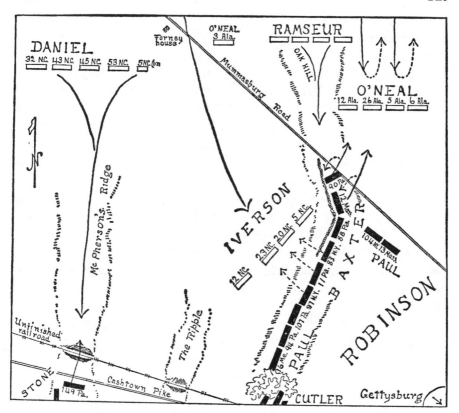

Rodes's confused attack from Oak Hill. July 1, 1863, 1:30 to 3:00 P.M.

From the commanding position on Oak Hill, Rodes watched Robinson's men aligning themselves in his front and misunderstood their movements, which were merely to secure the best defensive position available. He judged they were preparing an assault and sought to anticipate them. "Boys," he said to the 12th North Carolina, one of Iverson's regiments, "they are advancing upon us. Go ahead and meet them."[8]

Rodes's division was formed in an obtuse angle, with Doles and O'Neal facing south, Iverson facing southeast, and Daniel and Ramseur facing south in the rear. Iverson was attacking a Federal front that ran directly north and south, and therefore was approaching on an oblique line that put the brunt of the action on his left regiments, which were being supported by O'Neal. Iverson's line, from left to right, was made up of the 5th, 20th, 23rd, and 12th North Carolina regiments. The 12th, on the far right, had its flank in the air, except for the support it might expect from the advance of Daniel, who was much to the rear.

The line which Iverson was preparing to assail ran through the Forney farm, immediately south of Oak Hill. The farmhouse stood south of the Mummasburg road and the fields extended along the road for about a mile, the cultivated land being a quarter of a mile deep. It was bounded on the east by a stone fence which marked the Federal line, extending south about 550 yards from the road to a clump of timber north of the unfinished railroad.

The Federal defending line, from its right to left, or from the Mummasburg road to the stand of timber, consisted of the 90th Pennsylvania—with its right resting on the road—12th Massachusetts, 88th Pennsylvania, 83rd New York, 11th Pennsylvania, and 97th New York. They comprised Brigadier General Harry Baxter's brigade, excepting the 11th Pennsylvania, which was detached from Paul's brigade.

Even before Iverson could move out, O'Neal's brigade on his left had attacked prematurely and had been beaten back, leaving his left flank, which—owing to his oblique position—was the one heading his assault, grievously exposed. Baxter had seen O'Neal's advance and had quickly moved the 90th Pennsylvania and 12th Massachusetts to the right, changed their front to face northwest, stopped the Confederates with a destructive fire, and sent them reeling to the rear. The two Northern regiments then returned to their original position in time to meet Iverson.

Second Lieutenant Walter A. Montgomery of the 12th North Carolina, on Iverson's far right, could look down the line as the brigade went into action. It was two o'clock. The Federal position was half a mile ahead and the ground in front of it was barren of any protective features. Montgomery could not see a single bush or tree. But Iverson ordered his men forward with the words "Give them hell," and seemed to take little further interest in the matter.[9] He did not follow the advance or undertake to correct the brigade's faulty alignment. Nor had he or Rodes effectively reconnoitered what was in his front. The men were ignorant of the nature of the defensive line or the size of the force crouching behind the wall. Not a Federal flag showed above the parapet of rocks. Not a blue-capped soldier raised his head. Iverson, in a disastrous lapse from established practice, had neglected to send skirmishes ahead of his battle line.

"Unarmed, unled as a brigade, we went to our doom," said Captain Vines E. Turner of the 23rd North Carolina in the center of the line. "Deep and long must the desolate homes and orphan children of North Carolina rue the rashness of that hour."[10] One of Ramseur's soldiers, more blunt, charged that Iverson had been drinking and was "off hiding somewhere."[11]

The North Carolina regiments were close to the wall when the Federal line rose up and poured in a deadly fire at point-blank range. The 5th, on the left flank, suffered the greatest shock, but the blast caught also the 20th, the 23rd, and the two left companies of the 12th. Even the Federals were appalled. "We delivered such a deadly volley at very short range, that death's mission was with unerring certainty,"[12] said Lieutenant Colonel A. J. Sellars of Baxter's right regiment. This, the 90th Pennsylvania, aided by the 12th Massachusetts, was able to get in a destructive enfilade fire. Two regiments of Paul's brigade, on Baxter's left—the 16th Maine and 94th New York—also put in a raking fire.

All that Iverson's men could do was to run or hit the ground in the open, and the regiments were not of running material. The men found a shallow dip in the field about 80 yards in front of the stone wall. There, little protected from the Federals behind the wall and openly exposed to the flank fire, they tried to form a firing line. Lieutenant Colonel William S. Davis, commanding the 12th, saw a small bottom in a wheat field and moved his regiment into it, giving them the only worth-while protection along the front. He looked to the right and left and could see huge gaps in the Confederate line in both directions. Daniel's brigade was still far removed to his right rear.

"I was left alone without any orders," he said, "with no communication with the right or left, and with only 175 men confronting several thousand."[13] Owing to the exposure of this flank, Cutler's brigade near the railroad grading changed front and put an enfilade fire into Iverson's right, as had Paul.

The 20th North Carolina in the left center was pinned down and helpless. "I believe every man who stood up was either killed or wounded,"[14] said Lieutenant Oliver Williams, who was himself hit. This regiment had participated in a touching event, well remembered by both armies. At Fredericksburg in late 1862, after the Sharpsburg campaign, it had held a dress parade at which the band played "Dixie." Across the Rappahannock a Northern band heard and played back the song as a bit of camaraderie. The band of the 20th

North Carolina responded by playing "Yankee Doodle." Then both bands, as if by prearrangement, joined in "Home, Sweet Home." The chorus ran along the lines and both armies sang and wept.[15]

Now, many of the men, trapped in the most critical moment of the regiment's history, again were thinking of their North Carolina homes. The survivors never forgot the hour. They would inscribe in the regiment's records: "Initiated at Seven Pines, sacrificed at Gettysburg, and surrendered at Appomattox."[16]

Every commissioned officer of the 23rd North Carolina except one was either killed or wounded. "Unable to advance, unwilling to retreat, the brigade lay down in this hollow . . . and fought the best it could," Captain Turner said.

While the brigade was pinned down, alert General Baxter pushed out the 88th Pennsylvania and the 83rd and 97th New York to a point 80 yards due west of the stone fence and captured about 300 prisoners, including 200 of the 20th North Carolina, and the regiment's flag. The flag and some of the men were recaptured later in the day by Captain A. H. Galloway of the 45th North Carolina, of Daniel's brigade. Using their bayonets and gun butts as clubs, the Federals drove in forty-nine additional prisoners from the 23rd North Carolina and captured that regiment's flag.

Iverson apparently received only garbled accounts of what was happening, for he notified Rodes that one of his regiments had put up a white flag and gone over to the enemy.[17] The preposterous charge he later found to be untrue, although he adhered to an assertion that he had seen white handkerchiefs raised. Even this explanation, which is sometimes accepted, is doubtful. The North Carolina regiments did not record it.

Iverson said he found later that 500 of his men were lying dead and wounded in "a line as straight as a dress parade" and he exonerated the brigade "with one or two disgraceful individual exceptions."[18] But because of his false report, word spread over the army that a North Carolina regiment had surrendered en masse. It reached the 6th North Carolina of Early's division, where such irresolute men were cited as a warning by Lieutenant Colonel Samuel McDowell Tate.[19] No regiments served more gallantly than those so miserably led by Iverson. Rodes agreed that they "fought and died like heroes"; and he, too, reported that the dead and wounded lay on the field in a distinctly marked line of battle.[20]

After the battle rolled on elsewhere, Rodes, riding behind his line, thought he saw a regiment lying down to escape the fire of the Northern muskets. As he drew closer, he perceived they were all corpses.

Current regimental reports of the casualties were lost. Later returns showed 512 killed and wounded and 308 missing. Perhaps a more accurate estimate of the dead and wounded was made by Captain Turner, who placed the figure at 750. This would about check with the estimate of Lieutenant Montgomery of the 12th Regiment, who said between 350 and 400 were on hand when the brigade reassembled, out of 1,470 officers and men engaged.

Captain Turner reported that one of the privates of the 23rd was found dead, still clenching his musket, with five bullets through his head. That told the story of the leaden hail under which the men had lain. Lieutenant George B. Bullock of the 23rd said it was the only battle from Williamsburg to Appomattox where the blood actually ran in a rivulet, and it did just that at the bottom of the depression.[21] The brigade, and apparently with it the spirit of much of Rodes's division, was virtually destroyed. Daniel Harvey Hill, who had commanded the division in days of its greater glory, had never allowed a brigade to be sacrificed so needlessly.

Iverson was in such a distressful and played-out condition that Captain D. P. Halsey, his assistant adjutant general, had to reorganize the shattered regiments.[22] Iverson a little later was relieved from service in the Army of Northern Virginia. The steps are not quite clear. The North Carolinians refused to serve under him any longer. They attributed their catastrophe to the lack of a commander on the field. President Davis, some claimed, shielded Iverson from a court-martial. He was returned to Georgia, where later in the war he commanded a cavalry detachment.

The memory of Iverson's defeat lingered long in North Carolina, as Captain Turner had predicted. It was, perhaps, the North State's darkest hour. That night Lee's pioneers dug some shallow pits at the bottom of the depression behind Iverson's line in which the dead were buried in a few common graves. These came to be known over the Pennsylvania countryside as "Iverson's Pits." The unhappy spirits of the slaughtered North Carolina soldiers were reputed to abide in this section of the battlefield. Lieutenant Montgomery returned in 1898, thirty-five years after the battle, and learned from John S. Forney that a superstitious terror had long hung over the area. Farm laborers would not work there after night began to settle.[23]

Montgomery walked over the fields with Forney, who still owned and lived on the farm, as he had at the time of the battle.[24] They went to the pits, where the grass each year had shown a deeper verdure in springtime, and crops were luxuriant on years when the land was tended. Using the staffs they carried as pointers, they easily traced the edges of the pits by the more exuberant vegetation.[25] Though the bones had been disinterred during the general removal of the Confederate dead from Gettysburg to Richmond, the soil had been enriched with human flesh and blood.

Captain Turner of the 23rd Regiment visited the field that same year and dug into the empty pits. He found them "a veritable mine of war relics"—bullets, grapeshot, and shrapnel fragments released as the bodies of the soldiers had decayed.[26]

Montgomery noticed that Jessup Sheads had built a house on the site which the 97th New York, on Baxter's left, had occupied while it faced the 12th North Carolina. He said Sheads furnished wine to visitors to that part of the battlefield, and the arbors were on ground where the 12th North Carolina had left its dead.[27]

What remained of Iverson's brigade after the Federal descent on its left flank and the capture of the prisoners was saved by the arrival of Ramseur. Rodes had not thought to caution Ramseur against the same fate that befell Iverson's men. Ramseur was moving straight toward the stone wall when two lieutenants ran back and warned him,[28] suggesting that he trail off to the left and strike the right flank of the Federals.

That was the precise maneuver the brilliant young brigadier general made. Robinson saw the menace to his right and tried to change front to meet it, but Ramseur was quick and caught Baxter's men while they were thus engaged and before they could bring their guns into play. He held his fire until he could enfilade the entire line behind the stone wall, then delivered it with devastating effect.

Stephen Dodson Ramseur, Lee's youngest brigadier general—called the Chevalier Bayard of the war by the Richmond press[29]—was a handsome, black-eyed, highly intelligent graduate in the last class out of West Point before the states seceded. He was slim, erect, martial in his bearing, but boyish with his high, rounded brow, thick dark hair and an open, friendly manner that endeared him to his men. None sat with more grace or managed his horse with greater skill. His love was for the artillery and he always seemed a little reluctant that he was pushed ahead so rapidly in infantry commands.

A Lincolnton, North Carolina, youth, he had attended Davidson College when Daniel Harvey Hill was professor of mathematics there, and had applied for a cadetship at West Point with Hill's encouragement. Ramseur was twenty-five years old when given a brigade and had just passed his twenty-sixth birthday when Lee headed north, using him to head the invasion. He had led the charge at Malvern Hill and the advance for Jackson at Chancellorsville, being wounded in both attacks.

On one matter the army appeared to be agreed: that there was no more courageous brigade commander in the service. A memorial sketch apparently written by his old professor and commander, Harvey Hill, emphasized this quality, and stated that he "revelled in the fierce joys of strife," and that "his whole being seemed to kindle and glow amid the excitements of danger."[30]

Ramseur swept down the stone wall of the Forney farm from left to right, dislodged Robinson's division, one of the most stubborn commands of the Federal army, and pushed the two brigades back step by step slowly toward the seminary. Iverson and Ramseur had identical assignments; the one threw his brigade away, the other triumphed skillfully. In this action General Paul, commanding Robinson's First Brigade, was shot and permanently blinded in both eyes.

3. The Stand of the Bogus Bucktails

To the right, Daniel's brigade came into action after Iverson had been all but destroyed. Moving from the western slope of Oak Hill, Daniel had to travel a longer distance and, being the right brigade of Rodes's division, he had to make a contact with Pender's division of A. P. Hill's corps. The brigade had 2,100 men in five regiments and one separate battalion, all from North Carolina. While Iverson was confronting Baxter, Daniel skirted across the front of Cutler's brigade, passed through the hollow to Iverson's right, and moved toward the railroad cut and the Cashtown road, where he at once came under the fire of Stone's Bogus Bucktails, rated among the best marksmen of the Northern army.[31]

Stone's men had been under a constant pounding from Rodes's guns on Oak Hill and from Heth's batteries on Herr Ridge beyond Willoughby Run, and while the position was highly uncomfortable, Major Chamberlin considered the casualties not heavy because of the defective nature of the Southern ammunition. But the ammunition was good enough to force withdrawal of the Federal guns from the edge of the woods in Stone's rear.

Without knowing of the existence of the railroad cut, Daniel approached it and encountered a withering fire from the 149th Pennsylvania on the opposite side, which drove him back. Lieutenant Colonel Walton Dwight ordered the 149th to follow him across the cut. Dwight's men with great difficulty descended the embankment and clambered up the north side, where sliding shale slowed them.

But Dwight was the kind of man for whom the Pennsylvania mountaineers would go up the sheer sides of a precipice if he gave the word. He, too, had a combination of the varieties of courage. When Secretary Stanton closed the army to all visitors and issued a ban on passes, Dwight put in an application for a pass for an old man to visit his dying son. Stanton arbitrarily denied it and must have been stunned when Dwight stormed in with a blistering reproach. He told the domineering Secretary of War exactly what was on his mind: "My name is Dwight, Walton Dwight, Lieutenant Colonel of the One Hundred and Forty-ninth Regiment of Pennsylvania Volunteers. You can dismiss me from the service as soon as you like, but I am going to tell you what I think of you."[32]

Then he lit into Stanton with such vigor that the rebuked Secretary gave Dwight the pass and rescinded the entire order.

Dwight was now out in the open, with a resolute enemy in his front and the railroad cut in his rear. His men and Daniel's blazed away at each other. Doubleday watched the movement and thought it bold. Dwight fired two volleys, then charged with bayonets and pressed Daniel back farther, but the Carolinians returned and soon had the 149th scurrying to the other side. Daniel brought up a gun and stationed two of his companies to enfilade the railroad cut. Stone's men were held thereafter to the southern side. Stone, the gallant commander of the Bogus Bucktails, had come up to take charge of the movement and was heedless of his personal safety. While trying to extricate the regiment, he was hit by two bullets and carried out of the action. He was succeeded by Colonel Langhorne Wister of the 150th Pennsylvania.

Daniel's men now returned to the close-quarter fighting. With the 149th Regiment hard pressed, Wister called on his own regiment, facing west, to change front and face north along the roadway, a difficult maneuver which was nevertheless readily executed just in time for the

150th to pour a fire on Daniel at close range. The advancing Confederates were again driven into the woods. Fresh from the Carolina coast, the brigade was one of the best in the Southern army. Of it a regimental colonel said that "it never refused to advance when ordered and was never known to retire without command."[33]

Colonel Thomas S. Kenan, of the 43rd North Carolina, noted that Daniel handled the brigade "with consummate skill."[34] Now that he perceived Stone's markmanship, he broke up his close formations and sent in clouds of skirmishers close to the cut, where a destructive fire was exchanged with the 149th Pennsylvania, which Wister advanced. In this fighting Colonel Wister was shot through the face, and the Bogus Bucktails lost their second commander. Colonel Edmund L. Dana of the 143rd Pennsylvania took command. In the same fighting Lieutenant Colonel Dwight, of the 149th, and Major Chamberlin and Lieutenant Colonel H. S. Huiedekoper of the 150th were wounded.

Neither the Carolinians nor the Pennsylvanians had been able to gain an advantage after some of the hardest close-range fighting on the field, and the action now settled into a continuous exchange of rifle fire destructive to both commands. It was 2:30 P.M. The Bogus Bucktails had held their salient, but they had not yet felt the full impact of the forces being arrayed against them. Daniel's left meantime had engaged part of Paul and Cutler, indecisively, at longer range.

Rodes had attacked by his brigades in succession rather than in concert and by mid-afternoon three of them had met either with check or disaster. His battle had not opened any more auspiciously than Heth's. The brilliancy he had shown under Jackson at Chancellorsville had been lacking during the unusual opportunity for distinction that had been presented to his division by its timely arrival on Doubleday's flank at Gettysburg. Ewell, who was with him, had not helped. He was already disclosing that he was not aggressively commanding, but was merely accompanying his soldiers.

But new factors had entered the battle northwest of Gettysburg. Heth, who had not yet engaged the brigades of Pettigrew and Brockenbrough, had been restive under the restraint imposed on him by orders from Lee not to bring on a general battle. General Lee was now in the rear, in the neighborhood of Marsh Creek, and Heth rode back to him.

"Rodes is heavily engaged," he told the commanding general. "Had I not better attack?"

"No," he quoted Lee as replying. "I am not prepared to bring on a general engagement today. Longstreet is not up."[35]

Heth returned to his division, where he detected that the Federals were moving troops from his front to support those attacking Rodes. They were apparently Stone's men, on the bald crest of McPherson's Ridge, where they could be seen easily, changing front to fight Daniel. He reported this intelligence to General Lee, this time probably by courier, as he made no reference to a second trip to the rear. On the second request he received permission to resume his attack.[36]

The Battle of the Two Colonels

1. Zeb Vance Inspires a Regiment

Heth's assault was now about to precipitate one of the most gripping incidents of the Confederate War—the meeting of the 26th North Carolina Regiment of Pettigrew's brigade, commanded by the "boy colonel" Harry King Burgwyn, and the 24th Michigan of Meredith's Iron Brigade, led by an expatriate Virginian, Colonel Henry A. Morrow.

The episode manifested again that wars are most stubbornly contested between peoples of the same race and cultural heritage. Historically foreign wars have been made by governments, often as an expression of baffling statecraft. They have been a game which, in the words of Cowper, "were their subjects wise, Kings would not play at." Civil wars, on the other hand, are popular uprisings where each side sees the compelling necessity of its own stand. Distrusts between governments set off foreign wars; revolutions arise out of solemn popular convictions. Whipped-up hatreds attend foreign wars; civil strife is marked not so much by aversion as by a sense of righteousness felt deeply enough to tear a nation asunder.

So it was in the War between the States, where each side found a spiritual justification, transcending all emotion, in a belief that it fought in the sacred name of Freedom. Only this could explain the intensity, the firm resolution and the heedless personal sacrifice that distinguished this internecine struggle above all other American wars.

The 26th North Carolina Infantry, a name synonymous with blood,

death, and glory, had been Governor Zebulon Vance's regiment, recruited largely in the Piedmont counties, although two companies of
hillmen were among them. Vance was a mountaineer, a native of
Buncombe County, who had begun his career as a hotel clerk at Hot
Springs. His great natural force, with which his regiment came to be
imbued, was rated among the mountain dwellers as powerful as that
of his own French Broad River, which wrested and twisted its way
through the lofty barrier of the Great Smoky Mountains.

War had taken Vance from Congress to the command of a company, Buncombe County's hard-hitting Rough and Ready Guards,
which, in Ramseur's brigade, had been first across the Potomac of
Lee's army. A fall from an apple tree in early boyhood had broken
Vance's left hip and left him with a shortened leg and ambling gait.
This was more than compensated for by his intense ardor, superb
command of language, ready wit, and extraordinary capacity for making solid friendships. Soldier, Governor, United States Senator, Vance
enjoyed as have few other men in the country's history the abiding
affection of the people of his own state. A little later in the war he
would make an inspirational speaking tour of the different commands
of the Army of Northern Virginia. Jeb Stuart, who accompanied him,
declared that, measured by results, "Vance is the greatest orator that
ever lived," and General Lee was quoted as saying his visit to the
army was "worth 50,000 recruits."[1]

Such was the inspiring man who had met the impressionable youths
of the 26th Regiment. After electing Vance colonel the regiment had
gone on to choose Burgwyn, the camp instructor, its lieutenant colonel.
Almost immediately a good many judged that here the regiment had
made an appalling mistake. The young man was all intensity. The
regiment was literally snatched out of bed and shaken to attention.
"At first sight," said Corporal John R. Lane, who would soon rise
to become lieutenant colonel, "I both admired and feared him."[2]
Burgwyn, the son of a wealthy Northampton County planter, had
been educated by tutors and prepared for West Point, but had been
diverted to the University of North Carolina, where, like Pettigrew, he
had led his class, though he was graduated at the early age of eighteen.
His father, hearing the rumblings of the oncoming war, had influenced
him to continue his studies at Virginia Military Institute, where he
caught the attention of the austere T. J. Jackson, professor of artillery
and natural philosophy. Jackson gave him the top recommendation
one might expect from such a stern recluse, saying he would "make

an ornament not only to the artillery, but any branch of the military service."[3]

Vance inspired the regiment with his own tough, unyielding spirit, but he left the drill and military formalities to Burgwyn. The lieutenant colonel, twenty years old, conducted it with all the zeal of a V.M.I. cadet who had gratified "Old Jack." However cherished may have been the rugged independence of these Carolinians who had never recognized the frailest filaments of repression or restraint, war was something real to the diligent lieutenant colonel who meant to have a regiment that would obey him in battle. Something had been imparted to him from the intense light that burned in T. J. Jackson's pale-blue eyes.

Some of the men, looking on the war as a short-term lark that nobody needed to get excited about, grumbled at the martinet officer and swore that he would get the proper kind of attention when they fought their first battle. But they found in their first action that Burgwyn was the very prop they needed. He was in front when they advanced and in their rear when they retreated.

They perceived what it meant to have a coolheaded lieutenant colonel who knew how to conduct an engagement. Thoroughly disliked before the battle, Burgywn came out of it "the regiment's pride and joy."[4] The 26th went on to Virginia and took terrible punishment in the assault on Malvern Hill.

The test for Burgwyn came when Vance was elected Governor of North Carolina. He left the regiment in August 1862. The lieutenant colonel was still not twenty-one. The 26th was under Brigadier General Matt W. Ransom, who declared that he "wanted no boy colonel in his brigade."[5] The regiment decided to show its dander. The men made it known that they would have no other colonel than young Burgwyn, and petitioned to be taken out of Ransom's brigade. Hard-fighting D. H. Hill interceded; by all means Burgwyn should be promoted. Vance employed his influence. He knew the 26th needed Burgwyn. On his departure he had delivered a stirring speech: "It is fight to the end. All you can expect is War! War!! War!!!"[6]

So youthful Harry King Burgwyn was appointed colonel of the 26th by the Confederate War Department, field officers no longer being elected, and the regiment was assigned a little later to Pettigrew. John R. Lane, captain, but lately corporal, was appointed lieutenant colonel. The regiment knew what he would do for the soldiers. When they had charged up Malvern Hill he had carried inside his blouse the company's pay, wrapped in a newspaper. In the blood and excitement of the assault the package disappeared, and such were the demands of the wounded that night that he did not discover the loss until the next morning. Lee's army had been repulsed. Lane, unaware that McClellan also had retired during the night, set out alone to search the ground that had been saturated with Southern blood. Diligently he looked, and finally, half covered by dead and wounded, he found the packet of money, still wrapped and tied.[7] He hurried back and the company rejoiced with him.

One of the soldiers observed that Pettigrew and Burgwyn were "made for each other," being alike in their intensity, courage, zest for battle, martial bearing, and skillful horsemanship. Lieutenant Colonel Lane developed into a good drillmaster and the 26th came to vie with the 11th as "the best drilled regiment in the Confederate service."

2. The Factories Answer with Men

The 24th Michigan, which Burgwyn's regiment faced, had been born out of a Detroit riot. When Lincoln issued a call for 300,000 volunteers in the critical summer of 1862, the sentiments of Detroit, like those of other northern cities, were mixed, and the great mass meeting called together by the city authorities broke up in pandemonium. The Knights of the Golden Circle, augmented by refugee Confederates from the Canadian side of the Detroit River, had mobbed the meeting, drowned out the orations with catcalls, and finally wrecked the platform and driven off the speakers.

Ruffianism controlled the town. Sheriff Mark Flanigan and his deputies restored order to the shocked community. The good citizens determined to redeem their standing and display good faith to the nation by recruiting not only the six regiments called for under President Lincoln's proclamation, but also a seventh, a bonus regiment, which would prove to the world the city's loyalty to the cause.

The city judge, Henry A. Morrow, raised and led the regiment. Morrow had come to Detroit when a lad. Born in Warrenton, Virginia, he had been left an orphan without money or friends, and had made his way to Washington. There, being bright and courteous, he got a job as a Senate page boy, where the old soldier, General Lewis Cass, Senator from Michigan, who had raised himself by his own energies on a turbulent frontier, became attached to the young Virginian. Cass inspired him to read assiduously and encouraged him to move to Detroit and take up law.[8]

After reaching Detroit young Morrow enlisted as a private in a Michigan regiment and served in the Mexican War. Afterward he returned to Detroit, to begin a law practice, became recorder, and when the Recorder's Court was established in 1858, became its first judge.[9] Soon he was a familiar figure in Detroit public affairs, genial and pleasant, an excellent public speaker, an avid reader, and a respected jurist.

He was just the man to conduct a rapid, high-pressure campaign, sparkling with patriotism and publicity, to raise the bonus regiment. With the aid of Sheriff Flanigan, he had a full roster ready for muster into the Federal service in the remarkably short time of thirty days.

While he was making an eloquent appeal at a recruiting mass meeting, some wag in the crowd called out, "Why don't *you* enlist, Judge?"

"I'm going to," Morrow replied quickly.[10]

And he kept his word. When the regiment was organized the governor appointed him colonel. Sheriff Flanigan became lieutenant colonel.

On August 29, 1862, the 24th Regiment was assembled on the Campus Martius for departure to Virginia. The eyes of Michigan were on it and in performance it would have to excel. The ceremonies were elaborate. Local business houses had prepared a costly flag, with quilted stars on the blue field, inscribed with the words "24th Michigan Infantry,"[11] a regimental name destined to become as honored as that of any who ever carried the Stars and Stripes.

Colonel Morrow accepted the colors and the top officers took the swords that the admiring groups of citizens of Detroit presented—the lawyers to Morrow, and the deputy sheriffs to Flanigan.[12] Of the regiment's ten companies, eight were from Detroit, one from Plymouth and one from Livonia. Detroit even then had industrial pretensions and the factories had poured out their men. A public purse was collected to tide over families of the industrial recruits. Receptions and demonstrations occurred en route to the front, but the regiment was on its own when it was finally incorporated into the Army of the Potomac.

Rufus R. Dawes, then a major of the 6th Wisconsin, an Iron Brigade regiment, wrote from camp near Sharpsburg: "A fine new regiment has been added to our brigade . . . a splendid looking body of men . . . they are, as we were, crazy to fight."[13] A month later the brigade was at Warrenton, Virginia, without a single cracker. The veteran regiments, accustomed to scarcity, waited patiently for provisions to come up. The Wolverines were indignant at not being fed in their colonel's home town. They went about all day bellowing loudly, "Bread! Bread!" The balance of the brigade looked on contemptuously, but there was no contempt after the Detroiters had gone through the bloody battle of Fredericksburg. Dawes told the story in his letters home: "No soldiers ever faced fire more bravely. . . . Col. Morrow . . . enterprising, brave, and ambitious . . . stepped into a circle of the best and most experienced regimental commanders of the Army."[14]

3. Pettigrew Carries McPherson's Ridge

At a signal from Heth, Pettigrew advanced his brigade, numbering about 3,000 officers and men, a quarter of a mile across a wheat field, down the incline to Willoughby Run, and into McPherson's Woods, where the obstinate Iron Brigade that had scattered and captured Archer four hours earlier still waited.

Brockenbrough was on Pettigrew's left, moving against the McPherson farmhouse and outbuildings. At that point the Iron Brigade joined Stone's Bogus Bucktails, who held the Cashtown pike. Some remnants of Davis' brigade moved on Brockenbrough's left. Archer's survivors, commanded by Colonel Fry, marched on Pettigrew's right. Heth's line thus consisted, from left to right, of Davis, Brockenbrough, Pettigrew, and Fry. Opposed to them, from the Federal right to left, were Stone, Meredith, and Biddle. Meredith's regiments in the woods were, right to left, the 2nd and 7th Wisconsin, 24th Michigan and 19th Indiana.

Pettigrew appeared on his dapple gray, matching his trim, fresh uniform,[15] and rode forward with the men. "Oh, what a splendid place for artillery!" Colonel Burgwyn exclaimed to Lieutenant Colonel Lane, as the 26th moved out from Herr Ridge. "Why don't they fire on them?"[16]

The Southerners had scarcely gained momentum when Heth was hit. He had ordered the attack but knew nothing more about it until the next day. A Minié ball struck him on the head and rendered him insensible for thirty hours. Undoubtedly he would have been killed had his new hat not been too large. In Cashtown his quartermaster had exchanged Confederate script for Yankee headgear and offered Heth his pick. The one he selected was so big he had put a folded newspaper inside the sweat band. The bullet was slowed by the folds and did not penetrate his skull, although the impact took him out of the rest of the battle. Pettigrew assumed command of the division.

Meredith also went down early. He and his horse were hit by fragments of the same shell, and the horse rolled on him, causing severe internal injuries. Command of the Iron Brigade passed to Colonel Morrow, but he paid little attention to the brigade and continued to fight with his Michigan regiment.

Young Colonel Burgwyn was impatient as he marched his Carolinians in perfect alignment. While waiting in the wheat on the opposite hill, he had been conscious of the frightful loss of time. With a concerted attack Heth might have walked into Gettysburg. He attributed it to Hill's absence. The men had passed jokes as they waited. "Religious services were not held, as they should have been, owing to the absence of our chaplains."[17] In the woods 300 yards away they could catch glimpses of the tall, bell-crowned black hats of the Federal infantrymen, showing conspicuously through the green foliage. The hot sun was on their necks and the sweat ran down their arms and slickened their gunstocks. Off to the left Rodes's troops could be seen battling against Robinson. "Never was a grander sight beheld. The lines extended more than a mile, all distinctly visible to us."

Taking the center of the regiment, Burgwyn sent Lane to the right and Major John T. Jones to the left. The 26th moved at a quickstep, marching into action at attention, as on the drill ground. The standard-bearer, J. B. Mansfield, was four paces in front of the line, with four color guards on either side of the standard. All kept step and made a "pretty and perfect line."[18]

It was two o'clock when Pettigrew's soldiers struggled through the heavy underbrush and blackberry briers that still formed a barrier along the banks of Willoughby Run, after much threshing about of skirmishers and Archer's regiments. They came at once under the fire of Cooper's battery, posted on McPherson's Ridge to their right, between the Iron Brigade and Biddle. Cooper's guns were soon joined by those of Stewart's Battery B, of the 4th United States Artillery, stationed on the ridge behind the juncture of Stone and Meredith. After the battle this battery would claim that more men fell before its guns than before any other battery of the Federal army.

On crossing Willoughby Run, Burgwyn's men crowded to the center. Cooper's battery caused frightful loss from its enfilade position. Along the bank Burgwyn restored the alignment and the regiment moved ahead into the woods. For a moment bullets seemed to fill the air like hailstones. Then the men came face to face with the 24th Michigan and the two lines fired point-blank at each other. The smoke billowed in great white waves. The Federals receded and Burgwyn pressed on. Lane hurried from right to center.

"It is all right in the center and on the left," said Burgwyn. "We have broken their first line."

"We are in line on the right, Colonel," said Lane.[19]

Now the regiment began to work through the center of McPherson's Woods, a deceptive piece of ground a third of a mile in depth from Willoughby Run to the crest of McPherson's Ridge. After the first steep ascent the regiment passed over a rounded shoulder, then through a small valley about fifteen feet deep, with a dry bed of a stream at its bottom. Along this bed stood great oaks and chestnuts. The shoulder in front of the dry bed provided an excellent line of defense, while another defensive line ran only a hundred yards in the rear, where a stream fringed with thickets cut through another valley. Then the hill, heavily wooded, rose to the summit near which Reynolds had been killed. All through the woods the fighting raged as the Federals were forced back. Each stubborn halt was costly to both sides. By the time the North Carolina regiment reached the main Federal line at the crest of McPherson's Ridge, eight color guards and ten bearers of the colors had been shot down.[20]

Here Pettigrew and Burgwyn encountered determined and deadly resistance. While the two lines were blazing at each other, Captain W. W. McCreery, Pettigrew's assistant inspector general, rushed forward with a message from Pettigrew to Burgwyn. "Tell him," said Pettigrew, "his regiment has covered itself with glory."[21] What remained of it had also covered itself with sweat, grime, powder stains, and blood. McCreery was fired by the high zest of the attackers. Though he belonged with the staff, he foolishly seized the regimental flag, waved it back and forth, and rushed out in front of the line. He was shot instantly through the heart. Lieutenant George Wilcox of Company H ran forward and pulled the blood-covered flag from under the body; Wilcox had taken only a step when two bullets struck him. The Detroit factory hands had become deadly shots.

At this juncture Burgwyn's line hesitated. Stone was resisting Brockenbrough doggedly on the left, although still pressed by Daniel. To Burgwyn's right, the 47th North Carolina was locked in a desperate struggle with the 19th Indiana. The sweat on the rifle barrels and ramrods made it difficult to ram down the cartridges, and the attackers jammed the rods against stones to force the charges home.[22] The advancing line thus became undressed and ragged. Colonel George

H. Fairbault of the 47th tried to correct it as they passed through a wheat field to the right of the woods. Forty yards to the front a fresh enemy appeared, and the Carolinians went on with a rush. The regiment almost vanished as it ran ahead. "The earth seemed to open and take in that line," said Captain John A. Thorpe.[23]

The 47th overlapped the 19th Indiana and confronted Biddle, whom Thorpe said "deserved to command a corps." He related how a Federal officer rode rapidly forward carrying a large Federal flag. The Federals "swarmed around him as bees cover their queen." The mass of men was "acres big." Every Confederate gun turned on it and "seemingly shot the whole to pieces." The officer was Biddle. "It was with genuine and openly expressed pleasure our men heard he was not killed."[24]

Still farther on Pettigrew's right, the 52nd North Carolina felt the flank attack of Buford's cavalry, which guarded the extreme Federal left. The regiment formed a square to meet a charge of the horsemen, but Buford drew off and remained satisfied with long-range firing.

But the battle for the possession of McPherson's Heights, which commanded the main road by which Lee would have to reach Gettysburg, had developed into a duel mainly between two colonels, the boy Burgwyn and old Judge Morrow. Neither had any intention of giving way as long as men could stand.

In front of the 26th North Carolina, Colonel Morrow's men had been taking frightful punishment. Morrow's first volley had not checked Burgwyn's advance. The Carolinians "came on with rapid strides, yelling like demons."[25] He watched while the 19th Indiana was overpowered and pushed back, and to guard against a cross fire he swung his left companies back. Before the shift could be completed Burgwyn came storming against his front, and he was forced to another line in the rear.

Here on this last line occurred the final desperate fight between the two regiments. The crisis had been reached. Burgwyn told Lane the laudatory words received from Pettigrew and asked him to inform the men. Seeing the regiment waver, Burgwyn seized the flag as it fell from the hands of Lieutenant Wilcox and shouted, "Dress to the colors." Then he started forward with the flag. Private Frank Honeycutt of Company B ran from the ranks and requested the honor of advancing it. Burgwyn had turned to hand over the flag when a bullet struck his left side, passed through both lungs, spun him around with its force, and dropped him mortally wounded. He carried the colors down with him.[26] Honeycutt seized them, but almost instantly he was shot through the head. Thus for the thirteenth time in the attack the flag of the 26th North Carolina was on the ground. That should have been enough to end the mad vainglory of carrying the colors in battle. But the pride of showing the flag was to continue through this and future battles—and this and future wars—until the futility of the assignment had been adequately demonstrated. Eventually the colors came to be cased during battle.

Lane rushed to his fallen commander, the mere boy who had won the regiment's deep affection. He asked if he were hurt severely. Burgwyn's response was a pressure on Lane's hand. Then he got out a few words, "Tell the general my men never failed me."[27] The regiment was going forward and could not carry him back. That night they buried him, with a gun case for a coffin, beneath a large walnut tree near where he fell. He was twenty-one years old. The martinet drillmaster whom some of the men wanted to finish in the first battle died one of the most loved and admired officers in the Confederate army.

Only two days before the battle he had heard that some of his men had pilfered honey from a Pennsylvania farmer's beehive. He had found the owner and paid him for the honey.

Lane did not wait, but turning to right and left shouted to the remaining officers, "I am going to give them the bayonet. Close your men quickly to the left." At the center he found the colors still on the ground. He was raising them when Lieutenant Blair of Company I rushed out with earnest entreaty: "No man can take those colors and live." Lane shouted at him, "It's my time to take them now. 26th North Carolina, follow me!"[28] The thin line of survivors again let out the Rebel Yell and forged ahead. The last resistance broke. The Iron Brigade was swept from the crest of McPherson Ridge and pushed back to the entrenchments on Seminary Ridge.

Morrow's color-bearers had tossed their lives away as freely. By the time the third had fallen the regiment's ranks were so wasted that scarcely one fourth of it remained. Retreating to successive lines, Morrow had determined finally to stand and slug it out. He told Corporal Andrew Wagner of Company F to plant the flag where he pointed, but Wagner fell before he could obey the order. Morrow grabbed it up but Private William Kelley of Company E snatched it from his hand. "The colonel of the 24th shall never carry the colors while I am alive," said Kelley; almost instantly he too fell dead.[29]

Private Silburn Spaulding of Company K then carried the flag to the last stand in the barricade around the seminary. In all, nine color-bearers fell. At the end Morrow was shot. A Minié ball hit the top of his head and ripped along the skull, covering him with blood. He was left on the ground and the Confederates captured him as they advanced.

The firing had almost died away. Sergeant Charles H. McConnell of the 24th Michigan saw the commanding figure of Lieutenant Colonel Lane carrying the Confederate flag, and waited to take a parting shot. He rested his rifle against a tree only thirty paces away. The bullet crashed through Lane's jaw and mouth, and for the fourteenth time the flag of the 26th North Carolina fell.

Lane survived. Forty-four years later, when the Confederate monument was dedicated at Pittsboro, North Carolina, the last commander of the famous 26th Regiment, which claimed to have lost more men at Gettysburg than any other regiment of either army in any battle of the war, served as chief marshal. The old man rode a spirited horse at the head of the procession, sitting "erect as an Indian."[30]

The battle between the regiments ended more from extermination than exhaustion. Of the 496 officers and men who went in with the 24th Michigan, 399 were killed or wounded, a loss of 80 per cent.

"Our loss was very large," said Morrow, "exceeding perhaps the losses sustained by any regiment of equal size in a single engagement in this or any other war."[31]

The 26th North Carolina encountered not only the Michigan regiment, but at times in its advance the 19th Indiana and the 151st Pennsylvania, the right regiment of Biddle's command. The loss in killed and wounded was recorded in North Carolina annals as 82 per cent. Losses were heaviest in the two center companies, E and F, which marched at the sides of the colors. Company E on the right went in with 82 officers and men and ended the attack with 2 untouched. Company F, deer and bear hunters from the slopes of Grandfather Mountain, commanded by Captain R. M. Tuttle, later a Presbyterian minister, went in with 3 officers and 88 enlisted men. All were killed or wounded. Only Sergeant Hudspeth could report for duty after the fight, and he had been stunned for a time by an exploding shell. This company had three sets of twins and 5 of the 6 were left dead on

McPherson's Ridge. Company A of Ashe County went in with 92 and ended the fight with 15.

Pettigrew's adjutant general, Captain Young, was attracted by what he called "dreadful howls" from some of the wounded in the woods. He did not specify whether they were Federals or Confederates or both, but he approached several and found they were foaming at the mouth, as though mad, and were apparently unaware of their sounds. This was the only time during the war Young saw such a reaction; he attributed it to the shock of "a quick, frightful conflict following several hours of suspense."[32]

He gave his impression of the fighting: "I have taken part in many hotly contested fights, but this I think, was the deadliest of them all, not excepting the third day's charge on Cemetery Ridge; and never have I seen or known of better conduct on the part of any troops, under any circumstances, or at any time."[33]

After the battle Pettigrew wrote to Vance: "Their loss has been heavy, very heavy. . . . Your old command did honor to your association with them and to the State they represent."[34] Pettigrew might have added a line: Not a man of his brigade was taken prisoner.[35]

When Heth got around to aggregating his losses he said he began the action with 7,000 muskets and in twenty-five minutes lost 2,700 men.

The three Federal brigades found scant time behind their seminary entrenchments to collect stragglers and strengthen their lines. When Pettigrew's attack was spent, immediately behind came Pender's fresh division, moving against Doubleday's last stand on Seminary Ridge.

4. The Color Ruse of the Bucktails

When the Iron Brigade was beaten back to the seminary by Pettigrew's vehement attack, carrying Biddle with it, Stone and the remnants of Cutler were left exposed at the McPherson farm buildings and the railroad cut. Brockenbrough had been unable to dislodge them and had himself been momentarily repulsed. Now Daniel again aligned his brigade for a final decision with the Pennsylvanians, who were confronted by Brockenbrough on their left, Daniel on their right and the approach of Pender behind Brockenbrough in their front.

The spectacular stand of the Bogus Bucktails at their salient on the Cashtown road was made possible partly by a ruse perpetrated by Color Sergeant Henry G. Brehm of the 149th Pennsylvania volunteers, at the instigation of Colonels Stone and Dwight. In front of the angle of the brigade were two piles of fence rails formed at right angles, which had been made into a barricade by one of Buford's cavalry pickets on the night of June 30. The pile was fifty yards north of the Cashtown pike and 115 yards south of the railroad cut through Mc-Pherson's Ridge. Wheat stood waving in the fields around the barricade, but the rails were easily visible to the north and west.

When Rodes seized Oak Hill and sent his shells crashing through the old cherry trees in Stone's rear, Stone and Dwight pointed out the barricades to Sergeant Brehm and asked him if he could advance the colors to that point. Brehm agreed. Two thirds of the 149th lay along McPherson's farm lane facing west, and a third faced north along the Cashtown pike; the barricade was fully fifty yards from the closest point in the line. Crawling, Brehm led his color guard through the wheat and secured both the national and state flags to the fence rails. Almost immediately the Confederate artillery fire was lifted from the men in the line and directed against the colors. All through the afternoon, while Daniel's and Brockenbrough's men charged the Bogus Bucktails, the colors were held fast in their isolated position, seen easily from both Herr Ridge and Oak Hill, defiantly challenging the Confederate gunners and sharpshooters. Brehm and his color guard crouched in their holes and behind their rails, while the storm raged overhead. They held the position amid the bursting shells and hail of bullets. Even when Daniel's men finally burst in on him Brehm was reluctant to let his colors go.

"This is mine," said a Confederate, seizing a flagstaff.

"No, by God, it isn't," said Brehm, wielding his gun butt. But he and the color guard went down, all killed or wounded. They had drawn enough fire to annihilate the brigade, had it been dropped along the lane and roadway.[36]

The end had finally come for the Bogus Bucktails. One of the graphic contemporary pictures of the battle of the first day showed the thin line of survivors moving back along the Cashtown road at the double quick, with a Confederate brigade running abreast them on either side and another pressing their rear, all pouring a fire into them, to which they were replying as best they could. At the Ripple midway between McPherson's and Seminary Ridge, Stone's men undertook to make another stand but they were isolated and soon had to resume their retreat.

Never again did the army apply the term "Bogus" to Stone's Buck-tails. Today the traveler approaching Gettysburg on the Cashtown road sees as almost the first monument the figure of the Pennsylvania mountaineer holding his long deer rifle, stationed at the point where the 149th Regiment bent its line from McPherson's Lane to the Cash-town pike, at the hot corner of the first day's battle. There Stone's men stood for nearly five hours and there, as Doubleday asserted, most of them, true to their first promised shout, remained.

CHAPTER TWELVE

Through the Town

1. Two Georgia Brigades Converge

Henry T. Thomas, writing in later years of his glorious 12th Georgia Regiment, bemoaned the passing of the old order in the deep South. Change had come to the land of honeysuckle and wide verandas, where the mockingbird sang in the mimosa tree, the plover ran the meadow and the whippoorwill called in the moonlight.

One of the ancient customs that had well nigh disappeared was the event of hog killing in the first winter chill, when the lads blew up bladders, neighbors came to cook melts, chitterlings, souse and sausage, and the Negroes hovered about to share in the delightful tastes and odors of fresh pork frying on the hot stones.

Such was the rural society and luxurious times that had given way before "the Yankee, the western farmer and the New South,"[1] he complained, as he went on to tell the story of his intrepid regiment of Doles's brigade, one of the most celebrated bodies of men ever to come out of the red lands, and an aggregation typical of the culture and independent thought of central Georgia.

Although Thomas did not relate it, no man, not even Stonewall himself, could put a rein on the free spirit of the 12th. The regiment had given the Confederate high command "Clubby" Edward Johnson and had served in Johnson's brigade at the battle of McDowell. When Jackson had tried to retire it, the 12th had contemptuously ignored the orders and held to its exposed position on the forward side of

153

the ridge. A lank youth explained for his comrades that "we ain't cum all the way he'ah to Vuginia to run frum Yankees."[2]

The brigade carried a *sang-froid,* a devil-may-care attitude and a sensitiveness about points of honor characteristic of the Georgian plantation society. Life was not so dear it had to be husbanded. Officers brought their slaves as personal retainers, but punctiliously kept them in camp during the fighting, with firm admonitions not to venture near the firing line. In few instances in the army was there a closer affection between the brigade and its commander. George Doles, who would be so fortunate as to survive until Cold Harbor where his brigade met the main impact of Grant's attack, was justly rated "one of the bravest, best loved and most accomplished soldiers Georgia furnished to the Confederate army."[3] After he fell the men tried to express their love for him by adopting his daughter Minnie as the "daughter of the regiment."

Born and reared in the Georgia capital of Milledgeville, Doles became captain of the Baldwin Blues, one of the oldest and best-trained military aggregations of the state. His military proficiency was apparent to the soldiers who were his neighbors along the Oconee River, and when the war came and they were mustered into the Confederate service, they elected him colonel.

Doles, now thirty-three years old, was a handsome man with penetrating eyes under a lofty forehead. Like Pettigrew, he wore a beard but no sideburns and, also like Pettigrew, reflected a quiet self-assurance and a high order of intelligence. He had been wounded leading the charge at Malvern Hill and had been in the front line when Jackson rolled up the Federal flank at Chancellorsville, always showing a competence his superiors admired. Now he was moving again toward Schurz's Germans holding the line north of Gettysburg, the same troops he had confronted two months before at Chancellorsville.

Rodes had intended that Doles, on his left, should merely detain Schurz while Iverson and O'Neal delivered the main attack against Doubleday, but it was Daniel on his extreme right and Doles on his extreme left who carried the major fighting load of the division. The story of Doles's assault on Schimmelfennig was summed up quickly by the scribe of the 12th Georgia: "Our brigade charged with that soul-stirring rebel yell, which once heard on the field of battle can never be forgotten." The Yankees soon broke, and "fled in wild confusion, pursued by our shouting, exultant men."[4]

The attack was not quite so simple. Doles, menacing the gap between the First and Eleventh corps, which Schimmelfennig had been able to close partially with the batteries of Dilger and Wheeler, was confronting the better part of a corps with a single brigade. Moving across the open ground, he was without support on his left and was detached from O'Neal on his right, thus having both flanks open and dangerously exposed. Schimmelfennig advanced Von Amesburg's brigade to explore the gap between Doles and O'Neal, but the Georgian countered quickly by changing front, striking Von Amesburg and rolling him back on Schimmelfennig's second brigade, that of Kryzanowski, whose line ran across the fields between the Mummasburg and Carlisle roads. There the fences gave protection and Kryzanowski held.

Barlow, on Schimmelfennig's right, meanwhile observed that Doles's left flank was in the air and directed Von Gilsa to assail it. The opportunity was inviting. Doles, still confronting two divisions with his single brigade, seemed in danger of being overlapped and taken in reverse.

That was the situation at three o'clock when Early's division appeared along the Heidlersburg road, deployed across the hills on the opposite side of Rock Creek, moving rapidly toward Barlow's flank and rear. On Early's right the first of his brigades to come into contact with the Federals was John B. Gordon's, composed of six Georgia regiments. The Eleventh Corps in its exposed position thus suddenly found its flanks assailed by two converging Georgia brigades.

Early's march from Heidlersburg on the morning of July 1 had not been rapid, nor was there intimation of the battle until the head of his column was three or four miles northeast of the town. Then, after noon, firing was heard; however, because of freak atmospheric conditions the subdued roar sounded more like a cavalry engagement twenty miles distant than an infantry combat close at hand. Just then young Major John Warwick Daniel, Early's chief of staff (who in later life was elected five times to the United States Senate from Virginia), was seen riding at top speed to the front with directions to hurry the march. He described how Hill's corps was desperately engaged at Gettysburg, from which the infantry firing could finally be heard in heavy volume. The men stripped off their blankets, heaped them and other unneeded accouterments in piles to be gathered by the wagon train, and made the last mile toward Gettysburg at double-quick time.[5]

Near at hand they could see the clouds of white powder smoke floating over the town. When the division was formed in battle line Early ordered ten minutes' rest to let the men catch their breath.

Almost simultaneously with the appearance of Early northeast of Gettysburg, Pender's division of A. P. Hill's corps passed through Heth's exhausted troops and assaulted Seminary Ridge, where the remnants of the Federal brigades from McPherson's Heights had gathered behind the stone walls and bastions thrown up by the regiments that had waited there in reserve. Rodes at last pressed his brigades forward in unison, and for the first time during the scattered and intense fighting of July 1 the Confederate army managed to obtain something like concerted action. Lee was riding with his staff from Marsh Creek, still concerned over the prolonged firing ahead, which suggested that the "chance encounter" had turned into a major engagement. But the needed co-operation had now been arrived at between Hill on Herr Ridge and Ewell on Oak Hill.

Ewell could observe the advance of Early through the wheat fields on the opposite side of Rock Creek, Gordon on the right, Hays in the center, and Hoke's brigade, commanded by Avery, on the left, with Extra Billy Smith in reserve. A heavy mist began to fall, cooling the men after their hot march and momentarily obscuring the sun.

Early now re-formed his division after its brief rest, a pause which Jackson would have frowned on while other troops were fighting. Turning to his aide Daniel, he scurried off orders to Gordon, Hays, Avery and Smith to double-quick to the front and open the lines for the artillery to pass. Colonel Hillary P. Jones came thundering down with his four batteries, the horses at a run, and while he was getting his guns into position Gordon's clear voice rang out with its command, "Forward, Georgians!"[6]

The gleaming steel bayonets shone above the yellow wheat—"a silver wave across the cloth of gold," Major Daniel grandiloquently called it[7]—as Gordon moved west against the Federal flank and reached out to clasp hands with Doles's other Georgians attacking Barlow's division directly in front. Announcement of Early's arrival was carried the length of the Confederate line by the Charlottesville, Virginia, artillery opening fire at Early's personal command.

Early's extreme left regiment was the 57th North Carolina of Avery's brigade. "From our position," said Colonel Hamilton C. Jones, "we could see the Confederate and Federal lines arrayed one against the other in open ground, no breakworks, no fortifications, but

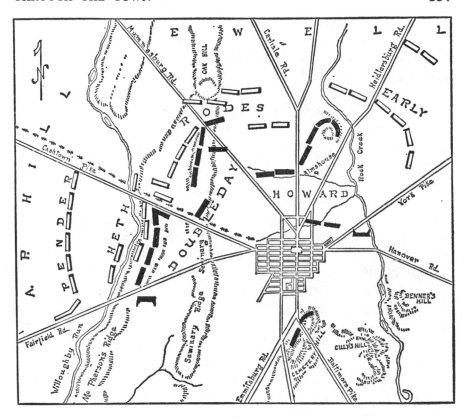

Concerted attack of Early, Rodes, Heth, and Pender.
July 1, 1863, 3:00 to 4:00 P.M.

they stood apart in battle array and were in plain view for two miles except where the line was lost in the depressions of the hills."[8]

That was the striking feature about this phase of the battle of the first day—the visibility of the entire battle line from both flanks of each army. Pender, attacking the seminary, could see Early's division assailing Barlow, and Avery's men on Early's left could look to the far right and see Pender. The foliage and buildings of 1863 did not obstruct the view.

What Colonel Jones observed as he stood on the left of the Confederate line sheds important light on the order of events during this phase of the battle. Far off to the right he could see a Southern brigade going into action. It must have been Perrin's, of Pender's division. White smoke billowed out from the Federal line, next there was a rattle of musketry, scarcely audible at that distance against the undertones of the artillery. "Then there came the expected yell, a rush, and the enemy's line broke," Jones said. While he watched, another brigade attacked in echelon, with the same yell, and again the enemy broke. This must have been Ramseur. Closer came the assaults and before each of them the Federal line gave way and the scattered blue-coated soldiers fell back toward the town.

"As the conflict neared our position," said Jones, "the effect was marvelous; the men were wild with excitement, and when their time came they went in with the wildest enthusiasm, for from where they stood they could see two miles of the enemy's line in full retreat. It looked indeed as if the end of the war had come."[9]

Robert Stiles, riding close to Early, noticed that the general's glossy black ostrich plume trembled and shimmered on the wide brim of his felt hat as though it were alive.[10] Major James McDowell Carrington, captain of the Charlottesville, Virginia, artillery, also with Early, found the general silent and absorbed, but uncertain enough about the attack to warn the artilleryman to be prepared to unlimber and provide a rallying point if Gordon should be severely handled. But the Georgian emerged through the great sycamores and willows and fell impetuously on Barlow at the Federal right.

By coincidence Barlow's right brigade was Von Gilsa's, which had been on Hooker's extreme right at Chancellorsville and had been the first to feel the shock of Jackson's flank attack. Perhaps it was this earlier experience that unnerved the Germans, for Gordon sent their line reeling back from its anchor on Barlow's Knoll, across the stream north of Gettysburg, past the almshouse, a group of brick buildings on the Heidlersburg road, where they halted momentarily, and into the outskirts of the town. The open fields northeast of Gettysburg were covered with their dead. Howard tried to save his right by hurrying Coster's brigade of Steinwehr's division down from Cemetery Ridge, but before the Federals could establish a second defensive line they were struck again by the brigades of Hays and Avery on Gordon's left.

Colonel Jones's command, the flank regiment of Early's division, encountered little resistance. Jones said the enemy broke at the first fire of the 57th North Carolina. "In fact, they scarcely waited to receive the fire,"[11] he asserted. The other regiments of Avery's brigade, the 6th and 21st North Carolina, experienced stiffer opposition and fought a bloody combat as they pressed ahead.

On reaching the field Gordon had at once noticed the threat to Doles by Von Gilsa's flanking movement. With what some have termed "savage cries,"[12] but what Gordon described as "a ringing yell,"[13] his men had fallen on Barlow's line, fought it hand to hand for a brief interval and had broken it. This placed his brigade obliquely in the rear of the Federal position. "Any troops that were ever marshalled would, under like conditions, have been as surely and swiftly shattered," said Gordon. "There was no alternative for Howard's men but to break and fly, or to throw down their arms and surrender."[14] Most of them chose flight and crowded down the road past the almshouse into Gettysburg. As Major Daniel described it, "The Federal flank had been shriveled up as a scroll."

Meantime Doles, being relieved from the menace of Von Gilsa by Gordon's attack, again assailed Von Amesburg and began the collection of prisoners among those unable to scurry back into Gettysburg.

Gordon rode ahead with his troops. The artilleryman Stiles observed the Federal retreat and described it as "pell-mell over the rolling wheat fields, through a grove, across a creek, up a little slope, and into the town itself."[15] Early's three brigades followed so rapidly that although Stiles brought his guns into battery several times, he could not fire because the two armies were so close together.

Stiles thought that Gordon at this moment was "the most glorious and inspiring thing I ever looked upon." He was riding "a majestic animal, 'whose neck was clothed with thunder,' " a coal-black stallion captured from one of Milroy's officers at Winchester. "I never saw a horse's neck so arched, his eyes so fierce, his nostrils so dilated." The speed of the Georgians was shown by the fact that Gordon rode at a trot, with the horse's head "right in among the slanting barrels and bayonets." He was bareheaded. "In a voice like a trumphet" he urged his men ahead. That sonorous voice would lead the last charge at Appomattox, by which time Gordon had risen to the command of half of Lee's army, and would long sound in the United States Senate halls, but never was it more inspiring than at this moment at Gettysburg. Stiles said he would not have risked a dime then against the independence of the Confederacy. He called to Gordon, "General, where are your dead men?"

"I haven't got any sir," Gordon bellowed back. "The Almighty has covered my men with His shield and buckler."[16]

Later in Richmond as Stiles aided the wounded, he asked one man what his outfit was. The man's face lighted up. "I belong to Gordon's old brigade, Captain," he said. "Did you ever see the gin'ral in battle?

He's the most prettiest thing you ever did see on a field of fight. It 'ud put fight into a whipped chicken just to look at him."[17]

In the Federal debacle an officer who had tried to rally the men was hit by a Minié ball; Gordon discovered him on his back with the afternoon July sun beating down in his face. All about him were Northern dead and he, too, appeared to be dying. Gordon dismounted, lifted his head, gave him water from his own canteen, and asked his name. He was Barlow, the Federal division commander, who did not appear likely to survive many hours. A ball had passed through his body near the spinal cord, paralyzing his legs and arms. Gordon had him carried to the shade, took a packet of letters he wanted destroyed and later, learning that Mrs. Barlow was with the Federal army, sent her a flag of truce for passage through the Southern lines. The Federal general survived, to command a division later in Grant's army.[18]

When Howard's men were scattered most of the Southern soldiers considered the battle won and Southern independence a virtual certainty. Carrington and his artillerists thought the wild yelling denoted victory. Just then Early ordered his guns advanced to the town. Carrington halted in the main street, unlimbered three pieces, and prepared his canister. But Early by that time thought the Federals were out of range.

In this battle, fought by two divisions of the Eleventh Corps mainly against two Georgia brigades, the Confederates were heavily outnumbered, even after Hays and Avery had brought their brigades into the attack. But Howard had placed his troops in a calamitous position, with a road—over which a Confederate division was approaching—leading to their rear. The fault was not so much in the troops as in their leader.

Doubleday, distrustful of the position from the start, had had little opportunity to influence Howard, who confided nothing and fought his own battle. The line, in Doubleday's opinion, was too far removed from the town and would have been more secure if it had been echeloned behind the right flank of the First Corps, with its right resting on the almshouse,[19] which was much easier to defend and much more difficult to turn than Barlow's Knoll. The Cemetery Hill position farther back would, of course, have been even safer.

As Gordon had now exhausted his ammunition and had stopped to refill his cartridge boxes, Early sent a summons to Smith. Impatient when he got no response, he repeated the order.[20] But Extra Billy was lost somewhere amid the white smoke clouds rolling off to the rear. He failed to appear, and it was not until later that Early learned he was off chasing a bugbear.

2. A "Steel Division" Assails the Seminary

West of Gettysburg, where first Buford, then Reynolds, and finally Doubleday had been doggedly holding off A. P. Hill since early morning, the Federal army enjoyed no such numerical superiority as Howard north of town. But the weakness of the First Corps lines had not been fully exploited and Doubleday had profited from the lack of coordination in the Confederate attack. Now, with most of his brigades already shattered, Doubleday was suddenly faced with the fierce onslaught of Pender's fresh division.

Pender's had been A. P. Hill's celebrated light division; its timely arrival on Lee's right had saved the army at Sharpsburg, and on the Peninsula it had been described as "made of steel, rather than flesh and blood."[21] It consisted of the North Carolina brigades of Lane and Scales, the Georgians of Thomas, and the South Carolinians of McGowan, these last being commanded at Gettysburg by Colonel Abner Perrin.

William Dorsey Pender, youngest among Lee's infantry division commanders, was an unusual combination of sweetness and gentleness with whirlwind military aggressiveness. He had the soft brown eyes of a dreamer but hit like a hammer in an attack. His love letters to his wife, written almost daily even during intense campaigning, show a deep religious faith and a compassion and softness altogether out of harmony with the fierce ruthlessness of the battlefield.

Both at Chancellorsville, after A. P. Hill was wounded, and at Gettysburg, Pender commanded a division, and while his term was brief in this enlarged responsibility, he obviously could not have given Lee a more impressive account of himself. Lee was later to bemoan the fact that he did not give Pender a corps. Had Pender rather than Hill led the Third Corps, and commanded it as closely at the scene of the fighting as was his custom, the story of Gettysburg might have been different. Because President Davis adhered so closely to the seniority system, Pender's promotion to major general had been delayed beyond what his friends felt were his deserts. Leadership of a corps was not thought about until after his death.

Medium tall, Pender was described by his brother as "well formed and graceful," but one of his early military feats suggests that he was a more muscular and powerful man than these words imply.[22] While campaigning against the Indians in the far Northwest, as a lieutenant of dragoons, he had ridden alone to bring up reinforcements at the battle of Spokane Plains, when he was suddenly intercepted and attacked by an Indian chief. He had no time to draw his sword and would have been killed had he not grasped his attacker's upraised arm, then his neck, and pinioned him. Holding the powerless Indian, he put spurs to his horse and galloped toward his men. When he reached them he picked up the Indian and hurled him back among the dragoons.

This was no puny young officer, whose voice was low and cultivated and whose words came in a soft Carolina drawl. One of his officers, First Lieutenant Benjamin H. Cathey of the 16th North Carolina, summed him up: "He was one of the coolest, most self-possessed and one of the most absolutely fearless men under fire I ever knew."[23]

He had been a close friend of Jeb Stuart at West Point and after their graduation in 1854 they had visited another classmate, Samuel Turner Shepperd, at the family's country seat, Good Spring, near Salem (now Winston-Salem), North Carolina. The distinguished father, Augustine Henry Shepperd, had represented his district nine terms in the United States Congress. At Good Spring Pender met the eldest daughter, Mary Frances Shepperd. They were married in 1859 and for the four years left to them—two years in the West and two under the Confederacy—their romance was one of pure beauty.

Pender, a regular army officer, had made no commitment until Lincoln called on North Carolina for troops to serve against other Southern states, whereupon he resigned his commission to become a lieutenant colonel and drill instructor at Camp Garysburg, North Carolina. Thereafter his rise, like Ramseur's, was rapid.

Mary Shepperd Pender, the congressman's daughter and general's wife, was a woman of gentle expression but strong convictions, as Pender's letters disclose.[24] Her devoutness made her reluctant to see the Southern army in the role of invader. Pender wrote her on June 24 from Shepherdstown, Virginia, a trifle apologetically: "Tomorrow I do what I know will cause you grief, and that is to cross the Potomac. . . . May the Lord prosper this expedition and bring an early peace out of it."

He had faith in the righteousness of his cause. Earlier he had written: "Take a few examples and see how hard and almost impossible it is to subdue a people determined to be free. The Netherlands whom Philip tried to crush; Spain against Napoleon. This country in '76. . . ."

In his last letter, from Fayetteville, Pennsylvania, where his division was resting after its march of 157 miles from the Rappahannock, he was confident but unsettled: "The people are frightened to death and will do anything we intimate to them. . . . I am tired of invasions for although they have made us suffer all that people can suffer I cannot get my resentment to that point to make me feel indifferent to what goes on here."

He knew enough about pillaging to understand that it ruined discipline. "But for the demoralizing effect plundering would have on our troops, they [the Pennsylvanians] would feel war in all its horrors." He would not be indebted to those he fought. "I have made up my mind to enjoy no hospitality of friendship from any of them," he declared.

"I never saw troops march as ours do. They will go 15 or 20 miles a day without having a straggler and sing (?)[25] and yell on all occasions. Confidence and good spirits seem to possess every one of them. I wish we could meet Hooker and have the matter settled at once." Thus Pender expressed his confidence.

Now Hooker's army was before him—as he had wished—though under a new commander, and Pender's turn had come. Most of the day the division had been waiting in the fields beyond Herr Ridge. On word from Hill at 3:30 P.M. his brigades in battle order crossed Willoughby Run.

Scales was on the left, Perrin in the center and Lane on the right, with Thomas in reserve. Pender's orders to them were to move through Heth's division and engage the enemy closely. In no circumstances were they to stop. "Rout him from his position."[26] Each brigadier was to manage his brigade according to his own judgment.

"Our men," said Perrin, "moved as bravely forward as any men ever did on earth. We charged over Pettigrews brigade; the poor fellows could scarcely rise to cheer us as we passed."[27]

Perrin's brigade had been built around South Carolina's famous Palmetto Regiment, which had been the first to enter Mexico City in the Mexican War, and in which its recently wounded commander, Samuel McGowan, had served as a private. Fighting alongside it in Mexico had been the 12th U.S. Infantry, commanded by the South Carolinian Colonel Milledge Luke Bonham, under whom Perrin served as a captain.

Bonham, McGowan, and Perrin, all from the back country of

western South Carolina, were close friends. Bonham was elected Governor of South Carolina in 1862 and left the Confederate Army. These old army comrades exchanged letters on confidential terms, one of which, from Perrin to Bonham, gives intimate observations on the battle of Gettysburg.

The Federal line at the seminary consisted of hurriedly constructed earthen breastworks and bastions of stone walls and rail fences. South of the seminary a stone wall began at the large brick house, the home of the Shultz sisters, Maria and Cornelia, and ran southwestwardly along the crest of Seminary Ridge. North of the seminary on the turnpike batteries which all day had exacted a heavy toll from the Confederates were still strongly posted when Pender began his attack. Pender's entire division was south of the turnpike, on which Scales rested the left of his brigade.

Here he struck the remnants of the Iron Brigade, now commanded by Colonel W. W. Robinson of the 7th Wisconsin, intermixed with survivors of Stone's Bucktails. Colonel Dawes with the 6th Wisconsin had reached the seminary by running down the railroad that had proved a cul-de-sac for his opponent earlier in the day, and waited for the oncoming assault. He gave a picture of Pender's approach: "For a mile up and down the open fields in front, the splendid lines of the veterans of the Army of Northern Virginia swept down upon us. Their bearing was magnificent. They maintained their alignment with great precision."[28] But the remnants of the Bucktails and the Iron Brigade still had fight left in them, and here perhaps they put in their most glorious performance. Strung out along Seminary Ridge, the men lay in the woods and kept up an incessant fire on the approaching gray lines.

Scales suffered fearful losses from what was described as a "sheet of flame"[29] spurting from the Federal riflemen and was arrested in front of the embankment. He was personally only seventy-five feet from the Federal guns when he was checked, wounded. His men hit the low places in the treeless plateau in front of the seminary and returned the fire without being able to close for a hand-to-hand encounter.[30] All the field officers of Scales's brigade except one were killed or wounded.

Lane had no better fortune on Pender's right. His brigade extended from the Fairfield road south to the McMillan house. Here one of Buford's cavalry brigades again guarded the Federal flank after a brief relief. The redoubtable Gamble, who had opened the battle for the Federal army, had gathered his remaining troopers to share in the final contest for Seminary Ridge, and had been given the critical position south of the Fairfield road. Here he seemed to threaten Lane both with an enfilade fire and with a cavalry charge, for which his troopers appeared to be preparing.

Doubleday had ordered a charge—a desperate undertaking against veteran infantry—but Buford did not attempt it. The menace from the cavalry, perhaps not great, was sufficient to disturb the young Confederate brigade leader, Lane. As one of Pettigrew's regiments had done earlier, he faced some of his regiments to the south and formed squares. Then he felt for the main Federal line on Seminary Ridge gingerly, maintaining little more than long-range firing against it and the Federal cavalry.

Although Scales and Lane were arrested, Perrin moved against the Federal center with an impact more characteristic of Pender's assaults. His men had received a whisky ration, unusual in the army, on the night before.[31] The South Carolinians were not to be denied. The hail of fire from the seminary works seemed less to retard than spur them on. In the words of Lieutenant Colonel Joseph N. Brown of the 14th South Carolina, "To stop was destruction. To retreat was disaster. To go forward was 'orders.' "[32] The intrepid Perrin was perhaps the most fortunate officer in the Confederate army. He came dashing through the ranks on his beautiful horse, his sword glinting in the late afternoon sun, and for the last 300 yards he personally led the charge over the open ground against the seminary.[33] Officers and men fell about him but he came through unscathed. Both sides fought with desperate earnestness, recognizing that possession of the seminary meant the command of Seminary Ridge and in turn the town of Gettysburg. The battle west of the town was in its decisive stage.

Biddle's Pennsylvania brigade, which all day had been meeting Heth's fierce onslaughts, was massed closely in the brick buildings and at the stone fence, and here the South Carolinians converged to make their most determined assault.[34]

3. The Palmetto Flag at the Diamond

It was approaching four o'clock. Doubleday's situation was desperate. His reserves were exhausted, and his thin, weak line was being hammered unremittingly; one flank was in immediate danger of being turned by the obstinate Daniel and enterprising Ramseur, and he was protected on the other only by a weak cavalry brigade.

Long ago he had sent his adjutant, Captain Richard F. Halsted, with urgent appeals to Howard, who was supposed to be commanding the entire battlefield. He besought assistance from Steinwehr's idle division on Cemetery Hill. But Howard tended to scoff at Doubleday's need, insisted that Halsted had been mistaking rail fences for advancing Confederates,[35] declined to order the First Corps to retire, and refused to send succor from Steinwehr. He did direct Halsted to find Buford, who was in feeble condition to give help; but Buford restored Gamble to the extreme left flank just in time to retard the advance of Lane.

Time had now run out for Doubleday west of Gettysburg. His lines were bent back on either flank by Pender's unabated pressure, leaving the seminary and its near-by buildings a salient. Ramseur, aided by O'Neal, was pressing Baxter and Paul and, with Daniel, coming to the assistance of Scales. And Perrin, at the center of Pender's assault, had now reached the salient at the seminary.

With a rush the South Carolinians carried the stone wall and barricades. The Federal line was broken and pushed back, "at first rapidly and disorderly, with our men close on them,"[36] said Colonel Brown. Cohesion was lost quickly in some of the First Corps units. In the pandemonium of the rout the Federal artillery limbered up and dashed off toward Cemetery Ridge and the fields south of Gettysburg, making a remarkable withdrawal with the loss of only two guns. These Perrin captured in his close pursuit, but he bemoaned the fact that Pender's other brigades had not kept pace with him. "If we had any support," he said in his confidential letter to Governor Bonham, "we could have taken every piece of artillery they had and thousands of prisoners."[37]

While Perrin had made the break through in the final assault, the alert Ramseur was not to be outdistanced. The Federals in his front could move neither to the right nor to the left because of the rout of the Eleventh Corps on the one hand and the loss of the seminary on the other; they could reach Gettysburg only along the unfinished railroad or the parallel Cashtown pike. "We had the Yankees like partridges in a nest," said one of Ramseur's men, "and the only way they could get out was up the railroad."[38] The entire brigade saw the situation in a twinkling and began shouting to the general, "Bring us a battery! Bring us a battery!" Ramseur turned to his courier and in a sudden outburst shouted, "Damn it, tell them to send me a battery! I have sent for one a half a dozen times." The words were scarcely out of his mouth before the devout young Presbyterian threw up both arms, looked upward and in the hearing of the entire brigade said, "God Almighty, forgive me that oath!"[39] As an almost immediate answer to one or the other of his entreaties, a battery rushed up and began throwing shells at the Federals retiring down the railroad. He and his brigade went off toward Gettysburg in hot pursuit.

"I could almost hear their bones crunch under the shot and shell," said Colonel Bennett of the 14th North Carolina.[40]

Nearly every regiment had men who performed deeds of great courage. The entire 16th Maine regiment played a heroic role. General Robinson selected it as the rear guard. It held the stone wall on the Mummasburg road, near the scene of Iverson's defeat, until it was engulfed. Said Abner R. Small, the adjutant: "For this little battalion of heroes, hemmed in by thousands of rebels, there was no succor, no hope."

When a Confederate officer was about to seize the flag the men crowded around it, clutched at it, tore it into bits, and secreted the small pieces in their clothing. Years later the flag of the 16th Maine was scattered in treasured fragments over the Pine Tree State. "In albums and frames and breast-pocketbooks" could be found the gold stars and silken shreds, "cherished mementoes of that heroic and awful hour."[41] The "Forlorn Hope" saved much of Robinson's division, then tried to extricate itself. "And so the Sixteenth Maine," said Adjutant Small, "was the last regiment that left the extreme front on the 1st of July—if four officers and thirty-six men can be called a regiment."[42]

The confused masses which had been the brigades of Cutler, Meredith, Stone, Biddle, Baxter, and Paul, straggled back, some into the town, most of them to the south of it and up the inviting slopes of Cemetery Hill. The retreat became so uncontrolled that one of Ramseur's officers grew apprehensive. "I was fearful their running troops would crush our little brigade," he wrote to his mother.[43] He, too, saw that some of the Federals were trapped. "We had them fairly in a pen, with only one gap open—the turnpike that led into Gettysburg—and hither they fled twenty deep, we all the while popping into them as fast as we could load and fire." In the town "we rushed pell-mell after them."[44]

This anonymous officer, whose letter home gave the North Carolina newspapers the first full account of Ramseur's attack, was in the skirmish line and pressed close to the Federals. "They hid by hundreds in houses and barns, and I had the felicity of capturing any number."[45] Ramseur's brigade was credited with capturing more than its own numbers in prisoners.[46] The same claim was made by Hays, and in both instances it was no doubt accurate.[47]

But the honor of being the first Confederates into Gettysburg went not to Ramseur, but to Perrin and the 1st South Carolina—the Palmetto Regiment, which repeated at Gettysburg its performance at Mexico City. Perrin knew that in battle one does not halt before a broken enemy. He did not tarry after capturing the seminary. The 14th South Carolina passed around the building at a rush, Colonel Brown conducting the left wing and Major Edward Croft the right, picked up the two Federal cannon, and marched on. It gave an artillery horse to Captain T. P. Alston of the 1st Regiment so that he might ride while leading the brigade's skirmishers into Gettysburg.

Perrin ordered the 1st and 14th regiments to make the entry and this they did simultaneously, with their flags unfurled.[48] The 1st South Carolina went down the Cashtown road to Chambersburg Street, the main east-west street, and thence to the Diamond, or public square. The 14th marched between North Boundary Street and the railroad embankment, until it reached Carlisle Street, the main north-south thoroughfare. The 14th then turned and marched toward the square.[49] As it moved south it passed a mounted figure under the shade trees. Pender had ridden up to give his compliments to the captors of Gettysburg.[50] The 14th did reach Carlisle Street ahead of any other troops, but at some distance north of the square, while the 1st, commanded by Major C. W. McCreary, got to the center of the town and there planted the Palmetto banner.[51] "The Yankee infantry," said Perrin, "literally swarmed through the streets."[52]

Pender had been momentarily concerned while observing, from Seminary Ridge, the close fighting and Perrin's rapid pursuit, in which his men appeared to mingle with masses of blue-clad soldiers. When Perrin dipped out of sight, Pender hastened ahead, met a lieutenant of the 12th Regiment, and expressed concern that the impetuous brigade might have been captured. "No, it is over the hill yonder," said the lieutenant.[53] Pender then stationed the 12th and 13th South Carolina between the town and the seminary to protect the right flank of the eager South Carolinians, and rode hurriedly into Gettysburg. Within a few minutes Ramseur's men appeared, entering farther to the north. Ramseur was followed a short time later by Hays of Early's division, coming in from the east.[54]

After the entry of Rodes, Pender withdrew the 1st and 14th South Carolina regiments to the position occupied by the balance of Perrin's brigade, between the town and the seminary.[55] Perrin's loss was heavy, about 600 out of 1,100. His largest regiment, the 14th, stormed the seminary with 475 and lost 200 in killed and wounded. The brigade proudly averred that it suffered no loss in prisoners.

Perrin wrote to Governor Bonham: "We captured the town of Gettysburg and hundreds of prisoners, thousands of small arms, two field pieces, . . . and four standards, two of which I intended to send to you to be placed in the State House at Columbia, but they made me turn them in here to be sent to Richmond, I suppose."[56] Among them were the corps standard of the First Army Corps and a beautiful flag presented to the 104th New York, the Wadsworth's Guards, by General Wadsworth.

Federal troops jammed into Gettysburg from north and west. The broad streets were soon congested, the alleys and yards were thronged with refugees, and milling, confused crowds tried to get out of the town as others sought to enter. At no time at Chancellorsville had there been such panic. As Doubleday rode through with his staff, citizens came out offering food and beseeching protection. "Pale and frightened women," he said, ". . . implored us not to abandon them."[57] Stone's Bucktails were among the last to yield their Seminary Ridge position and suffered heavily in prisoners. This was the brigade that had come under Ramseur's fire, and many were intercepted before they could gain the shelter of Gettysburg houses.[58]

Never was the Southern army in greater need of cavalry than at this instant of chaos in the Federal defense. Stuart on the field might have cut off the disorganized units from Cemetery Hill and doubled the number of prisoners taken. In such an instance, cavalry might function against fleeing soldiers, where it could make little impression on the solid ranks against which generals still liked to employ it. But the bag of prisoners captured in Gettysburg was impressive. Ramseur's officer placed the number at 7,300, with no doubt many duplications. The aggregate was perhaps nearer 5,000, the captures being made chiefly by Ramseur, Doles, Perrin and Hays. General Schimmelfennig was caught in the press, could not extricate himself, and had to hide under a woodpile for the next two days.

Of the brilliant actions in the fighting west of Gettysburg, the most sanguinary was the storming of McPherson's Woods by Pettigrew's brigade, and most conspicuous in that assault was the duel between the 26th North Carolina and the 24th Michigan. Second, if not equal, to this was Perrin's violent and triumphant attack on the seminary fortifications. At times it has been contended that Pettigrew did the hard chore and Pender's division only reaped the easy victory. That was far from the case; the casualty lists attest the true story.

Some other points are salient in considering the July 1 fighting. One is that Hill was tacitly, perhaps even covertly, looking for battle as well as for shoes. Ordinarily a full division is not employed for a foray or a reconnaissance, but in this case Hill consented not only to have Heth go to Gettysburg, but had Pender aroused by three o'clock in the morning with orders to follow him and give support. Manifestly something more than shoes was expected. Yet the full intention was not made clear to General Lee. The fact that Heth spent the balance of his life lamenting his role in bringing on the battle suggests that his own conscience was never eased or his conduct fully justified in his own reflections.

The defeat of the First Federal Corps west of Gettysburg could scarcely be attributed to the defeat of the Eleventh Corps north of the town. The First Corps was overpowered by superior numbers. Even had the Eleventh Corps held fast, the First could not likely have maintained its position another five minutes. It was cut in the center, not on the right flank where the Eleventh Corps crumbled. While Doubleday at the last minute did signal his units to fall back, the retirement was anything but voluntary. Some of both Wadsworth's and Robinson's regiments managed to retain a semblance of order, and a few colonels, like Dawes, insisted that their withdrawal was both prearranged and deliberate, and due wholly to the breakup of the Eleventh Corps. Perhaps in the frenzy of close fighting it seemed that way, but Doubleday's departure had few aspects of a calculated withdrawal.

North and west of Gettysburg the Federal army had fought two separate and distinct actions, under different commanders, to all practical effect. That was what Buford had in mind when in his midafternoon report to Pleasanton, who was with Meade at Taneytown, he wrote a pertinent closing sentence, "In my opinion there seems to be no directing person."[59]

Both forces gave way independently and at so nearly the same time that the one had substantially no effect on the other. The First Corps fought a prolonged engagement against heavy odds; the Eleventh disintegrated rapidly after being attacked by an inferior force.

Though entitled to acclaim, Doubleday got little more than demotion out of one of the great fights in American history, and after the battle he passed out of the Army of the Potomac, unwanted by Meade or Grant and unprotected by Halleck or Stanton. About the best tribute he received was from Colonel Dawes, who, prior to Gettysburg, in a letter home called him a "gallant officer" and said, "I saw him at Antietam . . . he was remarkably cool and at the very front of battle."[60] That was where he had been at Gettysburg.

The Southern, like the Northern army, fought the engagement without united leadership. Early's and Pender's divisions were well handled, Heth's and Rodes's poorly. The Confederate fighting was essentially by brigades and here the leadership was in most instances brilliant. Nothing better could have been asked of Gordon, Doles, Ramseur, Daniel, Pettigrew, or Perrin. Iverson, Archer, Davis, and, to a lesser extent, O'Neal were brigade failures. In the Federal army, the entire First Corps resistance was nothing short of heroic, and one brigade could with but difficulty be singled out above the others.

The Confederate victory at this stage was more impressive than that won two months earlier at Chancellorsville. There one Federal corps had been shattered; here two. On the Confederate side seventeen brigades had been brought to the field, four each by Heth, Early and Pender and five by Rodes. Two, those of Thomas and Smith, had not been engaged.

On the Federal side, fourteen brigades, including Buford's two cavalry brigades, were in line, although one of Steinwehr's had remained unemployed on Cemetery Hill. Ordinarily the Confederate brigades were stronger; thus approximately 22,000 Confederates with twenty batteries had fought 16,500 Federals with ten batteries. While the odds strongly favored the Confederates, they did not presage such a complete rout of the Federal army.

Great crowds of fugitives were making their way down the Baltimore road intent on nothing but escape. Some were arrested by the provost guard of the Twelfth Corps. Five thousand prisoners were in Confederate hands, while by a conservative estimate 4,000 were lying on the field or in hastily improvised hospitals. The Army of the Potomac had suffered a shattering blow.

CHAPTER THIRTEEN

High Ground and Golden Minutes

1. Early Shuns the Offerings of Fortune

Jubal Early stirred mixed emotions and remained an enigma both during the war and long after, when he became the manager of the notorious Louisiana Lottery, which probably blighted more Southern homes than were ever wrecked by Sherman's army.[1] He was rated by Sorrel, a competent judge, one of the best strategists in the Confederacy, yet Sorrel conceded that he lacked ability to handle troops effectively, while "his irritable disposition and biting tongue made him anything but popular."[2] He never married. He felt on the defensive when Ewell, after the capture of Milroy's army in Winchester, delegated him to speak to a group of women. "I never have been able to make a speech to one lady, much less to so many," he countered quickly.[3]

Having no family, Early devoted himself to causes and applied himself with unusual gusto to whatever he undertook. For a considerable period he campaigned against secession. He was among the most ardent supporters in Virginia of the old Federal union, though when the state seceded there was no doubt but that his extraordinary enterprise and irascibility would be thrown wholeheartedly into the cause of his native state.

While he was rated by some among the best scholars of the army—and his later writings and speeches were engaging, pungent, and voluminous—his conversation often was rough and ungrammatical and peppered by repeated oaths. At times he was epigrammatic. "The main use I have for a pioneer corps is to bury dead Yankees." Better examples were apparently unpublishable. Stiles judged him not a "superb magnetic leader like Gordon" nor could he "deliver quite as majestic a blow in actual battle as Longstreet," and summed him up: "Early was in some respects a bundle of inconsistencies and contradictions; of religion and irreligion; of reverence and profanity."[4] He admired both Lee and Jackson almost to the point of worship, but was the only officer ever heard to swear in Lee's presence. Lee's mild reproof, not without affection, was conveyed by treating Early as "my bad old man."[5] Had Lee been incapacitated so that Longstreet had to take over the command, Early would have been en route to an obscure sector the next morning, for Old Pete distrusted and despised him. After the war these two tough-fibered fighters enjoyed a lifelong quarrel, each intent on destroying the other, which came to involve in one manner or another almost all the surviving officers of the Army of Northern Virginia. It ended only with Early's death, as a recluse, thirty-one years after Gettysburg.

Early had turned lawyer after graduating from West Point, had gone back to the army during the Mexican War, then returned to law, and again resumed his military career when the states seceded. In Mexico he had contracted a rheumatism—probably arthritis—that for spells twisted and bent him[6] and made him appear one of the army ancients, although at Gettysburg he was only forty-six years old. But the soldiers usually called him "Old Jube" and the other officers respected his long, untrimmed beard and his years, even if many of them had little use for his character or personality. The war gave him several unusual opportunities but perhaps none approaching that which now fell to him as he sat astride his horse on Barlow's Knoll and watched the disorganized Federal soldiers streaming back into Gettysburg.

His division was still fresh. Gordon's losses were inconsequential; so were those of Hays and Hoke, while Smith had been unengaged. The artillery was well up. Colonel J. Thompson Brown, commanding the Second Corps guns, was under the impression the division would follow the defeated enemy and take the wooded hill (Culp's) on the left. He sent an officer to move with the division and find a road for the artillery.

Early rode into Gettysburg, passed the crowds of prisoners being taken to the rear, with virtually no guard, he noticed, and encountered Hays, who was forming a line along a street on the east side of the

town. Shells were dropping from Cemetery Hill. Federal sharpshooters still occupied some of the houses near the foot of the hill, and the
bluecoats had a skirmish line along its base. Early found it "very
apparent" that the hill held a force which had not participated in the
fight north of the town.[7] Avery meantime had placed his brigade
behind a low ridge on the Culp farm, where the rolling ground gave
protection from the Federals on Cemetery Hill. Thus Hays and
Avery were within striking distance of the heights in front, and Gordon
was close by.

This was a supreme instant for Early, although of course he could
not appreciate the great consequences of his actions to the cause of
Southern independence. Napoleon had a maxim: "The destiny of
States depend upon a moment."[8] Never did it have more pertinent
application than when Early stood on the outskirts of Gettysburg with
three fresh brigades and a fourth within reach and looked up at the
eminences immediately ahead of him.

Culp's Hill, to the left, was unoccupied. It was much later that
Wadsworth was able to collect there some of the scattered remnants
of his division and form a meager defending force around the nucleus
of the 7th Indiana Regiment, which had not shared in the fighting
west of Gettysburg. Seminary Hill held the distraught Eleventh Corps
refugees, estimated by Hancock after his arrival at 1,000 to 1,200
organized troops "at most." Howard had been distressfully unable to
re-form much of the Eleventh Corps as it passed over Cemetery Hill
and took to the Baltimore roads beyond.

Buford had his cavalry in solid formation on the fields to the right
of Cemetery Hill and gave some protection to that flank, but none in
front or on the Confederate left. Early was under no restraints. He
had at this stage of the battle received no orders to check his pursuit,
and certainly none of any nature applicable to his new situation. Nothing called for the perspicacity of Jackson. Early had routed an enemy,
and any textbook or any corporal would know the next move. The
enemy was making a fresh stand and there were still four and a half
hours of daylight, or time for half a dozen victories.

Napoleon had another dictum: "There is but one step between
triumph and ruin." That step Early now prepared to take, in the
wrong direction. Instead of ordering Hays and Avery to occupy the
high ground in their immediate front—as he was to order twenty hours
later when it bristled with bayonets—he groped about Gettysburg looking for either Ewell or Rodes, or both. He had not seen them that

day, and he wanted "to urge that we should advance at once upon the hill in our front, before the enemy could re-form."[9]

Early found neither general but encountered some of Rodes's soldier's, probably Ramseur's, on the other side of the town. Then he rode out the Cashtown road "to look at the position from that point of view and see if I could find Ewell or Rodes."[10] As Early rode west from Gettysburg, destiny was ticking off one of the great hours of the Confederacy. Jackson had made chance his handmaiden; Early became its servant. It seems in the case of Jackson that chance yielded to the strength of his character. However that may be, Early rode directly out of the arms of the fortune that had sought to embrace him, and cast himself on his irresolute corps commander, Ewell.

On the Cashtown road Early met one of Pender's staff officers and asked him to find A. P. Hill and say that if he would "send forward a division, we could take that hill."[11] Early was in error in contending that at this time none of Hill's troops had advanced beyond Seminary Ridge. Perrin's two regiments had preceded Ramseur. Apparently the South Carolinians had been withdrawn by the time Early reached the square.

Just then Colonel Abner Smead, inspector general of the Second Corps, rode up—Early does not make clear how far he had advanced toward the seminary when Smead appeared—with information from Ewell. Johnson's division was approaching and Ewell wanted Early's opinion where it should be placed.

Ewell meantime had ridden down the slopes of Oak Hill, followed closely by Trimble, who had been observing from the high ground where Oak Hill merges into Seminary Ridge. Everywhere were evidences of a great Confederate victory. The ground was covered with dead and wounded soldiers. Strewn about were rifles, muskets, haversacks, canteens, and large quantities of other equipment. Trimble had witnessed the flight of the Federals through the town and across the fields, and was fired by the sight. Before Ewell reached the square he and Trimble were joined by Gordon, whose eager spirit also had been fully aroused. Gordon was anxious for the chase, on which he could see that the fortunes of the day depended. As they rode into Gettysburg, Gordon was startled by the thud of a bullet hitting the corps commander, but Ewell jokingly remarked, "You see how much better fixed for a fight I am than you are. It didn't hurt a bit to be shot in the wooden leg."

Captain James Power Smith, Ewell's aide, placed Ewell's arrival at the town square at about five o'clock. He remained in the saddle beneath a shade tree, "chatted amiably with his men," and "pleasantly declined" a bottle of wine one of his young officers had brought up from a cellar.[12] Manifestly there was nothing pressing in the attitude or actions of the corps commander, and Captain Smith, who watched it all closely, agreed the events assumed a more critical importance in later reflection than at the time. "But even then, some of us who had served on Jackson's staff, sat in a group in our saddles, and one said sadly, 'Jackson is not here.'" Ewell was "simply waiting for orders" when every moment "could not be balanced with gold."[13]

2. Trimble Throws His Sword Away!

After dallying in Gettysburg, Ewell rode northeast to temporary headquarters at a farm near the almshouse. While in town he had received intelligence that Johnson's division was approaching and had dispatched Colonel Smead to find Early.

Lee's concentration had been impeded because the bulk of his army had to move through the single South Mountain pass and along the clogged Chambersburg-Gettysburg road. Johnson's division, which had reached Green Village on the night of June 30, was given the right of way over Longstreet, and on Wednesday July 1 moved through Fayetteville and over the gap to Cashtown. As they crossed the mountain the men heard the sound of distant artillery firing. Midway between Cashtown and Gettysburg Johnson sent Major Harry Kyd Douglas ahead with notice to Ewell that the division was "in prime condition" and ready to enter the line on its arrival.[14] When Douglas delivered the message he tried to convey something of Johnson's earnestness.

Gordon who was still with Ewell said he could join with Johnson in the assault, but Ewell demurred. Douglas quoted him: "General Lee told me to come to Gettysburg and gave me no orders to go further. I do not feel like advancing and making an attack without orders from him, and he is back at Cashtown."[15]

Gordon said nothing more. Ewell gave notice that Johnson should halt when he was well up and wait for further directions. As Douglas departed, Ewell's chief of staff said to him, in an aside:

"Oh, for the presence and inspiration of Old Jack for just one hour!"[16]

Trimble took note that the firing had now ceased, but he thought Ewell was moving about uneasily, "a good deal excited," and "seemed to me to be undecided what to do next."[17] Trimble decided this was a good moment to give advice: "Well, General," he said, "we have had a grand success. Are you not going to follow it up and push our advantage?"

Again Ewell referred to the lack of new orders from Lee. With the awful evidences of battle about him, he was going back to the instructions he had received early in the morning, which might or might not be applicable, according to a corps commander's views, to an altogether fresh set of conditions brought about by the expulsion of the enemy from Gettysburg.

Trimble was quick to see a discrepancy. "That hardly applies to the present state of things," he said, "as we have fought a hard battle already and should secure the advantage gained."

Ewell made no reply. Trimble judged him "far from composed." He was putting the brakes on the army when he should have been accelerating its movements. Trimble, recognizing this as "a critical moment," rode off for a closer view of Culp's and Cemetery hills. Quickly he returned and pointed to Culp's Hill.

"General," he said, "there is an eminence of commanding position and not now occupied, as it ought to be by us or the enemy soon. I advise you to send a brigade to hold it if we are to remain here."

"Are you sure it commands the town?" asked Ewell.

"Certainly it does, as you can see, and it ought to be held by us at once," Trimble asserted.

He did not record Ewell's response other than to say it was impatient.

Trimble's anger at this stage erupted. He had grasped in an instant what writers and historians have been speculating about for nearly a century, namely that the corps commander had grown timid.[18]

"Give me a division," he said, "and I will take that hill."

Ewell declined. His precise words were not given by Lieutenant McKim, the faithful recorder of many of the details of Gettysburg.

"Give me a brigade and I will do it," Trimble continued. When Ewell still declined, the despairing Trimble implored: "Give me a good regiment and I will engage to take that hill."

That too being denied, Trimble threw down his sword and stalked out of Ewell's headquarters in a huff, asserting that he would no longer serve under such an officer. He could do this, McKim explained, because he was merely acting as a volunteer aide to Ewell and had no established command. The Confederacy might have fared better with "old man Trimble" in command of the corps, or of Early's division. That would have been more practical than to yearn for the dead Jackson.

In the Confederate army, where private soldiers did not hesitate to express opinions, the general received some prompting. Major Daniel noted that when the men saw the delay and the hills ahead they shouted, "Let's go on!" Colonel Jones of Avery's brigade reflected a common viewpoint: "There was not an officer, not even a man, that did not expect that the war would be closed upon that hill that evening, for there was still two hours of daylight when the final charge was made, yet for reasons that have never been explained nor ever will be . . . some one made a blunder that lost the battle of Gettysburg, and, humanly speaking, the Confederate cause."[19]

Gordon was not a professional soldier and had merely risen from the command of the "Raccoon Roughs" of the northern Georgia hills, but he had better military intuition than some of the veteran officers of the old army and he understood the critical nature of the moment. A short time earlier he had looked down the lines and as far as he could see the enemy was retreating. Large numbers were throwing down their arms. Those farther away had fight in them still, but they, too, could be taken in flank. "In less than half an hour," he said, "my troops would have swept up and over those hills, the possession of which was of such momentous consequence."[20]

Gordon had, in fact, paid no attention to the first orders to halt. "Not until the third or fourth order of the most peremptory character reached me did I obey," he said. In later reflection he doubted that he would have obeyed even then except for the explanation that General Lee, who was several miles removed from the field, did not want to fight at Gettysburg.

While Early was talking with Colonel Smead on the Cashtown road, an aide from Extra Billy Smith arrived greatly excited, bringing word that Federal infantry and artillery were advancing along the York road, which would place them on the flank and rear of Early's division. Smith, according to Early's account of it,[21] said he would be unable to hold off this force; this was the reason he had not advanced when Early had sent for him during the attack on the Eleventh Corps. Early doubted Smith's accuracy but felt the troops would be disturbed by the report of an enemy on their flank, even if it proved untrue, so he sent a staff officer to Gordon directing him to take his brigade to the York road, and, in Early's words, stop the "stampeding." That ended the possibility of using Gordon against Culp's or Cemetery Hill.

Up to this time Early had not seen Ewell. He had just pointed out Culp's Hill to Colonel Smead as the place Johnson should occupy when another courier arrived, saying Ewell wanted to see Early in town. Ewell merely wanted to ask orally where Johnson should be placed and Early again pointed to Culp's Hill as the proper position. Then, according to Early's account, he urged that they should push ahead and occupy Cemetery Hill. This he had not done earlier, when the opportunity was most inviting. But Ewell suggested that they ride together toward the hill and reconnoiter it, which they did until they encountered the fire of Federal sharpshooters who still held the southern fringe of the town. Ewell then concluded that it would be best not to advance until Johnson arrived.

There is abundant information on this critical moment in the history of the Confederacy because Early in later years, smarting under the suggestion that perhaps he, and not Longstreet, was responsible for the Southern defeat, went to great length to build up a record, which, in the end, left a number of inconsistencies. While he urged Ewell to attack an hour or so after the Federals had broken, he explained in the record that he did not have a sufficient force for it; that the job could be done more readily from A. P. Hill's position; and that the Federal army was in such strength that an attack would have been doomed to failure, after all. He thought Smith was in a self-engendered panic, yet he emphasized in his account that an approach of the enemy on the York road was not improbable because Stuart had fought near Hanover the day before and Colonel White, his own cavalry leader, had reported an enemy infantry force on the Hanover road.[22]

Rodes now joined them, and while they awaited Johnson the three generals, Ewell, Rodes and Early, rode together out the York pike to probe into the nature of Smith's alleged encounter with the enemy. They could look down the road for two miles and on their arrival it was clear of troops. Early reaffirmed his first statement that he "placed no confidence in the rumor."[23] Rodes tended to believe it, and Ewell "seemed at a great loss as to what opinion to form." The reports of the enemy's presence on the road had come mainly from cavalry stragglers who Early thought were "waifs from the battlefield of Hanover."[24]

But while they looked and talked, far out to the right of the York road a line of skirmishers appeared, moving apparently in their direction. "There they come now!"[25] exclaimed Rodes. Blue and gray soldiers looked alike at that distance. Early answered in "somewhat emphatic language," which for him would mean a stronger than usual oath, that they must not be enemy skirmishers because Gordon, who was situated in that area, would fire on an enemy. Lieutenants T. T. Turner of Ewell's staff and Robert D. Early of Early's were sent out to investigate; they returned with the information that the skirmish line was Smith's, which Gordon was realigning. They found that Culp's Hill was unoccupied. Both armies were still being very casual.

Sunset was now at hand. Ewell departed and Early returned to the brigades of Hays and Avery on the eastern outskirts of Gettysburg. It was about 7:45 P.M. when he was again summoned by Ewell, for a conference with Lee.

3. Lee Wants the High Ground Taken

Daniel's brigade was resting with its left on the railroad cut at 4:00 P.M., after going through some of the toughest fighting and suffering some of the heaviest casualties of the battle. The men were much too exhausted to be sent after the fleeing Federals. Confederate guns on Seminary Ridge were testing the range to Cemetery Hill without committing themselves to a sustained bombardment, and were being answered by Steinwehr.

During this sporadic exchange Daniel's men saw a party of officers riding up the road from Cashtown. The horsemen drew up on Seminary Ridge where the pike reaches the summit, and their leader took up his glasses and looked down on the town of Gettysburg, then across at the range of hills.

Daniel's soldiers pulled themselves to their feet and took off their hats. There was no cheering—the Carolinians were too fagged out to manage anything except a salute, delivered more with their hearts than their hands. Colonel Thomas S. Kenan merely called his regiment to attention.[26] But all along the Confederate line passed a thrill of expectancy and elation, for General Lee had reached the field.

The commanding general had been progressing toward the firing line since early morning, halting from time to time to receive dispatches and maintain a headquarters where he might be reached by couriers.

The correspondent of the Savannah *Republican* was sitting on the wet ground west of Cashtown on the morning of July 1, his back against a tree, writing a story, when Lee passed. "He seemed to sniff battle in the breeze," the correspondent noted in his dispatch.[27] Longstreet had ridden with him for a time and found him cheerful.

At Cashtown he established temporary headquarters in an old house on the turnpike. On an inside door someone had nailed up a map of Adams County, Pennsylvania, of which Gettysburg is the seat. With his penknife Lee cut out the map, put it in his pocket, and carried it to Gettysburg. The incident has perhaps been unrecorded and there is no information about whether the map was of value or whether he paid anyone for it; if he did not, this was probably the only petty depredation he committed during the campaign.[28] When he set up headquarters around the Thompson House on Seminary Ridge later in the day he had a door taken off the hinges and laid across two braces, or chairs in a tent across the road; he used it for his map table during the battle.

Captain James Power Smith, Ewell's aide, made two trips in the late afternoon from Gettysburg to the seminary, and on the first he witnessed the arrival of the commanding general. Smith studied Lee carefully and reflected on his "superb physique," his quiet bearing, and his carefully cut gray uniform.[29] His felt hat had a medium brim, his boots fitted neatly, and everything about him was trim and military. "An unruffled calm upon his countenance" showed his concentration and control. He had stopped in the grass field to the north of the seminary, where, mounted on Traveler, he looked down the long slope toward the heights beyond Gettysburg. Federal soldiers were still streaming across the fields and climbing the heights.

The ubiquitous McKim was there, too. "I saw him sweep the horizon with his glasses, and noted he scanned that elevation [Little Round Top] with great attention."[30]

The whole panorama of the subsiding battle lay before him, the positions north of the town that had been carried by Early's arrival on the Federal flank; Oak Hill, which had been seized by Rodes; and the ground on which he stood, which had been the scene of the most stubborn fighting. He was quick to see the advantages of the high ground south of Gettysburg. He immediately directed Colonel Walter H. Taylor to inform Ewell that from the position he, Lee, occupied, he could see the Federals retreating over the hills in great confusion and without organization, and that it "was only necessary to press 'those people' in order to secure possession of the heights."[31] He wanted Ewell, if possible, to do this.

Taylor went immediately to Ewell and delivered the message, noticing that Ewell offered no objection to the orders conveyed, nor mentioned any obstacle to their execution. He received from Ewell information about the number of prisoners captured and returned to Lee to report that his message had been delivered. Taylor left several accounts of this transaction, all in substantially the same language. He returned to Lee with the impression that Ewell would carry out the orders. Lee would have been better served had Taylor waited and fretted Ewell until that general began the execution of the order. He could then have reported to Lee that the order had been complied with, not merely delivered.

Captain Smith had returned earlier and Ewell now sent him again to Lee. Possibly he passed Colonel Taylor en route, or possibly the message he carried was in the nature of an afterthought. He was directed to inform Lee that Early and Rodes thought they could go forward if supported by Hill on their right. South of the cemetery was a position which they felt should be taken at once because it commanded the cemetery. Whether this was the Round Tops or the extension of Cemetery Ridge is not clear, but Smith judged Ewell was thinking of the high ground immediately beyond the cemetery, and not of the more remote Round Tops.

On this trip he found Lee in a field some distance to the south. It was now five o'clock. Longstreet had ridden ahead of his troops and Lee and Longstreet had dismounted for a careful scrutiny of the terrain, especially the position south of the cemetery. Smith delivered his message and Lee wanted to know what position Ewell meant by "the ground to the south." He handed his glasses to Smith so that the captain might designate it. According to the captain, Lee said "the elevated position in front was, he supposed, the commanding position of which Early and Rodes spoke."[32] Then he added that some of "those people" were already there.

Smith thought they were cavalry scouts. But Lee continued that he did not have a force available to take this position. He asked Longstreet about the locations of the First Corps divisions, and was informed that the leading division, McLaws' was still six miles from the field. Lee then gave Smith his reply to Ewell: "He regretted that his people were not up to support him on the right; but wished him to take the Cemetery Hill if it were possible; and that he would ride over to see him very soon."[33]

As Colonel Taylor described Lee's message and as Captain Smith quoted his later instructions, Ewell was not cautioned against bringing on a general engagement prior to the arrival of Longstreet's troops. The only qualification carried by Taylor was "if possible," a condition that gave Ewell some discretion to weigh the chance of success before committing himself. The same qualification, "if it were possible," occurred in Lee's orders sent through Captain Smith. Any caution against bringing on a general engagement was clearly that imposed earlier in the day, as Taylor pointed out.

Lee's decision against an attack on the right with the troops already at hand, as well as his view that the position behind the cemetery was already occupied, resulted partly from the reconnaissance just made by his military secretary, Colonel Long. Long reported that Cemetery Hill was occupied in strength, part of the force being posted behind a stone fence near the crest of the hill, and the rest on the reverse slope. As he summed it up later, "In my opinion an attack at this time, with the troops then at hand, would have been hazardous and very doubtful of success."[34] That must have been an hour after Lee's arrival and almost two hours after Perrin had carried Seminary Ridge and after Early had halted in front of Culp's Hill and Cemetery Ridge.[35]

Anderson's division was close at hand, and there was restiveness among some of Pender's officers and men, as well as Early's, over the failure to take the ground on which the Federals had rallied. Major David Gregg McIntosh, commanding a battalion of Third Corps artillery, thought the army relaxed once it had captured the town, when it should have redoubled its efforts and made the assaults that proved so costly on the second and third days. His description of the situation is persuasive:

The Union troops driven into the town from different directions were wedged and jammed in the streets, and soon became a disorganized mass. Artillery and ambulances struggling to get through the tangled crowd added to the confusion. Had the fugitives been allowed no pause, and had the Confederates followed close on their heels, the very momentum of the flight, to say nothing of the contagion of panic, would have swept aside every support, and the pursuers could easily have rushed the Cemetery and surrounding heights.[36]

His main point was that concentrated Confederate artillery fire on Cemetery Hill would have been disastrous to the Federals and might have caused them to abandon the heights. Ample artillery was at hand. The two Third Corps battalions which had been at the front all day had suffered severely in casualties but still retained their fighting efficiency, each with a complement of 16 guns. Half these guns were rifled and Cemetery Hill was well in range. Garnett's battalion had just arrived fresh, and McIntosh estimated that between 30 and 40 guns could have been employed on Seminary Hill as they were in the great bombardment of July 3 before the Pickett-Pettigrew assault.

The decision was left to Brigadier General William Nelson Pendleton, chief of the army artillery, who had reconnoitered the woods to the right and along the ridge to the Fairfield road, his object being to find a position for Garnett's guns, which he had already ordered to the right. Cemetery Hill was in range from the Fairfield road position. Ramseur at that time came out of Gettysburg, now occupied by his troops, met Pendleton on Seminary Ridge at the Fairfield road crossing, and told him that if the batteries opened, they would draw a concentrated fire on his men, who were much exposed from Cemetery Hill. Only one side of this conversation is available, and Ramseur did try to press on that same evening. But Pendleton decided that unless his bombardment should be a part of a combined attack on Cemetery Hill "it would be worse than useless to open fire there."[37] That probably was a sound conclusion, although the onus of the decision should not have been placed on a single brigade general. Despite McIntosh's confidence in his guns, they would not likely have dislodged the Federal army unless followed by a strong infantry assault.

Pendleton may have been confused about Ramseur's request, which probably was not that he should refrain from drawing the enemy's fire, but that he should be careful about where he aimed his own. Doles's Georgians had just come under the fire of two Confederate brass pieces on Oak Hill and some had been killed, others wounded.[38] Three of Rodes's brigades were prepared to storm Cemetery Hill, and Ramseur no doubt was anxious to alert the Confederate artillery about the prospective attack. Doles registered a vigorous protest against the "indifference and neglect" of the battery commander who was careless with his shells.

The three brigades ready for the attack were those of O'Neal, Ramseur, and Doles. O'Neal, recovered to an extent after his repulse earlier, had ordered up artillery and formed in line with Doles, who had passed to the southern part of the town. O'Neal was preparing to begin the assault when he was recalled and directed to form his brigade north of the railroad.

A. P. Hill's report on the final phase of the first day's battle was almost an apology. The substance of it was that he—fighter though he

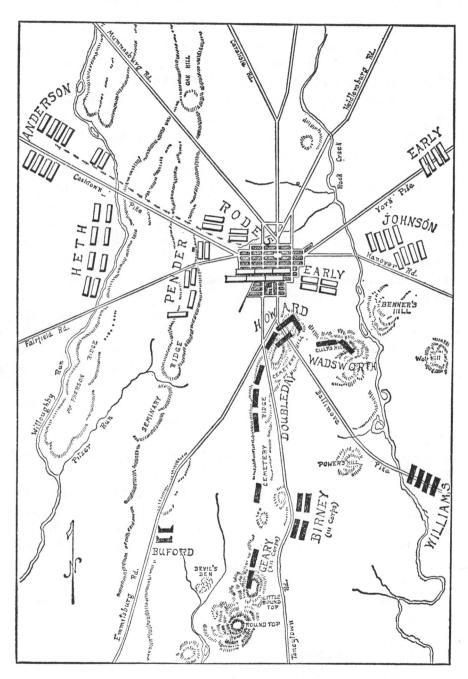

Armies at end of first day.

185

was known to be—was satisfied with half a loaf of victory at supper that night. It is true, as stated, that here the want of cavalry was seriously felt. But impressed with the belief that the enemy was "entirely routed," and with the exhaustion of his two divisions after six hours of hard fighting, "prudence led me to be content with what had been gained, and not push forward troops exhausted and necessarily disordered, probably to encounter fresh troops of the enemy."[39] He credited his corps with the capture of 2,300 prisoners and "the almost total annihilation of the First Corps of the enemy."

Ensign J. A. Stikeleather of the 4th North Carolina was on Ramseur's skirmish line. His letter to his mother, which reached the North Carolina press, said the Cemetery Hill position could have been carried readily with the loss of less than five hundred; that "Washington would have been evacuated, Baltimore freed, Maryland unfettered, the enemy discomfitted, and our victorious banners flaunting defiantly before the panic-stricken North." He told the attitude of the troops: "The simplest soldier in the ranks felt it. . . . But, timidity in the commander that stepped into the shoes of the fearless Jackson, prompted delay, and all night long the busy axes from tens of thousands of busy hands on that crest, rang out clearly on the night air, and bespoke the preparation the enemy were making for the morrow." This letter by a junior officer immediately after the battle contained perhaps the first attack on Ewell for the disastrous inaction of that evening.[40]

Longstreet meanwhile was surveying the country, especially the Federal position on the long ridge connecting the formidable hills at either end; chance, he noted, had provided the enemy with an exceptionally strong rallying place. Apprehensive that Lee might want to attack it, he returned to Lee and offered a counterproposal. The entire Confederate army, he suggested, could be moved by the right flank and put in position south of Round Top, where it would threaten to interpose itself between Meade and Washington. Meade would therefore be dislodged by strategy instead of assault.

Longstreet's account of this meeting is no doubt correct in general purport, but contains phrases that must have injected themselves into his thinking in later years.[41] After he had looked over the ground for five or ten minutes, he turned to Lee.

If we could have chosen a point to meet our plans of operation, [he said] I do not think we could have found a better one. . . . All we have to do is to throw our army around to their left, and we shall interpose between the Federal army and Washington. We can get a strong position and wait, and if they fail to attack us we shall have everything in condition to move back tomorrow night in the direction of Washington, selecting a good position into which we can place our troops to receive battle next day. Finding our objective is Washington or that army, the Federals will be sure to attack us. When they attack, we shall beat them, as we proposed to do before we left Fredericksburg, and the probabilities are that the fruits of our success will be great.[42]

Lee's reply was prompt: "No, the enemy is there, and I am going to attack him there."

Longstreet's account was written well after Lee's death; his phrase, "as we proposed to do before we left Fredericksburg," would have perplexed Lee had it been uttered on Seminary Ridge. Irrespective of what Longstreet may have proposed at Fredericksburg, Lee never committed himself arbitrarily to any plan, or felt bound by anything except the conditions immediately before him. So much he made clear, himself.

Longstreet was not a dissembler, and while he might maneuver a corps, the only approach he knew in conversation was frontal. He argued boldly, a trifle impudently, with Lee, contending that his proposal would give Lee command of the Washington roads.

"No," Lee answered again with finality, "they are in position and I am going to whip them or they are going to whip me."

Longstreet desisted but did not consider himself defeated. He would wait. As it developed, Lee did not brush Longstreet's project aside contemptuously. Later that evening he analyzed it more closely and apparently toyed with the notion of putting some modification of it into effect. Military comment has been well divided over the near-century since the battle about the feasibility of the turning movement. The difficulties would have been major. Lee still had no cavalry and did not know where the enemy was or would be. He could not undertake a prolongation of his right beyond Round Top so long as Ewell was gripped like a shepherd's crook around Culp's and Cemetery hills. He might have considered the plan more earnestly had he been able to shift Ewell to the far right, but Early always had so many impressive reasons against it.

What would have been the history of the Confederacy if he had made this turning movement? Perhaps it was possible for Lee to win the campaign either by the battle plan he adopted or by the strategy Longstreet proposed. Rarely in military matters is there but a single road to success. The execution is all-important. Victory in the end depends on the degree of skill and the force of character, and always a modicum of luck, behind any plan. A capable general considers all eventualities. When he has weighed the different factors he must select one plan, and only one, and then refrain from mulling over what might have happened had he chosen another.

Lee made his final choice on the basis of numerous cogent reasons. There are no means of comparing the battle of Gettysburg—the battle of history which he fought—with the might-have-been battle under Longstreet's flanking movement. That battle could have been lost, too.

None in the army understood the opportunities of the moment better nor grieved more bitterly than Gordon, who all through the late afternoon wanted only to be unleashed. That night he was unable to sleep. He mounted at 2:00 A.M. and with two staff officers rode to the red barn which Ewell and Early were using as a headquarters. Through the night he had heard the Federal soldiers with picks and shovels digging trenches on the hills, and the rumbling wheels of guns being put in position. He forecast to Ewell and Early that at daylight they would be able to see heavy works, guns, and infantry ranks frowning down on them, and he declared that he, even at that hour of two in the morning, could carry those works by a vigorous assault. After daylight, he said, it would cost 10,000 men.

Gordon seemed to detect an inclination on the part of the two superior officers to yield to his entreaty, but in the end his request was denied. "Those works were never carried," he said, "but the cost of the assault upon them, the appalling carnage resulting from the efforts to take them, far exceeded that which I ventured to predict."[43]

Johnson reached Gettysburg with his men "very much jaded from hard marching,"[44] in the words of Lieutenant McKim, who noted that it was still daylight as he entered the town. He was able to read a letter handed to him by Colonel Douglas.[45] And there was enough daylight to win a battle, although conditions had been altered vastly in the Federal army. Douglas thought Johnson was "spoiling for a fight"[46] because of the rapidity of his marching and he did expect to go immediately into action. He had covered twenty-five miles that day. Leaving the Cashtown road, the division followed the railroad cut and halted at the Pennsylvania College grounds while Johnson went to find Ewell. Some of the brigades passed straight on through to the position designated for them on Early's left. Johnson, never reluctant to fight even at a late hour, put his division in battle line. For what he referred to in later years as "some unexplained reason," he received orders from Ewell to halt.[47] He was not allowed the opportunity to assault Culp's Hill in the fading daylight of July 1.

Ewell, being an intelligent soldier, could not have been too happy with his management of affairs. After the war when a prisoner at Fort Warren, he told his fellow prisoner, Eppa Hunton, that "it took a dozen blunders to lose Gettysburg, and he had committed a good many of them."[48] Nobody has ever been in a strong position to dispute him. But Ewell's greatest deficiency, of course, was lack of foresight. He might have replied to his critics in the words of General Lee to an officer who was analyzing some of the mistakes of Gettysburg.

"Young man," said Lee, "why did you not tell me that before the battle? Even as stupid a man as I am can see it all now."[49]

CHAPTER FOURTEEN

Moonlight and Marching Columns

1. "The Damned Dutchmen . . . Ran Like Sheep"

L. L. Crounse, chief correspondent of the New York *Times* with the Army of the Potomac, brought the first objective account of the clash at Gettysburg to Taneytown and Meade's headquarters. Crounse galloped up in the midafternoon while the Cincinnati correspondent, Whitelaw Reid, was talking with the Federal commander in his tent.[1]

Meade had been getting sketchy reports all morning, but here finally was a more comprehensive, eyewitness version. Crounse said he had just ridden from the small town, ten to fifteen miles distant, where a battle of uncertain magnitude was still in progress. Reynolds had been killed and the air was heavy with Northern misfortune. He had hurried back to get access to a telegraph wire and file a preliminary dispatch. The other correspondents who had been moving close to headquarters must have obtained fill-ins, for all began writing stories on a Taneytown tavern porch. These dispatches were sent by messenger to Frederick, where communication with Washington and the North had been restored after it had been cut by Stuart. Then the newsmen galloped off toward Gettysburg.

En route they rode into the backwash of a great battle, into refugees with new rumors, distraught men and women with fresh eyewitness accounts. One was that "the damned Dutchmen of the Eleventh Corps broke and ran like sheep, just as they did at Chancellorsville." Another: "Wadsworth's division was cut to pieces . . . half of its officers killed." Still another: "We were driven pell-mell through

Gettysburg and things look black enough, I tell you."[2] The area of Two Taverns was filled with skulkers from the front. Frightened women were questioning the fleeing men about the battle. Prospects of Federal victory on Pennsylvania soil were anything but promising.

Through the early morning the Second Corps, Hancock's, had been marching up from Uniontown, where it had rested since the night of June 29. When it reached Taneytown at eleven o'clock, the men were allowed a coffee rest, which became extended as Meade awaited messengers from the front and pondered whether the battle ought to be fought at Gettysburg or along his more favored Pipe Creek. Buford's early-morning cavalry fight had indicated little, but shortly before one o'clock Meade had begun to comprehend the major nature of the engagement west of Gettysburg. He had heard of Reynolds' death and of the heavy pressure on the First Corps from the assembling Confederate army.

Meade might have gone himself to Gettysburg but he elected to send Hancock. The decision disclosed that he had not yet abandoned his intention of fighting along Pipe Creek and thought it more likely that the three corps which formed the left wing—the First, Eleventh and Third—would have to be brought back by the routes he had already specified, than that the rest of the army would go forward. But the severe nature of the fighting suggested that it might now be too late to withdraw. The final decision would have to be made on the basis of just what was happening at Gettysburg, and on whether the terrain offered defensive advantages for the army as inviting as those along Pipe Creek appeared to be.

Certainly if Meade judged his duty was at headquarters in the rear instead of on the fighting line, he could not have made a better choice of a substitute than Hancock. The fact that Hancock was junior to both the Eleventh and Third Corps commanders, Howard and Sickles, did not matter to Meade. His and the army's trust in Hancock was strong and he had full authorization to disregard rank in an emergency.

Meade kept Hancock at headquarters an hour, explaining his intentions and reviewing the orders already issued. He gave Hancock wide latitude at the front, to order the removal of the three corps and their trains to the rear for alignment behind Pipe Creek, or to establish a battle line at Gettysburg if he judged that expedient. These powers were fully as comprehensive as those of the commander in chief.

Hancock turned over command of the Second Corps to John Gibbon, the artilleryman who before the war had instructed the West

Point cadets in the use of the guns and had become McDowell's chief of artillery, then Meredith's predecessor as commander of the Iron Brigade. Although a Pennsylvanian by birth, he had been reared in Charlotte, North Carolina, and had three brothers fighting in the armies of the South, one of them, Dr. Robert Gibbon, being the surgeon of Lane's brigade. At two o'clock Hancock rode with his staff for Gettysburg, thirteen miles away. The time he required to cover this distance, almost two hours, is explained by the fact that he rode part of the way in an ambulance, so that he might study his maps. He sent his aide, Major William G. Mitchell, ahead to notify Howard of his coming.

Both Hancock and Mitchell placed the time of his arrival at three thirty; others thought the hour later. Doubleday said it was after Lee's arrival on the opposite hill,[3] which was at four o'clock. Lee and Hancock appear to have reached the field almost simultaneously, about four.

Rarely in warfare has the arrival of a single officer on a battlefield been more timely and consequential than Hancock's at Gettysburg. One of his subordinates gave the picture: before he came, "wreck, disaster, disorder, almost the panic that precedes disorganization, defeat and retreat were everywhere." After he appeared on Cemetery Hill, "soldiers retreating stopped, skulkers appeared from under their cover, lines were re-formed": in place of a rabble seeking Cemetery Hill as a sanctuary, an army with a purpose—under a leader who could lift it to extraordinary efforts—confronted the Confederates.

There was something dominating and inspiring about Hancock. The men of his corps were essentially the same as those of any other, but at the end of the war they could say that the Second had captured more enemy guns and more enemy colors than all the rest of the army combined. After Grant had taken command and had gone through the Wilderness, Hancock could tell him proudly that the corps had never lost a color or a gun, though oftener and more desperately engaged than any other. The Galena tanner was to use the corps cruelly at Cold Harbor, but it nevertheless finished the war, and with a record of a larger number of engagements and an aggregate of more killed and wounded than any other corps in the Northern armies.[4]

Hancock, one of twin brothers born in Montgomery County, Pennsylvania, owed his military eminence as much to his great industry as to his intelligence and striking appearance. He devoted the eleven years between 1850 and 1861 to assiduous preparation for the responsibilities of high command if it should ever come to him. He was so thorough that army detail work, which provoked some and baffled others, neither irritated nor bogged him down. He undoubtedly was one of the great soldiers of American history, though he never had the opportunity to command his own army, mainly because no commander of the Army of the Potomac from the Peninsula to Appomattox could dispense with him for an instant.[5]

McClellan had used the term "superb" in connection with his name, and the adjective was so fitting that the army adopted it and knew him thereafter as "Hancock the Superb," a difficult cognomen for any officer, but one he was able to handle with seemliness. The word "beautiful" is not ordinarily applicable to the male form, but it seemed to fit Hancock as it did Gordon. His mien and carriage were like those of a race horse at the starting line, and called for a stronger descriptive word than handsome.

Altogether, Hancock's aspect, poise, and common sense gave him an abundance of the quality of leadership, and officers and men turned to him instinctively. "One felt safe to be near him," said a junior. Young Frank Aretas Haskell gave a dramatic, though highly partisan, account of the Federal officers at Gettysburg. It contains some vivid word pictures, but he brought out his choice terms for Hancock, "the tallest and most shapely" of them all. Haskell was impressed with his innate ability to lead: "I think that if he were in citizens' clothes, and should give commands in the army to those who did not know him, he would be likely to be obeyed at once."[6]

That was not precisely the case, even though he was in uniform, when he arrived on Cemetery Hill to take over the duties that had proved such a heavy burden for Howard's shoulders. The senior officer demurred. As with most of these Gettysburg controversies, the versions of what happened vary widely, but Howard's attitude on the appearance both of Hancock and of Meade later that night seemed so intensely personal that he appeared to be thinking of his own rather than the army's standing.

Doubleday, who was near, said "quite a scene occurred" when he confronted Hancock. "Why, Hancock, you cannot give orders here!" Howard exclaimed. "I am in command and I rank you!"[7]

Hancock told of his orders from Meade, although his aide had already advised Howard of their scope. But, according to Doubleday, Howard still declined to recognize Hancock's authority.

Howard's own account shows a disposition to act either independently or as the officer who was directing. "All right, Hancock," he quoted himself as saying, "you take the left of the Baltimore Pike and I will take the right, and we will put these troops in line." He said his remarks were friendly, and Hancock "did as I suggested."[8]

Words almost identical with Doubleday's were attributed to Howard by Major Halstead, the First Corps adjutant general, who heard Howard exclaim: "No, I do not doubt your word, General Hancock, but you can give no orders here while I am here."[9]

Hancock explained that Meade had told him to select a field for battle; he thought the place where he stood was the strongest natural position he had ever seen. If Howard felt likewise, he would select it. Howard consented and Hancock said, "Very well, sir, I select this as the battle-field."[10]

Howard of course could not have truly commanded an army with Hancock present. Things did not work out that way in days when generals exercised immediate instead of remote control over troops and remained in their presence under the stress of battle. Expecting men to look to Howard would be like expecting them to go to Henry Dearborn for guidance with Andrew Jackson or Oliver Hazard Perry at hand. Men turned to Hancock's sureness where they would have recognized only Howard's insignia. In a supreme trial they would have sought strength and not rank.

The Maine artilleryman, Lieutenant Edward N. Whittier, went to Hancock for orders, found him unruffled by the confusion all around, and felt "his very atmosphere strong and invigorating." Whittier noticed that even after his long ride his linen was still clean and white. His sleeve was rolled back from his "firm, finely moulded hand." Everything about him imparted fresh courage to others.[11]

After his exchange with Howard, Hancock found Doubleday more co-operative. "General Doubleday," he said, "I command this field and I wish you to send a regiment over to that hill."[12]

Hancock had seen at once that Culp's Hill must be garrisoned or the Federal army would have to abandon Cemetery Hill. Like Trimble, he grasped instantly the paramount importance of the companion eminence on the right of Howard's position.

"My corps has been fighting, General, since ten o'clock," Doubleday entreated, "and they have been all cut to pieces."

"I know that, sir," said Hancock, "but this is a great emergency and everyone must do all he can." Hancock moved away, but taking no chances, he soon returned to find out whether his order had been followed. It had. Doubleday's regiments had been reduced to the size of companies, so he sent the remnants of the division under General Wadsworth.[13]

Wadsworth fortunately had a fresh regiment, the 7th Indiana of Cutler's brigade, which had been working its way up the Emmitsburg road after a day of guarding cattle and commissary trains. Although the regiment was fairly close on the south, the stratum of sultry air had deadened the sound of the firing. The first day's battle could be heard as far west as Pittsburgh, 180 miles away, but it passed unnoticed a dozen miles to the south and southeast. The day was mostly clear and in some localities the sun had dried the roads enough that marching columns stirred up dust. But the 7th Indiana was being drenched by a mountain shower when a messenger arrived with news of the battle.[14]

Marching rapidly to Cemetery Ridge, the regiment came alongside its division commander, General Wadsworth, sitting forlornly on a stone fence by the roadside. "His head bowed in grief, [he was] the most dejected woebegone person one would be likely to find on a world-around voyage," said Private Thomson of Company G.

Wadsworth said to the regiment, "I am glad you were not with us this afternoon."

Surprised, an officer declared that had the 7th Indiana been present they could have held their position.

"Yes," Wadsworth countered, "and all would now be dead or prisoners."[15] Just as after the first battle at Manassas, where he served on McDowell's staff, Wadsworth was as much overwhelmed by the humiliation of defeat as by the enormity of the losses.

The Hoosiers from the Ohio River towns found Culp's Hill much like the knobs and bluffs of southeastern Indiana, heavily timbered and strewn with rocks varying in size "from a chicken coop to a pioneer's cabin."[16] They went to work immediately felling trees and digging ditches while Major Ira G. Grover, their commander, personally conducted a patrol down the eastern slope.

Here he encountered an unsuspecting squad of scouts from the 42nd Virginia and brought in some prisoners.[17] Of far greater significance to the battle, however, his men gave notice to Johnson's newly arrived Confederate division that Culp's Hill was now in Northern hands, and corrected any impression the enemy may have held that the hill was open for the taking. Old Trimble had been correct hours earlier when he said it could be had with a regiment, but now it was held by an entrenched division. Also William's division of the Twelfth Federal Corps had come up to Rock Creek, close enough to give assistance.

Major Grover always believed that his bumping into the Virginia patrol was the decisive moment at Gettysburg, because it saved Culp's Hill for the Federals. Very likely Johnson, a more thorough man than Early, would have seized the hill had his patrols been able to work undetected to the summit. Although Ewell had restrained Johnson, he could scarcely have censured him for occupying high ground in his immediate front without becoming involved in a skirmish. But Grover showed him it was now occupied, and Johnson held off.

During the night an alarm was sounded on Culp's Hill, but it was found to be no more than the nightmare of a private of Company K, 7th Indiana, who let out wild yells that aroused several regiments to the left. They, half awake, thought the enemy was attacking and grabbed their guns. Some leaped over the breastworks and charged down the hill firing, while a few were seen "charging as vigorously to the rear."[18]

Stevens' 5th Maine Battery, which had blazed away all day against Heth, Rodes and Pender, was in position on the left of Culp's Hill, commanding the valley between it and Cemetery Hill. Hancock had seen it near the gate of the cemetery, called to Captain Stevens, pointed to the hill, and told him to "stop the enemy from coming up that ravine." "Fifth Battery, forward," said Stevens instantly, and the guns and caissons rolled across the plateau, east on the Baltimore pike until they found a lane that led to a house near Culp's Hill, and on to the summit.[19] They began dropping shells on Hays's Louisiana brigade even before the 7th Indiana arrived to give them infantry support.

Hancock stationed other batteries to command the Baltimore pike and the approaches from Gettysburg and Seminary Ridge. In half an hour he had a defense which he felt could hold the position, at least until darkness, although he conceded that had Howard been pursued vigorously he would have been driven beyond Cemetery Hill. Steinwehr had been on Cemetery Hill most of the day. He had neither put a protective patrol on near-by Culp's Hill nor been energetic in constructing fortifications.

Hancock later emphatically denied that Steinwehr threw up a lunette around each gun and built high, solid works around smooth, level gun platforms. All Hancock could find in the way of "works" were "some holes (not deep) dug to sink the wheels and trails of the pieces."[20] When he issued his orders to the artillery Hancock required his aide to listen carefully, then said: "I am of the opinion that the enemy will mass in town and make an effort to take this position, but I want you to remain until you are relieved by me or by my written order and take orders from no one." He was taking no chances of having the guns moved.

When his work was completed Hancock had a presentable line running from Culp's Hill on the right to the Round Tops. Williams' division was in the rear of Wadsworth. The other Twelfth Corps division, Geary's, had now arrived, and Hancock moved it to the left to occupy the ground toward Round Top and prevent a turning movement to his left. What remained of the First Corps beyond Wadsworth's division was used temporarily to strengthen Howard on Cemetery Hill. From time to time Hancock had sent back word to Meade: an oral message at 4:30 P.M., describing the position and informing the commanding general that it could be readily defended with good troops, followed by a message of the same purport in writing at 5:25 P.M.[21]

Major General Henry W. Slocum, commanding the Twelfth Corps, had finally reached the field; since he was Howard's senior there was no question about who would give orders after Hancock's departure. It was seven o'clock. Hancock transferred the command to Slocum and rode back to Taneytown to report to Meade. He soon met his own corps approaching under Gibbon, and halted it to serve as a rear guard; Hays's division went on to replace the battle-frayed Robinson on the left of the Eleventh Corps. Before morning the two other divisions were aligned to the left of Hays.

2. Meade Comes to Gettysburg at Last

Sickles' Third Corps, marching since it had been summoned by Howard, began to come up at seven o'clock, to be greeted by an appreciative Howard, who, as the New York *Herald* correspondent got it, said to the old Tammanyite: "Here you are—always reliable, always first."[22] The brigade of the Frenchman, Colonel Philip R. de Trobriand, plus the New Jersey brigade of Colonel George C. Burling, had been left behind to comply nominally with Meade's instructions for the Third Corps to watch the South Mountain pass near Emmitsburg.

For the balance of the corps the march was like a triumphal procession partly because the distinguished—even notorious—politician, Major General Daniel E. Sickles, always brought out the crowds, and partly because everyone in the countryside knew a battle was shaping up on which the course of the war would likely be determined. From Emmitsburg to Gettysburg the community centers and crossroads were filled with farm folk gathered to watch the soldiers pass. They cheered, waved hats and handkerchiefs. Flags were flown, and as evening came on lighted lanterns were hung hospitably at farmhouse gateways[23] while inside farmwives stood all day baking hot bread.

Ward's brigade of Birney's division, Third Corps, arrived at ten o'clock and bivouacked near the big red barn of the Codori farmhouse on the Emmitsburg road. The atmosphere was vaporous and smoky clouds scurried across the night sky, often obscuring the full moon. Colonel Elijah Walker of the 4th Maine laid out a bed of grass and leaves in a little clump of trees which two days later would be made famous for all time by the amount of blood shed there.[24] He was not yet asleep when orders came to establish a picket line connecting the Third with the First Corps pickets on the right and the Second Corps on the left. They went out to a rail fence two hundred yards west of the Emmitsburg road and heard the enemy pickets on the watch two hundred yards farther on. The division commander, Major General David B. Birney, saw the men assembling and whispered to a lieutenant, "I wish I were already dead."[25]

Carr's brigade of the Third Corps, coming up in the darkness, with the 26th Pennsylvania leading, marched by the wrong road and suddenly found itself inside the Confederate lines at Black Horse Tavern. Luckily it saw the error before the enemy could sound the alarm. It captured the picket into which it had blundered, about-faced quietly, groped until it found the proper road, and reached the Federal lines at midnight.[26]

Last to arrive before sunup was the Fifth Corps, which had already completed its day's march to Hanover, Pennsylvania, from Union Mills, Maryland, and had pitched its tents when at six o'clock orders arrived to continue to Gettysburg. The distance was thirteen miles and Major General George Sykes, who commanded, did not know the road, but a resident, a "country gentleman," volunteered to guide them. The corps trudged along until one o'clock and halted, feeling near enough to the battle zone to be available. At 4:00 A.M., without breakfast or coffee, it pushed on the remaining three miles to Gettysburg.[27]

The rapidity of some of these marches suggests that the Federal soldiers were traveling lighter than formerly. In the Chancellorsville campaign they had been laughed at by the Southerners as "too well fed, too well clothed, and have far too much to carry." What they carried was eight days' rations, sixty rounds of ammunition, a musket or rifle, woolen blanket, rubber blanket, overcoat, extra shirt, drawers, socks, and shelter tent, amounting to sixty pounds, an unconscionably heavy load for troops from whom upward of twenty-five miles in a single day might be expected. Thus while the roads behind the Confederates were littered with old shoes those behind the Federals as they advanced toward Gettysburg were strewn with brand-new overcoats, blankets, shelter halves, and anything else not useful in fighting.

Having fully determined to concentrate at Gettysburg, Meade ordered up the Third Corps brigades of De Trobriand and Burling that had been held at Emmitsburg; they arrived about 10:00 A.M., July 2. The Federal concentration was now complete except for the big Sixth Corps under Sedgwick.

The moon at the full[28] had proved a boon to the columns of the Federal army which was completing by night what Lee had accomplished largely during the day. By morning the Federals would overcome the numerical advantages which the Southerners had possessed on July 1. The task of concentrating in an advanced position had meant grueling marches, aching backs, and much confusion and disorganization, but had proved incalculably easier than a retrograde concentration behind Pipe Creek would have been in darkness. Meade at 6:30 P.M., when he had had time to reflect on the messages from Hancock, had decided to fight at Gettysburg. Any other course, he could see, would be a stunning blow to the Federal cause. A withdrawal on the night of July 1, even if sound strategically, would magnify the importance of that day's engagement and be of immense psychological advantage to the South. The Confederate victory of July 1 would quite justifiably assume proportions greater than those at Manassas and Chancellorsville. Lee might then detach Ewell to march on Harrisburg or Philadelphia.

These matters must certainly have passed through Meade's mind as he reflected on the inauspicious beginning of his term in the same uncomfortable shoes that had been worn by the dreary line of McDowell, Burnside, Hooker, others. So he determined, manifestly with reluctance, to abandon his Pipe Creek plans and fight on the field which chance had selected. He had surveyed the Pipe Creek line carefully and understood it, whereas, although he was a Pennsylvanian by family ties and had resided much in that state, he had never visited the Gettysburg area, could not visualize the terrain, and could only rely on Hancock's description of it.

The moon, described by some of the soldiers as pallid, was showing intermittently behind the racing clouds, giving a wan light through the towering sycamore trees that lined the Pennsylvania roadways, when sometime after 1:00 A.M. Meade's party of horsemen set out from Taneytown for Gettysburg. Why Meade delayed his departure so long is one of the curiosities of the battle, but probably one reason was that he imperatively needed some sleep. Earlier in the evening he had completed his marching orders for those elements of the army not already on the move: the Third Corps rear guard at Emmitsburg, the Fifth Corps at Hanover, and the Sixth Corps at distant Manchester.[29]

Meade reached the arched brick gateway into the cemetery between two and three o'clock in the morning, ahead of his escort. Howard, who was there, gave the time as "about 3 A.M.," but all he judged by was that it seemed so brief a time before daylight.[30] Howard was disturbed over the events of July 1. He met Meade just inside the gateway and was comforted by his chief's first kindly words. "I believed I had done my work well the preceding day," Howard explained later: "I desired his approval and so I frankly stated my earnest wish. Meade at once assured me that he imputed no blame."[31] He must have wondered at concern over a reputation when so many had died in the cause.

Sickles and Slocum joined Meade and Howard and spoke favorably, as Howard had, of the army's position. "I am glad to hear you say so, gentlemen," Meade responded, "for it is too late to leave it."[32]

The moon had now brightened. Meade decided he would not wait for daylight before inspecting the lines along which the battle would likely be joined. He was engaged in his tour when dawn came. Howard rode with him. As the sun rose Meade took the highest point in the cemetery and with his glasses looked across the dew-soaked fields to the lines of the Confederate army just beginning to stir on Seminary Ridge. This section was what Howard referred to as the army's left. Meade did not pursue his inspection to the region of the Round Tops.

When he completed it he made his preliminary decision, that the Federal army would attack with its right as soon as Sedgwick arrived with the Sixth Corps.[33] Meade had hurried off a messenger to the

Sixth around seven o'clock the evening before, and the corps would long since have been on the way.

3. Sedgwick Frolics and Waits

On the evening of July 1 Major General John Sedgwick sat at his headquarters under the towering trees near Manchester, Maryland. About the village and through the groves that extended down the valley lolled the members of the big Sixth Corps of the Army of the Potomac, enjoying a faint touch of breeze after a sweltering day.

Some were writing letters that would go to homes scattered from the Penobscot to the Wisconsin, for the corps that had lost heavily during Hooker's recent fiasco knew it was due for another battle. Some pitched mule shoes along the banks of the little streams where Sedgwick camped. But most of the men were merely lounging and resting.

Stocky General Sedgwick—"Uncle John" to the troops—labored over army papers in the dulling July twilight. Present for duty were about 15,000 officers and men. Lieutenant Colonel Martin T. McMahon, more of a companion to Sedgwick than a chief of staff, sat near by and helped with the calculations. Lee's army was in Pennsylvania to be sure, but that had no bearing on the paper work.

The corps had completed on the previous evening its rapid march from Virginia, via Poolesville and Westminster, Maryland, to its present camp site. The trains and baggage, except for ambulances and ammunition carts, had been left in Westminster. Now Sedgwick was learning that the situation of his corps in Manchester, consigned to a day of idleness while the balance of the Federal army plunged ahead to find Lee, was scarcely conducive to concentration on payroll vouchers.

Sedgwick had made his headquarters in the little brick Fort Hill school that had stood since 1803 on what had once been the old Indian trail from the Potomac to the Susquehanna River.[34] Manchester, partly on a ridge, is the high point between Harrisburg and Baltimore. Sedgwick could view from a summit near the school a great expanse of Maryland and southern Pennsylvania and see far away the soft mountain ridges between Gettysburg and Chambersburg over which Lee's army had that day been passing. But the road to Gettysburg was by way of Westminster,[35] thence northwest through Littlestown, a total distance of 35 miles. The position was almost isolated from the rest of the army. Meade could have sent his largest corps there only because Lee's advance had reached York, and Manchester was directly between York and Baltimore.

Sedgwick and McMahon inspected the camp, which lay along what in recent times has been known as the John Green farm, with its two springs and abundant timber. The corps commander observed with satisfaction that the men were rested and in good spirits. July 1 had been an extraordinary day. Nobody remembered anything more serene in the whole experience of this march-mad army. Most of the regiments had reached Manchester at the close of a hot June and had assumed that the corps would be on the move again at July daybreak.

But reveille sounded, the corps breakfasted, and to the surprise of the men, no orderlies shouted the familiar call to ranks with full packs. Details were assembled for fatigue and picket duty, and the balance of the troops fell out, nominally under regimental confines. The soldiers, anxious to use every minute of the unexpected leisure, mingled with the gathering crowds of the most appreciative population they had encountered since they had begun, fifteen months before, the march with McClellan on Richmond.

News spread rapidly over the Maryland hills that a sizable portion of the Federal army had halted at Manchester. On foot and horseback, in buggies, buckboards and wagons, more and more of the curious thronged in. Near-by houses discharged their residents. Farm wives began baking bread feverishly. Hawkers appeared, and soon the village took on the appearance and gaiety of a carnival or county fair.

Through the dimming years of succeeding decades the memory of those soldiers carried pictures of the gathering: girls in bright calico gaily swinging their bonnets from long ribbons; housewives bringing fruit and jelly; small boys begging permission to draw a bayonet, touch a gun, or test their teeth on a piece of army hardtack; peddlers droning their refrains through the crowds; wagoners selling jugs of apple and peach brandy. The young men of the district were gone, which prompted inquiries as to the location of different Union regiments. About these the Sixth Corps members had nothing more than guesses. The soldiers wrote their names and regimental units on their white paper collars and gave them to the girls as souvenirs, hoping for letters in return. They read old newspapers from near-by households; they lavished their pay so enthusiastically on tobacco and brandy that the supplies were soon short even in this Maryland section. They played poker and old sledge, cleaned equipment and tossed baseballs, but most of them simply sat chatting under the shade of the great oaks.[36]

Uncle John Sedgwick presided over the impromptu carnival with a mild indifference. His main concern was about the rye whisky and the brandy, distilled in abundance in the neighborhood. He issued orders for the arrest of anyone bringing liquor into camp. The men, he felt, were entitled to a good rest so long as Meade did not need them elsewhere. The Pipe Creek Circular showed the Sixth Corps already in position. The balance of the army, after it located Lee, would align itself on the Sixth and await a Confederate attack.[37] But any plan was likely to be changed; confirmation was long overdue from the army commander.

Sedgwick's attachment to the enlisted men was well understood in the Sixth Corps, even though it was never manifested by laxity or sentimentality. Uncle John had no family except his soldiers; he was one of the few bachelors among the senior officers. His affection for his men was hidden by a stern aloofness, although occasionally his genial spirit broke through and the soldiers and the general had a laugh together. In his own quarters Sedgwick was a jester and tease. Many in the army thought he might have had the high command succeeding Burnside if he had made any effort to line up friends in Washington. With Secretary Chase backing Hooker, opponents of the Chase faction had looked appraisingly at Sedgwick. But Uncle John seemed satisfied with the leadership of a division. He was a frank admirer of McClellan and could do nothing suggesting disloyalty to his memory,[38] which always hung broodingly over the army. He was contemptuous of officers who had politicians pleading their cases at the White House and in Congress. He was a soldier. He would stand on his record as a soldier, just as his grandfather had done under General Washington at Brandywine and Valley Forge.

His big frame, his military carriage, his wide, large-featured face, but more than these his solid self-assurance, gave him an instant power in an emergency. His leadership asserted itself naturally on the firing line, where he usually stripped off his epaulets and wore a private's blouse. He was an overflowing reservoir of confidence and strength. His shrewd Yankee wit was sufficiently penetrating to give its owner distinction among the officers of the high command. Yet Sedgwick at heart was placid and unpretentious. Secretly he longed for relief from the pounding of war and for peaceful retirement in the home he had left, when scarcely more than a boy, in a quiet Connecticut valley.

A peaceful man in an era of passion and turbulence! Few battles

had been fought in three decades of empire building and empire saving without the presence of this sturdy officer in the press of action.
Vera Cruz, Cerro Gordo, Churubusco, Chapultepec. His bravery had
given him three promotions in Mexico. Seminoles, Cherokees, Chey-
ennes; Utah, Solomon Fork, Grand Saline: he rarely missed Indian
or border skirmish. Usually he was in the front of the fight showing
his men how to be contemptuous of bullets.

Sedgwick had been born while the echo of Oliver Perry's guns
sounded from Lake Erie. His soul would pass as cannon roared at
Spottsylvania. And the thunder would rumble across the Connecticut
mountains as his neighbors lowered him into his final resting place,
peaceful at last, near the old family home in Cornwall Hollow.[39]

Thus, with Sedgwick looking on, the largest corps of the Union
army loitered in the Manchester grove, while less than thirty miles
away, as the crow flies, two other Union corps were being severely
handled in the first day of the battle beyond Gettysburg. The sound
of the battle was deadened; the men at Manchester knew nothing of it.

As daylight faded the crowds that had come to see the troops scattered again. The flag that had floated before headquarters was furled.
Campfires over which numerous chickens had lately sizzled were in
embers, and about the grove settled the stillness of a summer night.
The men along the company streets awaited the drumbeat that would
signal them to silence. The night of July 1, 1863, promised to be
peaceful for the big Sixth Corps, resting in bivouac. And at headquarters Sedgwick sat, shuffling papers with McMahon.

Faintly through the night came the distant rhythm of galloping
hoofs. The nearer clash of steel shoes sounded on gravel highway. The
picket challenged. Saddle leather groaned as the rider dismounted.
A dust-covered courier stood in Sedgwick's doorway. It was Trooper
Oliver of the army headquarters staff who had ridden down his second
horse to reach Sixth Corps headquarters with dispatches from General Meade.[40]

Sedgwick read and listened. The story of the first day's action at
Gettysburg was unfolded.

John Reynolds was dead. Even in the midst of momentous events,
how deeply does the personal touch one! The life of one man was as
nothing compared with the greater, endless purpose of the Union. Yet
Reynolds! Sedgwick's dear friend, who but yesterday was the ideal
soldier of the army; the fine equestrian who had excelled in the old

garrisons of the West, who sat his mount so handsomely, and could pluck a dime from the ground while riding at a gallop![41]

Reynolds was dead and the left wing of the Union army was shattered. The First and Eleventh corps had been broken and forced back. The town of Gettysburg had been captured. The balance of the Union army was concentrating to resume the battle in the morning. How soon, Meade asked, could the Sixth Corps be at Gettysburg?

Sedgwick looked at his watch. He calculated from his map the indirect road of thirty-five miles between him and the main army. He turned to the courier, Oliver: "Say to General Meade that my corps will be at Gettysburg at four o'clock tomorrow."[42]

As Oliver left the general's headquarters, he muttered to some nearby soldier, who was to embody his words in the Sixth Corps tradition, that such a march might just be possible, but he doubted that a corps—even the old Sixth—could do it.

Here was, indeed, a test for Sedgwick. The modest big-shouldered man may have felt that he had accomplished very little in thirty years of soldiering to disprove the early opinion of his former neighbors that the barefoot boy who had taught the Cornwall Hollow school could never become a real army officer. Senator Jabez Huntington had reflected that doubt when, with but a slight ring of conviction to the West Point examining board, he had guardedly predicted that young Sedgwick would "become of some service to the country."[43]

4. Sedgwick Encounters the Army Trains

Mellow and clear through the Maryland night sounded the headquarters bugle, followed by the crashing drum roll. Not tattoo, as the soldiers expected, but the sharp notes of assembly.

A few seconds of silence followed, then out from beneath the towering trees came the clank of rifles, bayonets and scabbards, the hissing of water on campfires, the drone of voices as the men unfastened their shelter halves, the shouldering of haversacks, the dull tramping of countless feet across the lumpy sod, and the heavy shouts of the sergeants bellowing, "Fall in! Fall in!"

The regiments were formed. The officers moved front and center to the brigadiers for instructions. Then out to the open pike moved the head of the big Sixth Corps, bound on a mission that none could guess.

Now despite the fact that, as an army ordinarily moved, he was two days' distant from Gettysburg, Sedgwick had made his calculations carefully; he knew his corps better than the courier Oliver. He had allowed ample time for these men of hardened legs and durable backs to reach the main army. Nevertheless, there were no moments to be wasted. To move a corps rapidly from camp to roadway involved a deal of logistics and was more difficult in darkness. The Sixth was, in fact, an army. It was organized and officered for action apart from the main body, such as it had fought at Marye's Heights and Salem Church in the Chancellorsville campaign. It had 36 infantry regiments, 8 batteries of artillery, and a cavalry complement, aggregating at full strength 18,000 officers and men. It was a blue monster whose rifles and cannon could belch a ton of lead at one breath. Its infantry units, without their trains, stretched ten miles on the roadway, and required three hours of marching time to pass a given point.[44] Its three divisions were commanded by Wright, Howe, and Wheaton. John Newton, who usually headed the third, had been rushed off by the dispatch from Meade to take command of the First Corps, superseding Doubleday.

But Sedgwick had based his promise on no more than the information he possessed when he quickly arranged his march. His head of column was already moving on the road to Taneytown when a later messenger specified the Baltimore pike direct to Gettysburg. It was a disconcerting command. A halt was ordered while Sedgwick and his staff hurriedly restudied their maps. Regiments were shunted across the fields; delays occurred in the darkness. Finally the column was readjusted.

But when the 98th Pennsylvania Regiment moved off again in the lead, the advance party encountered a much more serious obstacle. General Meade had ordered his huge supply trains back on Westminster, and now they sprawled along the turnpike, fifteen miles of slow-moving mules and wagons.[45] Sedgwick roared commands; messengers scattered through the night. Officers hurled oaths at teamsters and teamsters cursed at mules. Team were shunted into side roads. Nothing was more irksome to soldiers than the strain of the hobbled marching behind the teams. Some of the regiments still waited in the camp at Manchester, packs on, accouterments ready. Not until four o'clock on the morning of July 2 did the corps finally clear the town. At daybreak the regiments had covered an average distance of only six miles. Disaster loomed for the Northern army, for Sedgwick's word to Meade was surely broken.

A white sun rose over the eastern hills, promising another scorching day, but after such a night daylight of any nature was welcome to the Sixth Corps. There was a final delay which some of them sought to utilize for cooking breakfast. But the corps was now clear of its blockade and Sedgwick had no intention of giving his troops food when the fate of the Union depended on their marching. An officer rudely kicked over some of the coffeepots that were beginning to boil.[46]

Jauntily the 98th Pennsylvania stepped out at the head of the long column. Despite its Company A, the "Irish Wing,"[47] this regiment wore the name of the "German Regulars," so called because it had made a tenacious stand at Williamsburg. The corps artillery moved under Colonel Charles H. Tompkins, the 1st Massachusetts in the lead, followed by the 1st New York. (Captain Andrew Cowan, your words will live in granite at the high-water mark on Cemetery Ridge![48]) After the 3rd New York moved two batteries of the 1st Rhode Island and two batteries of the 2nd and one of the 5th United States Artillery. Infantry regiments were there with records that remain among the most resplendent in American military history. The Green Mountain Brigade, a heritage of the Revolution; Alexander Shaler's brigade (Lincoln with his own hand had fastened the brigadier's star on Shaler's shoulder). Young Emory Upton marched at the head of his regiment. Although only twenty-three years old, he was already known as the model colonel of the army.

The Sixth Corps was a trained, seasoned, formidable army, which Sheridan came to admire in later fighting in Virginia. (Seven years after Gettysburg Sheridan was an observer with the German staff when the French surrendered Metz. He told Prince Frederick Charles that if he had had one division of the Sixth Corps in Metz, he could have cut his way through the German iron ring.[49])

Thus was Sedgwick off to Gettysburg. At the head of the column, flying in the morning breeze alongside the Stars and Stripes, was the banner of the Greek Cross, the Sixth Corps emblem. The sunshine glinted off polished steel. Blue masses stood out on the white macadam roadway. Sedgwick's round, straw hat was pulled down over his dust-rimmed eyes. His jaw was set, his face as hard as the jutting rocks of his own Litchfield mountains.

Because of the absence of the farm boys, the harvest of 1863 was late. The wheat stood ripened, giving a golden hue to the rolling hills of what in any season is a section of unusual beauty. White clouds

rose up and filled the men's ears and nostrils, invaded the cartridge
boxes and settled in drifts around their shoulders. They had relief
from the crushed stone and gravel road at times where dirt side trails—
"summer roads"—had been worn over the level stretches by farmers'
buggies. The blazing sun sent ahead a shimmering haze on the white
pike. Uniforms dripped, men plodded ahead, sometimes silent, sometimes chanting the corps refrains:

> "The foremost in the conflict,
> The last to say, 'tis o'er.
> Who know not what it is to yield.
> You'll find the old Sixth Corps."[50]

Quick step and no rations. "It's hell, boys," shouted a barrel-
chested Philadelphia volunteer, "but if Lee's in Pennsylvania I'd walk
there on stumps." Mingled with the comments was the constant command of the junior officers to step lively and close up.

At length a stir passed along the winding column. Carried back
by "scuttle-butt," "latrine rumor," or in 1863 the "grapevine telegraph," the news went to the dozen Pennsylvania regiments. The
corps had reached the Mason-Dixon line.

Meade's orders for all commanders to address their men on the
crisis of the Southern invasion had been complied with in the Sixth
Corps units. The 93rd Pennsylvania had heard a speech from Colonel
James M. McCarter, a chaplain during the three months' service in
1861, who had become a line officer and the regiment's gallant commander at Fair Oaks, where he was wounded. Although almost an
invalid, he stayed in the saddle during the Gettysburg campaign. He
spoke unsupported from his horse and told the men with fiery elo-
quence of the stupendous issues that faced the Army of the Potomac
on Pennsylvania soil.

No cheer followed his remarks and there was no shouting now as
the men of the 93rd saw the green hills of their own state. The sentiments of the regiment had been stirred. The regimental colors were
unfurled. The drums beat the quickstep. The companies moved at
parade order. No reviewing officer could have desired a finer sight or
more even array of rifles at the "carry." To the time of their sharply
falling footsteps, the soldiers struck up the old, familiar song, and
passed into Pennsylvania singing, "Home, Sweet Home."[51]

Sedgwick was at the head of the column, a massive figure that seemed to bespeak the indissoluble Union. Mounted on his horse Cornwall, he paused at the side of the road to observe the corps as it passed him. An occasional bit of banter was tossed at the general from the ranks. "Get a fresh horse, Uncle John, and try to catch us," shouted a company wit. The general smiled and lifted his hat.

So it was, less than a year later, as he jested to steady a frightened soldier, Sedgwick was hit by a Southern marksman. The familiar smile was on his face as he lay dead in the Wilderness. There the men built a bower for his body out of pine-tree boughs. They covered all but his face with a flag and as they went into action they filed by as though passing in review, in their final reverence.[52]

As the march continued the men learned that their goal was Gettysburg, but the details of the first day's action were still unreported. The need for haste was obvious. Here and there men dropped limply. The column veered until they could be lifted into the shade along the roadside. Ambulances in the rear picked up as many of the stricken as possible. Wet uniforms weighed heavy, and backs ached with the dull hurt of exhaustion. Grime gathered on perspiring necks and the dust and mud made the blue regiments look much like the gray-and-butternut detachments Lee had led across the Potomac. Obviously there could be no halt for dinner and no chance to snatch food by straggling. Uncle John Sedgwick was in white-hot earnest.

Finally along the roadway began to appear traces of yesterday's engagement. Ambulances were rearward-bound. One of the muleteers hauling wounded thought he should have right of way on the road, and was dissuaded by a saber point at his throat. Another driver demanding the road with bread for the army saw it dumped into the ditches. Men going forward had first right; then ammunition. Food and wounded had to wait. At Littlestown, where they crossed the railroad, wounded gathered on the streets and in improvised hospitals. Gettysburg was ten miles away. Far to the west the undulating hills rose toward the tender outline of South Mountain. The men, silent now, moved grimly along. The sun beat in their faces. Two knobs at length stood out before them, one rising above the other. Still there was no sound of firing. The quiet was broken only by the heavy infantry tread and the groans of the lumbering caissons.

While the Sixth Corps marched, a tense nation awaited reports from Gettysburg. Throngs hovered about the telegraph and newspaper offices in Philadelphia and New York, discussing the drama of the invasion. In Washington Halleck clung to his telegraph wire, rushing

Stanton each message from Meade. Lincoln went to his room at the White House, got down on his knees, and burying his head in his arms, said to the Lord, "You know I have done all I can." Then he cried out, "Oh, God, give us a victory."[53] Strength seemed to reach him. Arising, he went to his office with a conviction that the invasion would be repelled and the Union saved.

And while the Sixth Corps marched, the balance of the Federal army remained in position on Culp's and Cemetery hills. The battle had not yet been resumed. Most of the officers were puzzled by Lee's inaction. They recalled the long quiet that had preceded Jackson's surprise attack just two months earlier at Chancellorsville. They remembered that Lee rarely struck where he was expected.

From the elevation of Little Round Top, scanning the roads, a signal officer saw far down the southeastern pike a haze and then distinctly a moving column. Officers seized their glasses and watched intently. "Cavalry," someone muttered. The remark caused consternation.[54] Was this Stuart in the Federal rear? Then some keen-eyed officer saw sunlight flashing from bayonets, and shouted that it was not gray calvary, but blue infantry. There was the flag and beside it the Greek Cross. "It is the Sixth Corps!" "The Sixth Corps has come!"

At two o'clock on the afternoon of July 2 Major General John Sedgwick reported to Meade at army headquarters, and the 98th Pennsylvania Infantry sucked the water of Rock Creek behind the Round Tops. Great cheers rolled down the Union line as word passed from division to division that the Sixth Corps had reached the field. They swept across the valley to Seminary Ridge, where the astute Lee, still having no information from his cavalry, mused and wondered.

At 4:00 P.M. the corps was well up and by five it was concentrated on the left flank of Meade's army, a reserve that made a battle feasible. Shortly before four while the men of the advance regiments were bathing their feet, the Southern bombardment suddenly erupted. The carnage of battle was to be continued; the future of America was to be determined. By one of the magnificent marches of warfare, the big Sixth Corps had reached the field of Gettysburg on time.

CHAPTER FIFTEEN

Lee's Attack Plans

1. Early Answers for the Second Corps

Why the long lull? On the evening of July 1, in the fading daylight, Lee rode through Gettysburg and out the Heidlersburg road to Ewell's headquarters at the Blocher farm northwest of Barlow's Knoll.

There he met Ewell, Early, and Rodes. Unfortunately, Johnson, perhaps the strongest of Ewell's division commanders and certainly neither so designing as Early nor as inhibited as Rodes, was posting troops and had no part in the consultations. Although the sun had set, the generals sat in the coolness of an arbor in the rear, where they enjoyed a relaxed conversation after a day of much anxiety, excitement, and physical exertion. There was common but unspoken assent that the battle of July 1 was now over; the talk should concern the next day.

Lee wanted information on three main points: the condition of the troops, the enemy's position, and the measures now to be deemed advisable. Early, a facile talker and skillful lawyer who knew how to present his case, took over as the Second Corps spokesman, with Ewell's tacit consent. Ewell merely affirmed what Early offered. Early became the only historian of the meeting,[1] and included Rodes as also in agreement with his propositions. The correspondent of the Petersburg *Express* who observed these two men at Orange Court House two months later might just as readily have obtained his thumbnail sketches from this earlier conference, for Early "seemed as one who could not be brooked in any thing he wished" while "General

Rodes is the most pleasant looking man I have seen in many a day."[2]
Rodes was certainly pleasant and harmonious at this conference, and
Early obdurate.

Lee made it evident at the outset that he had in mind a further
offensive against the Federal army. Nobody dwelt on defensive plans.
After he had heard a report on the condition and situation of the
troops, he asked the three generals conjointly, rather than the corps
commander in particular, one question: "Can you, with your corps,
attack on this flank at daylight tomorrow?"[3]

Early's answer was negative. Though he claimed to have been
pressing Ewell through the late afternoon to attack, he now shifted his
position. He said that he had reconnoitered in and about Gettysburg
both that day and when he had passed through en route to York on
June 26, and had observed: that the ground was steep and rough;
that the enemy was fortifying and concentrating in his front; and that
the houses and streets of the town would impede formation of a battle
line designed to move against the heights. It would be necessary to
attack from the left of the town, close up to the hills. The result would
be doubtful and success, if attained, would be attended by great loss.

Early clearly had a point when he said that the hills were being fortified and that the Federal army was moving to its own right in strength.
He had been unable earlier in the evening to have Hill's corps make
the attack on Cemetery Ridge and now he again called attention to
what he described as the more inviting aspect of the ground on the
other side of the town. The party must have moved to a vantage place,
for he pointed to the Round Tops, still discernible in the dusk, and
identified them as keys to the Federal position. He mentioned the
"more practicable nature of the ascents" on that side; an attack from
the Southern right flank, he said, would have better chances.

After Ewell and Rodes had concurred and Lee had seemed to agree
on the inadvisability of attacking with his left, Lee asked a disconcerting question: "Then perhaps I had better draw you around toward my
right, as the line will be very long and thin if you remain here, and the
enemy may come down and break through it?"[4]

The suggestion was critical in its bearing on the fortunes of the
army. Early did not reflect but "spoke at once in reply."[5] His main
objection was the loss of morale and equipment that would be en-
tailed. His men were elated with their success and should not be
compelled to give up the ground they had won. Some wounded were
not in a condition to be moved. The Gettysburg streets held stacks
of captured muskets that should not be abandoned.

Quite clearly Early wanted to stay where he was. Seeking to allay Lee's apprehension that the Federals might break the line, he declared the corps could repulse any force sent against it. He said it was more difficult for the enemy to come down than for the Confederates to go up to attack, although he did not elucidate. Again Ewell and Rodes concurred with Early's reasoning.

There is a hint, even as the story is related by Early, that Lee felt vaguely he was being pushed around a bit. He still was contemplative in his next remark: "Well, if I attack from my right, Longstreet will have to make the attack."

Then he paused and according to Early "held his head down in deep thought." When he looked up again, he added, "Longstreet is a very good fighter when he gets in position and gets everything ready, but he is *so slow*." The italics were Early's, and he explained, "The emphasis was just as I have given it, and the words seemed to come from General Lee with pain."[6]

The inconsistency of the remark with Eggleston's statement, quoted earlier, that Lee thought Longstreet speedier than Jackson is unimportant, because opinions will vary. But it is significant in that it showed Lee was forewarned and therefore might have found the means of forearming when he decided that Longstreet should begin the attack. Lee understood Longstreet better than some of the others could because he was, himself, more thorough than impulsive. Jackson had described Lee as "not slow" but "cautious." Lee must have known better than anyone else in the army that Longstreet would always be deliberate, and this was probably why the commanding general usually relied on him for the knockout punch rather than the first blow.[7]

Lee was far from satisfied when he departed from this anything but heartening conference. It showed him how fully Ewell had come under the dominance of the more sprightly minded Early. It is clear from the comment of Colonel Taylor that Lee had been intent on following up the success already gained; with the arrival of Johnson, Lee thought Ewell could go forward at dawn on the next day. What he obtained at the conference was a solid front of opinion that they should wait for Longstreet, who would then be employed against the enemy's "weak left."

One must wonder if more important to Early than the terrain was not the fact that Longstreet's corps had been resting at Suffolk while the balance of the army fought at Chancellorsville, and had not yet been engaged at Gettysburg. Certainly by the rule of rotation it was time for Longstreet to carry the major load of a battle. Early hinted broadly at this.[8] He had not reconnoitered the ground south of Gettysburg, was not familiar with the approaches to the Round Tops and could not have stressed the ease of making an attack there on the basis of any firsthand knowledge. He had reached Gettysburg late on June 26 and was too hurried then to have inspected the country south of the town with any care. Now he did not welcome the opportunity, which a soldier like Gordon probably would have leaped at, of moving to the far right himself and conducting the attack over the allegedly soft ground.

As it developed, Early's contentions left Lee with the necessity of planning the next day's operations with troops that had not yet reached the field, whose leader was known to be very methodical, if not, indeed, aggravatingly slow. Early's guile and reluctance had a profound bearing on the battle developments. Lee's active mind was comprehending all the possibilities. A few hours earlier on Seminary Ridge Longstreet had stubbornly reiterated his proposal for a flanking movement around the Federal left, by which Lee might interpose or threaten to interpose his army between Meade and Washington. The possibility of such a move, Lee later disclosed, was in his mind during his consultation with Ewell. Still, the move would be contingent on the shifting of Ewell and the willing co-operation of his subordinates, and that was not forthcoming.[9]

Early himself has provided perhaps the best analysis of Lee's method of command, which serves to explain not only his yielding in this July 1 conference, but also his transactions on the next day. According to Early, Lee "did not regard his officers as mere machines to execute his will," but as rational beings capable of reasoning and giving suggestions.

He had likewise a profound knowledge of human nature, and it was his custom to talk freely to officers about movements they were to make, get their views about the proper mode of making them, in order to ascertain whether they could be relied upon for the work in hand, adopt any judicious views they might suggest, and leave them under the impression that they were carrying out plans in the formation of which they had some part. . . .[10]

Lee knew that one of the first elements of success is "a confidence on the part of an officer entrusted with a movement in its feasibility." Early, it later developed, would apply this line of thought to himself but sparingly when dealing with the relations between Lee and Longstreet. The extreme of Lee's method can be found in his instructions in late April 1863, when he was informed that Hooker had crossed the Rappahannock: "Say to General Jackson that he knows just as well what to do with the enemy as I do."[11]

Manifestly, then, no plan for the attack on the morning of July 2 had been made when in darkness Lee rode back from Ewell's headquarters to his own on Seminary Hill. Longstreet meantime had returned to his camp beyond Marsh Creek with a distinct understanding that his corps should be brought up as quickly as possible in the morning, but without any orders for a sunrise attack.

Lee was purposely employing almost altogether verbal orders. His distrust of written directions in the presence of the enemy sprang from the well-near fatal loss of the orders in the Sharpsburg campaign, which revealed to McClellan how he had divided his army. Orders by word of mouth meant greater safety for the army, but greater confusion for historians who for nearly a century have had to feel their way hesitatingly and often with contrary judgment through a great mass of conflicting testimony about Lee's battle plans.[12]

2. A Headquarters Staff in a Cottage

Lee had his headquarters tents pitched in a field of grass just south of the Cashtown road on the reverse slope of Seminary Ridge. He conducted part of his work in the stone dwelling across the road, which even then was an old house, dating from 1779.

About the grounds were apple, plum, and cherry trees, while grapes grew over an arbor on the south side, screening the windows from the Cashtown road. The house was owned by Thaddeus Stevens, who rented it to the widow Maria Thompson, a slight, elderly woman, perhaps in her sixties, who volunteered to cook some of the meals for the Confederate officers. She had been indifferent when shells dropped near by, but the water in her cellar caused by the heavy rains of late June had finally persuaded her to seek better quarters in the town. Lee had offered to pay her rental but she declined it.

How he and his officers ate is a wonder. The little pine table on which Mrs. Thompson supposedly served them was only forty-one by forty-eight inches, and according to tradition not only Lee and his staff, but Longstreet, Ewell, Hood, Early, and others had their meals there at one time or another. Some of course must have eaten standing. Lee had scant time for sleep in his tent but he got some naps in a rocking chair.

Long after the battle some argued insistently that Lee did not use the Thompson house in Gettysburg; that he was seen much of the time elsewhere and observed riding over Seminary Hill as though coming from a headquarters farther behind the lines. The matter is of passing interest because of Lee's previous aversion to houses. But there is abundant testimony that he occupied the Thompson house for conferences and meals. Kyd Douglas, who tented with Colonel Taylor across the road, referred to it, as did couriers. The interior of the house was burned in the 1890s but was reconstructed, as the stone walls were left intact.

One room Lee used as an office and another as a reception room. The inadequacy of his staff is in no manner more clearly seen than from its ability to cramp itself into one or two tents and this simple stone house, measuring thirty by thirty-three feet. Lee tended to simplify the management of the army much as the private Confederate soldier simplified the load he carried on his back. He had no Berthier or Gneisenau, nor even a Rawlins to operate his headquarters or act in his absence. One of the amazing and, from a Confederate standpoint, distressing things about the battle was the amount of detail work Lee was compelled to carry personally in the midst of such a supreme trial of strength, and all this business was transacted in the cramped quarters of Mrs. Thompson's stone cottage. Needless to say, Lee had won some splendid victories with his meager staff, but the paucity of his headquarters assistance became more evident under the stress of Gettysburg.

After eating Mrs. Thompson's supper on July 1 Lee decided to do whatever he could to end Stuart's waywardness—the matter that had been causing him the greatest impatience and concern of the campaign. Having heard nothing, he was fearful, according to Longstreet, that his cavalry had been destroyed.[13] As Stuart did not seem able to find him, he would have to find Stuart. Lee asked the dashing raider, Harry Gilmore, who had accompanied Johnson, to send a good detail to headquarters and soon a Marylander, James D. Watters, was at hand with a squad of about eight men. All were mounted, as Lee had directed, on good horses.

Each man was given a copy of sealed orders to General Stuart. They were to scatter over the country and find Stuart as soon as possible. If they ran into danger of capture they were to destroy the orders but were to reach Stuart at all hazards and tell him to join Lee at Gettysburg with the least possible delay.[14] Watters happened to be the courier who found Stuart and brought him to headquarters, riding ahead of his men. Long afterward he told the story of the episode.

3. The Question of the "Sunrise Attack"

Lee must have thought he had been sold a peculiar bill of goods by Early and Ewell, because back in his headquarters that night he soon reversed his decision about letting his left remain idle. He sent Colonel Marshall with a message reopening the question of an attack on the heights, and summoning Ewell to headquarters. Johnson's division meantime was in position and its commander was optimistic about his ability to carry Culp's Hill, which he had found occupied soon after his arrival. Ewell, due to Johnson's opinion, reversed his own position and said he would attack. Though no time was set, this again dissuaded Lee from shifting Ewell to the far right. Ewell left Lee's headquarters about midnight. All that had really been decided was that Lee would continue the offensive in the morning after Longstreet's troops arrived.

No definite orders were issued for any corps. Yet one of the fixed popular misconceptions of American history is the belief that Lee at this night meeting ordered Longstreet to attack at daybreak on the morning of July 2. Early made it the crux of his case against Longstreet.

This writer on a recent visit to Gettysburg, where the battle is still continually analyzed and discussed, made it a point to inquire among residents in restaurants, stores, etc., why, in their opinion, Lee lost the battle. A majority answered that Lee lost because Longstreet failed to carry out orders for an attack at daybreak on the morning of July 2. Perhaps the most persistent controversy ever waged about the battle was that of the 1870s concerning this "sunrise attack." Lee, according to some of his officers, notably Early and Pendleton, ordered Longstreet to make it and lost the battle because Longstreet failed to comply. This has come to be almost the settled verdict of popular history.

Part of the uncertainty about the orders to Longstreet undoubtedly has resulted from a misunderstanding of Longstreet's actions on the night of July 1. The assumption has been that Longstreet was with Lee that night, and that Lee made his decision and imparted it to Longstreet. Longstreet himself contributed to this misunderstanding by saying in one of his accounts that he left Lee "quite late on the night of the 1st."[15]

The errors that crept into Longstreet's documents are no doubt attributable in part to his use of ghost writers, the most famous of whom was the Atlanta editor, Henry W. Grady. Grady likely contributed some of the striking passages in Longstreet's accounts. But the general used other writers too, because of his crippled right arm, and he apparently was not careful or experienced in editing and let errors creep through.

Longstreet may have meant merely that he left late in the evening of July 1. In another account he placed the time at seven o'clock. In still another he quite clearly suggests that he had no contact with Lee between the time he saw him on Seminary Hill in the evening, sometime between five and seven, and their meeting on the morning of July 2. Colonel Long told of Lee's addressing Longstreet and Hill on the "evening" of July 1 but specified no time. "Evening" is an indefinite word in the South.

But there is external evidence bearing on Longstreet's actions that is conclusive. He left Seminary Ridge and rode to his camp beyond Marsh Creek. He had progressed half a mile when he encountered Dr. J. S. D. Cullen, the Third Corps medical director, who said it was "about dark."[16] That, on July 1, would mean after eight, but in any case after seven-thirty. He traveled four miles or more to his headquarters and was moody. Fremantle rode back with him and left an account of it. The British correspondent Ross was traveling with Barksdale, near whom Longstreet camped. He said it was "pitch dark" when the fires were lighted for supper. Some doctors joined them, and Longstreet and his staff "presently came up" and confirmed news about the first day's fighting. This would place Longstreet's return from Gettysburg at around 9:30 P.M. More time would have been consumed at dinner. McLaws said he met Longstreet coming from Gettysburg that night about ten o'clock, which is more definite.

According to Longstreet's testimony, he was up the next morning while the stars were still shining. "It was still dusk," said Ross, when he went to the general's tent for breakfast.[17] Longstreet must have arisen sometime between three and three-thirty. The earlier time is usually used.

Considering that half an hour to forty-five minutes would have been required for normal night riding between Longstreet's and Lee's headquarters, it does not fit in that Longstreet could reasonably have attended any night conference with Lee. It would have involved a round trip in the middle of the night with no apparent purpose.

Had he felt that other business was necessary he would scarcely have returned to his camp in the early evening; had he been with Lee in a conference that did not end until around midnight, why would he have ridden five miles to get two hours' sleep and return by daybreak, when by remaining on Seminary Hill he might have got three or four? It does not appear that Lee called him. Lee's courier, F. S. Gore, left a letter saying he was sent that night to summon Ewell.[18] There is no reference to anyone's summoning Longstreet from Marsh Creek, and Lee did not mention his presence. Manifestly he was not there.

When, then, did Lee issue his orders for Longstreet to attack early on July 2, if at all? On this point Longstreet said that at the time of his departure from Lee on the night of July 1, "I believed that he had made up his mind to attack, but was confident that he had not yet determined as to when the attack was to be made."[19] Certainly if Longstreet had been ordered to attack, he or someone else would have known of it that evening. Here Longstreet's memories are well confirmed and to be trusted fully.[20] Not only was Lee uncertain that night about *when* the attack was to be made, but also *where,* as his later movements attest clearly.

When Longstreet met McLaws he said nothing about his division attacking in the morning, as he surely would have if Lee had ordered it at "sunrise."

As Lee went to sleep his last words to his secretary, Long, showed that indecision still existed.

"Colonel Long," he said, "do you think we had better attack without the cavalry? If we do, we will not, if successful, be able to reap the fruits of victory."[21]

Long thought it would be best to go ahead. The time when Stuart might come was uncertain.

4. *An Anxious General Roams the Lines*

How thoroughly unsettled Lee was is evident by his dispatch of Colonel Venable at sunrise with a further message to Ewell, inquiring again what Ewell thought of an attack from his position. Daylight permitted a better reconnaissance and Ewell might have new thoughts. That Ewell's reply was negative is suggested by Venable's statement that the corps commander "made me ride with him from point to point of his lines, so as to see with him the exact position of things."

Ewell was not likely to assent to an attack in Early's absence! Ven-

able did make it clear that the purpose of Lee's message—Lee was
explicit about this—was to determine whether he should move Ewell's
troops around to the right. The old question was thus reopened.
Lee's prudence still emphasized that Ewell's concave lines, largely
isolated from the rest of the army, were unsound and invited attack,
which, incidentally, Meade was at that instant considering. Venable
did not think when he went to Ewell that Lee was contemplating any
"sunrise attack." Manifestly his plans were still being formed.

Not satisfied with sending Venable, Lee soon followed. His first
concern was with his exposed left and with Culp's and Cemetery
hills. To carry those eminences would win the battle.

Ewell was engaged in his reconnaissance with Colonel Venable
when Lee reached the corps headquarters. Trimble, unemployed
since stalking away from Ewell on the previous evening, met the commanding general there. Lee wished to survey the country from an
elevation and get a view of the enemy's position.

The cupola on the almshouse was not so commanding as the cupolas
on the Lutheran Seminary or Pennsylvania College but it was the best
point in their vicinity. Lee and Trimble climbed to the top. They
had a good view of Culp's Hill and Cemetery Ridge and in the distance could see the Round Tops.

Lee turned to Trimble: "The enemy have the advantage of us in a
shorter and inside line and we are too much extended," he said. "We
did not or we could not pursue our advantage of yesterday and now
the enemy are in a good position."[22]

Those words—"we did not or we could not pursue our advantage of
yesterday"—were, for Lee, a rebuke, indicative of his deep displeasure
with the closing events of July 1. Anyone might see that Ewell "could"
have continued his attack, and therefore Lee considered it a matter
of neglect. In any event, he repeated the words several times that
morning, as he met Early, Rodes, and others.[23] Trimble said their
significance was impressed on him especially in view of Lee's statement at Hagerstown that he would fall on the enemy as he came up
and crush him in detail. That plan was not working out so readily as
he had a right to expect.

The precise hours at which Lee made his trips about the battlefield
that morning are difficult to determine and if they were known would
not be especially significant since they did not contribute either to the
development of plans or the progress of the battle. For the better part
of the morning Lee was groping for a means to launch a co-ordinated

offensive that would have the wholehearted support of his corps commanders; failing in this, he finally was compelled to make an arbitrary decision and order Longstreet to attack the Federal left forthwith. The hour at which the positive orders were issued was probably about eleven o'clock—it could scarcely have been earlier.[24] Too, that is the hour given by Colonel Taylor.

Lee's eagerness to have Longstreet's men on the field began to express itself soon after daybreak. Needless to say, no offensive could be undertaken anywhere until these fresh divisions were present. During the morning Lee made two visits to Ewell's lines on the left, passed along A. P. Hill's front, and was now and again in consultation with Longstreet, Hill, and others on Seminary Ridge. His anxiety to get the battle under way expressed itself not in any severity of tone or language, but in a restless wandering.

Lee was not in good physical condition on July 2. His difficulty may have been induced or aggravated by his mental distress. Several noticed his agitation, which was not dissimilar to that observed by Dr. Suesserott in Messersmith's woods near Chambersburg three days before.

Major Justus Scheibert of the Prussian Royal Engineers—who was on Seminary Ridge as an observer, as he had been at Chancellorsville, and whose admiration of Lee was almost boundless—made a revealing comparison of the commanding general's attitude in the two battles.[25] At Chancellorsville Lee was "full of calm, quiet, self-possession, feeling that he had done his duty to the utmost."

This calmness was wanting at Gettysburg, where:

Lee was not at his ease, but was riding to and fro, frequently changing his position, making anxious inquiries here and there, and looking care-worn. . . . This uneasiness . . . was contagious to the army, as will appear from the reports of Longstreet, Hood, Heth and others, and as appeared also to me from the peep I had of the battlefield.[26]

Lee's manner has sometimes been attributed to the wounding and capture of his son Rooney.[27] Rooney had received a leg wound at Fleetwood and had been taken to Hickory Hill, the home of W. F. Wickham near Richmond, to recuperate. The house was raided by Federal cavalry and Rooney was captured. But General Lee does not appear to have heard of the capture until he was at Williamsport after the battle of Gettysburg,[28] although he knew his son had been wounded. In no case could it have been the cause of such evident agitation. Lee as a soldier had steeled himself to loss. Moreover, the uneasiness was temporary. Scheibert emphasized that the general after the battle "resumed his accustomed calmness."

Longstreet treated the difficulty as emotional: "He seemed under a subdued excitement, which occasionally took possession of him when 'the hunt was up,' and threatened his superb equipoise." A Texan's view was that temperamentally Lee was a "game cock" when challenged by the enemy.[29] This was not far from the opinion of Heth, who looked on the commanding general as the most aggressive man of the army, "not even excepting Jackson."

Still, his agitation at Gettysburg was above any normal combativeness. Lieutenant Colonel Blackford offered what is perhaps the most plausible explanation, that Lee was suffering severely from diarrhea. That could explain also the unusual actions observed in Messersmith's woods by the Chambersburg physician. Blackford, after the army had been located for Stuart, rode ahead of the cavalry and was sent to report to Lee on some brushes that day with the Federals. A staff officer told him he could not see Lee, whom he had usually found accessible for such reports. So he made his report to either Venable or Taylor—he could not recall which—and then sat at headquarters half an hour relating some of the events of Stuart's long ride.

In that period Lee came out of his tent several times hurriedly and went to the rear, walking as though weakened and in pain. Blackford inquired and was informed that the general was suffering from diarrhea. This, he thought, could explain why some things were not pushed with their accustomed vigor on that day.[30]

The difficulty of diarrhea or flux was so common in the armies that it was often termed the "'old soldier's disease." Particularly was it present in the early fruit season, and the Confederate army, as we have seen, had been partaking freely all along the route. Early apples grown on Seminary Ridge were just ripening. They were being eaten heartily and it is not unlikely that Lee had been enjoying these and cherries, too. As we saw earlier, he had relished fresh raspberries in Maryland.[31]

The British correspondent Ross rode with Longstreet in the faint dawn to Gettysburg. Daylight had come when they mounted Seminary Ridge, where they met Lee. They "lay about for some time looking through glasses at the Yankees,"[32] who were so close that each individual figure could be distinguished.

Ross saw at once that it would be "a long time" before Longstreet's corps could be put into position, so he rode into Gettysburg with two doctors of Barksdale's brigade. They found the battlefield of July 1 well policed. Both Confederate and Federal dead had been buried and the wounded had been removed to hastily set-up hospitals. They met Ewell, "a gruff-looking man." They took note that the town had not been sacked, or even disturbed, and returned to find the generals still conversing on the ridge, having been joined by A. P. Hill and Heth.[33] Heth, wearing a bandage about his head, was not yet fit for action.

The Gettysburg district was finding the sudden descent of more than 150,000 men a severe strain on its water supply, and the wells were failing by the morning of July 2.[34] On Seminary Ridge Hill asked for a drink and one of the men brought him "some dirty stuff in a pail," with apologies; if he could wait, good water could be brought up from about a mile.

"Oh no, that will do very well," said the sickly general. It caused the correspondent Ross to understand that he was on a battlefield.[35]

Longstreet soon after his arrival again broached to Lee his plan for a flanking movement and found Lee no more receptive than on the previous afternoon. A hard loser, Longstreet urged as much as he thought a fairly tense situation would stand, then desisted. Lee had given it the most careful thought and decided against it. The two armies were face to face and a battle was the only solution for either of them.

Longstreet's corps, in its own view of things, was the main army. As one of Kershaw's brigade put it:

There was a kind of intuition, an apparent settled fact . . . that after all the other troops had made their long marches, tugged at the flanks of the enemy, threatened his rear, and all the display of strategy and generalship had been exhausted in the dislodgement of the foe, and all these failed, then when the hard, stubborn, decisive blow was to be struck, the troops of the First Corps were called on to strike it.[36]

Old Pete put it differently in addressing Lee: "My corps is as solid as a rock—a great rock."[37]

Mrs. Chesnut saw the troops two months after Gettysburg as they were going to Chickamauga: "Not one man was intoxicated; not one rude word did I hear." She felt a thrill of sympathy when "a knot of boyish, laughing young creatures" passed her.[38]

But these carefree youths had an *esprit de corps* and a confidence in their commander unsurpassed in the Confederate service. According to D. August Dickert, the brigade's scribe:

No battle was ever considered decisive until Longstreet, with his cool, steady head, his heart of steel and troops who acknowledged no superior, or scarcely equal, in ancient or modern times, in endurance and courage, had measured strength with the enemy. This I give not as a personal view, but as the feelings and confidence and pardonable pride of the troops of the First Corps.[39]

Now they were coming down out of the mountains to deliver the *coup de grâce* on a field where the other corps had fought brilliantly but without the power to put in the finishing blow.

Much of the day of July 1 they had waited idly at Greenwood while Johnson's division and then his long train—miles of caissons and wagons, including those of Rodes's division as well as his own, that had awakened Jacob Hoke as they rumbled through Chambersburg—had the right of way on the road to Gettysburg. The wagons broke and rutted the soft road and made it more difficult for infantry. Here was a signal example of Lee's inadequate staff work. Men should have been given preference. The fifteen miles of creeping vehicles kept McLaws' and Hood's divisions waiting by the roadside four to six hours and then slowed their progress when they were finally in column. Johnson, in turn, had been forced to wait until Anderson cleared the road ahead of him. The single pike was woefully inadequate for the great demands suddenly put on it, and it was employed in almost a haphazard fashion while Lee was figuratively wringing his hands for troops at Gettysburg.

George Pickett with his three Virginia brigades remained at Chambersburg. The task of guarding the rear and the army trains would normally have been Stuart's. Since he was missing, a division had to be sacrificed until Imboden could come over the mountains from Cumberland and McConnellsburg and relieve it. Here was an unfortunate, possibly a disastrous consequence of Stuart's absence. A whole division was kept away from Gettysburg at a time when it was most urgently needed.

McLaws' troops had not camped or marched compactly and some of them had not halted until 3:00 A.M. If a "dawn attack" had been ordered they could not have been present. Kershaw's brigade pulled up at what the general called midnight and some of the others

3:00 A.M., and from the eminence beyond Marsh Creek surveyed the sleeping Confederate army strung out toward Gettysburg, "a great sea of white tents, silent and still."[40] Kershaw's South Carolinians "learned with delight" that the Palmetto Regiment had planted the first flag in Gettysburg. A man coming up asked the scribe Dickert if he would have a drink. "You may have heard angel's voices," he recalled. "I was so tired, sleepy and worn . . . I said 'Yes, Yes!' " There was enough in the jug for Color Captain John W. Watts too.[41]

Longstreet gave Hood first place in the early morning march of July 2, and the Texan was in the lead as the First Corps began to reach Gettysburg.

5. *Hood's Men Stack Arms and Rest*

Hood's division had left Chambersburg at two o'clock on the afternoon of July 1, about the time Early and Pender were preparing their assaults. He lost only about four hours at Greenwood while Johnson's trains passed. But there were further delays. After moving only a hundred yards the command was halted and this irritating halting was repeated time after time, a process more tiring than straight marching.

Broken marching continued until 2:00 A.M. when Hood reached Cashtown. The men stretched out on the bare ground and almost immediately were asleep. Two hours later came the drum roll and in ten minutes the division was on the way to Gettysburg. It arrived at Lee's headquarters soon after sunrise.

Both Hood and his men clearly understood the urgency. Soon after daybreak Hood rode with his staff into the field where Lee was in consultation and reported to the commanding general. In a field a short distance back the troops were ordered to stack arms and rest until further notice.

Through the early morning Hood, Longstreet, and A. P. Hill were with Lee on the heights inspecting the Federal lines on the opposite ridge. Although it was a sultry July morning Lee had his coat buttoned to the throat.[42] He was walking back and forth under some towering trees and seemed to Hood to be both hopeful and "buried in deep thought." At one of his pauses he remarked to Hood: "The enemy is here, and if we do not whip him, he will whip us."[43]

That was a simple conclusion but one which some of his subordinates had not grasped yet. Their thought was not whether the army could gain a victory, but the method by which that victory could most readily be obtained. Defeat was not dreamed of. Longstreet heard

Lee's remark as he came up. When he had a chance he took Hood aside. They sat on the ground, leaning against a tree trunk, and Longstreet explained: "The general is a little nervous this morning; he wishes me to attack; I do not wish to do so without Pickett. I never like to go into battle with one boot off."[44]

Thus, as Hood observed, the morning of July 2 wore away.

Neither Lee nor Longstreet, who were together, seemed to be ready for Hood's troops after all the haste to get them there. They waited an hour and a half in the field, and when they were moved it was not into line for an attack. They were marched about a mile south to a valley where they could get water and fuel. The Texas brigade was ready for the skillet wagon to unload, fires were being built and the men were awaiting their issue of flour, when a small incident occurred that threw light on the status of Lee's attack plans at this hour, which was perhaps eight to nine o'clock.

A Confederate soldier, Private Ferdinand Hahn of the 4th Texas, wandered to the crest of the rising ground and saw a group of Confederate generals conversing. As a clerk in the Menger Hotel in San Antonio, he had become acquainted with many of the officers of the old army who were often at that famous hostelry during their tours of service in the Southwest. He moved up as close as he dared and identified Generals Lee, Longstreet and Hood, all of whom had stopped at the Menger. Sacrificing his breakfast, he stayed in hearing range for half an hour, then returned to his company loaded with information. Some of the men were still heating their skillet lids, on which to cook biscuits.

"You might as well quit bothering with those skillet lids, boys," said Hahn. "It'll not be twenty minutes before we are on the move again."

Several shot at him the same question: "What have you heard, Hahn?"

"Only this. I got up pretty close to General Lee and old Longstreet and Hood awhile ago, and while I stood there an officer rode up and, addressing General Lee, reported that the Yankees were moving troops to Round Top. General Lee at once turned his glasses in that direction and, after looking through them a minute or two, said: 'Ah, well, that was to be expected. But General Meade might as well have saved himself the trouble, for we'll have it in our possession before night.' That means, of course, that we'll have to take it, and to do it, we'll have to move from here as soon as Hood can send orders."[45]

True to his forecast, the brigade was called to attention within ten minutes, and for the next six hours Hood's division was on its devious journey, with many long waits, to a position from which it could launch its attack on the Round Tops.[46]

Longstreet's reserve artillery under Colonel E. P. Alexander was in camp at Greenwood and for some unaccountable reason had heard nothing about the battle being fought at Gettysburg sixteen miles away. Darkness brought the news, along with an order for the artillery to move at 2:00 A.M., and Alexander had his own battalion of 26 guns and the Washington Artillery of 10 guns, which together composed the artillery reserve, on the road punctually.

The moon was bright, the infantry was out of the way, and the marching was easy, and at an hour given vaguely as "about 8 or 9 A.M.,"—certainly much too late for an attack at sunrise—the guns were hauled into a woods in the vicinity of the battlefield.[47]

Alexander reported at once to Lee and Longstreet, who were together, showing no sign of haste, on a hill behind the Confederate position. He was informed that the enemy's left flank would be attacked; that he should take command of Cabell's and Henry's battalions, each having 18 guns, and his own, making a total of 62 guns; that the Washington Artillery should be placed in reserve and that he should reconnoiter the ground and co-operate with the infantry. He was cautioned against exposing the guns to the view of the signal station on Little Round Top.

Alexander did not get the impression that General Lee felt things were being delayed unnecessarily.[48] He made his reconnaissance, which consumed three hours.[49] The time must have been between ten and eleven o'clock when he went back for his battalion, and probably it was nearly noon before he had it at the schoolhouse near the Herr Tavern west of Willoughby Run.

6. *The Armies Are Finally Face to Face*

One reason for Lee's delay in ordering an attack on the Federal left was that he wanted a report on a reconnaissance on which he had sent one of Longstreet's engineers, Major J. J. Clarke, and Captain S. R. Johnston of his own headquarters. They left early, and while they were absent McLaws arrived, about eight o'clock, riding ahead of his men, who had given way to Hood on the road.

Lee showed him, both on the map and by pointing, the objective of the pending attack. The Confederates would move up the Emmitsburg road and take Cemetery Hill in reverse. Lee thought the Federal

army faced mainly to the north, with lines running east and west
across Cemetery and Culp's hills, but recessed on the left flank an
indeterminate distance. The attack would sweep up the east side of
the Emmitsburg road, with the Confederate left flank on the roadway.

When Lee asked McLaws if he could carry this line the Georgian
replied noncommittally that he knew of nothing to prevent it but that
he would like to take some skirmishers and reconnoiter the position.
Lee told him a reconnaissance already was in progress and he volunteered to join it. Longstreet here stepped in and declared forcibly
that he did not want McLaws to leave his division.

The corps commander seemed disturbed about the whole proposition. Nobody knows whether he was perturbed because the frontal
attack he opposed was becoming more and more inevitable, or was
merely piqued because Lee was issuing orders over his head to Mc-
Laws directly. That was what had caused A. P. Hill to explode against
Jackson, and it may have been a source of Longstreet's irritation here.
The compassionate Lee made no issue of the matter and Longstreet
prevailed. McLaws was not allowed to make his reconnaissance.

In one other matter there was danger of sparks flying between Lee
and Longstreet. The corps commander touched the map and told
McLaws where he should place his division when it came up.

"No, General, I wish it placed just opposite," Lee corrected him.[50]

Where either of them meant for McLaws to fall in cannot now be
determined, but soon Clarke and Johnston returned from their reconnaissance and the time had arrived for the attack. About all the information they had was that, sure enough, the Federal army occupied
the opposite ridge. They could not be so positive about Little Round
Top. They clambered up a shoulder—perhaps Vincent's Spur or Devil's Den—and could see no Federals on Little Round Top.

With respect to that eminence, Lee had already recognized what
many later-day students of the battle have ignored, that its occupation
by the Federal army was to be expected momentarily. The situation
here was different from Culp's Hill, where Confederates were at the
base. To reach Little Round Top they had to operate at a distance,
and Federal troops were always nearer, first Geary, then Sickles, Sykes,
and Sedgwick. Any Confederate advance against it was fairly certain
to be detected. Round Top, the larger and more heavily wooded eminence, might be approached under better cover.

Even though the Federals had left the summit of Little Round Top
unoccupied they probably could beat an enemy force to it. The first

baseman's foot is not on the bag but he can ordinarily get there in advance of the runner. Lee must have had that in mind when through his glasses he saw Federal troops moving in the direction of Little Round Top. Probably this was Sickles trying to find a good position around the base.

But the report of Major Clarke and Captain Johnston was of high significance in that it cleared the way for Longstreet to step off. Still, there was one more obstacle. Law's Alabama brigade, an essential part of Hood's division, was marching at top speed for the battlefield. Because Longstreet had not been allowed to "get his other boot on" by awaiting Pickett's arrival, he set down what he might have considered his bare foot about moving before he had Law. The Alabamians had left New Guilford at 3:00 A.M. and marched through without a break. They got to Gettysburg, according to Law, "shortly before noon," which meant they had marched twenty-four miles in less than nine hours. That Lee had become reconciled to the need for preparations could be seen from the permission he gave Longstreet to await Law's arrival. Longstreet called this the best marching in either army, and it did exceed anything except Sedgwick's march from Manchester. Sedgwick's was eleven miles farther and any soldier would say that the last eleven miles are the hardest.

Law found the balance of Hood's brigade in the Willoughby Run valley—they had not made much progress since Private Hahn brought back his news—and thus Longstreet had two full divisions at hand.

After Lee issued his orders he left to see Ewell again and explain his plan for the army to attack by brigades *en echelon*. Beginning on the army's far right, the attack would progress in sequence through Longstreet's corps, then A. P. Hill's. Ewell would not wait until Hill's nearest brigade attacked, but would get his signal from the sound of Longstreet's guns. As the observant E. P. Alexander pointed out, it was getting rather late in the day for an echelon attack. Such a method is good on some mornings. If it is begun in the afternoon, darkness may come before the last brigades can attack. Perhaps it would have been better for the entire army to attack in unison.

At noon, with Law coming in, Longstreet began his movement and the rest of the army awaited its turn. Lee and Meade faced each other with about the same degree of concentration. Lee was minus Stuart's cavalry and Pickett's Virginians. Meade still was waiting for the Sixth Corps. He had left French's 10,000 men back at Frederick, a rear guard that would have posed a problem for Lee in any flanking movement. After an inspection by Slocum, who recommended against it, Meade had abandoned any thought of taking the offensive against Lee's left.

Meade's peak campaign strength was 105,750 and Lee's 88,754, but as they faced each other on the field, with allowance for absenteeism from many causes, Meade's infantry and artillery aggregated probably 82,000 and Lee's 68,000. Infantry and cavalry, Meade probably brought to the battle area about 92,000 and Lee about 79,000 men. The Federal army had 354, the Confederate 272 guns.[51]

The high hope of the South for freedom, the firm determination of the North to preserve the Union intact—issues long argued in the legislative halls—were about to be resolved at last on the battlefield.

CHAPTER SIXTEEN

The Story of the Missing Canteens

1. The Guide Doesn't Know Where He's Going

Longstreet's two divisions now set out on as strange a march as was ever made on an American battlefield. They had been lying all morning in the depressions behind McPherson's and Herr's ridges. When the order came they were hurried back, some for the better part of three miles toward Cashtown, along the road they had traveled earlier that day in their hasty march to Gettysburg.

McLaws' division was in the lead, accompanied by Alexander's reserve artillery, while Kershaw, already well advanced, had first place among the brigades. Lee sent Captain Johnston, who had made the morning reconnaissance, as a guide. The artillery was dragged along. That it was to be a factor in preparing for the assault was inconsistent with the element of surprise if anything like Chancellorsville was to be duplicated. Yet stealth was, to Longstreet, a much more vital consideration than speed. Of time he appeared to have an abundance when he selected his long, devious route for reaching Meade's flank. But while he did not rush, neither were his actions so deliberately slow as to warrant a charge of sulking.

The march can be reconstructed with difficulty, because no two units covered the same distance and different routes must have been employed. In the beginning Longstreet's two divisions were spread over the country west of Gettysburg, with Law resting in the neighborhood of the McPherson farm—he said he was a mile from the town—and Kershaw, the forward element of McLaw's division, already was near Black Horse Tavern, where he had been most of the morning.

Approaching Seven Stars, the main body struck south along a little-used road following the course of Marsh Creek and leading to Black Horse Tavern, where the 26th Pennsylvania Regiment had stumbled into a Confederate picket on the previous evening. Johnston rode part of the time with Longstreet and part with McLaws, but he did not turn out to be a well-informed guide for either. Lee accompanied Longstreet for a time, having returned from visiting Ewell.

Johnston himself was appalled when he learned the others were relying on him for directions. He said later that he "had no idea that I had the confidence of the great General Lee to such an extent that he would entrust me with the conduct of an army corps moving within two miles of the enemy lines while the lieutenant general was riding in the rear of the column."[1]

Lee had asked Johnston to make a sketch of the country he had covered on his reconnaissance and on the basis of this map had appointed him to escort Longstreet. What he had covered in his reconnaissance, however, was the terrain east of Willoughby Run and the approaches to the Round Tops. Now he was traveling roads and byways apparently as unfamiliar to him as if they were in Africa or Massachusetts. Longstreet had a guide, to be sure, but a guide who had to feel his way, Indian-fashion, through the woods and valleys and hope for the best.

Johnston told Fitzhugh Lee that he did not even know where General Longstreet was going.[2] He thought he was there only to provide the benefit of the reconnaissance he had made earlier in the morning. He was not conducting the column, merely going with it.

From his position near Black Horse Tavern, Kershaw could look across the fields about two miles to the Emmitsburg road in the region of the Kerns house, southwest of the Round Tops. There, during the morning, he had witnessed the passage of a large Federal body, protected by flankers to the left, moving to join Meade's army.[3] This obviously was De Trobriand's brigade hurrying up from Emmitsburg— it arrived at 10:00 A.M. At noon or one o'clock—the hour was indefinite to Kershaw—he got the order to take the road leading along Marsh Creek, and to advance but remain concealed from the enemy.

Kershaw passed the Black Horse Tavern and "followed the road leading from that point toward the Emmitsburg Pike,"[4] which runs past the Plank farm to Willoughby Run, turns south, follows the west bank of the run, crosses it, and reaches the Pitzer schoolhouse about

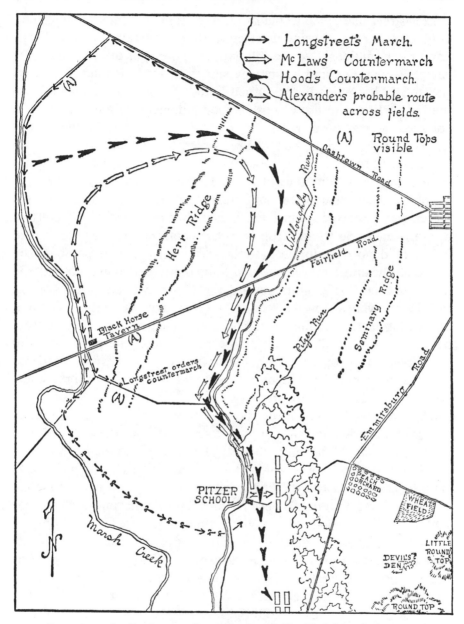

Longstreet's flank march. July 2, 1863, 12:30 to 3:45 P.M.

midway between the Sachs and Flaharty farmhouses. Kershaw went only a fifth of a mile, moving southeast, to the crest of the hill, where the road forked. If he had passed over the crest beyond this fork, he could have been seen from Little Round Top.

Longstreet had come to the front, and Captain Johnston explained to him the danger of being detected at the crest. Longstreet and Mc-Laws went cautiously up the hill and, sure enough, the wooded summit of Round Top and the craggy slopes of Little Round Top were clearly visible. When they returned both "manifested considerable irritation."[5] But Johnston was using good judgment for a guide who did not know where he was going. By passing around the shoulder of the hill and through a field, he told Longstreet, the column would still be hidden from the enemy, if the enemy should, indeed, be looking out from the Round Tops toward Black Horse Tavern.

Johnston said that when Longstreet went to the top of the hill his march was discovered, but there is no other evidence of it,[6] and the report from Little Round Top is to the contrary. If they were seen, it benefited no one, for Longstreet was disgusted and peremptorily called off the entire movement. He wanted another route. He ordered an about-face and a return toward the Cashtown road. This meant that Hood, who was in the rear of McLaws, now headed the column, and owing to the readjustment McLaws had to wait an hour before he could move at all. Alexander passed through the meadows with his artillery by a route he did not describe very clearly, and wondered why the infantry did not follow. He estimated that two to three hours were lost by the countermarch.[7]

On reaching the region of the Cashtown road again, Longstreet marched toward Gettysburg until he found another little-traveled road leading south and following generally Herr Ridge and the bank of Willoughby Run. He moved partly down this and partly along the bank until he came at last to the Pitzer school; he had been near this point at Black Horse Tavern. Thence he cut across country through Pitzer's and Biesecker's woods toward the Emmitsburg road.

A check of the distances involved in Longstreet's flank march shows that the route covered about thirteen miles. This does not mean all the troops marched that far, nor, indeed, that very many of them marched the full distance. But if the tail of the column on Willoughby Run had followed the route all the way to Black Horse Tavern, then retracted its steps to and along the Cashtown pike, and eventually reached the region of Round Top, it would have traveled thirteen miles or more, while those who assailed the Wheat Field would have gone almost thirteen miles.

Considering that McLaws lost an hour at the tavern while the tail of the column was being turned about and moved far enough ahead to release the front elements, and that broken terrain was traversed, Longstreet's men did some respectable marching that afternoon. It is reasonable to assume that the average soldier covered eight miles to reach his stepping-off place. That would mean a minimum of two and a half, and perhaps three hours. Where some mileage may have been saved by not using the roads, time probably was sacrificed by the slower pace in the rough woods and fields.

It is quite clear that Law's brigade could not have made this entire march and performed as nobly as it did during the remainder of the day. But what it did was not pleasant. "We moved very slowly," Law said, "with frequent halts and deflections from the direct course."[8] In the fields the two divisions doubled and moved abreast each other and at length Hood passed across the front of McLaws. This put Law's brigade on the extreme right of Lee's army.

From Kershaw's statement that Willoughby Run was dry,[9] it may be conjectured that the Confederates had to rely on the map Johnston had drafted hurriedly for Lee. The run had had plenty of water farther upstream because of the heavy June rains. Kershaw must not have been oriented on his map, or else was forgetful when he wrote in later years.

Kershaw's men were toiling along when Longstreet passed them "his eyes cast to the ground, as if in deep study, his mind disturbed." He had "more the look of gloom" than had ever been noticed before.[10] Obviously disconsolate, he was none the less submissive.

Did Longstreet unnecessarily delay the attack that should have been delivered in the morning? There are these points: Lee consented to await the arrival of Law's brigade before attacking.[11] Law came at noon.[12] The time of the delay is thus reduced to three and a half hours, from 12:00 until 3:30 P.M., when Hood was in position to begin his bombardment.[13] These hours are well accounted for by Longstreet's march behind the battlefield, as he groped for a good route by which to reach Meade's flank undetected. The afternoon may have been filled with mistakes, but not with stalling. Some have accounted the lost hours precious, but none can ever know.

The original fault unquestionably goes back to Stuart. Had he been playing his accustomed role he would have explored the roads and known the routes Longstreet should follow to gain the enemy flank. That was the purpose of cavalry. Also Lee did not have a large enough staff to make the necessary reconnaissance in a strange country, where he could draw but little on the civilian population either for guides or reliable information.

But with conditions as they were—without Stuart and without adequate knowledge—the fault in the main undoubtedly was Longstreet's. He should have investigated the routes in the wasted morning hours while Law was hastening to join him. He should have checked just how much Johnston knew before the column reached Black Horse Tavern and was about to be exposed.

Longstreet's ardor mounted as he went forward. He wanted to fall suddenly and unexpectedly on the Federal left and roll it up, as Jackson had done at Chancellorsville. All that was lacking was a touch of Jackson's ingenuity and intuition. In the end, nobody in the army was more impatient to begin than Longstreet,[14] and when he finally launched his divisions, nobody could have attacked more furiously.

Did Longstreet's march and countermarch impair Lee's chances of victory and damage the Southern cause? Careful critics are compelled to wonder, because there were events also on the Federal side of the valley, some of them errors of alignment that unquestionably assisted Longstreet's assault.

2. Sickles Finds Butternuts in the Woods

Cemetery Ridge, extending south from Cemetery Hill, loses elevation just as Seminary Ridge recedes immediately opposite it.

One of those large lumps of ground that seem to complicate battlefields rises at this point about midway between the two ridges. Colonel Long had observed the ground, had reconnoitered it as a position for Confederate artillery and was apprehensive the Federals would get there before Longstreet.[15] Some felt the Confederate line should rest here and continue along the Emmitsburg road instead of in the woods to the west along the lower Seminary Ridge.

At the summit of the hump, where the Emmitsburg road crosses it, a byroad leads back to the Taneytown road. At the southwest corner of the intersection was a peach orchard, opposite which was the Wentz farmhouse. This high ground, constituting a short ridge that commanded the depression between Cemetery Ridge and Little Round Top, might be used to advantage by either Confederate or Federal artillery; under certain conditions it might become the key to the battlefield, as the similar rise of Hazel Grove was at Chancellorsville.

Having little cover except the thin foliage of peach trees, it could be hammered by the artillery of either army and turned into a charnel house. It was not so much a place to be on as a place not to let the enemy hold. It could serve the Confederates better than the Federals because just west was Pitzer's woods, where supports would have cover, while on the eastern side were cultivated fields that afforded little protection to infantry. Should the main Federal battle line run through the Peach Orchard, a salient would be created, with neither face of the salient possessing any natural strength.

Meade's orders to Sickles contained some of the ambiguities that at times ruin battles or empires. He told Sickles to fall in on the left of the Second Corps, in the position that had been occupied by the Twelfth Corps during the night. Geary's division of the Twelfth Corps, by Hancock's instructions, had camped at the base and sent two regiments to the summit of Little Round Top, which gave security to the Federal left. Now Meade—and here was an uncertainty—told Sickles to extend his corps to the left to Little Round Top, "provided it was practicable to occupy it."[16] When Sickles extended his lines, he found he was not on high ground, but rather in a depression between Cemetery Ridge and Little Round Top, with fields made mushy here and there by the recent heavy rains. In front of this low land a creek, Plum Run, emerged to flow down a narrow valley into Rock Creek south of the battlefield.

Early in the morning Meade sent his son and aide, Captain George Meade, to Sickles to inform the corps commander where army headquarters would be located, and to ascertain if the Third Corps was in its proper position. Having been up most of the night, Sickles was taking a nap in his tent, so Meade, Jr., talked with Captain George E. Randolph, commander of the Third Corps artillery. Randolph went into Sickles' tent and came out with word that the corps was not in position and that Sickles had some doubt about where he should place it. The time was about 6:00 A.M.[17]

At 7:00 A.M. young Meade returned with more positive instructions for Sickles—to take over the position vacated by Geary. Geary had left at 5:00 A.M. to join the rest of the Twelfth Corps near Culp's Hill, but he had been so concerned about Little Round Top that he had sent a staff officer to describe it and request that, if troops were not to occupy it at once, Sickles should send a staff officer to see the ground. Sickles answered noncommittally that he would attend to the matter. Neither troops nor staff officer came, and Geary finally pulled out and left Little Round Top untenanted.

Birney, commanding one of Sickles' divisions, came up at 7:00 A.M. and extended his line to cover Little Round Top; all again appeared to be well. Still Sickles was dissatisfied, feeling that it would be harder to defend the valley if pounded by artillery than the elevation along the Emmitsburg road. He requested Meade to inspect the ground in person. When Meade did not come, Sickles about the middle of the morning rode to headquarters. Meade told him again that he was to occupy the position Geary had held on the previous evening. Sickles informed Meade, according to Meade's explanation of the conversation, that Geary had had no position so far as he could see, though in the neighborhood of his corps was good ground for artillery. He desired Meade to send a staff officer to see if it would not serve that purpose. This high ground was the Peach Orchard ridge.

When Sickles asked Meade if he were not authorized to align his corps in the manner he judged most suitable, Meade, by his own account of the conversation, replied, "Certainly, within the limits of the general instructions I have given you; any ground within those limits you choose to occupy I leave to you."

Meade then directed his chief of artillery, Brigadier General Henry J. Hunt, to look over the ground in question.

The New York *Herald* correspondent on the field, who claimed to have made the closest possible investigation of the meeting between Meade and Sickles and other phases of this episode, did not credit the commanding general with words so gentle. To Sickles' complaint that his front was exposed, Meade was quoted as replying: "Oh, generals are apt to look for the attack to be made where they are."

Meade was capable of sharpness and may have so worded it. Sickles did not take time to determine whether it was a jest or a jibe, but implored Meade to look over the ground himself. Meade, still concerned about his right, declined.

But Hunt went, looked over the situation, and tended to agree with Sickles that the high ground in front was superior to what he occupied in a direct line between Cemetery Ridge and Little Round Top.[18] Still, Hunt saw disadvantages and declined to issue any orders, until he could consult with Meade; orders would no doubt be forthcoming.

Careful and intelligent as Meade's course had been to that time, it is difficult to understand his stubborn reluctance personally to investigate his left flank. Perhaps he believed with Lee that the battle lines were running mainly east and west, and that the armies faced north and south. The Round Tops then would be too far in the rear to require more than garrisoning. Whatever was in his mind, Meade ignored Sickles' pleadings.

Meade was justifiably concerned about his right. He could not understand why Johnson would be coiled around him there unless the plan was to attack the soft underside of the Federal army along the Baltimore pike, a lifeline as essential to Meade as the Cashtown road was to Lee. But his left was worth a glance at least.

The afternoon rolled along and no orders came to Sickles. He learned that Buford's cavalry, which had been protecting the Federal left in the region of Round Top, had been ordered back to Westminster to recuperate. Thus the left flank of the army was exposed, and Ward's brigade of Birney's division became the left element of the army. Sickles remonstrated to Meade that Buford's withdrawal had left his flank naked, and Meade replied that he had not so intended and would have Buford recalled. But the cavalryman was well on his way toward Westminster and did not return to the theater; all the other cavalry, except a few corps details, was on the army's right.

Having no cavalry protection and with woods in his front that might hide a lurking enemy, Sickles sent out some of Berdan's regular army sharpshooters and a good Maine regiment, the 3rd, which all afternoon had been puzzled by what it considered the "unaccountable sluggishness"[19] of the Confederate army, the aggressiveness of which it knew from many other fields. Under Colonel Moses B. Lakeman the Maine men crossed the Emmitsburg road, moved west beyond the Sherfy house and entered the deep Pitzer woods, where on the previous evening the pickets of the 4th Maine Regiment had heard the soft drawling words of men obviously not Yankees. It was now twelve o'clock.

They had advanced less than a hundred yards into the heavy timber when ahead of them they detected skirmishers of what proved to be the 8th, 10th, and 11th Alabama infantry regiments of Wilcox's brigade, Anderson's division, Hill's corps.

Working with Berdan's sharpshooters, the Maine infantry drove these skirmishers back and soon unveiled three long enemy infantry lines, waiting 300 yards away. The Maine men claimed that the regular sharpshooters had taken all the trees and they had only the open spaces, but they looked on themselves as "one of the hardest fighting regiments in the Army of the Potomac." They declined to give way until they had battled Anderson's division for twenty-five minutes. Then they went back through the woods, across three quarters of a

mile of open farmland, reached Sickles' lines in the depression, and
reported to the corps commander that the main Confederate army
was not facing Culp's and Cemetery hills, or menacing Meade's right,
but was ready to step off from the woods directly in his front.[20]

3. Sickles Takes the High Ground

That was enough for the burly old politico-warrior who commanded
two of the army's most distinguished divisions. He had asked Meade
for help and had been treated cavalierly, at the very least. Now the
only things left to him were the drums and bugles. The Army of the
Potomac was about to witness one of the great sights of its spotted
and often spectacular career. It was three o'clock.

Across the open ground, three quarters of a mile in depth, moved
the two veteran divisions in battle order, drums beating the quick
step, flags waving, artillery rolling, heavily laden caissons growling on
their axles, cavalry patrols on the flanks, a cloud of skirmishers in
front. Old Dan Sickles was going to the war.

The right division, once Hooker's, was now commanded by Brigadier General Andrew A. Humphreys, commonly recognized as one of
the most capable general officers in the Federal Army. Meade had
wanted him for his chief of staff but did not judge it prudent to drop
Butterfield in the middle of a campaign. His grandfather had designed
and built the frigate *Constitution,* which had figured in great moments
of American history. Humphreys, a Pennsylvanian, had become an
engineer after being graduated from West Point, but he could not be
spared from infantry commands, where he was repeatedly cited for
gallant and meritorious service.

Sickles' other division was led by the Alabama-born David B.
Birney. It had been commanded earlier by one of the most gallant
of Americans, Major General Philip Kearny, who had been killed at
Chantilly. The tradition and spirit of this soldier of fortune, who had
fought on three continents, still hung over the division; long after the
war the legend persisted that he might be seen at night riding a white
horse through the sky or across the Jersey meadows, calling his men
to follow him in quest of glory.

One of his old regiments, the 20th Indiana raised at Lafayette,
became known as the "Fighting Three Hundred." They were mostly
farmers' sons, clerks, and Lafayette high-school boys, and they liked
to say that they were all Western-born except Patrick Maloney, who,
when he enrolled and was asked about his birthplace, replied, "I was
born in Ireland, sir, but I think Indiana is me native state."[21]

The Hoosiers were observers on the Peninsula when Kearny, punctilious in his military requirements, saw several officers of another command loafing by the roadside. Thinking they were of his division, he admonished them for straggling—he had a stinging tongue. They listened to him courteously, then one saluted and said with quiet dignity that the general was mistaken and they did not belong to his command.

"Pardon me, gentlemen," Kearney said apologetically. "I will take steps to know how to recognize my men hereafter."

On returning to headquarters he devised a diamond-shaped piece of red cloth for all of his division to wear on their caps. The soldiers called it the "Kearny Patch." The division wore it and eventually the corps adopted it.[22] The idea spread and when Hooker took command he assigned to each corps its identifying insignia. The custom has prevailed in the American army to the present day, though the patches are now worn on the sleeve.

From no point along the line was the advance of Sickles' ten thousand soldiers a more spectacular sight than at Hancock's position on Cemetery Ridge. Hancock had just ridden up and dismounted, and was talking with Brigadier General John C. Caldwell, commanding his 1st division, Colonel Patrick Kelly, commanding the 88th New York, and Colonel Richard Byrnes of the 28th Massachusetts. A few minutes after three o'clock, many of the soldiers were playing euchre while others were toasting hardtack and frying bacon. The day was warm and now clear; open fields stretched away to the Emmitsburg road. Suddenly the Second Corps men detected a commotion on their left. They dropped their cards and hardtack and crowded to where they could witness the simultaneous and orderly movement of this great body of men. "How splendidly they march!" "It looks like a dress parade, a review."[23]

Hancock leaned on his sword and rested one knee on the ground. He watched with surprise, even with some amusement. The placement of the Third Corps half to three quarters of a mile in advance of the main line left a great gap between it and his left. Grave as this was, it was almost ludicrous. Turning to the other officers, he smiled and said, "Wait a moment, you will see them tumbling back."[24]

But it was more than a moment. An hour passed before he called quietly, "Caldwell, get your division ready."[25]

The period of grace allowed the Third Corps at its Peach Orchard salient was due to Lee's plan of attacking *en echelon*. The storm had not yet broken on the far Federal left. Sickles would be given enough time to align his men, post his artillery, and make ready for the enemy. He leveled fences to facilitate the movements of his troops and to provide a field of fire. Birney's division was on the left, stretched thin from the orchard to the great hump of rocks in front of Little Round Top called the Devil's Den. He could not reach back as far as Little Round Top, and so it was left uncovered. The line ran along the front of a wheat field and faced southwest.

Humphrey joined Birney north of the Wentz farmhouse and ran along the Emmitsburg road, facing northwest. This left a sharp angle, or salient, at the Wentz house and the Peach Orchard. The advance of the corps had invited Confederate fire, and now the shells crashed through the Peach Orchard and apple trees farther up the road. The men hugged the ground, knowing it was a prelude to an infantry attack. The 3rd Maine had not been permitted to rejoin its brigade, Ward's, which was on Birney's left at the Devil's Den, but had been retained with Graham after it had come back from Pitzer's woods. It faced along the Emmitsburg road behind the orchard fence. It was 3:45 P.M.

Colonel Lakeman could look out to the south across the country beyond the Emmitsburg road, and there he saw the gray ranks and glistening bayonets of heavy masses of Confederate infantry moving far on the left. Hood's division was marching toward the Round Tops. Lakeman hurried off word to Captain Randolph, the artillery chief of the Third Corps, who threw some shells at the distant gray columns. Thus the battle of July 2 was opened.[26]

Meade, meantime, had called a council of his corps commanders at his headquarters cottage just behind the lines on the Taneytown road. There appears to be little basis for the contention that he intended at this stage to retreat to his Pipe Creek line, though he did not seem warmly attached to the position. Nothing had happened to make his situation worse, and much to improve it, since he had reached the field. The Sixth Corps was coming up and formidable works had been constructed on Cemetery and Culp's hills, where artillery had been skillfully placed to enfilade the approaches. The arrival of the Sixth Corps allowed him to shift his reserves. The bulk of the corps was placed on his right, where the Fifth Corps had been in support. He moved the Fifth to the left and the units were marching or resting behind the Round Tops while the council was in progress.

Sickles was not prompt to answer Meade. He was busy arranging his new lines. But at a final peremptory summons he left the work to Birney and Humphreys and rode more than a mile to the rear.

At the door of the headquarters he was met by Meade, who had heard the voice of Longstreet's guns opening far down the line to his left. "General, I will not ask you to dismount," Meade said to Sickles. "The enemy are engaging your fronts. The council is over."[27]

Under the pressure of Longstreet's guns Meade at last rode with Sickles to inspect the lines along the wheat fields and at the Peach Orchard salient. With him rode Brigadier General Gouverneur K. Warren, chief engineer of the Army of the Potomac, whom he hurried off to Little Round Top to make certain it was garrisoned. The conversation with Sickles has been variously reported. Meade is alleged to have berated Sickles. But the New York *Herald* correspondent talked with "several officers" who heard him; their version was probably more accurate than the account after the wording had been polished up for the official reports or for exhibits in the Meade-Sickles controversy that followed.[28]

"Are you not too much extended, General?" Meade inquired. "Can you hold this front?"

"Yes," replied Sickles, "until more troops are brought up. The enemy are attacking in force and I shall need support."

Meade again indicated his uncertainty about the amount of front covered by the corps, which was stretched thin indeed.

Sickles said, rather defensively, "General, I have received no orders. I have made these dispositions to the best of my judgment. Of course I shall be happy to modify them according to your views."

"No," said Meade, "I will send you the Fifth Corps and you may send for support from the Second Corps."

"I shall need more artillery," said Sickles.

"Send for all you want to the artillery reserve," Meade told him. "I shall direct General Hunt to send you all you ask for."[29]

Such was the situation at the time Longstreet's blow was delivered against the Federal left.

Had Longstreet's delay been disastrous, or had his attack been delayed until the happy hour when the Third Corps would be caught isolated and exposed? A short time before, Longstreet could not have attacked up the Emmitsburg road because it was merely a no-man's-land between the two armies. There would have been nothing to attack. A short time before, Birney's troops covered Little Round Top and, even moderately defended, it would be impregnable. The Federal line ran straight along Cemetery Ridge. Longstreet would have had to change front and deliver his blow across three quarters of a mile of open land to reach the Third Corps line.

Longstreet's slowness did indeed seem fortunate. If he could launch a strong assault and Lee could follow it with timely companion assaults by Hill and Ewell, the battle might be won between four o'clock and darkness. This much is clear: that if Sickles erred in marching to the Peach Orchard, Longstreet was lucky in having delayed his attack.

Sickles has been called a Bully Boy,[30] and the name is apt if it implied guts and gusto. While Gettysburg ended the war for many, it merely began it for Sickles. Always there was divided sentiment about the prudence of his move. The intolerant Frank Aretas Haskell, Gibbon's aide, attacked him because "he was neither born nor bred a soldier," which might have been said about many of the regular officers, and as "a politician and some other things"—"a man after show and notoriety, and newspaper fame, and the adulation of the mob!"[31] These comments occurred in a private letter which was published during Sickles' lifetime. Two months before Gettysburg Sickles had seen Chancellorsville lost because he was pulled back unnecessarily from Hazel Grove. He was taking no chances. Spunk was a good thing to infuse in the Army of the Potomac, which from the beginning had woefully needed some fighting souls among the officers, whether they carried the union cards of the regular army or not.

In a survey of 56 generals who participated, Colonel John B. Batchelder, the official governmental historian of Gettysburg in the generation after the battle, found the opinion respecting Sickles' advance about equally divided. But Meade condemned him both in his official report and later, and the army tended to side with Meade, which gave the Bully Boy a lifelong issue. In the end, fighting all the way, he won handily because he outlived his detractors and went down swinging at the age of ninety-five. He got fifty years of argument, political appointment, and glory out of one afternoon of fighting, but never a monument—like the other corps commanders—on the battlefield.

In all that time the only man to reduce the controversy to its proper proportions was Lincoln. The President had to pass on Sickles' request for a court of inquiry to determine the fairness of Meade's charges that he brought on the battle before the Federal commander was prepared and thereby endangered the whole army and cause. Lincoln met him thus:

Sickles, they say you pushed out your men too near the enemy, and began the fight just as that council was about to meet, at three o'clock in the afternoon of the battle. I am afraid that what they say is true, and God bless you for it. Don't ask us to order an inquest to relieve you from bringing on the battle of Gettysburg. History will set you all right and give everybody his just place, and there is glory enough to go all around.

Sickles' advance was unsound, though none can be certain how he would have fared in his old position. The one at the Peach Orchard meant a ragged battle line. With all his importuning for guidance from headquarters, the blame is scarcely assessable against the corps commander alone. The old veterans, in their stories of the affair, usually said he "stuck out like a sore thumb." He offered Longstreet a pretty target and distressed his fellow corps commanders, but he did succeed in getting the two armies locked in a combat from which they could not emerge until they were reeling and spent, and until the future courses of the two governments were fairly determined. That much Sickles contributed, and it is rarely judged an outrage of grave proportions when a general whose commanding officer is preoccupied, believes his purpose on a battlefield is to go forward and fight.

4. Hood Discovers an Exposed Flank

As soon as he received notice from Longstreet that he would attack the enemy's left, General Hood sent Lieutenant John McPherson Pinckney, of Hempstead, Texas, with a detail of five others from the 4th Texas Infantry, Robertson's brigade, to determine the Federal army's position and locate its flank.

They crossed the Emmitsburg road, scouted through the woods, climbed to the summit of Round Top, looked down on the Federal army with its trains and artillery reserve that had been parked with a scant guard in the rear of the Round Tops, and discovered that its flank was in front of these eminences. Thousands of Federal soldiers could be seen along lines extending to the north but none were on the summits.

Pinckney sent two of his scouts in haste to Hood with a message that the left flank of the Army of the Potomac was in the air and that behind it were trains and artillery parks which might be made an easy prize by a prompt movement to the south and to the rear of Round Top. He urged that the high points, Round Top and Little Round Top, be occupied by the largest force possible.[32]

Pinckney's scouts reached Hood just as Longstreet had finally got

his and McLaws' divisions into line for the assault. It was approaching four o'clock. Hood saw at once the importance of the intelligence
and hurried to the corps commander a request that the impending assault, instead of being directed up the Emmitsburg road and toward
the Federal concentration already detected at the Peach Orchard,
should envelop the enemy left, pass around Round Top, and take the
trains in the rear.

No more difficult question could have been presented to Longstreet
at this moment. The turning movement recommended by Hood,
though more limited, was of the nature he had been urging on Lee
ever since he reached the field, and in his bluff and uncompromising
manner he had insisted to a point where their relations were becoming strained.

Longstreet has been severely censured by some writers for not
at once revising his entire attack plan; at least, he should have halted
Hood until he could again consult with Lee. It may be easily imagined that Lee, having waited what seemed almost interminably for the
sound of Longstreet's guns, and finding the day slipping away from
him, would have been provoked in the extreme had the attack again
been checked to submit a modified version of the proposal that he had
rejected again and again in the last two days. Such a last-minute
delay would have seemed a mere pretext, and would have given him
ample grounds for relieving Longstreet of his command.

These considerations must have passed through Longstreet's mind,
for he flatly rejected Hood's recommendation. Accounts vary, but
the story as told by Hood has become the accepted version. Hood
said that after receiving the intelligence from his scouts he opened with
some of his guns and developed the Federal line, which had its left
resting on or near Round Top and ran concavely to the Emmitsburg
road, with a considerable force on high ground near a peach orchard.[33]

All the difficulties of an attack across a country strewn with great
boulders and broken by sharp ravines, which would disorganize and
scatter an attacking force, now impressed themselves on Hood; he
perceived also that an assault on the Peach Orchard and up the
Emmitsburg road would expose his force to an enfilade fire from the
main Federal line running from Cemetery Hill to the region of the
Round Tops. He consequently judged it his duty to report even at
this late hour that an attack up the Emmitsburg road was unwise,
and to suggest the envelopment of the enemy's flank and rear.

Longstreet's reply was prompt and blunt: "General Lee's orders are to attack up the Emmitsburg Road."

Hood was not satisfied, having by now developed a strong conviction against the direct assault. He sent a second aide to Longstreet, only to receive the same unyielding and unelaborated answer: "General Lee's orders are to attack up the Emmitsburg Road."[34]

Clearly Longstreet judged that his province of discretionary action had been so sharply circumscribed that all he could do was to obey Lee's words implicitly. Hood meantime continued to explore with his batteries. If, as he thought, the enemy now occupied Round Top, it would be impregnable. It could be defended, he believed, without gunfire. The enemy would merely have to roll the huge boulders down the mountain side as his men started up. So he sent his adjutant general, Colonel Harry Sellars, whom he judged an officer of great ability, to explain the hazards and request Longstreet to come and inspect the ground himself.

Sellars returned with the same monotonous answer. Major John W. Fairfax of Longstreet's staff followed with equally emphatic notice that General Lee's orders would have to be obeyed.

Hood's disappointment was keen. "After this urgent protest against entering the battle of Gettysburg, according to instructions—which protest is the first and only one I ever made during my entire military career—I ordered my line to advance and make the assault."

As he moved out, Longstreet rode up. Hood again voiced regret that he was not being allowed to take Round Top in flank. He quoted Longstreet as replying: "We must obey the orders of General Lee."[35]

The evidence from Hood is not one of a sulking Longstreet. Though Longstreet had now discovered that his own views were strongly and independently supported by a division commander regarded as one of the best strategists and fighters in the army, he expressed neither personal satisfaction nor bitterness over Lee's rejection of them. The picture obtained from Hood is one of co-operation, not pique. Hood's reports were enlightening, yet they contained nothing that might not have been assumed by Longstreet when he made his initial recommendations. Longstreet would have moved the entire army whereas Hood would begin with a division, perhaps even a brigade. But Lee's plan was bolder and more aggressive. He would strike where the enemy was, not where he was not.

Another interesting account is available. William Youngblood, of

Birmingham, Alabama, a courier, said that Lee was present at the final meeting of Longstreet and Hood just before Hood's division went into action. He said that Lee shook hands with both generals and said "God bless you" as they departed. He heard Hood beg Lee to be allowed to send a brigade around the right of Round Top, through a pass or ravine which his scouts had described to him, that would lead to the enemy's rear, apparently the depression between Round Top and Little Round Top. Hood insisted that he could flank the Federal army and attack Round Top from two sides. But Lee had personally decided against Hood.

Youngblood quoted Lee's words: "I cannot take the risk of losing a brigade. We must do the best we can. When the signals are given you, General Hood, advance your men and do the best you can."[36]

The statement of a scout, made voluntarily when the incident was under discussion, cannot be disregarded. Also even a general may be forgetful about the details of how his proposal came to be rejected. Youngblood's account is persuasive, for one reason, because it places General Lee at the point where he might be expected when the main attack was launched. The commanding general would not normally be five or six miles away when Hood was about to make the decisive movement of the day at the opposite end of the line. Nobody was riding behind Lee with a notebook on July 2 and his movements cannot be reconstructed, but he saw Longstreet repeatedly and must have been near by at the time of the assault. Possibly Hood received a first report while Lee was there and had more complete information later that caused him to repeat his pleas to Longstreet.

One thing is certain: there was ample notice to Hood and, in turn, to his subordinates, that the flanking movement around Round Top was not favored by the commanding general.

Hood launched his attack with his right brigade, Law's, from the neighborhood of the Bushman farm, between the Emmitsburg road and Round Top. The Round Tops are two craggy mountains, the smaller a spur of the larger, and they are about 1,000 yards apart on a line from summit to summit. Little Round Top is more accessible mainly because it is 120 feet lower, but the ascent of both is steep and rugged except on the eastern side of the larger, where the drop is sheer. Superficially Little Round Top came to be rated as having greater military value, partly because artillery could be drawn up its sides more readily, but mainly because the Weikert brothers, Charles and John, had taken off the timber in the fall of 1862 to help meet the war's ravenous demands for lumber. Round Top was heavily wooded; Little Round Top was a bald crag. Visibility was difficult through the trees from Round Top; it was open and easy from Little Round Top.

That accounted for the placing of a Federal signal station on Little Round Top instead of Round Top, which commanded more of the surrounding country. The trees on Round Top also seemed to make it unsuitable for posting guns.

5. Colonel Oates Looks from Round Top

Brigadier General Evander McIver Law, a professor of history and belles-lettres, was twenty-six years old at the time of Gettysburg. A South Carolinian, he had a heritage of in-the-woods fighting. His grandfather and two great-grandfathers had been soldiers under Francis Marion and one had lost his life while serving in the "Swamp Fox's" little band. General Law had taught at Kings Mountain Military Institute, then had established a military school at Tuskegee, Alabama, of which he was principal when the war came. From his captaincy of the Alabama Zouaves to his command of the Alabama brigade of Hood's division, his service had been brilliant and his promotion rapid. Now, after Hood, he was the senior officer in what would probably have been rated, by public opinion in the South, Lee's outstanding combat division.

Law had opportunity to rest his brigade only a few minutes after its march of twenty-four miles to the battlefield. Then he fell in with Hood, marched and countermarched, and eventually reached the far right of Lee's army in the woods in front of Round Top.

Law's brigade was formed with the 44th and 48th Alabama on the right, the 47th and 4th on the left and the 15th Regiment, commanded by Colonel William C. Oates, in the center. Robertson's Texas brigade was next in line to the left, then "Tige" Anderson's Georgians. "Rock" Benning with another Georgia brigade was in the rear of the center as a division reserve.

Irrespective of the long delay that had attended Longstreet's preparations, the attack signal came a few minutes too soon for Oates's 15th Alabama. The line had been formed at 3:30 P.M.[37] and shortly thereafter Hood drew fire from Federal batteries in the Devil's Den region in front of Little Round Top. During this bombardment which destroyed any remaining element of surprise, and while the regiment was awaiting the attack signal, the canteens were found low on water.

Colonel Oates detailed two men from each of his eleven companies to take the canteens to a well about 100 yards in the rear—probably that of the Snyder or Bushman farm—to supply the regiment with fresh water before it went into battle against the formidable-appearing hills ahead. The twenty-two water carriers would have returned in another five minutes, but, as Oates pointed out, it was never the custom to ask the colonels if they were ready. When it was time to attack, then attack it was, without question. He wanted to await the water detail, but "the order was given and away we went."[38]

When the detail discovered that the regiment had gone on, it tried to follow, but it went in the wrong direction, inclining to the left. The twenty-two men entered a woods and shortly found themselves inside the Federal lines, prisoners, carrying virtually every canteen of the regiment.[39] The day was hot, cloudless, sticky, and in such an assault water was as essential as cartridges.

Oates moved the regiment along but found that Law had recessed his two right regiments, the 44th and 48th, then had sent the 44th to participate in the attack on the Devil's Den and had dropped the 48th back as a reserve. This put the 15th on Lee's far right flank—under Lee's plan of attack, the step-off regiment of the army. Oates noted that the Texans and Benning were moving *en echelon*. He compared the Confederate line to the rim of a half-opened fan. When Law struck the base of the Round Tops, which were treated as a single mountain in much of the Confederate comment, each brigade would hit the enemy a flank or quartering blow. That plan, however, was deranged somewhat by Sickles' advance and now the brigades were compelled to assail Sickles' line in front and not obliquely.

Oates complained that Law's skirmishers, five companies from two regiments, were commanded by two captains instead of one field officer. They did not work in harmony, but finally bore to the right, passed around Round Top, and reached the eastern side. Both captains, A. O. Dickson, of Brooksville, and J. Q. Burton, of Opelika, Alabama, confirmed this.[40] Oates complained that had these companies continued entirely around the mountain and joined him he could have captured the Federal ordnance trains behind Round Top.

As Hood's and Law's other regiments pressed ahead, they made a half left wheel in order to assault Birney's line, but the skirmishers ahead of Oates continued straight ahead against Round Top. Oates thought that an informed field officer would not have allowed this to happen, but the regimental commanders did not know the objective

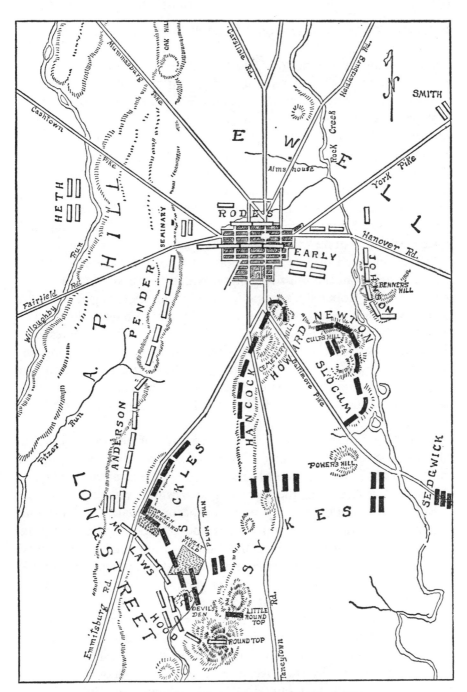

Attack on Federal left. July 2, 1863, 4:00 P.M

251

of the attack until they were on the march. Oates followed the skirmishers.

Law finally rode alongside Oates, to tell him that his regiment was
the right of the army, that he should go up the valley between the
two Round Tops, feel for the Federal left flank, and do it all the
damage possible. He said also that the 47th Alabama on his immediate left had been ordered to guide on the 15th and act under Oates's
orders.[41]

Oates emerged from the woods, crossed Plum Run without stopping for water, and entered the heavy woods in front of Round Top,
where he found himself confronted by the 2nd United States Sharpshooters under Major Homer S. Stoughton, part of Sickles' command,
posted behind a stone wall close by the southern face of Round Top.

Oates continued despite the fire but noticed that he was being deprived of aid from the 48th Regiment, which was marching off in the
rear to support Robertson's brigade, already warmly engaged at Devil's
Den. A second round from the sharpshooters brought down Lieutenant Colonel I. B. Feagin and some of the men, and Oates concluded that he would have to oust these marksmen before going any
farther, which he did by swinging to the right with the 15th and part
of the 47th, and moving against the front of the sharpshooters with
the balance of his command.[42] This took him farther south and farther
from the gap between the Round Tops.

Then followed what must have been one of the most onerous
labors of the war, the advance of the two Alabama regiments up the
south side of the Round Top Mountain in the face of an annoying and
often effective fire from the retreating sharpshooters.

Here the mountain is steep and treacherous. Oates said his men
caught hold of the ledges and bushes and clambered over the giant
boulders in the face of the enemy bullets, while the sharpshooters
took cover and fired from crags and rocks "thicker than gravestones
in a cemetery."[43] Most were vastly larger than gravestones, and behind them whole squads might hide and fire in volleys.

Only young men as lightly equipped as these Southern regiments
could have made the ascent even if freed from harassment by expert
riflemen. But they were fortunate in that here the sharpshooters belied
their name and usually shot over the heads of the oncoming Confederates. Halfway up the mountain they abandoned the battle, divided,
passed around the waist of Round Top, and disappeared, apparently
issuing into the heavily wooded trough between the two Round Tops.

Colonel Oates was now alone on Round Top with two regiments, one having no water. He moved Company A to protect his right and continued the toiling journey up the southern face of the mountain, which is more difficult of ascent than the western. Hanging onto the bushes and clutching the edges of stones, the two regiments made their way finally to the summit.

During this tortuous struggle the 15th had ceased to think of blue-coated enemies, of rocks, bushes, the great oak trees that rose above them, or anything except one vital element—water and their missing canteens. Many fainted on the final lap, succumbing to heat and thirst. Oates halted them at the rocky peak, his right resting where the observatory now stands. The ascent is such that this point cannot be reached even today by motorcar, but only by a winding pathway, which meanders up the western face. One who climbs to the summit can appreciate the difficulties of the Alabamians, opposed halfway by sharpshooters and afflicted by an increasing intense craving for fresh water.

As Colonel Oates looked out through the trees, he saw below him Devil's Den, which Robertson's Texans were beginning to assault. The smoke of battle billowed away slowly, to hang like a cloud in the heavy upper strata of air. He saw the long battle line of Sickles' corps running like a thin ribbon from Devil's Den to the Peach Orchard, then bending and following the Emmitsburg road to the northeast. Farther away he could see the town of Gettysburg sprawling on the plain between Oak and Cemetery hills, while the flat land stretched away to the north as far as eye could reach.

Immediately beneath him, as though he could throw a stone to its summit, was Little Round Top. North of it, but within artillery range, was Cemetery Ridge, dense with Federal troops, and behind it the busy little white house, with its adjutants and couriers, where Meade had his headquarters.

As the commander of the 15th Alabama gasped at the view, he saw something else even more clearly. Guns planted on Round Top would make Little Round Top untenable. He could visualize their explosive shells falling into Birney's line and the abundant Federal artillery from Devil's Den to the Peach Orchard. In fancy he could see the Federal army dislodged from Cemetery Ridge, and the long gray column on the road again, marching on Washington. He could picture his Alabamians on Pennsylvania Avenue; the new red flag with its blue cross and eleven white stars floating above the Capitol; Southern independence ratified at the cannon's mouth; the war ended and the boys going back to the loamy plantations of the Alabama black soil belt, free and independent at last.

Let Law give him cannon on Round Top and the battle of Gettysburg was won!

Law's brigade had marched twenty-four miles and Oates's regiments had ascended without water the steep sides of a rugged mountain, carrying their muskets, ammunition, and haversacks. Few men, according to Oates, would have been able to climb it even without accouterments. "Greater heroes never shouldered muskets than these Alabamians," he said. It was, indeed, a superb accomplishment. Now they required rest.[44]

The two regiments had been halted five minutes when Captain L. R. Terrell, Law's assistant adjutant general, appeared on horseback, having picked his way through the boulders on the southeast side of the mountain, which is close to the sheer face, an extraordinary feat of horsemanship. Terrell had been the author of a report charging the 55th North Carolina with the loss of a gun at Suffolk, which caused Colonel John Carr Connally to demand satisfaction. Terrell, to give it, had specified double-barreled shotguns loaded with buckshot. But the matter had been adjusted. Now Connally had fallen maimed near the railroad cut in the very first fighting at Gettysburg, and Terrell had entered into a leading role at a high point of the battle, where he might be able to give greater purpose to Connally's sacrifice.

His first inquiry was why Oates had halted his men. The answer was before him: they were exhausted. Terrell brought information that Hood had been wounded, that Law now commanded the division, and that Law wanted Oates to press ahead immediately, turning the Federal left and capturing Little Round Top. Oates explained his present position. He pointed out the near-precipice on the northern and eastern sides, and the difficult nature of the ascent over the stones and through the timber on the west. The enemy, he declared, could reach the summit only by the long wooded slope on the northwestern side, where the pathway now winds to the observatory, which approach, he insisted, could in half an hour be converted into a Gibraltar that he could hold against ten times his numbers. It should be occupied with artillery without delay; being higher than Little Round Top, it commanded the entire battlefield.[45]

The question of whether or not artillery could have been drawn to the summit of Round Top has often been answered in the negative.

But artillery, in the course of war, has been taken up difficult ascents. Wolfe in his quest for glory dragged two fieldpieces up the cliff at Anse du Foulon and fired grape on the Heights of Abraham.[46] Napoleon pulled his artillery over the Alps.

The Confederate army happened to have an engineer officer on the field who was an expert in such matters. He had served as guide for the advance of Twigg's division of Winfield Scott's army at Cerro Gordo, over what young Lieutenant Ulysses S. Grant would later call "chasms so steep that men could barely climb them" and "animals could not."[47] They broke down the guns and drew them up the opposite slopes piece by piece, by ropes slung from the tops of the cliffs. The engineer who picked out the route and supervised the operation could easily have shown how guns might be taken to the summit of Round Top.[48] He was probably not more than a mile away and his name was Robert E. Lee.

Oates urged that Round Top be held; though Terrell agreed it no doubt would be the best thing to do, he had no authority to change old or initiate new orders. Oates understood. Had the adjutant sanctioned it, he would have remained on what he regarded as the key to the battlefield until he could consult General Law.[49] But Law was on the left of the division, where Hood's other brigades were beginning to close with Birney, and Terrell's own mission was to urge Oates to hurry on and drive everything in front of him.

Here again may be seen how the inadequacy of Lee's and, in turn, Longstreet's staff hampered these generals in the conduct of the battle. The high command had no representative on the far right. No liaison was maintained. From the times Oates went into action against the sharpshooters on Round Top, until the morning of July 3, when on his part of the field the battle was over, he did not have contact with a single general or any staff officer except Captain Terrell, who merely brought a reiteration of his orders.[50]

If the Confederate soldiers who were lost a few minutes later in the assault on Little Round Top could have been concentrated to hold Round Top, and had Law devoted his main effort to dragging a battery to or near the summit, the story of the battle on the Confederate right surely would have had a different ending. More trees than the Weikert brothers had felled on Little Round Top in an autumn could have been cut by 500 Alabama axmen before sundown. Who could doubt that had Meade looked out on a well-supported battery on Round Top before going into his council of corps commanders that

night, he would have reflected even more earnestly on the advantages
of his Pipe Creek line and the prudence of withdrawing the badly
hammered Federal army?

Oates, in compliance with his orders, moved his command down
the northwest side of the mountain, meeting not a single squad of Federal soldiers. Perhaps it was with the descent of these Alabama regiments from Round Top, step by step, that the cause of Southern independence languished. The Confederates passed to the rear of what
has become known as Vincent's Spur, a toss-up of earth and rocks
between the Round Tops. Less than 300 yards away was the great
park of Federal trains, the supply and ordnance wagons of the army
that had been concealed behind these hills at the time the main battle
line was presumed to be farther north at the town. Oates thought
them an easy prize, so he detached Company A of the 15th Alabama,
Captain Shaaf, to pick them up.[51] A single regiment from Early's
division, which Lee had wanted to shift to the right but which Ewell
and Early had held tenaciously on the left, would have proved con-
venient for the Confederate cause on the right at this juncture.

With all but this one company, Oates moved toward Little Round
Top. At a ledge of rocks forming a natural bastion he came up
against four regiments—the 16th Michigan, 44th New York, 83rd
Pennsylvania, and 20th Maine—composing the brigade of Colonel
Strong Vincent, of Barnes's division, Fifth Federal Corps.

They had, according to Oates's calculations, been in position ten
minutes—the ten minutes he had lost resting his men on the summit
of Round Top because the 15th Alabama had been compelled to step
off without its canteens.[52] Longstreet's assault may have been sorrow-
fully delayed on the afternoon of July 2, because of thoroughness,
sluggishness, recalcitrance, coincidence or other cause, but finally it
had been launched five minutes too soon for Oates to recover his canteens and get his Alabamians on top of Little Round Top.

CHAPTER SEVENTEEN

The Prize of Little Round Top

1. A Decision on the Far Flank

Although Little Round Top had defenders hurrying to it from front and rear, the man who first reached the menaced peak was Colonel Strong Vincent, whose quick energy prevented Law from turning the left of the imperiled Northern army.

Vincent was on the Taneytown road in the rear of Round Top, awaiting orders near the home of John Weikert, when a messenger sped up from Sykes looking for Brigadier General James Barnes, who commanded the division of the Fifth Corps that included Vincent's brigade. Barnes was hard to find that day and, according to Oliver Wilcox Norton, Vincent's bugler and flag-bearer, had not been seen since morning, was not at the head of the column, and "if he gave an order during the battle to any brigade commander I fail to find a record of it in any account I have read."[1]

So Vincent intercepted the orders from Sykes to Barnes to send a brigade to Little Round Top, and declared he would take the responsibility of getting one there.

Vincent, who was not long out of Harvard, had been warmly admired by most other officers because he had made his regiment, the 83rd Pennsylvania, so precise and splendid in drill that McClellan had rated it first in Porter's division. That was an achievement for one who had prepared himself in the liberal arts and his father's iron foundry at Erie, Pennsylvania, instead of at military school. But

257

Strong Vincent's personality was like his first name and would have marked him for advancement in any citizen army.

His young wife, a skilled equestrienne, had visited him on the Rappahannock and their long horseback rides, their gaiety, and their striking good looks made them familiar figures to the army, greatly admired for their ideal love. Vincent had passed his twenty-sixth birthday on the march north toward Gettysburg. All the while he knew the desperate nature of the impending battle. Near Hanover, on the evening of July 1, as he watched the flag of his beloved 83rd Pennsylvania unfurled at headquarters after the long march, he took off his hat and said prophetically to a staff officer, "What death more glorious can any man desire than to die on the soil of old Pennsylvania fighting for that flag."[2]

After telling Colonel James M. Rice of the 44th New York to bring up the brigade, Vincent dashed ahead to find a position, which he selected with an eye on the slope instead of the summit. It would require his men, if they had to fall back, to go toward rather than from the peak, and would allow reinforcements coming up on the other side of the mountain to form a line above him. That is precisely what happened. General Warren had been seeking other help. When he reached Little Round Top after leaving Meade, he caused a rifled battery at the base to send a shell into the woods east of the Emmitsburg road, which he suspected of concealing the enemy. He caught the gleam on the gun barrels and bayonets of Hood's men as the shell whined overhead, and learned, as Sickles had earlier, how the Confederates were massed on Meade's left, when they were supposed to be clustered around Gettysburg. Warren rushed off word to Meade, who ordered Sykes to secure the hill with the Fifth Corps.

The results came rapidly. Before Warren descended, First Lieutenant Charles E. Hazlett brought up a battery of rifled cannon and planted two of them—all he could find room for—on the summit, with Warren's help. The horses were lashed ahead but the straining men supplied most of the motive power, pulling and pushing at the spokes of the gun-carriage wheels and tugging them around the boulders and jutting ledges. Warren and Third Corps stragglers lifted one to the top.

When the guns were up, Warren, not knowing that Vincent was already beneath him in the woods to the left, descended the forward slopes of Little Round Top and almost at once caught the rear of Weed's brigade of Ayer's division, Fifth Corps, moving west on the

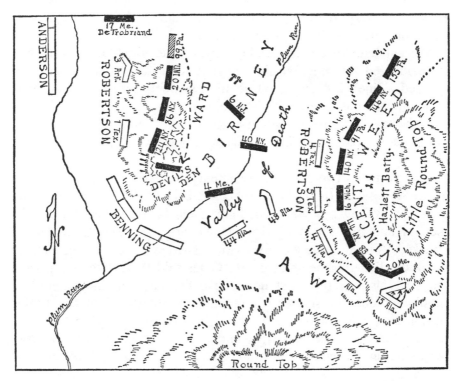

Defense of Little Round Top and Devil's Den. July 2, 1863.

Peach Orchard road to support Sickles. Warren's old regiment, the
140th New York, was last in the column, under command of the scholarly Colonel Patrick H. O'Rorke.

Warren, "apparently greatly excited," spoke to O'Rorke in his
"usually impulsive style."[3] The colonel replied that he was expected
by his brigade commander.

"Never mind that," said Warren; "bring your regiment up here and
I will take the responsibility."[4]

That was all the young colonel required. He had distinguished himself in the Rochester, New York, schools and had been first in the
class of 1861 at West Point, in which the cavalryman, George A.
Custer, now one of Pleasanton's brigadier generals, stood last.
O'Rorke's perception was quick; he saw Warren's need and responded.
When Weed learned the cause of O'Rorke's about-face, he took his
entire brigade to Little Round Top. Much as Vincent had anticipated,
the reinforcements came in above him and soon his line of battle,
drawn around the waist of Little Round Top, was being supported by

Hazlett's battery, then by O'Rorke above him, and finally by Weed's entire brigade, which fell in on his right.

Vincent had tossed the bridle rein of "Old Jim" to Norton, had reconnoitered the mountainside on foot for a few minutes, and had selected a line of strength before his regiments arrived.[5] The most critical post went to the 20th Maine, commanded by Colonel Joshua Chamberlain, a former Bowdoin professor, for whose stanchness during the next hour and a half Congress would vote him the Medal of Honor.

Oates with his two Alabama regiments that had passed over Round Top now assailed the right of Vincent's brigade, and were joined on their left by Law's other Alabamians from beyond Devil's Den and the 4th and 5th Texas of Robertson's brigade. The Confederates attacked Vincent's rocky citadel with desperate drive, seeking both to break the Federal line and turn it. Oates said the first greeting from the Federals was the most destructive fire he ever encountered; it shook but did not shatter his regiments. He drove in the Maine skirmishers, who could be seen through the smoke dodging from tree to tree, then advanced his right and overlapped the left of the 20th Maine Regiment, which constituted the extreme left flank of the Federal army.

Oates hoped, prayed, and cried out for support. Here was what chance does not often award a regimental officer, a second opportunity to win a great battle. Before him was the Federal flank he had been ordered to find and strike with all his power. Where now were some good Confederate regiments to help hit and destroy it? Where merely one regiment which might prove sufficient? This was what Oates believed: "If I had had one more regiment we could have completely turned the flank and have won Little Round Top, which would have forced Meade's entire left wing to retire."[6]

Even the five companies of skirmishers that had gone around the mountain to the east side and then disappeared would have helped. But there was not enough power to make the flanking movement effective. Chamberlain promptly refused his left companies and the Maine regiment held, though it was badly mauled and its front was subjected to a destructive enfilade fire. "The edge of the fight swayed backward and forward like a wave,"[7] Chamberlain said. Captain Howard L. Prince of the 20th used similar words: "Again and again was this mad rush repeated, each time to be beaten off by the everthinning line that desperately clung to its ledge of rock."[8] The regiment consisted of lumberjacks and fishermen from the rocky coast.

Strong Vincent exposed himself recklessly and fell early. His last words were typical: "Don't yield an inch." That night Meade sent a telegram to President Lincoln, who issued his brigadier general's commission, dated from the field. President Charles W. Eliot of Harvard recalled Vincent's student days: "He was one of the manliest and most attractive persons that I ever saw." Longstreet later acknowledged him as the man who saved Little Round Top and the Federal army.[9]

Oates was now in the front rank, fighting over the blood-stained rocks on which his two regiments were being wasted away by the burning yellow spurts from the Federal muskets. Often the lines surged so close together that neither side had time to load. They battled with bayonets, gun butts, and stones. Small parties broke through both lines and fought until beaten down. For a moment the Alabama colors floated over the Federal defenses. The Maine colors seemed certain to be lost, but when the next cloud of black smoke lifted, the flag was aloft, attended by no more than a single color sergeant, Andrew J. Tozier. He was holding his little sector alone.

Chamberlain had prepared for the fight by calling up the pioneers and provost guard, releasing the company prisoners, putting every spare man on the firing line. The sick list responded, dropping their pills and taking up their muskets.[10] Still the line looked knife-thin in many places.

Farther to the Confederate left the fight raged with equal fury. Gallant, gray-haired Lieutenant Colonel M. J. Bulger, commanding the 47th Alabama, was shot through the lungs. The old squire knew little of drill and nothing of discipline but had more than ample courage to compensate for those wants; although fifty-eight years old, he was unchallenged in the leadership of his regiment. As an Alabama delegate he had voted against secession; none now supported the Southern cause more ardently. He sat with his back against a tree, stranded when his line was driven back.

A captain of the 44th New York demanded his surrender and threatened to shoot him if he did not immediately hand over his sword.

"You may kill and be damned," said the lieutenant colonel, who had seen enough years not to worry about a few more when his men were dying about him.

He declined to yield except to an officer of equal rank. Colonel

Rice was brought forward to gratify the old colonel's whim in what were regarded his last moments. But he astonished his captors by living, and living lustily. The next year he was exchanged and was promoted to full colonel; after the war he graced heartily the town of Dadeville, Alabama, until 1900, when he expired at the age of ninety-five.[11]

2. *The Lone Star Over Devil's Den*

While Law's brigade assailed the brigades of Vincent and Weed, an equally desperate battle was being fought along the banks of Plum Run, on ground that came to be known as the "Valley of Death," and about Devil's Den, a citadel as rugged as but lower than Little Round Top. When Robertson attacked it was held by Ward's brigade, Sickles' corps, consisting of New York, Pennsylvania, Maine and Indiana regiments.

Two of Robertson's regiments, the 4th and 5th Texas, were helping Law on Little Round Top, while his other two regiments, the 1st Texas and 3rd Arkansas, threw themselves against Devil's Den, where a little later they were joined by Benning's Georgians. Robertson directed the Devil's Den attack personally,[12] while on the front slope of Little Round Top his other regiments, like the Alabamians farther around the mountain, fought on their own, without a brigadier general.

Devil's Den is no more than a sharp fissure, though the name is usually applied to the great mass of rocks that rise into a hill about it, and which are separated from Little Round Top by the narrow valley of Plum Run. In all directions were boulders, ranging in size, by a Texan's comparison, from that of a hogshead to a small house.

The Federals had managed to get Captain James E. Smith's 4th New York Battery in position at Devil's Den, on the extreme left of Sickles' line, with the 4th Maine and 124th New York in support. Four guns were on the crest and two were 75 yards in the rear. The battery opened with destructive fire, one shell killing or wounding 15 men.

Private James O. Bradfield, Company E, 1st Texas, described the Devil's Den fighting as "one of the wildest, fiercest struggles of the war,"[13] and none who was there disputed him.

The Texas brigade had a kind of symbol of its spirit in a jolly youth under twenty, Will Barbee, who served as a courier for Hood, and whom Private Bradfield described as "a reckless daredevil" utterly without fear. When a battle was joined he managed to get to the firing line and the soldiers had learned to watch for him. Now, as the fight grew desperate, someone called, "Here comes Barbee!"

The men saw the high-spirited lad dash up on a little sorrel, waving his hat. His horse fell but he "hit the ground running," grabbed a gun, jumped on top of a high rock behind which there were already many wounded, stood erect, exposed and fearless, and began firing. Below him the wounded loaded and passed up their guns, and he blazed away at any exposed bluecoat. Bradfield, a few paces away, knew that no man could live in the leaden hail where the lad stood.

Finally Barbee was knocked off with a wound in the leg. But he crawled back. Then he was hit in the other leg; again he got to his exposed perch. At length he was wounded so severely that he could not climb back unaided. He was last seen "crying and cursing" because the boys would not restore him to his place of danger.[14]

In front of Little Round Top and on its forward slopes the reckless charges continued. Colonel Van H. Manning, commanding the brigade's Arkansas regiment, was wounded, and Colonel R. M. Powell of the 5th Texas was riddled. Major Rogers took command of the 5th.

John Haggerty, a courier for Law, rode up the slope. He said: "General Law presents his compliments and says hold the place at all hazards."

"Compliments hell!" roared Rogers. "Who wants compliments in such a damned place as this? Go back and ask General Law if he expects me to hold the world in check with the Fifth Texas Regiment."[15]

When the fighting was at its hottest the men noticed a pint-sized private of the 3rd Arkansas behind a stump, biting the cartridges, aiming, and firing as rapidly as he could, all the while, between bites and shots, singing lustily:

> "Now let the world wag as it will,
> I'll be gay and happy still."[16]

Private Joe Smith of the 4th Texas was feeling the heat when he went in. He soaked a white handkerchief in Plum Run, tied it around his head, and started. When they buried him, they counted eleven holes through the neat white target.

Private Bradford complimented the Federals on their bravery at Devil's Den. But the Southern fire was too hot. Benning's Georgia brigade came up—"Old Rock, that peerless hero," the Texan called him.[17] It was 5:30 P.M. Benning walked back and forth along the front of his line issuing only one order: "Give them hell, boys—give them hell."[18] As the near-by private Bradford observed, the boys were following instructions. Within twenty-five minutes after the Georgians struck the 20th Indiana, it lost its Colonel John Wheeler, shot through the temple in the first fire, and 146 of its 268 men.

The Federal line bent in the Plum Run valley, then broke on Devil's Den. As Bradford put it: "The Lone Star flag crowned the hill and Texas was there to stay."[19] It was six o'clock.

Meade threw in two fresh Fifth Corps brigades, and the advance up Plum Run Valley was checked, but the Texans and Georgians held grimly to Devil's Den until the last gun was fired at Gettysburg. Benning captured about 300 prisoners and three of the six guns of Smith's battery, one having been disabled. His loss was heavy, among the dead being two of his regimental commanders.

3. The Retreat Is Made up the Mountain

From the eastern to the southern and western slopes of Little Round Top the battle rolled, with the same resolute vigor being displayed on both sides. On the western face the Texans and Law's other Alabamians battled Weed's brigade. The Texans and O'Rorke met head-on and in the first blast O'Rorke and 27 of his officers and men were killed. Warren had greatly admired the youthful colonel who answered his summons. "He was glorious," Warren said in simple tribute.

The battle lines wavered up and down the hill, like ribbons fluttering in the wind. The Federal commander, Brigadier General Stephen Hinsdale Weed, twenty-nine years old, a native of New York City and an artillery specialist at and after West Point, was on the bald summit of Little Round Top, exposed to the Confederate sharpshooters now concealed among the rocks of Devil's Den. He was hit and killed almost instantly. Captain Hazlett was standing beside him and stooped to catch any words he might utter. In an instant Hazlett, too, was shot dead. He did not speak, but Lieutenant Colonel David T. Jenkins, of the 146th New York, who stood near by, thought he heard Weed say, "My sister."

While the fighting surged up and down the slopes and among the giant boulders of Little Round Top, marked by charge and countercharge and frightful carnage all along the line, the final decision was to be reached on the flank where Oates battled Chamberlain.

On another advance, Oates found the fire so destructive that his line inclined forward as it moved—he compared it to a man trying to walk against a heavy wind. Oates saw his brother, Lieutenant John A. Oates, fall mortally wounded close by. The loss of officers was appalling. But the gallant regiment with a shout made its final charge against the ledge of rock where it had already spilled so much blood. Oates used his pistol "within musket length," but the Maine soldiers would not be dislodged. "Five times they rallied and charged us," he said. As he looked back on this fighting, he thought the outcome of the battle was decided in this deadly struggle amid the rocks on the far left of Meade's army.[20]

The Confederate position was rapidly becoming desperate. It was 6:30 P.M. Stoughton's sharpshooters appeared from nowhere and threatened the Alabama rear. Oates said, "The blood stood in puddles in some places on the rocks." Still hoping for reinforcements, he told his captains: "Return to your companies; we will sell out as dearly as possible."[21] But soon with better judgment he ordered a retreat. Chamberlain saw the fagging of the Southern pressure and called for the bayonet. Oates claimed the retirement was by his order, but this spirited bayonet charge was persuasive also. Oates described his retirement: "When the signal was given we ran like a herd of wild cattle."

Dismounted Federal cavalrymen in the rear near Stoughton's sharpshooters were nearly crushed by the Confederates as they passed over and through them. Some of the troopers were grabbed by the collars and carried off prisoners. Alongside Oates was an Alabama private whose windpipe had been severed by a bullet; his breath screeched through his open throat as he ran. Captain D. B. Waddell, regimental adjutant, had been on the extreme Confederate right. He escaped but some of his men were cut off and captured. Oates thought he lost 40 or 50; Chamberlain thought he captured 400 or 500. The Federals probably picked up the companies of skirmishers that disappeared on the back side of Round Top. They vanished from sight and from the accounts.

Captain Shaaf rejoined the 15th Alabama with Company A that had been looking hungrily at the Federal trains without having quite the dash to move against them or the judgment to rejoin the regiment during the emergency on the slopes of Little Round Top. Shaaf had seen guards in the woods, some of the sharpshooters perhaps, and one Maine company, and had hesitated.

On Round Top Oates stopped Chamberlain with a determined stand and formed a line for a time along the lower northwestern slope. Then, in one of the amazing episodes of the battle, he retired to the very summit of Round Top. His men toiled a second time up the rugged slopes as though they had not marched twenty-four miles to the field, marched and countermarched for four or more miles getting into position, lost their canteens, and fought one of the most desperate battles of American history, all in a single day.

On the crest of Round Top Oates made an effort to re-form his survivors. But the men were scattered and the heat was still intense; numerous details were helping the wounded. Finally the gallant commander whose spirit had been the dominating factor of the attack on Little Round Top went down, overcome by exertion and heat. When he was revived by his physician, he ordered the regiment to form a line at the foot of the mountain. Darkness was coming on. The extreme right regiment of Lee's army rested at the base of Round Top on the night of July 2.

That night the Texans on Devil's Den could hear the bluecoats talking and working on Little Round Top. According to Private Val C. Giles, 4th Texas, the Yankee officers on top of the ridge were "cursing men by platoons," and in reply the men were telling the officers to "go to a country not very far from them." Something approaching hell could be found anywhere near by. The lines in some places were fifty yards apart. Giles thought there was not much good spirit on this sector that night. "Both sides were whipped and all were mad about it."[22]

Robertson's brigade (formerly Hood's) had helped win Devil's Den, but its regiments had been stopped on the slopes of the higher hill on the Federal left. The battle here was summed up succinctly, from the Texas viewpoint, in one of the postwar orations: "At the first roll of the war drum, Texas sent forth her noblest and best. She gave the Army of Northern Virginia Hood's matchless brigade—a band of heroes who bore their country's flag to victory on every field, until God stopped them at Little Round Top."[23]

There were other versions of why the Confederates failed to take the hill. Colonel Elijah Walker of the 4th Maine, fighting in the Plum Run valley, thought that if Benning had gone to Law's rather than Robertson's support the Confederates would have carried Little Round Top as they did Devil's Den. Hood had placed Benning in the rear to serve as Law's support, but in the advance through the woods and smoke the front-line units could not be readily identified. Emerging, Benning followed what he thought was Law's brigade. It proved to be Robertson's, and when Robertson called for help he responded. It was a natural but probably a costly error.

Longstreet, far off to the left, never knew until after the battle— years later, according to Oates—that two of his regiments had passed over the summit of Round Top. Oates took into action what he regarded "the finest and strongest regiment in Hood's division," numbering 500 officers and men, and came out with 223, a loss of more than 50 per cent.

Colonel William Calvin Oates, of Abbeville, Alabama, was twenty-seven years old when he became the main factor in the Confederate attack on Little Round Top. He was wounded six times in the war and lost his right arm at Petersburg, but being a man of capacity as well as courage, went on to serve his southern Alabama district seven terms in Congress, was governor of his state, and commanded a brigade at Camp Meade, Pennsylvania, in the Spanish-American War. With his left hand he wrote a gripping account of the desperate battle for the Round Tops. He omitted only one thing: He never did tell when his Alabamians finally got some water.

That evening the Federal army awoke to the importance of big Round Top. Colonels Rice and Chamberlain met Colonel Joseph Fisher, commanding a Pennsylvania brigade of Crawford's division, Fifth Corps, and they concluded that if the enemy should fortify it, Little Round Top would have to be abandoned. The decisions in both armies on this far flank were being made that day by junior officers.

Rice ordered Chamberlain to take the 20th Maine up the mountain. At 9:00 P.M. Chamberlain began the slow ascent, guided by the moonlight streaming through the foliage. At the summit his men captured 25 prisoners, then labored to construct a defensive line. The stone wall they built still shows that the New Englanders knew their rock work even by moonlight. Later they were joined by the 83rd Pennsylvania and 44th New York, and the extreme left of Meade's army was at last secure.

CHAPTER EIGHTEEN

Crushing the Orchard Salient

1. McLaws' Belated Attack

John Clark Ridpath, biographer and historian in the generation following the Confederate War, in writing his *Life and Work of James A. Garfield,* described the incessant volume of orders transmitted from headquarters during the battle of Chickamauga, where the future President served as chief of staff to the Federal army commander, Rosecrans.

He contrasted this with Gettysburg, where few orders were issued, and said Meade "had little to do with the battle." The country around Gettysburg being open, the division commanders merely stationed troops where they would do the most good.[1]

This was a pertinent observation, but the striking fact often lost sight of is that it applied to Lee's army even more than to Meade's, and still more pointedly to Lee's corps. After the fighting was begun, at few points did the corps commanders exercise more control over the action than the greenest corporal. About all they could govern was the time at which the different divisions or brigades might be sent in; once a command was embattled the soldiers took over and the top generals became simply onlookers. Eager observer Fremantle noted that throughout the battle of the afternoon of July 2, Lee sent only one message.[2]

Longstreet, in the decades after the battle, was made the object of some just and many trumped-up criticisms—"jaundiced and malicious charges,"[3] one of his men called them—but his main error was largely overlooked. It was that of withholding McLaws for an hour and a half, under the unfortunate echelon plan of attack, while Hood fought unaided, with almost unprecedented fury, against the two Federal corps of Sickles and Sykes, and ultimately some of Hancock and Sedgwick as well.

Here, at a point where he had full control, Longstreet let his temperamental slowness hold sway. Instead of allowing McLaws to follow Hood in a matter of minutes, he restrained the Georgian and in turn his impatient brigadiers. The sharp edge of Hood's attack was dulled to butter before the lieutenant general gave the signal that sent in McLaws, and this tardiness slowed the rest of the army.

Hood had been wounded severely in the arm twenty minutes after the action commenced. Knocked from his horse, he was compelled to leave the field. The wound was a calamity to the Confederacy on more than one count. It deprived Lee's right wing of the supervision of a combat leader of great courage, experience, and mental agility, and left it under the professor of belles-lettres, McIver Law, an excellent young general, but lacking in Hood's inspirational and rugged combat qualities and experience in divisional command.[4]

The wounding of Hood also had a more far-reaching effect, for it sent him to his first recuperation in Richmond, to be followed by a second after he lost his leg at Chickamauga. There he established a circle of ardent friends; his winning personality even warmed chill President Davis. His conversation around the capital—with his critical analysis of the conduct of the Gettysburg campaign—stamped him in the civilian mind as a man who knew how to lead an army and win a battle. The result was his appointment later in the war to replace Joseph E. Johnston commanding the army confronting Sherman. Here again one of Lee's capable division leaders showed that although he possessed a full measure of courage and dash, he lacked the moderating qualities of caution and discernment required for high, independent command; thus, in more ways than one, was the Confederate War lost on the field of Gettysburg.

McLaws was more phlegmatic than Hood. He possessed a Grant-like stolidity but had strong compensating points, such as reliability and some of Grant's doggedness, which made his division as hard to dislodge as any in the army. His complexion was swarthy, his hair was very black, and his eyes were "coal black," according to the good reporter, Robert Stiles. He was short and compact, with big, square shoulders, deep chest, and large, muscular arms, and Stiles thought that "of his type, he is a handsome man." But in dealing with him one thought more of his tenacity than his grace, for impassiveness and unflinching fortitude seemed to show all over him. Stiles compared him to the Roman centurion who stood at his post in Herculaneum until the lava flowed over and engulfed him.[5]

Born and reared in Savannah, McLaws had been a student at the University of Virginia when he received an appointment to West Point. After his mature traits began to assert themselves, he was found to have the same deliberate tendencies as his West Point classmate and present commander, Longstreet, though, unlike Longstreet, who rarely showed a tender side and shunned paper work, he was fond of detail and innately sentimental. On the Rappahannock he and Barksdale would go to the river-bank at night and listen wistfully to the Federal bands playing the familiar old army songs.[6] Stiles told of riding with him through camp. He made "quite a notable figure on his small white horse,"[7] but his men went on with their work, cleaning equipment and guns, and paid no attention to him unless questioned. They were respectful but not enthusiastic. He was not the most brilliant of Lee's division commanders. Because of his persistence he was perhaps the superior of Early or Richard H. Anderson or Heth, though not equal to Hood, Johnson, or Pender. And he was an officer who could probably get more out of a situation than either Ewell or A. P. Hill.

Hood went in at four o'clock, McLaws at five-thirty. McIver Law contended that he halted the advance of Hood's division because of lack of support on his left. He went to Kershaw, who commanded McLaws' right brigade, found he had received no attack orders, urged him to move forward, and thus initiated the attack of McLaws' entire division.[8] Kershaw, however, said he stepped off at a signal from Cabell's artillery, which opened about four o'clock.[9] The brigade leaped over a stone wall, and Kershaw thought they moved with "great steadiness and precision." Longstreet walked on foot with Kershaw at the head of the South Carolinians until they reached the Emmitsburg road. They could hear on their left Barksdale's drums beating the assembly to take up the echelon attack in due season. They marched east, then wheeled to face Birney's line and the Federal battery east of the Peach Orchard.

McLaws was moving in the form of a right angle against the Peach Orchard salient. Kershaw, supported by Semmes, faced north to attack past the Rose house to the Wheat Field. Barksdale, with Wofford in his rear, faced east and attacked the Peach Orchard and Wentz farm. Kershaw came into line on the left of Hood's left brigade, commanded by Brigadier General George Thomas Anderson,[10] who had been assailing the right of Ward's brigade west of Devil's Den while Robertson and Benning were pressing back its center and left. Kershaw attacked at 5:30 P.M.[11]

Kershaw's cultured sensibilities may have influenced the South to call that first major battle of the war Manassas instead of Bull Run. According to a Richmond report, he had asked Beauregard to change the name of the stream because "Bull's Run was so unrefined." Beauregard countered with: "Let's try to make it as great a name as your South Carolina Cowpens."[12]

Manassas prevailed, though probably for other reasons. Kershaw had written up his independent account of the battle and made it public without reference to Beauregard, who was astonished, but Mrs. Chesnut, often the final arbiter of such matters, explained, "He meant no harm. He is not yet used to the fine arts of war."

Now, two years later, Kershaw had learned that the "fine arts of war" usually simmered down to spirited rushes and rapid volleys, matters in which his South Carolinians had become expert. He began against De Trobriand, who was worthy of the best South Carolina could offer. The emotional Frenchman, heedless of his own danger, rode up and down in front of his line, unaccompanied even by an orderly, exhorting his men to hold. The division commander, Birney, was in De Trobriand's rear, while Bully Boy Sickles roamed the lines insensible to the devastating fire from the Southern cannon.[13]

The battle of the Wheat Field and Peach Orchard was rendered complex by the converging of numerous brigades from both armies over a period of three hours. For an hour Anderson and Kershaw assaulted De Trobriand with great vigor and scant success. The Wheat Field was a triangular parcel of land about 400 yards on each of the three sides, defended in front by the 17th Maine, 5th Michigan, 110th Pennsylvania, and, at the Peach Orchard, by the 3rd Michigan and 3rd Maine, linking De Trobriand with Graham. The 17th Maine had the advantage of a stone wall at the southern edge of the field, where it had already met the successive attacks of Robertson and Anderson of Hood's division before Kershaw assailed the right of De Trobriand's line.

The two brigades of Barnes's division remaining after Vincent had rushed to the defense of Little Round Top—those of Sweitzer and

Tilton—were sent by Sykes to the aid of Birney and fell in on De Trobriand's right. Kershaw and Anderson attacked in concert and at six o'clock they were supported by the resolute advance of Paul Semmes's Georgia Brigade of McLaws' division, which came in on Kershaw's right. The Confederate pressure asserted itself. Semmes, whose brother, Raphael Semmes, was commanding the Confederate cruiser *Alabama* at that hour making for the South African coast, fell mortally wounded at the first fire. But Barnes's brigades were pushed back and De Trobriand's flank was threatened.

The miserable showing made by Barnes at this juncture was the source of complaint, denial, and recrimination. Certainly the brigades which later fought with great resolution under a new commander, failed to stand in the Wheat Field under Barnes. The New York *Herald* correspondent on the scene wrote that after Barnes gave way he refused to go back into line, while De Trobriand asserted that he fell back even before being engaged. Birney stated that when he saw Barnes withdraw without firing a shot he remonstrated, but without effect.[14] Barnes's retirement enabled Kershaw to advance through the woods on the west side of the Wheat Field and threatened De Trobriand's exposed flank and rear, at the very moment when McLaws' other brigades became menacing.

The Frenchman found great difficulty in disengaging his troops from their fierce struggle in front. "Third Michigan," he cried, "change front to right! I give ze order three or four times. Change quick, or you will be gobbled up. Don't you see you are flanked? Ze whole rebel army is in your rear."[15]

Birney, fearful that his entire line was about to collapse, ordered a charge by the 17th Maine, which was momentarily effective and gave the 17th and the 5th Michigan a position halfway across the wheat. Barnes's two brigades remained from 100 to 300 yards in their rear.

Sickles was watching the action near the Trostle house behind the Peach Orchard-Little Round Top road when he was hit by a cannon ball that shattered his leg. Captain M. J. Foote of the 70th New York, Sickles' old regiment, fearful that the men might be affected on the Third Corps line, formed a detail of a sergeant and six soldiers, who quickly covered the corps commander with a blanket and carried him into the Trostle farmhouse. His leg was amputated above the knee that night and he passed out of the Army of the Potomac. When Meade heard he had fallen he rode hurriedly to Hancock and placed him in command of the Third Corps as well as his own.

On the Confederate side, Robertson and "Tige" Anderson were wounded. Colonels in both armies were taking over the brigades.

Meade had already directed his cavalry commander, Pleasanton, at about 5:00 P.M., to get together what cavalry and artillery he could find, take a position in the rear, and be prepared to cover a retreat of the army from Gettysburg.[16] It was a wise precaution, because the battle was not developing satisfactorily for the Federal commander and it was good judgment to be prepared for the worst.

Birney meantime had called desperately on Hancock for help and now at 6:40 P.M. Caldwell's division, consisting of the brigades of Cross, Zook, Kelly, and Brooke, reached the region of the Wheat Field.

Colonel Patrick Kelly commanded the famous Irish Brigade, formerly led by Brigadier General Thomas Francis Meagher, that flew the green flag with golden harp alongside the Stars and Stripes from Manassas to Gettysburg and on to Appomattox. Possessing a preponderance of Catholics among its members, the brigade chaplain was a Catholic priest, the Reverend William Corby.

On every side was evidence of the desperate fury of the battle. As the Irish Brigade prepared to enter, the men were drawn up in column of regiments, with arms "at order" so that Father Corby might give absolution. Major St. Clair A. Mulholland, commander of the 116th Pennsylvania, which was attached to the brigade, described the striking ceremony.[17] Hancock stood close by, surrounded by his staff and high officers from other commands. Father Corby, mounted on a large rock, explained that absolution could be obtained if each individual made an act of sincere contrition and resolved to confess his sins at the first opportunity. He declared that the Catholic Church would refuse Christian burial to the soldier who turned his back on the enemy and deserted his flag. The men dropped to their knees, the chaplain stretched out his right hand, and spoke the words of general absolution. For many it was their last prayer. Said Mulholland, "It was awe-inspiring."[18]

Across to their left the battle roared around Little Round Top and the Peach Orchard. Caldwell moved his eager division toward the Wheat Field in the center of the distressed Federal lines.

Hancock looked on fondly as Caldwell went in. As Colonel Edward E. Cross, commander of the 1st Brigade, who had led the 5th New Hampshire in earlier battles, passed with his four trim regiments, Hancock called out to him, "Cross, this is the last time you'll fight without a star."

The laconic colonel did not even halt. "Too late, general. This is my last battle." Ten minutes later he was dead.[19]

Zook was in the lead. As they approached the Wheat Field, his way was blocked by the disorganized troops of Barnes's division. "If you can't get out of the way," stormed Zook, "lie down and we will march over you."

Birney, who was close at hand, also gave blunt orders for Barnes's troops to lie down, and Zook's brigade passed over their prostrate bodies as they went into line on De Trobriand's left. Zook began an advance through the Wheat Field and was driving the enemy when he was shot dead. Samuel Kosciusko Zook, of New York City, was a native of Chester County, Pennsylvania, who as a young man had won notice by his discoveries and inventions in electricity and had got into the army by prewar service in the New York State Militia.

Caldwell's division had marched south from Cemetery Ridge and had deployed in front of Little Round Top, then swept up to the Wheat Field, with each brigade joining the action as it arrived. After Cross and Zook, Kelly went in on their right and was soon at close quarters with Kershaw. Mulholland said his regiment, armed with smooth-bore muskets, was firing "buck and ball," consisting of one large ball and three buckshot, with which "a blind man could not have missed his mark."[20] Brooke made a spectacular charge through the wheat. After fifteen minutes the fresh Federal division prevailed, and the brigades of Kershaw and Semmes were driven back. The old Third Corps line was maintained and in some places advanced.

De Trobriand's wearied regiments passed to the rear through Caldwell's line. The 5th Michigan and 17th Maine had stood as sacrifices during some of the fiercest fighting of the battle. One soldier of the 3rd Maine was picked up with 48 wounds.[21]

That night when De Trobriand was making his inspection he came to the bivouac of the 5th Michigan and saw the pitiful little group of survivors. He inquired about others and was told, "These only are left." Quickly his eyes filled with tears, and he exclaimed with all his Gallic fervor, "Oh! My little Fifth! My little Fifth! I would rather command you than to command a division."[22]

2. Barksdale's "Most Magnificent Charge of the War"

But the battle of the Peach Orchard and the Wheat Field was about to take a new turn. Under the *en echelon* plan, the attack passed to Longstreet's only Mississippi brigade, commanded by William Barksdale.

The big Mississippian possessed a national but not everywhere an enviable reputation. This was not so much because of his ardent championship of the Southern cause in Congress, but because he was reputed to have walked to the Senate chamber with his fellow veteran of the Mexican War, Representative Preston S. Brooks, and looked as though he might hold off interference at the time Brooks rained the vengeful blows of his gutta-percha cane on the head of Massachusetts Senator Charles Sumner. Identities may have been mistaken.[23] A friend who accompanied Barksdale in Mexico commented, "What a noble, generous heart beat in that broad bosom!" Although a quartermaster with the Mississippians in Mexico he could be seen coatless, with a big sword, at the very front when fighting was promised.[24]

The Virginia artilleryman Stiles said Barksdale's was the brigade "I knew and loved best of all in Lee's army";[25] he felt safe when it supported his guns. The Mississippians were described as "irrepressible" by a Southern observer,[26] and the careful scribe Jacob Hoke, who tried to detect the distinguishing characteristics of soldiers from the different states as they passed through Chambersburg, decided "those from Mississippi and Texas were more vicious and defiant. . . ."[27]

As he waited for an opportunity to attack, Barksdale was nettled by Longstreet's delay and irritated by the battery that Graham had put up at the Peach Orchard, which kept his men pinned down only a quarter of a mile away. Longstreet passed along the lines.

"I wish you would let me go in, General," said Barksdale. "I would take that battery in five minutes."

"Wait a little," Longstreet replied. "We are all going in presently."[28]

"Presently" was not good enough for Barksdale, but he bore the orders. Longstreet objected when the men began tearing down a fence, saying it would draw the enemy fire, but when he rode off they leveled everything in front of them. Some, contemptuous of the Federal artillery, roamed about getting water and cherries. They began to hope when Alexander brought up twenty or more guns to their immediate rear. The guns were unlimbered behind the hill and the infantrymen rolled them up by hand. The delightful roar and stomach-shaking concussion were suddenly experienced as the guns were unloosed on the Peach Orchard, where Graham's bluecoats were scooping the earth with their bayonets and fingernails and hiding behind fences. After an hour or so the Mississippians heard an order for the guns to cease firing, and they knew their moment at Gettysburg had come.[29]

Barksdale rode along the line hatless. The great shock of sandy hair that had tossed in the halls of Congress was now white, a beacon for his brigade. When he rode he leaned forward as if trying to push his horse faster. "He had a thirst for battle glory," said one of his men. It was generally noticed that the fury of conflict kindled in him an incandescence that warmed all near by. His brigade was in line, with Colonel Benjamin Grubb Humphreys, planter, lawyer, and legislator, commanding the 21st Mississippi on the right. Humphreys had been dismissed from West Point after the great Christmas Eve riot of 1826, when the army authorities demonstrated that letting off steam was reserved for the liberal-arts colleges. A man of marked leadership, he was the first governor of his state after Appomattox.

The roar of Law's battle sounded on the far right, and nearer at hand Kershaw and Caldwell were locked in a deadly, unyielding struggle. It was six o'clock. Barksdale had about 1,500 avid soldiers who thought the war might be ended here.

The clearest, most ringing voice was Humphreys', and as he called his regiment to attention it brought the men up "like an electric shock."[30] Barksdale moved out in front of his old regiment, the 13th, and took his place before the flag. The men cast off their scanty packs —a blanket and a change of underwear—and each regiment heaped them and assigned a single guard to them. The field and staff officers dismounted. Orders were that none below the rank of brigadier general might ride because, as the brigade chronicler naïvely observed, "the government had a great deal of difficulty replacing the horses."[31] Then the drum rolled and Barksdale started, his shock of white hair waving in the evening breeze. The men let out the savage rebel yell, took the double-quick and, as they emerged from the timber, rushed the two rail fences lining the Emmitsburg road. The fences seemed to disappear as if by sorcery.

George Clark, of Wilcox's Alabama brigade, immediately on Barksdale's left, observed the unbroken line at the salient and called it "the most magnificent charge I witnessed during the war," and so it came to be termed in Mississippi annals.[32] Clark, later a Waco, Texas, judge, declared Barksdale seemed to be fifty yards in front of his men. John S. Henry of the 17th Mississippi quoted a Northern colonel as saying, "It was the grandest charge that was ever made by mortal man."

Captain G. B. Lamar, Jr., aide of McLaws, who carried the step-off orders to the brigade, said Barksdale's face "was radiant with joy." The general's long white hair reminded Lamar of the white plume of Henry of Navarre.[33] The enraptured captain watched him as far as his eye could follow, still out in front. "I have witnessed many charges marked in every way by unflinching gallantry . . . but I never saw anything to equal the dash and heroism of the Mississippians," Lamar said.

The British correspondent Ross who had been trailing Longstreet up and down the lines, was on hand to witness Barksdale's attack:

It was a glorious sight. The men who had been lying down sprang to their feet and went in with a will. There was no lagging behind, no spraining of ankles on the uneven ground, no stopping to help a wounded comrade. Not one fell out of line unless he was really hurt. . . . The guns in the Peach Orchard were pounced upon, and half of them taken in a thrice, whilst the others limbered up and made off. Hundreds of prisoners were captured, and everything was going so satisfactorily for a time we hardly doubted the enemy would be driven from his very strong position on the hills in front.[34]

Graham's brigade had plenty of spunk. It, too, had been pinned down, not for an hour, as Barksdale's men estimated the length of the bombardment, but for two hours according to Captain E. C. Strouss of the 57th Pennsylvania. When the enemy line was seen emerging from the woods, Graham's men did not wait. The 57th and the 114th Pennsylvania ran forward across the Emmitsburg road to meet them. The 57th jumped into the Sherfy house and outbuildings. About them the battle raged furiously for a time, and then the Mississippians swept on, having captured many trapped in the house and barn.

When the 114th Pennsylvania retired from the Sherfy buildings in front of the 18th Mississippi, the only avenue of retreat was up the Emmitsburg road. Captain A. W. Given, who had taken command when the higher officers fell, conducted the regiment, closely pressed by the enemy. Soon the road was filled with dead and wounded. One of the wounded officers of the 114th, prostrate on the road, witnessed a Confederate battery dash up with its guns. When the officer in charge saw the dead and wounded, he stopped the horses, had his men lift the dead to the side and carry the wounded into a cellar, probably that of the Klingle or Rogers house. He left them with a supply of water and said he would return after he had "caught the rest of the Yankees."[35] Who he was they never knew. He was off again quickly with his guns.

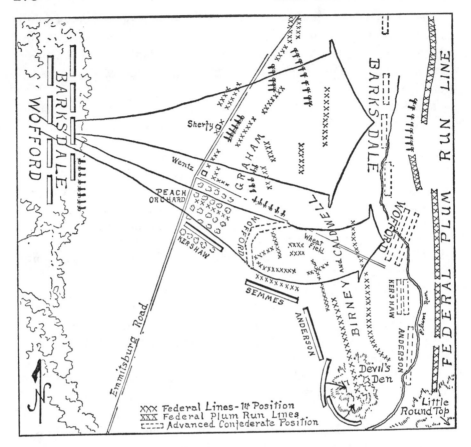

Break-through of Barksdale and Wofford at the Peach Orchard.
July 2, 1863.

The 141st Pennsylvania, stationed immediately behind the Wentz house, went in with 9 officers and 200 men. In "several minutes" it lost 6 officers and 145 men. After the regiment retreated a battery dashed up and unlimbered in the Wentz yard. The young gunner in charge dismounted and looked over the familiar surroundings. Sergeant Henry Wentz had come home from the South, wearing a gray uniform.[36]

The 68th Pennsylvania was at the angle. Here General Graham, personally directing the firing line, was wounded and he was carried to the rear. He insisted on returning and this time he was pitched to the ground when his horse fell; being stunned, and weak from loss of blood, he could only grope about when he rose. The attack of the 21st Mississippi passed over him and he was captured.

A native of New York City, Charles Kinnaird Graham had already built a career in the Navy when war came. He had served in the Gulf in the Mexican War, then had become a civil engineer at the Brooklyn Navy Yard. When he volunteered for the army, 400 coworkers followed him and he organized the 74th New York Regiment of Sickles' Excelsior Brigade.

As about 1,000 prisoners were being taken back by Major Fairfax, of Longstreet's staff, Graham among them, the Southern Artillerist William M. Owen talked with him. Fairfax had ordered a courier to dismount in order that the wounded Federal general might ride. Graham asked the name of the officer who had led the charge against his brigade. "Our generals do not do that sort of thing," Owen quoted him as saying.[37]

"It was a terrible afternoon in that orchard," said Private Alfred J. Craighead of the 68th Pennsylvania, which faced south at the corner.[38] In the orchard 12 of the regiment's officers were killed or wounded, leaving but 4 to extricate the regiment in the retreat. Colonel A. H. Tippin of the 68th took command of the brigade when Graham was captured. The 105th Pennsylvania, called the "Wildcat Regiment," left half its men along the Emmitsburg road.

Graham's men fought gallantly and retired slowly, pressed step by step by the relentless Barksdale, who stayed in front, all the time calling, "Forward, men, forward!" Eventually the Federal retirement became a rout. Barksdale drove straight ahead, indifferent to his flanks.

As Longstreet had escorted Kershaw, so he accompanied Wofford's brigade that followed Barksdale. It attacked the flank of Birney and Caldwell, left exposed by the rout of Graham. The courier William Youngblood, who accompanied Longstreet, said the general's attention was so occupied trying to see what Hood's troops were doing farther to the right that he did not notice how far he had advanced in front of Wofford's line. Youngblood had to warn him to save him from capture, and they checked their horses to let the infantry pass.

Wofford, a native of Habersham County, Georgia, had become a prosperous plantation owner and lawyer in Cassville, Georgia, before the war. He published the weekly newspaper and opposed secession to the very end. He had been a captain under Scott in Mexico.

Kelly's Irish Brigade was battling Kershaw and Semmes when Major Mulholland noticed a column passing from the Peach Orchard toward his rear. It looked like Confederates. Uneasy, he reported it to Kelly, who sent him to inform one of Zook's regiments a short distance behind in support. This regiment moved fifty yards and discovered that the column was indeed Confederate. It was Wofford's brigade coming in on Barksdale's right and threatening to cut off Birney and Caldwell.

Sickles' old line had now been penetrated in two places—at Devil's Den by Robertson and Benning and at the Peach Orchard by Barksdale followed by Wofford. Between these two points Graham's fragments and the remnants of Birney still faced Anderson, Kershaw, and Semmes. Being all but surrounded, the entire Federal line suddenly collapsed. Some units managed a fairly orderly withdrawal to the east side of Plum Run; others broke into a rout. "We were in a trap," said Mulholland. "A line of the enemy was advancing on the Wheat Field from the South, and Wofford's brigade . . . was closing in from the North."[39] He told his men of the 116th Pennsylvania to look to their own safety in the region of Little Round Top, furled the regimental colors, and moved down the corridor between the two lines of Confederates. Cross and Brooke were extended beyond Wofford's advance and were not critically exposed, but Kelly and Zook "were completely surrounded, and the only way out of the trap was to pass down between the two lines of the enemy."[40] Caldwell's division managed to extricate itself at frightful loss. The disorganized units found security behind Ayres's fresh division of the Fifth Corps, consisting largely of Regular Army troops.

Barksdale advanced about three quarters of a mile and came to Plum Run, behind which was a slight ridge. The Federal chief of artillery, Hunt, who in going about the field had been attracted by defensive positions much as a bootblack is by a pair of dirty shoes, had noted this ridge and labeled it the Plum Run line, keeping it in mind as a possible substitute for the Peach Orchard in its front or Cemetery Ridge in its rear. Here Barksdale hit something solid. Only the redoubtable West Point rioter, Colonel Humphreys, got his Mississippi regiment across Plum Run, where it ran smack into three fourths of the Federal army being rushed forward by Meade.

In the new line were elements of Burling's New Jersey brigade of General Humphreys' division, called back from the Emmitsburg road, but mainly some of Hancock's fresh troops. Burling had seen Barksdale in front of his men and assigned a company to pick him off. The new Federal line came out of the elderbushes along the creek and poured a withering fire into Barksdale's front, which was ragged and disorganized by the long advance over rough, broken ground. Barksdale fell; the Mississippians recoiled, then retreated.

Private J. C. Lloyd of the 13th Mississippi, who was close to Barksdale, was hit by a Minié ball; as the retreat passed over him a comrade stopped long enough to make a sling for his arm. Left between the lines, he heard a weak voice speaking on his right, and, turning, saw Barksdale on the ground. He crawled over and held his canteen to the general's mouth, but there was no water. The canteen had been pierced by a ball. He ran back for litter bearers, wandered into the Northern lines, escaped in the thick smoke, made a wide circuit, and got back to a field hospital the Confederates had set up in a barn. Meanwhile the Federal line had advanced and the general could not be reached.[41] That night Barksdale was found in front of a Vermont regiment. On the next morning he died.[42]

Meade continued to rush reinforcements to his imperiled left wing, stripping his center and right heedlessly in the supreme emergency. Soon most of the Federal army was marching rapidly toward the Round Tops. Ayers was brought up from the Baltimore pike half a mile west of Rock Creek to the defensive line established behind Devil's Den. Part of Gibbon's division marched from Ziegler's Grove on Cemetery Ridge to Hunt's Plum Run line. Newton, commanding the First Corps, sent in the weakened divisions of Doubleday and Robinson. Finally Meade ordered the Twelfth Corps, posted behind the walls and trenches it had been constructing on Culp's Hill, to hurry to the left, and it moved quickly, leaving a single brigade behind. Two Sixth Corps brigades were rushed to the left.

Longstreet was not much in error in saying Hood and McLaws faced upward of 50,000 soldiers. Said Longstreet with pride: "History records no parallel to the fight made by these two divisions on the 2nd of July at Gettysburg."

CHAPTER NINETEEN

Cemetery and Culp's Hills

1. Humphreys Extracts His Division

Humphreys, commanding the remaining division of Sickles' corps after the defeat of Birney, was left strung out along the Emmitsburg road destitute of support on either side. Graham's survivors, who had guarded the Peach Orchard on his left, were streaming back beyond Plum Run, their leader captured, their organization destroyed, their effectiveness ended. His right, far out in front of the main Federal line, was suspended, resting on no more than a fence corner where a lane ran south of the great red barn of the Codori farm. The lower part of this barn, a center of the fighting on July 2 and 3, was of stone and provided good shelter; the upper was wood, painted red, after the Pennsylvania Dutch custom established in Colonial times. It served as a landmark readily seen from almost every part of the battlefield.

Humphreys' position clearly was untenable. He stood alone, far out in front of the army. Before he had much opportunity to appraise it or attempt a withdrawal, he was hit by two brigades of A. P. Hill's corps—Wilcox' and Lang's—who were prompt to attack after Barksdale went in on their right.

Meade and Hancock, well aware of the danger, took measures to save Humphreys, who began a withdrawal which he hoped to keep systematic and unhurried, but which in time became chaotic. Hunt had combed the field for guns and now brought up 40, chiefly from the artillery reserve, and opened on the advancing Confederates to give

Humphreys time. Hancock detached Willard's brigade from Hays's division and then reinforced it with three regiments from Harrow's brigade, Gibbon's division—the 106th Pennsylvania, 15th Massachusetts, and 1st Minnesota—to help fill the yawning gap between Humphreys and his own Second Corps, the unemployed portions of which were still back on the main line—almost theoretical at this stage—that ran from Cemetery Hill across the low ground to Little Round Top. Meade, seeing the approach of Lockwood's brigade, a newly-attached New York and Maryland unit, placed himself at its head and led it into position.

The troops assailing Humphreys, who threatened to overlap his right and sever him from Hancock, were the fresh division of Major General Richard S. Anderson, who had reached the field too late on July 1 to take part in the battle. For most of the day Anderson's men had been lying in the woods west of the Emmitsburg road, waiting for the attack order to reach them as it moved through the succession of brigades. Of Hill's three divisions, Anderson was on the right, Pender on the left connected with Rodes of Ewell's corps in the town, and Heth, commanded by Pettigrew, was in reserve behind them on Seminary Ridge. As Anderson attacked, the order of his brigade from right to left was Wilcox, Perry, Wright, Posey, and Mahone. Perry was suffering from typhoid fever, and his small Florida brigade was commanded by Colonel David Lang, of the 8th Florida.

Anderson, whose influence on the progress of the battle promised to be of the first significance, was an officer who, as Sorrel pointed out, was loved so warmly by all who knew him that they hesitated to criticize him; yet he was, in fact, indolent. Longstreet had been able to get good service out of him when he commanded a brigade and he had performed well with a division in a defensive role at Chancellorsville. But Gettysburg was his first battle under Hill, who lacked Longstreet's blunt firmness and was likely at times to be so temperamental or erratic as to leave a slothful subordinate indisposed where Longstreet would have enforced action. Sorrel rated Anderson's capacity and intelligence as excellent: "but it was hard to get him to use them."

At about 6:15 P.M. on July 2, he arrived at the greatest opportunity of his career, when the question of his capacity was to receive its clearest test. Meade had been weakening his center, along with his right, by the dispatch of troops to succor his hard-pressed left, and somewhere there must be soft spots. Hancock, who manned the Federal line here, could expect no further service that day from Caldwell, and thus one third of his corps was gone. He had been using elements of his other two divisions piecemeal to bolster the endangered line, and while Gibbon's division was fairly intact, it had been left with a long front between Howard—who was still licking his wounds on Cemetery Hill—and the mass of the army that had been concentrated on the Plum Run line. If Anderson should hit with all his power, he was likely to discover something worth exploiting somewhere along his front.

Perhaps one of the tragedies of the battle, from the Confederate standpoint, was that in the alignment of the divisions, in which the order of their arrival was highly influential, Pender was not on Hill's right in place of Anderson, where he would have followed McLaws. But Pender remained on the ground he had won, and Anderson, coming later, was stationed on his right and ahead of him in the progress of the battle from Lee's right to left.

Anderson's brigades were to attack "individually and successively," and in that manner they began. Wilcox, an officer from the old Regular Army, was a bit on the shelf as a brigade commander alongside the zestful young men who in their twenties were giving Lee such outstanding performance, and he was disquieted at being passed over for divisional command. He always turned in a creditable, rarely a brilliant performance. His Alabama troops were as good as could be found in the army but things seemed not to work out for the best for their commander.

Wilcox, followed by Lang on his left, drove Humphreys ahead of them as they advanced to the base of Cemetery Ridge, all the time meeting a devastating artillery fire from guns on the crest of the ridge and musketry from behind the stone walls. Wilcox passed the Emmitsburg road about 300 yards south of the Codori house, while Lang brushed the farm buildings with his left flank as he advanced, passing over ground that would be traveled a day later by Kemper of Pickett's division.

Even the most adept of generals may lose their discretion in a supreme emergency. Humphreys, laboring desperately to extricate his division, had ordered the brigade of Colonel William R. Brewster, formerly Sickles' "Excelsior Brigade," to change front to the rear, an army method of saying things were getting too hot and the men had better get out, presumably in an orderly way at a double-quick, but in usual practice at a run. Hancock had sent reinforcements, and the 19th Maine of Harrow's brigade was lying in the grass in the rear of the Excelsiors, who, when they received the "change front to the rear" order, seemed about to break into a rout. Humphreys hurried back to Colonel Francis E. Heath of the 19th Maine, 150 paces in the rear, and asked him to have his regiment stand up and stop the Excelsiors with their bayonets.

Heath apparently thought that was not what his boys had come down from the Maine woods to do and declined to obey Humphreys— although the reason given later was that he did not want his own men disorganized by the broken troops. Humphreys then rode down the Maine line and ordered the men, over their colonel's head, to give his fleeing men the bayonet. Heath immediately countermanded the order; it is not difficult to know which officer the men obeyed.

Humphreys, enraged, ordered Colonel Heath to the rear, but the colonel, who had been stationed by Hancock, said firmly, though still respectfully, "I was placed here by an officer of higher rank [than you] for a purpose," he said, "and I do not intend to go to the rear. Let your troops form in the rear and we will take care of the enemy in front."[1]

The Excelsior men were now passing; some in good spirits shouted to the Maine regiment, "Hang on, boys! We will form in your rear."

They did that, but when Hancock tried to put Humphreys' division into the hole that had been left by the departure of Caldwell, the division had virtually been dissipated. Said Hancock, "I directed General Humphreys to form his command on the ground from which General Caldwell had moved . . . which was promptly done. The number of his troops collected was, however, very small, scarcely equal to an ordinary battalion, but . . . composed of the fragments of many shattered regiments."

Wilcox and Lang were not fortunate enough to strike a soft spot, but they moved ahead, firing and advancing until about 7:00 P.M. Colonel Lang claimed his command routed everything in its front until it reached a small stand of timber in front of the main Federal line. Here he called a halt to allow his wearied men to rest briefly. Wilcox's attack had fallen principally on Brewster's Excelsiors, while Lang attacked the brigade of Joseph B. Carr, a mixed command composed of Massachusetts, New Hampshire, New Jersey, and Pennsylvania regiments. The battle waged by these two brigades, which had comprised Humphreys' forward line along the Emmitsburg road, was more destructive to the Federals than the assailants, and Lang, who was applying a pressure on Carr's front and flank, declared that at no time in the war had he seen so many dead Federal soldiers on the ground over which he passed.[2]

2. The Georgians Perch on Cemetery Ridge

Anderson's next brigade was commanded by Brigadier General Ambrose R. Wright, who had enlisted in the 3rd Georgia regiment as a private at the beginning of the war. A poor boy from Jefferson County, Georgia, he had literally reared himself by his hoe handle, working a small patch of land while he studied at night by the light of a pine knot. He became an Augusta lawyer and a man of great force in Georgia public affairs, who did not wait for a commission when the sudden call to arms was heard. He was president of the state senate for a period in 1863 and presided while on furlough, but returned to the army after the session. At Sharpsburg he had been wounded critically in the breast and at Chancellorsville had been hit in the knee with a piece of shrapnel, but he was in his full vigor at Gettysburg, commanding his four Georgia regiments with all the fervor of a natural-born leader fighting in the cause of independence.

Wright took up the march at about six-forty-five across the long stretch of open ground between the woods west of the Emmitsburg road and the ridge where the center of the Federal army now rested. He crossed the road north of the Codori house; there the ground is undulating but exposed to artillery and infantry fire from Cemetery Ridge, and men were soon dropping from his ranks. His brigade front was about 400 yards, and his attack was directed at a battery which opened on him from Gibbon's position between the small clump of trees and Ziegler's grove on the crest of the ridge to the north. His brigade would just fit the distance between the clump and the grove.

The excitable Frank Aretas Haskell, Gibbon's aide-de-camp, described the advance: "The whole slope in our front is full of them; and in various formation, in line, in column, and in masses which are neither, with yells and thick volleys they are rushing toward our crest."

"On they came like the fury of a whirlwind," said Captain John E. Reilly of the 69th Pennsylvania, Webb's brigade of Hancock's corps.[3] The guns at which Wright aimed his charge were Lieutenant T. Fred Brown's 1st Rhode Island Battery, behind which was the 69th Pennsylvania, while the remainder of Webb's brigade was over the crest in the vicinity of Meade's headquarters.

Wright swept up the hill, captured the Rhode Island guns, and stood with his brigade on the crest of Cemetery Ridge, at almost the exact spot that would be the focal point of Lee's attack on the Federal center on the following day. While Wright's lodgement is often called a penetration of the Federal center, that was not precisely the case, because Webb's brigade of Gibbon's division, which manned the line at this point, was largely behind instead of on the crest, and had to be reckoned with before Wright might claim an actual piercing of the Federal army. But he was inspired by a sight of the Baltimore pike, loaded with refugees leaving the battlefield.

The instant was one of the critical moments of the battle for General Lee, and a continuation of the attack by brigades *en echelon* would have held a distinct promise of breaking the weakened Federal center. But Wright was alone and unaided on the ridge. On his right Wilcox and Lang faltered. While Lang was in the small woods reforming his command, he saw what he described as a heavy column thrown against Wilcox that forced him back.[4] This was a portion of Harrow's brigade. Hancock personally directed the 1st Minnesota, a small regiment which made one of the gallant sacrifice charges of the battle and lost close to 75 per cent of its numbers.[5] Wilcox's retreat was followed by that of Lang, who held to his trees until he saw the Federals 100 yards in his rear. Unable to find a defensible line in the open fields over which he had passed, he was compelled to retreat to the woods west of the Emmitsburg road.

Lang lost some men as prisoners in his withdrawal. One of them was a big Floridian named Lewis Thornton Powell, alias Lewis T. Paine, who was sent to Baltimore wounded. He escaped, deserted, got into civilian clothes, and became so captivated by John Wilkes Booth that he offered himself as Booth's devoted follower; eventually he was a principal in the plot to assassinate Lincoln, his own role being the knifing of Secretary of State Seward.

Wright's spectacular assault was doomed to failure. His was a single brigade a mile in advance of Lee's main army. His thrust could not be regarded a heavy blow from the shoulder, with the weight of the body behind it, but more a hard cuff from the wrist, which annoyed but did not rock Meade severely. But it was enough of a shock that a supporting, straight-from-the-shoulder follow-up blow could have knocked the Federal army off Cemetery Ridge.[6]

Webb's brigade made certain it was the Confederates, not the Federals, to be knocked off the ridge. While the 69th Pennsylvania assailed Wright in front, the 106th Pennsylvania moved against his right, exposed by Lang's retirement. Lieutenant Colonel W. L. Curry had the 106th Pennsylvania put three effective volleys into Wright's flank, then ordered a bayonet charge.

Hancock was hurrying up other troops, and Wright's brilliant exploit now seemed likely to be turned into a disaster for the courageous Georgians. Soon they were all but surrounded, but before Curry's attack reached them, they abandoned their captured guns and fairly cut their way out of the circle. They halted at a fence at the bottom of the hill, delivered a volley, and continued their retreat, only to be caught by the shells as the bombardment reopened on them from Cemetery Ridge. A second time they faced about, re-formed and battled off their pursuers.

Wright was followed closely by units of Doubleday's division and by the 106th Pennsylvania, which before reaching the Emmitsburg road captured Colonel William Gibson, and a number of his 48th Georgia Regiment. Colonel Curry halted his Pennsylvanians along the road, threw out skirmishers, and sent back to Webb for orders. The brigade commander recalled the regiment. It was about seven-thirty.

If any small-unit action controlled the outcome of the battle, it was perhaps the affair in no man's land brought about when Curry left behind two companies, to be deployed as skirmishers, connecting with the skirmishers of the 1st Delaware Regiment at the Bliss house and barn in the field west of the Emmitsburg road.

Posey advanced his Mississippians belatedly, after Wright had been beaten off, and was arrested by the 1st Delaware skirmishers, whom he finally ousted from the Bliss buildings. His fire drove back one of the Pennsylvania companies which it took in flank, but the second company came up to relieve its comrades. Brigadier General Alexander Hays, seeing this fighting far out in front of the army about midway between the two lines, sent five companies of the 12th New Jersey, which, with the help of the spirited Pennsylvania company, assailed and recaptured the Bliss farm buildings. That was enough for Posey. Though his brigade had not been hurt much—he lost 92 prisoners in the barn—he did not attempt a further movement. Longstreet had escorted his brigades in, but neither Hill nor Anderson, who were not far removed, gave Posey orders or encouragement.

So the Confederate advance was stopped at the Bliss farm.[7] Here Lee's echelon plan broke down completely. The small action proved one of the most consequential of the battle. When Posey tarried,

Mahone on his left withheld his attack and would heed no entreaties from the troops engaged. Pender's division still farther to the left was governed by the advance of Mahone. Both Anderson and Hill appeared lacking in the necessary enterprise at the moment when a resolute attack by Posey and Mahone, acting together, would have had an excellent chance to penetrate the enemy line. Anderson, of course, should have used his brigades in some sort of concert. The *en echelon* plan ordinarily would be more effective if brigade followed brigade in prompt succession, but would be foredoomed to failure under lackadaisical management, by which it might become a series of individual attacks by isolated brigades, each being repulsed in turn by the whole enemy army.

Another important aspect of the Bliss farm fight was that by discouraging Posey, it left Hancock free to watch the right of the Federal army; he possessed enough unengaged troops to send assistance if needed. The 106th Pennsylvania had not been back in its old position many minutes before a call came for it to join Carroll's brigade and go to Howard's assistance on East Cemetery Hill. Certainly Carroll could not have been spared had Posey and Mahone attacked. Wilcox insisted that had Posey and Mahone been sent in at the time he dispatched his adjutant to Anderson for help, the Federal line could have been broken. The opportunity was even more promising when Wright captured the battery and held the crest of the ridge.

At least one southern correspondent with the army saw that here a great opportunity to win the battle was cast away. An analysis of the action in the center, made five days after the battle and published by the Richmond *Enquirer,* is as clear an explanation of the failure of Hill's corps as any that has yet been written. It embodies the essential facts.[8]

Pender, anxious to participate and sensing that Anderson's left brigades were not entering the action, rode to the right of his division to ascertain the cause. Perrin was certain that Pender did not mean to be held back by the faltering Mahone. But he was hit in the leg by a shell fragment just at the moment of decision. While the wound was severe, it was not of a fatal type. Pender was carried back, placed in an ambulance and started next day on the journey to his North Carolina home. At Staunton, Virginia, there was a hemorrhage of the wound. His brother came and he appeared to improve, but a second hemorrhage necessitated amputation of the leg. He died within a few hours after the surgery.[9]

General Lee, believing that Pender was about to go in with his division at the time he was wounded, attributed the loss of the battle to his fall: "I shall ever believe if General Pender had remained on his horse half an hour longer we would have carried the enemy's position."[10]

Major Joseph A. Englehard, Pender's adjutant general, spoke for the division when he said, "Seldom has the service suffered more in the loss of one man."[11] The misfortune was indeed akin to the loss of Jackson and in view of the critical moment at which Pender fell, probably fully as significant to the Southern cause.

Ewell's corps on Pender's left was not included in the plan to attack *en echelon,* but was to be governed by the sound of Longstreet's guns. The guns had been sounding since four o'clock—and now they were subsiding—but Ewell had not moved.

As the battle was dying on the far left of the Federal army, the brigade of Colonel William McCandless, of Brigadier General S. Wiley Crawford's division, Fifth Corps, which included the original "Bucktails," advanced across Plum Run and applied enough pressure on Longstreet to cause him to realign his right division. That night he retained the ground from which he had ousted Sickles, but lay close to the Federals only where his far right held Devil's Den and rested on the base of Round Top.

When Longstreet rode back from the lines in the early night, he was still trailed by the British correspondent Ross, to whom he declared, "We have not been as successful as we wished."[12] Then he attributed the lack of success to the wounding of Hood and the death of Barksdale.[13] Ross and Longstreet tied their horses to a fence, used their saddles as pillows, and that night slept on the meadow.

3. Hays and Avery Attack at Sundown

The flaming sun of July 2, 1863, that had looked down on some of the most sanguinary fighting of modern warfare, gradually sank into a red sky after a torrid day. Twilight was creeping across the battlefield. Far off to the right the angry booms could still be heard from Longstreet's guns. Bursts of infantry fire told that the attack on Meade's center had subsided but was not yet spent.

It was seven-thirty. The Carolinians in the hollow of the Culp spring were thinking of home. The candles and pine knots would soon be lighted on far-off farms. The delicate pink afterglow would be crowning the bold summits of the Blue Ridge. Corn must be tossing with full tassel in the Piedmont bottoms. The hungry Yadkin still ate the yellow hills. Families would be lingering at the supper tables watching the day die out of the sky. In countless North Carolina homes the mother was reserving an empty chair, as something of a devotion or fetish or symbol of her hope, against the day when her boy would be returning from Lee's army. Now that Lee had carried the war into the unscathed regions beyond the Potomac, word of his movements was awaited with taut expectancy. North Carolina listened, anxious, uncertain.

On East Cemetery Hill the heavily manned Federal line rose above the town of Gettysburg. The batteries of Weidrich, Ricketts, and Reynolds swept the green approaches across the undulating acres of the Culp farm. The regiments of Von Gilsa's brigade, the German immigrants to New York, who had been flanked by Early on the afternoon of July 1, manned the stone works and trenches which followed roughly the crest of Cemetery Hill. From their elevated position these Federal troops could look down on the valley of Rock Creek, through which the evening dusk was stealing, and on the red homestead and outbuildings of the farm of the Pennsylvania Dutchman, William Culp, one of whose sons, by a play of chance, was fighting across the fields in the army of the South, while another was fighting in the army of the North.

There, in the wheat field near the Culp house, on the outskirts of Gettysburg, the Northern soldiers could observe in the twilight the forming of a Southern assault column.[14] It was composed of the three infantry regiments of Hoke's North Carolina brigade and Hays's five demi-regiments from Louisiana, all of Early's division. The intrepid Hoke, whose soldiers, by their tenacity, were later to give to North Carolinians the name of "Tar Heels,"[15] was absent. He had been wounded at Salem Church, and his brigade was commanded by the senior colonel, Isaac E. Avery, of the 6th North Carolina.

This regiment, which had been a part of Bee's brigade at the first battle of Manassas, had been partly an outgrowth of the North Carolina Military Institute at Charlotte. There many of its members had come under the inspiration of the devout soldier, author, mathematician, and hard fighter, Major General Daniel Harvey Hill, who had presided over this institution in the days before the war.

Hoke's, or Avery's, brigade consisted at Gettysburg of the 6th, 21st and 57th North Carolina Infantry regiments. It was weakened by the detachment of the 54th Regiment, which had been sent back to Staunton, Virginia, as the escort for the prisoners of Milroy's army captured by Lee at Winchester.

Forming on the right of Avery was the brigade of Brigadier General Harry T. Hays, known as the Louisiana Tigers, and composed in heavy measure of French-speaking Creoles. They had been commanded formerly by Dick Taylor, and with him had won glory under Stonewall Jackson in the Valley. A gay, dashing, guitar-playing aggregation, they could march and fight all day, then sing and dance around the campfires the greater part of the night.

All during the day of July 2 these two brigades had been lying near the Culp spring, in a treeless hollow, or in the open wheat under a sweltering sun.[16] Major James F. Beall of the 21st North Carolina Regiment witnessed the delight with which the men hailed the attack order when it finally ended the almost insufferable suspense. Ewell had at last acknowledged Longstreet's guns and in the approach of darkness was bestirring himself.

The clear notes of the bugle called across the fields. The North Carolinians moved out in sharp alignment, marching toward the valley that divides Culp's and Cemetery hills. Colonel Hamilton C. Jones of the 57th North Carolina, the center regiment, noted the striking manner in which the men kept their order, guiding right on the Louisianians. Years later he applied to the advance the single descriptive word—"beautiful."[17]

The federal artillery greeted the movement with sudden blasts from both Culp's and Cemetery hills. "Really," said Major Beall, "the enemy's artillery, reopening at the going down of the sun, fell like music on our ears."[18] It heralded the moment of decision. The Maine artillery lieutenant, Edward N. Whittier, using a French ordnance glass, had taken the range during the afternoon on all of the positions in front of Culp's Hill and now he blazed away with case shot. The six guns of his battery fired simultaneously, startling the Massachusetts regiment at the base of Culp's Hill, which could not yet detect the Confederate approach over the broken ground.

Whittier then ordered the guns to fire at will. Although the range was measured and the firing unusually rapid, the attacking line moved firmly ahead. It crossed fences and stone walls and worked over the rising ground behind the Culp homestead. Loading and firing as they advanced, and slowed at times by the 6 guns looking directly down on them from Culp's Hill and the 16 others of the three batteries on Cemetery Hill, the Confederate force required almost an hour to pass the 700 yards of rocky and uneven ground between the Culp house and the wall and trenches at the base of East Cemetery Hill.[10] Here, with a dash and shout, they crashed through the first Federal line.

The first assault proved costly. The brigade commander, Colonel Avery, had bravely but imprudently ridden his horse. He was the only mounted man in the column and was among the first to fall.[20] Just as his men reached the Federal line at the base of the hill, he was hit by a musket ball that passed through his neck and shoulders and knocked him from his mount. The attack swept on without him and it was some time before the brigade knew he had fallen. Prostrate and alone, he perceived that his wound was mortal. His shoulder and right arm were shattered. But he took a lead pencil and paper from his pocket and scribbled a note to his fellow officer, Lieutenant Colonel Samuel McDowell Tate, who had succeeded to the command of the 6th Regiment when Avery took the brigade. The faltering handwriting showed life was ebbing. The message merely said, "Tell my father I fell with my face to the enemy."[21] Nothing needed to be added. The place where he fell was marked by his men, but more enduring than their marker, which long ago was lost or obliterated, were the words of the note which spoke so truly the spirit of the Southern army.

The 57th North Carolina restored its alignment that had been broken by the rough terrain. The brigade wheeled to the right and looked up the hill toward the main Federal wall and breastworks. The commander of the 57th, Colonel Archibald Campbell Godwin, was now the senior officer and assumed command of Hoke's brigade. A native of Nansemond County, Virginia, he had heard the call of gold when the precious metal was discovered in California and, at the age of nineteen, had trudged across the continent on foot. He had been among the few able to turn the lure into abundant yellow washings and had amassed wealth. But when Virginia seceded he hastened eastward, leaving most of his tangible assets behind. Colonel Hamilton C. Jones, writing in later years, bestowed on him the ultimate accolade: "A Virginian in command of a North Carolina regiment and afterwards a North Carolina brigade, he was as much beloved and admired by those under him as if he had been a North Carolinian, or they Virginians."[22] He fell a year later, at Winchester.

It was now 8:20 P.M. Darkness came on rapidly after eight-fifteen. Hays, by virtue of his seniority, commanded the two brigades. Creoles from the Louisiana bayous, together with descendants of the British,

Scottish, and German pioneers who had pushed down the mountain valleys or westward across the North Carolina plains and Piedmont, now began together their ascent of East Cemetery Hill. Hays thought his command was saved from annihilation by the gathering darkness and the smoke which billowed down the hillside from the three batteries on the summit and the infantry brigades firing rapidly from three directions. The heavy locust trees afforded some protection. But speed had bearing on the success. The charge up the steep incline was impetuous. Breaking through a second Federal line halfway up the hill, the storming party appeared to gather strength as it pressed forward. With a confident shout the men at length reached the crest.

Von Gilsa's German New Yorkers broke.[23] They had not expected such internecine fury in New World fighting. The Federal Corps commander, Howard, was standing on East Cemetery Hill with Major General Schurz. "Almost before I could tell where the assault was made," said Howard, "our men and the Confederates came tumbling back together."[24] The North Carolina and Louisiana troops poured over the Federal entrenchments. Daniel Harvey Hill could have asked no better from his old cadets. Godwin, the prospector, was finding the gold of victory in these Pennsylvania hills.

The situation on the Federal front was rendered critical by the flight of Von Gilsa's brigade. Colonel Andrew L. Harris, commanding another of Howard's brigades, ordered the 17th Connecticut Regiment to fill the hole left by the disappearance of Von Gilsa. The movement of the 17th Connecticut in turn left an opening in Ames's front and through this gap rushed the 6th North Carolina and 9th Louisiana. They pushed out on the plateau occupied by the Federal artillery. Here they struck another of Ames's regiments, the 75th Ohio, and rolled back the right companies, causing the balance of the regiment to change front and face to the right. The other North Carolina and Louisiana regiments continued the battle in their front at the summit.

The Federal artillery, deprived of infantry support, fought desperately but ineffectually. Some of the cannoneers seized abandoned infantry muskets and jabbed and rammed at their assailants with the butts, while others fought with handspikes, clubs, and stones. The swabbers wielded their sponge staffs and swung them in wide arcs. Storming past the guns of Weidrich's New York battery, the North Carolinians unloosed a volley point-blank into Ricketts' light Pennsylvania artillery. "Over the wall and into the midst of the guns they came," said the Federal Colonel J. P. S. Gobin, "and around these

raged the conflict with whatever was in reach to fight with."[25] Two
of the batteries were overrun and the guns captured. Some of Ricketts'
pieces were spiked. Howard was fearful that the Confederates would
carry off all this precious artillery and scurried about for reinforcements. Hays hoped to turn it on its owners, given a little assistance
and time.[26]

Suddenly the shouting stopped. Hays noticed that the uproar of the
guns died away. There were moments of quiet and suspense on the
crest of Cemetery Hill. "At that time," said Hays, "every piece of
artillery that had been firing at us was silenced."[27]

It was an instant of which the people of the South who had been
eagerly awaiting reports from Pennsylvania might well take note. Here
was a high point, possibly *the* high point, of Lee's invasion of the
Free States.

"We had full possession," said Captain Ray, "of East Cemetery
Hill, the key to General Meade's position."[28]

But there was a Federal general of quick perception and action only
a quarter of a mile from the point of the Confederate break-through.
Hancock, who had just saved the Federal center following the defeat
of Sickles, now, more by intuition than direct information—"a happy
inspiration," a Federal officer called it[29]—sensed the menace on his
right. Although Howard had not asked him for assistance, Hancock
ordered Colonel Samuel S. Carroll, commanding a brigade of Ohio,
Indiana, and West Virginia troops, augmented by the 106th Pennsylvania that had just returned from beating off Wright, to hasten to East
Cemetery Hill. Then he added the 71st Pennsylvania as insurance.[30]

Carroll was a young officer of great verve and dash, a West Point
graduate born in the District of Columbia, whose war service was
marked by a succession of promotions for gallantry on nearly every
major field of battle. His brigade was in instant motion. Night had
now fallen. Although a moon had risen and lighted the fields at inter-
vals, the East Cemetery plateau, wooded, was in darkness. Carroll
had no guide, but he led his men directly toward the flashes from the
Confederate infantry fire across the plateau.

The moment of final decision had arrived. Howard was collecting
remnants of the First and Eleventh corps. Nearest at hand was Colonel Kryzanowski's brigade of 800 men, who went in at the double-
quick. Newton began to extend the line of the First Corps to enable
Howard to shorten his front.

The 6th North Carolina had formed behind the stone wall that had earlier marked the Federal line. Twice the Federal advance was driven back by infantry volleys. Anxiously the Carolinians looked for reinforcements. None came.

Hays heard the approach of Carroll's brigade through the darkness but held his fire. He had been warned that he possibly would encounter other Confederate units in his front. Longstreet had attacked on the far right and might come crashing through the Federal lines. Johnson was assailing Culp's Hill on the left. Rodes presumably would be giving support close at hand, to be followed by Lane with Pender's division. This mass of infantry advancing through the darkness might be the forward elements of Longstreet's or Rodes's triumphant line. The memory of how Jackson had been shot by his own men hung heavily over the army.

Hays waited hesitatingly until Carroll had fired his third volley. Even then he would not have replied, perhaps, except that Carroll's men were now so close that the flash of their muskets revealed their blue uniforms. Then Hays ordered his men to return the volleys.

But the brigades of Hays and Godwin had been wasted and exhausted. The feeble fire which the men could offer checked the oncoming Federals only momentarily. Hays found the enemy overlapping him and moving toward his rear. The rear of the North Carolinians was likewise threatened. Reluctantly he ordered a retreat. Godwin called back his regiments in concert, forced to abandon a greater fortune in fame than he had ever left in gold in California. The survivors of the two brigades retired 75 yards to another fence, then dropped back to their original position near the Culp farm buildings. Hays brought back 4 Federal flags and 100 prisoners.

Here Gordon had held his supporting brigade, awaiting word from Early before following the assault up the hillside, but Early had not cared to risk his sole available reserve. His only other brigade, Smith's, had been sent to the far left to watch for the approach of Stuart. Said Captain Neill W. Ray of the 6th North Carolina: "By not supporting Hoke's brigade of North Carolina and Hays' brigade of Louisiana in the storming and capturing of Cemetery Hill, the battle of Gettysburg was lost. I do not know whose fault it was, but I feel assured in saying it was not the fault of the assaulting column."[31] In writing to Governor Vance about the 6th Regiment, Lieutenant Colonel Tate declared: "Such a fight as they made in front of the fortifications has never been equalled." Then with pride he said, "This regiment has had a reputation, you know."[32]

That was the story. Half a mile in front of the main Confederate lines, two brigades again had fought hand to hand unaided, until almost surrounded by reinforcements rushed up from three Federal corps.

Very likely they would have effected a permanent lodgment on East Cemetery Hill had Rodes provided the expected assistance on the right. Through the afternoon before the advance the negotiations went back and forth to establish concert of action between Early and Rodes. Late in the day Rodes did make ready. His division occupied the town of Gettysburg, and he found it impossible to advance in battle order through the streets. He, too, was concerned about his right, and about the co-operation of Lane, of Hill's corps, who had taken command of Pender's division.

Rodes finally disentangled himself from the streets and notified Lane that he would attack at nightfall. Ramseur and Doles advanced their brigades toward Cemetery Hill at about the time Hays and Avery left the Culp farm but had much farther to travel. That Ramseur's men were in high spirits was suggested by their countersign: "North Carolina to the rescue."[33]

Word passed through the ranks that the attack would be made just as the moon rose. Pocketbooks and last messages were given to the surgeons. "We marched boldly forward, sweeping through the tall wheat," said a lieutenant. They reached the base of the hill with the graveyard above them, facing the opposite slope of the same broad elevation Early's brigades were assailing from the other side. At the base a low command passed along the two brigades for the men to lie down. Ramseur was crawling ahead personally to inspect the position his troops were to assail. The brigades waited in suspense. The moon went behind a cloud. Someone said, "Boys, if I come out of this battle alive, I'm coming out with a Yankee canteen."[34] A Confederate canteen "leaked like a sifter," being two simple tin plates often fastened insecurely.

Finally Ramseur returned. He had reconnoitered, then conferred with Doles; together they had concluded that the fortifications on the front of the hill, with numerous batteries ready to pour in a direct and enfilade fire, made an assault impractical. The order ran along the line: "Fall back without noise." Again, with nobody of higher rank at hand, the important decisions were being made by brigadier generals. But scarcely were two brigadier generals better qualified to pass judgment on the full capabilities of their troops.

"Our general saw the foolhardiness and madness of the attempt," said an officer writing home. "For that act there are many Carolina mothers . . . who should pray blessings on his head."[35]

The best Rodes could do that late hour was to consolidate a line along an abandoned road bed facing the hill and await the coming of morning.

Responsibility for the failure rested first with Ewell and then with Early. Ewell had not established with Rodes the imperative need for Rodes and Early to attack simultaneously nor had he co-ordinated their movements. He does not appear to have given any personal, on-the-spot supervision. Early had sent his brigades into a most desperate undertaking without certainty that they would be assisted, and then had withheld Gordon while the impetus of the assault was being wasted on the plateau and among the stone fences at the summit. With Gordon's help, the army might have obtained a lodgment on Cemetery Hill for the night, subject to exploitation at dawn by Rodes or by Pickett's fresh division.

Either the attack should not have been made or it should have been supported. Lack of careful preparation and lack of follow-through— the second a fault that would plague Early and ultimately lead to his dismissal from the command of an army—explained the repulse of Hays and Godwin. Two small brigades could not do more. Early had failed to seize the heights on the previous afternoon when the opportunity was most inviting. Now he had compounded that error by wasting some of the South's best soldiers against them.

The penciled note Tate wrote Governor Vance at the first opportunity after the assault was in compliance with his promise to the 6th North Carolina: "to acquaint you with the truth, that history may speak truly of them." He distrusted Early and said that since Avery had been killed "we have no friends" who would tell of their action. The official report Early was yet to write was already suspect. Tate explained that he knew it had not been written, but he still felt free to attack it as a "monstrous injustice." An irascible general does not inspire confidence. "I know the disposition so well that I look for no special mention of our regiment," he said. Then he summed up the account of how the regiment and the 9th Louisiana had planted their colors on the heights: "The enemy stood with a tenacity never before displayed by them, but with bayonet, clubbed musket, sword and pistol, and rocks from the wall, we cleared the heights and silenced the guns. In vain did I send to the rear for support. . . ."[36]

The day would come when North Carolina regiments would chant of their dislikes:

"Old Jimboden's gone up the spout,
And old Jube Early's about played out."[37]

But in July 1863 Jube was making some peculiar decisions for Lee's left wing at Gettysburg.

4. Old Man Greene Holds the Trenches

Lieutenant Randolph H. McKim, aide and spiritual counselor to the devout Brigadier General George H. Steuart, stood on the far left of Lee's army, east of Benner's Hill, on the afternoon of July 2 and held his watch in hand. It was approaching four o'clock.

He was counting the artillery discharges after Longstreet opened his bombardment on the other flank of the army, and he found that Longstreet was firing at a rate of 180 guns a minute. Considering that Alexander had put only 46 guns into batteries on the Confederate right, and that each gun had to be swabbed, loaded, and rammed between discharges, either some astoundingly rapid firing was in progress or some woefully poor arithmetic was involved in the gentle McKim's calculations.[38]

But the point was that Ewell, who has often been excused for delaying his attack on the score that he could not hear Longstreet's bombardment, could not have escaped it with a feather bed over his head. He must have been at that time in his Hanover road headquarters north of the Culp buildings, between Gettysburg and Rock Creek, where he had moved from the almshouse to be closer to his troops. But wherever he was along his lines, the bombardment, so easily heard by McKim and by the Federals across the Rock Creek Valley on Culp's Hill, was surely audible to him and to his staff, who should have been on the alert for it.

This bombardment, under Lee's orders, was the signal for Ewell to launch an assault on Meade's right, sustaining Longstreet's assault on the Federal left. Ewell's attack was an imperative part of Lee's battle plan. After the commanding general had reluctantly assented to the entreaties of Ewell and Early that their corps be retained in its extended position on the army's left, encircling Meade's right even to overlapping part of his rear, he had assigned to Ewell a role of easy execution but of profound bearing on the Southern army's prospects of victory. Ewell's duty was simple and clear: when Longstreet attacked on the right, Ewell would attack sharply on the left to prevent Meade from shifting troops to bolster his left after Longstreet assailed it. The advantage Meade would have in moving fresh units to points of danger had been clear to Lee when he looked out with Trimble from the almshouse cupola. He had taken every precaution to neutralize that advantage when he finally developed his plan, the main feature of which was the simultaneous attack on the two flanks, followed by the attack *en echelon* by brigades moving from the right to the center of the army.

The record of Ewell's personal activities at this stage of the battle remains hazy: apparently his movements were not sufficiently emphatic for anyone to take especial notice of them. For more than twenty hours Johnson's division lay in attack formation east of Rock Creek, mainly north of the Hanover road, Nichols on the right, Jones in the center, and Steuart on the left, with Walker, commanding the Stonewall Brigade, drawn up perpendicularly behind Steuart. He faced east in the woods just beyond a little stream that meanders southward and joins Rock Creek directly east of Culp's Hill. Steuart's brigade was thus on Lee's left flank, with the Stonewall Brigade in support. Steuart at his closest point was a mile from the eastern face of Culp's Hill, which under Johnson's attack plan—when it was finally put into effect—he was to assail; he was six miles, following Lee's long front, from Longstreet's right, but only about two miles away as the crow flies.[39]

While Johnson's division idled through the hours, McKim held religious services. The men, awaiting attack orders, seemed thankful for this divine worship. For many it was their last.[40] Not until after 6:00 P.M., when Meade was stripping his right of troops to support his left and center, did Ewell order Johnson's division into motion. Not until about seven-forty-five—at best three hours late—had the regiments worked their way to the eastern face of Culp's Hill. Most of the intervening period had been devoted to Ewell's artillery preparation, which was being wasted against the vacant hillside and empty trenches that in the afternoon had housed the Twelfth Corps divisions of John W. Geary and Alpheus S. Williams, now off to their left giving Meade the margin of security he needed against Hood, McLaws, and Anderson. They had moved out about six-thirty, and their old lines were vacant by seven.

Johnson's artillery was commanded by youthful Major Joseph W.

Latimer, who rimmed the crest of Benner's Hill with guns. The Federals replied and the exchange gave the illusion of activity on Lee's left, but the six batteries Ewell had put into position on Benner's Hill were stark targets on the open crest, being shielded by nothing resembling embankments or lunettes, or any natural protective ridges, or the stone fences so common in this Pennsylvania section, and having not even a covering of timber for the gun crews. The Federal artillery across the sharp valley of Rock Creek had the security not only of the heavy woods and numerous natural citadels, but also of stone and log fortifications on which Wadsworth's and Slocum's men had been laboring incessantly, part of them for more than twenty-four hours.

The result of the exchange was unfortunate for Ewell's guns. Instead of making a quick assault—which would have complied with Lee's orders and held the Federal infantry in place—he undertook a sustained bombardment, allowed the Federal infantry to avoid him, and ended with most of his artillery silenced and his gun crews crippled. Among the mortally wounded was the competent young commander, Major Latimer, who had been a sophomore at the Virginia Military Institute when war broke and was not yet twenty-one when he fell. He was hit while withdrawing the guns. By Ewell's orders, one battery was left in its exposed position to cover Johnson's infantry advance.

Meade, in his anxiety to save his left from Longstreet's crushing blows, had denuded his right recklessly. Culp's Hill had been garrisoned strongly after the arrival of Slocum's corps. Wadsworth's division of the First Corps already was on the summit when Slocum took his position in the early morning of July 2. Wadsworth held the left of the crest, looking north and west toward Cemetery Hill and Gettysburg. Slocum, whose corps included only two divisions, extended Wadsworth's line on the right. Geary's division was on Wadsworth's right, curving around with the convex crest of the hill and facing east, and Williams' division was to the right of Geary. Williams' reached along the broken, wooded shoulder of Culp's Hill, passing in front of a spring in a grove near the Henry Spangler homestead, but continuing along Rock Creek through the woods to McAllister's Mill. The length of the Twelfth Corps line from its juncture with Wadsworth to its termination in a marshland near the mill was slightly less than a mile.

Largely on the insistence of Brigadier General George S. Greene,

Geary's division had devoted the morning and early afternoon to building entrenchments, which, when completed, were formidable barricades of logs, fence rails, cord wood, and rocks. Greene's brigade of upstate New Yorkers was on Geary's left, joining Wadsworth, which proved to be a fortunate coincidence for the Federal army because of Greene's dogged character. Slocum objected strenuously to Meade's order stripping his right wing and baring the entire east face of Culp's Hill to an enemy known to be lurking in heavy force in the woods on the other side of Rock Creek, and was able to wring permission from Meade to leave a single brigade.[41] The order to move the entire Twelfth Corps has commonly been characterized with one word—"suicidal." Having Geary's division on the march toward him no doubt gave Meade comfort while Longstreet was hammering on his left, but the division remained unemployed and actually was not needed. Two brigades, Candy's and Kane's, became confused, strolled down the Baltimore pike, moving farther and farther from the battlefield, and accomplished nothing except to get lost.[42] Williams' division gave Meade valuable help in his repulse of Anderson, and Lee's army would have been well served had he been kept engaged on Culp's Hill by Ewell.

Greene's brigade, being on Geary's left and next to Wadsworth, naturally was selected to remain behind. For three hours that night the fate of the battle and possibly the destiny of the Federal cause hung on the stanch shoulders of "Old Pop" Greene, whose sturdiness had much to do with saving the hill for the Federals when its loss would have been calamitous.

Pop Greene was in his sixty-third year, probably the oldest Northern fighter on the field after the guerilla John Burns had been hauled off to his place of safety. His New York youths, mostly under twenty-one, looked on him as an ancient out of the Revolution or the War of 1812, though he had not graduated from West Point until 1823 and was a hardy man who spent most of his time in the saddle. He outlived many of these soldiers who had thought a bullet would hurry to get him before his normal time ran out; he died in his ninety-eighth year and retained the West Point longevity record until early in 1958.[43]

Greene was a native of Warwick, Rhode Island. He stood second in his class at West Point, where he instructed for a time; after years of dull garrison duty in the West, he resigned to build railroads and other works, among them the reservoir in Central Park, New York,

and the enlarged High Bridge over the Harlem River. On the outbreak of war, he became colonel of the 60th New York, recruited
along the St. Lawrence River.

Greene's five New York regiments on Culp's Hill aggregated 1,310,
of whom 70 were officers. To have stretched them over the Twelfth
Corps's old front would have meant a musket every four feet, or a
line as thin as skirmishers. Greene did extend his front more than
a fourth of the distance, into the rifle pits that had been dug by
Kane's brigade; then he set his men to digging a traverse at the end
of his line, turning back to his right and facing south. When the thin
line was manned Greene had a single rank, with no reserve, with only
about one foot between elbows. The Federals could hear in their
rear the attack being made on Cemetery Hill by Hays and Avery;
finally in the rapidly approaching darkness Johnson's four brigades,
Jones and Steuart in front, followed by Nichols and Walker, were seen
descending the opposite slope and entering the waters of Rock Creek.
It was 7:45 P.M.

The creek was waist-deep, but the Confederates held their lines and
began in the twilight to work their way up the rough, eastern slope of
Culp's Hill, which though not so precipitous, resembled Little Round
Top and had the same importance to Meade's right as the other eminence had to his left. Culp's Hill rises above Cemetery Hill which is
due west and looks down to the southwest on Cemetery Ridge, behind
which was Meade's headquarters. Scattered around were the reserve
artillery and ammunition trains. More important still, the hill commanded the Baltimore pike, Meade's avenue to Baltimore and Washington, which many of his less stalwart soldiers were already employing. Possession of Culp's Hill was essential to Meade's safety. He
might lose other positions and still hold his lines, but not Culp's Hill.

Steuart, on the Confederate left, kept the 1st North Carolina in
reserve as a flank guard, then worked up the hill until he struck
Greene's line in Kane's old rifle pits. Darkness was coming on rapidly,
but the engagement soon grew heated. Because of the dim light the
lines drew close, and Steuart's losses became so heavy that he sent
Lieutenant McKim to bring up his reserve regiment. McKim, using
the flash of the muskets as a guide, led the Carolinians up the incline
until he encountered a line of troops 100 yards ahead. They were
discernible through the thick foliage and fading light only by their gun
flashes, which seemed to be directed downhill. He had the regiment
open fire, only to learn an instant later that he was firing on the 3rd

North Carolina, Steuart's right flank regiment.[44] This anguishing
mistake delayed but did not unnerve Steuart.

On Steuart's right Brigadier General John M. Jones led his Virginia brigade, supported by Nicholls' Louisianans, commanded by
Colonel J. M. Williams in Nicholls' absence, against Greene's left.
Here for more than two hours the battle raged in the dusk, then the
darkness, with intense fury. Pop Greene would not be pushed aside.
He retained his mount, riding back and forth behind his lines through
the trees and boulders. Four times Jones charged the entrenchments,
but each time the thin line held, and Jones was forced back to the
foot of the hill, only to re-form his lines for another assault.

Greene meantime called for help. One of the closest regiments
was the 6th Wisconsin, which Wadsworth sent. All day the First
Corps officers in groups on Culp's Hill had watched Longstreet's distant assault, and gained the bitter impression that Meade was being
defeated on his left. About dark they heard the Rebel yell sound suddenly on their right. The desperate nature of the battle there was
speedily apparent. A staff officer directed Colonel Dawes to take his
regiment and find Greene. When approached, Old Pop, who in his
fighting clothes looked more like a farmer than a general, wrote
his name and brigade on a card in the darkness and handed it to Dawes
to identify himself. The incident suggests the intensity of the firing. But
he managed an audible order that put the Wisconsin men behind some
breastworks which, by a quick descent, they recovered from Confederates already entering them. Dawes was followed by the 14th Brooklyn, and Greene's left began to take on strength.

On his right he was less successful. Steuart's flank skirmishers
overran the empty trenches reaching toward McAllister's Mill, then
the Marylander again worked his way up the hill to Greene's immediate front. He found Greene's entrenchments to be five feet thick,
made of earth and heavy logs and protected by abatis. Old Greene
had built railroads, bridges, canals, and was a specialist on entrench-
ing, as his works showed. Steuart's men had been fighting in front
of them for two hours when, at nine-thirty, by a sudden assault, the
1st North Carolina and 1st Maryland regiments burst into the works.
As Lieutenant Green Martin, Company B, 1st North Carolina, led in
the storming party, he received a mortal wound.[45]

Johnson now had a lodgment on Culp's Hill and easy access to the
soft underside of the Federal army. He had part of Greene's trenches,
but the traverse protected the Federal flank and prevented it from

being turned. In the darkness, or fitful moonlight, neither Steuart nor Johnson knew at first of the full prize that was open to their taking. Two hundred yards beneath them, in easy musket shot, was the Baltimore pike, the jugular vein of Meade's army. Hancock and the entire Cemetery Ridge position could be taken in reverse. Surely the ridge could be carried from the rear with any kind of co-operation from Hill's corps in its front. One factor, and only one, nullified the importance of Steuart's achievement—it came at 9:30 P.M. Even in the darkness Johnson might have set off a panic by driving into Meade's reserve ammunition trains and thus notifying the Federal army that he was operating in its rear. His troops were ample for the purpose. The Stonewall Brigade had scarcely been scratched, Jeb Stuart had finally reached the battlefield, and Extra Billy Smith, who had diligently completed the restful duty of watching for him on the York pike, was now available for battle service.

Skirmishers from the 1st North Carolina managed to locate the Baltimore pike and sent back word to Johnson that it was within musket shot.[46] Johnson tried to get Smith's brigade in motion but Smith lacked orientation. Darkness paralyzed him and he stopped.

The two armies settled down to await the coming of daylight. Spangler's Spring gave water to both blue and gray soldiers. Water details of both armies exchanged banter as if they were all on a school picnic. Nobody wanted to deny anyone water, even if he had to be disemboweled with a bayonet the next morning.

Confederate McKim became quite worked up over the assertion that the trenches his chief, Steuart, occupied were those from which the Federal troops had been withdrawn. The withdrawal orders, he asserted, *"came from the men of Steuart's Brigade, and they were delivered at the point of the bayonet."*[47] The Confederate dead in front of the captured works told the correct story.

Late at night the Twelfth Corps brigades began moving back to the right and to their amazement found Confederates in their old entrenchments. Kane and Candy came back first from their goose chase down the Baltimore pike, and eventually Williams. All they could do was lie in the fields north of Power's Hill, reach up to Greene's right and wait. Ewell was aware that the hard part of the battle was still ahead of him. He had lent Extra Billy Smith's brigade of Early's division to Johnson, and followed it now with the brigades of O'Neal and Daniel from Rodes's division. Clearly something would erupt on Culp's Hill on the morning of July 3.

Through the early part of the night Johnson's soldiers trying to sleep on the hill heard the rumbling of artillery on the Baltimore pike, the sound receding instead of advancing. They reported it to Ewell, and the corps commander for a time expected to wake up the next morning and find the Federal army gone. The noise stopped soon after midnight.[48] Could it have been the beginning of a Federal withdrawal? Some of the officers of both armies went to their graves believing so. It was, in any event, an unexplained mystery that seemed to be a part of one of the dramatic episodes of the battle, enacted by the Federal officers while the soldiers slept.

CHAPTER TWENTY

The Council and the Captain

1. The Corps Commanders Vote on a Plan

Sometime about 11:00 P.M. Meade called a council of corps commanders to review the fortunes of the army and recommend the course for the next day.

That he called the council was evidence of his uncertainty. It had become almost axiomatic to behind-the-lines observers that councils were vacillating, pusillanimous, and pretty certain to come up with the wrong decision.

Lincoln was not impressed with them; neither Lee nor Jackson had held them. But in the Army of the Potomac they had become something of a fixture and they were not wholly unrelated to the checkered nature of that army's career. Meade's council, it developed, had positive opinions about what should be done, whereas the commanding general seemed uncertain. It made bold, concise recommendations which Meade accepted. It reversed the old proverb that "councils never fight."

There is much to suggest that Meade wanted to withdraw to his Pipe Creek line on the night of July 2, and the evidence is sufficiently cumulative not to be brushed aside lightly. Certainly it is not conclusive, but the contention of some of his own officers that he preferred withdrawal is a valid part of the Gettysburg story. He did not retreat and he did not at any time issue an order to retreat; consequently, he is entitled to full credit for staying on the field and slugging it out with Lee on the third and decisive day of the battle. But quite

307

naturally he was uncertain about the wisdom of this course, and surely there was reason for him to be uncertain.

The Army of the Potomac had, indeed, been severely handled. The First, Eleventh and Third corps had been broken up, and while the survivors had been reassembled to an extent, troops that had been so thoroughly routed and disorganized are rarely fully serviceable in the same battle. The loss of field and company officers had been staggering. The Second and Fifth corps had fought hard battles, and they too had suffered heavily in loss of men and officers. Meade's casualties for that day alone were around 8,000 killed and wounded, plus an indeterminate number of missing. The First and Eleventh corps losses on the first day aggregated nearly 9,000 in killed and wounded, and thus the army had lost 17,000 plus the missing, which would include upward of 5,000 prisoners. That night Meade estimated his combat strength at 58,000, based on the reports of his corps commanders.[1] The figure seems approximately correct. It shows how his great army was being hacked away.

Two corps were fresh, the Sixth and Twelfth. The Sixth, with the exception of Shaler's brigade, was concentrated, that night, on the left, about the Round Tops, and gave ample protection to that flank. The Twelfth was on Meade's right, poised to undertake the recovery of its old Culp's Hill position on the coming of daylight.

Butterfield, Meade's chief of staff, testified before the Committee on the Conduct of the War that Meade had ordered him on the morning of July 2 to draw up a retreat order and had taken pains to see that he was uninterrupted in an upstairs chamber until he could complete the work. But the conference at which this was to be considered was the one rudely broken up by Longstreet's attack on Sickles. Prior to Meade's hasty departure to the front at the time Longstreet struck, Butterfield had completed the withdrawal order and handed it to Meade. There was no doubt about this order. John Gibbon read it, and checked on the map the towns it mentioned.[2] But here again, as in Meade's instructions to Pleasanton—to be prepared to cover a retreat—the commanding general was merely taking precautions, as any conservative general might under similar circumstances. The only thing peculiar about this order was that it was later discovered that all the copies had been destroyed. According to Assistant Adjutant General Seth Williams, none could be found among his records, and: "it must have been destroyed within a day or two after it was prepared."[3] The destruction of this order—by whom none ever knew—

was one of the weak points in the long insistence by Meade's close followers that he never had the remotest thought of retiring from Gettysburg.[4]

Some of Meade's partisans came to believe that there had never been such an order; that Butterfield conjured up the whole notion. Of course, Meade did not intend to use the order except in an emergency. Even while it was being drafted, he sent Halleck a dispatch at 3:00 P.M., ending: "If not attacked, and I can get any positive information of the position of the enemy which will justify me in so doing, I shall attack."[5] That did not look as if he were considering a withdrawal. But Lincoln in his blessing to Sickles clearly believed that a withdrawal that afternoon was under consideration.

Meade sent another dispatch to Halleck at 8:00 P.M.—while the fighting on his right was at its height but before he had lost the Culp's Hill trenches: "I shall remain in my present position tomorrow, but am not prepared to say, until better advised on the condition of the army, whether my operations will be of an offensive or defensive character."[6]

Why did Meade, after sending these two messages to Halleck, then call a meeting of his corps commanders to pass judgment on the very question of whether he should or should not remain at Gettysburg and continue the battle? Meade had been around long enough, of course, to know that consistency and achievement do not always work together under the same yoke. Did he change his mind abruptly after he lost the Culp's Hill trenches? His actions that evening do not give a clear picture of his impulses. One thing was elucidated by Birney: that when Meade began the council, he stated that he would be governed by the verdict of his corps commanders.[7] That in itself was a surprising acknowledgment for a commanding general locked in a desperate engagement about which he, at headquarters, would be presumed to know more than anyone else on the field.

The main room in the quaint little headquarters house was ten feet by twelve, and into this crowded Meade, Butterfield, the wounded Warren, Newton (First Corps); Hancock and Gibbon (Second); Birney (Third); Sykes (Fifth); Sedgwick (Sixth); Howard (Eleventh); and Slocum and Williams (Twelfth). Adjutants and couriers hovered outside. Meade seemed to look on Williams as an uninvited guest at a wedding, and the men of "Pap" Williams' division learned of this and described it as "droll,"[8] apparently believing Williams capable of advising God himself in a pinch; but Slocum thought he was still commanding the right wing and brought along Williams as commander of the Twelfth Corps, though Meade had not understood it that way and thought Slocum's wing assignment had ended. Pleasanton was not there, being engaged, as he explained, in making arrangements for the army's withdrawal, a task that held him until midnight.[9]

A rickety bed stood in one corner and a cheap pine table in the center, and thus, with candles providing the only light, the council began talking. The generals leaned against the walls, some lolled on the shaky bed, some sat on the floor, and all were composed. They were "as modest and unpretentious as their surroundings," and "as calm, mild-mannered and as free from flurry or excitement as a board of commissioners met to discuss a street improvement," according to the report Williams carried back.[10] There was a wide range in the capacity of these officers of fairly equal rank, as would be the case in any army, but Meade must have known that the opinions of Hancock, Sedgwick, Slocum, and Newton would have a broader base and be more closely reasoned than those of Sykes, or Howard, or some of the others.

Unfortunately, no actual minutes were kept. Butterfield recorded the votes on a yellow slip which years later was found among Meade's personal papers, and by this tally sheet it is known that every corps commander voted in favor of remaining on the field.[11] The votes were taken in writing and the most succinct statement was that of Slocum: "Stay and fight it out." Prior to the vote, much talk dwelt on the possibility of Lee's undertaking a flank movement to Meade's left—the plan Longstreet had proposed. Newton, who was looked on by many as the best engineer and one of the best infantry commanders in the army, anticipated the flank movement and also saw faults in the details of the line which ought to be corrected; but he voted against withdrawal. Gibbon quoted him as saying, "This is no place to fight a battle in."[12]

All the time Meade expressed no opinions and made few comments of any nature.[13] Warren was asleep in a corner, said nothing, and apparently heard nothing. Hancock's views coincided with Slocum's. In the discussion, he said the Army of the Potomac already had retreated too much.

When Meade announced his decision after the voting, different generals heard him say different things. Gibbon heard him say, "Such then is the decision." Slocum, whose integrity none could doubt, heard him say: "Well, gentlemen, the question is settled; we will remain here, but I wish to say I consider this no place to fight a battle."[14]

Doubleday was not present but was so close to Butterfield that the source of his information is not to be doubted, and he was positive in his assertion: "There can be no question that, at the council referred to, General Meade did desire to retreat."[15] Doubleday presented some attractive reasons why this would not have been bad judgment; he felt that the enemy was weak on ammunition, was too far from base, and was too exhausted to pursue; that the Army of the Potomac could be refitted where Lee could not; and that it would be the safer course not to risk a complete defeat by remaining on the field, when withdrawal might win the campaign even if it lost the battle.

Birney, as he rode back from the council, told his adjutant, Major J. B. Fassitt, that Meade had said Gettysburg was no place to fight in.[16] Unhappily, one of the methods followed in this and the Sickles controversy was to impeach the character of some of those who questioned the full measure of Meade's discernment. The whole matter might have been kept minor except that such a controversy makes good newspaper copy. When the question of whether Meade did or did not want to leave Gettysburg got into the press, Meade's son and aide circulated among the generals who had been at the council and found that most of them had not heard Meade express dissatisfaction with the battlefield. The wording of the younger Meade's question was either not penetrating enough or too penetrating: he said the commanding general (Meade) desired a short statement "giving your recollection of what transpired at the council," and mentioning "whether he at any time insisted on a withdrawal of the army from before Gettysburg."[17] The word "insisted" was of course out of place. Nobody ever contended that Meade "insisted" on a withdrawal. Had he done so, the army most certainly would have been withdrawn, for he commanded.

Hancock refused to make any statement to such a query. He had appeared before the Committee on the Conduct of the War, and although he had said nothing there about the withdrawal issue, he declined to elaborate on his testimony. He held himself aloof from all these petty controversies. No answer was received from Slocum. Those who thought Meade had wanted to withdraw, or had been toying with the notion, included Slocum, Birney, Pleasanton, Butterfield, Doubleday, and, respecting the afternoon conference, Sickles. So many high-ranking officers manifestly would not have been engaged in a cabal against Meade's reputation. Those who had not heard him express dissatisfaction included Sedgwick, Newton, Sykes, Williams, Gibbon, and Howard.

The issue had some bearing on how close the Federal army was to retreating on the night of July 2; irrespective of Doubleday's argument, retreat would have lost the battle and possibly the war. There are, however, other interesting aspects. Meade decided to stay, but was it altogether, or even mainly, because of the vote of his corps commanders?

The controversy, the lack of minutes of the council, and the uncertainty about what was said, even by the commanding general, left open to question the exact nature of what went on behind Meade's lines during the middle hours of the night of July 2, when Ewell's scouts heard the receding rumble of artillery wheels and Pleasanton was so busy making withdrawal arrangements that he could not attend the council. The suggestion believed by many in the South that Meade was actually beginning a withdrawal has been a subject of interesting speculation. According to this belief, or deduction, it was not the council of war that kept him on the field, but a minor incident which had occurred that afternoon on the other side of the mountains.

2. *Lee's Letters Are Found in the Mailbag*

Captain Ulric Dahlgren had a roving Federal cavalry squadron, which on July 2 he took across South Mountain at the Monterey Pass, led through Waynesboro, and halted at Greencastle, where he was greeted much as if he were a conqueror, to the gratification of his pride and vanity.

He had just reached the age of twenty. His father, Admiral John Adolf Dahlgren, after whom the big, bottle-shaped, smooth-bore naval guns were named, was one of Lincoln's close confidants, whom the President, with his tinkering and inventive instincts, delighted to visit. Ulric was well acquainted with all the great figures of Washington whom the President brought to Admiral Dahlgren's house, stopping on visits to the Navy Yard, and probably could have had any type of military career he desired. But he had entered the dashing cavalry arm and was serving as a foot-loose patrol of Kilpatrick's division around Gettysburg.

Young Dahlgren was about to engage in an exploit that would fascinate the army and the capital, enliven the newspaper columns, win him a jump promotion over two grades, from captain to colonel, and ultimately lead to his death in circumstances that left him one of the figures in the Federal Army most odious to the South.

The sight of Dahlgren's blue column, in the rear of Lee's army, aroused the citizens who had watched so long the passing of the Southern host. The entire Greencastle population was brought to the streets. Dahlgren, accepting their cheers for a time, ordered them back into their houses and restored the town to a normal appearance. Then he hid his troopers around the corners of the public square, making ready to intercept any communications on that afternoon between Lee's army and the Confederate capital, for he was on the main route. With the trap set, he climbed to the belfry of the Dutch Reformed Church and surveyed the surrounding country with his glasses.

Sure enough, a Confederate cavalry company was approaching from the south. It was not well led and came into town blindly, without even outriders or an advance party. Jeb Stuart had contributed so much already to Lee's discomfiture that it seems superfluous to mention other instances. But if Stuart had been on hand properly discharging his duties, one of which was to protect the army's communications, Lee's rear would not have been exposed to the molestation of such small Federal bodies as Dahlgren's. Robertson, Jones, and Imboden were supposed to be watching, but their forces were limited and Stuart's vigorous leadership was lacking.

As the Confederate troop came into the square, Dahlgren's men dashed out suddenly with a shrill yell, fired their pistols, and, more by the impetuosity of their assault than by their numbers, threw the Southern column into disorder and flight.[18] The prisoners included 3 officers and 14 men.

Then Dahlgren discovered what a treasure of intelligence he had captured. The detachment was bringing up the official Richmond mail addressed to General Lee, and even a cursory examination disclosed to the Federal cavalry captain its significance. Dahlgren set out at once for Meade's headquarters, about thirty-five miles away. So concerned was he lest he encounter another body of Confederates and have his packet wrested from him, on leaving Waynesboro, he split his command and had part of the men form a barricade on the eastern hill by piling wagons and farm equipment across the roadway. He crossed again over Monterey Pass, moved by Emmitsburg, and finally handed the Confederate mailbag to Meade's chief of staff, General Butterfield. Butterfield read the letters and went at once to

Meade. The hour is uncertain, but it must have been near midnight.

The correspondence showed that Lee's force on Seminary Hill was the full load of the invasion.

Lee would not receive the reinforcements of Corse's, Jenkins', or Cooke's brigades. He would have to detach men from his own army to keep his communications open. Beauregard would not establish a second front in Virginia threatening Washington. This highly important phase of Lee's planning—the assembly of an actual army, or "an army in effigy," at Culpeper, to menace the Federal capital from the south while Lee was on its flank in Pennsylvania—had collapsed.

All this was clear from the correspondence. Meade need not worry about any sudden foray on Washington, or the arrival of reinforcements for Lee, or operations against his own rear, or anything except the embattled Confederate army in his immediate front. The reading of these dispatches bolstered Meade's confidence; if, as some have felt, it had been as limp as a wisp of smoke, it quickly came as stiff as a gun barrel.

Lee's recommendation had been given rather cavalier treatment in Richmond. The captured correspondence, soon published in the Northern press, showed that Jefferson Davis had not been diligent to create an army at Culpeper. Though Lee had proposed it in his letter of June 23, Davis had never heard of the idea when Adjutant General Cooper went to discuss it with him on the night of June 28. The government was behind with its correspondence. Instead of threatening Washington, Davis was fearful about Richmond with Lee away.

All that the Richmond authorities would have had to do was pull together the brigades and regiments scattered through Virginia and the Carolinas. But they did not recognize what Lee had emphasized: that every man who could be spared had to be thrown into this great invasion effort. A New York *Herald* story dated July 3 told that a member of Longstreet's staff had been captured heading south, on his way, he said, to Culpeper, "to ascertain what had become of Beauregard's army." It merely had never been born.

Colonel Edward A. Palfrey, of New Orleans, claimed to have obtained, second-hand of course, Dahlgren's own account of what had happened respecting the dispatches. In summary: when Dahlgren saw their importance, he rode to Meade's headquarters, arriving shortly after midnight, and found Meade consulting with his corps commanders. Meade, according to this version, had already resolved to withdraw to Pipe Creek, but a perusal of the captured dispatches caused him to change his plans abruptly. The artillery was ordered back into position. Palfrey found his own conclusions verified to some extent, or to his own satisfaction, by the unusual preferment given young Dahlgren by Lincoln and Stanton.[19] It appeared they thought he had performed an unusual service indeed. It is a fair speculation—but only a speculation—that young Dahlgren told Lincoln and Stanton how he delivered the captured dispatches just in time to hold Meade on the battlefield; and that Lincoln's response, as in the instance of Sickles, was an impulsive "God-bless-you-for-it" attitude. The only solid fact is that Captain Dahlgren became Colonel Dahlgren almost on the spot.

The bounty of fortune and glare of fame were strong stimulants for the young man, whose story should be completed. In the following March Colonel Dahlgren, still not twenty-one, led part of a cavalry attack on Richmond. Next morning William Littlepage, thirteen, saw a "dead Yankee" in the ditch and searched for a watch, but all he found was a cigar case and memorandum box. In the box was enough to show it was Dahlgren's body, together with orders by Dahlgren for his men to release the Belle Island prisoners, cross the James River to Richmond and "destroy and burn the hateful city, and not allow the Rebel leader Davis and his traitorous crew to escape." Another admonition was: "The men must keep together and well in hand, and once in the city it must be destroyed, and Jeff Davis and Cabinet killed."[20] The orders were a burst of individual braggadocio, of course, but they united the South, stiffened the resistance, and probably contributed to many Northern casualties.

About the rumbling of the guns there could be little doubt. Pickets in the midst of a deadly battle do not manufacture information and then have it verified by other attentive scouts. Steuart's men reported it; Ewell had the account to him verified; Nicholl's Louisiana brigade must have heard it also, because the story was current in New Orleans after the war and Palfrey declared there were men in that city who would testify to its correctness.[21]

Is it possible they heard Candy trying to get back to Culp's Hill? This wandering brigade that had marched down the Baltimore pike never knew where it was going or where it had been. Said Captain Joseph A. Moore of the 147th Pennsylvania:

It seemed to be a night of bewilderment to all, for I have failed to discover any two members of the 147th whose views coincided on the route traversed.[22] It was a night of slow, tiresome, roundabout maneuvering, through fields, over fences, now on the pike; then a whispered halt! a rest for a few minutes; the men asleep! Wake up! a forward march. . . .

But all the while Candy's men were coming closer to Culp's Hill and the rumbling artillery was moving farther and farther away.[23] Were they Federal guns or phantom guns? Was it the apparition of unconquered Stonewall rolling his specter caissons over the Pennsylvania hills on a long flank march behind the Federal lines? Many great battles have had their mysteries. Gettysburg has "The Strange Case of the Retiring Artillery."

3. The Wandering Cavalryman Returns

Lee's headquarters cottage that night was crowded with officers, some seeking orders, some greeting friends from other commands, some responding to the summons of the commanding general; adjutants coming and going; altogether a pack that made passage inside the little house difficult. Outside, crowds of soldiers hovered in the neighborhood, those who liked to gossip about what the army's next move might be, drawn to the headquarters like yokels to a magician's tent.

At ten o'clock soldiers were cooking supper along the streets of the town, obviously in top spirits as a result of the battle progress that day. An unidentified officer summoned to headquarters found it crowded with staff officers who had assembled from all parts of the battlefield. At eleven o'clock a stir of muffled excitement and suspense passed over the crowd as two muddy, fatigued generals, with staffs, dismounted on the Cashtown pike, walked through the short yard and entered the headquarters building. The long-missing J. E. B. Stuart, followed by Fitzhugh Lee and Major Henry B. McClellan, Stuart's adjutant, was reporting his arrival to the commanding general.

Only one account is known to exist of the meeting between Lee and Stuart and it is far from satisfactory. It was set down fifty-two years after the battle by Brigadier General Thomas T. Munford, who was not present but who had the information from Major McClellan. Munford, one of Stuart's colonels in the Gettysburg campaign, wrote from Roanoke, Virginia, July 24, 1915, to Mrs. Charles H. Hyde, of Lookout Mountain, Tennessee, that McClellan had told him the meeting was "painful beyond description."[24]

Lee had raised his arm—there was no suggestion that he intended to strike Stuart, but more likely, it seemed, in a gesture—and said, "General Stuart, *where have you been?* Not one word from your command has been received by me! Where have you been?"

Stuart, according to McClellan, "wilted." He told Lee the course he had followed and, in what would appear an appeal for mitigation, added, "I have brought you 150 wagons and their mule teams."

"Yes, general, but they are an impediment to me now! Let me ask your help. We will not discuss the matter longer."

Lee then gave Stuart directions for his part in the battle of the next day, and Stuart left. On the same page of this letter, but in a different hand, was a memorandum note that Munford said McClellan had quoted one more of Lee's remarks: "I have not heard a word from you for days, and you the eyes and ears of my army."

Lee at first reflected wrath, then great tenderness, the notation added.

The account does not fit conveniently into one's conception of Lee's character, in which self-control was the dominant note. Considering the lapse of more than half a century before it was written down, the wording cannot be looked on as in any respect exact. Stuart surely could not have attached great importance to 150 wagons (the correct number was 125) when the army had thousands. Nor would Lee have called them an impediment now, however much they may have slowed the cavalry earlier.

Remembering how George Cary Eggleston had observed that Lee spoke in crisp, compact, even epigrammatic sentences, one is more inclined to accept the conventional story of the meeting, in which Lee, when the cavalry commander presented himself, looked at him and said, "Well, General Stuart, you are here at last."[25]

For those who knew Lee, there could scarcely have been stronger censure.

Stuart had reached Gettysburg without difficulty after Lee's scout had found him. Colonel R. L. T. Beale, of the 9th Virginia Cavalry, who attended Dickinson College at Carlisle and knew the territory brought down the wagons, the pitiful little exhibit of achievement Stuart had to offer. There was not a modicum of what he loved most—glory.

After Stuart had left, Powell Hill reached the headquarters, where he went about shaking hands with friends he had not seen since leaving Virginia. Apparently he was in the best of spirits and showed no trace of his illness of the last few days. Battle always exhilarated him.

It is not clear, but apparently Hill (of all people!) was receiving congratulations on the day's work. Lee was busy in his office room, but Hill's voice carried to him over the hubbub. The affection of the commanding general for his singular subordinate was warm and genuine, almost fatherly. He attached no blame to Hill for stopping the army's attack when it reached the middle of his corps.

Lee made his way through the crowd of other officers and clasped Hill by the hand. "It is all well, General," he said. "Everything is well."[26]

Then he and Hill walked away from the others—they must have gone into the little back room Lee was using for an office—and talked together for a quarter of an hour. This was about the nearest Lee came to holding a "council of war" that night. Longstreet was sleeping on his saddle; Ewell was preparing for the bloody battle the next morning on Culp's Hill.

The unidentified officer whom Lee had summoned commented that the general looked well, which may have meant that he was recovering from the diarrhea Blackford had found disturbing him earlier in the day. The line of people waiting to see Lee must have looked like the patients in the office of a popular country doctor on a Saturday morning. General Lee was busy with a plan for evacuating the wounded, work a competent staff should have discharged smoothly without ever bringing it to the commanding general's notice.[27] But he dropped everything when Colonel Marshall announced this caller. He thought that this man and a Captain Brockenborough were well acquainted with the upper Potomac fords and he wanted them to go with General Imboden, who was expected to arrive in the morning with his cavalry brigade from Chambersburg, and start a convoy of wounded for Virginia. Lee's staff had been remiss even in the most ordinary of secretarial duties, because Lee had been misinformed and was wasting his time with officers who were intimately acquainted with the fords of the Rappahannock, not the Potomac. An adjutant might have learned this by one or two questions, before showing them in; in fact, a competent adjutant would have acquainted himself with the purposes of most of Lee's callers.

When the mistake was discovered, Lee was advised that the expert on Potomac fords was a man named Logan, from Winchester, Virginia, serving in Rodes's division. He turned at once to Marshall or Taylor—both staff members were with him—and said, "Hunt up Mr. Logan and send him to me at once."[28] It was then 1:00 A.M.

With all this detail, how much attention was Lee actually allowed to give to the renewal of the battle on the morrow? He has been pictured as morose on the night of July 2, believing he was about to be defeated.[29] That obviously was not the case. He was mired down in office work.

"He was full of business," said his caller, "and his strong mind and intellectual energies were taxed to their utmost." This man went on to describe the surrounding scene: "The fences all around the head-quarters were lined with soldiers who had participated in the struggle of the day, relating their experiences. The writer remained with these until the morning sun appeared on Friday, July 3."[30]

That would be the way in such a gregarious, high-spirited army. Men about to continue on the next day one of the hardest fights of human history would prepare themselves by staying up all night talking about it.

4. The Sleepy Armies Fight to Exhaustion on Culp's Hill

Had Ewell possessed prescience, time, and ample men—had Pickett's, a fresh division, been thrown around to Lee's left, augmented by Stuart's newly arrived cavalry—Ewell might have exploited the breech made by Steuart's brigade in the Federal defenses on Culp's Hill, driven past the Baltimore pike and the Taneytown road, and hit the center of the Federal army in its rear.

The soldiers might pray for an hour of Jackson, who would have supplied all the intuitive judgment needed, but even Stonewall would have needed some good brigades. As it developed, Ewell's attack did not go past the flank to the mushy Federal rear—which must have been sensitive and yielding—but directly against the entrenched line, which was as firm as the great boulders amid which it was anchored.

Ewell possessed none of these prerequisites of prescience, men, and time, least of all time. Before he was astir on the morning of July 3, Slocum was ahead of him.

If, on this far flank of the armies, the Southerners were led hesitantly by Ewell, they possessed in Johnson one of their most stubborn fighters. They were opposed by one of the toughest of the Federals—Major General Henry W. Slocum, who would never fight until he had to, and then, as the saying went about army favorites, he confused himself with a wildcat.

He had been a colonel at First Manassas and ended the war heading two corps as commander of the Army of Georgia, and all the time the men serving under him never lost a stand of colors or a gun. Some liked to say it was because Slocum preferred maneuvering to battling—even maneuvering to keep out of sight when hard assignments were in prospect. The instance of his coolly refusing to answer Howard's call to come to Gettysburg without orders on July 1 was an example. The aggregate of the record, however, was different.

Slocum, an upstate New Yorker and West Point graduate (he roomed with five-year-man Sheridan and yet was an honor student), went into the artillery, but while serving at Fort Moultrie he kept his active mind occupied by reading law in the office of the eminent South Carolina judge, B. C. Presley. In 1857 he left the army and hung out his shingle in Syracuse, New York, where he became county treasurer and then a state legislator. There was something independent, even perverse, about him. He wore only a mustache in an army that decreed whiskers. Being an ardent Republican before the war, he became after the war, at a time when almost anybody could be elected under the Republican label, a Democrat, because, though he had been second in command of Sherman's "Bummers," he did not like the "scorched-earth policy" the radicals of Congress were applying to the defeated South. A hard fighter, he was a magnanimous winner; he resigned from the army with the coming of peace, became a Brooklyn lawyer, amassed a tidy fortune, and left a more enviable record than those generals who, like Grant, were ambitious above their talents.

In arranging his battle plans for July 3, Lee had told Ewell to attack on the Federal right as a cover for an assault he was planning against the center, but here was where Ewell lacked time.

Slocum had been up all night making arrangements. Powerful batteries already had been ranged along Power's and McAllister's hills, commanding the valley of Rock Creek and the south and east face of Culp's Hill. The Confederate guns, on the other hand, had been left far behind. They could not be drawn over the rugged ground, and with no cannon Johnson faced the prospect of an uneven battle.

The summer dawn was showing faintly when Brigadier General John W. Geary drew his service pistol and fired a single shot into the air.[31] It was 3:45 A.M. At once an inferno of artillery fire was turned loose on the Confederates rousing themselves in the old Federal trenches or lying in groups at the east base of Culp's Hill. Then the infantry brigades of Candy and Kane let out a rapid rifle fire, which McDougall, Colgrove, and the Eastern Shore Marylanders under Lockwood, in-

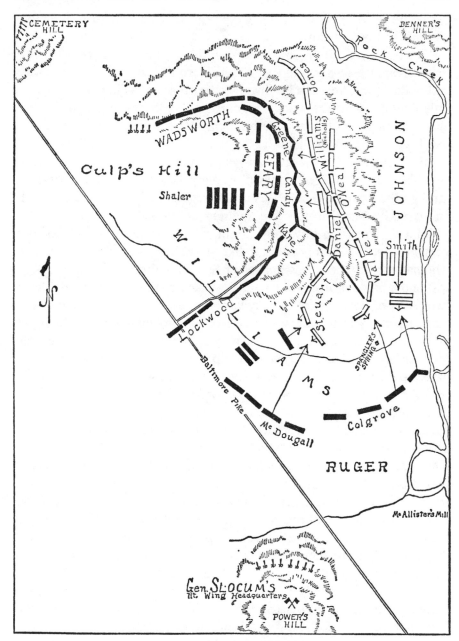

Battle of Culp's Hill. July 3, 1863.

cluding the Federal 1st Maryland, quickly joined. Virtually none of
Slocum's men had had sleep since reaching Gettysburg, and many of
them, lying prone on the firing line at this early hour, fell asleep with

the battle roaring about them. Company officers had to move along the line and prod them.

"We can see no Rebs to fire at," complained a private of the 147th Pennsylvania. He was told that orders were to keep firing "continually and without intermission"[32] through the trees in their front, across a little field and into the woods beyond. There Johnson's Confederates had been planning to do some attacking themselves, but the initiative had been stolen from them.

Pap Williams, whose division was commanded by Brigadier General Thomas H. Ruger, a West Point graduate who had come up through the command of a Wisconsin regiment, was on Geary's right and quickly shared in this pre-daylight fighting.

John W. Geary, a huge man, built solidly, whose size did not prevent him from carrying himself like a soldier, was a Pennsylvanian who had already been postmaster of San Francisco, governor of Kansas, and a colonel in the Mexican War. After the war he would serve two terms of governor of Pennsylvania. At times he was given a wide berth by many in the army because of his violent temper, which was an antisocial characteristic in a man nearly six feet, six inches tall.

Since Slocum had returned to Culp's Hill by way of the Baltimore pike, he was inside the arc that had been thrown around Culp's Hill by Johnson. Geary had taken position on Greene's right, and Ruger continued the line to Spangler's Spring. They faced the old Federal trenches still held at the coming of daylight by the Southerners. Kane's little brigade numbered about 650. Brigadier General Thomas L. Kane had been absent on sick leave for several weeks, but when action was promised, he appeared in an ambulance and tried to command from his bed. His strength was not sufficient and Colonel George A. Cobham, 111th Pennsylvania, who later fell before Atlanta leading his regiment at Peach Tree Creek, took the command.

As a prelude to their infantry attack, the Federal artillery blasted the trenches along the southeast shoulder of Culp's Hill, then Geary advanced on Johnson's right and center while Ruger undertook a flanking movement across the marshy ground and small stream that flowed from Spangler's Spring. Scarcely had this attack been beaten off when Johnson, in desperate fury because he could not answer the destructive Federal artillery fire, responded with an infantry assault along his front. The Confederates came on in three close lines.

"The enemy advanced steadily," said Captain Moore of the 147th Pennsylvania, "and in splendid order, and was certainly under the impression that Lee's hopes depended upon their success." When their columns were less than 100 yards from the Federal position, Geary's long line poured a "deliberate and most deadly fire" into them. Moore said it was with "well-aimed precision, such as old veterans alone could do."[33] The assaulting column was well-nigh destroyed.

McKim wrote in his diary:

The men were mowed down with fearful rapidity. . . . It was the most fearful fire I ever encountered, and my heart was sickened with the sight of so many gallant men sacrificed. The greatest confusion ensued—regiments were reduced to companies and everything mixed up. It came very near being a rout."[34]

McKim made another and a revealing entry in his diary: "The storm of shot and shell was terrible, yet I went to sleep in the midst of it several times."[35]

On this assault Johnson's men obtained a clear view by daylight of the Baltimore pike, littered with the behind-the-lines debris, loaded with wagons and refugees, enlivened by squadrons of cavalry dashing about to check stragglers continually trying to escape from the battlefield. The sight inspired Johnson to redoubled efforts.

Captain Joseph Matchett of the 46th Pennsylvania, McDougall's brigade of Ruger's division, maintained that Johnson had actually reached the pike the night before but, fearing a trap, hesitated and pulled back. He attributed the apprehension to the intervention of providence. "They were made afraid when there was nothing to fear."[36]

Now Ruger's men in turn assaulted the line of Steuart and Walker. Colgrove's brigade made a bloody, impassioned charge. This attack showed how the desperate nature of the fighting caused the soldiers of both armies to forget all else, including any sense of time. The 27th Indiana had begun firing at 3:50 A.M. It helped make the assault on the Confederate works and was beaten off with heavy loss. Later when officers and men tried to establish the time of the assault, some thought it was as early as five and some as late as ten o'clock in the morning.[37] In the attack the 27th moved with the 2nd Massachusetts.

"It cannot be done. It cannot be done," said the Hoosier Colonel Silas Colgrove, commanding the brigade, muttering to himself, when he got the attack order. "But if it can be done," he added, "the 2nd Massachusetts and 27th Indiana can do it." He questioned sharply the adjutant who brought the order, and when assured it was genuine, he declared, "It is murder, but it is an order. Up men, over the works! Forward, double-quick!"[38]

Near the Confederate line the three right companies of the 27th seemed to be knocked over together, and a withering volley hit the rest of the line. "The air was alive with singing, hissing and zipping bullets." They pressed on, but fell short of their objective and the survivors of the two broken regiments had to be recalled. That was much the story with regiments of both armies all along the line.

For seven hours the battle of Culp's Hill rolled up and down the rocky slope, with neither side content to remain on the defensive, and both insisting on carrying their attack to the heart of the enemy's position. Now and again, as the battle would lull momentarily, Johnson would try vainly to catch the sound of Longstreet's battle, which he presumed was raging far off to his right.

Random bullets flew high through the air, passed over Culp's Hill and sang, almost spent, through Hancock's ranks on Cemetery Ridge about a mile away. On Cemetery Hill the men followed Slocum's fight by the sound of the firing and "almost held their breath in anxiety." But Longstreet remained silent in front of them.

Big Geary charged back and forth along the lines like a bull trying to find a gap in a tight fence, while on the opposite side "Clubby" Johnson limped about cursing, admonishing, praying. Back in Richmond, War Clerk Jones had written: "Instead of a sword he goes into battle with a stout cane in his hand, with which he belabors any skulking miscreant found dodging in the hour of danger."[39] But Johnson's tongue must have been sufficient, though some of the men began to call him "Fence Rail" Johnson, which suggested he used his big stick as a bar.

When the battle opened in the morning, the Confederate brigades that had been engaged until ten o'clock on the evening before found themselves short of ammunition. The 3rd North Carolina had but two rounds, and the men hunted about among the dead and wounded and temporarily replenished their supply. Steuart sent a staff officer and a detail across Rock Creek to the reserve ammunition wagons, which were parked a mile and a quarter away, near where Johnson had launched his attack. They emptied boxes of cartridges into a blanket, swung the blanket on a fence rail, and carried the load over the rocks and through the bushes to the front.[40]

The sun came up, burned off a thin morning mist, and beat down with a heat more intense than that given off by the thousands of gun blasts and the hot Federal cannon. Nobody on the firing line got a minute's relief in seven hours of intense fury. The battle here was without any general movement or form, other than that each side fought with the desperate determination to exterminate the other or drive him from the slopes of the hill.

Major Henry Kyd Douglas, concerned that Extra Billy Smith might not get his brigade up in the proper place, had galloped back at 5:00 A.M. and helped the old politician. Smith was "cool and deliberate—too much so, just then,"[41] but he put his men into line. Ewell, in compliance with Lee's orders, although without effort to co-ordinate his movement with any Longstreet might be making, ordered a final attack all along Johnson's line. Daniel brought his shredded brigade up from Rodes's line to support Steuart and both he and Steuart, looking at the forbidding hill in front of them, deplored the attack order. The line Steuart would have to assail was that of the traverse trench running almost at right angles to his own line. Behind this was a sort of ravelin giving the Federals two parallel entrenched lines, each heavily manned. Steuart remonstrated, but when the time came he jumped from the trenches with his men, formed a line of battle on the other side, ordered bayonets fixed, and, drawing his sword, charged up the hill at the head of his brigade. The brigade was checked on a flank but reached to within twenty or thirty paces of the Federal entrenchments before being beaten back. By this time Culp's Hill was being called by the Confederates the "Hill of Death."

"That last charge on the third day was a cruel thing for the Third," said Colonel S. D. Thurston, of the 3rd North Carolina.[42] At the end of the fight it had 77 muskets out of 300, a loss of almost 75 per cent.

When time came for a withdrawal, Johnson's men were not pursued. The firing seemed to stop by mutual agreement. Both armies were exhausted. It was 11:00 A.M. Johnson retired slowly to the foot of the hill, then formed a new line along the west bank of Rock Creek, which he held for the remainder of the day. Slocum did not undertake to dislodge him.

When the results were reviewed, it was recognized that Culp's Hill had been the scene of some of the most determined, sanguinary fighting of the war. Geary always thought that the main battle of Gettysburg was won by Meade's army on Culp's Hill.

Kane's brigade found 500 dead Confederates in its front. Somewhere among them was a squat little man, Wesley Culp, a private in Company B, 2nd Virginia, of the Stonewall Brigade. He was twenty-four and because he was only five feet tall, Colonel Douglas had had a special gun made for him.[43] Where he fell he could look at the house where he was born. Like Henry Wentz, he had gone to Virginia to sell Gettysburg carriages and Southern eyes made him stay.

CHAPTER TWENTY-ONE

Pickett, Pettigrew, and Trimble

1. Arrival of the Virginians

At two o'clock on the morning of July 2 the long roll sounding in the Chambersburg streets aroused Pickett's men, and well before dawn they were on the road—dusty that morning—marching toward the battlefield with which their name will forever be associated.

The division was the smallest in Lee's army because the two veteran brigades of "tough old bull-terrier" Montgomery D. Corse and "ardent" Micah Jenkins[1] had been left to defend Richmond—temporarily, by Lee's intentions. Had Pickett received his missing brigades, his division would have numbered about 8,000, instead of less than 4,800 at Gettysburg,[2] and the difference might have been decisive.

Pickett had been busy in Chambersburg while awaiting the coming of Imboden's cavalry to relieve him as the rear guard for Lee's army. All liquor had been kept under lock in the courthouse.[3] He had destroyed the railroad and railroad shops, depots, and all public machinery, though he had reluctantly followed Lee's orders respecting private property. Now that most things made of iron had been twisted, rolling stock flattened, turntables burned, the last cattle rounded up, and the country cleaned of provisions, he regarded his duty done and his rear-guard service ended. He was happy, as he passed the ruins of Thaddeus Stevens' Caledonia Iron Works, to see that Early had made a delay there unnecessary.

Pickett's division, after the detachment of Jenkins' Georgia Brigade, was all-Virginian. As it took up the march, Garnett headed the column. Brigadier General Richard Brooke Garnett, forty-four years old, was a somewhat pathetic figure for whom keen sympathy existed in Lee's army. A West Point graduate who had remained in the old Federal service, he was, under the Confederacy, an officer about whom one of Jackson's most embittered personal battles had centered; the unforgiving Stonewall had pursued it almost to the point of persecution.

Garnett was an able soldier, the son of an Essex County plantation owner, whose devoted twin brother had given his life in nursing sufferers in the yellow-fever epidemic in Norfolk in 1855.[4] Richard was of the same selfless and courageous mold, but too easy in his attitude to suit his zealous commander. Garnett had first incurred Jackson's displeasure in the mid-winter Romney campaign of early 1862, on which Jackson pressed his poorly clad men so mercilessly through the snow that the discipline of Loring's division broke down, a storm of public criticism was aroused, and in the charges and recriminations, Jackson submitted his resignation, which he withdrew only after the intercession of Governor Letcher. Garnett commanded the Stonewall Brigade in the campaign and had his brush with Jackson when he rested his cold and hungry men as they toiled over the mountains. Jackson rode up, demanded the reason for the delay, and reprimanded him curtly.[5]

This should have been warning to Garnett that Jackson would expect the ultimate with scant thought of the men as long as they had an ounce of strength left to give for the cause. At the battle of Kernstown, where Jackson had not imparted his plans to his subordinates, Garnett fought with great bravery and ordered a retreat only when the line was broken elsewhere by a superior Federal force. His officers thought the withdrawal justified, but Stonewall was enraged and believed it lost the field for him. He was unsparing thereafter in his efforts to keep Garnett out of any command in the Confederate service. He relieved the brigadier general and preferred charges. The case dragged on for months, much to Garnett's distress, because Jackson never was in one place long enough for a court-martial to convene.[6] Finally Lee, short of trained officers as usual, assigned Garnett to Pickett's brigade for the Sharpsburg campaign, after Pickett had been wounded at Gaines' Mill, and the charges against him were pigeonholed in the light of his unfailing diligence.

But his spirit had been crushed by the reproaches of his severe commander and stirred by a deep sense of injustice, and he believed

Jackson guilty of deliberate falsehoods. When Pickett became a major general in September 1862, Garnett retained the brigade permanently as a part of Pickett's division.

Garnett's charitable nature was disclosed when he grieved over Jackson's death and marched as a sincere mourner in the procession of generals who followed the great leader to his grave, but Pickett's widow and biographer felt that "the sensitive mind of the brave general . . . never recovered from what he regarded as a stigma upon his military career."[7] That was the reason, she felt, and probably Pickett had the same belief, why Garnett insisted on leading the brigade at Gettysburg at a time when he was scarcely strong enough, after a debilitating illness, to sit on his horse. Nothing in his animated conduct suggested his physical weakness. He gave his orders with vigor and rode the lines with apparent enthusiasm. The only hint was that he wore his heavy blue overcoat[8] on the hot summer day.

Walter Harrison, inspector general of Pickett's division, thought that Garnett's whole purpose was to expose himself, even unnecessarily, "to wipe out effectively, by some great distinction in action, what he felt was an unmerited slur on his military reputation."[9] Eppa Hunton said of him simply, "He was one of the noblest and bravest men I ever knew."[10]

Armistead's brigade followed Garnett. Probably no officer in the army was more spirited and none possessed a more martial family background than Brigadier General Lewis A. Armistead. Like Wilcox, who was a career soldier of comparable rank out of the old army, he was somewhat above the average age of Lee's brigadier generals. But this, as in Wilcox's case, appeared due to chance instead of any reluctance by superiors to trust him. In this army of extraordinarily able brigade commanders, Armistead, by his courage, experience, and good judgment, would have stood in nearly everyone's top group.

Armistead's family had left its name on some of the peaks of American history. His uncle, Major George Armistead, had commanded Fort McHenry and kept the flag flying in Baltimore harbor during the attack by the British fleet September 13-14, 1814, which inspired Francis Scott Key to write "The Star-Spangled Banner." His grandfather had served under Washington. His father, Captain Walter Keith Armistead, an army engineer who had graduated in the second class at West Point, had laid out the defenses of Norfolk, Virginia, in the War of 1812. The gallant defense of Norfolk and the American victory in beating off a formidable British expedition headed by Major

General Sir Sidney Beckwith, June 1, 1813, had heartened the country at one of the most depressed moments of its history.

The Armistead family was from New Market, Virginia. Though Lewis was born in New Bern, North Carolina, he entered West Point from Virginia, and would have been graduated in 1838 had he not been expelled in his junior year because he wielded a plate effectively against Jubal Early's head. Early's scalp was merely cracked and there would be no basis for any supposition that this might have permanently affected Early's military judgment; nor did it retard Armistead's career, for, despite his ejection, he went in the service with a commission. His father had become the army's chief engineer and a brevet brigadier general, and was closely associated in the Florida wars with blunt old Zachary Taylor under whom Lewis became a second lieutenant in the 6th Infantry in 1839.

Young Armistead showed unusual bravery in the Mexican War and won repeated citations and brevets. He was on garrison duty with his good friend Hancock at Los Angeles when war came in 1861, but when the decision had to be made, he crossed the continent with Albert Sidney Johnston and cast his fortunes with Virginia.

Third in the column was the brigade of handsome James Lawson Kemper, thirty-nine years old. His only military experience had been as a volunteer captain in Mexico, though he reached Taylor's army too late for the battle of Buena Vista. He had graduated from Washington College (now Washington and Lee) at Lexington, Virginia, and studied law in Charleston; had turned to a legislative and legal career, served ten years in the Virginia House of Delegates, and for a term was Speaker. He volunteered on the outbreak of the war, commanded the 7th Virginia at First Manassas, served in turn under Early, Longstreet, and A. P. Hill, and finally was assigned under Pickett.[11]

Some of Pickett's men had been stationed beyond Chambersburg and a march of about thirty miles was ahead of them, but they left the town with loud shouts and with "more spirit and élan" than their leader had ever before observed in them.[12] The hot July sun burned their faces as they marched over the mountain. At Cashtown they heard the "sullen booming" and learned, in the staccato language of a behind-the-lines quartermaster, that the army had: ". . . been fighting for two days—driving the Yankees all the time—got 6,000 prisoners already—hurrah for Lee! . . ."[13] Soon they passed "acres of bluecoat prisoners" in a field and came upon a beautiful, "splendidly caparisoned black charger" which had been General Reynolds' mount. Within four miles of the battlefield in the late afternoon the division bivouacked, and the men "fell asleep to the lullaby of deep reverberations from the battle front."[14]

Pickett had ridden ahead to report to Longstreet. Being punctilious about the formalities, he did not go to Lee, but sent Harrison, his inspector general, to advise the commanding general of his presence and the proximity of his troops. Harrison reached Lee on Seminary Ridge while he was watching Anderson's brigades going into action. It was probably about 7:00 P.M. He told Lee that Pickett had marched twenty miles that day but with two hours' rest would be ready for use on any part of the field. Lee apparently was sanguine about the progress of the battle. At about that time Longstreet had signaled to him: "We are doing well."[15]

"Tell General Pickett," he said, "I shall not want him this evening; to let his men rest, and I will send him word when I want them."[16]

2. Lincoln's Protégé is Longstreet's Favorite

The drum roll sounded at 3:00 A.M. on the morning of July 3, and in the predawn blackness Pickett held a conference with his three brigadier generals—a "heart to heart powwow," he called it.[17] Pickett had not been apprised of the battle plans and the "powwow" turned out to be more frolicsome than somber. "Old Man Armistead," who was all of forty-six, and a widower like Pickett, though not a suitor, took a ring from his little finger, handed it to the love-smitten division commander, and said, "Give this little token, George, please, to her of the sunset eyes." In writing about it to his sweetheart, Pickett gushed with sentiment: "Dear old Lewis—dear old 'Lo' as Magruder always called him, being short for Lothario."

Whiskered, thoroughly military, ripened in middle age, Lewis was anything but a blade. Pickett, however, was in the clouds with thoughts of "My Sallie," the beautiful young LaSalle Corbell, whom he would marry after the Gettysburg campaign, and he must have looked on all the world as lovers. Longstreet, in after years, in his life long diligence to protect Pickett, told of his subordinate's devotion to the military profession, "tolerating no rival near the throne," except for the "beautiful, charming and talented lady"[18] he was courting.

Sorrel was not certain but that the lady held the scepter and military duty sat on the footstool, remembering how Pickett, while at

Suffolk, would steal off to see her without leave, asking him to cover up with Old Peter in case of difficulty. Sorrel was fearful an emergency, or movement of the corps, might occur while the general was A.W.O.L., but Pickett's need to go was desperate.

Typically Sorrel would say, when Pickett came to him, "No, you must go to the Lieutenant General."

"But he is tired of it and will refuse; and I must go, I must see her. I swear, Sorrel, I'll be back before anything can happen in the morning."[19]

Sorrell would not allow himself to be persuaded, but Pickett went nevertheless.

"Nothing could hold him back from that pursuit," according to Sorrel, who added, "I don't think his division benefited by such carpet-knight doings in the field."[20]

Pickett said he would take Armistead's ring to John Tyler, the Richmond jeweler, and have it made into a breastpin, "set around with rubies and diamonds and emeralds," with Sallie as the pearl. As they parted, Pickett grasped Armistead's hand. "Good luck, old man," he said warmly, as he rode off through the dawn to find Longstreet.[21]

For a time rain threatened northwest of Gettysburg. Clouds and mist hung low over the countryside. The order of march to the field was Kemper in the lead, followed by Garnett and Armistead, a normal rotation for the day which accounted for the assault order that placed Kemper and Garnett in the line and Armistead in support. At 7:00 A.M., the division was strung out behind Seminary Ridge, part of it in a field of rye. In front of the men was a long line of artillery, silent after the heavy duty of the day before; on the far left the roar of Slocum's artillery and the incessant rattle of musketry were the only indications that a battle was in progress.

The sun burned through the mist and soon the day was hot and humid. "Few believed they would be killed," said David Johnston of the 7th Virginia, but an exception was the colonel of that regiment, W. Tazwell Patton, known everywhere as one of the courageous, tough fighters of the army. He always had a presentiment that he would be hit, and he usually was, and his men knew that some day the bullet would be final.[22] His great-nephew, Lieutenant General George S. Patton, Jr., would be outstanding in the Second World War.

Marching with Armistead was the adjutant of the 9th Virginia, James Frank Crocker, of Isle of Wight County, Virginia, through whom a nostalgic pathos must have stirred, for he was returning after thirteen years to the scene of his scholastic triumphs at Pennsylvania College in Gettysburg. Now he could look out from Seminary Hill on the little town with its tree-lined streets, and see the college tower and long building ahead of him. Perhaps some of his old professors were in its halls. Crocker looked across at the Federal heights and told a group of the officers that it would be "another Malvern Hill."

Lee's attack plan was simple—to use Pickett's fresh division as the shock troops in an effort to break the Federal center. The Confederate commander had to continue the battle. He could not withdraw after two days of successful fighting. His attacks on Little Round Top and Culp's Hill had caused the Federal army to concentrate on its flanks; hence, its weakest point must be its center. The many advantages gained on July 2 convinced him that victory was possible on the third. He was no more inclined to favor Longstreet's enveloping movement around the Federal left than on the first day. The battle was joined and he would fight it to a decision on this ground.

Pickett and Pettigrew would advance on the same line. Pettigrew now commanded Heth's division. Two brigades would be added from Pender and two from Anderson. Stuart would be sent to Meade's rear to aggravate and pursue the Federals in case Pickett and Pettigrew achieved a break-through.

At 8:00 A.M. Pickett was summoned by Longstreet to the crest of Seminary Ridge, where he found the corps commander in a conversation, only one degree removed from heated, with General Lee. Pickett quoted Longstreet's words overheard as he came up:

Great God! Look, General Lee, at the insurmountable difficulty between our line and that of the Yankees—the steep hills—the tiers of artillery—the fences—the heavy skirmish line. And then we'll have to fight their infantry against their batteries. Look at the ground we'll have to charge over, nearly a mile of that open ground there, under the rain of their canister and shrapnel.[23]

Lee answered in what Pickett described as "his firm, quiet, determined voice, "The enemy is there, General Longstreet, and I am going to strike him."[24]

Longstreet's approach was rough, but that could not have impaired Lee's judgment. There is wonder that he could have been won to a hazardous alignment of his army by Early's persuasiveness, but rejected Longstreet's cautioning peremptorily. The reason undoubtedly was that being locked in battle, he would accept no less than a final decision.

Lee, Longstreet and Pickett rode along the line of Pickett's infantry. The men had been ordered to lie prone so as not to attract the attention of the enemy signal station clearly seen on Little Round Top, and had been told not to cheer. They merely lifted their caps as Lee and the others passed. Pickett, at his first opportunity, went off to write another letter or add a paragraph to his sweetheart:

Well, my darling, their fate and that of our beloved Southland will be settled ere your glorious brown eyes rest on these scraps of penciled paper—your soldier's last letter, perhaps.[25]

With Lee, Longstreet, Pickett and Armistead in close proximity on Seminary Ridge, about to launch an attack, it would have been natural for all of them to think back sixteen years to the storming of a citadel even more forbidding than the slopes of Cemetery Ridge.

Engineer officer Lee had provided the plan by which Scott had reached Mexico City. As Scott's army faced the towering fortress of Chapultepec, which seemed impregnable, Lieutenant Armistead was at the head of the 6th Infantry storming party. He was first to jump into the formidable ditch surrounding the castle and among the first to fall wounded. Near by was Lieutenant Hancock of the 6th, and a few paces behind, carrying the American flag, was Lieutenant Longstreet, who fell grievously wounded. As the colors dropped they were snatched up by Lieutenant George E. Pickett—newly from the academy—and carried forward.[26] In the words of Longstreet, Pickett "was first to scale the parapets" and "was the brave American who unfurled our flag over the castle."[27] For raising the Stars and Stripes and also the regimental flag of Longstreet's and his own 8th Infantry over the heights that gave the Americans Mexico City, Pickett, a low-ranking lieutenant, was brevetted captain.

Pickett maintained a fairly even level of mediocrity as a general, but when he rose it was to unusual heights. "A singular figure indeed!" exclaimed Sorrel, who retained through his life the memory of the day when the erect, well-built man of medium height, with a neatly fitted uniform and an elegant riding whip, reported to Longstreet to command a brigade in his division. His appearance, according to Sorrel, was "distinguished and striking." But what amazed the chief of staff was his extraordinary hair. "Long ringlets flowed loosely over his shoulders, trimmed and highly perfumed." That was not the most of it. His beard, likewise curly, was fragrant in the extreme, giving out, as Sorrel put it, the "scents of Araby."[28] In an army so stingy of time that Jackson would not let Garnett feed his men, where sleep was rationed scantily, and every moment had to be employed in the cause of independence, Pickett found ample leisure for arranging his coiffure and primping, as well as for writing his lengthy love letters. Still—apparently to Sorrel's surprise—he made in many respects a good brigadier general.

Pickett had been born in Richmond, Virginia, but owed his army career to a foxy Springfield, Illinois, lawyer, Abraham Lincoln, who procured his appointment to West Point from Illinois by interceding with Representative John Todd Stuart, of the Third Illinois District. Lincoln had served with Stuart in the Black Hawk War and had joined him as a law partner when, a melancholy, near-destitute young politician of twenty-eight years, he had first gone to Springfield. Stuart was a first cousin of Mary Todd.

Another of Lincoln's close friends was Andrew Johnston, a Springfield lawyer, who later returned to practice in Richmond, Virginia. The attachment between Lincoln and Johnston was based on the aspiration of both to write poetry. They exchanged their compositions, among them being Lincoln's famous poem of twenty-two verses on "A Bear Hunt," written when he was thirty-seven.[29]

Johnston's nephew, George Edward Pickett, came to Springfield to study law under his uncle, and Lincoln took a fancy to the frank, sensible young man. Pickett, not desiring to excite his uncle's choler, made Lincoln his confidant when he developed an aversion to lawbooks. His cousins, Harry Heth, Basil Duke and John Hunt Morgan, all of whom became Confederate generals, were talking of West Point, and when Pickett imparted to Lincoln his secret ambition to go there, the shrewd lawyer soon came up with the appointment from Congressman Stuart.

Thereafter, even in the grip of a deadly war, Pickett always spoke reverently of Lincoln,[30] and Lincoln used no harsher term about Pickett than "the rascal."[31]

Longstreet had met Pickett first at West Point,[32] and had been with the 8th Infantry when Pickett joined it as a second lieutenant in 1846. "In memory I can see him," wrote Old Peter affectionately thirty-five years after Gettysburg, "of medium height, of graceful build, dark, glossy hair, worn almost to his shoulders in curly waves, of wonderous pulchritude and magnetic presence. . . ." His temperament was "open, frank and genial," and never did he by one word blame or censure his superior officers.[33]

When Sorrel took orders in an emergency, he could see how the corps commander always looked after Pickett "and made us give him things very fully; indeed, sometimes stay with him to make sure he did not get astray." That and the perfume caused Sorrel to summarize: "Such was the man whose name called up the most famous and heroic charge, perhaps, in the annals of war."[34]

But there were pinnacles, as at Chapultepec. His humanitarian service was extraordinary among the Northwest Indians, where he learned the language and dialects of the tribes, taught them, translated for them the Lord's Prayer and some of the American hymns and airs, and became known to the Nootkams and Chinooks as the "Great Chief," all of which indicated that the garrison years—which wore down many regular officers and sent some of them to the bottle— were not wasted by Pickett.

In the dispute with Great Britain over San Juan Island in Puget Sound, he refused to be budged with his sixty-eight men when threatened by a British naval force with a thousand, and said to his men calmly, "We will make a Bunker Hill of it."[35] War was averted and Pickett remained on San Juan until he resigned his commission to go with the Confederacy.

Yet despite Chapultepec and other Mexican engagements, in all of which he showed his mettle, and his resolution at San Juan, there was in the minds of some a question about Pickett's personal courage. Eppa Hunton rode along the lines at Suffolk with Pickett and his staff, past a position exposed to enemy fire, and noticed that Pickett, and his staff after him, lay flat against the necks of their horses, which amazed the colonel, who considered it showed a very bad example for the troops. Hunton, though he knew it was imprudent, rode "bolt upright in my saddle," and wondered about his general.[36]

3. Alexander Brings up the Guns

With staff and orderlies riding the lines, Lee's party was large enough to command the attention of enemy sharpshooters, and occasionally the Federal artillery threw a shell at them. Scattered about were the dead, wounded, and wreckage of the July 2 battle. The pleading eyes of a Federal Zouave, mortally wounded, seemed to beseech Lee's aid and compassion, but he was beyond the help of either the commanding general or physicians working over the field.[37] Although the dead were being buried, the number was so large that not much progress had been made in the early morning.

West of the Wheat Field Lee and Longstreet encountered General Wofford. The morning had advanced considerably, because Wofford placed the meeting as "before the artillery opened fire." He would scarcely have done so if it had been some hours before the bombardment, which opened at one. As they looked over the terrain Wofford told Lee he had nearly reached the crest of Cemetery Ridge on July 2. Lee asked him if he could go there again.

"No, General, I think not," Wofford replied.

"Why not?" asked Lee.

"Because, General, the enemy have had all night to entrench and reinforce. I had been pursuing a broken enemy and the situation is now very different."

Lee rode on without contradicting Wofford; still, he was not dissuaded. His confidence in the striking power of his army was strong. He seemed to have special trust in Pickett's Virginia division. When it had passed through Richmond for Drewry's Bluff in February, War Clerk Jones noted in his diary: "General Lee writes that this division can beat the army corps of Hooker, supposed to be sent to the Peninsula. It has 12,000—an army corps 40,000."[38] Jones may have been a little askew with his figures, but probably not about Lee's reliance on Pickett's men.

Meantime Lieutenant Colonel E. Porter Alexander had received orders before daylight to post the artillery to cover an assault, and he was busy assembling guns. Dearing's battalion of artillery had come up with Pickett, giving the corps a welcome addition. Longstreet had placed Alexander in charge of the First Corps artillery without notifying Colonel J. B. Walton, commander of the Washington Artillery and the ranking artillery officer of the corps. Friction was averted until the brooding years after the battle. Now Alexander, as Longstreet's personal representative, labored diligently all morning to arrange an impressive artillery line in front of the infantry. He was an officer given to action, and he stirred the artillerists to unusual efforts. He put 75 pieces along the First Corps front, the right of the line resting on the high ground at the Peach Orchard that had been wrested from Sickles, and the left joining the artillery of Hill's corps, which would take part in the bombardment of the Federal center.

Despite the potentially explosive situation with Colonel Walton, the

Washington Artillery was brought up from reserve near the Cashtown road and put in the middle of the line. Alexander had all the artillery animals that had been taken to the rear for pasture and forage returned to the front to move the guns into position and give mobility in the impending action. Caissons that had gone to the reserve trains for fresh ammunition supplies were brought forward. Guns were drawn over from Devil's Den.[39] He borrowed from General Pendleton, chief of the army's artillery, seven 12-pounders of Richardson's Battalion of the Third Corps artillery. He looked over the ground behind the lines carefully, found a safe spot for these guns, and put them by as a reserve so they would be available to accompany Pickett's troops on the advance. If the other batteries should be disabled or depleted of ammunition, here at least would be seven pieces with fresh horses and full ammunition chests, ready to support the infantry at the critical moment of the battle.[40]

Aware that an army operating so far from its base is never flush with ammunition, Alexander restrained the First Corps artillery from firing that morning while he looked as best he could into the reserve situation. Apparently the ammunition was a matter to which Chief of Artillery Pendleton had given little attention, for no inventory had been kept as the battle progressed, and Lee unknowingly was just about to begin his supreme effort with no certainty that his infantry could expect sustained artillery support.

According to Alexander, each piece carried in its limber and caisson between 130 and 150 rounds, including canister, which would be useful only to a limited extent in bombarding lines nearly a mile away. Artillery at the time of Gettysburg was firing a wide range of ammunition, including solid shot, explosive shells and shrapnel of different types, rifled projectiles, canister, case shot, grape. The rounds carried with each piece would be enough for rapid firing for no more than an hour and a half. The question that remained was what was in the reserve ordnance trains. Alexander calculated that the maximum reserve taken into Pennsylvania was 100 rounds per gun but he doubted that the amount exceeded 60 rounds, the practice in the Richmond area having been to carry only 50 rounds in reserve per gun.[41] Pendleton gave neither Lee nor Longstreet, on whom Lee imposed the over-all command of the assault, information on the condition of the ordnance reserve and such information was vitally important considering that the army had been fighting for two days and must have expended a considerable part of its supplies. Lee's staff must share in the blame for this appalling oversight, but the responsibility would seem to be more directly chargeable to the chief of artillery.

Alexander's horror can be imagined when at about eleven o'clock all of Hill's 63 guns began sportive firing at the Bliss barn in their front, where skirmishers of both armies had been carrying on desultory fighting.[42] The barn had little tactical value, but when the Federal artillery joined in the battle between the skirmishers, Colonel Lindsay Walker, commanding Hill's artillery, replied capriciously, with Hill interposing no objection. The artillery combat lasted half an hour, the barn was blown to bits, the skirmishers retained pretty much their respective positions, and it should have been obvious that the Confederate Third Corps management was thinking more about letting off steam than conserving powder in order to win a battle. By about eleven-thirty this firing died away. The Culp's Hill engagement had ended at eleven, and an expectant silence settled over the two long ridges crowded with the hostile armies.

Pender's two brigades assigned to participate with Pickett and Pettigrew were those of Lane and Scales, both composed entirely of North Carolina troops. Scales had been wounded on the first day and the command had passed to Colonel William L. J. Lowrance, of the 38th North Carolina.

Brigadier General James Henry Lane, twenty-nine years old, filled competently the highly difficult role of a Virginian leading North Carolina troops. The antipathy between the two states, which was usually expressed mildly but seethed on occasions, was a heritage of colonial times, when North Carolina planters, possessing no adequate seaport north of Wilmington, had been forced to use Norfolk, an irritating expedient from which the Carolinians felt they suffered at the hands of astute Virginia traders. Though the hostility, ordinarily latent, had been largely laid aside in the war, it was being fanned into flame at the time of the Gettysburg campaign because of the politically inept appointment by President Davis of a Virginian to be Confederate tax collector in North Carolina.

Lee's march into Pennsylvania commanded little more attention in the North Carolina press than this gaucherie of the Richmond government. In Raleigh the appointee, the "chief Tithingman," was referred to in no more deferential fashion than "a person by the name of Bradford,"[43] and when it was made known that a wounded North Carolina officer had been rejected, a demand was set up that "foreign mercenaries must be withdrawn from the state."[44] Resolutions were adopted, the people were informed that South Carolina or Georgia would not submit to such an indignity, and the storm subsided only when the appointment was withdrawn. It set the stage for the later exchanges between individuals in the two states over phases of the third day at Gettysburg.

But Virginian Lane held the strong affections of a North State brigade that was being chaffed by the rest of the army because the fire of one of its regiments, the 18th North Carolina, had brought down Stonewall Jackson at Chancellorsville.

The 18th North Carolina carried a heavy burden of sadness for its role in this tragedy and grieved in common with all the Confederate cause. The regiment made no effort to shift the blame; the only explanation was that they had been told to fire at anyone coming down the road and did so.

The temper of the men with whom Lane had to deal could be seen from their reaction to a rebuke by A. P. Hill when, half an hour after Jackson was wounded, he reproved them for firing at a noise and, incidentally, hitting him in the calf of the leg.

A backwoodsman in Company B, 18th North Carolina, talked back to Hill. "Everybody knows," he said, "that the Yankee army can't run the Light Division and one little general needn't try it."[45]

Hill merely limped down the road.

Stonewall Jackson had given the brigade its greatest tribute after the battle at Cedar Run, August 9, 1862, where it had plugged the gap when the Stonewall Brigade had fallen back. Jackson had not used words. He had ridden to the brigade, then Branch's, and silently removed his cap and dropped it on the ground in front of the men.[46]

The brigade, known as "the flower of the Cape Fear section," had petitioned after Sharpsburg—where its early commander, Lawrence O'Brien Branch, was killed—to have Lane, then colonel of the 28th North Carolina, promoted to brigadier general. He was born on a Virginia plantation, educated by tutors, and stood second in his class at V.M.I.; then studied science three years at the University of Virginia and returned to V.M.I. to become assistant professor in the departments of mathematics and tactics. He went on to the North Carolina Military Institute, where he held the chair of natural philosophy and military tactics at the outbreak of the war. He became major of the 1st North Carolina, of which Daniel Harvey Hill was colonel. On reaching Virginia in 1861, Lane conducted the scouting party which encountered the enemy and brought on the battle of Bethel, the first of the war. He served thereafter in all the major engagements and surrendered with Lee, and thus, possibly alone of all Lee's officers, represented the story of the Confederate army from Bethel to Appomattox.[47]

Lane was the senior brigadier general of Pender's division, and took command when Pender fell, but Lee, having a surplus major general in Trimble, assigned him to command the brigades of Lane and Lowrance (formerly, Scales's).

The selection of brigades appears to have been made at random, and Lee obviously did not have prudent guidance either from Hill or any of his subordinates closely acquainted with the condition of the corps. Lane's brigade was a proper choice. Being on Pender's right flank in the July 1 attack on the Seminary, it had been occupied casually by Buford's cavalry, and had suffered only minor losses. Scales, on the other hand, had lost heavily. Not only was the brigade commander out of the action, but every field officer except one had been wounded. Captains were commanding regiments and sergeants companies.

Mahone's brigade of Anderson's division, and Thomas' of Pender's division had scarcely been under fire. Posey's brigade of Anderson's division was comparatively fresh. These brigades might have been used to provide the initial impetus to Hill's attack, along with Lane, thus leaving Pettigrew's division (Heth's) in support. Rodes, who had lent O'Neal and Daniel to Ewell, could help but little. He had two brigades in good condition in Ramseur and Doles. But they were holding Gettysburg and the line to the right of the town and were the reliance against a Federal offensive from Cemetery Hill that might threaten to break Lee's army and isolate Johnson and Early. If they were to be used with Pickett, it would be necessary to replace them with other troops.

Longstreet's two divisions other than Pickett's, those of Hood and McLaws, had carried most of the fighting load of July 2, and were reduced to not much more than 50 per cent of their striking power. They had lost heavily in officers and were manning thinly the long line from the base of Round Top to the Peach Orchard. Any brigade that might be withdrawn for concentration with Pickett would leave a gap that might be inviting to the Federals whose skirmishers were in close contact with the Confederate front. Longstreet's line extended over relatively flat ground quite different from the Federal position on the Round Tops and Cemetery Ridge. It possessed few strong defensive features, and if it was to be maintained during the thrust at the Federal center, the troops of Law (Hood) and McLaws were no more than adequate for the task. Lee seemed to recognize this tacitly during his conversation with Wofford, whose brigade remained in as good condition as any in the two divisions. When he left Wofford without giving him any indication that he was expected to attack following Pickett, it was obvious that Lee did not expect a forward movement by his entire right wing, as has often been contended. No such movement was ordered and apparently none was considered, unless, of course, the center of the Federal army should be broken, when such a success would become a signal for a general advance all along the line. Longstreet did ride over and tell Law to be prepared to follow Pickett, but a threat by the Federal cavalry made it imperative that he hold his lines.

Merritt's and Farnsworth's brigades of Kilpatrick's Federal cavalry division appeared in the rear of Law's Division, Farnsworth having passed in full view between Plum Run and the Round Tops at about eleven o'clock, and taken position in the open country beyond Round Top. Law was compelled to detach Robertson's brigade to protect his exposed flank. It was apparent that a weakening of the Confederate right would be exploited promptly by a vigilant enemy cavalry.

Thus it may be seen that Lee had no abundance of unemployed troops from which to make selections for his column of assault, but Anderson's two fresh brigades, Mahone and Posey, plus Thomas, would have seemed a more logical choice than Pettigrew's depleted division, which two days before had taken merciless punishment when it ousted the Iron Brigade from McPherson's Heights.

No troops in the army were of stancher material than Pickett's, but the bulk of the commands of Pettigrew and Trimble were inured in more recent fighting. Pickett's division had been on duty around Richmond, Petersburg, and in North Carolina—"picnic grounds," the others called these theaters—and had not been engaged at Chancellorsville.

Part of Pettigrew's own brigade likewise was from the "picnic grounds," and had never been with the Army of Northern Virginia; part had served in the Peninsular campaign and all had been tested and found steadfast on July 1. Pettigrew's other brigades were Archer's, which had been long with the army and had distinguished itself at Chancellorsville; Brockenborough's, formerly C. W. Field's, a veteran brigade that had served in A. P. Hill's division; and Davis', which included veteran regiments. The brigades under Trimble—those of Lane and Lowrance—were composed of veterans long a part of the Army of Northern Virginia.

The selection of Pettigrew's division to deliver the shock of the attack alongside Pickett's fresh troops disturbed Colonel Venable, who said "they were terribly mistaken . . . in this planning."[48] "They" could have referred only to Lee, the nearest the staff officer could come to personal criticism of his chief. Continuing, he said the division had suffered more than was reported on the first day and had not recuperated. As proof that Davis had gone almost into Gettysburg, he said "Rodes found dead Mississippians on the wooded hill just above the town."[49] The division had been sadly battered but it did no complaining. Hill might have been expected to protect it, but he is not known to have put in any protest. What was needed was not a division of different character, but one fresher and with larger numbers.

Colonel Taylor, who was with Lee during the morning discussion with Longstreet, said the plan as he understood it was for two divisions to make the assault while the remaining divisions moved forward to support them.[50] This does not answer the vital question of whether the supporting divisions were to move forward before or after Pickett, Pettigrew, and Trimble had broken the enemy's line. If before, then Lee intended a forward movement of his entire army. At no time did he order such an advance. What he ordered was an attack by Pickett reinforced by "two divisions of the Third Corps."

Taylor did not give the wording of the order he thought Lee intended, but merely said it was the result of the conference "as understood by me." That neither Hill, who was in Lee's company during the assault, nor Longstreet made an effort to advance anything except the designated units—Pickett, Pettigrew, and Trimble—is fairly good evidence that they did not understand that Lee contemplated a broad movement of the entire army ahead of the break-through.

4. Lee Designates the Troops and Objective

Responsibility for the timing of the attack of July 3 had to be shared jointly by Lee and Longstreet because the two were together much of the morning. Lee had seen neither Longstreet nor Pickett on the night before, and he had not settled on the attack until he made his reconnaissance, though he had stated his general purpose at the time Pickett joined him and Longstreet on Seminary Ridge.

As the hour approached eleven, timing became less consequential than careful preparation, for Johnson's attack and defense on Culp's Hill had petered out and unless Lee initiated a fresh supporting movement—which he did not contemplate and for which he scarcely had the troops—the full responsibility of engaging the Federals would be left to the column of Pickett, Pettigrew, and Trimble. So long as the attack was not to be co-ordinated with other movements, the hour was not of the first significance. Johnson on the far left had been unable to await the arrival of Pickett, because the Culp's Hill battle of July 3 was begun not by him, but by Slocum.

Now that Lee and Longstreet had ridden the lines, they returned to a point in front of Pickett's troops. It was clear that Lee had not altered his desire to undertake a massed infantry offensive against Meade's center and he was prepared to issue his attack orders. He formally designated the objective and selected the troops that were to participate. The objective has always been known as the "clump of trees," though in July 1863 the clump consisted mainly of an umbrella-shaped tree, with a few scrub oaks about it and bushes running along a stone wall. Two trees, apparently maples not much larger than saplings, stood north of the clump; elsewhere the hill was bald.

Pickett would have the forward role, with Pettigrew, followed by Trimble, advancing abreast him on his left, and Wilcox and Perry *en echelon* on his right. Longstreet was still blunt in his objections to a frontal assault. He told Lee he had examined the ground on his right—his nerve must have been unbounded to have alluded to this subject again—and thought the best plan would be to move to the Federal left in a wide flanking movement. The record of conversation that ensued is Longstreet's.

"No," said General Lee, "I am going to take them where they are on Cemetery Hill. I want you to take Pickett's division and make the attack. I will reinforce you by two divisions [Heth's under Pettigrew and Pender's under Trimble] of the Third Corps."

"That will give me fifteen thousand men," Longstreet responded. "I have been a soldier, I may say, from the ranks up to the position I now hold. I have been in pretty much all kinds of skirmishes, from those of two or three soldiers up to those of an army corps, and I

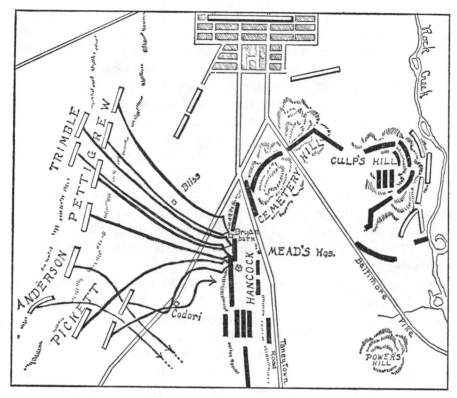

Launching the assault of July 3, 1863.

think I can safely say there never was a body of fifteen thousand men who could make that attack successfully."[51]

Lee was disturbed, if not angered. As Longstreet described it, he "seemed a little impatient at my remarks, so I said nothing more."[52] That was the last contact, before the attack, between the commanding general and his ranking subordinate. Nothing suggests that Lee ever thought of entrusting the attack to other supervision than Longstreet's, though many in later years have wondered why he did not. It would have been just as easy for Lee to lend Pickett to Hill as it was to lend Pettigrew and Trimble to Longstreet. That he did not evidenced how fully he retained confidence in Longstreet's pre-eminent ability to handle a large-scale assault.

Those capabilities the First Corps commander had demonstrated fully on the afternoon of July 2. On the basis of what had transpired since the army had reached Gettysburg, could Lee have committed the main attack to Hill or Ewell, or Early or Rodes? He needed Jackson, of course, but it is as well to say he could have used Napoleon, Soult, or Ney, or any other military figure out of the past. He had to work with the tools at hand. Unquestionably Longstreet, partial as he had been from the beginning to the flanking movement, had conducted on the afternoon of the second the hardest fighting on the field and possibly the hardest of the war, and had been partially successful against vastly superior numbers. There was no reason why Lee should doubt his effectiveness, even though it had been necessary to overrule him in ordering the frontal assault. The situation on the third was not different from what it had been on the second, when Longstreet had fought well an action with which he was not sympathetic. After the battle was joined, his strong competitive instinct— the will to win—as well as his devotion to the cause always asserted themselves.

As Lee left Longstreet and Pickett he was heard to say, largely to himself, "The attack must succeed."[53] He knew he was staking almost everything on it. He rode to an elevated position about the center of the Confederate line where he could witness the assault. Correspondent Ross noted that the entire morning had been devoted to reconnaissance and consultation by the top generals.

Longstreet assumed command over the brigades assigned to him from Hill's corps, though the transaction was little more than nominal. Pettigrew reported to him, then aligned his troops on Pickett's left.

Longstreet next told Alexander to find a position from which he could readily observe the effect of the Confederate artillery fire on the center of the enemy's line. The signal for the opening of the bombardment which Longstreet would order personally, would be two shots from fieldpieces of the Washington Artillery fired in quick succession, upon which the guns would open all along the line and converge their fire on the Federal lines running approximately a quarter of a mile along Cemetery Ridge from Ziegler's Grove to the umbrella-shaped oak beyond the Codori farm buildings. When Alexander saw that the Federal batteries were silenced or crippled, he would advise Pickett, who on this notice would launch his assault. Longstreet showed Pickett where his troops should rest during the bombardment, then rode to the crest of the ridge with him and pointed to the objective Lee had designated.

"He seemed to appreciate the severity of the contest . . ." said Longstreet, "but was quite hopeful of success."[54]

Pickett in fact was elated. Alexander went to him just before the bombardment and found Pickett "entirely sanguine" about the success of the attack and "congratulating himself on the opportunity."[55] He had had no recent chance at distinction.

For a lieutenant general Longstreet was singularly reluctant to assume the responsibility for an attack he knew to be inevitable. Scarcely to his credit was his effort to impose it on a young subordinate. Alexander, who had found a good place for observation at the left of his artillery line, where a point of woods stood out toward the Federal position, was talking with General Wright when he received a note from Longstreet. The corps commander said that if the fire did not drive off the enemy "or greatly demoralize him so as to make our efforts pretty certain," he would prefer that Pickett not be advised to make the assault. Longstreet added that he would rely a great deal on Alexander's judgment.[56]

The lieutenant colonel of artillery had the spunk to repel Longstreet's effort to charge him with the final accountability for the major movement of the entire battle. Alexander discussed the situation with Wright, then wrote Longstreet saying he would be able to judge the effect of his fire only by the return fire of the enemy, because the Federal infantry was but little exposed and smoke would cloud the field. Then he passed the responsibility back to his chief: "If, as I infer from your note, there is any alternative to this attack, it should be carefully considered before opening our fire, for it will take all the artillery ammunition we have to test this one thoroughly, and, if the result is unfavorable, we will have none left for another effort."

Alexander then gratuitously, and, as some commanders might have judged, almost impertinently, affixed his own opinion about the assault: "And even if this is entirely successful it can only be so at a very bloody cost."[57]

Longstreet replied at once, but still left the decision to Alexander. The intention, he asserted, was to advance the infantry if the artillery drove the enemy off, or had "other effect such as to warrant us in making the attack," a contingency which he did not explain. Then he said that when that moment arrived Alexander should advise Pickett "and of course advance such artillery as you can use in aiding the attack."[58]

The alert Alexander perceived that Longstreet had again put the load of the decision on his shoulders. It was noon or later. "I felt it very deeply," said Alexander, "for the day was rapidly advancing . . ." and whatever he was to do had to be done promptly.[59] His only consolation was General Wright, who on the previous evening had stood on the very ground Pickett had as his objective. Wright told Alexander that the difficulty was not so much in reaching and taking Cemetery Ridge, but in holding it, because the entire Federal army was massed in the shape of a horseshoe and could shift troops and reinforce points rapidly, which a long attacking line could not. Alexander felt partly reassured, because he had heard, from some source he did not name, that Lee intended to employ his entire army in the assault, and that would mean ample support for the attacking column.

But before replying to Longstreet's last note, Alexander rode back to see Pickett, who was in good spirits and eager to go ahead. When Alexander returned, his mind was fully made up that *"if the artillery opened Pickett must charge."*[60] It was one chance or nothing. He wrote Longstreet a final note showing the full scope of his own responsibility, which was no assurance, such as Longstreet seemed to demand, that the bombardment would guarantee the success of the infantry:

"General: When our artillery fire is doing its best I shall advise General Pickett to advance."[61]

CHAPTER

TWENTY-TWO

At Fearful Price

1. *"Times When a . . . Life Does Not Count"*

The day that had begun with heavy mists in the valleys had retained a vaporous, almost steaming hotness, uncomfortable both to the long lines of expectant Confederates lying in the woods and rye and of Federals beneath the violent sun in the open fields and pastures. Though the temperature was recorded at only 87 degrees in the shady town, the humidity made it seem like 100 on the rolling meadows.

White, billowy clouds lay lethargic on the western and northern horizons, but the sun beat down with such fury that Meade's men here and there put up their shelter tents for shade. Some thought that the battle was over and Lee would withdraw behind the mountains; others that he would renew and perhaps intensify his desperate efforts to pierce the Federal army. On the Confederate side, where the men were cooking bean broth and salt pork, to which they had been forced when the battle ended foraging, the conviction was still strong that the fight would be pressed relentlessly until they carried the opposite heights.

It was one o'clock. The midday bell would just be ringing on the Mississippi plantation, calling in the field hands from laying by the cotton. The sweet fragrance of the clematis hung over Tennessee verandas. Scant patches of Carolina tobacco were ready for the harvest. Dull, heavy summer lay across the South, where the Alabama cattle ruminated beneath the water oaks and the hot mists rose from the Georgia swamps.

At one o'clock Longstreet, in final capitulation to Lee's orders, sent notice to Colonel Walton to fire the signal guns and at 1:07—timed exactly by those who like to record the precise hour of great events—a field piece from the Washington Artillery spoke. It seemed to silence the hosts scattered about the battlefield, and to give notice that something momentous was impending. There were sixty seconds more of suspense,[1] another gun, and then all in both armies knew it was the hour of final decision, for the earth shook and a holocaust of flame and shell sprang from the Confederate woods.

If anyone on the Federal side was surprised about the point along the lines where, it was at once apparent, Lee was concentrating his fire, it was Meade himself. Meade had told Gibbon after his council of war on the night of July 2 that the enemy would attack again on July 3 and would strike him at the Federal center.[2] But he had not held long to that conviction. He was overheard to tell Hancock and others, at about 9:00 A.M. on July 3, that he did not think the center was the danger spot. The reasons he gave were that the artillery had an unobstructed field of fire in his front; that the Confederates were not partial to attacks in the center; and that he could reinforce his center very rapidly from his wings.[3]

Meade anticipated another attack on his left, where he held heavy masses of the Fifth and Sixth corps and remnants of the Third.

On the Federal side, at one o'clock, the generals had just seated themselves at Gibbon's field headquarters for a mess of stewed chicken garnished with cucumber pickle.[4] The top rank of the army was there: Hancock, Meade, Newton, Pleasanton, and others. The generals had procured cracker boxes and blankets; the staff officers sat on the ground. Though it is not related in the graphic accounts written about this luncheon, probably the staff ate the backs and wings and more pickle than chicken. Then the generals and aides who had finished lighted cigars and began to rehash the events of the day before. Meade reiterated his view that if the enemy attacked it would be the left, and Hancock ventured that it would be the center.

The answer was not long delayed. A gun spoke from across the wide, shallow valley, then another, and suddenly the air above them erupted with countless explosions, spreading panic among the lolling crowd, sending the generals scurrying to their commands, frightening the servants who had spread the meal, and filling the whole region with the din of roars, moans, and shrieks—"the voice of the rebellion," young Haskell termed it.[5] An orderly who had been serving the butter was cut in two. The Federal guns—80 along this immediate line, perhaps 200 in all from the Cemetery to Little Round Top—answered, and almost before anyone was certain of what had happened, the greatest cannonade in the annals of the North American continent was upon them.

Only to the artilleryman Alexander did the volcanic prelude to the assault carry a sweet refrain, which provoked a simile: "As suddenly as an organ strikes up in church, the grand roar followed from all the guns. . . ."

Correspondent Samuel Wilkeson of the New York *Times,* who continued his dispatches though his son had been killed in the July 1 fighting under Barlow, was at Meade's headquarters, where the Confederate shells burst and screamed "as many as six a second, constantly two a second," and "made a very hell of fire that amazed the oldest officers." Horses of the aides and orderlies hitched near by plunged about in pitiful panic.[6]

After the firing, Wilkeson found sixteen horses dead at the headquarters, still fastened by their halters, and giving the appearance of being "wickedly tied up to die painfully." An ambulance careened by at top speed, drawn faithfully although one horse had a hind leg shot off at the hock. As the cannonade continued, the army seemed to disappear. "Not an orderly, not an ambulance, not a straggler was to be seen upon the field swept by this tempest of orchestral death, thirty minutes after it commenced." Camp followers and skulkers were disappearing down the Baltimore pike; the soldiers had dug in until the violence passed.

The shells that hit in the region of Meade's little white house were in large measure wasted, for they had cleared the ridge and passed over the heads of the soldiers. The commanding general was forced to evacuate his headquarters and find space with Slocum on Power's Hill. But these high explosives that struck the rear of the army blew up caissons, dismantled guns, and disrupted the army's supply lines.

Here and there on the ridge men and horses were blown into bits, to become a part of the flesh and blood that before nightfall would saturate acres of this sod. In direct hits the slaughter was frightful; General Webb said a Federal battery lost twenty-seven of its thirty-six horses in ten minutes.

A gruff colonel who never showed weakness was told he would be hit if he persisted in standing in the open. A shell fragment tore his cheek and knocked out two teeth. Someone asked solicitously if he were wounded.

"No, sir," he barked; "just had a tooth pulled."[7]

He fought till the battle ended.

Each side employed a greater concentration of artillery than Napoleon ever achieved. This artillery bombardment seemed to fall on both Northern and Southern armies like brimstone showers descending in an inferno. The air was rent with sickening blasts. Bursting shells tore and seared the flesh and threatened to destroy life as completely as a wave of fiery lava creeping down a mountainside.

While the cannonade was at its height, the Federal soldiers were witness to a breath-taking incident. The men were hugging the unsteady earth, digging with bayonets and fingernails, crowding in behind the stone walls, when a horseman followed by a small staff appeared at the north end of the Second Corps line where the Taneytown road crossed Cemetery Ridge, and began moving deliberately down the crest. When the men could look up, they saw it was Hancock riding the lines, to inspire confidence for the attack. Shells burst above and around him and solid shot struck and rolled with its ominous thud. Beside him the Second Corps flag, the clover leaf, was carried by Private James Wells of the 6th New York Cavalry. Hancock did not stop until he had reached the far left of his line, a distance of perhaps three quarters of a mile.[8]

One of his brigade commanders said, "General, the corps commander ought not to risk his life that way."

"There are times," replied Hancock, "when a corps commander's life does not count."[9]

Across the valley where the Confederate army waited, some of the 7th Virginia noticed that the sun, brilliant when the cannonading was begun, soon was clouded and almost darkened by the enveloping smoke issuing from the numerous guns.[10] Company D of this regiment claimed something of a distinction, in that it believed its abortive efforts early in the war to shout in unison at the drillmaster's demand—efforts that turned into a raucous discord—gave birth to the "Rebel yell," which was often considered an imitation of the Indian war whoop. The company had been organized in Pearisburg and drilled by the town doctor, W. W. McComas, a captain in the Mexican War. They had first emitted their blood-curdling whoop before the banquet where the town of Pearisburg assembled to see them off, never dreaming that in its chilling effect on the enemy, this spine-tingling shout would come to have more worth than a round of bullets.

The eager school lad David E. Johnston had run all the way home and back, two and a half miles in the country, to get his uncle's consent, fearful that the rolls would be filled without him. Now a seasoned soldier, he was lying in a rye field, suffering from lack of water, and filing away the picture of his surroundings in his memory: "Turn your eyes whithersoever you would, there was to be seen . . . guns, swords, haversacks, human flesh and bones, flying and dangling in the air or bouncing above the earth, which now trembled beneath as if shaken by an earthquake."[11]

Dr. Joseph Hold of the 11th Mississippi, Davis' brigade, anticipated that the afternoon would be busy and set up his dressing station early in a shelter behind Seminary Ridge about a mile from Gettysburg. When the cannonade opened and the Federals' guns replied, stretcher bearers, crouching low, began bringing in the wounded. Among the first was an athletic young man with reddish golden hair, "a princely fellow," the doctor called him, with a calm manner and delightful smile, one of that gay, turbulent company that had left with the University Greys of Oxford to form Company A of the 11th Mississippi.

The physician examined the left arm, torn off at the elbow, and offered encouragement.

"Why, doctor, that isn't where I am hurt." The boy pulled back a blanket and showed where a shell had ripped deep across his abdomen, carrying away much that was vital. "I am in great agony," he said, still smiling. "Let me die easy, dear doctor."

But before the lad drank the cup containing the concentrated solution of opium, the doctor held up his right arm so he could write: "My dear mother. . . . Remember that I am true to my country and my regret at dying is that she is not free . . . you must not regret that my body cannot be obtained. It is a mere matter of form anyhow. . . . Send my dying release to Miss Mary. . . ." He signed, JERE S. GAGE, Co. A, 11 Miss. By that time the letter was covered with blood.

Then he raised his cup to a group of soldiers. "I do not invite you to drink with me," he remarked wryly; then with fervor, "but I drink a toast to you, to the Southern Confederacy and to victory."[12]

His was a code to die by, as well as live by.

But men adjust themselves even to the stunning concussions of a great bombardment. The prolongation of the cannonade finally brought an easy contempt of it. The 16th Vermont was not only at the point of the concentrated Southern fire, but was lying almost beneath the muzzles of the Federal guns. Colonel W. G. Veazey said that many of them, "I think the majority, *fell asleep*," and it was all he could do to stay awake himself.[13]

A Southern soldier, waiting for the command to advance, rested a careless foot in the fork of a small tree and dozed. A shell hit and so mangled his ankle that he knew it would have to be amputated. He looked at the mutilated leg and drawled: "Boys, I'll be damned if that ain't a thirty-day furlough!"[14]

Despite the havoc from the shells, the main body of the infantry on both sides survived, and was not materially impaired in fighting ability. Consuming though the cannonading seemed to be, and charred and pitted as the land was, the infantrymen of both armies crawled from their holes, shell craters, heaps of fence rails, and stone walls, and up, it seemed, out of the bowels of the earth, singed, shaken, bruised, but with lines intact. And the soldiers in the ranks of both undoubtedly said to one another that after all the blowing and puffing of long-range battle, the decision would only be reached when the infantrymen came face to face.

2. "If Old Peter's Nod Means Death . . ."

While the Confederate soldiers had been awaiting the lifting of the bombardment, Pickett had been scribbling prose poems of his love. In them he told about the signal guns, the unloosing of the fearful volcano of shot and shell, the low-spoken orders, and of how his Virginians were to lead the assault. "Oh, God, in mercy help me as He never helped before!"[15]

How Pickett found time to write these lines is one of the astonishing things of the battle, but he gave a concise running account of his actions:

I have ridden to Old Peter. I shall give him this letter to mail to you and a package to give to you if—Oh, my darling, do you feel the love of my heart, the prayer, as I write that fatal word "if"?

Old Peter laid his hand over mine and said: "I know, George, I know—but I can't do it, boy. Alexander has my instructions. He will give you the order." There was a silence, and his hand still rested on mine, when a courier rode up and handed me a note from Alexander.

Now, I go; but remember always that I love you. . . . I will keep up a brave heart for Virginia and for you, my darling."[16]

All this was presumably inscribed just before the step-off. That Pickett was able to fit it into so portentous a moment reveals an abnormal sense of high personal drama and emotionalism. At such a time his full thoughts might have rested on firing the elation and looking to the preparedness of his men. One cannot remotely picture Oliver Hazard Perry writing anything like these transports of passion as he prepared his fleet down to the duties of the last cabin boy to fight the British on Lake Erie.

The lines composed before the attack were supplemented by additional details written on the following day. Pickett told of riding up to Longstreet: "I found him like a great lion at bay. I have never seen him so grave and troubled. For several minutes after I had saluted him he looked at me without speaking."[17]

Alexander had estimated that the average distance was 1,400 yards. His first intention had been to wait until his guns and Hill's got the range, which he calculated would take ten to fifteen minutes, then signal Pickett to advance, but the Federal return fire proved so heavy that he felt the infantry would be unable to face it over such a long distance in the open under a hot sun; so he sustained the bombardment in the hope it would develop a more inviting situation. More time went by with no abatement of the intense firing on either side. Correspondent Wilkeson timed the cannonade at one hour and forty minutes.

Alexander calculated that the critical moment had come, and would soon pass. He wrote Pickett the note received in Longstreet's presence, saying: "If you are coming at all you must come immediately or I cannot give you proper support; but the enemy's fire has not slackened materially, and at least eighteen guns are still firing from the Cemetery itself."[18]

Just then the Federal batteries in the cemetery limbered up and drew off—to replenish their ammunition, it developed—and within five minutes after Alexander had written Pickett the Northern fire slackened all along the line. He was not sure yet what it meant, whether a withdrawal or only a change of position, but he judged the Federals had suffered and he was encouraged.

Varying reasons are ascribed for the slackening of the Northern artillery, but the most logical appears to have been that Warren from his customary point of observation on Little Round Top saw that it was only molesting and not damaging the Confederates greatly, while it was filling the level ground with smoke. Under the cover of this cloud they might reach close to the Federal lines undetected. He advised Meade, who told Chief of Artillery Hunt. Hunt also wanted to reload his caissons and lure the Southerners into attack in the belief that the Northern artillery was largely silenced.

Alexander waited five minutes longer, then hurried a courier to Pickett with an urgent note: "For God's sake come quick; the eighteen guns are gone."[19]

Pickett was still with Longstreet. He showed the note to his commander and asked if he should obey.

"He looked at me for a moment, then held out his hand. Presently, clasping his other over mine without speaking, he lowered his head upon his breast. I shall never forget the look in his face nor the clasp of his hand when I said: 'General, I shall lead my division on.' "[20]

Pickett had started away when he remembered his letter to LaSalle Corbell. He wrote across the corner of the envelope: "If Old Peter's nod means death then good by and God bless you, little one." Handing over the missive, he asked Longstreet to mail it, and saw the tears shining on the old soldier's cheek and beard. Said Pickett: "The stern old War Horse, God bless him, was weeping for his men. . . ."[21]

"I could not speak," said Longstreet on a visit to Gettysburg years later. "I merely gave a nod of assent, and then the tears rushed to my eyes as I saw those brave fellows rush to certain death."[22]

Now that Pickett was ready, Alexander sent for Richardson's seven 12-pounders to come up from their haven, prepared to move out with the infantry and carry on the indispensable function of shelling the Federal lines at the last minute before the Southern infantry struck. To his consternation the guns were gone. Pendleton, who had contributed so little to the preparation, now had interposed his authority, innocently perhaps but blunderingly, in a manner almost certain to foredoom the attack to failure. Without informing Alexander, the chief of artillery had removed Richardson's pieces. He had sent four of them to some other section of the field and the other three had disappeared at the same time.[23] Alexander could not find them. It was too late to replace them effectively with other guns because of the low ammunition supplies in the caissons.

As Pickett left Longstreet, Cadmus Wilcox came up to him, drew a flask, and offered liquor. "Pickett," he said, "take a drink with me. In an hour you'll be in hell or glory."[24]

Pickett said he had promised the young lady back in Virginia that he would not touch spirits.

He went back to his division and rode down the line. Randolph A. Shotwell of the 8th Virginia, Garnett's brigade, thought he looked cool, "rather dandyish in his ruffles and curls," well mounted, and "ready to ride to death if need be."[25]

Garnett was drawing at a cigar to show his unconcern.[26] "Have you any further instructions?" he asked.

"No, Dick," said Pickett. "I don't recollect anything, unless it is to tell you to make the best kind of time in crossing the valley. It's a hell of an ugly-looking place over yonder."[27]

Then Pickett stood in front of his division and gave the final word: "Charge the enemy, and remember old Virginia." His voice was clear and strong as he spoke the order: "Forward! Guide center! March!"[28]

After Pickett had left him, Longstreet rode to Alexander's observation post, and the artilleryman explained the situation: his ammunition was low and he feared he could not give Pickett the required assistance, especially since Richardson's 12-pounders had disappeared.

Longstreet, deeply agitated, spoke sharply. "Go and stop Pickett right where he is and replenish your ammunition."[29]

Alexander said the ordnance wagons were nearly empty, with not 20 rounds remaining per gun, too scant an amount for much to be expected of it; meantime, the enemy would recover from the shelling already delivered.

"I don't want to make this charge," Longstreet declared emphatically. "I don't believe it can succeed. I would stop Pickett now, but that General Lee has ordered it and expects it."[30]

Further remarks showed he wanted some excuse for calling off the whole attack.

But Longstreet and Alexander had lost control. As they talked the turf trembled about them and the long line of gray infantry broke from the woods. First came Garnett's Virginians, the general in front, his old blue overcoat buttoned tightly around his neck. Abreast was Kemper's trim line marching majestically into the open fields, the fifes piping "Dixie," the ranks in nearly perfect alignment. Far off to the left could be heard the drum rolls of the Carolina regiments— Pettigrew and Trimble were in motion. The hour of the generals had passed. The infantrymen from the Richmond offices and Pearisburg farmlands, the "greys" from the halls of "Old Miss" and the "flower of the Cape Fear section," had taken the Confederate cause into their hands.

3. The Shells Go "Whicker, Whicker"

Pickett's men were cheered by the begrimed cannoneers as they passed through the artillery and took up the tramp down the long slope and up the companion ridge toward the hostile army, barricaded and waiting.[31] As they left the woods, the "hell of an ugly place" ahead seemed much more than a mile, although the average distance was about three fourths that. Along Pettigrew's line the artillerymen had been cutting fuses for a mile and a quarter, and Pickett would have to regulate his advance until these more distant troops could fall in beside him and give the assaulting party an unbroken front.

Said Crocker:

As the lines cleared the woods that skirted the brow of the ridge and passed through our batteries, with their flags proudly held aloft, waving in the air, with polished muskets and swords gleaming and flashing in the sunlight, they presented an inexpressibly grand and inspiring sight.[32]

The vast body of men was now in the gentle, open valley midway between the lines, and for an instant the two armies on the ridges seemed enthralled, spellbound. Then the Federal artillery opened, firing first solid shot, next explosives and finally, as the column drew nearer the works, canister.

Though Lee was more an inspirational than a book general, the model for the massed infantry assault of Pickett, Pettigrew, and Trimble, following a thorough artillery preparation, was supposed to have been Macdonald's frontal attack at Wagram, where Napoleon had concentrated his artillery stealthily, delivered a concentrated cannonade, and had then broken the center of the enemy line by the weight of Macdonald's numbers. But Napoleon was not assailing troops of the same character and stability possessed by these Northern soldiers.

The gray-coated marchers learned abruptly that the Federal cannon had by no means been silenced. The massing of flags along the heights —scores of them fifty paces apart—told of the presence of hostile infantry in heavy numbers, and the sudden resumption of the full-scale cannonading gave notice that the artillery was ample for a stout defense.

Harassing to Pickett's entire force and especially destructive and impeding to Kemper on the right was the battery on Little Round Top, which with its excellent view of the field, kept the range and threw its shells and canister with devastating effect.

Far down the lines Oscar McMillan, whose handsome house on Seminary Ridge had been taken over by the Confederates, viewed the awesome panorama from the summit of Little Round Top. He had seen the approach of the battle and calculated that denuded Little Round Top, shorn of its timber, would be the best point of observation, and there he passed the first three days of July, observing the struggle with the anxiety of a violent Unionist, feeling that the arm of the Lord was slow to action. Now as Pickett's men filled the fields he was on his knees, with arms stretched toward Heaven, and the delighted Federal gunners heard between their firings his shouted exhortations and recommendations to Jehovah!

One of Pickett's soldiers described an oncoming shell—first the boom of the Yankee cannon, then a shriek in the air that sounded like a frightened horse neighing, "a kind of a whicker, whicker, whicker."[33]

Crocker saw a shell explode in the left company of his regiment; he said, "Men fell like ten-pins in a ten-strike." But the survivors did not even break step. In a surge of emotion he described it: "My God! it was magnificent—this march of our men."[34]

He asked himself what inspired them to such courage, and answered: "It was the fervor of patriotism—the high sense of individual duty."

When Robert W. Morgan was hit on the right instep by a Minié ball, he stopped to examine the wound and another ball tore his other foot from toe to heel. He made crutches of his own musket and an abandoned one and hobbled to where his Negro servant, Horace, could carry him on his back to a wagon that would take them home to Virginia.[35]

Dabney Tweedy was carried back on a stretcher, his blood spurting, and all the while he sang an anthem.[36] Charlie Jones, a private who had been ahead of the officers at the step-off, saying "Come on, boys, let's drive away those Yankees,"[37] was killed early.

While in Chambersburg, David E. Johnston of the 7th Virginia had had a dream in which he saw himself bleeding on a battlefield, his left side mangled by an exploding shell. Now he lay bleeding on the field, but it would be three days before consciousness returned for him to know an exploding shell had shattered his left side.[38]

The assaulting column consisted of 41 regiments and one battalion, excepting the supporting brigades of Wilcox, Lang, Thomas and Perrin, who did not reach Cemetery Ridge. Nineteen of the regiments were from Virginia, 15 from North Carolina, 3 each from Tennessee and Mississippi, and one regiment and one battalion were from Alabama.

The Codori house and its outbuildings were the only obstructions apart from the Emmitsburg pike, which seemed a sunken roadway, perhaps a trap, as the men approached. The skirmishers in front of them pulled down part of the fence, piled the rails into a breastwork, and in the long grass began firing at the Federal line as they awaited the advance of their own main body.[39]

Looking back, they could see Pickett riding over the crest of Seminary Ridge and coming into the open. Noticing that his skirmishers had stopped, he sent his brother, Charles Pickett, to tell them to keep 120 yards ahead of the attacking column.[40]

Garnett, with a big voice issuing from his frail body, rode ahead of his line regulating the pace, admonishing his men not to move too rapidly. From the skirmish line Captain Shotwell obtained one of the rare views of the Confederate advance: the "glittering forest of bright bayonets," the column coming down the slope "in superb alignment," the "murmur and jingle" and "rustle of thousands of feet amid the stubble" which stirred up a cloud of dust "like the dash of spray at the prow of a vessel."[41]

In front of Pickett flew the blue banner of the Old Dominion with its motto, *"Sic Semper Tyrannis,"* and the Stars and Bars of the Confederacy (the red battle flag with its blue cross not yet being in general use). The regimental flags flapped. A soft warm wind was blowing from the land they loved.

4. A Green Vermonter Reassures Hancock

While infantrymen might scorn the artillery when under cover, such was not the case when they were advancing in the open field. There the long lines were exposed targets, especially sensitive to unanswered artillery fire on their flanks. When Pickett started, Alexander hurriedly tried to scrape together an artillery support for him, but what he could get was low on ammunition and promised little.

The Federal center on Cemetery Ridge was held by two of Hancock's divisions, those of Gibbon and Hays, and, ranging south, by Doubleday's division of the First Corps, which had been joined by Stannard's Vermont brigade that had not participated in the First Corps battle of July 1. Beyond Doubleday's left were remnants of Hancock's other division, Caldwell's, and then the Third, Fifth, and Sixth corps.

The Federal line at the clump of trees was commanded by Brigadier General Alexander S. Webb, twenty-eight years old, an honor graduate of West Point in the class of 1855, who had fought at First Manassas and all battles of the Army of the Potomac. As chief of staff of the Fifth Corps in the Sharpsburg and Chancellorsville campaigns, he had been so conspicuous that he was promoted to general and assigned to command the Philadelphia Brigade, of Gibbon's division, Hancock's corps. Webb's grandfather, Samuel B. Webb, had been one of the little band of minutemen who stood with Captain Jonas Parker on Lexington Common, April 19, 1775; his father had been a regular army officer, a diplomat, then a newspaper editor in New York City, where Alexander was born.[42]

Pickett's most sensitive point was his right, where Kemper advanced with his flank in the air, riddled by the Federal guns on Little Round Top. Pickett, seeing this ghastly exposure, sent repeated messages to Wilcox and Lang to come up, but as they had not possessed quite the impetus to go up abreast Wright on the afternoon of the second, so they now became lost in the smoke and drifted farther and farther to their right, leaving a gap between themselves and Kemper wide enough for Meade to throw in a division had he been near by and so minded.

What happened was that an alert Vermonter, with a relatively green brigade, detected the great opportunity of the day and seized it promptly. Brigadier General George J. Stannard, whose men had performed brilliantly on the afternoon before, recapturing a battery under the eyes and at the personal request of Hancock, was in Doubleday's line on the left of Gibbon. Before July 2, the brigade had never come under fire and since it had enlisted for only nine months and the term was almost expiring, Newton, the uncertain First Corps commander, had put two veteran lines of battle behind it. Kemper had been making directly for Stannard, but as he crossed the Emmitsburg road he suddenly changed front and moved off to his left, both to close a gap that had developed between him and Garnett and to converge on the clump of trees. This took him directly across the front of the 14th Vermont, of Stannard's brigade, which poured a withering fire into his flank. After moving about 300 yards to his left, Kemper changed front to the right, again faced the main line of the Federal army, and advanced on the clump of trees. Here Kemper's men broke out with the wild Rebel yell and started up the incline to the Federal works.

Stannard now executed a bold maneuver, which he was enabled to do because Wilcox and Lang were offering Kemper no protection. He threw his Vermont brigade forward and changed front, so part faced north, perpendicular to the main Federal line facing west, and immediately on Kemper's flank. In this new position, his left was more than 300 yards in front of the Federal position.

Hancock, close by, observed this individualistic movement by the Vermonters and was apprehensive that it would leave a hole through which an enterprising enemy lurking behind the smoke might pass. But Stannard vouched that he could get back in time to meet any troops on Pickett's right. From this position the brigade threw a deadly fire into Kemper's flank, which no troops in the world could have withstood.[43]

Kemper meantime had seen the critical situation on his right and had ridden back to Armistead. "General, hurry up," he said. "My men can stand no more."[44]

Armistead turned to his 1st Regiment and ordered, "Colonel, double-quick." From a fast step the men broke into a run, then a fast charge.

But Kemper was no longer a participant. He was knocked from his horse critically wounded, and the report went through the army that he had been killed.[45]

Meanwhile, Garnett had pushed straight ahead, maintaining an even pace. He continually called, "Faster, men! Faster, but don't double-quick." At the Emmitsburg road he struck the Federal skirmish line, which, in the words of an observer, he swept away "like trash before the broom." His men began a scattering fire but he galloped along the line ordering, "Cease firing," and the remarkable discipline of the brigade caused it to shoulder arms again and move ahead.[46]

Garnett was across the road climbing the slope toward the stone wall when he saw far on his right a long blue column—apparently Stannard's—coming up on Kemper's unguarded flank. If the works ahead of him were to be carried it would have to be done quickly,

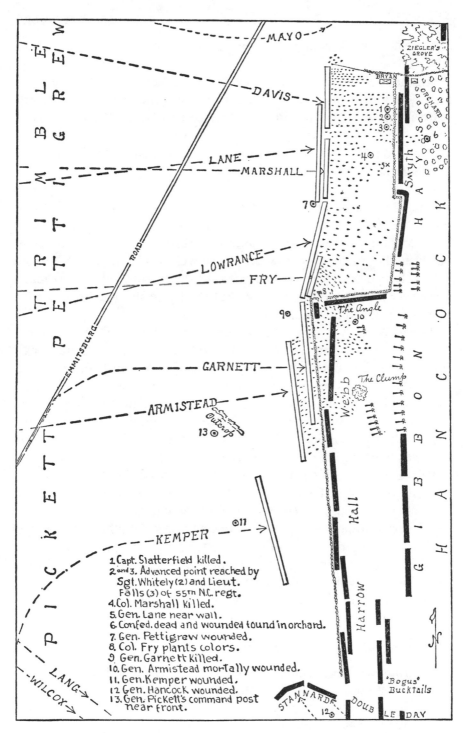

Assault by Pickett, Pettigrew, and Trimble.
July 3, 1863, 3:00 to 3:30 P.M.

before these flankers hit Kemper's right, exposed by the inertia of Wilcox.

As they neared the Federal works, Garnett's men could see the flags above them but no bluecoats to fire at. But when Garnett was halfway up the slope the Federal line rose. Their polished muskets shone for a moment in the sunlight, then a great, devastating blast spurted from the crest, a cloud of smoke rolled out, and much of the Confederate column seemed to sink into the ground.[47]

Garnett was not close enough yet for the charge. He rode the line steadying the men: "Don't double-quick. Save your wind and ammunition for the final charge." The words were scarcely spoken when his men noticed that he was covered with blood. Still he rode, but his head began to drop toward his horse's neck. Then horse and rider fell together. Garnett had been hit in several places—how many none ever knew—and did not rise, but the horse struggled back to his feet and galloped down the hill.[48]

James W. Clay of the 18th Virginia was hit by a shell a hundred yards below the clump of trees and stumbled blindly into some rocks, from where he could see Garnett on his black horse ahead of his brigade as it approached the stone wall. The general was waving his black felt hat with its silver cord, cheering on his men, his sword still sheathed at his side, when he collapsed and fell.[49] Captain Archer Campbell, 18th Virginia, had been hit with a ball that broke his arm and was lying beside Clay when Garnett's horse, a jagged hole in his shoulder, came dashing down the hill in frenzied flight.

Clay was puzzled that his general's body was never found, for Garnett's new uniform beneath his old overcoat was adorned with the Confederate wreath and general's star, and he wore officer's boots and spurs. He judged it "inexplicable that his remains were not identified."[50] But one wonders about the blue overcoat, probably a heritage from his days with the Regular Army before the war. Because of it, could this gallant officer who gave his life at the supreme moment of the Confederacy sleep in an unmarked Federal grave?

5. A General Falls Inside the Works

But Armistead was coming up. Garnett's men could hear the thud of their feet on the sod just behind them, while above them the canister and grape sounded, as Captain H. T. Owen described it, like the whirring of a flock of quail rising in sudden flight.

The blue flanking column on the right meantime had well-nigh destroyed Kemper and now poured its fire into Garnett's and Armistead's men. These two brigades, tangled and confused, rushed the stone wall, clubbing muskets and jabbing with bayonets. None had time to load. At the front was Armistead. The Federal artillery fired its last round, the guns shotted to the muzzle, when the Virginia soldiers were but a few feet from them.

As strong runners seeing the goal ahead draw together their reserve powers for a burst of supreme effort and speed more swiftly across the finish line than at any point on the back course, so these daring soldiers, their objective just before them, impelled themselves to efforts which a few minutes earlier they would have judged beyond their powers, and pushed, clambered, jumped, and fell across the wall.

Armistead was in front of them. Just before they had begun this final dash he had walked along the line with final words of cheer. He had met on his left a mounted man, probably Garnett, who leaned from his horse that they might have a final word before making the rush together. Then "Old Lo" Armistead had plunged ahead, and Garnett had fallen. He put his black hat on his sword point and held it aloft for the whole brigade to see.[51] When he was over the wall, about 150 of his men rushed pell-mell behind him.

Here, face to face, the general could see whom he was fighting. He called back, "It's the Philadelphia Brigade. Give them the cold steel, boys."

That was his last order. He put his hand possessively on the Federal cannon into which his men had charged, as though his thought was to turn it about, but at that instant, with his hat on his sword and his hand on a gun, he fell mortally wounded, fairly riddled with bullets. Some of them came from revolvers fired at arm's length.

An unidentified Federal colonel, who admired Armistead's courage and saw his peril, was at that very instant trying to ride into him and knock him down, to save him from the hail of bullets.[52] The story that he pitifully sent word to Hancock that he had chosen the wrong side appears to be apochryphal.[53] When Armistead fell the command of his brigade passed to Colonel William R. Aylett, grandson of Patrick Henry. Half of those who crossed the wall with Armistead were killed.

As Armistead was being carried back, Captain Harry Bingham of Hancock's staff met the bearers and asked if he could be of help. Armistead requested that Hancock send his spurs and watch to his relatives. This Hancock did. Old Lo's sword had been taken where he fell.[54]

All along the line the Confederate regiments were approaching the wall, their ranks thinning at every step. The whirring canister and sheets of rifle and musket fire withered their line away. As Armistead's men poured over the barrier, Webb's Pennsylvanians—a thin front line for such a critical sector—were driven back, but the triumph for the small party inside the Federal works was short-lived.

What Pickett needed mainly was support coming up behind him. Had another division—the brigades of Mahone, Thomas, and Posey—been close in his rear, it is not unlikely he would have carried the heights. But while Armistead was having his flash of triumph inside the Federal lines, help was being rushed to Webb from all directions. Hall's brigade of Gibbon's division came up at a run. Hancock transferred a part of Harrow's brigade at double-quick. Doubleday swung into action. Part of the Third Corps hastened. Webb formed his men into a second line, and the threat of a more serious break-through at this point rapidly vanished.

When Webb's regiments gave way before the impact of Garnett and Armistead, the onrush of new Federal defenders to the threatened salient was so impetuous that most of Harrow's and Hall's regiments lost all form and became masses of individuals seeking only to repel their desperate assailants. The nearest of Harrow's regiments, the 19th Maine, charged "wildly," its scribe recorded, "with little regard for ranks or files." The men fired as they ran and in their anxiety "thrust their rifles over the shoulders, under the arms and between the legs, of those in the front ranks of the melee." As Hancock explained it, "the men of all the brigades had in some measure lost their regimental organization, but individually they were firm." Harrow's men moved past the south end of the little copse to the wall in front, still held by the Confederates, where "by sheer strength," the enemy was pushed beyond the wall.

The defense, quite as much as the attack, was sublime in its heroism. Young Lieutenant A. H. Cushing, commanding Battery A of the 4th U. S. Artillery, was at his guns when hit in the abdomen by a bursting shell. All of his pieces had been disabled except one. Holding his intestines back with one hand, he helped run his remaining gun down to the stone wall, and shouted to his general, "Webb, I will give them one more shot."

After the gun spoke he called again: "Good-by." Then he fell dead across his last cannon.

Before Cushing fell or his battery was disabled, Cowan dashed up near by with his 1st New York Battery that had moved with the Sixth Corps from Manchester, and issued his orders to give them "double canister at ten yards," the words which were chiseled on the battery's monument on Cemetery Hill. Double canister meant ninety-eight iron balls, each about an inch in diameter. In a single charge, canister was packed in seven layers of seven balls each. A double charge—the balls would spread like shot from a shotgun—was certain to make havoc of anything in its front.

Hancock was with Stannard, looking down on the masses of Confederate infantry—Pettigrew's and Trimble's men, who were pressing up the hill some distance to his right—when he was hit in his right thigh. The bullet passed through the pommel of his saddle and carried wood fragments and a nail into the deep wound. He reeled and would have fallen had not Stannard's aides caught him and laid him on the ground, where he bled so profusely that his life seemed endangered. Stannard jumped from his horse and made a tourniquet with his handkerchief and pistol barrel. With the flow of blood checked, Hancock remained where he was, refusing to allow the men to move him to the rear until he could determine the outcome of the assault.[55]

Meantime Harrow's brigade had come to the assistance of Stannard and joined in the attack on Kemper's survivors. With their leader down and virtually all their field officers gone, this remnant of a splendid brigade was sent flying to the bottom of the hill.

When Wilcox and Lang made their closest approach to the Federal lines and began a desultory firing against Caldwell's division on Doubleday's left, Stannard's Vermont brigade repeated the maneuver it had employed against Kemper, and poured a fire of musketry into their flank while the canister and Caldwell's men were tearing up their front. Caught in this crossfire, they retired rapidly, leaving many prisoners with Stannard. Stannard himself was wounded in the upper leg soon after Hancock and, like Hancock, refused to leave the field.

6. Planting the Tennessee Flag on the Wall

The Pickett-Pettigrew-Trimble assault of July 3 had some of the aspects of Longstreet's attack *en echelon* of July 2, in that while the brigades of the Confederate line approached the Federal works in a well-dressed line, the critical fighting moved from the Confederate right to the left and was without essential concert.

Pickett's battle was waning as Pettigrew's began, and Pettigrew in turn had shot his bolt when Trimble put in his greatest effort. Yet the impression often conveyed that only Armistead's soldiers stormed the wall and penetrated the Northern works does not spring from the events of the battle. The "high-water mark" is more symbolic than actual, because the conformation of the Federal line caused three of Pettigrew's and both of Trimble's brigades to strike the Northerners farther in advance than Pickett and nearer the summit of the ridge.

The Pettigrew-Trimble march across the open fields was as stirring and magnificent as the inspiring advance of Pickett's Virginians. One of the group of Confederate officers observing on Seminary Ridge said Pettigrew's front as it burst from the woods appeared to cover twice that of Pickett's. These officers, thrilled by the sight, thought from the way the column filled the plain that it must be Hill's entire corps. They shouted, "Here they come! Here they are! Hurrah!"[56]

The words, except the last, were almost exactly those that were running along the Federal line as this splendid force, coming into line with Pickett and giving the assaulting column a front of three quarters of a mile, appeared through the smoke.

When Captain Randolph A. Shotwell on the skirmish line first saw Pettigrew's column, it was nearly half a mile to the left and rear of Pickett. It met the storm of shell which "fairly melted away the two left brigades," those of Mayo and Davis. "Pettigrew's old brigade . . . and the remnants of Archer came on with springing steps,"[57] not far behind the left of Pickett's line.

Pettigrew's column had to travel a longer distance than Pickett's and move diagonally across the field in order to converge on the umbrella-shaped tree.[58] The ground was less undulating than that traversed by Pickett, and though in Pickett's case the protection was scant, in Pettigrew's there was none at all. This terrain was particularly exposed to the batteries in the cemetery and Ziegler's Woods, which sent in an oblique fire.[59] Colonel W. H. Swallow observed that the first Federal fire shook them as if they had been "struck by some unseen power, some great physical body." The column reeled and halted momentarily. When the smoke cleared they were moving steadily ahead again though the ground behind was covered with the fallen. Reaching the Emmitsburg road, they had no dead space and came directly under the fire of the blue line behind the stone wall on the crest.

The tough old filibusterer, Colonel Birkett Davenport Fry, who had led Heth's advance to Gettysburg on July 1, commanded Pettigrew's right brigade, Archer's Alabama and Tennessee survivors of the first day's battle. Though there had been apprehension because of the distance between Pettigrew's and Pickett's divisions at the beginning, the gap was skillfully closed by Fry and Pettigrew. The timing proved exact, for according to some of the Confederate observers, Fry's right met Garnett's left precisely at the Emmitsburg road and they moved up the slope abreast, both suffering staggering losses as they advanced.

Federal observers thought the juncture was not so neatly done—there was considerable crowding of Pickett into Pettigrew, resulting in confusion for Pickett and a slackening of the assault.

Pettigrew's own brigade, led by Colonel James K. Marshall of the 52nd North Carolina, was on Fry's left, then came Davis and Brockenborough. This last brigade was commanded by Colonel Robert M. Mayo of the 47th Virginia. The time required to climb the front of Cemetery Ridge seemed interminable, but as Fry and Marshall neared the crest the men let out a shout and ran forward toward the wall. Trimble was close behind them, in the rear of the right of Pettigrew's division. As Fry and the left of Garnett struck the wall together, a Virginia lieutenant and a Tennessee captain shook hands. "Virginia and Tennessee will stand together on these works," the Virginian said.

Where these brigades met, the wall formed an angle, and turned back to the east for a distance of about 80 yards. Then it turned again to the north. Thus the section of the wall hit by Kemper, Armistead, and Fry was 80 yards closer than the section hit by Marshall and Davis. As Fry's Tennesseans clambered over the wall following the mixed commands of Kemper and Armistead, Marshall and Davis rushed past them and struck the wall ahead. Here they menaced the flank of Webb, facing Fry and the Virginians. But they were in turn critically exposed on their right and encountered a destructive fire from Webb and Hancock's oncoming supports.

The 14th Tennessee had marched from Clarksville, its point of concentration in northwest Tennessee in 1861, with 960 men. It had moved across virtually all of the battlefields of Virginia and counted 365 bayonets when it went into the first day's fight at Gettysburg. The battle on McPherson's Heights had reduced it to only 60 men, commanded by a captain, L. B. Phillips. Here where the wall turned, at what came to be known as the "bloody angle" of Gettysburg, all but three of these remaining 60 fell.

The requiem was indeed affecting:

Thus the band that once was the pride of Clarksville has fallen. . . . A gloom rests over the city; the hopes and affections of the people were wrapped in the regiment. . . . Ah! what a terrible responsibility rests upon those who inaugurated this unholy war.[60]

In front of the wall Colonel Marshall, leading Pettigrew's men, was shot and fell dead from his horse. Pettigrew's hand was shattered by a ball but he paid no attention. Along the wall nearly all of the Virginia colonels were killed. Though Armistead had broken through and some of Garnett's men had swarmed in, the only colors planted on the Federal works were those of the gallant Fry, who took in the 1st and 7th Tennessee and the 13th Alabama, then fell, wounded and remained a prisoner when his men were killed or forced back.[61]

But the Confederate attack was not yet spent. Old Man Trimble, who, Kyd Douglas said, had enough fight in him "to satisfy a herd of tigers,"[62] was coming up behind Pettigrew.

7. *"All Hell Can't Take It"*

Trimble was at disadvantage, commanding at this high point a demi-division he had scarcely seen before, replacing the wounded General Pender. He had time before the firing of the signal guns to ride down the line and talk to the different regiments, saying he would lead them against Cemetery Hill at three o'clock. His timing was accurate, and from his position the advance of the long line of Confederate soldiers with their fluttering banners was steady and inspiring. Soon Trimble, who had marched in rear of Archer and Marshall, obliqued to the left to the rear of Mayo, whose brigade, destitute of flank protection, was suffering from the enfilade fire and, like Kemper on the other flank, was beginning to disintegrate.

Major J. A. Weston, 33rd North Carolina, of Lane's brigade, thought the attack would have succeeded if artillery had been pushed forward with the infantry. As he saw it, Pickett's men struck the Federal line ahead of Pettigrew or Trimble, owing to the terrain and fences, and for a time held the ground they had taken, but finally fell back under the tempest of fire.

As Trimble's men came up to Pettigrew's, someone cried, "Three cheers for the old North State," and both of his brigades let out a shout.[63] Turning to his aide, Trimble declared, "I believe those first fellows are going into the enemy's line!"[64] Trimble, his command merging with Pettigrew's, then struck the wall, with Lane and Lowrance battling on after Pettigrew had been slaughtered and forced back following Pickett. These two brigades—Lane and Lowrance—

went to the wall with a rush, but were met by volleys from the second Federal line.

Trimble was wounded near the fence, while encouraging his men to storm it, and fell into enemy hands, but he remained an observer of the assault.

With Trimble down, Lane was now fighting the battle virtually unaided. On his left the enfilade fire had become so destructive that he directed Colonel Clark M. Avery, commanding the 33rd North Carolina, to change front and face the new enemy.

Avery nearly exploded. "My God, General," he shouted, "do you intend pushing your troops into such a place unsupported, when the whole right has given way?"[65]

Lane looked to his right and saw that Pickett's line of battle was gone. No Confederate troops were visible there. Avery meantime was at the stone wall, his men firing and cheering, but Lane called them back.

Said the general: "My brigade, I know, was the last to leave the field, and it did so by my order."[66]

Professor James H. Lane, mathematician and scientist, devoted his life to teaching in Virginia, North Carolina, and Missouri, except for the four years he was a colonel and general in the Confederate army. No doubt the educational years were the more constructive, but his most intense moment was about 3:30 P.M. on July 3 when his brigade closed on the Federals on Cemetery Ridge. Captain John H. Thorpe, of the 47th North Carolina, Pettigrew's old brigade, saw him on horseback at the wall, urging his men forward with his hand, as though trying to push them over. Blood spurted from his horse and they went down together.[67] Smoke obscured the picture for Thorpe, but Lane was up again quickly to try again and then to take the skeleton of his brigade slowly back across the long valley over which it had moved with high ardor only half an hour before. He was unscathed.

Lowrance had a story similar to Lane's of the sustained attack by Trimble, and declared that at this stage all others had apparently forsaken his men and Lane's. "The two brigades, now reduced to mere squads, not numbering in all 800 men, were the only lines to be seen upon that vast field, and with no support in view, the brigade retreated."[68]

Lane and Lowrance retired in fair formation. Major Weston was emphatic that there was no disorder. In Trimble's words they fell back "sullenly and slowly, in almost as good order as they had advanced."[69] Trimble summed it up: "If the troops I had the honor to command today couldn't take that position, all hell can't take it."

Then he described the clash: "At the fence the exposure was dreadful. The incessant discharge of canister, shell and musketry was more than any troops could endure. The brigades of Pender, yielding ground, began to move back slowly and in good order, not even breaking ranks."[70]

Looking across, Trimble saw from where he lay wounded that the battle had ended in front of Pickett. Of his own men he said, corroborating Lane: "I know these brigades were the last troops to leave the field." He cited an axiom: "No single line of infantry without artillery can carry a line, protected by rifle pits, knapsacks and other cover, and a numerous artillery, if the assaulted party bravely avails itself of all its advantages."[71]

All along the lines the Federals had captured numerous prisoners and sheafs of regimental flags. Lowrance's 38th North Carolina reversed the normal process by capturing 30 Federal prisoners beside the works and shooting many, but the regiment's own loss was staggering. Company A had two survivors; the entire regiment only 40, commanded by a lieutenant. Two months earlier the regiment had been a factor in Jackson's flank march at Chancellorsville. Now it was virtually gone.

When the cleanup was begun in front of the Federal position, some of the wounded Confederates were found to be still angry. One, mortally wounded, declined defiantly to allow the 69th Pennsylvania relief workers to take him to a hospital. He said he wanted to die where he fell.[72] Said Major St. Clair A. Mullholland: "In front of the Second Corps the dead lay in great heaps. . . . Out on the field where Longstreet's Corps had passed, thousands of wounded were lying."[73] As there were no means of reaching them, many lay between the lines until the second day, when Lee's army had gone.

8. The General Was with His Men

One baffling question for later years was: Where was Pickett? Colonel Eppa Hunton, commanding the 8th Virginia, said, "No man who was in that charge has ever been found, within my knowledge, who saw Pickett during the charge."[74] Hunton was not observant or well advised, for Pickett was not missing. One account said he was behind a "ledge of rocks" about 100 yards in the rear of "where the division was just prior to the charge." One of Hunton's men said he carried water to Pickett and his staff, but the location described was so vague that it might have been either near Seminary Ridge or where the brigades re-formed after crossing the Emmitsburg road. Hunton was told by General L. L. Lomax, the Confederate representative on the Gettysburg Commission, that although there had been frequent references to this ledge, no such ledge had ever been located.[75] Nothing that answers the exact description is to be found on the ground over which Pickett's division attacked.

In analyzing the question of Pickett's whereabouts Hunton made a strong point that neither Pickett nor any of his staff, all mounted, was killed or wounded, nor were any of the horses injured, whereas, he asserted, "every man who was known to have gone into the charge on horseback, was killed or wounded or had his horse killed."[76] Garnett and Kemper were good examples. Hunton himself was wounded near the red Codori barn. He conceded that several of Pickett's staff said Pickett accompanied the men, but Hunton could not learn how far.

The question was booted about in later years and the impression was strong that Pickett went at least as far as the Codori barn, which is certainly as close to the front line as the division commander ought to go.[77] Near the barn is some dead space, protected from Cemetery Ridge, and whether Pickett was there, in the field, or behind the stone foundation of the barn probably depended on when a courier or orderly happened to reach him. The rock foundation of the barn may have been what Hunton's soldier meant as a "ledge of rocks" to which he carried water.

Captain W. Stuart Symington, one of Pickett's aides, said that Pickett ordered Armistead to move up to the left as he advanced and the left became exposed; that would have been after the division was near the Federal wall. Pickett was therefore following the action closely. Captain R. A. Bright, also of Pickett's staff, gave more exact information. Pickett and four of his staff rode on the right of Armistead's brigade until they reached the Emmitsburg road, which at the Codori farm was about 400 yards from the copse of trees that marked the objective of the assault. Here Pickett sent Bright back to Longstreet to tell him he could carry the heights but could not hold them without reinforcements. When Bright returned he found Pickett "between the Emmitsburg Road and Cemetery Heights." That would mean closer than the Codori barn. Pickett then sent Bright, Symington, and Captain E. R. Baird, also of his staff, to urge Wilcox to come up; Bright on his return from that unsuccessful mission, found him "near the descent of the last hill, facing the Federal works." This was close indeed to the enemy line—closer than a major general would ordinarily venture in an attack in the open fields.

About 100 yards beyond the Codori barn the ground sinks to an old stream bed. In this depression, up which Kemper had moved across the front of Stannard's brigade, troops were not visible to watchers on Seminary Ridge, where Lee and Longstreet were anxiously trying to observe. Between the depression and the Federal wall, about 300 yards, the gentle incline is broken by an outcropping of rocks, scarcely a ledge, though rough and protruding. The land here is untillable and unsuited even for pasture and is covered with low hemlock, scrub oak, and wild cherry.

This is most likely, though not certainly, the point to which Pickett advanced personally, and in such case he is entitled to the full honor of leading his desperate charge. From here the enemy lines were just 100 yards distant. This may have been what the water carrier had in mind as the ledge, and it might readily be termed "the last valley in front of Cemetery Ridge," where Bright said he found his commander. Lomax must have been looking for his ledge too far in the rear.

Another mission on which Pickett sent his aide, Bright, was to Dearing's battalion, to ask it to open and protect the left flank of the assaulting column. He brought back word that Dearing had only three rounds but had opened with them at once.

When the attack was finally reviewed after the battle it was found that each of the three commands—Pickett, Pettigrew, and Trimble—had entered the enemy line at some point.

Dead and wounded of both Pettigrew's and Trimble's divisions were found in the orchard beyond the stone wall. The well-known justice of the North Carolina Supreme Court in later years, then Captain J. J. Davis of the 47th North Carolina, Pettigrew's brigade, was captured inside the wall.[78] The fact that Pettigrew and Trimble attacked the stone barrier where it was 80 yards recessed from the wall assailed by Pickett took those two commands closer to the heart of the enemy position. A review of the claims of the different units shows that the troops which probably advanced the farthest were Captain E. Fletcher Slatterfield's company of the 55th North Carolina Regiment. The regiment was commanded by Captain George Gilreath. At this point, where the high tide of the Confederacy surged and receded, Slatterfield fell.[79]

Members of Davis' brigade, this company was part of the regiment that pursued Cutler's men north of the railroad cutting on the first day of the battle. The point of farthest advance was established—at least to the content of North Carolinians, and to the apparent satisfaction of the Gettysburg battlefield authorities of that day—when Lieutenant T. D. Falls, of Fallstown, Cleveland County, North Carolina, and Sergeant Augustus Whitley, of Everitts, in Martin County, visited the terrain, made affidavits about the point they had reached, and had it marked by the Gettysburg Commission.[80] This testimony, according to Adjutant Charles M. Cooke, of the 55th, had other corroboration.

Taken with the advance of Lane and D. H. Hill in the pre-Manassas affair on the Peninsula, and the fact that Cox's brigade fired the final round of the Army of Northern Virginia, this bold feat of the 55th Regiment went to establish North Carolina's most cherished tradition of its part in the Confederate War: "First at Bethel, farthest at Gettysburg and last at Appomattox."

Unhappily for the North Carolinians, the principal press accounts of the battle were from the Richmond correspondents. In one of the first conspicuous dispatches to the *Enquirer*, Pettigrew's command, containing some of the stanchest veteran regiments of the army, was termed "raw troops," and Pickett's defeat was attributed to Pettigrew's "faltering." North Carolina has not yet recovered.[81]

This impression worked its way into early Southern history and no doubt influenced the writing of some of the official army reports prepared within a few months after the battle. Longstreet's tended to exonerate Pickett and blame Hill's troops,[82] and Pickett's was so bitter that Lee declined to receive it and requested that it be rewritten.[83] The assault, much to the annoyance of North Carolina participants and the state's postwar writers, came to be known as "Pickett's charge" without ever a reference to Pettigrew or Trimble. That name is probably a historical fixture, though Pickett commanded little more than a third of the attacking column and performance was equally courageous all along the line.

Going into the attack with both flanks in the air foredoomed the movement to failure, and the troops naturally faltered first at the two extremes of the line. This was no reflection of the right under Kemper nor the left under Mayo. No troops could have withstood the enfilade fire while assailed by artillery and musketry in their immediate front. It was not the character of the units but their positions which caused the disintegration that eventually affected the entire assaulting force.

Many factors contributed to the repulse apart from the terrain and inadequate numbers: improper organization of the movement, inadequate staffwork, the faltering of Wilcox and Lang, the failure of Hill to move Thomas and Perrin into close support of the left flank of the column, and, by no means last, Pendleton's inexcusable blunder of depriving the assaulting column of well-stocked artillery that could have helped keep the Federal flankers in check.

9. *"The Task Was Too Great for You"*

As Shotwell of the 8th Virginia was dragging himself up Seminary Ridge after the heartbreaking experience in the valley, he saw a horseman observing alone, and as he approached, was surprised to find it was the commanding general. Shotwell gave a brief picture of Lee at this moment. "His bridle rein was carelessly upon his horse's neck, and in the whole attitude of the trim, soldierly figure was an air of sadness, weariness, regretfulness, akin to depression, such as I had never known in him before."

Shotwell saluted Lee and was about to pass on when the general stopped him. "Are you wounded?" Lee asked.

"No, General," he replied, "only a little fatigued; but I am afraid there are but few so lucky as myself."

"Ah! yes," said Lee. "I am very sorry—the task was too great for you. But we mustn't despond. Another time we shall succeed. Are you one of Pickett's men?"

"Yes, sir."

"Well, you had better go back and rest yourself. Captain Linthicum will tell you the rendezvous for your brigade."

An officer came up at a gallop and told Lee a division—Shotwell was so filled with emotion that he did not get the name, but it was more likely Wright's brigade than a division—was coming into line behind the ridge, and Lee gathered up his reins. "It is well," he said. "Those people over yonder seem to be advancing, and I am becoming a little anxious."[84]

The advance Lee detected was only heavy waves of skirmishers, but they might have heralded a more general movement of Meade's army.

Shotwell had one other touching experience. When he found Linthicum, "our soldier-parson," the captain was standing with his head resting on the neck of a horse, weeping for the man whose blood covered the saddle—his dear friend General Richard S. Garnett.[85] Dick Garnett now was with Stonewall Jackson, and if the stern old genius had been looking down at the assault on Cemetery Ridge it is likely he had already wiped the slate clean for Garnett's retreat at Kernstown.

Lee was at his greatest in this moment of adversity. He made no effort to shift the least part of the blame. "It was all my fault," he repeated again and again as officers came to him. Then he urged them to "do the best we can toward saving what is left us."[86] Already he was looking toward other battles and offering his soldiers resolution instead of remorse.

The Confederate army was indeed in peril when the troops of Pickett, Pettigrew, and Trimble came streaming back, but Longstreet allowed no moments to escape him. He anticipated that the Federals would pursue quickly, Meade at their head. But neither Longstreet nor Lincoln a little later seemed to understand that Meade—who had been selected because he was a safe, cautious general, temperamentally the opposite of Hooker—would go on being cautious and safe to the end.

Longstreet rode the line of his batteries to inspire a resolute defense, determined that his last gun would be sacrificed if necessary in repelling a counterattack. He was not so sparing of ammunition but that he opened on the dense waves of skirmishers and they were soon driven back. That night Law and McLaws were withdrawn from the base of Round Top to Seminary Ridge, and Johnson was retired from Benner's Hill to Seminary Ridge and Oak Hill to make the defensive line more compact.

Lee remained at the line of guns on the fringe of the woods where he awaited the soldiers returning from the assault and spoke to them cheeringly. Meade at that time left his Power's Hill headquarters and rode to Little Round Top, greeted by swelling cheers all along the line. Lee heard them and told a lieutenant to ascertain their meaning, but nothing gave evidence of the counterattack he feared.[87] The Federal army clung to its ridge as though it, too, was spent, and all Meade attempted was a gingerly reconnaissance by a brigade of the Fifth Corps. Could Meade at this moment have attacked successfully? Who knows? If so, his losses would have been terrific, for he in turn would have had to cross the open ground and charge up the slope. The Confederacy, at fearful price, had made its great thrust for freedom, and Meade's army had repulsed it; both sides seemed to recognize that enough blood had been poured already across these Pennsylvania hills.

Of Pickett's fifteen regiments only one field officer escaped injury. He was Lieutenant Colonel Joseph C. Cabell, who survived to fall near Richmond. Seven colonels were dead in front of their men and an eighth was mortally wounded; all the others were casualties. The loss in company officers and noncommissioned officers, while unrecorded, was undoubtedly as severe. True to his presumption, Colonel Patton fell at the wall.

One of the pathetic pictures of the Confederate War was that of Pickett back on Seminary Ridge, dismounted, holding his reins, his hat off, reporting to Longstreet, "General, my noble division is swept away."

That was substantially the case, for the retreat of the survivors, virtually without officers, degenerated into a rout.

Though some of the attacking column, maddened by the repulse, pleaded to be taken back again[88] and Lane heartily invited a Federal counterattack so his men might return some of the favors handed to them along the wall,[89] most of the soldiers knew that for them the battle was over. They stumbled across the fields distraught, winded, assailed from the rear by rapid Federal fire. What destroyed their morale utterly was this return journey across nearly a mile of open country covered with the bodies of their comrades, while shells still exploded overhead and men were dropping about them.[90] Facing the firing guns had been easier than having them at their backs.

Even with a Malvern Hill in its record, the Army of Northern Virginia had experienced no such sanguinary repulse. Efforts to stop the refugees on Seminary Ridge were abortive. Regimental and company formations had been lost; there was no longer a division, or brigades, or regiments. There were merely groups of battle-shocked men seeking shelter from the ghastly carnage. Several hundred yards beyond Seminary Ridge the remnants came to a country road running down a valley, which would lead eventually to a juncture with the Fairfield road. Because of a bluff on one side and a swamp on the other, the fleeing men had to converge and pass through a defile. Here, in the blind frenzy that overtakes men in flight, they threw away much of their equipment—blankets, haversacks, and guns. Efforts by the handful of officers to halt them were as unsuccessful as they had been on Seminary Ridge. Finally some of the privates themselves saw the unreasoning nature of their retreat. Standing firm, they soon brought others into their group until they formed a guard of about thirty men across the road and checked the rout. Sorrel called it "a sight never before witnessed—part of the Army of Northern Virginia in full, breathless flight."[90]

Pickett was weeping without restraint. A man of his high emotions could not control the tears even in front of his soldiers. Riding after his men, he came to the volunteer guard barring the roadway and said, "Don't stop any of my men. Tell them to come to the camp we occupied last night." Then, a pitiful and solitary figure, unaccompanied by aides or orderlies, he rode back toward his old camp on Marsh Creek.

Charles Marshall of Lee's staff came along after Pickett departed, set up a patrol several hundred yards to the rear along a small stream, and kept it there until sunset. By that time the frenzy of the defeat had subsided, and Marshall marched the assembled group back to Seminary Ridge, where Lee spoke kindly to them.

Pickett next morning on Marsh Creek mustered 800 men in place of the approximately 4,800 who had followed him into battle. The division, now calmed, was put in charge of about 4,000 Federal prisoners and started for Virginia.[91] The last to reach the battlefield was the first to depart.

But while the survivors marched away, their name lingered. Pickett's division had been denied the aura of victory, but it had been chosen by fame to identify eternally what is probably the most renowned infantry assault of Anglo-Saxon history—an assault that was "the high-water mark of the Rebellion" and of a type of warfare more akin to chivalry than to the fighting of our present day.

10. The Cavalry Charges Around

Stuart's part in the effort to break the Federal center on July 3 was entirely negative. He took his troopers to the far Confederate left, between the York and Hanover roads, and fought inconclusively at the Rummel farm with Gregg's Federal cavalry, augmented by Custer's brigade of Kilpatrick's division.

The action, begun by dismounted pickets, gradually drew in the heavier columns until Stuart had about 6,000 and Gregg about 4,000 on the field. After a series of charges and countercharges, compared by one of the contestants to "the crash of ocean waves breaking on a rock-bound coast,"[92] the tide receded and there was not an unusual amount of driftage left on the shore. Stuart pulled off when it was obvious that he could not reach the rear of Meade's army and that it had not been broken. He saw unengaged Federal horsemen massing on his flank and knew a bitter and prolonged fight was promised.

Like all the other elements of the Gettysburg campaign for Stuart, this battle in the Federal right rear was barren of glory. It was all he did at Gettysburg and it was worth no more than his pitiful exhibit of 125 wagons, the fruit of his long ride around the Federal army. Wade Hampton was severely but not critically wounded. Stuart retired in the late afternoon and fell in on Ewell's flank.

More spectacular but altogether vain was the attack by the Federal Brigadier General Elon J. Farnsworth, who had worn his star only four days, against some of Law's regiments on the far right of the Confederate army. Farnsworth had passed to the Confederate flank with Kilpatrick, and Law had added Tige Anderson's Georgia brigade as a flank protection. Robertson's 1st Texas Regiment was close by and Benning's Georgians were in supporting distance. Skirmishers of the 1st Texas were so close they overheard the Federal cavalry planning the charge, then an angry voice exclaiming, "If you are afraid to attack, by God, I will lead the charge myself."

Law said he learned later that Kilpatrick was the speaker and that Farnsworth, who knew the harebrained nature of the movement, would not have made it on his own judgment.

Captain H. C. Parsons of the 1st Vermont Cavalry was close when Kilpatrick gave the order and noticed Farnsworth's emotion as he replied, "General, do you mean it? Shall I throw my handful of men over rough ground, through timber, against a brigade of infantry? The 1st Vermont has already been fought half to pieces; these men are too good to kill."[93]

Parsons quoted Kilpatrick's reply in words similar to those overheard by the Texans: "Do you refuse to obey my orders? If you are afraid to lead this charge, I will lead it."

"Take that back," cried Farnsworth in high passion, rising in his stirrups and facing his superior boldly.

Kilpatrick was apparently the one who lacked personal courage in such an encounter—though he was intrepid enough in action—and sidled away from his affronted subordinate. "I did not mean it; forget it," he said.

The ability of the cavalry to break infantry began to pass with the introduction of gunpowder, but Kilpatrick did not seem to realize this; according to one of his officers he thought the cavalry could "fight anywhere except at sea." The ground here was anything but suited to cavalry, being covered with great rocks, lined with stone walls and spotted with clumps of timber.

Farnsworth took two of his regiments, the depleted 1st Vermont and the 1st West Virginia, out of the woods near the base of Round Top and threw them against what a near-by Federal cavalry colonel judged was the best-guarded spot along the entire Confederate line.[94] Anderson's brigade was astride the Emmitsburg road watching Merritt's cavalry brigade which had come up from Emmitsburg and driven in his skirmishers. Farnsworth dashed pell-mell against the front of the 1st Texas, in line between the road and Round Top, and was repulsed, but his front extended beyond that of the enemy; the 1st Vermont, overlapping the Texans, rode on until it found itself between the Confederate artillery and their main line, Farnsworth riding with it.

Law had already ordered the 9th Georgia, Anderson's brigade, from the Emmitsburg road, and it came at a run. He told an aide to find the first available regiment and throw it across Farnsworth's path and the aide brought up the 4th Alabama. Law then ordered Colonel Oates of the 15th Alabama to close the gap on the flank of the 1st Texas where Farnsworth had entered.

The gallant Federal cavalryman was now enclosed, and what his charge consisted of was riding in large circles around the fields, dashing himself here and there against the infantry, seeking an escape. Riding north up the valley he struck the 4th Alabama first, recoiled, moved against the Confederate batteries with their infantry supports, which tore his little command apart at close range, and then circled again in an effort to emerge at his point of entry. Here he struck the Alabamians, bounced back once more, and gained temporary security in the woods, from where about six of his troopers worked their way out past the flank of the 1st Texas.[95]

Most of Law's division, including its commander and General Benning, watched the frantic efforts of the Federal cavalry leader, who could be distinguished by a linen havelock worn over his military cap. Benning said it was as if enacted in an amphitheater. When Farnsworth reached the woods he rode dauntlessly with a handful of men to the 15th Alabama. Flourishing his pistol, he called on the lieutenant commanding the firing line to surrender. He received a volley that emptied most of his saddles, killed his horse, and wounded him in several places. As the lieutenant approached him and demanded his surrender, Farnsworth put his pistol to his head and blew out his brains. His reason can only be surmised. Possibly he believed that all that remained for him was the scorn of his superior, Kilpatrick. That part of the command which had not entered behind the Confederate lines retired in good order.

Colonel Frederick C. Newhall of the 6th Pennsylvania Cavalry, Merritt's advance regiment, which was near by, said later that if Kilpatrick really dared Farnsworth to charge, "it was a crime."[96] About this there could be little doubt, because part of a good cavalry brigade was tossed away capriciously, against the attacking officer's advice, and it seemed largely to embellish a general's swashbuckling. Newhall appeared to believe the story, which was adequately attested, but hoped it was not true that this brave general "rode to his death with that contemptible taunt goading him."

Some of the Confederates who interviewed the prisoners told Benning the attackers "were all drunk."[97] That probably was not the case, but the conclusion is understandable because of the senseless nature of the attack. Nothing was better managed, according to observer Benning, than the manner in which Farnsworth was hemmed in and repulsed. His attack was the final episode of the battle.

That night it rained.

CHAPTER TWENTY-THREE

Retreat to Virginia

1. "I Cain't Find No Rear"

The rain fell in such torrents that, as War Clerk Jones observed, it "washed the blood from the grass all night,"[1] while the historian of the Army of the Potomac, J. H. Stine, thought the heavy cannonading of the three days had so agitated the elements as to unleash the violent storms.[2]

The gods of the thunder, challenged by the blasts of the guns, shot giant bolts with rumbles and reverberations across the hills, deluged the valleys and, except when the eerie flashes lighted the ghostly fields, covered the country with "a darkness like that of Egypt."[3] Canvas gave scant protection, and the Confederate army lay in gloomy silence, drenched, with the rain beating in their faces and depressing any remaining battle ardor for the moment.

The rain finally slackened, reserving some of its torrents for the succeeding days, and although the mud mired down the artillery, Lee was able to withdraw his two wings so that his line ran straight along Seminary Ridge.

Johnson extricated himself skillfully from his remote and always hazardous position hooked around Meade's right, where an enterprising antagonist possessing interior lines might have concentrated an overwhelming force against him. He began his withdrawal at 1:30 A.M., July 4, and conducted it so quietly that it was undetected by Federal pickets only fifty yards away.[4] The noise of the rain must have helped him in his stealth, but it was not likely Slocum would have tried to interfere in the darkness.

Early followed him, then Rodes. When day broke, the Federals on Culp's and East Cemetery hills looked out on the empty Confederate lines, which they could not yet know for certain presaged the death of the Southern cause. But the Federal soldiers had notions.

Where the skirmish lines were still close enough for conversation a Northern soldier called across to a Southern picket, "Hello, Johnnie, have you got any butter?"

"No," the Confederate answered. "Why?"

"Because," the Yank went on, "you'll need it to slide back into the Union on."[5]

Victory and defeat are not always matters of men and bayonets, but often conditions of the mind. All through the night of July 3 the Confederate soldiers thought they would continue the fight in the morning. So did Meade. Few in the ranks were defeated or, in any event, prepared to recognize it. But as the day of July 4 wore on and Lee's intentions became apparent, the Southern army came to understand that the campaign in Pennsylvania had failed, and Meade to know that he had won a great victory.

On the night of July 3 Lee summoned Imboden to headquarters. The cavalry officer arrived about eleven only to learn that Lee was at Hill's headquarters. There Imboden found him and Hill seated on camp stools examining the Adams County map by the light of a single candle, talking earnestly, carefully preparing for the withdrawal of the army, which Hill's corps would commence. Lee directed Imboden to return and await him at army headquarters, which the commanding general reached about one o'clock. The skies had cleared temporarily, for Imboden said Lee could be seen approaching slowly by the moonlight, but he was so exhausted he could scarcely alight. After the cavalryman had assisted him he rested himself against his horse, his arm across the saddle, and stood for a time looking at the ground as though too fatigued to go further.

Sympathetically Imboden broke the silence with a word of understanding. "General, this has been a hard day for you."

"Yes, it has been a sad, sad day for us," Lee responded, his thoughts as always on the army. He gave Imboden clear instructions for the conduct of the wounded to Virginia, specifying the route via Chambersburg and Williamsport to the Potomac.[6]

The rain resumed soon after noon on July 4 and, according to Imboden, "the meadows became small lakes; raging streams ran across the road . . . the storm increased in fury every minute." At 4:00 P.M.

Imboden moved by the Cashtown pike with the long train carrying the thousands of wounded soldiers—seventeen miles of them, a slow-moving convoy that required thirty-four hours to pass a given point.

Lee's spirits were restored after the painful task of evacuating the wounded. Hill's artilleryman, McIntosh, thought the greatness of his character was never more clearly revealed than at this time when his plans had crashed: "He never appeared more serene than on the days succeeding the battle."[7]

All day July 4 the two armies faced each other, sickened by their appalling losses, bogged down in mud and water, each watching for the other to disclose its intention. Ewell entrenched along the ridge northwest of Gettysburg and awaited the Northern army, and though Lee's artillery was short of ammunition, the infantry had plenty for another engagement.

But Meade had decided with finality against attacking Lee on Seminary Ridge. Hancock had written him from his stretcher just after Pickett was repulsed, urging a counterattack. The Federal cavalry chief, Pleasanton, had ridden up to Meade, congratulated him, then badgered him.

"General," Pleasanton said, "I will give you half an hour to show yourself a great general. Order the army to advance, while I will take the cavalry, get in Lee's rear, and we will finish the campaign in a week."

Meade's reply was typical. "How do you know Lee will not attack me again? We have done well enough."[8]

On the gloomy night of July 4 Hill's drenched corps marched, followed by Longstreet, then Ewell. All moved by the Fairfield road toward Hagerstown, which gave protection to the trains going by the Cashtown route. Meade could not shift toward Lee's left and unblock Washington. Just as on Lee's approach to Gettysburg, too many men had to move along a single road, and it was not until ten o'clock on the morning of July 5 that Ewell was on the way from Seminary Ridge. Gordon's brigade, the rear guard, left Gettysburg at noon, unmolested.

Dickert, of Kershaw's brigade, described the retreat: ". . . down mountain sides, through gorges and over hills, the army slowly made its way. No haste, no confusion. . . . The rain fell in torrents, night and day. The roads were soon greatly cut up, which in a measure was to Lee's advantage, preventing the enemy from following him too closely."[9]

Lee, according to his custom, fell in with Longstreet and when the correspondent Ross observed them at Bream's Tavern on the Fairfield road, they were standing apart, talking earnestly, while the staff officers huddled around the fire that was a protection from the chill rain, or, exhausted, slept with the rain beating into their faces, using logs or fence rails for pillows.[10]

Lee said later that he considered countermanding his retreat order because of the rain. He declared he would not have left his position if he had anticipated such dreadfully bad weather."[11] But the wagon trains would be endangered if the army did not follow. Quite obviously he still had unbounded confidence in his men and accepted defeat with deep reluctance.

Ross talked with him and Longstreet at Hagerstown, where the commanding general expressed opinions of interest because they were his first recorded after the battle. He said he would not have attacked had he known that Meade had been able to concentrate his entire army, and he complimented Meade on this achievement. He had not intended, in fact, to bring on any full-scale battle, but, "led away, partly by the success of the first day, believing that Meade had only a portion of his army . . . and seeing the enthusiasm of his own troops, he had thought that a successful battle would cut the knot so easily and satisfactorily that he had determined to risk it."

He attributed his lack of knowledge about Meade to Stuart's absence. The fact that he had been forced to wait three days at Chambersburg had deprived him of the advantage he had secured at the beginning of the invasion. As Ross interpreted his views, Lee felt that if he had not been compelled to wait—and the absence of the cavalry was what slowed him—he could have taken the entire army into the Susquehanna valley, following Ewell, threatened Philadelphia, and severed the Army of the Potomac from the north except by sea. Meade could not have menaced his communications seriously without exposing Baltimore and Washington. "He might have taken a position where it would have been very difficult for Meade to attack him; and without further fighting, by merely maintaining his army near Harrisburg or some other central point, incalculable results might have been secured."[12] That was essentially Longstreet's "defensive tactics" proposal made at the beginning of the campaign.

Lee reached the Potomac on July 7 and found the river in flood and his pontoons destroyed by raiders operating against his rear from French's force at Frederick. He constructed works extending from

Conococheague Creek near Hagerstown, to the Potomac, then awaited either attack by Meade or a recession of the river.

Meade straggled up on July 12, reconnoitered Lee's strong lines, and, against Lincoln's specific injunction to "call no council of war," called a meeting of the corps commanders on the night of July 12. All but two—Howard and Wadsworth, the temporary First Corps commander—opposed an attack, a judgment to which Meade for the time yielded. But after another reconnaissance on July 13, with the rain still pouring, he decided to attack on the fourteenth. When he moved out on the morning of the fourteenth, Lee had gone.

Lack of flour more than lack of ammunition impelled Lee to cross.[13] Adequate supplies for his artillery had been brought up from Winchester on July 9. Meade, too, recognized that Lee's caissons were now loaded. His information, though he regarded it as scanty, was that ammunition trains had been ferried to Williamsport.[14] Why Lee's staff and chief of artillery had not brought up ammunition from Winchester and made it available to him at Gettysburg is an unanswered question. There must have been time while Lee waited at Chambersburg before the battle.

Lincoln was deeply disappointed that Lee was allowed to "escape," and Halleck's telegram reflecting the President's view was so severe that Meade tendered his resignation, which was declined.

The question of whether an attack by Meade might have succeeded will, of course, never be answered. Lee had a larger force than that with which he withstood McClellan at Sharpsburg. He was entrenched in a superior position and his men were eager to retaliate for Gettysburg. It seems unlikely Meade could have done much better than Burnside did at Fredericksburg. That the spirit of the army was by no means crushed could be seen by the attitude of the officer interviewed by Ross: "We will fight them, sir, till hell freezes over, and then, sir, we'll fight them on the ice."[15]

Even when across the river some still thought Lee had really won. Surgeon Welch wrote to his South Carolina wife from Bunker Hill:

We drove the Yankees three miles from the battlefield to a long range of high hills, from which it was impossible to dislodge them. General Lee had to fall back to keep them from getting the advantage."[16]

How the in-the-ranks Federals regarded it could be seen from the letter from Josiah Williams of Putnamville, Indiana, about how he found things when he rejoined his regiment, the 27th Indiana, from the hospital.

Gettysburg was an awful fight the boys saying it was more terrific than anything they ever saw, which is emphatically some. Men laying in piles, our Regiment losing 100 in about 3 minutes in a charge made upon the Breast-works. . . .[17]

Though Meade did not attack before the crossing, his artillery was annoying while the Confederate army had its back to the river. Mc-Kim told a story of a servant who came too close to the lines, where his master admonished him.

"Caesar, what are you doing here?" asked the Confederate officer. "Have I not ordered you always to keep in the rear when the fighting is going on?"

"Yes, Marster," the Negro answered, "I know you is told me dat. But I declar' fo' God, I'se look ebery whar on dis here battle field dis day, and I cain't find no rear."[18]

Heth, restored to duty, covered Lee's crossing. His depleted division was north of the river on the morning of July 14, while Pender's, closer to the stream, was preparing to cross. Heth's men had marched all night and were asleep. Heth put out no pickets, although Pettigrew set up a guard for his own brigade.

While his exhausted men napped, Pettigrew examined the lines. His aide, Captain Louis G. Young, met him on foot in the rear center of his command. While they talked, Heth rode by and told him his brigade would be the rear guard. Pettigrew expressed regret that he had been given no artillery but told Young to arouse the men, which the captain did.

Just then Pettigrew and Young noticed a body of cavalry on rising ground a mile distant and inquired of Heth about its identity. The general said that if it should be an enemy party it could be driven off easily. While Heth and Pettigrew were watching, another small cavalry squadron rode out of the woods only 500 yards distant, flying the United States flag. Heth, for some reason, thought they could not be the enemy but were displaying a captured flag in a spirit of braggadocio. Said Young: "It was difficult to believe sane men would attack as this small body of cavalry did."[19]

The bold Federal squadron rode close to Pettigrew's soldiers, who were only awaiting orders to fire, demanded their surrender, and dashed about firing their revolvers. Pettigrew was tossed from his startled horse. One of his arms was still weak from a wound received at Seven Pines and the other was in a sling from the hand injury suffered at Gettysburg.

His troops meantime formed a line along a fence. When he arose he directed them calmly and the Federal cavalrymen began to fall. One of them took a position on the flank where he fired so effectively that Pettigrew ordered his men to get him. They apparently did not hear, so he started at the man with his own pistol and, heedless of his danger, tried to get so close he could not miss. Before he could fire the Federal trooper shot him in the abdomen. His wound was mortal and he died three days later at Bunker Hill, Virginia, probably the last casualty of the Southern army in the campaign. All North Carolina mourned him.[20]

The small attacking party was annihilated by the Confederate fire. Correspondent Ross called them "forty tipsy cavalrymen,"[21] and others claimed they were drunk, though it is hard to see how that could be determined with all of them dead. It is probable they were only foolhardy.

2. Some Reasons for Victory and Defeat

Meade approached many of his decisions gropingly, owing probably to his brief tenure in command. In the end, his decisions seemed to be unfailingly correct.

He gave battle at Gettysburg instead of along his more favored Pipe Creek line; the Gettysburg position with its interior lines was a major element in his success. He remained on the defensive at every stage, which proved good judgment. When he won he prudently conserved his victory. Unlike many past generals initially successful in dealing with a resourceful adversary, he did not chance spoiling success by an ill-conceived and hastily arranged counterattack or, a little later, by an assault on strongly fortified lines.

In the conduct of the battle, Hancock was as vital a factor as Meade himself—and it was to Meade's credit that he knew how to employ so capable a subordinate; he knew when not to yield to his views, as on the afternoon of July 3 when Hancock, being a more daring warrior, counseled a counteroffensive. As the battle progressed, Hancock's quick decisions and prompt actions meant on more than one occasion the difference between defeat and victory.

It is true that Meade might have won more decisively by taking the offensive. He wisely decided, at an hour when defeat would have meant disaster to the Federal cause, that a victory in hand, even though it did not destroy his adversary, was preferable to risking his own badly battered army further, when there was nothing in the history of Lee's generalship or that of the Army of Northern Virginia which gave much promise that by a frontal attack that army could be captured or destroyed.

Probably the preservation of the union depended a great deal at this hour on Meade's conservatism. He had the sense to recognize that after three days of fighting, he possessed, not striking power, but position.

Lee offered no apologies for his failure at Gettysburg, and needed none; it was a part of his greatness that after the war he refrained from the temptation that besets generals to write accounts of justification and explanation. His words were not required to tell why the Confederacy lost the war and why he did not win it.

But Lee did fail to dislodge his opponent in the decisive battle of the war, and it is pertinent to examine the reasons. Perhaps no battle has been subjected to such searching analysis, yet even at this late date it seems that part of the blame has been misassessed and that some of the areas—such as Lee's selection of his subordinates and the composition of his own staff—have been looked on as sacrosanct by many Southern writers and have been ignored by many Northern.

Of the factors which contributed to Lee's defeat, this writer has listed some which appear outstanding. They are:

Inadequate staff work. This was at the heart of Lee's battle problems and accounted for most of his earlier difficulties. It was evident at the outset in the loose wording of the orders given to Stuart, which deprived Lee of his cavalry. The inadequacy of his staff was present at every hour at Gettysburg, in the inability of the commander to enforce his will on his subordinates and dominate the action as a victorious general must do. Lee needed as chief of staff a soldier of the stature of Hood, Johnson, Gordon, or Benning, with appropriate rank and a sufficient number of subordinates to make certain that (1) the commanding general was informed of all developments on the field (like the value of garrisoning Round Top), and (2) that the commanding general's main purposes were not flouted because of minor developments (like the stoppage of the *en echelon* attack by the Bliss farm skirmish). As it was, after giving his orders to his corps commanders, Lee lost all control of the battle action. This chief of staff should not only have taken over the detail work, but should have maintained close contact with the War Department in Richmond, keeping it informed of the army's condition, causing it to respond to Lee's suggestion for an "army in effigy," and insisting on the forwarding of Pickett's missing brigades.

Failure of Ewell and Early to follow their advantage of July 1. This appears to have been the major tactical error of the battle, for quick pursuit of a broken enemy almost certainly would have deprived Meade of his Cemetery Ridge position, necessitated his concentration behind Pipe Creek, and given Lee a significant psychological victory on July 1, instead of merely a preliminary advantage that was a prelude to defeat. Lee himself might have ridden more speedily to Gettysburg and assumed a more vigorous control of the action on his arrival. He did not need to await Longstreet when a broken, fleeing enemy was before him.

Absence of the cavalry. This led to the battle in circumstances that were not of Lee's choosing, deprived him of intelligence about Meade's concentration, and severely handicapped him at every turn both in the campaign and on the battlefield. A typical instance of the latter was Longstreet's groping flank march of July 2 without cavalry guide and over terrain no cavalry had reconnoitered.

Failure to transfer Ewell's corps to the army's right. After Ewell and Early had missed the opportunity to take Culp's and Cemetery hills at the close of the first day's fighting, Johnson was allowed to beat his division and three additional brigades to pieces against the Culp's Hill citadel without maintaining any concert with the balance of the army. Lee had recognized from the almshouse cupola on the evening of July 1 the weakness of his strung-out, concave line and had urgently desired a more compact, straight line of battle along Seminary Ridge. But he had allowed himself to be induced by the glib, persuasive lawyer, Jubal Early, to maintain his faulty position. With Ewell on his right he might have rolled up Meade's army on July 2, and he could always have imposed more of a threat of a flanking movement around Meade's left, about which the Federal commander seemed sensitive.

Pender's fall on July 2. The loss at a critical moment of this intrepid officer, who had demonstrated on July 1 how ably he could conduct an attack, was a cause of defeat which Lee himself mentioned, although inadvertently or through error in reporting, he placed Pender's fall on the wrong day. Lee's thought was clear enough.

Had Pender not been mortally wounded, it is fairly certain the attack of July 2 would not have petered out in the center of the army, even if the brigade on Pender's immediate right (Mahone's) had remained unemployed. The success of Wright showed that if Pender had hit the Federal center with his customary impact, the Federal line there, weakened by the transfer of troops to the Wheat Field, very likely would have yielded. Hancock would not have been able to send Carroll's brigade to the succor of Howard when East Cemetery Hill was assailed by the brigades of Avery (Hoke) and Hays. Surely the fall of Pender came at an unhappy moment for Lee's fortunes.

Ewell's failure to attack in concert with Longstreet on July 2. Had he done so, the Federal left could not have been reinforced by the Twelfth Corps, and the center might have been further weakened, with a resultant greater opportunity for the brigades of Wright, Wilcox, and Lang.

The capture of Lee's correspondence. This was undoubtedly a strong factor in holding Meade on the battlefield on the night of July 2, when there were valid inducements in his mind to suggest retirement to Pipe Creek. Merely by maintaining his position—by standing firm—he was able to win a great victory.

Longstreet's attack on July 2. While the delay in this attack is generally advanced as a reason—often as *the* reason—for Lee's defeat, two factors are ignored. The first is the historical misconception that Lee ordered a sunrise attack by Longstreet or that Longstreet could have had his troops in hand had Lee so ordered. The second is that the Federal army would not have been unprepared.

Meade had achieved as good a concentration as Lee on the morning of July 2. He had garrisoned Little Round Top, first with Geary, then with Birney. It was vacated on the afternoon of July 2, when Longstreet attacked. The Federals were always closer and could reach it first if it were threatened.

In many respects it seems that Longstreet's attack was delivered, fortuitously more than by intent, at exactly the right moment, because it was at the only time he was likely to catch Sickles' Third Corps so grievously exposed. Earlier than three o'clock Longstreet would have been compelled to attack a more compact Federal line, over a long stretch of open fields, in the same unfavorable circumstances that attended Pickett, Pettigrew, and Trimble a day later.

By attacking when he did, Longstreet disrupted Meade's entire army, shattered some of its best divisions, and brought it so close to defeat that if Ewell had supplied the co-operation which Lee expected, and if Hill had not faltered when less than half his forces were engaged, it is highly likely that the Federal army, already brought to the verge of defeat, would have been dislodged.

The long and vindictive campaign against Longstreet carried on for a generation was initiated by Pendleton and Early on the false premise that Lee had issued a "sunrise attack order." Longstreet was able to refute this easily from the records and Lee's own staff. But the ground continually shifted in the criticism, and Early, a vindictive assailant, finally goaded Longstreet, who was for a long period indifferent, into indiscretions that aligned much sentiment against him. His political defection had already alienated many. His loss of prestige had its inception not so much in what he did or failed to do at Gettysburg, but in defending his course at Gettysburg. His fame among his contemporaries would have been greater had his pen been more discreet.

A review of Early's extensive writing on this subject in the *Southern Historical Society Papers,* and of Pendleton's original attack, leaves a disinterested reader wondering if the case against Longstreet was not built out of an acute need by these two generals for self-justification of their own conduct during the battle, and perhaps it was an unconscious acknowledgment that they themselves had played no small role in causing Lee's defeat. Certainly Lee never attached blame to Longstreet, nor was the affection he maintained for this peculiar, blunt, domineering subordinate ever moderated, even to the very end.

Finally, the mass assault of July 3. Lee could not know until he tested it how hard it would be to break the Federal center on July 3. After it was over, it was easy to see that too much had been expected from the troops. Before, the assault seemed feasible to him, even if not to Longstreet. The cost was staggering and the failure as complete as Grant's comparable mass attack at Cold Harbor in 1864. These assaults, with others in the War between the States, were part of the costly exactions warfare demands to demonstrate how its established methods become obsolete before many are aware of it. The massed infantry attack over open ground against veteran adversaries was ended, as might have been clear from Andrew Jackson's tremendous victory at New Orleans, but the fact had not been manifested repeatedly and conclusively.

Nevertheless, Pickett and Pettigrew had an outside chance. It was not the case that a mere handful under Armistead reached the enemy lines. Large numbers of assailants surged up to the wall. Had the flanks been protected and an artillery complement been supplied to help keep back the flanking parties, it is not unreasonable to believe that the assaulting column might have gained a lodgment on the crest. What would have happened then, if they could have held or been ejected, would have depended on Longstreet's readiness to send in more troops. Still, in the light of what happened, the attack was a ghastly failure that had better never have been made, and Lee was the first to concede this.[22]

Whether from lack of experience in high command or lack of innate ability, the shortcomings of Ewell and A. P. Hill were critical; compared with them, the deficiencies of Longstreet were indeed venial. Neither Ewell nor Hill at this stage of the war—and it was the decisive stage—knew how to conduct a large-scale attack, and in this Longstreet, with his pugnaciousness, tenacity, and above everything else his supreme desire to win, was superb.

The question occurs, with all the opportunities of hindsight, whether Lee would not have found greater advantage in not attacking on July 2, but in holding his position on Seminary Ridge after bringing Ewell around and forming a straight line with its left flank on Oak Hill. Public opinion and fretting from Washington would have compelled Meade to assail him. There is some misunderstanding that Lee was compelled to attack—that he, being the invader, was committed to the offensive. Many great campaigns have been won by invading armies that fought on the defensive as at Crécy, Agincourt, Senlac and Marengo. Lee had plenty of food and enough powder and could wait. His herds were large—he lost 12,000 head of cattle, and 8,000 head of sheep on his retreat—and when the cavalry arrived it could have rounded up more.[23]

Lee saw the possibility of ending the campaign in a few quick strokes, and quite boldly he responded to that invitation. His troops performed to the full measure of his expectations. Had he achieved a victory, everything he did would have seemed correct. Still great generals do not make victories as often as victories seem to make great generals. As it was, he came so close to success that at several points an additional brigade, like that of Corse or Jenkins, might have changed the outcome of the battle.

That was his own view. When he next saw Micah Jenkins in Virginia, he said, "Jenkins, if I had had your brigade at Gettysburg I would have won."[24]

Probably the best summary of why he lost was his own, contained in a letter written in 1868 to an author contemplating a school history, in which, after referring him to the official accounts of the battle, Lee said:

Its loss was occasioned by a combination of circumstances. It was commenced in the absence of correct intelligence. It was continued in the effort to overcome the difficulties by which we were surrounded, and it would have been gained could one determined and united blow have been delivered by our whole line. As it was, victory trembled in the balance for three days, and the battle resulted in the infliction of as great an amount of injury as was received and in frustrating the Federal campaign for the season.[25]

Charles Francis Adams, a competent Northern authority, thought that in view of the chances always present in warfare: "The Gettysburg campaign was . . . timely, admirably designed, energetically executed, and brought to a close with consummate military skill."

Adams brought out likewise that no hostile force ever invaded an enemy country and retreated "leaving behind less cause for hate and bitterness than did the Army of Northern Virginia in that memorable campaign."[26]

Thousands of battle deaths and nearly twenty-two months of desperate fighting remained before the results of the battle of Gettysburg were confirmed. Victory was not always thereafter a stranger to Lee's army. But the attrition of the South set in and the war rolled on through the Wilderness toward Appomattox. When the fighting had ended it was clear that the Confederate cause was at high tide when it surged against the stone walls and Federal trenches on the crest of Cemetery Hill.

Notes

Chapter One: SUBSTITUTES FOR GENIUS

[1] James P. Crocker, "My Personal Experiences in Taking up Arms," *Southern Historical Society Papers,* XXXIII, 113.

[2] *Ibid.*

[3] Mary Boykin Chesnut, *A Diary from Dixie,* 258.

[4] George Cary Eggleston, *A Rebel's Recollections,* 150.

[5] G. Moxley Sorrel, *Recollections of a Confederate Staff Officer,* 23.

[6] *Southern Historical Society Papers,* V, 176. (Hereinafter *S.H.S.P.*)

[7] *Ibid.*

[8] Eggleston, 153. The italics are his.

[9] William M. Owen, *In Camp and Battle with the Washington Artillery of New Orleans,* 176.

[10] Sorrel, 113.

[11] *Ibid.*

[12] Eggleston, 150.

[13] Sorrel, 37.

[14] *Ibid.*

[15] *Ibid.,* 38.

[16] Henry Heth, *S.H.S.P.,* IV, 151, quotes Lee as saying to him, ". . . you, and all my officers know that I am always ready and anxious to have their suggestions."

[17] Richard Taylor, *Library of Southern Literature,* XII, 5205. (Hereinafter *L.S.L.*)

[18] *Ibid.*

[19] *Official Records of the Union and Confederate Armies,* XII, Part III, 9. (Hereinafter *O.R.*)

[20] Taylor, *L.S.L.,* XII, 5205.

[21] June 19, 1863.

[22] Randolph H. McKim, *A Soldier's Recollections,* 134.

[23] John B. Gordon, *Reminiscences of the Civil War,* 157.

[24] McKim, 134.

[25] Washington *Post* interview, June 11, 1893.

26 *Ibid.*

27 Heros von Borcke, *Memoirs of the Confederate War for Independence,* II, 262.

28 Glenn Tucker, *Poltroons and Patriots,* II, 652.

29 Richmond *Examiner,* July 31, 1862, uses the phrase.

30 James C. Birdsong, *Brief Sketches of North Carolina Troops . . . ,* 54. A major asked Hill if he knew Burnside. "Ought to," said Hill. "He owes me $8,000." J. B. Jones placed the amount at $10,000.

31 Richmond *Examiner,* June 28, 1862.

32 Richmond *Whig,* July 11, 1862.

33 Sorrel, 89.

34 Sorrel thought Longstreet largely forgot and became reconciled with Hill, but his later statements, as in the Washington *Post* interview, June 11, 1893, show a lack of warmth.

35 Charleston *Mercury,* September 25, 1862; cited by Douglas Southall Freeman, *Lee's Lieutenants,* II, 148n.

36 Henry Kyd Douglas, *I Rode with Stonewall,* 146f, relates the incident and thinks Jackson "was thoroughly justified."

37 *O.R.,* XIX, Part II, 643.

38 *The Annals of the War, by Leading Participants North and South,* 703. (Hereinafter *Annals.*)

39 Washington *Post,* July 11, 1893.

40 *Ibid.*

41 *Battles and Leaders of the Civil War,* III, 245n. (Hereinafter *B. and L.*)

42 Sorrel, 135.

43 Although born in South Carolina, Longstreet spent much of his early and late life in Georgia and is properly accredited to that state. He was appointed to West Point from Alabama. Hood, born in Kentucky, became a Texan during his army service there.

44 Walter Clark, ed., *Histories of the Several Regiments and Battalions from North Carolina in the Great War, 1861-65,* I, 293ff. (Hereinafter *N.C. Regts.*)

45 Longstreet, *B. and L.,* III, 245n. Longstreet said D. H. Hill was the superior of A. P. Hill "in rank, skill, judgment, and distinguished services." The record supports him strongly.

Chapter Two: THE GRAY HOST UNLEASHED

1 J. B. Jones, *A Rebel War Clerk's Diary,* I, 272.

2 *Ibid.,* 274.

3 The riot details are from J. B. Jones, I, 284-285, or Josiah Gorgas, *War Diary,* 29.

4 Gorgas, 29.

5 J. B. Jones, 286.

6 *Ibid.,* 293, 328. Jones, who saw President Davis often, wrote: "I think he has been ill every day for several years, but this (May 19, 1863) is his most serious illness." Gorgas, 47, said July 2 that the President's physician was seriously alarmed.

7 J. B. Jones, I, 380.

8 *Ibid.,* 314-315.

9 *Ibid.,* 314.

10 *Ibid.,* 325.

11 *S.H.S.P.,* IV, 120.

[12] *Ibid.*, 153.

[13] Gorgas, 26.

[14] Colonel G. F. R. Henderson, "Review of General Longstreet's Book . . . " *S.H.S.P.*, XXXIX, 105.

[15] *Annals*, 415-416; James Longstreet, *From Manassas to Appomattox*, 332.

[16] *Annals*, 416

[17] Gordon, 139.

[18] *S.H.S.P.*, IV, 52.

[19] Charles Marshall, *Papers*, 10.

[20] McKim, 133.

[21] *Ibid.*, 134.

[22] *Ibid.*

[23] *N.C. Regts.*, I, 717.

[24] McKim, 137.

[25] J. B. Jones, I, 315.

[26] *S.H.S.P.*, IV, 152.

[27] June 19, 1863.

[28] John West, *A Texan in Search of a Fight*, 74-75.

[29] *Ibid.*, 75.

[30] *Ibid.*, 76.

[31] *Ibid.*

[32] Spencer Glasgow Welch, *A Confederate Surgeon's Letters to His Wife*, 53.

[33] *S.H.S.P.*, XIX, 314.

[34] Isaac R. Trimble, "The Campaign and Battle of Gettysburg," *Confederate Veteran*, XXV, 209.

[35] *Ibid.*, 209-210.

[36] *Ibid.*, 210. Lee issued his orders against plundering while at Berryville, Va., June 21, but they were not printed until the army reached Chambersburg, Pa.

[37] *O.R.*, XXVII, Part III, 882.

[38] *Ibid.*, 881-882.

[39] Albert J. Beveridge, *Abraham Lincoln*, I, 433. Myrta L. Avary, *Recollections of Alexander H. Stephens*, 21. Lincoln and Stephens were among the seven Whig Congressmen who organized the "Young Indians," a group to advance the candidacy of Zachary Taylor for the presidential nomination.

Chapter Three: THE ARMY CROSSES

[1] *N.C. Regts.*, I, 718.

[2] *Ibid.* This was the company raised by Governor Zebulon Vance of North Carolina at the outbreak of the war, which he headed as captain.

[3] Jacob Hoke, *The Great Invasion*, 97ff. Halleck to Hooker, June 18, 1863, *O.R.*, XXVII, Part I, 50.

[4] Richmond *Examiner*, July 3, 1863.

[5] *Ibid.*

[6] Hoke, 96.

[7] *Ibid.*, 95ff. Hoke quotes notes prepared by Dr. Philip Schaff saying the passage in St. Matthew 24:6, "and ye shall hear of wars and rumors of wars" was arranged in climatic order, since the rumor often was worse than war itself.

[8] Brigadier General Albert Gallatin Jenkins knew many Northerners, having been graduated from Jefferson College, at Canonsburg, Pennsylvania, in 1848, and Harvard Law School in 1850. Although but thirty-two at the time of the Gettysburg campaign, he had served two terms in Congress, representing his

western Virginia district, then had been a delegate to the provisional Confederate Congress in 1861. Commissioned brigadier general August 1, 1862, he would survive until the battle of Cloyds Mountain, in May 1864. One of the Chambersburg newspapers said of him: "He graduated from Jefferson college in this state, and gave promise of future usefulness and greatness. His downward career commenced some five years ago, when in an evil hour he became a member of Congress from Western Virginia, and from thence may be dated his decline and fall." Quoted by LaSalle Corbell Pickett, *Pickett and His Men,* 263, the paper being unidentified.

9 During McCausland's raid on Chambersburg in 1864, the house was burned and the farm devastated. McClure did not nurse his loss. As the editor years later in the Philadelphia *Times,* he published without bias the stories of participants on both sides. The series is one of the outstanding collections of source material on the war. Many of the articles were collected later in the well-known volume, *The Annals of the War.*

10 Hoke, 110.

11 Robert Stiles, *Four Years Under Marse Robert,* 199.

12 *O.R.,* XXVII, Part II, 297-298.

13 Richmond *Examiner,* July 3, 1863.

14 Hoke, 112.

15 *Ibid.,* 135.

16 *Ibid.,* 136.

17 *Ibid.,* 138.

18 Information from Dr. Jacqueline Bull, Archivist, Margaret I. King Memorial Library, University of Kentucky, based on William H. Townsend, *Lincoln and the Bluegrass* and Thomas M. Green, *Historic Families of Kentucky.*

19 Marshall, 199.

20 Reprinted in Richmond *Examiner,* July 7, 1863.

21 *O.R.,* XXVII, Part III, 914. Marshall, 200.

22 Marshall, 201.

23 W. W. Blackford, *War Years with Jeb Stuart,* 222.

24 Marshall, 202.

25 *Ibid.,* O.R., XXVII, Part III, 913.

26 Marshall, 204.

27 *Ibid.,* 206. *O.R.,* XXVII, Part III, 915.

28 Marshall, 208.

29 *Ibid. O.R.,* XXVII, Part III, 923.

30 Blackford, 222.

31 H. B. McClellan, *The Life and Campaigns of Major General J. E. B. Stuart,* 316-318.

32 Blackford, 223-224.

33 *Ibid.,* 223.

34 *O.R.,* XXVII, Part III, 931.

35 *Ibid.* Lee thought the plan would be the best protection against marauding parties.

36 *Ibid.,* XXVII, Part III, 946.

37 Eppa Hunton, *Autobiography,* 87.

38 Katharine M. Jones, *Heroines of Dixie,* 173.

39 Owen, 234.

40 J. F. J. Caldwell, *History of a Brigade . . . ,* 97.

41 *Ibid.*

42 Welch, *Letters,* 57.

43 Fitzgerald Ross, *A Visit to Cities and Camps of the Confederacy,* 31.

[44] *Ibid.*

[45] *Ibid.*, 33. He said, "I do not recollect ever to have seen a drunken private soldier in the South. . . ." Only once or twice had he seen an officer a little "tight."

Chapter Four: FEASTING ON NORTHERN PLENTY

[1] The stories of "Darling Nellie Gray" and "Dixie" are taken from Emilius O. Randall, "High Lights of Ohio Literature," *Ohio Archeological and Historical Society Publications,* XXXVIII, 269 (hereinafter *O.A. and H.S.P.*), and C. B. Galbreath, "Song Writers of Ohio," *O.A. and H.S.P.,* XIV, 180-192. For his account of the introduction of "Dixie" in New Orleans, Galbreath cited the article by Dr. G. A. Kane in the New York *World* in 1893, which told of Patti's zouave march and how the Washington Artillery had the tune set to a quickstep by Romeo Meniri. Emmett in 1895 made a triumphal tour through the South as the author of "Dixie."

[2] Sorrel, 57-58, noticed that early in the war the soldiers at Centerville sang mainly "Lorena," "Maryland," and "Dixie." There was back-home feeling that "Dixie" did not have the proper dignity and that the South should have a national anthem. "I Puritana" was discussed. But the soldiers adopted "Dixie," made it their favorite, and decided the question.

[3] John B. Hood, *Advance and Retreat,* 54. Although the "Yellow Rose of Texas" was set to the tune of the "Song of the Texas Rangers" (W. L. Fagan, *Southern War Songs*), Hood did not mention it at the crossing, nor has reference to it been found elsewhere during the Gettysburg campaign.

[4] William C. Oates, *The War Between the Union and the Confederacy . . . ,* 198.

[5] *Ibid.*

[6] *Ibid.*

[7] West.

[8] Joseph B. Polley, *Hood's Texas Brigade . . . ,* 147.

[9] *Ibid.,* 148.

[10] *Ibid.*

[11] Sorrel, 177.

[12] *Ibid.,* 178.

[13] *Ibid.,* 179.

[14] Randolph A. Shotwell, *Our Living and Dead,* IV, 81. (Hereinafter *O.L. and D.*)

[15] D. Augustus Dickert, *History of Kershaw's Brigade,* 288.

[16] *Ibid.,* 230.

[17] Ross, 35.

[18] *Ibid.,* 35-36.

[19] *Ibid.,* 37.

[20] George Pickett, *Soldier of the South,* 41. (Hereinafter *Soldier of the South.*)

[21] *Ibid.,* 43.

[22] *Ibid.*

[23] *Ibid.* In *Blue and Gray . . . ,* 107, Colonel William R. Aylett, with whose Virginia regiment Pickett was moving, said, "Struck by her courage and loyalty, Pickett with hat off, gave her a military salute, my regiment presented arms, and we cheered her with a good old-fashioned rebel yell. . . ."

[24] *Soldier of the South,* 48.

25 *Ibid.*

26 *O.R.,* XXVII, Part I, 65.

27 Owen, 241.

28 Gordon, 146.

29 Douglas, 245.

30 Stiles, 199.

31 Ross, 40. See the claim of the Virginia company in Chapter 22.

32 Trimble left the story of these transactions in the Ms. later published in *Confederate Veteran,* XV, 210ff.

33 Hoke, 161.

34 *Ibid.,* 164

35 *Ibid.,* 197-198. A request for the needy was made by Mrs. Ellen McClellan, who gained easy access to Lee. She wrote an account of the visit, giving a colloquy with the general, from whom, on departing, she asked an autograph. "He replied: 'Do you want the autograph of a rebel?' I said, 'General Lee, I am a true Union woman, and yet I ask for bread and your autograph.' The General replied, 'It is to your interest to be for the Union, and I hope you may be as firm in your principles as I am in mine.' He assured me that his autograph would be a dangerous thing to possess, but at length he gave it to me. Changing the topic of conversation, he assured me the war was a cruel thing, and that he only desired that they would let him go home and eat his bread there in peace. All this time I was impressed with the strength and sadness of the man."

36 Sorrel, 178.

37 Hood, 55.

38 Sorrel, 73.

39 Eggleston, 141.

40 W. H. Stewart, *A Pair of Blankets,* 94.

41 Eggleston, 142.

42 Sorrel, 74.

43 Chesnut, 264.

44 Eggleston, 142-143.

45 Arthur J. L. Fremantle, *Three Months in the Southern States,* 242ff.

46 A. L. Long, *Memoirs of Robert E. Lee,* 29.

47 Benjamin Harvey Hill, Confederate Senator from Georgia, related his conversation with Lee, speaking before the Southern Historical Society in Atlanta, February 18, 1874. The address is published in *L.S.L.,* VI, 2397.

48 Hill said in thought after the conversation, "Surely Washington is no longer the only exception." *Ibid.*

49 Hood, 17.

50 Long, 31.

51 *Ibid.*

52 J. William Jones, *Life and Letters of Robert E. Lee . . . ,* 27.

53 Marshall, XXIV.

54 *Ibid.,* XXV.

55 *Ibid.*

56 *Ibid.,* XX. Lee was able to poke a bit at the press. He told Senator Hill that a mistake had been made at the start of the war. "What mistake is that, General?" the Senator asked. "Why, sir," said Lee, "at the beginning we appointed all our worst generals to command the armies and all our best generals to edit the newspapers." *L.S.L.,* VI, 2397.

A Northern estimate was published in the *Sunday School Herald,* of Dayton, Ohio, XIV, 466 (1906), which told that Lee participated in the camp prayer meetings. Under the heading of "Anecdotes of the Great," it said: "Lee never spoke a scurrilous word of the Federal army. . . . He was a man of clean

lips. One has said: 'A soldier would as soon have thought of kissing the lips of a raging volcano as of telling a coarse jest in his presence.' "
[57] Ada C. Lightsly, *The Veteran's Story*, 5.

Chapter Five: A MISSIVE AMONG THE ROSES

[1] Hoke, 170.
[2] *O.R.*, XXVII, Part II, 465.
[3] *Ibid.*
[4] York was the capital from September 30, 1777, until June 27, 1788. There the Articles of Confederation were adopted.
[5] Early in his official report, *O.R.*, XXVII, Part II, 466, said the town authorities came out on the night of June 27 and surrendered to Gordon. But Smith's brigade entered first. Stiles, the chronicler of the event, was at the head of the column.
[6] Stiles, 202.
[7] *Ibid.*
[8] *Ibid.*, 203. The same author pictures Smith as he appeared on the march. He carried a blue cotton umbrella under his arm. He sat his horse by the roadside, smiling and "actually bowing to the artillerymen" who were passing, giving them the hearty greeting "which had, for more than a generation, proved irresistible on the hustings of the Old Dominion." *Ibid.*, 194.
[9] *Ibid.*, 202-204, gives the account of Smith's entry and speech.
[10] *Ibid.*, 206, tells the familiar story of the Lutheran delegation in Carlisle that asked Ewell if their pastor might pray according to his practice for the President of the United States. "Certainly, pray for him," replied Ewell. "I don't know of anybody that stands more in need of prayer."
[11] Gordon, 141.
[12] *N.C. Regts.*, III, 412.
[13] The Confederates spent liberally in York as elsewhere. York had had experience in an earlier generation with depreciated currency, for there $10,-000,000 of "Continentals" were printed in the Revolutionary War.
[14] *N.C. Regts.*, III, 412.
[15] Gordon, 142.
[16] *Ibid.*, 142-143.
[17] *O.R.*, XXVII, Part II, 467.
[18] Tucker, II, 592.
[19] Gordon, 143-144.
[20] *O.R.*, XXVII, Part II, 466.
[21] Gordon, 147.
[22] *O.R.*, XXVII, Part II, 466.
[23] J. D. Hufham, Jr., "Gettysburg . . . ," Wake Forest *Student* (April 1897), 451.
[24] *Ibid.*, 454.
[25] *N.C. Regts.*, II, 233.
[26] *Ibid.*
[27] Hufham, 454.
[28] Stephen D. Ramseur, Ms. letters, Southern Historical Collection, University of North Carolina Library, Chapel Hill, N.C.
[29] Henry W. Thomas, *History of the Doles-Cook Brigade*, 7.
[30] *Ibid.*
[31] This came to be known as the "battle flag" and is the one commonly recognized and displayed throughout the South. Though the flag over Jackson's

casket was of the new design, it was largely white. Most flags at Gettysburg
were either the Stars and Bars or the state flags, which the Southern regiments
cherished dearly. Henry A. London, historian of the 32nd North Carolina,
N.C. Regts., II, 524, said the flag was made from the design adopted condition-
ally by the Confederate Congress a few weeks earlier. It is at times challenged
that the Confederacy ever adopted an "official" flag, but the battle standard had
full recognition.

32 This account of the ceremony follows London in *N.C. Regts.,* II, 525ff. The
flag of the new design was flown over Castle Thunder in Richmond, June 22,
1863. Richmond *Examiner,* June 23, 1863.

33 McKim, 163.

34 John O. Casler, *Four Years in the Stonewall Brigade,* 240.

35 *Ibid.*

36 McKim, 163.

37 *Ibid.,* 166.

38 This account of the New York *Herald* correspondent's trip through Lee's
army was republished in full, without comment, in the Richmond *Examiner,*
July 18, 1863.

Chapter Six: HOOKER AND MEADE PURSUE

1 *O.R.,* XXVII, Part I, 31.

2 *Ibid.,* 34.

3 *Ibid.,* 35.

4 *Ibid.*

5 Charles F. Benjamin, War Department official, in his paper, "Hooker's Appointment and Removal," *B and L.,* III, 239ff., says, 240, that Stanton "knew"
there were two Hookers in the same man, one "an excellent officer, mentally
strong, clever and tireless, and charming (almost magnetic) in address. It was
the other Hooker on whom he wished to take no chances."

6 Meade, who commanded the rear guard on the retreat from Chancellorsville,
sent an emergency request for additional orders. His adjutant found that
Hooker was sleeping and could not be disturbed, and the adjutant had to take
a mere repetition of old orders from Hooker's chief of staff, Butterfield. Couch,
second in command, retired also. Reynolds said, when applied to, "Tell General Meade that someone should be waked up to take command of this army."
Isaac R. Pennypacker, *Life of George Gordon Meade,* 125.

7 His dispatch was published June 23, 1863.

8 *O.R.,* XXVII, Part I, 55.

9 Hooker's correspondence with Halleck on Harpers Ferry is assembled in
Stine, 443-444.

10 *Ibid.,* 444.

11 General Hardie's delay in reaching Meade's headquarters was due to the
disorganized state of affairs in Frederick. Benjamin, *B and L.,* III, 242n., says
no provost marshall had been appointed and streets and roads were "thronged
with boisterous soldiers, more or less filled with Maryland whisky, and many of
them ripe for rudeness or mischief."

12 Colonel Henry S. Huidekoper in *Pennsylvania at Gettysburg,* II, 1097.
Hancock in a letter to John William Wallace, president of the Historical Society
of Pennsylvania, March 4, 1880, thought it was well established historically that
Reynolds had been offered the place. *Reynolds Memorial,* 94. Benjamin, *B. and
L.,* III, 240, thought Halleck sounded him.

[13] *Pennsylvania at Gettysburg,* II, 1097.

[14] George B. McClellan, *McClellan's Own Story,* 140.

[15] Benjamin, *B. and L.,* III, 241, says Lincoln, Stanton, and Halleck in a conference after Chancellorsville concluded that "both the check at Chancellorsville and the retreat were inexcusable, and that Hooker must not be intrusted with the conduct of another battle." That Lincoln entered into such a compact is to be strongly doubted because his later course was so sharply inconsistent with such a decision. Not only did he urge on Hooker an aggressive pursuit of Lee, which would have involved fighting, but also it would have been clear to him that a successor to Hooker ought to have the advantage of familiarizing himself with the duties of high command as much as possible in advance of a battle. If Lincoln had positively decided within a few days after Chancellorsville that Hooker could not fight again, he would have removed Hooker promptly, or else taken the responsibility before history of retaining a feared general for his own protection, so that the mistake of the selection would not be emphasized. It appears that Hooker's lackadaisical handling of the army after leaving the Rappahannock was the deciding factor in bringing Lincoln over to the view of Stanton and Halleck.

[16] George Gordon Meade, *Life and Letters,* II, 3.

[17] *Ibid.,* I, 373.

[18] *Ibid.,* 365.

[19] *Ibid.,* 364.

[20] *Ibid.*

[21] *Ibid.,* 367.

[22] *Ibid.,* 366.

[23] The Meade sketch follows Meade, I, 1-11, and Pennypacker, 11-17.

[24] Meade, I, 264.

[25] Carl Sandburg, *Abraham Lincoln. The War Years,* II, 335.

[26] Barton H. Wise, *The Life of Henry A. Wise . . . ,* 367.

[27] Meade, I, 367.

[28] Joseph W. Keifer, *Slavery and Four Years of War,* II, 25.

[29] George B. McClellan, 137.

[30] This was a mine case in California; Stanton claimed in a conversation with General H. W. Hitchcock that it was his partner who had a personal controversy with Halleck. George B. McClellan, 137n.

[31] *Ibid.,* 137.

[32] Frank Moore, ed., *The Rebellion Record,* 86. (Hereinafter *Rebellion Record.*)

[33] *Ibid.,* 86-87.

[34] *Ibid.*

[35] *Ibid.*

[36] *B. and L.,* III, 242.

[37] Oliver O. Howard, *Autobiography,* I, 395.

[38] Abner Doubleday, *Chancellorsville and Gettysburg,* 114-115. Butterfield told him a review would mean the loss of Harrisburg and Philadelphia.

Chapter Seven: CONCENTRATION

[1] Sorrel, 164.

[2] *Ibid.,* 156-157.

[3] *Ibid.,* 161. *B. and L.,* III, 249.

[4] Sorrel, 164.

[5] *Ibid.*

[6] Marshall made it clear that Lee thought Hooker was still in Virginia. The commander was becoming anxious that Hooker might move in strength on Richmond. "I heard General Lee express this apprehension more than once while we lay at Chambersburg." Marshall, 217-218.

[7] *Ibid.*, 218.

[8] *Ibid.*, 219.

[9] There is a possibility of confusion in towns. Middletown is eight miles west of Frederick. Middleburg, near the juncture of Pipe Creek with the Monocacy River, is northeast of Frederick. Meade was actually moving toward Middleburg, not Middletown.

[10] *Annals,* 439.

[11] This writer many years ago talked with an older resident of the Great Falls neighborhood who remembered Stuart's horsemen riding along the canal towpath twelve miles from Washington and was struck by the zest and fine appearance of the men despite their hard riding. Blackford, 224, tells of the crossing.

[12] Blackford, 225.

[13] *Ibid.*, 224.

[14] *Ibid.*, 225.

[15] *Ibid.*

[16] *Rebellion Record,* 85.

[17] *Ibid.*

[18] Blackford, 225.

[19] Randolph H. McKim, "Gen. J. E. B. Stuart in the Gettysburg Campaign," *S.H.S.P.,* XXXVII, 210, says it would have been natural for Stuart to go to Gettysburg since he had been instructed that one column of Lee's army would move by that point. McKim thought Stuart's proper course was by Littlestown to Gettysburg, which he could have reached by 11:00 A.M., June 30, to take his position in front of Lee's army.

[20] Blackford, 225. *Pennsylvania at Gettysburg,* II, 887. The 2nd North Carolina Regiment struck the 18th Pennsylvania Cavalry, which, in its first engagement, suddenly found itself in hand-to-hand combat. After giving way, it rallied and with the 5th New York drove the Carolinians back on their reserves.

[21] *Pennsylvania at Gettysburg,* II, 888.

[22] Colonel W. H. Swallow, *Southern Bivouac,* November 1885, thinks the juncture could have been made around East Berlin, four miles north of the York pike. Hoke, 253-254, who cites Swallow, makes the point that Early had not been alerted on Stuart's ride around the Federal army and was not expecting him, but heard Stuart's guns at Hanover. As Stuart crossed Early's trail, not an inhabitant informed him that Confederate infantry had passed a short time before.

[23] Blackford, 228.

[24] Colonel David Gregg McIntosh, of Hill's artillery, told the story of Marshall's declaration that Stuart should have been shot. Marshall, some years after the war, attended a small dinner party of Confederate officers, who were startled when Lee's chief of staff said he had tried to have Stuart court-martialed. " 'Who?' everyone exclaimed, 'not Jeb Stuart,' 'Yes, Jeb Stuart,' he said."

Then he made a statement which McIntosh put down in writing the next day. It told of his great difficulty in getting a report from Stuart on the Gettysburg campaign, for which Lee was pressing him. It was necessary to have all the reports from subordinates before Lee could complete his own report. Finally Stuart's was received and Marshall could go ahead. McIntosh's memorandum continued to quote Marshall: " 'I then concluded my report to General Lee. In doing so I dealt with Stuart in the plainest language; in fact, I had told him before I thought he ought to be shot.

" 'General Lee was unwilling, however, to adopt my draft. I had explicitly charged him with disobedience of orders, and laid the full responsibility at his door.' "

Marshall then reviewed the orders Stuart had received and proceeded: ".... in declining to adopt his report General Lee did not question its accuracy, but said he could not adopt my conclusions and charge him with the facts as I had stated them unless they should be established by a court martial." David Gregg McIntosh, *Review of the Gettysburg Campaign,* 27ff.

[25] Marshall, 217.

[26] Marshall, 229, says the Southern army could have reached Gettysburg June 29. Although a good road center, it was not of high value then, for Lee's objective was not to take Gettysburg but to defeat the Federal army.

[27] Suesserott letter, Hoke, 205.

[28] Mrs. McClellan's letter, Hoke, 197-198.

[29] Stiles, 227-228.

[30] Hoke, 217.

[31] *Ibid.,* 226.

[32] *O.R.,* XXVII, Part III, 420.

[33] Trimble, *Confederate Veteran,* XV, 211.

[34] *Ibid.*

Chapter Eight: PETTIGREW'S ENCOUNTER

[1] *N.C. Regts.,* III, 236.

[2] *Ibid.*

[3] W. N. Pickerill, *History of the Third Indiana Cavalry,* 81. Buford report, *O.R.,* XXVII, Part I, 926.

[4] J. B. Jones, I, 209.

[5] *Ibid.*

[6] Major General Matthew F. Maury, quoted by Kemp P. Battle, *History of the University of North Carolina,* I, 507.

[7] Battle, I, 504, 729.

[8] Chesnut, 63-64.

[9] *Ibid.,* 284, 24n.

[10] Walter Clark, *General James Johnston Pettigrew, C.S.A.,* 5.

[11] *S.H.S.P.,* IV, 157.

[12] *N.C. Regts.,* I, 506.

[13] *Ibid.,* 587. Leventhorpe rose to Major General in the Confederate service.

[14] *O. L. and D.,* IV, 82.

[15] *N.C. Regts.,* III, 88.

[16] *Ibid.,* V, 115.

[17] *Ibid.*

[18] This Federal regiment, which thus had the first contact with Confederates in Gettysburg and in the next day suffered the first casualty and first loss of life in the battle, was recruited in southeastern Indiana, mainly from Dearborn, Switzerland, Harrison, Jefferson, Fayette, Rush, Shelby, and Marion counties. Watlington Mss. Indiana State Library.

[19] *Indiana at the Fiftieth Anniversary of Gettysburg* (Report of State Commission), 42.

20 *N.C. Regts.*, II, 342.
21 *S.H.S.P.*, IV, 157.
22 *N.C. Regts.*, V, 116.
23 *Ibid.*
24 *Ibid.*, 117.
25 *Ibid.*

Chapter Nine: McPHERSON'S HEIGHTS

1 Bragg on assigning Fry in 1864. *Dictionary of Alabama Biography,* 619.

2 The weather on the first day was variable and governed by local conditions. The Iron Brigade historian says there were puddles on the road but no thick mud. The lack of mud is further attested by the rapidity of the marching in both armies. Mist is mentioned locally in both morning and afternoon, though some of the men spoke of the clear, hot, sunshiny day. The 20th Indiana, coming up from Emmitsburg, was drenched by a mountain shower. But over most of the area from Manchester to Chambersburg the day was cloudy, hot, and sticky and in some areas the roads were dusty. Such is the best possible interpretation of the many seemingly inconsistent references to the weather of July 1 in regimental and brigade accounts.
  Dr. Michael Jacobs made observations in Gettysburg and recorded that from June 15 to July 22, 1863, there was not an entirely clear day. The 2:00 P.M. temperatures were: July 1, 76; July 2, 82; July 3, 87. These were probably shade temperatures. Frequent references by soldiers to the intense heat, "broiling sun," in *Pennsylvania at Gettysburg* I, 317, and the road "aglow with fiery rage," *ibid.*, II, 653, suggest higher temperatures and humidity in roads and fields. During July 1 the sky at Gettysburg was covered with stratus clouds; the afternoons of the second and third were largely clear. From scrapbook of clippings, Gettysburg National Military Park library.

3 *Confederate Veteran,* XIV, 308.

4 The best account of Archer's march noticed is that of Private E. T. Boland, 13th Alabama, of Brewton, Alabama, in *Confederate Veteran,* XIV, 308f.

5 Richmond *Enquirer,* July 15, 1863.

6 *S.H.S.P.,* XIV, 6.

7 A. C. Weaver, *Third Indiana Cavalry . . . ,* 4-5.

8 Clark, *Pickett's Charge a Misnomer,* 3.

9 The writer, on a day when the visibility was probably about like that of July 1, 1863, found that the seminary cupola affords an excellent view of the roads reaching Gettysburg from the north, west, and south, along which the armies were converging. As an observation point it is in many respects superior to Little Round Top on which the Federal army relied during the last two days of the battle.

10 Rosengarten in *Reynolds Memorial,* 29.

11 *Ibid.,* 29-30. Captain James A. Hall, commanding the Maine light artillery battery, said he heard Reynolds dictate a message to Meade: "Buford just now reports that he finds a small force of the enemy's infantry in a point of woods near Gettysburg, which he is unable to dislodge, and while I am aware that it is not your desire to force an engagement at that point, still I feel at liberty to advance and develop the strength of the enemy."

12 Robert K. Beecham, *Gettysburg, the Pivotal Battle of the Civil War,* 62.

[13] *Maine at Gettysburg,* 16.

[14] Beecham, 64.

[15] Lincoln was attached to Meredith, one of the few Indiana generals. When the President reviewed the army before Hooker's spring campaign, the Cincinnati *Gazette* correspondent gave the story. As Meredith passed, his men at that time comprising the 4th Brigade of the 1st Division, First Corps, they showed their excellent discipline and condition. Hooker proudly pointed them out to Lincoln: "This is the famous Fourth Brigade," he said.

"Yes," Lincoln replied, "it is commanded by the only Quaker General I have in the army." Rufus R. Dawes, *Service with the Sixth Wisconsin Volunteers,* 131n.

[16] *Ibid.,* 29. Julia Ward Howe in Henry Steele Commager, *The Blue and the Gray,* 571-572.

[17] McIntosh, 44.

[18] Meade address to Pennsylvania Reserves, *Reynolds Memorial, 57. Annals,* 210.

[19] *Ibid.,* 32. Heth in an address at Bunker Hill, Virginia.

[20] "The 19th Indiana at Gettysburg," Ms. Indiana State Library.

[21] *Confederate Veteran,* XIV, 308.

[22] *Ibid.*

[23] Beecham, 66.

[24] *Ibid.,* 67.

[25] Stine, 460. Halstead in *B and L.,* III, 285, gives substantially the same language.

[26] *Indiana at Antietam,* 119.

[27] "Old Graybeard" was not a man to be intimidated. In Washington recovering from the wound he received at Gainesville, he bought a new uniform and went to Secretary Stanton's office to pay his respects. After a long wait he got in, but before he could speak, Stanton roared, "What in the hell are you doing in Washington? Why don't you go to your regiment, where you are needed?"

"If I had not been shot and a fool," Cutler replied, taken aback, "I would never have come here. Good day, Mr. Secretary." Dawes, 177.

[28] *N.C. Regts.,* III, 297.

[29] *New York at Gettysburg,* III, 992. Pierce said the orderlies informed them as they came up that "the Rebels are thicker than blackberries beyond the hill."

[30] Dawes, 167-168.

[31] *Ibid.,* 169.

[32] *Reynolds Memorial,* 32.

[33] This account of the formation of the Bucktail Brigade is largely from a paper by Sergeant William R. Ramsey, *Pennsylvania at Gettysburg,* II, 757.

[34] Charles King, *The Iron Brigade,* 311. *Pennsylvania at Gettysburg,* II, 738.

[35] *Pennsylvania at Gettysburg,* II, 746.

[36] *Ibid.,* 746-747.

[37] *Ibid.,* 936.

[38] *Ibid.*

[39] *Ibid.,* 739.

[40] Major General Abner Doubleday, left in command on the field after the death of Reynolds, had led the First Corps after Reynolds took command of the left wing. But no event in the war won him the attention he received for pulling the lanyard that fired the first shot in the defense of Fort Sumter. And that was minor compared with his recognition as "the father of baseball," from having stepped off at Cooperstown, New York, according to the accepted version of the

origin of the game, the baseball diamond, of such well-calculated dimensions that it has never been changed. He helped in the introduction of baseball among the soldiers and thereby did much to establish it as a national sport.

Chapter Ten: OAK HILL

1 Doubleday, 135, called it "baleful intelligence," in which Howard magnified a forced retreat of two regiments "into the flight of an entire corps, two-thirds of which had not yet reached the field."

2 Biddle says Howard was atop the Fahnestock Building, which is still Gettysburg's skyscraper. It gave about as good a view as the college cupola, which he visited also. The view today is obscured by the larger amount of building and apparently a larger growth of timber in some areas.

3 Doubleday, 126.

4 Horace Greeley, *American Conflict,* II, 373.

5 Edmund R. Brown, *27th Indiana Volunteer Infantry . . . ,* 365. Slocum reached Gettysburg at 7:00 P.M., *O.R.,* XXVII, Part I, 115. This was the hour of Sickles' arrival, but Sickles marched farther after hearing from Howard.

6 *Pennsylvania at Gettysburg,* I, 428.

7 Pennypacker, Meade's sympathetic biographer, says, 156, "Howard had just come through a bitter experience at Chancellorsville that should have been sufficiently impressive of the catastrophes that might be looked for along roads leading to army flanks."

8 *N.C. Regts.,* I, 634.

9 *Ibid.,* II, 239.

10 *Ibid.,* II, 235.

11 Wake Forest *Student,* April 1897, 451.

12 *Pennsylvania at Gettysburg,* I, 488.

13 *N.C. Regts.,* I, 637.

14 *Ibid.,* II, 119.

15 J. B. Jones, I, 290-291. *N.C. Regts.,* II, 113.

16 *N.C. Regts.,* II, 111.

17 Lieutenant Walter A. Montgomery, historian of the 12th North Carolina, said Iverson "did not at any time go on the fighting field." *N.C. Regts.,* I, 637.

18 *O.R.,* XXVII, Part II, 579.

19 *Ibid.,* 486.

20 *N.C. Regts.,* II, 237.

21 *Ibid.,* 238.

22 *O.R.,* XXVII, Part II, 554.

23 *N.C. Regts.,* I, 637.

24 Forney had gone on the gold rush in 1849, returned to Pennsylvania in 1859, and bought 150 acres. His house no longer stands, but this writer noticed in 1957 the iris persisting around its site on the Mummasburg Road.

25 An examination of the territory made by the writer in 1957 failed to disclose the location of the pits, and no one was found in Gettysburg who knew of them. At one point a possible trace seemed to remain in a slight depression, but this may have resulted from some later working of the land.

26 *N.C. Regts.,* II, 238.

27 *Ibid.,* I, 634.

28 They were Lieutenants Crowder and Dugger, *N.C. Regts.,* II, 237.

29 Cited in Daniel Harvey Hill, editor, *Land We Love,* V, 2.

30 *Ibid.*, 1.

31 Stone's fire was described by one opponent as the most destructive ever witnessed, *N.C. Regts.*, I, 42.

32 Doubleday, 144n. The statement is judged to have been made orally. No correspondence by Dwight to Stanton can be located in the National Archives or the Pennsylvania State Library.

33 *N.C. Regts.*, III, 255.

34 *Ibid.*, 5.

35 *S.H.S.P.*, IV, 158.

36 *Ibid.*

Chapter Eleven: THE BATTLE OF THE TWO COLONELS

1 William S. Burgwyn, "Zebulon Baird Vance," *H.S.L.*, XII, 5555.

2 *N.C. Regts.*, II, 306.

3 Unidentified Raleigh, N.C., news story in *N.C. Regts.*, II, 405.

4 *Ibid.*, 329.

5 *Ibid.*, 334.

6 *Ibid.*

7 *Ibid.*, 333.

8 The Christian Clemens *Papers,* Detroit Public Library, contain a clipping apparently from a Niles, Mich., newspaper of February 1891, telling of Morrow's death at Hot Springs, Ark. This is the only biographical sketch found giving facts of his early life, and it is the source of this account.

9 Detroit *Free Press,* January 5, 1908.

10 *Ibid.*

11 Robertson, *Michigan in the War,* 439. This flag was carried until lost at Gettysburg.

12 *Ibid.*, 438-439.

13 Dawes, 101.

14 *Ibid.*, 112.

15 *N.C. Regts.*, II, 343.

16 *Ibid.*, 369.

17 *Ibid.*, 350.

18 *Ibid.*, 351.

19 *Ibid.*

20 *Ibid.*, 352

21 *Ibid.*

22 *Ibid.*, III, 89.

23 *Ibid.*

24 *Ibid.*, 90.

25 *Michigan in the War,* 441.

26 *N.C. Regts.*, II, 353.

27 *Ibid.*

28 *Ibid.*, 375.

29 *Michigan in the War,* 441-442.

30 *Confederate Veteran,* XV, 504.

31 *Michigan in the War,* 442.

32 *N.C. Regts.*, V, 119.

33 *Ibid.*, 120.

34 *Ibid.*, II, 356.

35 Heth, *O.R.,* XXVII, Part 2, 638, said Pettigrew's brigade "Fought as well, and displayed as heroic courage as it was ever my fortune to witness on a battle-field."

36 J. H. Bassler, "The Color Episode . . . ," *S.H.S.P.,* XXXVII, 266ff.

Chapter Twelve: THROUGH THE TOWN

1 Thomas, 608.

2 R. L. Dabney, *Life and Campaigns of Lt. Gen. Thomas J. Jackson,* II, 73; cited in G. F. R. Henderson, *Stonewall Jackson and the American Civil War,* I, 299. The quotation has been given a colloquial form.

3 Thomas, 47.

4 *Ibid.,* 9.

5 *N.C. Regts.,* III, 413.

6 Address by Major John W. Daniel in J. William Jones, compiler, *Army of Northern Virginia, Memorial Volume,* 102-103.

7 *Ibid.*

8 *N.C. Regts.,* III, 413-414.

9 *Ibid.,* 414.

10 Stiles, 210.

11 *N.C. Regts.,* III, 414.

12 The term the Count of Paris employs to describe the rebel yell.

13 Gordon, 151.

14 *Ibid.*

15 Stiles, 210.

16 *Ibid.,* 211.

17 *Ibid.,* 212.

18 Barlow, a native of Brooklyn, had been first in his class at Harvard, graduating in 1855. He was a reporter on the New York *Tribune,* a lawyer, then a private at First Manassas. After that battle he returned to New York to hang out his shingle, not for clients, but for recruits. They came to a regimental level and he became colonel, then brigadier general. Thus the private at First Manassas was a division commander at Gettysburg. His wife contracted a fever working in army hospitals and died in 1864. *New York at Gettysburg,* III, 1353-1355.

19 Doubleday, 141.

20 *S.H.S.P.,* IV, 254.

21 William P. Snow, *Southern Generals, Their Lives and Campaigns,* 378.

22 Most of the material for this sketch is from the biography of Pender by Hugh B. Johnson, Jr., of Wilson, N.C., published in the *Wilson Daily Times.* It is in the Southern Historical Collection, University of North Carolina Library, Chapel Hill, N.C.

23 *N.C. Regts.,* I, 764-765.

24 Pender's letters here quoted are from the original Ms. in the Southern Historical Collection, University of North Carolina Library, Chapel Hill, N.C.

25 The word is not clearly distinguishable.

26 Varina D. Brown, *A Colonel at Gettysburg and Spotsylvania,* 78.

27 Perrin letter, July 29, 1863, in M. L. Bonham, *A Little More Light on Gettysburg,* 522. University of South Carolina Library, Columbia, S.C.

28 Dawes, 175.

29 Varina D. Brown, 79.

[30] Scales visited the field with Dawes in 1882 and said the fire of one of the batteries was the most destructive he had encountered in the war, Dawes, 175n.

[31] Caldwell, 98.

[32] Varina D. Brown, 80.

[33] *Ibid.*

[34] After Biddle was wounded, the brigade was commanded by Colonel Theodore B. Gates of the 20th New York.

[35] Doubleday, 146.

[36] Varina D. Brown, 81.

[37] Bonham, 522. Perrin, in Bonham, 523, placed the blame for the loss of the battle on Anderson. "His failure to us was the cause of the failure of the campaign," said Perrin, who did not know whether it was Anderson's or Hill's fault. But he was angered to observe that the enemy he drove from the seminary went into action without molestation on Cemetery Hill. "The very batteries which we had run off and which we saw them take off through Gettysburg, were the first to fire a shot from the new position," he said. "The first shell fired by them from that position was aimed at my brigade." Not only Perrin, but others complained of Anderson's slowness. The Richmond *Enquirer* account filed from near Hagerstown July 8 said that Anderson's division halted unnecessarily more than three hours at Cashtown, although it could hear the firing ahead. If Anderson had pushed on, the enemy could probably have been captured and certainly the army would have been able to "get possession of the mountain range" on which the Federals were located. "Fatal blunder!!" The scribe said he learned that all brigade commanders were anxious to advance but that Anderson would not consent.

[38] Wake Forest *Student,* April 1897, 451f.

[39] *Ibid.*

[40] *N.C. Regts.,* I, 719. Many of Ramseur's men were overcome by the heat in this pursuit.

[41] *Maine at Gettysburg,* 47.

[42] *Ibid.*

[43] Raleigh, N.C., *Semi-Weekly Standard,* August 4, 1863. The writer was described as "a gallant young officer of the 2nd North Carolina, Ramseur's Brigade."

[44] *Ibid.*

[45] *Ibid.*

[46] J. Bryan Grimes, "Gettysburg," *Papers,* 3.

[47] *O.R.,* XXVII, Part II, 479.

[48] Varina D. Brown, 82.

[49] Colonel Joseph N. Brown, 3, affirmed it of his personal knowledge that the 1st and 14th South Carolina regiments were first in the town, and gave the details of their entry.

[50] Varina D. Brown, 82.

[51] Adding to much other testimony, B. G. Benson, of Augusta, Ga., wrote to his brother from near Hagerstown July 7, saying a dispute had arisen as to what troops entered Gettysburg first, and said there was no room for doubt, as the 1st South Carolina was already in the middle of the town when he saw the next troops coming up a side street. *Reminiscences,* 173.

[52] Bonham, 522.

[53] Varina D. Brown, 82.

[54] This was the only brigade of Early's division to enter Gettysburg. *S.H.S.P.,* IV, 254.

[55] Colonel Joseph N. Brown, 3, said when they withdrew they observed troops

coming up on the left and Perrin inquired who they were. A staff officer told
him it was Rodes's division. According to Brown, Perrin "showed displeasure on
account of their going in and taking the place captured by us."

56 Bonham, 522.

57 Doubleday, 149.

58 *Pennsylvania at Gettysburg,* II, 753.

59 *O.R.,* XXVII, Part I, 925.

60 Dawes, 115. At the dedication of the 143rd Pennsylvania monument at
Gettysburg, Doubleday was referred to as "a soldier of fine military attainments
and personal courage." *Pennsylvania at Gettysburg,* II, 695.

Chapter Thirteen: HIGH GROUND AND GOLDEN MINUTES

1 How the offer to head the Louisiana lottery affected another outstanding general of the Confederacy was altogether different. Major General Dabney
Herndon Maury was offered $25,000 a year to become president of the lottery.
"The temptation was a terrible one," he said. "I was almost penniless, and there
was no prospect of my being otherwise. Twenty-five thousand dollars a year
was wealth which to me seemed fabulous." He told no one, tossed all night
without sleep, and at dawn decided to reject the offer. "I had never done anything which was not honest, and I determined it was too late to begin in my old
age. Sleep was easy to me then. . . ." He wrote a letter of refusal and never
regretted it. Richmond *Dispatch,* January 14, 1900. *S.H.S.P.,* XXVII, 335ff.

2 Sorrel, 55.

3 Freeman, *Lee's Lieutenants,* III, 27, cites Hotchkiss Ms. *Diary,* 213.

4 Stiles, 189.

5 *Ibid.*

6 Sorrel, 55.

7 *S.H.S.P.,* IV, 254.

8 The Wilmington, N.C., *Daily Journal* with keen penetration saw the significance of the lack of celerity at Gettysburg and in its July 18, 1863, issue
quoted this and the Napoleonic maxim which follows.

9 *S.H.S.P.,* IV, 254.

10 *Ibid.,* 255.

11 *Ibid.*

12 *S.H.S.P.,* XXXIII, 144.

13 *Ibid.*

14 Douglas, 247.

15 *Ibid.* Lee was at Cashtown when Johnson's division marched through and
had not ridden past them on the roadway, so Douglas was satisfied he had not
arrived.

16 *Ibid.*

17 Trimble, *Confederate Veteran,* XXV, 211. The conversation is as he
reported it in his manuscript.

18 Trimble's account ended here, but the story was carried on by McKim,
S.H.S.P., XL, 273.

19 *N.C. Regts.,* III, 414.

20 Gordon, 154.

21 *S.H.S.P.,* IV, 255.

22 *Ibid.,* 256.

23 *Ibid.*

24 *Ibid.*

[25] *Ibid.*

[26] *N.C. Regts.*, III, 5-6.

[27] Reprinted in Raleigh *Semi-Weekly Standard,* August 4, 1863.

[28] Related to the writer by a resident who had purchased this property and learned from earlier owners the incident of Lee's occupancy. The fact that Lee took it suggests it may have been a map made in 1857, which gives details down to individual houses and their occupants.

[29] *S.H.S.P.,* XXXIII, 140-141.

[30] McKim, 176.

[31] *S.H.S.P.,* IV, 127. Walter H. Taylor, *Four Years with General Lee,* 95. *O.R.,* XXVII, Part II, 318.

[32] *S.H.S.P.,* XXXIII, 145.

[33] *Ibid.* The wording and subsequent events cause wonder if Ewell did not see in Lee's promised arrival an excuse for withholding the attack until Lee could take charge. When Lee arrived, it was too late.

[34] *S.H.S.P.,* IV, 66.

[35] Colonel Joseph N. Brown had just withdrawn the 14th South Carolina from Gettysburg when General Lee arrived. Lee congratulated Perrin on "his splendid achievement" and Brown observed that "it was not too late then to have followed the retreating Federals." Later he asked himself the perplexing questions about Lee: "Might he not once in his illustrious life, with the great responsibilities resting on him, viewing the almost impregnable heights in an enemy's country far from his base, with such fearful odds against him, have hesitated who never hesitated before? It was his first battle without Stonewall Jackson and might he not have felt as never before the want of that rushing torrent which always carried everything before it when that celebrated hero was at the helm? Others felt it." Joseph N. Brown, *The Battle of Gettysburg,* 3.

[36] McIntosh, 52.

[37] *O.R.,* XXVII, Part II, 349.

[38] *Ibid.,* 583.

[39] *S.H.S.P.,* II, 225.

[40] Raleigh *Semi-Weekly Standard,* August 4, 1863.

[41] There appears little material difference in Longstreet's various accounts, the purport of all being that he strongly favored a flanking movement.

[42] *B. and L.,* III, 339. Other statements of the same nature are in Longstreet, *From Manassas to Appomattox,* 358f., and *Annals,* 421-422.

[43] Gordon, 155-157.

[44] *S.H.S.P.,* V, 291.

[45] McKim, 193.

[46] Douglas, 247.

[47] *Annals,* 308-309.

[48] Hunton, 98.

[49] *S.H.S.P.,* V, 175.

Chapter Fourteen: MOONLIGHT AND MARCHING COLUMNS

[1] *Rebellion Record,* 87-89.

[2] *Ibid.*

[3] Doubleday, 143.

[4] *Pennsylvania at Gettysburg,* II, 1075-1076.

[5] "Hancock received a brigade early in the formation of the Army of the Potomac. He was a man of the most chivalrous courage, and of a superb pres-

ence, especially in action; he had a wonderfully quick and correct eye for ground and for handling troops; his judgment was good, and it would be difficult to find a better corps commander." George B. McClellan, 140.

6 Frank A. Haskell, *The Battle of Gettysburg,* 381-382.

7 *B. and L.,* III, 285. Doubleday, 151.

8 Howard, I, 418.

9 *B. and L.,* III, 285.

10 *Ibid.*

11 Edward N. Whittier, *The Left Attack (Ewell's) at Gettysburg,* 316.

12 Doubleday, 151.

13 Hancock on his arrival found only 1,000 to 1,200 organized troops "at most" on Cemetery Hill. Hancock to Fitz Lee, *S.H.S.P.,* V, 169.

14 Thomson, *Seventh Indiana Infantry . . . ,* 162.

15 *Ibid.*

16 *Ibid.,* 163.

17 *Ibid.*

18 *Ibid.,* 165.

19 *Maine at Gettysburg,* 88-89.

20 Hancock to Fitz Lee, *S.H.S.P.,* V, 172.

21 *O.R.,* XXVII, Part I, 366.

22 New York *Herald,* March 12, 1864.

23 Francis A. Osbourn, *"Fighting Three Hundred," the Twentieth Indiana Infantry,* 13.

24 *Maine at Gettysburg,* 159, 179-180.

25 Whittier, 340.

26 *Pennsylvania at Gettysburg,* I, 196. General Humphreys, *O.R.,* XXVII, Part 1, 531, contended that the route via Black Horse Tavern was intentional.

27 William H. Powell, *The Fifth Army Corps,* 509-510.

28 The phase of the moon has sometimes been questioned. The moon was at the full on the night of July 1, 1863. Letter to author from U.S. Naval Observatory, January 6, 1958.

29 *O.R.,* XXVII, Part I, 115. Meade gave different times from those of some observers. He said he broke headquarters at 10:00 P.M. and arrived at 1:00 A.M. July 2.

30 Howard, I, 423.

31 *Ibid.*

32 *Ibid.,* 424.

33 According to Pleasanton, Meade was "strongly impressed" that his right was weakest. *Annals,* 454.

34 The old schoolhouse was used as a tractor barn when the writer visited the site in November 1957. At Manchester the writer talked with Miss Cecelia Shower, 93 years old, whose father had often told of Sedgwick's halt there, and who, with her sister-in-law, gave information about Sedgwick's camp and headquarters site. An indication of how the countryside assisted Sedgwick was seen in the statement of Mrs. John Green that her grandmother cooked bread and had it taken 5 miles to Sedgwick's camp.

35 One of the reasons assigned for Meade's delay at Taneytown was that he wanted to wait until the Sixth Corps came up and therefore gave Sedgwick orders to move by Taneytown. Later, deciding to leave for Gettysburg, he ordered Sedgwick to take the Baltimore pike, the more direct road from Westminster to Gettysburg. Pennypacker, 151. That necessitated a readjustment of the head of the column, which had not moved far from Westminster. It cut across the fields from the Taneytown road to the Baltimore-Gettysburg pike. Meade directed Sedgwick to shunt all the trains out of the road and make a

forced march. *Ibid.* Sedgwick calculated the distance as 35 miles, *Annals,* 211, but some units, countermarching, probably covered 37 miles, as some regimental accounts attest.

36 Lieutenant Colonel James W. Latta, 119th Pennsylvania Infantry, said, "The day at Manchester was a novel one; we had no such experience before or after." He described it as a carnival and said the friendly population had never seen so many soldiers. "Men and maidens, matrons and children, afoot and in wheeled vehicles, gathered from far and near for the opportunity to witness the sudden increase of male population. No thought was abroad that scarce forty miles away mortal strife was waging hotly." *Pennsylvania at Gettysburg,* II, 652.

37 Brevet Major General Alexander Shaler, *ibid.,* I, 187.

38 *B. and L.,* III, 239. When Henry Breckenridge, assistant secretary of war in the Woodrow Wilson administration, accepted the Sedgwick equestrian statue at Gettysburg, he emphasized Sedgwick's modesty and pointed out that "when it seemed that Sedgwick could have had command of the Army of the Potomac by simply stretching forth his hand, he would not make the move" *Proceedings at Dedication of Statue at Gettysburg* (Hartford, Conn.), 69. (Hereinafter *Conn. Proc.*)

39 *Ibid.,* 52, says: "As the coffin was being lowered to its last resting place, a distinct peal of thunder like the roll of distant artillery reverberated along the hills a most solemn requiem to the buried soldier."

40 Latta in *Pennsylvania at Gettysburg,* II, 652. The time of the messenger's arrival is placed at nine o'clock in several accounts, slightly earlier in others.

41 Colonel Henry S. Huidekoper, 115th Pennsylvania Infantry, said, "He (Reynolds) was a superb horseman, and was so much at ease in the saddle as to be able to pick up from the ground, at full speed, a silver ten-cent piece, and to dismount by vaulting, his hands on the pommel." *Pennsylvania at Gettysburg,* II, 1097.

42 Latta, *ibid.,* II, 652.

43 Letter from Senator Huntington, 1833; *Conn. Proc.,* 31.

44 The description of the corps is from Sergeant A. T. Brewer, 61st Pennsylvania. *Pennsylvania at Gettysburg,* I, 378.

45 *Ibid.,* 377.

46 *Maine at Gettysburg,* 366. The 5th Maine got no halt for breakfast or dinner. An officer of the 93rd Pennsylvania kicked over the coffee pots. *Pennsylvania at Gettysburg,* I, 506.

47 Sergeant F. J. Loeble, 98th Pennsylvania Infantry. *Ibid.,* I, 528.

48 The 1st New York Battery under Captain Cowan was stationed close by the High Water Mark and helped repulse Pickett's assault on July 3. The inscription on the monument includes the words used by Cowan.

49 *Pennsylvania at Gettysburg,* I, 373.

50 *Ibid.,* II, 677.

51 Chaplain J. S. Lane, *ibid.,* I, 506.

52 *Conn. Proc.,* 48-50.

53 Address of Maj. Gen. O. O. Howard at National Republican Club, New York. In *Lincoln Day Addresses, 1887-1909,* 280-281, Lincoln related the incident to General Sickles, who told it to Howard.

54 Charles C. Coffin, cited in *Pennsylvania at Gettysburg,* I, 378.

Chapter Fifteen: LEE'S ATTACK PLANS

1 This account of the conference is almost wholly from Early's long report, *S.H.S.P.,* IV, 271ff.

2 *Grayjackets*, 230. Rodes, though born in Lynchburg, Virginia, came into the army with Alabama troops. A graduate of V. M. I., he became a civil engineer and just before the war moved to Tuscaloosa, Alabama, from where he was elected colonel of the 5th Alabama Regiment. That unit became a part of Ewell's brigade. He was a man of soldierly appearance but, according to Stiles (45), had a habit of chewing or holding the ends of his long mustache in his lips.

3 *S.H.S.P.*, IV, 271.

4 *Ibid.*, 272.

5 *Ibid.*

6 *Ibid.*, 273-274.

7 Fitz Lee quotes General Lee, *S.H.S.P.*, V, 192, as saying to the Reverend Mr. Jones that "General Longstreet, when once in a fight, was a most brilliant soldier; but he was the hardest man to move I had in my army."

8 Early said, *S.H.S.P.*, IV, 293: "It was very natural that Longstreet's corps should be selected to assume the initiative on the second day at Gettysburg. Neither of his divisions had been at the recent battles of Chancellorsville and Fredericksburg, except McLaws, and that division, with the exception of Barksdale's brigade, had not been as heavily engaged there as the other corps."

9 Marshall, 252.

10 *S.H.S.P.*, IV, 275.

11 Robert E. Lee, *Recollections and Letters*, 95.

12 At Chambersburg, Marshall mentioned to British correspondent Ross the calamity of the lost order at Antietam, which he looked on as a greater misfortune to the South than the fall of New Orleans. He said it was lost through the carelessness of a general of division (D. H. Hill, who denied responsibility) who "singularly enough" had lost an order of equal importance just before the Seven Days' Battles around Richmond. In the second instance the order had been found on a prisoner captured at Gaines' Mill, who, not understanding its importance, had not sent it to headquarters. Marshall did not mention Hill by name. Ross, 46.

13 *Annals*, 435.

14 McIntosh, 28, obtained the story from Watters when Watters was judge of the Third Judicial District of Maryland.

15 *Annals*, 422.

16 *Ibid.*, 439.

17 Ross, 49.

18 In Lee's Headquarters Museum on Cashtown pike (Lincoln Highway).

19 *Annals*, 422.

20 Because of the long-standing and popularly accepted belief that Lee ordered this "sunrise attack," some statements of headquarters officers, or others in a position to have informed opinions, to Longstreet may be cited to help establish the facts. While taken from context, the meaning is not distorted.

Charles Marshall: "I have no personal recollection of the order. . . . It certainly was not conveyed by me, nor is there anything in General Lee's official report to show the attack of the 2nd was expected by him to begin earlier, except that he notices that there was no proper concert of action on that day." *Annals*, 437. *A. S. Long:* "I do not recollect of hearing of an order to attack at sunrise, or at any other designated hour. . . ." *Ibid.*, 438. *Charles S. Venable:* "I do not know of any order for an attack on the enemy at sunrise on the 2nd, nor can I believe that any such order was issued by General Lee." *Ibid.*, 438. *Walter H. Taylor:* "I never heard of the 'sunrise attack'. . . . If such an order was given you I never knew of it, or it has strangely escaped my memory.

I think it more than probable that if General Lee had had your troops available the evening previous . . . he would have ordered an early attack; but this does not touch the point at issue." *Ibid.,* 437. *Alexander:* "No orders whatever were given to Longstreet that night."

Fully as conclusive as all this is the statement by McLaws that when he saw Longstreet returning from Gettysburg on the night of July 1, he made no reference to any attack orders. Had Lee directed him to attack at daybreak, certainly he would have told the general who would have to do it.

Colonel Taylor in another statement gave a résumé that was as sensible as any on this situation: "I cannot say he (Longstreet) was notified on the night of the first, of the attack proposed to be made on the morning of the second, and the part his corps was to take therein. Neither do I think it just to charge that he was alone responsible for the delay in attacking that ensued after his arrival on the field. I well remember how General Lee was chafed by the non-appearance of the troops, until he finally became restless and rode back to meet General Longstreet, and urge him forward; but, then, there was considerable delay in putting the troops to work after they reached the field and much time was spent in discussing what was to be done, which, perhaps, could not be avoided. At any rate, it would be unreasonable to hold General Longstreet accountable for this. Indeed, great injustice has been done him in the charge that he had orders from the Commanding General to attack the enemy at sunrise on the second of July, and that he disobeyed these orders." *S.H.S.P.,* IV, 130-131.

[21] Burke Davis, *Gray Fox,* 229.

[22] *Confederate Veteran,* 209f.

[23] *Ibid.*

[24] E. P. Alexander, *Military Memories of a Confederate,* 391, says the orders were issued "about 11 A.M." The attack order was issued after Lee's return from his second visit to Ewell, where he had been rebuffed continually in his desire to attack or pull Ewell's corps around to his right.

[25] *S.H.S.P.,* V, 90.

[26] *Ibid.,* V, 92.

[27] Doubleday, 111, says Lee's son was serving as a hostage, because President Davis had determined to hang a Federal captain, but feared Rooney Lee would be hung in retaliation.

[28] That was implied in his letter to his wife, R. E. Lee, 101.

[29] Polley, 153.

[30] W. W. Blackford, 231.

[31] Sanger, in D. B. Sanger and Thomas R. Hays, *James Longstreet,* 163, says that Lee was sick and asked if he was too ill and exhausted to command his army.

[32] Ross, 50.

[33] *Ibid.,* 51-52.

[34] *Ibid.,* 52.

[35] *Ibid.,* 52-53.

[36] Dickert, 234.

[37] *Ibid.*

[38] Chesnut, 241.

[39] Dickert, 234.

[40] *Ibid.,* 230, 232.

[41] *Ibid.,* 230.

[42] Hood, *Advance and Retreat,* 57. This again suggests an indisposition, for it was hot in the early morning.

[43] *Ibid.*

44 *Ibid.*

45 Polley, 155.

46 The common soldier's viewpoint may have been reflected by Polley, 155, when he said Lee had not yet decided where Longstreet's men should advance, and "If at this hour he betrayed anger and disappointment, it was not at the failure of Longstreet's command to be up sooner (how could they!)" nor at the deliberation of Longstreet's movements, but at Ewell's failure to seize Culp's Hill and the delay of the officers he had sent on a reconnaissance. "Not until they reported to him, which was close on to mid-day, did he announce his plan to Longstreet."

47 E. P. Alexander, "Causes of Southern Defeat at Gettysburg," *S.H.S.P.,* IV, 101.

48 *Ibid.*

49 *B. and L.,* III, 359.

50 *S.H.S.P.,* XXVII, 57. McLaws told of the incident in an address in Savannah, Ga., April 27, 1896.

51 Comte de Paris, *History of the Civil War,* 240-242, made a careful estimate of numbers as does *B. and L.,* III, 440. These estimates are made from these sources.

Chapter Sixteen: THE STORY OF THE MISSING CANTEENS

1 *S.H.S.P.,* V, 183-184.

2 *Ibid.*

3 *B. and L.,* III, 331.

4 *Ibid.*

5 *Ibid.,* 321.

6 The Little Round Top signal station reported to Meade at 4:00 P.M. that the only enemy infantry visible was on the extreme Federal left moving toward Emmitsburg. This could scarcely have been Longstreet's column, but more likely was one of Hill's regiments being sent as a flank picket to the Kerns house *B. and L.,* III, 320.

7 *S.H.S.P.,* IV, 99-102; *B. and L.,* III, 359.

8 *B. and L.,* III, 320.

9 *Ibid.,* 332.

10 Dickert, 235.

11 *Annals,* 422. Freeman, who is most critical of Longstreet's actions on July 2, concedes, *Lee's Lieutenants,* III, 115, that Lee consented to Longstreet's awaiting the arrival of Law.

12 *B. and L.,* III, 319.

13 Oates, 206.

14 *Annals,* 423.

15 *S.H.S.P.,* IV, 68.

16 Hoke, 574, in his appendix, "Did General Sickles Disregard an Order from General Meade on July 2nd, 1863?"

17 Powell, 517.

18 *B. and L.,* III, 301.

19 *Maine at Gettysburg,* 130.

20 *Ibid.,* 129.

21 Osbourn, 1.

22 *Ibid.,* 13. *Pennsylvania at Gettysburg,* I, 349.

23 *Pennsylvania at Gettysburg,* II, 622.

24 *Ibid.,* 623.

25 *Ibid.*

26 *Maine at Gettysburg,* 130-131.

27 Historicus in New York *Herald,* March 12, 1864.

28 *Ibid.*

29 *Ibid.*

30 *Time* Magazine, May 7, 1956, 118.

31 Haskell, 367.

32 Pinckney, who headed this scouting venture, was a descendant of Charles Cotesworth Pinckney, author of the statement, "Millions for defense but not one cent for tribute." (Oration in House of Representatives, April 29, 1906, by Robert Lee Henry, Representative from Texas and great-great-great-grandson of Patrick Henry.) He was eulogized also by Representatives John Nance Garner and Alexander White Gregg of Texas. Gregg gave the story of his scouting venture, from which this account is drawn. Pinckney was serving in Congress at the time of his death.

General Law, *B. and L.,* 321, tells of sending a scouting detail to the summit of Round Top, which raises the question of whether two such parties went out or whether Law intercepted Pinckney and received his report on his return. Law had not been on the field during the morning, as had Hood, and while he dwells in detail on the scouts from his brigade, it seems impossible that he could have made an extensive reconnaissance during the short time he was in front of Round Top prior to the assault. He may have been forgetful, or was speaking as the division commander, which he soon became when Hood was wounded.

33 Hood, *Advance and Retreat,* 57-58.

34 *Ibid.,* 58.

35 *Ibid.,* 58-59.

36 Longstreet Papers, Southern Historical Collection, University of North Carolina Library, Chapel Hill, N.C.

37 Oates, 206.

38 *Ibid.,* 212.

39 *Ibid.*

40 *Ibid.,* 207-208n.

41 *Ibid.,* 210.

42 *Maine at Gettysburg,* 255. Oates gave as another reason for ascending Round Top that he was pushed to the right by the 47th Alabama on his left. *O.R.,* XXVII, part II, 392.

43 Oates, 211.

44 *Ibid.*

45 *Ibid.,* 212.

46 Francis Parkman, II, 287-307.

47 U. S. Grant, *Personal Memoirs* . . . , I, 132-133.

48 Snow, 25. Robert Selph Henry, *The Story of the Mexican War,* 284.

49 Oates, 212. In late years, vehicles of the Gettysburg National Military Park have been driven to the summit of Round Top.

50 *Ibid.,* 213.

51 *Ibid.,* 214.

52 *Ibid.*

Chapter Seventeen: THE PRIZE OF LITTLE ROUND TOP

1 *Pennsylvania at Gettysburg,* I, 461.

2 *Ibid.,* 462. Oliver W. Norton, *The Attack and Defense of Little Round Top,* 285.

3 Powell, 523.

4 *Ibid.,* 524.

5 *Pennsylvania at Gettysburg,* I, 461-462.

6 Oates, 215.

7 *Maine at Gettysburg,* 256.

8 Norton, 90.

9 *Ibid.,* 283, 287-288.

10 *Maine at Gettysburg,* 254n.

11 Oates, 217.

12 Jerome Bonaparte Robertson, commander of the Texas Brigade, was one of the most humane men in Lee's army, who, except for occasional excursions into warfare, was a beloved country doctor in Washington County, Texas. He was 48 years old at the time of Gettysburg. Born in Kentucky, he was apprenticed as a hatter, went to St. Louis, bought his release, and though virtually unschooled, won the favor of a St. Louis physician who taught him, and, upon removal to Owensboro, Ky., made him an office assistant. This tutoring enabled him to enter Transylvania University. After graduation in medicine, he was practicing in Owensboro when the Texas revolution against Mexico excited his compassion and caused him to raise a Kentucky company for Sam Houston's army. He remained in Texas to practice medicine thirty-four years. He took time out for fighting Indians, raised a company for the 5th Texas on the outbreak of war with the North and rose from captain to general. When the war ended he returned to medicine in his home town of Independence, Tex., and later moved to Waco.

13 Polley, 169.

14 *Ibid.,* 171-172.

15 *Ibid.,* 174.

16 *Ibid.,* 175.

17 Henry Lewis Benning, one of the able men of the Confederacy, probably would have been offered a place in President Davis' cabinet had he not organized a regiment in Columbus, Ga., his home, and become colonel at the first clash of arms. Lawyer, legislator, judge of the Georgia Supreme Court, he was industrious and capable and a citizen of the highest integrity, who has been compared in character to Calhoun. He worked diligently for secession, a cause for which he retained hope to the very end. He lost his only son in the war, but was survived by 5 daughters. Fort Benning, 9 miles south of Columbus, Ga.—of 220,000 acres—perhaps the largest U.S. army post in area and number of troops in the country, is named in his honor.

18 Polley, 168.

19 *Ibid.*

20 Oates, 219. At Appomattox, Chamberlain commanded the brigade, including the 20th Maine, which received the surrender of Lee's army. *Maine at Gettysburg,* 286.

21 Oates, 219.

22 Polley, 175-176. The confidence of Robertson's men was unshaken. Private West wrote later, ". . . I do not believe the combined Yankee army can subjugate the Texas brigade. . . ." West, 99.

23 Polley, 172. The orator and occasion are not identified.

Chapter Eighteen: CRUSHING THE ORCHARD SALIENT

1 John C. Ridpath, *Life and Times of James A. Garfield,* 145.

2 Moore, *Civil War in Song and Story,* 320.

³ J. S. McNeilly, "Barksdale's Mississippi Brigade," *Publications of the Mississippi Historical Society,* XIX, 231.

⁴ John Bell Hood—his classmates called him Sam Hood at West Point, though the inquisitive Mrs. Chesnut could not learn why—had "the face of an old Crusader," whose "whole appearance [was] that of awkward strength." Chesnut, 299. Venable, of Lee's staff, had been on many fields and said he had often heard of the "light of battle shining in a man's eyes," but had seen it only once, when he carried Lee's orders to Hood in a hot corner. "The man was transfigured. The fierce light in Hood's eyes I can never forget." That was when the battle was joined. But Blackford, 210, told how he was unwilling to shell the Federals by surprise. He was tall, blond, and blue-eyed, and reserved almost to the point of shyness. In his pocket he always carried a Bible his mother had given him. He was 32 years old at Gettysburg.

His brigade, a long way from Texas, did not have the clothing replacements enjoyed by some of the other commands. Mrs. Chesnut described it as it passed through Richmond: "Such rags and tags. . . . Nothing was like anything else. Most garments and arms were such as had been taken from the enemy. Such shoes as they had on. . . .

"They did not seem to mind their shabby condition. They laughed, shouted and cheered as they marched by. . . ." Chesnut, 231. These were the men now about to assail the Devil's Den and Little Round Top.

⁵ Stiles, 223.

⁶ J. B. Jones, I, 290-291.

⁷ Stiles, 223.

⁸ *B. and L.,* III, 325.

⁹ *Ibid.,* 334. Though Cabell opened at four, he signaled Kershaw much later.

¹⁰ "Tige" Anderson's brigade had been Bartow's at First Manassas and included the 8th Georgia, the first regiment incorporated into the Confederate service after the government was organized at Montgomery, Ala. Bartow, then chairman of the House Military Affairs Committee in the first Confederate Congress, arranged the induction with President Davis. It included his Savannah company, the Oglethorpe Light Infantry, named in honor of General James Oglethorpe. Bartow was killed at First Manassas. "Tige" Anderson served long as chief of police of Atlanta after the war.

¹¹ Kershaw was from Camden, S.C., a town that gave the Confederate army 5 generals. There young men grew up under the inspiration of Baron DeKalb, who fell with 11 wounds in the Revolutionary War battle at Camden. Kershaw had entered Mexico City with the Palmetto Regiment and had fought in Virginia beginning at First Manassas.

¹² Chesnut, 63.

¹³ DeTrobriand, duelist, poet, novelist, soldier, was born in Tours, France, came to the United States on a dare, married a New York heiress, and after life abroad, returned to New York and became one of the city's literary group of the 1850s. In 1861, elected colonel of the "Gardes Lafayette," he became naturalized, and soon proved he was even more adept at arms than letters. The Federal army did not contain a more romantic or perhaps a more stubborn soldier.

¹⁴ Historicus, in New York *Herald,* March 12, 1864, made the charges and said Barnes's disorganized troops impeded Zook's advance. Barnes answered sharply March 21, 1864. Historicus said April 4, 1864, that he had redoubled his research and "found his picture not only correct, but in nearly every detail and incident exact," and added statements by Birney and deTrobriand. The articles are in Meade, II, 324ff.

¹⁵ *Michigan at Gettysburg,* 76.

16 Pleasanton in Washington *Post,* February 8, 1883. Meade, II, 397.

17 *Pennsylvania at Gettysburg,* II, 623.

18 *Ibid.*

19 *Ibid.,* 624.

20 *Ibid.,* 625.

21 L. W. Minnigh, *Gettysburg, What They Did Here,* 151.

22 *Michigan at Gettysburg,* 102.

23 This is stated in the official *Biographical Directory of the American Congress,* 815, and since each House is the judge of the conduct of its own members, the findings in such a publication might be judged conclusive! But the Congressman who stood closest by Brooks was Representative Laurence M. Keitt of South Carolina, with whom Barksdale may have been confused. Barksdale's name does not appear in the detailed account of the incident the writer has examined, but the matter is left open even in such a standard biography as *D.A.B.*

24 Reuben Davis, *Recollections of Mississippi and Mississippians,* 237.

25 Stiles, 185.

26 *Ibid.,* 223.

27 Hoke, 209.

28 Owen, 245.

29 McNeilly, 235-236.

30 *Ibid.,* 236.

31 *Ibid.,* 238.

32 *Ibid.,* 241.

33 *Ibid.*

34 Ross, 55-56.

35 *Pennsylvania at Gettysburg,* II, 612-613.

36 Hoke, 337. W. C. Storrick, *The Battle of Gettysburg . . . ,* 52-53.

37 Owen, 246.

38 *Pennsylvania at Gettysburg,* I, 394.

39 *Ibid.,* II, 627.

40 *Ibid.*

41 Meridian, Miss., *Dispatch,* August 3, 1914, in McNeilly, *Publ. M.H.S.,* XIX, 238-239.

42 Col. William T. Nichols of the 14th Vermont learned from a prisoner that Barksdale was mortally wounded in front of the line, sent a detail and took him to a temporary hospital. G. G. Benedict, *Vermont at Gettysburg,* 9. A ball had pierced his breast and both legs were bloody with wounds.

Chapter Nineteen: CEMETERY AND CULP'S HILLS

1 *Maine at Gettysburg,* 292 and note.

2 *S.H.S.P.,* XXVII, 195.

3 *Pennsylvania at Gettysburg,* I, 404. Haskell, 373.

4 *S.H.S.P.,* XXVII, 194.

5 The losses of this regiment, frequently stated as the heaviest in relation to the number of engaged, are scarcely comparable with those of larger regiments, but more readily with some of the company losses. The 24th Michigan and 26th North Carolina, larger regiments, lost more heavily, as did the 14th Tennessee, which, with 3 left out of 365, undoubtedly suffered the highest percentage of casualties of the battle. The divisional adjutant, Haskell, placed the loss of the 1st Minnesota at "more than two-thirds."

6 Wright returned to the Georgia legislature in the autumn of 1863, quite apparently because of the dislike he developed for Anderson after that general's

failure to support him at a critical moment of the battle. After the session he returned to different rolls in the armies.

[7] This writer camped on the Bliss farm in 1922 as a newspaper correspondent covering the re-enactment by General Smedley Butler with the Marine Corps of the assault of Pickett's division, with President Warren G. Harding and other officials as spectators.

[8] The July 8 dispatch from Hagerstown to the Richmond *Enquirer* (published July 23) was severe: "But although orders were preemptory that all of Anderson's Division move into action simultaneously, Brig. Gen. Posey commanding a Mississippi brigade and Brig. Gen. Mahone commanding a Virginia brigade failed to advance. The failure of these two to advance is assigned, as I learn upon inquiry, as the reason why Pender's Division of Hill's Corps did not advance—the order being that the advance was to commence on the right and be taken up all along the line. Pender's failure to advance caused the division on his left, Heth's, to remain inactive.

"Here we have two whole divisions, and two brigades of another, standing idle spectators of one of the most desperate and important assaults that has ever been made on this continent—fifteen or twenty thousand armed men resting on their arms, in plain view of a terrible battle, witnessing the mighty efforts of two little brigades (Wright's and Wilcox's, for Perry had fallen back overpowered) contending with the heavy masses of Yankee infantry, and subjected to a most deadly fire from the enemy's heavy artillery, without a single effort to aid them in the assault, or to assist them when the heights were carried. . . . It was now apparent that the day was lost—lost after it was *won*—lost, not because our army fought badly, but because a large portion *did not fight at all*."

[9] Perrin, a good soldier, saw the full measure of his commander's ability: "In my humble judgment he was the best general officer in the army." Perrin to Bonham, 522.

[10] *S.H.S.P.,* IV, 154. The date of Pender's fall is confused in Lee's statement, being placed on July 3. But his meaning was clear, and applicable to the second, the proper date. The error could have been typographical, or Lee's, or Heth's, who recorded the conversation.

[11] *O.R.,* XXVII, Part II, 658.

[12] Ross, 56.

[13] That view was shared by Private West, who had ideas on the disastrous nature of Hood's loss: "I believe the wounding of General Hood was the greatest misfortune of the day. . . . If a considerable force had been thrown around the mountain to our right, the enemy would have been routed in half an hour. Baltimore would have been ours and the New York riots would have been as famous as the battle of Bunker Hill." West, 96.

[14] Edward N. Whittier, commanding a Federal battery on Culp's Hill, gives the picture of the opening of the assault from which this account has been drawn. He times it at between 7:30 and 7:45 P.M. and said the sun had dropped behind the Cumberland mountains. Whittier, 329.

[15] Applied to Hoke's division in 1864. Wasler, North Carolina *Folklore,* July 1957, p. 9.

[16] *N.C. Regts.,* II, 136.

[17] *Ibid.,* III, 415.

[18] *Ibid.,* II, 136.

[19] Whittier, 330. The twilight was a delaying factor.

[20] Colonel Avery, 35 years old, was the youngest of 4 brothers from Morganton, N.C., in the Confederate armies. His grandfather, Waighstill Avery, the first attorney general of the state, was a signer of the Mecklenburg Declaration of Independence.

21 Oration at Kingston, N.C., February 20, 1864, at Masonic Demonstration in honor of Colonel Avery.

22 *N.C. Regts.,* III, 421.

23 Whittier, 332, said they "disappeared at the first approach of the enemy and left their front open." Also *N.C. Regts.,* I, 355.

24 Howard, I, 429.

25 *Pennsylvania at Gettysburg,* II, 919.

26 *O.R.,* XXVII, Part II, 480. Hays in his report said: "Arriving at the summit by a simultaneous rush of my whole line, I captured several pieces of artillery, four stand of colors, and a number of prisoners."

27 *Ibid.*

28 *N.C. Regts.,* I, 313.

29 Hunt in *B. and L.,* III, 313. Birney in Meade, II, 414, said it was sent "at the sound of the firing."

30 *Pennsylvania at Gettysburg,* I, 551. Howard, who had seen the 106th Pennsylvania in a stand at Sharpsburg, said to his artillery officer, "Major, your batteries can be withdrawn when that regiment runs away."

31 *N.C. Regts.,* I, 314.

32 *O.R.,* XXVII, Part II, 486.

33 Raleigh, N.C., *Semi-Weekly Standard,* August 4, 1863.

34 Wake Forest *Student,* XVI, 451.

35 Raleigh, N.C., *Semi-Weekly Standard,* August 4, 1863.

36 *O.R.,* XXVII, Part II, 485-486.

37 *N.C. Regts.,* II, 258.

38 McKim, 184.

39 The air distance from Benner's Hill to the Wheat Field is slightly more than 2 miles.

40 McKim, 184.

41 *New York at Gettysburg,* III, 1335.

42 Kane's brigade was commanded at that time by Colonel George A. Cobham, Jr., of the 111th Pennsylvania.

43 On January 10, 1958, Maj. Gen. Henry Clay Hodges, Jr., became 97 years, 6 months, and 23 days old, and on that day passed Greene's and set a new longevity record for a West Point graduate.

44 McKim, 196.

45 *N.C. Regts.,* I, 148.

46 *Ibid.*

47 McKim, 196. The italics are his.

48 Colonel Ed A. Palfrey, "Some of the Secret History of Gettysburg," *S.H.S.P.,* VIII, 522f.

Chapter Twenty: THE COUNCIL AND THE CAPTAIN

1 Other factors were Stuart's arrival and the coming of Pickett's division, which equalized conditions or threw the scale a bit in Lee's favor in the matter of fresh troops, taken with his brigades that had not been heavily engaged. But Meade's over-all strength was much greater than Lee's, though he considered himself to be outnumbered. He testified (*Life and Letters,* II, 365) that he had in all arms about 95,000 men and that Lee had 95,000 infantry, 4 or 5,000 artillery and 10,000 cavalry. This would mean a total of about 110,000. The estimate of 58,000 is from the minutes of the meeting. *O.R.,* XXVII, Part I, 73-74. *B. and L.,* III, 314.

2 *B. and L.,* III, 411.

3 *Ibid.*

4 *Ibid.* Hunt, writing to Webb, January 12, 1888, said Meade "did tell me, July 2d, that he feared we were in no condition to fight at Gettysburg, but in this matter he did give me his reason, so far as it concerned me—'lack of ammunition (artillery).'" Hunt told him there was none to throw away, but enough, and that seemed to satisfy him. Hunt did not say if there were reasons pertinent to others, as Meade's words might imply, but he declined to accept the charge that Meade wanted to withdraw. *Journal of the Military Service Institution of the U. S.*, XLV, 54.

5 The withdrawal order was never issued, and that must have salved Meade's conscience when he testified before the Committee on the Conduct of the War that "he had no recollection of ever having directed such an order to be issued, or ever having contemplated the issuing of such an order." *B. and L.*, III, 410-411. On the second occasion he denied ever having intended or thought to withdraw the army unless future developments might make it necessary.

6 *O.R.*, XXVII, Part I, 72.

7 After Chancellorsville, Meade wrote: "Who would have believed a few days ago that Hooker would withdraw his army, in opposition to the opinion of a majority of his corps commanders? Yet such is absolutely and actually the case." Meade, I, 372.

8 Edmund R. Brown, 377.

9 Writing the Committee of Congress, October 16, 1865, Pleasanton said Meade "had so little assurance of his own ability to maintain himself, or on the strength of his position," that he gave the order for Pleasanton to prepare to cover a retreat. Meade, II, 403-404.

10 Edmund R. Brown, 376.

11 *O.R.*, XXVII, Part I, 73-74.

12 *B. and L.*, III, 313. With so many in a room, confusion was inevitable, and none would likely catch all remarks.

13 *Ibid.*

14 Slocum to Doubleday, February 19, 1883. Meade, II, 398.

15 Doubleday, 185n.

16 Meade, II, 398.

17 *Ibid.*, 413. Some of the replies are in II, 399ff.

18 Hoke, 180-183. Oates, 194. *O.R.*, XXVII, Part I, 75.

19 *S.H.S.P.*, VIII, 522.

20 *Ibid.*, XXXVII, 351. The circumstances under which they were found by a lad looking for a watch on the body of a dead cavalryman, did not lend credence to the charge that the papers were forgeries, though they were by no means orders from responsible authorities.

21 *Ibid.*, VIII, 522.

22 *Pennsylvania at Gettysburg*, II, 717.

23 Captain J. M. Robertson brought up a Federal artillery brigade and moved it back 2 miles on the Baltimore pike to camp for the night. Meade, II, 406, *O.R.*, XXVII, Part I, 1021. But this, the only large movement known in the area except Kane's and Candy's, was much earlier in the evening.

24 Gen. Thomas T. Munford, Ms. letter to Mrs. Charles F. Hyde, Southern Historical Collection, University of North Carolina, Chapel Hill, N.C.

25 Thomason, 440.

26 Hoke, 355.

27 The comparison is appropriate with a great British general, Henry V, of whom a contemporary said, "He transacts all his affairs himself." John Richard Green, *History of England*, I, 549.

28 Hoke, 356.

[29] H. J. Eckenrode and Bryan Conrad, *James Longstreet, Lee's War Horse,* 200-201.

[30] Hoke, 356.

[31] Haskell, p. 385, claims to have heard Meade express displeasure over Geary's attack as "not ordered and not necessary" because Geary's position was already good and the works he assailed were valueless. He said he had heard Meade say he sent an order to have the fighting stopped, but it was not delivered until the Confederates had been beaten back. Haskell either must have been mistaken or the remark was a reflection of Meade's generalship, for Culp's Hill was essential to the Federal army.

[32] *Pennsylvania at Gettysburg,* II, 717.

[33] *Ibid.,* 718.

[34] McKim, 188.

[35] *Ibid.*

[36] *Pennsylvania at Gettysburg,* I, 308.

[37] Edmund R. Brown, 379.

[38] *Ibid.,* 380.

[39] J. B. Jones, I, 100.

[40] McKim, 201.

[41] Douglas, 249.

[42] *N.C. Regts.,* V, 195.

[43] Douglas, 250.

Chapter Twenty-one: PICKETT, PETTIGREW, AND TRIMBLE

[1] Walter Harrison, *Pickett's Men . . . ,* 98.

[2] *O.R.,* XXVII, Part III, 910. Pickett reported from Berryville on June 24 that his three brigades aggregated 4,795 men.

[3] Charles T. Loehr, *War History of the Old First Virginia Infantry Regiment . . . ,* 35.

[4] Harrison, 18.

[5] G. F. R. Henderson, *Stonewall Jackson and the American Civil War,* I, 190.

[6] *Ibid.,* 244, 253. Freeman, *Lee's Lieutenants,* I, 318.

[7] LaSalle Corbell Pickett, 212.

[8] Alexander, *S.H.S.P.,* IV, 108. The overcoat must have been a relic of Garnett's U.S. Army days.

[9] Harrison, 20.

[10] Hunton, 84.

[11] Biographical material on Pickett's three brigadier generals is largely from Harrison and LaSalle Corbell Pickett.

[12] Randolph A. Shotwell, "Virginia and North Carolina in the Battle of Gettysburg," *O. L. and D.,* IV, 87.

[13] *Ibid.,* 86.

[14] *Ibid.*

[15] Snow, 103.

[16] Harrison, 86.

[17] The ensuing conversation is from *Soldier of the South,* 54-55.

[18] LaSalle Corbell Pickett, XI.

[19] Sorrel, 155-156.

[20] *Ibid.,* 156.

[21] *Soldier of the South,* 55.

[22] David E. Johnston, *Four Years a Soldier,* 250.

23 *Soldier of the South*, 55-56.
24 *Ibid*. Pickett said Lee spoke in "his firm, quiet, determined voice."
25 *Ibid.*, 56.
26 Henry, *Story of the Mexican War*, 361.
27 LaSalle Corbell Pickett, XI.
28 Sorrel, 54.
29 Beveridge, I, 385.
30 LaSalle Corbell Pickett, 128.
31 *Ibid*.
32 *Ibid.*, XI.
33 *Ibid.*, XI-XII.
34 Sorrel, 54.
35 LaSalle Corbell Pickett, 112.
36 Hunton, 85.
37 Snow, 103.
38 J. B. Jones, I, 261.
39 Two batteries were taken from Law, *Pennsylvania at Gettysburg*, II, 844.
40 Alexander, *S.H.S.P.*, IV, 103.
41 *Ibid*.
42 *B. and L.*, III, 362.
43 Raleigh, N.C., *Semi-Weekly Standard*, July 3, 1863. The first article was headed "Gross Injustice to North Carolina."
44 *Ibid*.
45 *N.C. Regts.*, II, 38.
46 *Ibid.*, 71.
47 Lane, mentioned but slightly in the histories of Lee's army, was entitled to the comment of Captain Octavius A. Wiggins of the 37th North Carolina: "General James H. Lane . . . was all that a true soldier could be upon a battlefield. Nothing could excite him and when he put his troops in battle he always went with them. Always enjoying good health and miraculously escaping a mortal wound, he kept close to his brigade and passed through as many battles as any person in the Confederate army, dearly beloved by his entire brigade."
48 Taylor, *Four Years*, 103.
49 *Ibid*.
50 *Ibid.*, 104.
51 *B. and L.*, III, 342-343.
52 *Ibid*.
53 *Southern Bivouac*, February 1886; Hoke, 336.
54 *Ibid.*, 343.
55 *S.H.S.P.*, IV, 105.
56 *Ibid.*, 104.
57 *Ibid.*, 104-105.
58 *Ibid.*, 105.
59 *Ibid*.
60 *Ibid.*, 106. Alexander used the italics.
61 *Ibid*.

Chapter Twenty-two: AT FEARFUL PRICE

1 The signal was to be shorter but a friction primer failed, causing delay with the second gun. *B. and L.*, III, 362n.
2 *Ibid.*, 314.

3 Haskell, 390, 387.

4 *Pennsylvania at Gettysburg,* II, 629. Haskell, 391f.

5 *Ibid.,* 395.

6 Wilkeson's dispatch, a near classic, is quoted in *Civil War in Song and Story,* 333, and Hoke, 364.

7 Osbourn, 16.

8 *Pennsylvania at Gettysburg,* II, 629-630.

9 Rhodes, 238.

10 Johnston, 252.

11 *Ibid.*

12 Maud Morrow Brown, *The University Greys . . . ,* 38-41.

13 *Vermont at Gettysburg,* 14. Dickert, 200, says most of Kershaw's South Carolinians slept during the cannonade.

14 Dickert, 201.

15 *Soldier of the South,* 57.

16 *Ibid.*

17 *Ibid.,* 60.

18 *S.H.S.P.,* IV, 107.

19 *Ibid.,* 108.

20 *Soldier of the South,* 60. The words vary slightly in different accounts.

21 *Ibid.,* 60-61.

22 Philadelphia *Times* interview in Minnigh, 149.

23 *S.H.S.P.,* IV, 106. Alexander made no complaint in his account, saying the guns might have been lost, but "I always feel like apologizing for their absence." He thought it a "brilliant opportunity" for this artillery escort.

24 LaSalle Corbell Pickett, 302.

25 Shotwell, *O.L. and D.,* IV, 90.

26 Harrison, 98, says Garnett was "in no physical condition to be on the field."

27 Shotwell, *O.L. and D.,* IV, 90.

28 *Ibid.,* 91.

29 *S.H.S.P.,* IV, 108.

30 *Ibid.*

31 Shotwell, *O.L. and D.,* 90. The cannoneers crawled on top of their guns to witness the march and assault.

32 *S.H.S.P.,* XXXIII, 129.

33 William H. Morgan, *Personal Reminiscences of the War,* 53.

34 Crocker, *S.H.S.P.,* XXXIII, 129.

35 Morgan, 167.

36 *Ibid.,* 166.

37 *Ibid.*

38 Johnston, 196.

39 *O.L. and D.,* IV, 91.

40 *Ibid.*

41 *Ibid.*

42 *New York at Gettysburg,* III, 1365.

43 J. H. Stine, *History of the Army of the Potomac,* 527-528.

44 *S.H.S.P.,* XXXIX, 186.

45 Kemper was left partially paralyzed on the field; though permanently disabled, he served a useful later career and became governor of Virginia. Kemper wrote to Colonel W. H. Swallow: "I was nearly up to the Federal line, so near I could easily see the faces and the expression on the countenances of the Union men, and I thought I could identify the individual soldier that shot me." Quoted in letter from Swallow, Hoke, 372n.

46 Captain H. T. Owen in Philadelphia *Times,* cited in Hoke, 386-387.

47 *O.L. and D.,* IV, 93.

48 *Confederate Veteran,* XIV, 81.

49 *Ibid.*

50 *Ibid.*

51 *S.H.S.P.,* XXXIX, 186-187.

52 *Pennsylvania at Gettysburg,* I, 410.

53 The account that Armistead, while lying on the ground wounded, made the call of the widow's son, a fraternal appeal for help, and then sent to his old army friend such words as "Tell Hancock I wronged him and wronged my country" (Stine, 531) is so far out of character and inconsistent with what he was telling his men a few minutes earlier, that it would be questioned and probably discarded as apocryphal even if the circumstances under which the story originated were less doubtful.

Armistead fell in the midst of a group of five Federal soldiers, only one of whom, Private Wildemore of the 71st Pennsylvania, claimed to have caught words spoken in a whisper by Armistead, asking help and saying, as Wildemore repeated the words to his comrades, that "he is the son of a widow." Wildemore was wounded almost at once and the others, understanding the fraternal implications of the call, carried Armistead back, where he died. The story frequently given, that he met death penitently and apologetically, implying that he performed a mental flipflop in favor of those who had just filled his body with lead, and pitifully called for help, is difficult to accept on the available evidence of whispered words heard by only one of five men. Armisteads do not die that way.

54 Sergeant Michael Specht, 72nd Pennsylvania, got the general's sword and kept it until he was commissioned lieutenant, wore it until the end of the war, and in 1906, at a reunion in Gettysburg, returned it to the veterans of Pickett's division.

55 Stine, 528-529.

56 Swallow, *Southern Bivouac,* February 1886. Hoke, 396.

57 *O.L. and D.,* IV, 92.

58 Pickett had moved forward from the reverse slope and waited at a point in the woods nearer than Pettigrew.

59 This was evident to the writer from walking over the ground traversed by both commands.

60 *Civil War in Song and Story,* 220.

61 Shotwell of the 8th Virginia, after Garnett's repulse, looked over and thought the North Carolinians had gained a lodgment on the crest. He seized a musket and hurried over but before he could join them they were beaten back. *O.L. and D.,* IV, 94.

62 Douglas, 212.

63 *S.H.S.P.,* IX, 29.

64 *O.L. and D.,* IV, 57.

65 *Ibid.,* III, 462. *N.C. Regts.,* II, 564.

66 *N.C. Regts.,* II, 566.

67 *Ibid.,* III, 91.

68 *Ibid.,* II, 566.

69 *Ibid.,* 563.

70 *Confederate Veteran,* XXV, 213.

71 *O.L. and D.,* IV, 57.

72 *Pennsylvania at Gettysburg,* II, 631.

73 *Ibid.*

74 Hunton, 98.

75 *Ibid.*

76 *Ibid.*, 98-99. Hunton dictated his memoirs in his eighty-second year, then published them privately, but they show how he retained strong recollections of the battle. He appears forgetful in one point particularly, as Pickett, *Soldier of the South,* 70, said, or strongly implied that he dismounted. Pickett's words were: "Poor Dick Garnett did not dismount, as did the others of us. . . ."

77 When this writer witnessed the re-enactment of the charge by the Marine Corps in 1922, Pickett was represented as going to the Codori barn.

78 Walter A. Clarke's pamphlet, "Pickett's Charge a Misnomer," 7.

79 *N.C. Regts.,* III, 299.

80 *Ibid.*

81 Joseph A. Englehart, adjutant of Pender's division, said the troops with him struck the wall at the point farthest to the front. "I leaned an elbow upon one of the guns of the enemy to rest, while I watched with painful anxiety the flight of Pickett's right." Grimes, Papers, Southern Historical Collection, University of North Carolina Library, Chapel Hill, N.C.

82 Longstreet felt it necessary to defend himself from N.C. strictures resulting from his report, as in *B. and L.,* III, 353.

83 *Soldier of the South,* 62, said the report originally stated "without reserve" the reasons why he believed the charge proved disastrous. The same or similar material was contained in one of Pickett's letters, but it was omitted from those Mrs. Pickett published. J. Bryan Grimes said that by having the division commander alter his report, Lee "saved Pickett from being torn to pieces by his critics." Papers. Pickett did not file an amended report.

84 *O.L. and D.,* IV, 95.

85 *Ibid.*

86 Lee must have made this remark a number of times. Fremantle, the British observer, thought his face was "placid and cheerful" and showed no disappointment. He assured the soldiers: "All this will come right in the end, we'll talk it over afterwards; but in the meantime all good men must rally." Fremantle, 315. Sorrel, 173, mentioned Lee's "extreme agitation" on witnessing the repulse, and quoted him: "It's all my fault. I take it all—get together men, we shall yet beat them." Sorrel added: "I saw no man fail him." Loehr of the 1st Virginia heard him say to Pickett: "General, your men have done all that men can do. The fault is entirely my own." Loehr, 38. Neither then nor at any later time did Lee blame any of his subordinates for the failure of the assault.

87 Fremantle, evidently a free-handed reporter given to quick, superficial impressions, as in congratulating Longstreet on Pickett's success, when Longstreet was already fully aware of the failure, told of Lee reproving an artillery officer who put spurs to his horse when it was frightened by an exploding shell. Alexander gave an account of the incident. The officer, Lieutenant F. M. Colston, was directed by Lee when he heard the cheering, to ascertain if the enemy showed indications of advancing. The lieutenant's horse, used to accompanying Alexander's horse, and as bound by habit as army horses often became, did not want to leave alone. The lieutenant, anxious to be off, did spur him and Lee did object to it. *S.H.S.P.,* IV, 110. He must have been deeply perturbed beneath his calm exterior. But the officer obviously was more zealous than cruel.

88 Behind the lines, when Pickett rode among his survivors, some were thoroughly defeated, some were angry. "General, let's go it again," shouted Charlie Belcher of the 24th Virginia. Loehr, 38.

89 *S.H.S.P.,* IX, 29.

90 Sorrel, 172. The nature of Pickett's rout was soon known in Richmond. Gorgas recorded, 50, on July 17, that the division was wholly scattered and could not be rallied until far in the rear.

[91] *O.L. and D.,* IV, 95.

[92] Stine, 548.

[93] *B. and L.,* III, 394. The conversation follows.

[94] *Pennsylvania at Gettysburg,* II, 845.

[95] This account is summarized mainly from General Benning in *S.H.S.P.,* IV, 176f and Col. F. C. Newhall, *Pennsylvania at Gettysburg,* II, 835f.

[96] *Pennsylvania at Gettysburg,* II, 846.

[97] *S.H.S.P.,* IV, 177. H. L. Parsons of the 1st Vermont Cavalry said Farnsworth fell dead with "five mortal wounds." This differs from the general version.

Chapter Twenty-three: RETREAT TO VIRGINIA

[1] J. B. Jones, I, 373.

[2] Stine, 555. According to the notes of Professor Michael Jacobs there was a thundershower beginning at 6:00 P.M. July 3, another at 6:00 A.M. July 4, and others in the afternoon of July 4.

[3] *Ibid.*

[4] McKim, 189.

[5] Lightsly, 5.

[6] *B. and L.,* III, 420-421.

[7] McIntosh, 79.

[8] *Annals,* 455.

[9] Dickert, 256.

[10] Ross, 69f.

[11] *Ibid.,* 73.

[12] *Ibid.,* 80-83.

[13] Ross, 87, says many were disappointed at the decision to return to Virginia. Their view had been that Lee was merely awaiting supplies to resume the offensive. But Ross thought news of the surrender of Vicksburg may have decided Lee to cross. The losses in both armies were staggering and about equal. Colonel William Allen, *S.H.S.P.,* IV, 34, aggregated Lee's loss at 22,928, made up of Longstreet, 7,659; Ewell, 6,087; Hill, 8,982; and cavalry, 200. From his study he placed Meade's loss at 23,186. The official returns of killed, wounded, and missing give Lee's loss as 20,448 and Meade's as 22,990. Paris, 313 and 298. The final figures of the official records vary little from these totals.

[14] Meade, II, 365.

[15] Ross, 89.

[16] Welch, 59.

[17] Ms. letter, Indiana State Library.

[18] McKim, 190.

[19] *O.L. and D.,* I, 30.

[20] *Ibid.,* 29-31.

[21] Ross, 87.

[22] Alexander, "Causes of Southern Defeat . . ." *S.H.S.P.,* IV, 99, who was one of the best Southern analysts of the cause of the repulse, thought Lee could have taken a position covering Fairfield and maneuvered to force Meade to attack. He added: "They had never driven us from the field since the war began."

[23] Captured by the Sixth Corps, *Sedgwick Memorial,* 38.

[24] Frank M. Mixon, *Reminiscences of a Private,* 41.

[25] R. E. Lee, 102.

[26] Charles Francis Adams, *Lee's Centennial,* 23.

Bibliography

ADAMS, CHARLES FRANCIS. *Lee's Centennial.* Address at Lexington, Va., January 19, 1907. Boston, 1907.

ADAMS, JOHN G. B. *Reminiscences of the 19th Massachusetts Regiment.* Boston, 1899.

ALDERMAN, EDWIN ANDERSON, and JOEL CHANDLER HARRIS, editors-in-chief. *Library of Southern Literature.* 16 vols. Atlanta, 1907-1909.

ALEXANDER, E. P. "Causes of Southern Defeat at Gettysburg," *Southern Historical Society Papers,* IV, 97.

————. *Military Memories of a Confederate.* New York, 1907.

ALLAN, WILLIAM. "General Lee's Strength and Losses at Gettysburg," *Southern Historical Society Papers,* IV, 34.

————. *The Strategy of the Gettysburg Campaign.* Military History Society of Massachusetts. Boston, 1903.

————. "Gettysburg," *Southern Historical Society Papers,* IV, 76ff.

The Annals of the War, by Leading Participants North and South. Philadelphia, 1879.

ASHE, SAMUEL A. *History of North Carolina.* Raleigh, 1925.

————. *The Charge at Gettysburg.* Raleigh, no date.

————, editor-in-chief. *Biographical Dictionary of North Carolina from Colonial Times to the Present.* Greensboro, 1907.

AVARY, MYRTA LOCKETT, editor. *Recollections of Alexander H. Stephens.* New York, 1910.

AVERY, ISAAC WHEELER. *History of the State of Georgia from 1850 to 1881.* New York, 1881.

BACHELDER, JOHN B. *Repulse of Longstreet's Assault.* New York, 1870.

————. "Letter on Gettysburg," *Southern Historical Society Papers,* V, 173.

BALCH, WILLIAM RALSTON. *The Battle of Gettysburg.* Harrisburg, 1885.

BANES, CHARLES H. *History of the Philadelphia Brigade.* Philadelphia, 1876.

BARTLETT, NAPIER. *A Soldier's Story of the War, Including the Marches and Battles of the Battalion of Washington Artillery.* New Orleans, 1874.

BASSLER, J. H. "The Color Episode of the 149th Regiment, Pennsylvania Volunteers in the First Day's Fight at Gettysburg," *Southern Historical Society Papers,* XXXVII, 266.

BATES, SAMUEL P. *The Battle of Gettysburg.* Philadelphia, 1875.

BATTINE, CECIL. *The Crisis of the Confederacy.* London, 1905.

BATTLE, KEMP P. *History of the University of North Carolina.* 2 vols. Raleigh, 1907.

Battles and Leaders of the Civil War. 4 vols. New York, 1884.

BEECHAM, ROBERT K. *Gettysburg, The Pivotal Battle of the Civil War.* Chicago, 1911.

BELLAMY, F. J. *War Diary of Co. A, 3rd Indiana Cavalry.* Ms. Indiana State Library.

BENEDICT, G. G. *Vermont at Gettysburg.* Burlington, 1870.

BENNING, HENRY L. "Notes on the Battle of Gettysburg," *Southern Historical Society Papers,* IV, 176.

BENSON, BERRY GREENWOOD. *Reminiscences.* Ms. Augusta, Ga., 1863.

BEVERIDGE, ALBERT J. *Abraham Lincoln.* 2 vols. Boston, 1928.

BIDDLE, CHAPMAN. *The First Day of the Battle of Gettysburg.* Philadelphia, 1880.

BILL, ALFRED HOYT. *The Beleaguered City.* New York, 1946.

BILLINGS, JOHN D. *Hard Tack and Coffee or the Unwritten Story of Army Life.* Boston, 1887.

BIRDSONG, JAMES C. *Brief Sketches of North Carolina Troops in the War Between the States.* Raleigh, 1894.

BLACKFORD, W. W. *War Years with Jeb Stuart.* New York, 1945.

Blue and Gray—Reunion of Philadelphia Brigade and Pickett's Division. Philadelphia, 1906.

BOND, W. R. *Pickett or Pettigrew.* Weldon, N.C., 1888.

BONHAM, M. L. *A Little More Light on Gettysburg.* Pamphlet at University of South Carolina Library, apparently extract from article in Mississippi Valley Historical Review. No date or place.

BORCKE, HEROS VON. *Memoirs of the Confederate War for Independence.* 1886. Republished, New York, 1938.

BOWEN, J. J. *The Strategy of Robert E. Lee.* New York, 1914.

BRADFORD, GAMALIEL. *Confederate Portraits.* Boston, 1917.

BRATTON, JOHN. "Tribute to General Dick Anderson," *Southern Historical Society Papers,* XIII, 419.

BROCK, R. A. *Robert E. Lee: Soldier, Citizen, Christian Patriot.* Richmond, 1897.

BROOKS, U. R. *Stories of the Confederacy.* Columbia, S.C., 1912.

BROWN, EDMUND R. *The 27th Indiana Volunteer Infantry in the War of the Rebellion.* No place, 1899.

BROWN, JOSEPH N. *The Battle of Gettysburg.* Anderson, S.C., 1901.

BROWN, MAUD MORROW. *The University Greys (Co. A, 11th Mississippi Infantry Regiment)*. Richmond, 1940.

BROWN, VARINA D. *A Colonel at Gettysburg and Spotsylvania*. Columbia, S.C., 1931.

BURGWYN, WILLIAM S. "Unparalleled Loss of Company E, 26th North Carolina, Pettigrew's Brigade, at Gettysburg," *Southern Historical Society Papers*, XXVIII, 199ff.

––––––. "Zebulon Baird Vance," *Library of Southern Literature*, XII, 5555.

CALDWELL, J. F. J. *History of a Brigade of South Carolinians Known First as Gregg's and Subsequently as McGowan's Brigade*. Philadelphia, 1866.

CANDLER, ALLEN D., and CLEMENT A. EVANS. *Georgia: Comprising Sketches of Counties, Towns, Events, Institutions, and Persons*. 3 vols. Atlanta, 1906.

CARRINGTON, JAMES MCDOWELL. "First Day on the Left at Gettysburg," *Southern Historical Society Papers*, XXXVII, 326-337.

CASLER, JOHN O. *Four Years in the Stonewall Brigade*. Guthrie, Okla., 1893.

CATTON, BRUCE. *Glory Road*. Garden City, N.Y., 1952.

CHESNUT, MARY BOYKIN. *A Diary from Dixie*. New York, 1905.

CLARK, CHIEF JUSTICE WALTER. Memorial address, Bunker Hill, W. Va. *General James Johnston Pettigrew, C.S.A.* Address at the unveiling of the memorial marble pillar and tablet to General Pettigrew near Bunker Hill, Sept. 17, 1920. Pamphlet, no other date or place.

––––––. *Pickett's Charge a Misnomer*. Address before North Carolina Confederate Veterans Association, Durham, N.C., August 24, 1921. Pamphlet, no other date or place.

––––––, editor. *Histories of the Several Regiments and Battalions from North Carolina in the Great War, 1861-65*. 5 vols. Raleigh, 1901.

COMMAGER, HENRY STEELE. *The Blue and the Gray*. Indianapolis, 1950.

CONFEDERATE, A. *The Grayjackets: and How They Lived, Fought and Died for Dixie*. Richmond, 1867.

Confederate Veteran. 40 vols. (1893-1932). Nashville, Tenn.

COX, WILLIAM E. *Life and Character of General Stephen D. Ramseur*. Raleigh, 1891.

COX, JUDGE WILLIAM RUFFIN. *Life and Services of General James H. Lane*. Richmond, 1908.

CROCKER, JAMES P. "My Personal Experiences in Taking up Arms" (an address before Stonewall Camp, Confederate Veterans, Portsmouth, Va., Feb. 6, 1889), *Southern Historical Society Papers*, XXXIII, 111ff.

––––––. "Gettysburg—Pickett's Charge" (an address, same camp, Nov. 7, 1894), *Southern Historical Society Papers*, XXXIII, 111ff.

CURTIS, GEORGE W. Address at dedication of statue of Major General John Sedgwick at West Point, Oct. 21, 1868. New York, 1869.

CURTIS, O. B. *History of the 24th Michigan of the Iron Brigade*. Detroit, 1891.

DALBIAC, COLONEL P. H. *American War of Secession: Chancellorsville and Gettysburg.* London and New York, 1911.

DANIEL, FREDERICK S. *Richmond Howitzers in the War.* Richmond, 1891.

DANIEL, LIZZIE CARY. *Confederate Scrap Book.* Richmond, 1893.

DAVIS, BURKE. *Gray Fox.* New York, 1956.

DAVIS, JEFFERSON. *A Short History of the Confederate States of America.* New York, 1890.

DAVIS, REUBEN. *Recollections of Mississippi and Mississippians.* Boston and New York, 1889.

DAWES, RUFUS R. *Service with the Sixth Wisconsin Volunteers.* Marietta, Ohio, 1890.

DETROBRIAND, REGIS. *Four Years with the Army of the Potomac.* Translated by George C. Dauchy. Boston, 1889.

DICKERT, D. AUGUSTUS. *History of Kershaw's Brigade.* Newberry, S.C., 1899.

DOUBLEDAY, ABNER. *Chancellorsville and Gettysburg.* New York, 1882.

DOUGLAS, HENRY KYD. *I Rode With Stonewall.* Chapel Hill, N.C., 1940.

DOWD, CLEMENT. *Life of Zebulon B. Vance.* Charlotte, N.C., 1899.

DRIVER, WILLIAM R. *Pickett's Charge at Gettysburg.* Boston, 1903.

EARLY, JUBAL A. "A Review by General Early," *Southern Historical Society Papers,* IV, 241.

———. "Causes of the Defeat of General Lee's Army at the Battle of Gettysburg," *Southern Historical Society Papers,* IV, 49-87.

———. "Supplement to General Early's Reply," *Southern Historical Society Papers,* IV, 282ff.

———. "Reply to Count of Paris," *Southern Historical Society Papers,* VI, 12-22.

ECKENRODE, H. J., and BRYAN CONRAD. *James Longstreet, Lee's War Horse.* Chapel Hill, N.C., 1936.

EGGLESTON, GEORGE CARY. *A Rebel's Recollections.* New York, 1875.

EVANS, CLEMENT A. *Confederate Military History.* 12 vols. Atlanta, 1899.

FAGAN, W. L. *Southern War Songs.* New York, 1890.

FARLEY, JOSEPH PEARSON. *West Point in the Early Sixties, with Incidents of the War.* Troy, N.Y., 1902.

FLEMING, FRANCIS P. "Florida Brigade at Gettysburg," *Southern Historical Society Papers,* XXVII, 192ff.

FREEMAN, DOUGLAS SOUTHALL. *Robert E. Lee: A Biography.* 2 vols. New York, 1935.

———. *Lee's Lieutenants.* 3 vols. New York, 1942.

FREMANTLE, ARTHUR J. L. *Three Months in the Southern States.* New York, 1864.

GALBREATH, C. B. "Song Writers of Ohio." *Ohio Archeological and Historical Society Publications,* Vols. XIII and XIV. Columbus, 1904 and 1905.

GALBREATH, E. C. Ms. Notes for Family. Indiana State Library.

GETTYSBURG BATTLEFIELD COMMISSION. Ms. entries entitled *A Record of the Position of Troops on the Battlefield.* At Gettysburg National Park.

GETTYSBURG NATIONAL MILITARY PARK. Scrapbook of newspaper clippings.

GORDON, JOHN B. *Reminiscences of the Civil War.* New York, 1903.

GORGAS, JOSIAH. *The Civil War Diary of General Josiah Gorgas.* Edited by Frank E. Vandiver. University of Alabama Press, 1947.

GRANT, ULYSSES S. *Personal Memoirs of U. S. Grant.* 2 vols. New York, 1885.

GREELEY, HORACE. *American Conflict.* 2 vols. Hartford, Conn., 1867-1869.

GREEN, JOHN RICHARD. *History of England.* 4 vols. World's Best Histories Series. New York and London, no date.

GRIMES, J. BRYAN. "Gettysburg," Ms., *Papers,* Southern Historical Collection, Chapel Hill, N.C., 1911.

———. "The Truth is Let Out as to Gettysburg," Raleigh *News and Observer,* August 6, 1911.

GRIFFIN, CLARENCE W. *History of Old Tryon and Rutherford Counties, North Carolina 1730-1936.* Asheville, N.C., 1937.

HAMLIN, PERCY GATLING. *Old Bald Head (Ewell): The Portrait of a Soldier.* Strasburg, Va., 1940.

HANCOCK, MRS. WINFIELD SCOTT. *Reminiscences of Winfield Scott Hancock.* New York, 1887.

HARRISON, WALTER. *Pickett's Men, A Fragment of War History.* New York, 1870.

HASKELL, FRANK ARETAS. *The Battle of Gettysburg.* From vol. 43, The Harvard Classics. New York, 1910.

HAYS, LOUISE FREDERICK. *History of Macon County, Georgia.* Atlanta, 1933.

HENDERSON, G. F. R. of British Army. "Review of General Longstreet's Book, *From Manassas to Appomattox,*" *Southern Historical Society Papers,* CIV, 117.

———. *Stonewall Jackson and the American Civil War.* 2 vols. London, 1911.

HENRY, ROBERT SELPH. *The Story of the Mexican War.* Indianapolis, 1950.

———. *The Story of the Confederacy.* Indianapolis, 1931.

HETH, HARRY. "Gettysburg" (An account of the opening of the engagement), *Southern Historical Society Papers,* IV, 151.

HILL, BENJAMIN HARVEY. *Tribute to Lee and Davis. Library of Southern Literature.* Vol. VI, Atlanta, 1907. From address delivered before Southern Historical Society, Atlanta, Feb. 18, 1874.

HILL, DANIEL HARVEY, editor. *The Land We Love.* Charlotte, N.C. (A monthly magazine, May 1866-March 1869.)

HILLSBORO *Recorder,* a newspaper. Hillsboro, N.C., 1863.

HOKE, JACOB. *The Great Invasion.* Dayton, O., 1887.

HOOD, JOHN B. *Advance and Retreat.* New Orleans, 1880.

———. "Gettysburg," *Southern Historical Society Papers,* IV, 145.

HOWARD, OLIVER O. *Autobiography.* New York, 1907.

HUFHAM, J. D., JR. "Gettysburg (Being an Account of the Experiences of a Veteran, Told by Himself)," Wake Forest (N.C.) *Student,* April 1897.

HUIDEKOPER, H. S. *A Short Story of the First Day's Fight at Gettysburg.* Philadelphia, 1906.

HUNTON, EPPA. *Autobiography.* Richmond, 1933.

HURST, M. B. *History of the Fourteenth Alabama Volunteers.* Richmond, 1863.

HYDE, THOMAS W. *Following the Creek Cross.* Boston, 1894.

Indiana at Antietam. Indiana Monument Commission report. Indianapolis, 1911.

Indiana at the Fiftieth Anniversary of the Battle of Gettysburg. Indianapolis, no date (1913?).

IRBY, RICHARD. *Historical Sketch of the Nottoway Grays, Afterwards Co. G, Eighteenth Virginia Infantry.* Richmond, 1878.

IREDELL *Express,* a newspaper. Statesville, N.C. 1863 file.

The Iron Brigade at Gettysburg. Cincinnati, 1879.

JACOBS, MICHAEL. *Notes on the Rebel Invasion of Maryland and Pennsylvania and the Battle of Gettysburg.* Philadelphia, 1864.

JOHNSTON, DAVID E. *Four Years a Soldier.* Princeton, W. Va., 1887.

———. *The Story of a Confederate Boy in the Civil War.* Portland, Ore., 1914.

JONES, CHARLES E. *Georgia and the War.* (Brief biographies of Georgia officers.) Atlanta, 1909.

JONES, J. B. *A Rebel War Clerk's Diary.* 2 vols. Philadelphia, 1866. New edition, Howard Swigget, editor. 2 vols. New York, 1935.

JONES, J. WILLIAM, secretary of the Southern Historical Society. *Life and Letters of Robert E. Lee: Soldier and Man.* New York and Washington, 1906.

———. *Personal Reminiscences, Anecdotes, and Letters of General Robert E. Lee.* New York, 1875.

———, compiler. *Army of Northern Virginia, Memorial Volume.* Richmond, 1880.

JONES, KATHARINE M. *Heroines of Dixie.* Indianapolis, 1955.

KEIFER, JOSEPH WARREN. *Slavery and Four Years of War.* 2 vols. New York and London, 1900.

KING, CHARLES. *The Iron Brigade.* New York, 1902.

KINGSBURY, T. B. "North Carolina at Gettysburg," *Our Living and Dead,* I, 193. Raleigh, 1874.

KIRKLAND, FRAZER. *The Picture Book of Anecdotes of the Rebellion.* Hillsdale, Mich., 1887.

KNIGHT, LUCIAN LAMAR. *Georgia Landmarks, Memorials and Legends.* 2 vols. Atlanta, 1913.

LANE, JAMES H. "History of Lane's North Carolina Brigade," *Southern Historical Society Papers,* Vols. VII-X.
————. "Letter to J. William Jones on Gettysburg," *Southern Historical Society Papers,* V, 38.

LEE, FITZHUGH. *General Lee.* New York, 1894.
————. "A Review of the First Two Days' Operations at Gettysburg and a Reply to General Longstreet," *Southern Historical Society Papers,* V, 168ff.

LEE, ROBERT E. (son of General Lee). *Recollections and Letters of General Robert E. Lee.* New York, 1904.

LIGHTSLY, ADA CHRISTINE. *The Veteran's Story.* Meridian, Miss., 1899.

Lincoln Day Addresses, 1887-1909. The National Republican Club, 2nd ed., Copy No. 278, New York.

LOEHR, CHARLES T. *War History of the Old First Virginia Infantry Regiment, Army of Northern Virginia.* Richmond, 1884.

LONG, A. L. *Memoirs of Robert E. Lee.* London, 1886.

LONGSTREET, HELEN DORTSCH. *Lee and Longstreet at High Tide.* Gainesville, Ga., 1905.

LONGSTREET, JAMES. *From Manassas to Appomattox.* Philadelphia, 1896.

LONGSTREET PAPERS. Southern Historical Collection, University of North Carolina Library. Chapel Hill, N.C.

LOSSING, BENSON J. *Pictorial History of the Civil War.* 3 vols. Hartford, Conn., 1874.

Maine at Gettysburg. Portland, Me., 1898.

MARSHALL, CHARLES. *Papers.* Edited by Major General Sir Frederick Maurice. Boston, 1927.

MARTIN, DR. R. W. "Armistead at the Battle of Gettysburg. Extracts from letters to Rev. James Poindexter," *Southern Historical Society Papers,* XXXIX, 186-187.

Maryland at Gettysburg. Baltimore, Md., 1891.

MAURICE, SIR FREDERICK. *Robert E. Lee, the Soldier.* Boston, 1925.

McCABE, JAMES D., JR. *Life and Campaigns of General Robert E. Lee.* New York, 1866.

McCLELLAN, GEORGE B. *McClellan's Own Story.* New York, 1887.

McCLELLAN, H. B. *The Life and Campaigns of Major General J. E. B. Stuart.* Boston and New York, 1885.

McDANIEL, J. J. *Diary of the Battles, and Incidents of the Seventh South Carolina Regiment.* No date or place.

McINTOSH, DAVID GREGG. *Review of the Gettysburg Campaign.* No date or place. University of South Carolina Library. (Similar or same article in *Southern Historical Society Papers,* XXXVII, 74ff.)

McKIM, RANDOLPH H. "The Gettysburg Campaign," *Southern Historical Society Papers,* XL, 253-295.

————. "Steuart's Brigade in the Battle of Gettysburg," *Southern Historical Society Papers,* V, 291.

————. *A Soldier's Recollections.* New York, 1910.

————. "Gen. J. E. B. Stuart in the Gettysburg Campaign," *Southern Historical Society Papers,* XXXVII, 210ff. (A Reply to Col. John S. Mosby.)

McNEILLY, J. S. "Barksdale's Mississippi Brigade at Gettysburg: The Most Magnificent Charge of the War," *Publications of the Mississippi Historical Society,* XIX, 231-265.

MEADE, GEORGE GORDON. Life and Letters of George Gordon Meade. 2 vols. New York, 1913.

MEREDITH, SOLOMON. Defense of General Sol Meredith against the False and Infamous Slanders of George W. Julian. Indianapolis, 1866.

Michigan at Gettysburg. Report of Monuments Commission. Detroit, 1889.

MINNIGH, L. W. *Gettysburg: What They Did Here.* Gettysburg, 1954.

MIXON, FRANK M. *Reminiscences of a Private.* Columbia, S.C., 1910.

MONTGOMERY, WALTER A. *Life and Character of Major General W. D. Pender.* Memorial address, May 10, 1894. Raleigh, 1894.

MOORE, FRANK, editor. *The Rebellion Record.* Vol. VII. New York, 1864.

————, collector and arranger. *The Civil War in Song and Story.* New York, 1889.

————. *Women of the War.* Hartford, Conn., 1866.

MORGAN, WILLIAM HENRY. *Personal Reminiscences of the War, 1861-65.* Lynchburg, Va., 1911.

MOSBY, J. S. *Stuart's Cavalry in the Gettysburg Campaign.* New York, 1908.

MUNFORD, GEN. THOMAS T. Ms. letter to Mrs. Charles F. Hyde. Southern Historical Collection. University of North Carolina Library, Chapel Hill, N.C.

NEW JERSEY STATE PUBLICATION. *Report of Gettysburg Battlefield Commission.* Trenton, 1891.

New York at Gettysburg. 3 vols. Albany, 1900.

NEW YORK STATE PUBLICATION. *Major General James S. Wadsworth at Gettysburg and Other Fields.* Albany, 1916.

NEW YORK *Herald.* Files for 1862-1863.

NEW YORK *Tribune.* Files for 1862-1863.

NICHOLS, G. W. *A Soldier's Story of His Regiment (61st Georgia).* No place, 1898.

"The 19th Indiana at Gettysburg. The Thrilling Story of a Great Regiment in a Great Battle." Typed Ms. Indiana State Library.

NORTON, OLIVER WILLCOX. *The Attack and Defense of Little Round Top.* New York, 1913.

————. *Strong Vincent and His Brigade at Gettysburg.* Chicago, 1909.

OATES, WILLIAM C. "The Battle on the Right," *Southern Historical Society Papers*, VI, 172.

———. *The War Between the Union and the Confederacy and Its Lost Opportunities, with a History of the 15th Alabama Regiment and the Forty-eight Battles in which It Was Engaged.* New York, 1905.

Official Records of the Union and Confederate Armies. Washington, 1882-1900.

Ohio Archeological and Historical Society Publications. Scattered issues. Columbus.

OSBOURN, FRANCIS A. *"Fighting Three Hundred,"* the Twentieth Indiana *Infantry.* No place or date.

Our Living and Dead, a magazine. New Bern and Raleigh, 1873-1876.

OWEN, WILLIAM M. *In Camp and Battle with the Washington Artillery of New Orleans.* Boston, 1885.

PALFREY, COL. ED A. "Some of the Secret History of Gettysburg," *Southern Historical Society Papers,* VIII, 521.

PARIS, COMTE DE. "Battle of Gettysburg," from *History of the Civil War in America.* Philadelphia, 1886-1912.

———. "Gettysburg," *Southern Historical Society Papers,* V, 87.

PARK, CHARLES B. "Notes, Gettysburg Battlefield, June 21, 1913. Compiled from Established Data under Direction of Judge Walter A. Montgomery, member North Carolina Historical Commission." Ms. 1913. University of North Carolina Library, Chapel Hill, N.C.

PARK, R. E. *Sketch of the Twelfth Alabama Infantry.* Richmond, 1906.

PARKMAN, FRANCIS. *Montcalm and Wolfe. (France and England in North America,* vol. II.) Boston, 1899.

PECK, RUFUS H. *Reminiscences of a Confederate Soldier.* Fincastle, Va., no date.

PENDER, WILLIAM DORSEY. Ms. Letters and papers. Southern Historical Collection. University of North Carolina Library, Chapel Hill, N.C.

Pennsylvania at Gettysburg. 2 vols. Harrisburg, 1904.

PENNYPACKER, ISAAC R. *Life of George Gordon Meade.* New York, 1901.

PHILADELPHIA BRIGADE ASSOCIATION. *Reply of the Philadelphia Brigade Association to the Foolish and Absurd Narrative of Lieutenant Frank A. Haskell.* Philadelphia, 1910.

PICKERILL, W. N. *History of the Third Indiana Cavalry.* Indianapolis, 1906.

PICKETT, GEORGE. *Soldier of the South.* Letters. Arthur Crew Inman, editor. Boston, 1928.

PICKETT, LASALLE CORBELL. *Pickett and His Men.* Atlanta, 1899.

PINCHON, EDGCUMB. *Dan Sickles, Hero of Gettysburg and "Yankee King of Spain."* New York, 1945.

PINCKNEY, JOHN MCPHERSON. *Proceedings in the House of Representatives in Memory of Representative John M. Pinckney, December 5, 1905.* Washington, 1907.

POLLARD, E. A. *Southern History of the War.* 2 vols. in one. New York, 1866.

————. *The Early Life, Campaigns, and Public Services of Robert E. Lee, etc.* New York, 1870.

POLLEY, JOSEPH BENJAMIN. *Hood's Texas Brigade. Its Marches, Its Battles, Its Achievements.* New York, 1910.

POWELL, WILLIAM HENRY. *The Fifth Army Corps.* New York, 1896.

PULLEN, JOHN J. *The Twentieth Maine.* Philadelphia, 1957.

RALEIGH *Semi-Weekly Standard.* Raleigh, N.C. Files for 1863.

RAMSEUR, STEPHEN DODSON. Ms. Letters. Southern Historical Collection. University of North Carolina Library, Chapel Hill, N.C.

RANDALL, EMILIUS O. "High Lights of Ohio Literature," *Ohio Archeological and Historical Society Publications,* XXVIII. Columbus, Ohio, 1919.

"REGULARS AT GETTYSBURG," series by different officers, *Journal of the Military Service Institution of the United States,* XLIV and XLV. Governor's Island, 1909.

REID, WHITELAW. *Ohio in the War. Her Statesmen, Generals and Soldiers.* Columbus, 1893.

Reynolds Memorial—Addresses Before the Historical Society of Pennsylvania. Philadelphia, 1880.

RHODES, JAMES FORD. *History of the Civil War.* New York, 1917.

RICHMOND *Examiner.* Files for 1863.

RICHMOND *Inquirer.* Files for 1862-1863.

RICHMOND *Whig and Public Advertiser.* Files for 1863.

RIDPATH, JOHN CLARK. *Life and Times of James A. Garfield.* Cincinnati, 1881.

ROBBINS, W. M. "Longstreet's Assault at Gettysburg," *Histories of the Several Regiments and Battalions from North Carolina in the Great War, 1861-65,* V, 101.

ROBERTSON, JOHN, compiler. *Michigan in the War.* Lansing, 1882.

ROCKWELL, W. S. *The Oglethorpe Light Infantry of Savannah in Peace and in War.* Savannah, 1894.

ROSS, FITZGERALD. *A Visit to Cities and Camps of the Confederacy.* Edinburg and London, 1865.

SANDBURG, CARL. *Abraham Lincoln. The War Years.* Vol. II. New York, 1939.

SANGER, D. B., and THOMAS R. HAY. *James Longstreet.* Baton Rouge, 1952.

SCHEIBERT, JUSTUS (of Prussian Royal Engineers). Letter to J. William Jones, Secretary of Southern Historical Society, *Southern Historical Society Papers,* V, 90.

SCHOULER, JAMES. *The History of the Civil War.* New York, 1899.

SCRIBNER, THEODORE T. *Indiana's Roll of Honor.* Indianapolis, 1866.

SEDGWICK, MAJ. GEN. JOHN. *Proceedings at Dedication of Statue at Gettysburg.* Hartford, Conn., 1913.

SHIELDS, DAVID. "Story of Longstreet's Assault," from Prof. Nixon papers, Southern Historical Collection, Chapel Hill, N.C.

SHOTWELL, RANDOLPH A. "Virginia and North Carolina in the Battle of Gettysburg," *Our Living and Dead,* IV, 80ff.

SMITH, JAMES POWER. "General Lee at Gettysburg," *Southern Historical Society Papers,* XXXIII, 135ff.

SNOW, WILLIAM PARKER. *Southern Generals, Their Lives and Campaigns.* New York, 1866.

SORREL, G. MOXLEY. *Recollections of a Confederate Staff Officer.* New York, 1905. Reprinted, Jackson, Tenn., 1958.

Southern Historical Society Papers. 49 vols., chiefly Vols. 4 and 5. Richmond, 1876——.

STACKPOLE, EDWARD J. *They Met at Gettysburg.* Harrisburg, 1956.

STEELE, MATTHEW FORNEY. *American Campaigns.* 2 vols. Washington, 1909.

STEVENS, GEORGE T. *Three Years in the Sixth Corps.* New York, 1870.

STEWART, W. H. *A Pair of Blankets.* New York, 1911.

STIKELEATHER, J. A. Ms. Recollections of the Civil War in the United States. Among J. Bryan Grimes papers, Southern Historical Collection. Chapel Hill, N.C. Olive, N.C., 1909.

STILES, ROBERT. *Four Years Under Marse Robert.* New York, 1903.

STINE, J. H. *History of the Army of the Potomac.* Washington, 1893.

STORRICK, W. C. *The Battle of Gettysburg, The Country, The Contestants, The Results.* Harrisburg, 1947.

STROUDER, A. C. *Roster and History of 19th Ind. Reg. of Inf.* Muncie, 1907.

SYPHER, JOSIAH R. *History of the Pennsylvania Reserve Corps.* Lancaster, 1865.

T. K. B. (No name). "North Carolina Generals," *Our Living and Dead,* III.

——. "Another Witness: Gettysburg," *Our Living and Dead,* III, 45.

TALCOTT, T. M. R. "Review of Stuart's Cavalry in the Gettysburg Campaign, by Colonel John S. Mosby," *Southern Historical Society Papers,* XXXVII, 21.

TAYLOR, RICHARD. "Reminiscences of Secession, War and Reconstruction" advance sheets, *Southern Historical Society Papers,* V, 136ff.

——. *Destruction and Reconstruction.* New York, 1879.

TAYLOR, WALTER H. *Four Years with General Lee.* New York, 1877.

——. General Lee, His Campaigns in Virginia. Norfolk, 1906.

——. "Gettysburg," letter to J. William Jones, *Southern Historical Society Papers,* IV, 124.

THOMAS, HENRY W. *History of the Doles-Cook Brigade.* Atlanta, 1903.

THOMASON, JOHN W., JR. *Jeb Stuart.* New York, 1930.

THOMSON (of Co. G). *Seventh Indiana Infantry in the War for the Union.* Indiana State Library.

THURSTON, EDWARD N. "Memoir of Richard H. Anderson, C.S.A.," *Southern Historical Society Papers,* XXXIX, 152.

TOOMBS, SAMUEL. *New Jersey Troops in the Gettysburg Campaign.* Orange, N.J., 1888.

TRESCOT, WILLIAM HENRY. *Memorial of the Life of J. Johnston Pettigrew, Brigadier General of the Confederacy.* Charleston, 1870.

TRIMBLE, MAJOR GEN. ISAAC R. "The Campaign and Battle of Gettysburg" (from an original Ms. in possession of his grandson), *Confederate Veteran,* XXV, 209ff.

————. "North Carolinians at Gettysburg, IV, *Our Living and Dead,* 53ff.

TUCKER, GLENN. *Poltroons and Patriots.* 2 vols. Indianapolis, 1954.

TURNER, GEORGE EDGAR. *Victory Rode the Rails.* Indianapolis, 1953.

VEIL, CHARLES H. Letter to General Reynolds' orderly. Mimeograph copy in material of Jacob M. Sheads at Gettysburg.

WALKER, C. IRVINE. *Life of Lieutenant General Richard Heron Anderson of the Confederate States Army.* Charleston, 1917.

WALTON, J. B. "Longstreet's artillery at Gettysburg," *Southern Historical Society Papers,* V, 47.

WARD, DR. B. F. Co. K, 11th Mississippi Regiment Papers. Southern Historical Collection, Chapel Hill, N.C.

WASHINGTON *Post.* Scattered issues, 1893–1934.

WASLER, RICHARD. "That Word 'Tar Heel' Again" in North Carolina *Folklore,* a magazine. Chapel Hill, July 1957.

WATLINGTON, WILLIAM. Typed Ms. "The Third Indiana Cavalry." Madison, Ind., 1915.

WEAVER, A. C. *Third Indiana Cavalry, a Brief Account of the Actions in which They Took Part as Seen by Comrade A. C. Weaver, late Saddler and Brevet Commissary Sergeant of Company A.* Greenwood, Ind., 1919.

WELCH, SPENCER GLASGOW. *A Confederate Surgeon's Letters to His Wife.* New edition with additional illustrations and letters. Marietta, Ga., 1954.

WEST, JOHN C. *A Texan in Search of a Fight.* Waco, 1901.

WHITE, HENRY A. "Gettysburg Battle, Some Literary Facts Connected Therewith," *Southern Historical Society Papers,* XXVII, 52.

————. *Robert E. Lee of the Southern Confederacy.* New York, 1897.

WHITTIER, EDWARD N. *The Left Attack (Ewell's) at Gettysburg.* Military Historical Society of Massachusetts. Boston, 1903.

WILCOX, C. M. "Letter on Gettysburg," *Southern Historical Society Papers,* IV, 111.

WILEY, BELL IRVIN. *The Life of Johnny Reb.* Indianapolis, 1943.

WILMINGTON *Daily Journal.* Wilmington, N.C. Files for 1862–1863.

WISE, BARTON H. *The Life of Henry A. Wise of Virginia 1806-1876* (by his grandson). New York, 1899.

WISE, JENNINGS CROPPER. *The Long Arm of Lee.* Lynchburg, Va., 1915.

YOUNG, LOUIS G. "Pettigrew's Brigade at Gettysburg," *Our Living and Dead,* I.

————. "The Death of Brigadier General J. Johnston Pettigrew of North Carolina," *Our Living and Dead,* I.

Acknowledgments

The author is indebted to many for generous help given during the research and writing of *High Tide at Gettysburg*, especially to gracious staff members at the following libraries where I conducted research: University of North Carolina Library, Chapel Hill; North Carolina Department of Archives and History, Raleigh; University of South Carolina Library, Columbia; South Carolina State Archives, Columbia; Emory University Library, Emory University, Georgia; Alderman Library, University of Virginia, Charlottesville; Virginia State Library, Richmond; Library of Congress, Washington; New York Public Library, New York; Indiana State Library, Indianapolis; Sondley Reference Library, Asheville; Gettysburg National Military Park Library, Gettysburg.

Additional help in response to inquiries was received from the Alabama Department of Archives and History, Montgomery; University of Kentucky Library, Lexington; State of Mississippi, Department of Archives and History, Jackson; Burton Historical Collection, Detroit Public Library, Detroit; National Archives, Washington; Department of the Army, Washington; Pennsylvania State Library, Harrisburg; State Historical Society of Wisconsin, Madison.

Thanks are expressed also to the North Carolina Department of Archives and History for permission to use textually portions of papers on Pettigrew's and Hoke's brigades I read before meetings of the North Carolina Literary and Historical Association at Cullowhee and Raleigh, N.C., and published partially in the April 1958 issue of the *North Carolina Historical Review*, entitled "Some Aspects of North Carolina's Participation in the Gettysburg Campaign."

The *American Heritage* magazine for permission to use textually an article purchased by that magazine entitled "The Sixth Corps Goes to Gettysburg."

Major General John DeF. Barker, U.S. Air Force, retired, a student of military history, for reading the original draft and making valuable suggestions, though he is in no manner accountable for conclusions or factual matter.

Dr. Frederick Tilberg, historian, and Dr. Harry Pfanz, assistant historian, of the Gettysburg National Military Park, for suggestions and material. Dr. Pfanz read and criticized proofs, and made pertinent recommendations out of his store of detailed information about both battle and battlefield, but he is responsible for neither textual matter used nor conclusions reached.

Jacob M. Sheads, history professor at Gettysburg High School, an enthusiastic student of the battle, accredited guide, and authority on Adams County, Pennsylvania, history, who was helpful in conversations and visits about the battlefield.

It is to the Virginia Historical Society, Richmond, that I owe thanks for permission to use material from the Southern Historical Society Papers.

Emory University librarian G. R. Lyle and his staff and Dr. Bell I. Wiley, Emory University professor and historian, who made suggestions of material while I was at Emory University Library, where I engaged in two fairly extended periods of research and covered files of the Southern Historical Society Papers.

For similar help I desire to thank Miss Mary Thornton, North Carolina Collection, and Dr. James W. Patton and his staff, Southern Historical Collection, University of North Carolina Library, Chapel Hill.

My thanks for permission to use excerpts are also due to A. C. McClurg & Co., for *Gettysburg, the Pivotal Battle of the Civil War* by Robert K. Beecham; Continental Book Company, Inc., for *A Confederate Surgeon's Letters to His Wife* by Spencer Glasgow Welch (reprinted with additions, 1954); Appleton-Century-Crofts, Inc., for *A Diary from Dixie* by Mary Boykin Chesnut (1905); Longmans, Green & Co., Inc., for *A Soldier's Recollections* by Randolph H. McKim; The State-Record Company, successor to the State Company, for *A Colonel at Gettysburg and Spotsylvania* by Varina D. Brown; the University of Alabama Press, for *The Civil War Diary of General Josiah Gorgas* edited by Frank E. Vandiver; McCowat-Mercer Press, Inc., for *Recollections of a Confederate Staff Officer* by G. Moxley Sorrel; Maud Morrow Brown, author of *University Greys;* Charles Scribner's Sons, for *Memories of a Confederate* by E. P. Alexander, for *Life and Letters* by G. G. Meade, and for *War Years with Jeb Stuart* by W. W. Blackford; The University of North Carolina Press, for *I Rode with Stonewall* by Henry Kyd Douglas; Houghton Mifflin Company, for *Soldier of the South* by George Pickett; Neale Publishing Company and John L. Gammel, for *Hood's Texas Brigade* by Joseph Benjamin Polley; State Historical Society of Wisconsin for *The Battle of Gettysburg* by Frederick Aretas Haskell; Eppa Hunton IV for *Autobiography* by Eppa Hunton.

Dorothy Thomas Tucker, my wife, accompanied me on numerous trips to Gettysburg. From the long-ago accounts by her grandfather, Henry C. Wheeler, of Dillsboro, Indiana, 7th Indiana Infantry, she was able to locate the stone on which he sat after he was wounded on Culp's Hill. She drew the maps in this volume, executing them as we outlined them together, giving due deference to the John B. Bachelder maps, but examining numerous others, and in instances of more limited engagements using our own sketches and the measurements we made on the field.

I am indebted to many with whom I discussed phases of this battle, who gave impressions or lent books and pamphlets. Writing on a remote North Carolina farm is quite different from writing next door to a well-stocked library and the loan of material has been greatly appreciated, the lenders numerous.

Among those of whom I should make especial mention are Mrs. George Ditchburn, Miss Margaret McMillan and Mrs. Emma Sheffer, all of Gettysburg; Colonel James Ripley Jacobs, retired, author of historical works on the regular army, of Easley, S.C.; Colonel Paul Rockwell, writer and military student, of Asheville, N.C.; Frank L. FitzSimons, historian and banker, Hendersonville, N.C.; the late Clarence W. Griffin, Forest City, N.C., historian; Stanley P. Barnett, retired Cleveland, O., newspaper editor, of Tyron, N.C., for the loan of his set of *Official Records;* Miss Mary L. Davis, Hendersonville, N.C., for pamphlets collected by her father, a Union army veteran; and David Schenck, Greensboro, N.C., for permission to quote from the personal letters of his great-uncle, General Stephen Dodson Ramseur.

Index

Rank indicated is the highest held during the Gettysburg Campaign. All abbreviations are standard, except for the following: c., captured; k., killed; m.w., mortally wounded; w., wounded. A particular military unit—company, regiment, brigade, division or corps—will be found at the appropriate level under either Army of Northern Virginia or Army of the Potomac.

Adams, Charles Francis, 395
Alexander, Col. E. P., 2nd day, 227, 229, 234, 275, 299; 3rd day, 337-339, 346-348, 351, 355-357, 360
Alston, Capt. T. P., 168
Ames, Brig. Gen. Adelbert, 294
Anderson, Brig. Gen. George T., 2nd day, 249, 271-272, 280; w., 273
Anderson, Maj. Gen. Richard H., 2nd day, 283-285, 288, 300, 302; 3rd day, 333, 342; *see also,* 11
Archer, Brig. Gen. James J., 1st day, 103, 112, 171; c., 112-113, 116, 144; *see also,* 95, 101
Armistead, Brig. Gen. Lewis A., 2nd day, 329, 332; background, 329-330; 3rd day, 332, 334, 362, 364-366, 369-370, m.w., 365; *see also,* 331, 373, 393
ARMY OF NORTHERN VIRGINIA
FIRST CORPS (Longstreet), 66; 1st day, 182-183; 2nd day, 223, 225, 229, 235, 245-246; 3rd day, 337-338, 345, 372
  McLAW'S DIVISION, 23, 224; 1st day, 182; 2nd day, 231, 246, 270; 3rd day, 341-342
  Kershaw's Brigade, 224-225; 2nd day, 231, 274
  Semmes's Brigade (Bryan), 2nd day, 271-272, 274
  Barksdale's Brigade (Humphreys), 2nd day, 274-275
    13th Mississippi, 2nd day, 281
    17th Mississippi, 2nd day, 276
    18th Mississippi, 2nd day, 277
    21st Mississippi, 2nd day, 276, 278
  Wofford's Brigade, 2nd day, 279-280

McLAW'S DIVISION—*Cont.*
  Cabell's Artillery Battalion, 2nd day, 227, 270
  PICKETT'S DIVISION, 229, 319; 2nd day, 298, 327, 330, 333-348; 3rd day, 337-338, 343-344, 354-379
  Garnett's Brigade (Peyton), 2nd day, 327-329; 3rd day, 332, 360-362
    18th Virginia, 3rd day, 364
  Armistead's Brigade (Aylett), 2nd day, 329; 3rd day, 364-366, 368
    9th Virginia, 2nd day, 332
  Kemper's Brigade (Mayo), 3rd day, 362, 367
    7th Virginia, 3rd day, 332, 352, 359
  Dearing's Artillery Battalion, 3rd day, 337, 374
  HOOD'S DIVISION (Law), 23; reaches Gettysburg, 225-227, 229; 2nd day, 242, 249-250, 258, 270, 279; 3rd day, 341-342
  Law's Brigade (Sheffield), 2nd day, 229, 235, 248-250, 254, 260-261, 264
    4th Alabama, 2nd day, 249
    15th Alabama, 2nd day, 249-253, 256, 265
    44th Alabama, 2nd day, 249-250
    47th Alabama, 2nd day, 249, 252, 261
    48th Alabama, 2nd day, 249-252
  Anderson's Brigade, 2nd day, 249, 271
  Robertson's Brigade, 42; 2nd day, 252-253, 264-267; 3rd day, 342
    3rd Arkansas, 2nd day, 262-263

449

Suggested reading list:

"Bayonet! Forward": My Civil War Reminiscences by General Joshua Lawrence Chamberlain

The Passing of the Armies: The Last Campaign of the Armies by Joshua Lawrence Chamberlain

Lee: A Biography by Clifford Dowdey

Crisis at the Crossroads: The First Day at Gettysburg by Warren Hassler

The Great Invasion of 1863 or General Lee in Pennsylvania by Jacob Hoke

Gettysburg to the Rapidan by General Andrew A. Humphreys

A Diary of Battle: The Personal Journals of Colonel Charles S. Wainwright 1861-1865 edited by Allan Nevins

The Attack and Defense of Little Round Top, Gettysburg, July 2, 1863 by Oliver W. Norton

Sickles the Incredible: A Biography of General Daniel Edgar Sickles by W. A. Swanberg

Soul of the Lion: A Biography of General Joshua Lawrence Chamberlain by Willard Wallace

Through Blood and Fire at Gettysburg: My Experiences with the 20th Maine Regiment on Little Round Top by Joshua Lawrence Chamberlain

The Killer Angels: A Novel About the Four Days of Gettysburg by Michael Shaara

At Gettysburg or What a Girl Saw and Heard of the Battle by Tillie (Pierce) Alleman

WORLD FANTASY AWARD–WINNING AUTHOR

NNEDI  OKORAFOR

AKATA WARRIOR

":Nnedi Okorafor writes glorious futures and fabulous fantasies.
Her characters take your heart and squeeze it; her worlds open
your mind to new things."

—NEIL GAIMAN

PRAISE FOR AKATA WARRIOR

A *New York Times* Editors' Choice Selection
2018 Locus Award
An NPR Best Book
A *Booklist* Editors' Choice Selection
A *The Root* Best Book
A CCBC Choice Book
A Tor Best YA Science Fiction Fantasy Book
A PopSugar Best Book

★ "The reader gets tangled up in Sunny's journey in the most delicious of ways. The lush world and high-stakes plot are fun, imaginative, timely, and authentic. Sunny as a character is beautiful, strong, and resilient, and her host of friends and allies are well-drawn and compelling, adding to the magic of the story. Okorafor's novel will ensnare readers and keep them turning pages until the very end." —*Booklist*, starred review

★ "Fans of *Akata Witch* will fall again for the wondrously intriguing fantasy world in modern-day Nigeria in this imaginative sequel . . . Don't miss this beautifully written fantasy that seamlessly weaves inventive juju with contemporary Nigerian culture and history." —*School Library Journal*, starred review

"Okorafor invents wild, fantastical creatures and worlds but she has a rarer gift too: She can describe the effect of using magic—the emotional and physiological repercussions of it—so viscerally, it's as if it were a fever we'd contracted ourselves . . . The action sequences are enthralling. In the most memorable one, Sunny must ask a favor from a house-size female spider who is so terrifying, even Tolkien's Shelob would want to wait in the car . . . Okorafor describes Sunny's moments of anguish beautifully,

as well as her feelings of kinship and wonder. This is a novel about a girl who's just trying to find her place in the world, when she's called upon to save it."   —*The New York Times Book Review*

"*Akata Warrior* is Nnedi Okorafor's sequel to her award-winning novel *Akata Witch*, and it is longer and better than its predecessor . . . As always, Okorafor effortlessly blends in critiques and observations of modern culture, reflecting on police brutality; the casual, familial misogyny in even the most modern households; and the cultural misunderstanding that can put Africans and African Americans at odds. This book, although written for young adults, is sophisticated in parsing out these adult issues, and it is a salve for grown-ups who may see themselves reflected in these very real, funny kids."

—*The Washington Post*

"The sheer joy of something like the Akata series is the feeling that I simply have not read this before, and that is so rare . . . It's fantasy, yet it comes from a cultural place that isn't the stuff we've already seen 1,000 times before."   —Neil Gaiman

"A compelling and often terrifying version of one of fantasy literature's most enduring traditions, [a perilous quest] recast in a thoroughly original way."   —*Chicago Tribune*

"If you think Eleven is cool, wait until you meet Sunny . . . A rich and beautiful story brimming with imagination and enchantment, *Akata Warrior* is the kind of coming-of-age story Eleven and the gang could appreciate and readers will love."   —Bustle

"If your niece or nephew was too young for Harry Potter mania (tear), introduce them to Sunny Nwazue, aka the Hermione of a new generation. *Akata Warrior*, which just came out this fall, is the second book in the series. Better pick up the first book, *Akata Witch*, too, just to be safe."   —HelloGiggles

"This new YA novel brilliantly mixes fantasy and today's Nigeria to create a new enticing world." —PopSugar

"Mythology, fantasy, science fiction, history, and magic blend into a compelling tale that will hold readers spellbound." —Chicago Review of Books

"*Akata Warrior* is the sequel to Nnedi Okorafor's *Akata Witch*, which has been hailed as 'the Nigerian Harry Potter.' It's a flattering comparison—but it doesn't give enough credit to Okorafor's wild imagination, with which she's crafted a magical world all her own." —MPR News

"Okorafor has created two thoroughly engaging worlds in her books—that of Nigeria today, and the world of spirits, masquerades and secret languages that her main characters alone are able to navigate. The power of this book lies in the fact that she makes both worlds so vividly real, dangerous and intriguing, meaning that readers will be invested in Sunny's battles in both worlds." —RT Book Reviews

"Sunny's story has shifted from what was largely a tale of initiation and education (with even a few echoes of Harry Potter) into a full-blown epic . . . Okorafor offers a clear-eyed view of the real Nigeria . . . This is a book about kids trying to learn the world even as they need to battle a few cosmic terrors along the way. *Akata Warrior* turns out to indeed be the epic that *Akata Witch* seemed to promise, and it's a pretty spectacular one at that." —*Locus* magazine

"A charming adventure stocked with a house-sized spider, an Afro comb gifted by a goddess, and a giant flying rodent—one who loves hip-hop." —*Kirkus Reviews*

"*Akata Warrior* swiftly synthesizes the lessons and knowledge of the first book into a heart-racing story of resilience and a determination

to save the world. This title is a unique coming-of-age story, coupling the distinct experience of the cultural duality as both African and African-American with lessons of love, loyalty, and the pains of adolescent insecurities. While readers will eagerly turn page after page in this quick-paced and imaginative title, the true joy lies in Okorafor's subtly devised cliffhanger, leaving a distinct opening for what we can only hope will be more magic and adventure in a third installment."

—*Bulletin of the Center for Children's Books*

"It's no wonder that this series is being dubbed 'the Nigerian Harry Potter.' Full of magical realism, endearing camaraderie, and creepily exciting adventures, fans of J.K. Rowling and Rick Riordan will no doubt devour this spicy arrangement. Award-winning author Nnedi Okorafor brilliantly parallels her books with popular Euro-fantasy, but she is no copycat. This fresh and funky series is only comparable because it demonstrates the best possible aspects an author can create within a book: an engaging connection between reader and characters with an investment in the characters' predicament and outcome, all within a captivating environment."   —Compass Book Ratings

"Nnedi Okorafor's talented use of the pen is the gift that keeps on giving."   —OkayAfrica

"Okorafor's imagination never ceases to amaze me, nor does her story-telling ability. The layers of story in this installment in Sunny's adventure were complex and revealed so much about Sunny, her family, and her friends. Sunny's coming-of-age continues and weaves so perfectly with the brilliantly alive storylines of the people, spirits, and creatures around her—including her wasp artist, Della—and was captivating from page one."   —*Wandering Bark Books*

"You don't want to miss a moment of this intoxicating blend of fantasy, horror and Nigeria."   —*Waking Brain Cells*

BOOKS BY
NNEDI OKORAFOR

Zahrah the Windseeker

The Shadow Speaker

Long Juju Man

Akata Witch

Akata Warrior

Who Fears Death

The Book of Phoenix

Lagoon

Kabu Kabu

Binti

Binti: Home

Binti: The Night Masquerade

Chicken in the Kitchen

The Girl with the Magic Hands

NNEDI ✺ OKORAFOR

AKATA WARRIOR

speak

SPEAK
An imprint of Penguin Random House LLC
375 Hudson Street
New York, New York 10014

First published in the United States of America by Viking,
an imprint of Penguin Random House LLC, 2017
Published by Speak, an imprint of Penguin Random House LLC, 2018

THE LIBRARY OF CONGRESS HAS CATALOGED THE VIKING EDITION AS FOLLOWS:
Names: Okorafor, Nnedi, author.
Title: Akata warrior / Nnedi Okorafor.
Description: New York : Viking, 2017. | Sequel to: Akata witch. | Summary:
Now stronger, feistier, and a bit older, Sunny Nwazue, along with her
friends from the Leopard Society, travel through worlds, both visible
and invisible, to the mysterious town of Osisi, where they fight in a
climactic battle to save humanity.
Identifiers: LCCN 2016055398 | ISBN 9780670785612 (hardback)
Subjects: | CYAC: Supernatural—Fiction. | Magic—Fiction. | Secret
societies—Fiction. | Albinos and albinism—Fiction. |
Blacks—Nigeria—Fiction. | Nigeria—Fiction.
Classification: LCC PZ7.O4157 Ah 2017 | DDC [Fic]—dc23
LC record available at https://lccn.loc.gov/2016055398

Speak ISBN 9780142425855

Printed in the United States of America

Design by Jim Hoover
Set in LTC Kennerley

10 9 8 7 6 5 4 3

Dedicated to the stories that constantly
breathe on my neck. I see you.

NSIBIDI FOR "LOVE"

CONTENTS

LET THE READER BEWARE
THAT THERE IS JUJU IN THIS BOOK.

ONYE NA-AGU EDEMEDE A MURU AKO:

Let the Reader Beware

Greetings from the Obi Library Collective of Leopard Knocks' Department of Responsibility. We are a busy organization with more important things to do. However, we've been ordered to write you this brief letter of information. It is necessary that you understand what you are getting into before you begin reading this book. If you already understand, then feel free to skip this warning and jump right into the continuation of Sunny's story at Chapter 1.

Okay, let's begin.

Let the reader beware that there is juju in this book.

"Juju" is what we West Africans like to loosely call magic, manipulatable mysticism, or alluring allures. It is wild, alive, and enigmatic, and it is interested in you. Juju always defies

definition. It certainly includes all uncomprehended tricksy forces wrung from the deepest reservoirs of nature and spirit. There is control, but never absolute control. Do not take juju lightly, unless you are looking for unexpected death.

Juju cartwheels between these pages like dust in a sand-storm. We don't care if you are afraid. We don't care if you think this book will bring you good luck. We don't care if you are an outsider. We just care that you read this warning and are thus warned. This way, you have no one to blame but yourself if you enjoy this story.

Now, this girl Sunny Nwazue lives in southeastern Nigeria (which is considered Igboland) in a village not far from the thriving city of Aba. Sunny is about thirteen and a half now, of the Igbo ethnic group, and "Naijamerican" (which means "Nigerian American"—American-born to Nigerian parents, as if you couldn't consult the Internet for that information). Her two older brothers, Chukwu and Ugonna, were born in Nigeria. Sunny, on the other hand, was born in New York City. She and her family lived there until she was nine, when they moved back to Nigeria. This means she speaks Igbo with an American accent and says "soccer" instead of "football." It also means she has to sometimes deal with classmates calling her "*akata*" when trying to get on her nerves.

"*Akata*" is a word some of us Nigerians use to refer to and, more often, degrade black Americans or foreign-born blacks. Some say the word means "bush animal," others say it

means "cotton picker," others say "wild animal" or "fox"—no one can agree. Whatever the meaning, it's not a kind word. Ask anyone who has ever been called an *akata* by Nigerians for the reasons Nigerians call people *akata* and you won't find one person who enjoys the experience.

Oh, and Sunny also happens to have albinism (an inherited genetic condition that reduces the amount of melanin pigment formed in the skin, hair, and/or eyes), but that is neither here nor there.

Let the reader be aware that a year and a half ago, Sunny Nwazue finally became conscious of her truest self and was officially brought into the local Leopard society. For clarity, let us quote the staple tome *Fast Facts for Free Agents* by Isong Abong Effiong Isong:

> A *Leopard Person goes by many names around the world. The term "Leopard Person" is a West African coinage, derived from the Efik term "ekpe," "leopard." All people of mystical true ability are Leopard People.*

We Leopard folk go by many other names in many other languages. A core characteristic of being a Leopard Person is that one of your greater natural "flaws" or your uniqueness is the key to your power. For Sunny, it was in her albinism. She's slowly learning what this means. Also, to be a Leopard Person is to have a spirit face; this is your truest face, the one

that you will always have. And to expose your spirit face to people is like trotting around in public in the buff. Sunny is slowly getting used to the existence, privacy, and power of her spirit face (whose name is Anyanwu), as well.

Last year, Sunny learned that she was a free agent, one where the spirit of the Leopard had skipped a generation. Free agents don't have Leopard parents who have taught them who they are from birth. A free agent knows nothing of Leopard society—be it other Leopard People, knowledge of juju and the mystical world, or exposure to mystical places like Leopard Knocks. They have just become aware of their Leopardom and know what it is to have their world become chaos.

Sunny learned about her Leopardom when she was twelve. Her mysterious grandmother on her mother's side was the Leopard Person in Sunny's family, and if that grandmother hadn't been murdered by the student she was mentoring, she'd have brought Sunny in properly.

Be aware that Sunny's world is now occupied by mystical people and also beings only Leopard People can see, such as masquerades, *tungwas*, bush souls, ghost hoppers, and so on. This is especially true in the local Leopard society haven called Leopard Knocks, an isolated piece of land conjured by the ancestors and surrounded by a rushing river inhabited by a sneaky, vindictive water beast. The entrance to it is a bridge as narrow as an old telephone pole that runs over the river.

Understand that in order to appreciate this book, you must

comprehend what a masquerade is and is not. Masquerades are not men dressed in elaborate masks and costumes of raffia, cloth, beads, and such. Here is a quote about them from the book *Fast Facts for Free Agents* by Isong Abong Effiong Isong:

> *Ghosts, witches, demons, shape-shifters, and masquerades are all real. And masquerades are always dangerous. They can kill, steal your soul, take your mind, take your past, rewrite your future, bring the end of the world, even. As a free agent you will have nothing to do with the real thing, otherwise you face certain death. If you are smart, you will leave true masquerades up to those who know what to do with juju.*

> *Masquerades come in many sizes; they can be the size of a house or a bumblebee. They can even be invisible. They can be a dusty sheet draped over a heap of moths, look like a mound of dried grass, take the form of a spinning shadow, have many wooden heads. You really can never know until you know.*

Please note, however, that when the author of the book just quoted, Isong Abong Effiong Isong, was a teenager, she harassed a Mmuo Ifuru (flower masquerade) dwelling in her garden one too many times. That masquerade went on to make Isong's life a living hell for three years, and Isong's bias

against them is reflected in her book. Not all masquerades are angry, mean, evil, or dangerous. Many are quite kind and beautiful; some are neither, wanting nothing to do with living beings, and so on.

Know that the more Sunny learns to read that Nsibidi book she bought last year, the more she will see. Nsibidi is a magical writing script from southwestern Nigeria. One must read deep Nsibidi with great care and skill; Nsibidi words carelessly read can lead to death. Be aware that as you read about Sunny, your own world may shift, expand, clarify, and grow more vibrant. No need to check beneath your bed every night, but you might want to make sure all the books in your bedroom are truly books.

Beware because this young lady Sunny has close friends who work juju as well. And when the four of them are together, they can save or destroy the world. Chichi is the girl who lives with her mother in the small hut sitting between the big modern houses, despite the fact that she is royalty from her mother's side and that her absent father is a famous highlife and afrobeat singer. Chichi could be older or younger than Sunny, who knows, who cares? Chichi may be short in stature, but her mouth and strong will rival the most successful market woman. Chichi's photographic memory and intense restlessness are the keys to her personal talent.

Orlu, who's almost fifteen, is the boy next door whom Sunny didn't talk to until destiny blossomed. Orlu is calm with an even temperament, qualities Sunny kind of likes in a

boy. His dyslexia led him to his astounding ability to instinctively undo any juju he encounters. The best way to know if there is magical trouble is to watch Orlu's hands.

Sasha, who's fifteen, is from African America, the South Side of Chicago, to be exact. His parents sent him to Naija (slang for "Nigeria") because of his issues with authority, especially authority in the form of police. He's like Chichi: fast, hyper-intelligent, and he can remember like a computer. He's trouble in the Lamb (non-magical) world, but beautifully gifted in the Leopard world.

Understand that not long after entering the Leopard society, Sunny, Orlu, Chichi, and Sasha had to face a nasty ritual killer named Black Hat Otokoto, who was intent on bringing Ekwensu, the most powerful, ugliest, evilest masquerade, to the mundane world. Since they're all still alive, you can assume that things didn't go completely wrong with their encounter. Lastly, Sugar Cream, the head librarian at the Obi Library (the focal point of Leopard society), has, to Sunny's delight, finally agreed to be Sunny's mentor.

This book claims nothing, save that it strives to tell the story of the further comings and goings of this free agent girl named Sunny Nwazue.

Sincerely,

The Obi Library Collective of Leopard Knocks'
Department of Responsibility

1

TAINTED PEPPERS

It was stupid to come out here at night, especially considering the disturbing dreams Sunny had been having. The dreams Sunny suspected were not dreams at all. However, her mentor, Sugar Cream, had challenged her, and Sunny wanted to prove her wrong.

Sunny and Sugar Cream had gotten into one of their heated discussions; this one was about modern American girls and their general lack of skills in the kitchen. The old, twisted woman had looked condescendingly at Sunny, chuckled, and said, "You're so Americanized, you probably can't even make pepper soup."

"Yes, I can, ma," Sunny insisted, annoyed and insulted. Pepper soup wasn't hard to make at all.

"Oh, sure, but you're a Leopard Person, aren't you? So *your* soup should be made with *tainted* peppers, not those weak things the Lambs like to grind up and use."

Sunny had read a recipe for tainted pepper soup in her *Fast Facts for Free Agents* book but really, truthfully, honestly, she couldn't live up to Sugar Cream's challenge of making it. When making tainted pepper soup, if you made the tiniest mistake (like using table salt instead of sea salt), it resulted in some scary consequence like the soup becoming poisonous or exploding. This had discouraged Sunny from ever attempting to make it.

Nevertheless, she wasn't about to admit her inability to make the soup. Not to Sugar Cream, whom she'd had to prove herself to by defeating one of the most powerful criminals the Leopard community had seen in centuries. Sunny was a mere free agent, a Leopard Person raised among Lambs and therefore ignorant of so much. Still, her chi who showed itself as her spirit face was Anyanwu, someone great in the wilderness. But really, what did it matter if you had been a big badass in the spirit world? Now was now, and she was Sunny Nwazue. She still had to prove to the Head Librarian that she was worthy of having her as a mentor.

So instead, Sunny said she'd leave the Obi Library grounds, despite the fact that it was just after midnight, to go pick three tainted chili peppers from the patch that grew down the dirt road. Sugar Cream had only rolled her eyes and

promised to have all the other ingredients for the soup on her office desk when Sunny returned. Including some freshly cut goat meat.

Sunny left her purse and glasses behind. She was especially glad to leave her glasses. They were made of green feather-light plastic, and she still wasn't used to them. Over the last year, though being a Leopard Person had lessened her sensitivity to light, it hadn't done a thing for her eyesight. She'd always had better eyes than most with albinism, but that didn't mean they were great.

After her eye exam last month, her doctor had finally said what Sunny knew he'd eventually say: "Let's get you some glasses." They were the type that grew shaded in the sunlight, and she hated them. She liked seeing true sunshine, though it hurt her eyes. Nevertheless, lately her eyes' inability to keep out sunlight had begun to make the world look so washed out that she could barely see any detail. She'd even tried wearing a baseball cap for a week, hoping the bill would shade her eyes. It didn't help at all, so glasses it was. But whenever she could, she took them off. And this was the best thing about the night.

"I hope the goat meat is hard for her to get at this hour," Sunny muttered to herself as she stomped out the Obi Library's entrance onto the narrow dirt road.

Not a minute later, she felt a mosquito bite her ankle. "Oh, come on," she muttered. She walked faster. The night

was hot and cloying, a perfect companion to her foul mood. It was rainy season, and the clouds had dropped an hour's worth of rain the day before. The ground had expanded, and the trees and plants were breathing. Insects buzzed excitedly, and she heard small bats chirping as they fed on them. Back the other way, toward the entrance of Leopard Knocks, business was in full swing. It was the hour when both the quieter and noisier transactions were made. Even from where she was, she could hear a few of the noisier ones, including two Igbo men loudly discussing the limitations and the unreasonable cost of luck charms.

Sunny picked up her pace. The sooner she got to the field where the wild tainted peppers grew, the sooner she could get back to the Obi Library and show Sugar Cream that she indeed had no idea how to make tainted pepper soup, one of the most common dishes of Nigeria's Leopard People.

Sunny sighed. She'd come to this field several times with Chichi to pick tainted peppers. They grew wild here and were not as concentrated as the ones sold in the Leopard Knocks produce huts and shops, but Sunny liked having functioning taste buds, thank you very much. It was Chichi who always made the soup, and Chichi liked it mild, too. Plus, the tainted peppers here didn't cost a thing, and you could get them at any time, day or night.

It was the time of the year when the peppers grew fat, or so Orlu and Chichi said. Sunny had only learned of Leopard

Knocks' existence within the last year and a half. This was far from enough time to know the habits of the wild tainted peppers that grew near the fields of flowers used to make juju powder. Chichi and Orlu had been coming to Leopard Knocks all their lives. So Sunny was inclined to believe them. The peppers loved heat and sun, and despite the recent rains, there had been plenty of both.

When she reached the patch, she gathered two nice red ones and put them in her heat-resistant basket. The small patch of tainted peppers glowed like a little galaxy. The yellow-green flash of fireflies was like the occasional alien ship. Beyond the glowing peppers was a field of purple flowers with white centers, which would be picked, dried, and crushed to make many types of the common juju powders. Sunny admired the sight of the field in the late night.

She had been paying attention; she even noticed a *tungwa* lazily floating yards away just above some of the flowers. Round and large as a basketball, its thin brown skin grazed the tip of a flower. "Ridiculous thing," she muttered as it exploded with a soft pop, quietly showering tufts of black hair, bits of raw meat, white teeth, and bones on the pepper plants. She knelt down to look for the third pepper she wanted to pick. Two minutes later, she looked up again. All she could do was blink and stare.

"What . . . the . . . hell?" she whispered.

She clutched her basket of tainted peppers. She had a

sinking feeling that she needed all her senses right now. She was light-headed from the intensity of her confusion . . . and her fear.

"Am I dreaming?"

Where the field of purple flowers had been was a lake. Its waters were calm, reflecting the bright half moon like a mirror. Did the peppers exude some sort of fume that caused hallucinations? She wouldn't be surprised. When they were overly ripe, they softly smoked and sometimes even sizzled. But she was not only *seeing* a lake, she smelled it, too— jungly, with the tang of brine, wet. She could even hear frogs singing.

Sunny considered turning tail and running back to the Obi Library. *Best to pretend you don't see anything,* a little voice in her head warned. *Go back!* In Leopard Knocks, some-times the smartest thing to do when you were a kid who stumbled across some unexplainable weirdness was to turn a blind eye and walk away.

Plus, she had her parents to consider. She was out late on a Saturday evening and she was in Leopard Knocks, a place non-Leopard folk including her parents weren't allowed to know about, let alone set foot on. Her parents couldn't know about anything Leopard related. All they knew was that Sunny was not home, and it was due to something simi-lar to what Sunny's mother's mother used to do while she was alive.

Sunny's mother was probably worried sick but wouldn't ask a thing when Sunny returned home. And her father would angrily open the door and then wordlessly go back to his room where he, too, would finally be able to sleep. Regardless of the tension between her and her parents, Sunny quietly promised them in her mind that she would remain safe and sound.

But Sunny's dreams had been crazy lately. If she started having them while awake and on her feet, this would be a new type of problem. She had to make sure this wasn't that. She brought out her house key and clicked on the tiny flashlight she kept on the ring. Then she crept to the lip of the lake for a better look, pushing aside damp, thick green plants that were not tainted peppers or purple flowers. The ground stayed dry until she reached the edge of the water where it was spongy and waterlogged.

She picked up and threw a small stone. *Plunk.* The water looked deep. At least seven feet. She flashed her tiny weak beam across it just in time to see the tentacle shoot out and try to slap around her leg. It missed, grabbing and pulling up some of the tall plants instead. Sunny shrieked, stumbling away from the water. More of the squishy, large tentacles shot out.

She whirled around and took off, managing seven strides before tripping over a vine and then falling onto some flowers, yards from the lake. She looked back, relieved to be a safe

distance from whatever was in the water. She shuddered and scrambled to her feet, horrified. She couldn't believe it. But not believing didn't make it any less true. The lake was now less than two feet from her, its waters creeping closer by the second. It moved fast like a rolling wave in the ocean, the land, flowers and all, quietly tumbling into it.

The tentacles slipped around her right ankle before she could move away. They yanked her off her feet, as two then three more tentacles slapped around her left ankle, torso, and thigh. Grass ground into her jeans and T-shirt and then bare skin on her back as it dragged her toward the water. Sunny had never been a great swimmer. When she was a young child, swimming was always something done in the sun, so she avoided it. It was nighttime, but she definitely wanted to avoid swimming now.

She thrashed and twisted, fighting terror; panic would get her nowhere. This was one of the first things Sugar Cream had taught her on the first day of her mentorship. Sugar Cream. She'd be wondering where Sunny was. She was almost to the water now.

Suddenly, one of the tentacles let go. Then another. And another. She was . . . free. She scrambled back from the water, feeling the mud and soggy leaves and flowers mash beneath her. She stared at the water, dizzy with adrenaline-fueled fright. For a moment, she bizarrely saw through two sets of eyes, those of her spirit face and her mortal one. Through

them, she simultaneously saw water and somewhere else. The double vision made her stomach lurch. She held her belly, blinking several times. "But I'm okay, I'm okay," she whispered.

When she looked again, in the moonlight, bobbing at the surface of the lake was a black-skinned woman with what looked like bushy long, long dreadlocks. She laughed a guttural laugh and dove back into the deep. *She has a fin*, Sunny thought. She giggled. "Lake monsters are real and Mami Wata is real." Sunny leaned back on her elbows for a moment, shut her eyes, and took a deep breath. Orlu would know about the lake beast; he'd probably know every detail about it from its scientific name to its mating patterns. She giggled some more. Then she froze because there was loud splashing coming from behind her, and the land beneath her was growing wetter and wetter. Sunny dared a look back.

Roiling in the water was what looked like a ball of tentacles filling the lake. The beginnings of a bulbous wet head emerged. Octopus! A massive octopus. It tilted its head back, exposing a car-sized powerful beak. The monster loudly chomped down and opened it several times and then made a strong hacking sound that was more terrifying than if it had roared.

The woman bobbed between her and the monster, her back to Sunny. The beast paused, but Sunny could see it still eyeing her. Sunny jumped up, turned, and ran. She

heard the flap of wings and looked up just in time to see a huge dark winged figure zip by overhead. "What?" she breathed. "Is that . . ." But she had to save her breath for running. She reached the dirt road and, without a look back or up, kept running.

The pepper soup smelled like the nectar of life. Strong. It was made with tainted peppers and goat meat. There was fish in it, too. Mackerel? The room was warm. She was alive. The pattering of rain came from outside through the window. The sound drew her to wakefulness. She opened her eyes to hundreds of ceremonial masks hanging on the wall—some smiling, some snarling, some staring. Big eyes, bulging eyes, narrow eyes. Gods and spirits of many colors, shapes, and attitudes. Sugar Cream had told her to shut up and sit down for ten minutes. When Sugar Cream left the office to "go get some things," Sunny must have dozed off.

Now the old woman knelt beside her, carrying a bowl of what Sunny assumed was pepper soup. She was hunched forward, her twisted spine making it difficult for her to kneel. "Since you had such a hard time getting the peppers, I went and bought them myself," she said. She slowly got up, looking pleased. "I met Miknikstic on the way to the all-night market."

"He . . . he was here?" *So that* was *him I saw fly by,* she thought.

"Sit up," Sugar Cream said.

She handed Sunny the bowl of soup. Sunny began to eat, and the soup warmed her body nicely. Sunny had been lying on a mat. She glanced around the floor for the tiny red spiders Sugar Cream always had lurking about in her office. She spotted one a few feet away and shivered. But she didn't get up. Sugar Cream said the spiders were poisonous, but if she didn't bother them, they would not bother her. They also didn't take well to rude treatment, so she wasn't allowed to move away from them immediately.

"There was a lake," Sunny said. "Where the tainted peppers and those purple flowers grow. I know it sounds crazy but . . ." She touched her hair and frowned. She was sporting a medium-length Afro these days, and something was in it. Her irrational mind told her it was a giant red spider, and her entire body seized up.

"You're fine," Sugar Cream said with a wave of a hand. "You met the lake beast, cousin of the river beast. I don't know why it tried to eat you, though."

Sunny felt dizzy as her attention split between trying to figure out what was on her head and processing the fact that the river beast had relatives. "The river beast has family?" Sunny asked.

"Doesn't everything?"

Sunny rubbed her face. The river beast dwelled beneath the narrow bridge that led to Leopard Knocks. The first time

she'd crossed the bridge it had tried to trick her to her death. If Sasha hadn't grabbed her by her necklace, it would have succeeded. To think that that thing had family did not set her mind at ease.

"And then it was Ogbuide who saved you from it," Sugar Cream continued.

Sunny blinked, looking up. "You mean Mami Wata? The water spirit?" Sunny asked, her temples starting to throb. She reached up to touch her head, but then brought her hands down. "My mom always talks about her because she was terrified of being kidnapped by her as a child."

"Nonsense stories," Sugar Cream said. "Ogbuide doesn't kidnap anyone. When Lambs don't understand something or they forget the real story of things, they replace it with fear. Anyway, you're still fresh. Most Leopard People know to walk away when they see a lake that should not be where it is."

"Is there something on my head?" Sunny whispered, working hard not to drop her bowl. She wanted to ask if it was a spider, but she didn't want to irritate her mentor any more than she already had by nearly dying.

"It's a comb," Sugar Cream said.

Relieved, Sunny reached up and pulled it out. "Oooh," she quietly crooned. "Pretty." It looked like the inside of an oyster shell, shining iridescent blue and pink, but it was heavy and solid like metal. She looked at Sugar Cream for an explanation.

"She saved you," she said. "Then she gave you a gift."

Sunny had been attacked by an octopus monster that roamed around using a giant lake like a spider uses its web. Then she'd been saved by Ogbuide, the renowned deity of the water. *Then* she'd seen Miknikstic, a Zuma Wrestling Champion killed in a match and turned guardian angel, fly by. Sunny was speechless.

"Keep it well," Sugar Cream said. "And if I were you, I'd not cut my hair anytime soon, either. Ogbuide probably expects you to have hair that can hold that comb. Also, buy something nice and shiny and go to a real lake or pond or the beach and throw it in. She'll catch it."

Sunny finished her pepper soup. Then she endured another thirty minutes of Sugar Cream lecturing her about being a more cautious rational Leopard girl. As Sugar Cream walked Sunny out of the building into the rain, she handed Sunny a black umbrella very much like the one Sunny used to use a little more than a year ago. "Are you all right with crossing the bridge alone?"

Sunny bit her lip, paused, and then nodded. "I'll glide across." To glide was to drop her spirit into the wilderness (Leopard slang for the "spirit world") and shift her physical body into invisibility. She would make an agreement with the air and then zip through it as a swift-moving breeze.

She had first glided by instinct when crossing the Leopard Knocks Bridge for the third time, hoping to avoid the river

beast. With Sugar Cream's subsequent instruction, Sunny had now perfected the skill so expertly that she didn't emit even the usual puff of warm air when she passed people by. With the help of juju powder, all Leopard People could glide, but Sunny's natural ability allowed her to glide powder-free. To do it this way was to dangerously step partially into the wilderness. However, Sunny did it so often and enjoyed it so much that she didn't fret over it.

"You have money for the funky train?"

"I do," Sunny said. "I'll be fine."

"I expect you to prepare a nice batch of tainted pepper soup for me by next week."

Sunny fought hard not to groan. She'd buy the tainted peppers this time. There was no way she was going back to the field down the road. Not for a while. Sunny held the umbrella over her head and stepped into the warm, rainy early morning. On the way home, she saw plenty of puddles and one rushing river, but thankfully no more lakes.

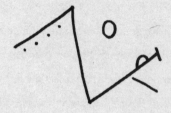

NSIBIDI FOR "NSIBIDI"

*This book will never be a bestseller. The language
in which it is written is much like that of the
highest level of academia. It is selfishly exclusive
by definition. It is self-indulgent. This is the
nature of anything written in the mystic juju-
rooted script known as Nsibidi.*

*You can hear me. You are special. You are in
that exclusive group. You can do something most
Leopard People cannot. So shut it down, turn it
off, power down, log off. You feel the breeze; it
is warm and fresh. It smells like palm and iroko
leaves, damp red soil; they have not started drill-
ing for oil here. There are few roads, so leaded
fuel has not poisoned the air. There is a dove in
the palm tree on your right, and it looks down at
you with its soft, cautious black eyes. A mosquito
tries to bite you and you slap your arm. Now
you scratch your arm because you were too slow.*

Walk with me . . .

—*from* Nsibidi: The Magical Language
of the Spirits

2

YAAAAWN

"In social studies we learn about history, geography, and economics. We put it all together so that we can study how we live with one another," Mrs. Oluwatosin said as she sat in her chair at the front of the class. "But in many ways, social studies class is all about *you*. It should help you look at yourself and ask, 'Who am I? And who do I want to be when I am an adult?' So today, I want to ask you all: Who do you want to be? What do you want to do when you grow up?"

She paused, waiting. No one in the class raised a hand. Sunny yawned, pushing up her glasses for the millionth time. She was too busy navigating an intense magical world to figure out what she wanted to be when she grew up. She'd only

managed two hours of sleep after she'd returned home. And those two hours were plagued by thoughts of the giant lake-dwelling octopus that had tried to grab her. *What the hell was its problem?* she wondered for the millionth time. She'd been too sluggish to bother with breakfast, and though she'd finished all her homework, she could barely remember what she'd done. Beside her, Precious Agu raised a hand. Mrs. Oluwatosin smiled with relief and nodded for her to speak.

"I want to be president," Precious said with a grand smile.

There was a pause, and then the entire class burst out laughing.

"You can't be president when you are not rich," Periwinkle said from the other side of the room.

"What will your husband think?" a boy beside him asked. They slapped hands.

Precious cut her eyes at them and turned away, hissing. "You people are still living in the Dark Ages," she muttered.

"Because we live on the Dark Continent," Periwinkle retorted, and the class laughed harder.

"Quiet!" Mrs. Oluwatosin snapped. "Precious, that is a fine idea. Nigeria could use its first female president. Hold on to your dream and study hard, and you may be the one to make it come true."

Precious seemed to swell with pride, despite the snickering of the boys. Sunny watched all this through her groggy haze. She liked Mrs. Oluwatosin. She had just joined the faculty at Sunny's exclusive secondary school, and she was

a welcome addition; she was the type of teacher who truly believed in the potential of her students.

Periwinkle raised his hand. When Mrs. Oluwatosin called on him, he said, "I want to be chief of the police force."

"So that people can be dashing you money all over the place?" Jibaku asked.

More laughter.

Periwinkle nodded. "I plan to have many, many wives, so I'll need to make extra money to keep them all happy." He winked at Jibaku, and she sucked her teeth and rolled her eyes.

"You'll be lucky to even have one wife," she retorted. "With your fat head."

Sunny chuckled, resting her chin on her hands. Jibaku's meanness was certainly funnier when it wasn't aimed at her. She shut her eyes for a moment, feeling sleep try to take her. In the darkness behind her eyes she felt that thing again, like something was pulling her to the left and something else was pulling her to the right. It was unsettling, but for a moment she tried to analyze it. Doing so made her stomach lurch. She felt her body sway and was about to open her eyes when she heard snoring.

Oh no! I'm asleep, she thought, quickly opening her eyes, sure people would be staring at her. No one was, thank goodness. Apparently her snoring had been in her head.

"Orlu," Mrs. Oluwatosin said. "What do you want to be when you grow up?"

Sunny perked up. Orlu was at the front of the class so she

couldn't see his face. She'd barely had a chance to say hello to him this morning, but it seemed Orlu had gotten a fine night's sleep. She wondered what his mentor, Taiwo, had him doing last night and how he'd been able to return early enough to sleep well.

"A zoologist, I think," he said. "I love studying animals."

"Very nice," Mrs. Oluwatosin said. "That's an excellent career. And an exciting one, too."

Sunny agreed. Plus, Orlu was already like a walking encyclopedia when it came to creatures and beasts, magical or non-magical.

"Sunny? What about you?"

Sunny opened her mouth and then closed it. She didn't know what she wanted to be. *A professional soccer player?* she thought. *I'm good at that.*

For the past few months, she'd been playing soccer with her male classmates when they gathered in the field beside the school. Proving to them that she was worthy enough to play with them had been easy. All she had to do was take the soccer ball and do her thing; it came as naturally as breathing.

However, it was explaining how she could have albinism and yet play in the pounding Nigerian sun that was trickier; she certainly couldn't tell them that her ability to do this was linked to her being a Leopard Person. "My father had a drug delivered from America that makes me able to be in the sun," she told the boys who asked. She was such an excellent soccer player that they all accepted her answer and let her play.

When she was on the field, she was so so happy.

But being a soccer player wasn't a career. Not really. Not for a girl. And honestly, did she want to make such a spectacle of herself for a living? If she played, she'd play for Nigeria, and she'd stand out too much, having albinism. She frowned, her own thought stinging her. *I'm not really good at anything else*, she thought. "Um . . . I . . . I don't know, ma," she said. "I'm still figuring it out."

Mrs. Oluwatosin chuckled. "That's okay, you have plenty of time. But let yourself think about it. God has plans for you; you want to know what they are, right?"

"Yes, ma," Sunny said quietly. She was glad when Mrs. Oluwatosin moved on with the lesson. Considering the chaos of last year, Sunny wasn't quite sure if she wanted to know what "God had planned" for her. *I would be surprised if God took notice of me at all*, she thought tiredly.

"That lake beast and the river beast clearly have a thing for you," Sasha said that afternoon in Chichi's mother's hut. "What'd you do to them in your past life?" He laughed loudly. Chichi snickered, plopping down onto his lap and leaning back against his chest. She was carrying a large heavy book, and Sasha wheezed beneath her weight. "Jesus, Chichi, you trying to kill me?"

"Oh, you'll live," she said, kissing him on the cheek and nuzzling it with her nose. With effort, she brought the book

up and began to flip through the pages. Sunny rolled her eyes but smiled. It was so nice to be around her friends after all that had happened in the last twenty-four hours.

"The lake beast is of the genus *Enteroctopus*," Orlu said. "They're born and raised in the full lands by large extended families. Most of them venture out into the world moving with their bodies of water. Why was it in Leopard Knocks?"

"What are 'full lands'?" Sunny asked.

"Places that mix evenly with the wilderness," he said. "A few places in Nigeria are known full lands: Osisi, Arochukwu, Ikare-Akoko, and sometimes Chibok gets a little full. Full places are a little bit of here and a little bit of there, layered over and meshed with each other."

"A beast attacked her in Leopard Knocks," Chichi said. "Who cares *why* it was there? Things come and go all the time for whatever reason. I'm more interested in who *saved* you! Hey, can I see the comb?!"

Sunny plucked it from the front of her hair and handed it to Chichi. As soon as it was out of her hair, she was very aware of it not being there. The comb was rather heavy, but it was a nice kind of heavy, comforting. The oysterlike coloring went well with Sunny's thick blonde Afro.

"What's this? Metal or shell?" Chichi asked.

Sunny shrugged as she got up. "I have to go home."

Chichi handed the comb back to her, and Sunny tucked it into her hair. She slapped hands with Sasha, and Chichi

gave her a hug. "Are you all right?" Chichi asked.

"Yeah," she said. "It didn't get me; I'm alive."

"Don't know why that thing goes after you when it can more easily catch smaller weaker prey," Chichi said, pinching one of Sunny's strong arms.

Sunny smiled but looked away from Chichi. Sunny'd always been somewhat tall, but even she had to admit, she'd become quite strong. It was probably all the soccer she was playing with the boys, but there was something more to it, too. She wasn't bulking up like a body-builder, but there were . . . changes, like being able to squeeze someone's wrist into terrible pain, being able to kick the soccer ball so hard that it hurt if it hit anyone, and being able to lift things she hadn't been able to lift last year.

"You want me to work some juju on it to humiliate all of its ancestors and deform every single one of its offspring?" Sasha asked.

Sunny smiled, pausing to consider. "Nah," she said. "I'll let karma handle it."

"Juju works better and faster than karma," Chichi said.

Sunny walked out and Orlu followed her, gently taking her hand. When Sunny let go of his hand as she stepped onto the empty road, Orlu said, "See you tomorrow."

Sunny smiled at him, looking into his sweet eyes, and said, "Yeah."

You're not yet reading this correctly if this is your first time reading Nsibidi. Keep reading. It will come. But you can hear my voice and that's the first step. I am with you. I am your guide. Nsibidi is the script of the wilderness. It is not made for the use of humankind. However, just because it is not made for us does not mean we cannot use it. Some of us can. Nsibidi is to "play" and it is to truly see. If you lose this book, it will find you again but not without forcing you to suffer a punishment . . . if you deserve it. Don't lose this book . . .

—*from* Nsibidi: The Magical Language
of the Spirits

3
HOME

Sunny's oldest brother, Chukwu, sat in his Jeep in front of the house staring at the screen of his cell phone as he furiously typed a text. Sunny watched him as she quietly crept closer. He was frowning deeply, his nostrils flared. He'd discovered his potential to easily bulk up last year, and his recently swollen biceps and pectorals twitched as he grasped the phone.

"What is wrong with this silly girl?" he muttered as Sunny leaned against the Jeep with her arm on the warm door. She didn't need to worry about dirt. As always, it was spotless. Sunny suspected he paid some of the younger boys in the neighborhood to wash it often. Chukwu had gotten the Jeep three weeks ago, and he would take it with him to the University of Port Harcourt in five days.

He didn't see her standing there. He never saw her. Since they were young, she could do this to him; to her other brother, Ugonna; to her father. She never crept up on her mother. Something in her, even when she was three years old, told her never to do that.

Sunny rolled her eyes. This was her oldest brother. Reeking of cologne. Wearing the finest clothes. His hair shaved close and perfect. Seventeen years, soon to be eighteen, and already adept at juggling four girlfriends he'd leave behind in less than a week. Going on five if he could convince the one he was texting to go out with him this weekend. Sunny read as his fingers flew over the touch screen.

Just try me, he typed. **U kno u interested, cuz u kno I show you a gud time.**

Sunny was glad that she'd never gotten that into texting. Look how it stupid it made you sound! Plus, she didn't need it. She only used her cell phone to call her parents to let them know where she was. When you knew juju, a lot of technology seemed primitive.

"Are you serious?" she finally said, when she couldn't stand watching him make an ass of himself any longer.

He screeched and jolted, dropping his cell phone on his lap. Then he glared at Sunny. "Shit! What is wrong with you?"

Sunny giggled.

"I hate when you do that!"

On his lap, his phone buzzed. He picked it up. "This is private. Go cook dinner or something. I'm hungry. Make yourself useful."

"Don't you have enough girlfriends?"

He flashed a toothy grin, quickly texting the girl back. "It's just so *easy*. I can't help myself."

"Stupid," Sunny muttered, walking toward the house.

"Where are you coming from all sweaty like that?" he asked her, looking up.

She'd been playing soccer with the boys. Chukwu's soccer group was older, so he had no idea she was playing now. If he did, Sunny didn't know how she'd explain. Really, she had more to worry about with Ugonna, who was sixteen. Sometimes her age mates played with the boys from his age group. Thankfully, he wasn't that interested in soccer. Thus, so far, so good.

"None of your business," she said over her shoulder, quickly going inside.

Her parents wouldn't be home for a few hours. Her mother was on call and had sent a text to all of them describing what they could eat. And their father always came home late on Thursdays. Ugonna was at the kitchen table nibbling on an orange. He had a pencil in his hand. He was drawing again. Sunny considered leaving the kitchen, but she was hungry.

Ugonna had always liked to draw; he'd sketch things like smiling faces and vague images of girls, trees, cars he liked,

and gym shoes. But in the last year, after discovering an instruction website on the Internet, he'd gotten more serious
with his skill. Instead of going out with his friends, he began
to spend more and more time at the kitchen table, drawing.
He was best at drawing faces and abstract images of forests.

Some of these abstract drawings reminded Sunny of
the Nsibidi she was learning to read. Not that they looked
the same, but they carried a similar energy. His drawings
didn't literally move as the Nsibidi in her book did, but they
seemed to move. The trees seemed to blow, the insects on the
branches *seemed* to walk.

Then last month, he'd drawn what she'd been dreaming
about since a week after facing Ekwensu. The city of smoke.
It was a good drawing. Their mother had thought it was so
beautiful she'd had it framed. Sunny had to look at that image
on the family room wall every day now whenever she wanted
to watch TV or exit the house. The dreams themselves were
horrible enough.

They were worse than the vision of the world ending.
The dreams were what happened *as* it ended. A city of smoke
that rippled as it burned, that looked almost like another
world entirely. It was like seeing through the eyes of a god.
The first time she'd had the dream, she'd woken up, run to
the bathroom in the dark, and vomited into the toilet. The
second time, a week later, she'd fallen sick hours afterward
and been unable to leave the house for two days while fight-

ing a horrible case of malaria. The third time, she woke crying uncontrollably. She'd told no one about the dreams. Not even Sugar Cream. Yet her non-Leopard brother was drawing it, and her mother had framed and hung it on the family room wall.

"Hey," she grunted, walking quickly past Ugonna to the refrigerator.

"Good afternoon," he said, not taking his eyes from what he was drawing.

She opened the fridge, her belly growling horribly. She hadn't eaten breakfast, had forgotten her lunch, hadn't had enough money to buy a snack during lunch, didn't feel like asking Orlu yet again; essentially, she hadn't eaten since the pepper soup Sugar Cream had given her last night after the attack. She brought out three ripe plantain.

"Is Chukwu still in his Jeep?" Ugonna asked.

"Yeah."

"His head is so big," Ugonna said. "I don't know why Mummy and Daddy had to buy him that! He's staying in the government hostel, how's that even going to look?"

"Dad tried," Sunny said with a shrug. Chukwu was going to make a big splash at the university. Not only had he been one of the top students in his graduating class, he was the best soccer player in the area. Still, his father wanted his oldest son to really experience university life. Thus, instead of having Chukwu stay in one of the cushier private

student hostels off campus, he'd insisted Chukwu stay at the more stripped-down government-owned hostels on campus. He'd have to stay in one large room with five other students. Chukwu had angrily protested, but he finally shut up when he learned that their mother had bought him the used Jeep.

Ugonna chuckled. Sunny did, too. She slit the black-yellow plantain skins and peeled them off. Then she sliced the plantain up into thin, round, slightly diagonal pieces and put them into a large bowl. She fired up a deep pan of hot oil and then dumped the plantain into it to fry. As she did all this, she resisted the urge to look at what her brother was drawing. Yet again she wondered how it was that he'd drawn that horrible burning city. He wasn't a Leopard Person. Was someone working some sort of juju on her? On her family?

She frowned, flipping the frying plantain over. She dished out the first batch and placed the hot slices on a plate covered with three paper towels. She picked one up and bit into it. Her mouth filled with saliva as it savored the tangy, sweet fried fruit that was so much like banana but not like banana at all. Perfect.

She focused on making the plantain and not on the talk she planned to have with Sugar Cream tomorrow night. Not on the fact that she had been keeping such deep secrets from her friends. From Orlu, in particular, it was the most difficult. Soon, she'd tell them. All three of them would hit the roof.

She put the plate of plantain in the middle of the table.

"You want some?" she asked, placing several on her plate.

Ugonna looked at the plantain, then got up to get a plate. "Thanks."

They both ate plantain and watched a Nollywood movie on the kitchen TV. Minutes later Chukwu joined them. As they laughed at the stupid woman who was so dumb that she'd left her baby in the taxi cab, Sunny glanced at Ugonna's drawing. It was of a tricked-out Viper with a sultry-looking woman draped on the hood.

She smiled and enjoyed her plantain and her brother.

That night, Sunny lay on her bed, gazing at the photo of her grandmother. Her grandmother, the only one of all her relatives who was a Leopard Person, the only person she could have talked to about all things Leopard. Where Sunny was albino, having pale skin, hair, and eyes, her grandmother was indigo black with closely cropped black hair. Sunny held the photo closer and looked at the juju knife her grandmother held to her chest.

It was particularly large, almost like a pointed machete, and looked made of a heavy raw iron. And both edges were notched with many sharp teeth and etched with deep designs. *Did they bury you with it?* Sunny wondered. *Did you even have a body to burn after Black Hat murdered you?* She shut her eyes. It was late and she was tired. This was not a

place to go in her mind right before bed. She put the photo aside and unfolded the only other item that had been in the box with the letter from her grandma, the thin piece of paper with the Nsibidi symbols on it.

Sunny tried to read it yet again. When she felt the nausea setting in, she folded it back up. She shut her eyes, willing the nausea to pass. The first time, she hadn't heeded her body's warning; she kept trying and trying to read it. She wound up vomiting like crazy. It was so much that her father was overcome with wild worry no matter how much her mother, who was a medical doctor, assured him that Sunny was okay.

"What's wrong with taking her to the hospital, anyway?" he kept angrily asking, as he stood at her bedside with her mother. "*Kai!* This is a regular illness, isn't it? Then the cure is regular!" Eventually the nausea did pass, leaving Sunny with the nagging question of what the Nsibidi on the piece of paper said. She'd have to get better at reading Nsibidi in order to find out. She glanced at the piece of paper just for a brief second. Then she put all her grandmother's things away and grabbed her book *Nsibidi: The Magical Language of the Spirits* instead.

She wasn't ready to read her grandmother's complex Nsibidi page, but she *had* gotten a lot better at reading Nsibidi. Each day, she got better and better at "reading" Sugar Cream's book—particularly when she was rested, had eaten a good meal, and managed to go most of the day without talk-

ing to anyone. One did not simply read Nsibidi as one read a book or even music. Nsibidi was a magical writing script. It had to call you, and it only called those who could and wanted to change their shape.

Shape-shifters who saw Nsibidi would see the symbols moving and even hear it whispering. Sunny had experienced this the moment she picked up the book of Nsibidi at random in Bola's Store for Books last year. And though the book had cost some heavy *chittim* (Leopard currency that could only be earned by acquiring knowledge), it was worth it. It was her first lesson in mastering a Leopard art. Learning to read Nsibidi was initially intuitive, forcing the reader to reach deep within and understand that the symbols were alive and that they were shape-shifters, too. And when Nsibidi symbols changed shape for you, the whole world shifted.

The first time it happened had been two weeks ago, after Sunny thought she'd already learned to read Nsibidi. She'd managed to get through the first page, which was basically an introduction to the book, or at least, this was what she thought. Sugar Cream wrote that her book would never be a bestseller. So few could "hear" Nsibidi and even fewer wanted to listen. She said that Nsibidi was more a language of the spirits than one for the use of humankind. Then she began explaining how the book was split into sections. The book was quite thin, so the sections were very short. This was as far as Sunny had gotten.

For some reason, no matter how much she turned the wiggling symbols over in her head, unfocused her eyes, and strained to "hear" what the whispers were saying, she could get no further in her reading. She'd hit a wall.

Sweating and frustrated, she'd set the book down on her bed, the thick pages open. She leaned against the pillows on her bed.

"Come on," she tiredly whispered.

Understanding that first page had been deeply satisfying. With all that she'd experienced in the past year, here was something she felt made sense. Every part of her being loved and wanted to learn Nsibidi. And it seemed as if the understanding came to her *because* of this. It was exhausting, mentally taxing and frustrating, but she loved it. So it came. Then she hit this wall.

Now, as she looked at the thin book with thick cream-colored pages and maroon, almost jellylike symbols that wiggled and sometimes rotated, shrank, and stretched, she relaxed. She sighed.

"It will come," she whispered. She relaxed more. Her heartbeat slowed. She had other homework to do. Nsibidi was her friend, not a lion to tame or anything else to beat into submission. She was about to go get something to eat. Her stomach felt empty, though she had just eaten dinner.

"Sunny," she heard someone softly whisper.

When she looked at her book, she felt cool, soft hands press her cheeks to steady her head.

"Hold," the voice said.

Everything dropped. Away.

Nothing but the whispering symbols.

Oral and written words combined.

There was warmth on her face, like sunshine.

Sunshine now, not before her initiation into the *Ekpe* society. The Leopard society. The sunshine didn't burn.

She walked along a path, wild jungle to her left, wild jungle to her right. Drums beat but she could hear Sugar Cream's voice clearly; Sunny saw the symbols dancing before her when Sugar Cream called them, burrowing into the dirt when spoken, swirling into a tornadolike cycle when uttered.

"This book's titled *Nsibidi: The Magical Language of the Spirits*. But this book is tricky. Like me, it shape-shifts. It goes by another name, an inside name for those who can read it. *Trickster: My Life and My Lessons*, by Sugar Cream, is its inside name, its true name. This book is a part of me. It is wonderful that you are here and you are hearing. It is good."

Sugar Cream went on to tell/show Sunny that this jungle was where she grew up. She was introducing an old fluffy baboon from a clan that she called the Idiok when Sunny suddenly came back to herself. She had to blink several times to get her eyes and mind to focus. There was knocking at the door, and she glanced at her cell phone's time. Two hours had passed! She'd turned *one* page.

"Sunny?" her mother called again. Sunny tensed up. No one in her family knew a thing about a thing. They could

not, by both juju and Leopard law. Among many other issues, this sometimes made reading the Nsibidi book difficult. Her mother knocked on the door. "What are you doing in there?"

Chink, chink, chink, chink! Ten heavy copper *chittim* fell onto the floor in front of Sunny's bed. The Leopard currency dropped whenever knowledge was earned, and these were the most prized kind. Shaped like curved rods, *chittim* came in many sizes and could be made of copper, bronze, silver, or gold—copper being the most valuable and gold being the least. No one knew who dropped them or why they never injured anyone when they fell.

Sunny jumped up and quickly grabbed the *chittim* and piled them in her purse. Yes, she'd learned something big, and she knew she could look into the book and "hear" Nsibidi in the same way again. "Wow," she whispered, putting her heavy purse beside her, the *chittim* inside clinking loudly. The pain in her belly hit her then, and she doubled over. Hunger, but a terrible aggressive hunger. She cleared her throat and tried to sound normal. "I'm just studying, Mom."

Her mother tried to open the door. "Why is the door locked, then?"

Sunny dragged herself to the edge of her bed. She placed her feet on the cool floor. "Sorry, Mom," she said, forcing herself to stand.

When she opened the door, her mother stared at her for

a long time. She searched Sunny's face, sniffing the room, listening for anything, anything at all. Sunny knew the routine. The unspoken between her and her mother increased every single day. But the love remained, too. So it was okay. "I'm . . . I'm okay, Mom," Sunny stammered. She smiled the most fake smile ever.

"Are you sure?" her mother whispered. Sunny wrapped her arms around her. At thirteen and a half, Sunny was as tall as her mother's five foot eight.

"Yes, Mom," she said. "Just studying . . . really hard."

"It's ten o'clock. You should get ready for bed." Her mother glanced over Sunny's shoulder at the book on her bed that was not a textbook.

"I will," Sunny said. "After I eat something."

"But you just ate dinner."

"I know. But I'm hungry again, I guess. A little."

"Okay, o," her mother sighed. "There's plenty of leftover plantain."

Sunny grinned. "Perfect." She could never eat enough fried, juicy, sweet, scrumptious yummies. When she finished, she brushed her teeth again and returned to her room. She shut off her light, fell back into bed, and was asleep within thirty seconds. Five minutes later, she was dreaming about the end of the world . . .

❤ ❤ ❤ ❤

The city was burning so furiously it looked like a city of smoke. She witnessed it from above the lush green forest. She was flying. But she was not a bird. What was she? Who am I? *she wondered.*

It was always like this here. She could smell it as she rushed toward the burning city. She did not smell smoke, however. The wind must have been tumbling away from her. She smelled flowers, instead. Sweetness, as if the trees below were seeding the air with pollen.

She tried to stop, but the force that she was riding wanted to go toward the city. She was a mind in a body that had other plans. There were spiraling edifices. Smaller structures on the ground, bulbous like giant smoky eggs. All of it undulated with smoke. This was the end. Was this Lagos? New York? Tokyo? Cairo?

Closer.

She felt like screaming. She didn't want to look anymore. But she had no body to look away with. It was like reading Nsibidi. Nsibidi? *she thought, panicky.* What is that?

She was too close to the burning city. Soon she'd be upon it. What were those flying out of it? Bits of incinerating building? They looked like bats. Demons.

She could feel her heart beating. Slamming in her chest; it wanted out. My heart? I have a heart? *She was shaking. She was falling now. The forest trees crashing toward her . . .*

Her body jerked as she hit the floor. Her eyes shot open as she thrashed in the darkness. The floor was hard. Familiar scents. She calmed. Her scent. She touched her mashed up Afro; she'd forgotten to take out the comb Mami Wata had given to her. Then she climbed back into bed and lay there until she slept a restless, yet thankfully dreamless sleep.

4

READING NSIBIDI
IS RISKY

Saturday evening, Sunny went to see Sugar Cream in the Obi Library as usual. She was used to crossing the bridge to Leopard Knocks alone. The river beast made her nervous, but each and every time, she stared it down as she crossed. Even this time. It lurked just beneath the surface, a shadow the size of a house with eyes that glowed a dull yellow. Watching. Waiting. For what, Sunny didn't know. But when she brought forth her spirit face, and Anyanwu filled her up with confidence, poise, and courage, she didn't care. She dared the river beast to do its worst; then she'd have a reason to kick its backside once and for all.

When she arrived at Sugar Cream's office at around eight

P.M., her mentor was not there yet. One of the ancestral masks on the wall, the red one with inflated cheeks and wild eyes, opened its mouth and silently laughed at her. Another stuck its tongue out. The masks were so annoying. They were like having a chorus of children behind Sugar Cream's back who jeered and made fun of her as she was scolded or when she made mistakes.

"Oh, stop it," she said to the long-faced ebony mask that narrowed its eyes and sucked its teeth at her as she went to Sugar Cream's desk. There was a note on it. *Sit. We will practice gliding today. So clear your head. I will return shortly.*

Sunny groaned. "Sit" meant "Sit on the floor in front of her desk." She sighed, scanning the dark wooden floor. She spotted four of the large red spiders scrambling across the floor. There were always a few. Where they were going, Sunny didn't know, but they were *always* going somewhere. They were like scary ugly ants that were spiders.

She slowly sat on the floor. She shut her eyes and took a deep slow breath. She blocked out the spiders and took another deep slow breath. Unfortunately, as her mind cleared, it made room for the very thing she wanted to stop thinking about. Her dream. The smoking city. She frowned, trying harder to clear her mind. Sweat beaded on her forehead as the dream lost its sharp edges and began to grow fuzzy in her mind.

Her body began to relax. Her heartbeat slowed. Well-

being. Nothing else. It would last about thirty seconds. So far, this was how long she could hold it. But this half minute was bliss. Ten seconds. A smile spread across her lips. Fifteen seconds. She began to hear that soft, slow hum again. It came from beneath her feet, beneath the floor—deep, deep, deep. It was beautiful. Eighteen seconds, she felt something scratchy.

Her eyes shot open, and she looked at her hand. One of the red spiders was crawling onto her pinky and ring finger.

"Eeeeeeeeee!" she screeched, flinging it off. It landed on the floor and ran toward Sugar Cream's desk. Sunny was on her feet, still in mid-screech when her eyes fell on the woman sitting behind the desk.

"Good evening," Sugar Cream said. Today, she wore a creamy yellow dress with a creamy yellow headwrap. The yellow bangles on her wrists clicked as she shifted her position.

"Spider! It was . . ." Sunny was so disoriented that she was out of breath and babbling. Anything but relaxed.

"You must have been deep in meditation," she said in Igbo. "I think it was going to check your pulse to make sure you were still alive." Behind her, the red mask laughed silently. "What would you like to discuss today?" Sugar Cream asked.

Sunny knew that whatever she answered was rarely taken into consideration, but she appreciated the question. She considered telling her about the dream. *But it was just a dream, really*, she thought. *I don't have any evidence.* When it

came to the vision of the end of the world she'd seen while gazing into the flame of a candle two years ago, there were other elders who had also seen a similar vision. It wasn't just her. But then again, maybe others were having the dream, too. Maybe. A dream was a lot flimsier than an actual vision that one had while lucid and awake. She'd seen Black Hat slit his own throat, and then she'd faced Ekwensu very recently. Really, it was normal to have a few nightmares. She decided to go in another direction.

"How about teaching me more about reading Nsibidi," she said, slowly sitting back down. "I think . . . I think I've had a major breakthrough." She told Sugar Cream about her Nsibidi reading experience, and Sugar Cream was pleased.

"Finally," she said, smiling bigger than Sunny had ever seen her smile since starting her mentorship with the Head Librarian. Normally, Sugar Cream was so subdued and stoic. "Reading Nsibidi is not something I can teach you. Good, good, good. We can do more now."

"But why does it take so much from me?" Sunny asked. "I felt like I would die of hunger. I don't know how I was able to hide the pain from my mother."

"Trust me, your mother noticed." Sugar Cream chuckled. "But she's learning to accept what you are, even if she doesn't know exactly *what* you are, and that's good and safe for you both." She arched her back in her plush leather chair and shifted to the side. Sugar Cream's spine was curved in a

dramatic S shape and thus, no chair was really made to suit her type of body. Sunny wondered why she didn't just have a special chair made for her. "Reading Nsibidi is give and take," she continued. "It gives you experience and knowledge, and in return the magic drinks your energy. This is fine if you replenish right afterward. Do what you've been doing. Read a tiny bit, then go eat well, sleep, relax. Don't go arguing with your brothers or watching something annoying on television, because next thing you know, you'll pass out and make a fool of yourself."

Sunny laughed.

"And expect a few nightmares now that you have un-locked the key to truly reading Nsibidi."

"Nightmares?" Sunny asked, her entire body prickling.

"Reading Nsibidi is similar to gliding through the wilder-ness in many ways," she said. "It, too, involves leaving your body. This will scare you, even if what you are reading is not scary. Your mind compensates by giving you nightmares."

"Oh," Sunny said.

Sugar Cream grew serious and held up a bony index fin-ger, locking Sunny with her eyes. "Reading Nsibidi is risky. You're a free agent and for you to do this is not as rare as it is a bad combination. People have died from reading too much, Sunny," she said. "Beware of books written in excellent Nsi-bidi; you have to be truly strong to read them. Otherwise, you could get sucked into the story or the lessons or the in-

formation. When you return to yourself, it is only to wish this current life goodbye. Your body will have withered to bones; you'll have nothing left. It's not a good way to pass to your next life."

The sheet of Nsibidi her grandmother had left must have been that dangerous type of Nsibidi. She didn't know what it said, if it was fiction or nonfiction, but she knew how she felt when she tried to "read" it.

Sugar Cream stood up. "Now, then," she said. "Today, we're going for a walk."

"Where?"

"The tainted pepper patch," she said.

Sunny felt her entire body seize up.

"See the way you just reacted?" Sugar Cream asked. "It's not good to live a life dictated by fear. That is a lesson you especially must learn right here and now. Otherwise, you'll be miserable." She laughed. "Your spirit face is courageous and strong; do you want her to be ashamed of you?"

Sunny followed Sugar Cream out the door. Fine. *But I better not see even a small pond,* she thought.

5

AUNTIE UJU AND
HER JUJU

By Monday, despite what Sugar Cream said and the fact that
there was no lake beast near the tainted pepper patch, Sunny
was back to fretting about her dream. Outside it was raining and the humidity made everything indoors damp. After
school it was still raining, and Sunny had to meet Orlu at the
school's front door. They walked off into the rain. Neither of
them had an umbrella.

Sunny grumbled, grasping her juju knife in her pocket.
She brought it with her everywhere, even to school, though
she'd never use it for anything there. They reached the slick
road, and Orlu started walking the other way, away from their
homes. Sunny sighed. She could use a healthy dose of Orlu's

quiet presence today. Chichi and Sasha might be around, but they might not be. Those two were always either at the market shopping for fresh juju powders or off in their "secret place" creating them. These days, aside from being boyfriend and girlfriend, Sasha and Chichi were like partnered mad scientists, always reeking of crushed flowers, having stained fingers and constant pleased and half-crazy grins on their faces. Sasha's hair had even grown twice its length, as if he were taking some kind of magical vitamins. The braids at the ends of his cornrows reached down his back now.

Sunny had hoped she and Orlu could go to her house and study together at the kitchen table while they listened to the rain. However, she'd forgotten, it was the day when Orlu went to visit his auntie in a nearby village.

"Can I go with?" she suddenly asked.

Orlu looked at her with raised eyebrows, rain dripping down his face. "Why?"

She shrugged. "If it's a problem, then . . ."

"No," he said. "It's fine. It's just . . . will your parents be okay with it?"

"I'll call," she said. "It should be fine."

"All right. But, let me warn you now, I love my auntie, but she's . . . she's very set in her ways."

Two minutes from the school, they managed to catch a *danfo*. The banged-up small bus was packed with sullen soaked people, and all the seats were taken. Sunny and Orlu

squashed in with the people standing in the aisle. Orlu put an arm around Sunny when the jerky motion of the bus nearly threw her into the man sitting beside her.

The ride was only ten minutes. And despite having to stand, Sunny wished it were longer. As they drove, the rain began to come down harder. When they got off, it was like stepping into a waterfall. "Wish we could use an umbrella spell," Orlu muttered. But both of them knew this would only get them a trip to the Obi Library for punishment. All it would take was one Lamb seeing them walk down the street with not a drop touching their skin or clothes or backpacks.

His auntie's house was large and white with a green roof, surrounded by a thick white fence. Orlu knocked on the gate, and the gate man quickly opened it for them.

"Good afternoon," the gate man said. Then he ran back under the shelter of his gate man post. As they walked up to the house, Orlu suddenly stopped. "My auntie is a Lamb," he blurted.

"Okay," Sunny said. "So?"

Orlu shrugged.

"Orlu, I'm a free agent," she said. "You think I'm going to judge you for having Lamb relatives?"

He smiled sheepishly. "True," he said. "Come on, let's get out of this rain."

A young woman opened the door for them. "Good afternoon, Orlu," she said. She paused, looking Sunny over. Then

her smile turned into a smirk. "You have got to be Sunny Nwazue."

"Kema, stop," Orlu said.

"Hi," Sunny said. Kema took her hand and shook it firmly.

"He talks a lot about you," Kema said. She touched the Mami Wata comb Sunny wore in her Afro. "Pretty comb."

"Thanks," Sunny said, nervous. If his auntie wasn't a Leopard, was Kema? What happened when Lambs touched gifts from Mami Wata?

"Where's Auntie?" Orlu asked.

Kema's smile lessened. "She's in the living room, watching a movie. She's not doing all that great today. Might be the rain."

Orlu took Sunny's hand. "Come on."

Sunny could smell Orlu's auntie before she saw her. A mix of cigarette smoke, expensive perfume, palm oil, and illness. She was sitting in front of a large flat-screen television, staring blankly. She wasn't much older than Sunny's mother and she was a healthy plump, with a face painted with bright makeup. Her eyelids were a deep purple, her eyebrows were shaven off and redrawn in the shape of thick black bars, her lips were a blood red, and her skin was flawless with light brown foundation. She clearly bleached it, for her light brown face was a great contrast to her dark brown neck and arms. She wore a white blouse and stylish black pants.

A Nollywood film was on, and a woman wearing a bad wig was shouting at another woman with an equally bad wig. When the second woman's eyes grew wide, and she slapped the other woman, Orlu's auntie didn't even react. The volume was way too high, and Orlu immediately turned it down. She did not react to this, either.

"Good afternoon, Auntie Uju," he softly said, kneeling in front of her and taking her hand.

Sunny's eyes began to water, and she suddenly felt like sneezing. Then she did. She nearly jumped as Auntie Uju suddenly looked at her. Sunny took several steps away from the woman; the look on her face was full of venom.

"Who is *this*?" Auntie Uju snapped.

"Auntie," Orlu said. "This is Sunny. She's my . . ."

"She is albeeno," she said, her face curling with disgust.

"Yes, Auntie," Orlu said. "That's obvious."

"Good afternoon," Sunny softly said, holding out a hand. The woman seemed ready to explode; best to tread lightly. Sunny's nose tickled again, and before she could take the woman's hand, she sneezed. Then she sneezed again and again.

"*Kai!*" his auntie exclaimed, staring at Sunny, who was holding her snotty nose.

"I'm sorry," Sunny said, embarrassed.

"Look at this evil girl!" his auntie shouted. "Look at her! Like ghost. She'll bring illness, poverty, bad luck into the house! Child witch full of witchcraft!"

"Auntie, come on," Orlu pleaded. He glanced at Sunny

apologetically. "Relax. This is my friend. My best friend. She . . ."

"*This* is your best friend?!" his auntie exclaimed, with bulging shocked eyes. She turned to Sunny with such a mean scary look, scrunching her painted face, that Sunny jumped back. "Go and die!" she shouted at Sunny.

Sunny whimpered. "What? I . . ."

"Our father, who art in heaven, ooooo," she suddenly started to wail. She held her hand in the air, jumped up, and stamped her foot as she shouted, "Fire! Fire! Fire! Be gone!"

"Auntie!" Orlu exclaimed, taking her shoulders and trying to get her to sit down.

But this only agitated his auntie more. "Fire! Fire! Fire! BE GONE!"

Sunny jerkily turned and walked out of the room. She moved down the hall, breathing heavily. She would not shed a tear in front of that crazy woman. She wasn't about to give her *that* satisfaction. She'd encountered this kind of thing many times. If Sunny cried, the woman would think her shouting and carrying on had caused Sunny to feel guilt for her "evil witchcraft."

Sunny stopped at the doorway and brought her shaky hands to her face. "But I am a witch," she whispered to herself. Though she was not a witch in the sense of what the woman and so many other delusional Nigerians believed. Leopard People had nothing to do with all of that. That stuff didn't even exist.

Why is it always about my being albino? she thought. *I never do anything to anyone, but yet they think I'm bad.* Her eyes stung as the tears came.

"Are you all right?" Kema asked, coming out of the bathroom.

"Fine," Sunny mumbled.

"Sunny," Orlu said, running up. "I'm sorry about that. Don't feel badly. Auntie Uju is not right in the head. She suffers a sort of dementia."

Sunny couldn't help the tears now. Nor could she help the sneezing. She looked at Orlu, wanting to ask the question that was on her mind. But Kema was there. Kema ran into the bathroom and brought Sunny a bunch of toilet paper.

"Thanks," Sunny said, blowing her nose. She sneezed again. "I think I should leave."

Orlu followed her out, and they stood at the front door as Sunny blew her nose again. Orlu handed her more of the toilet paper Kema had given him. "Sorry," he said.

Sunny only shook her head. "It's not the first time," she said. "People go crazy on albino people more often than you want to imagine."

"My auntie is involved in Mountain of Fire," Orlu said.

"So I noticed."

"I should have known this would happen, I guess. I'm just so used to you that I . . . I don't see your albinism as more than just part of what you are. I forget that other people . . . have issues."

"Like your auntie."

"Yeah," he said, sticking a foot in the rain.

"Orlu, you said she wasn't Leopard."

"She's not."

"Is Kema?"

"No. It's my uncle."

"Why does that room reek of juju powder?"

"That's why you're sneezing?" he asked.

"Yeah. Duh."

"My uncle thinks her dementia is . . . not natural. So he puts all these protective spells in the house. But as you can see, they don't work."

"Because maybe it *is* natural."

"Yes. It runs in her side of the family."

They were silent for a while. Orlu took her hand and squeezed it. "I'm sorry."

Sunny shook her head. "It's okay."

"Do you want me to ride back with you?"

"No, visit with your auntie. She needs you."

Kema came up the hall with an umbrella. "Here. Take," Kema said, handing it to Sunny. "Give it back to Orlu later." This was the second time someone had handed her a black umbrella in less than a week.

"Thanks," she said, taking it. She held it over her head and walked into the heavy rain. She stood waiting for a *danfo* for a half hour. The black umbrella was a godsend.

6

IDIOK'S DELIGHT

You are walking in virgin jungle. It has never been touched by shovel, brick, mortar, or tire. This place is full. Years back it was assumed to be an Evil Forest. Too evil a place for people to even dump the dead bodies of suicide victims, unwanted twins, murderers, and other people who were considered by Igbo and Ibibio traditional societies to be abominations. The Idiok baboons told me all of this when I was too young to really understand. But they have a way of teaching where the knowledge that is planted within you blossoms when you are ready to understand it. This is their own special way of teaching that human beings are still not able to master. I was taught in this way. Parts of this book are based on information they told

me and experiences I had when I was under the age of three. It is clear to me as day.

This small patch of forest I show you was haunted. People believed that if you stepped even two feet inside, you would never be able to find your way out. Maybe this was true for Lambs. Superstitions are like stereotypes in a lot of ways. Not only are they based on fear and igno-rance, they are also blended with fact. This place was the physical mundane world and the wilderness all in one. This was why these baboons loved it, for they were Leopard People, too. And for centuries, generation after generation, they made this place their home. Here they were safe and here they could speak with their ancestors, spirits, and other creatures of the wilderness.

You can smell the purity in the air, can't you? Stop and touch the leaves on this bush. Run your hand over them. They whisper, and if you look closely, you'll see that that brown cricket with the long antennae just walked through the leaf. You will not find it again. Spir-its who do not like to be seen become unseen when they are accidently seen.

That is me, sitting with those four baboons. They told me that when I tell my story I should leave their names out of it. The baboons have names but not in the sense that we have names. Their names are not just their identities; they carry bloodline. Unlike with human

beings, their names are the same as their spirit faces. So they don't share their names so freely. See the large one with the matted fur; he likes to swim in the ocean often, and the salt mats his hair and makes him smell like the sea. Many were sure he was close with Mami Wata. He taught me my first juju, which was how to open a coconut without losing the water. My first jujus were with Nsibidi, not powder or a knife.

The one with the patch of red fur near her eye hated me from the moment she saw me. She tried to tear me apart, but the others would not let her. She taught me how to climb trees by letting me fall. Then, impressed that I didn't die, she taught me how to climb the highest tree in the forest. It led to a place in the sky where you could walk because it was also the wilderness. Strange fruits grew there that only she and I enjoyed eating. The small one with the mangled leg was my best friend. We slept in the same nest until the day I was taken to live with humans.

And the fourth one with the white-gray fur is an elder. He is the oldest of the entire clan. No one knows how old he is, but his memory of Nsibidi is unmatched. Some say that his great skill with the language and storytelling is why he lives so far beyond everyone else. He moves slowly and only eats the softened fruits, but he could make the entire clan disappear if in danger. He is known throughout the wilderness. He speaks regularly

with masquerades, and these powerful spirits love him because he can drop into the wilderness completely and return to the living world as if he were a ghost. As a matter of fact, that is his nickname, "Ghost." I know his true name and that used to make several of the others jealous, for only I and his companion, an old baboon elder who rarely left her nest, knew his true name.

I am about three years old. See me there beside the tree, sulking. The brown-skinned, naked little girl with a bracelet made from tiny shells, the one with the matted hair had found near the seaside. My arms are around my chest, my chin to my neck. Even having been raised by baboons, I still exhibit human traits. I know I am human. They made sure I understood that. The Idiok do not believe in lies. It is two weeks before the seventeen-year-old boy who would become my father would find me. I was happy the day before, but this day I am not.

I am so young, but Ghost has shown me the faces of my parents. I've seen humans before, from afar, as they drive past in their cars or hurry past our forest. I've listened to them speak and even picked up some of their words, to the Idiok's delight. But when Ghost made those signs before my face, something happened to me. I began to recall how I got there. I believe my parents were murdered. And this is why I am sulking. It is too much for someone as small as me.

However, stand here. Watch me. I will not stay

upset for long. I am a young child and the world is beautiful to me. But I will remember. That is one of the powers of Nsibidi. Memory. When you close this book, think of—

"Sunny!" her mother called.

Sunny came back to herself and leaned against her bed's pillow, her copy of Sugar Cream's *Nsibidi: The Magical Language of the Spirits* on her lap. She could smell the fresh leaves and pure dirt. It was warm and humid, and a breeze was blowing. She could hear the calls and chirps of strange birds. But the human mind often denies when it can't understand. *How can baboons teach a magical language?* she wondered. It was ridiculous. The entire book was all ridiculous, but cool, too. She'd ask Sugar Cream directly about this. And maybe she'd ask about Ghost and the Mami Wata baboon. And maybe she'd ask how one even *writes* a book in Nsibidi. She laughed. Sugar Cream had very strange origins, indeed. And "reading" about it was making Sunny feel equally strange. She yawned. Her body felt sluggish and thick.

"Sunny?!" her mother said, opening her door.

"Yes, Mom."

"Chukwu's leaving. Come say goodbye."

"Oh!" Sunny said. She'd been so wrapped up in her book that she'd lost track of time. Had two hours passed already?

She slowly got out of bed, closing her eyes for a moment and then opening them. She shook herself. "Wake up, Sunny," she said. She jumped up and down. It helped, but not much. She'd been "reading" her Nsibidi for two hours. Nothing could chase away the fatigue but a nap. She'd have to play it off.

Sunny's brother's Jeep was full of suitcases. "I can't wait," Chukwu declared. "First semester, I'll have chemistry and biology classes. I will show them what I am made of." His best friend, Adebayo Moses Oluwaseun, sat in the passenger seat. The two had been friends for years, but in the last year they'd become inseparable. Both were good soccer players, though Sunny's brother was easily better. And both had discovered weightlifting at the same time.

"I was going to say that you should watch for armed robbers on the road, but you two look too dangerous to bother." Their father laughed.

Adebayo flexed a muscular arm. "No bullet can penetrate my flesh," he said.

Chukwu laughed hard, and they both exchanged a look, sharing some sort of inside joke.

"Just drive carefully and quickly," Sunny's mother said. "Get to campus before dark."

"Mummy, campus is a half hour away," Chukwu said. "It's morning."

"Better to be safe," she said.

"Sunny," Chukwu said, smirking. "Stay out of my room."

"As if I have a reason to want to go in that smelly place," she said, leaning against the house. Her legs felt so weak. She sat down on the curb, gazing at her brother. He was really going off to university. "Wow," she said to herself.

"Ugonna, stay away from my side of the room," Chukwu said, waving a dismissive hand at Sunny.

"*Your* room?" Ugonna said. "You don't *have* a room anymore, and I have a big one."

"We'll see about that when I visit for Christmas," Chukwu said, starting the Jeep.

"Call when you get there," their mother added, opening the door and hugging him in the driver's seat.

"Study hard, my son," his father said, clapping him on the shoulder.

Sunny leaned to the side, her hand in the dirt, as they all watched him drive through the gate onto the road. Then he was gone. Sunny frowned, her mind jumping to what she'd just "read" in her Nsibidi book, that the Idiok who'd adopted Sugar Cream were Baboon Leopard People, and they all had the same name as their spirit faces. *That is just . . . bizarre,* she lazily thought. Then she laughed and slowly got up. *Good luck, Chukwu.*

7
THE NUT

Later that day, Sunny dribbled the soccer ball between her bare feet as she ran toward Ugonna. She moved it faster and faster the closer that she got to him. As she approached, Ugonna prepared to challenge her. As she did so, she watched his face shift from smiling to frowning.

"Shit," he exclaimed.

She kicked the ball to the left when she got to him, doing a quick whirl and catching it easily as she shot around him.

"Damn it!" he exclaimed, turning around to watch her.

She slowed down, working the ball with her feet. She flipped it onto the top of her foot and tapped it three times. Then she bopped it to her knee where she bounced it.

"Maybe you should try out for Arsenal."

Sunny's smile grew even broader. "They don't allow women." She popped the ball onto her head and then back to her feet. Then she kicked it to her brother.

"You can show them how to make an exception," he said, clumsily dribbling the ball between his feet.

"Maybe," she said, looking up at the shining evening sun. She'd gotten her Leopard teammates at the Zuma Cup in Abuja and then the group of boys from school to make exceptions, who said she couldn't do it a third time? "Maybe."

A car pulled up to the gate. It was Uncle Chibuzo, their father's oldest brother. He drove his shiny green BMW into the compound and parked it beside their father's black Honda.

"Ugonna, Sunny, how are you?" he asked, hopping out.

"Fine," they both said, each giving him a hug.

"How is school? Studying hard?"

"Yes, sir," Ugonna said.

"Always," Sunny said.

"I hear your brother went off to university today."

"Yes," Ugonna said. "He's probably meeting his hostel mates right now."

"You should be proud."

"We are," Sunny said. She gently kicked the soccer ball up, kneed it, and caught it in her hands.

"You are pretty good," Uncle Chibuzo said. "You want to be like your older brother?"

"No," Sunny said. "He's not as good as me."

Uncle Chibuzo laughed heartily. Too heartily. *Pff, he has no idea*, Sunny thought, annoyed. She wished he'd been there when she'd made five goals in a row last week playing with her classmates.

"This way," Ugonna said, taking the lead.

Their father had been expecting their uncle, and he was already waiting in the living room. As they greeted each other, slapping hands and laughing, Sunny and Ugonna tried to sneak away.

"Sunny," Uncle Chibuzo said, "bring kola."

Ugonna silently laughed, covering his mouth. And as Sunny turned away, she rolled her eyes. The ceremony of breaking the kola nut, more simply called "breaking kola," always relegated her to servant because she was always the youngest girl in the house. "Whatever," she muttered, going to the kitchen.

She placed a kola nut on the small wooden plate. Then she added a large dollop of peanut paste and a small pile of alligator pepper on the side. She brought it out to her uncle and father and tried her best not to look as irritated as she felt.

"Ah, kola has come," her uncle ceremoniously said, smiling wide with all his teeth.

"Very good," her father added.

Ugonna just stood there, clearly as impatient to have this over and done with as Sunny. She stood before her uncle be-

cause the kola was always presented to the oldest man in the room. She held the plate steady so that the balls of alligator pepper wouldn't roll off.

"Look at you presenting it like a miserable human being," her uncle snapped. "Wake up. This is not just something your elders do. It's an important ritual. You young people don't know anything."

Sunny wanted to heavily protest. She wanted to say that she knew more old ways than he *ever* would. She'd faced *real* masquerades and had her own juju knife, for goodness sake.

"Kola is important," her uncle said. "Not just to Igbo, to *all* Nigerians. The Yoruba grow it, the Hausa chew it, Igbos talk and talk about it. For us, Ndi Igbo people, the kola nut, the *oji*, symbolizes pure intention. It connects us to our ancestors. *Oji* is the channel of communication beyond the physical world and into the spirit world. Nothing starts without breaking kola."

He picked up the pinkish-yellow kola nut and broke it into four parts. "Four lobes," he said. "Very good."

He took a piece, scooped up some peanut paste with it, then some alligator pepper, and handed the plate back to Sunny as he ate it. Sunny next offered the plate to her father who did the same. When she served Ugonna, she refused to look at his smirking face. If he had been younger than her, she'd still have had to serve him, for maleness outdid age in Igbo culture. *Ridiculous*, Sunny thought as she

always did when she got stuck serving the kola nut when her father had visitors.

She took her piece, dipped it into the peanut paste and then the pepper, and angrily crunched the combination. The bitter taste came from the fact that kola was full of caffeine. It used to be the ingredient in Coca-Cola that gave it its flavor and caffeine. The bitterness, the heat of the pepper, and the peanut flavor was always an explosion to her taste buds. She focused on that instead of her irritation.

Sunny studied well into the night, riding the caffeine wave of that one piece of kola nut. When she finished, she brought out the box from beneath her bed and opened it. Her kola nut buzz gave a kick to her curiosity. *I wonder*, she thought, bringing out the sheet of Nsibidi. She put it down, turned off by the idea of vomiting kola nut if she tried to read it. Then she picked it up again. She took a deep breath and then quickly unfolded it.

She looked at the symbols and nothing happened. She sighed, irritated. Nothing happening was even worse than feeling the nasty nausea. "Great," she muttered, still straining to "read" the Nsibidi. "Now I don't even—" The symbols started shifting. Her belly flipped with surprise; she grasped the sheet more tightly. "They're looking back at me," she whispered, feeling her lips go numb and her ears begin to

plug up. She was being thrust high into the air or deep into the water. There was a strange smell, but it wasn't unpleasant. The smell was sweet and grassy—oily, too. Her belly rumbled and roiled.

Then Sunny heard the voice of her only Leopard relative, who'd been so powerful and loved and secretive and then brutally slain by her best student Black Hat Otokoto. Sunny's belly stopped rioting, the rising nausea disappearing. Her grandmother sounded almost exactly like Sunny's mother. The same high voice and rapid way of speaking. Then a strange place opened before Sunny—a city with beautiful stone buildings all etched with intricate designs. Mosaics, engravings, stone that contained mineral veins in natural, colorful, fractal patterns. Tall buildings that stretched high into the sky, but the buildings were rivaled by equally ambitious and strong trees, some palm, some more like fat baobab trees and hefty ebony trees. The roads were red packed dirt. And there was a small sunflower-yellow stone house with a stone roof . . .

The House is here. Yes, it smells like flowers, too. This surprises me. I love flowers. Everything here is stone, built to last. If it is wood, the trees will take offense and then take it apart. The winds can be strong in this place when it rains. A house must be solid and heavy, too. The front door is round and made from the wing of a giant Ntu Tu beetle. It's clearer than glass

but won't break no matter what you do to it. That door is old, but it is not the oldest part of the house. Inside, you will find books, you will find heat, and flowers that have grown on the ceiling since the house was built.

Sunny, this is a place where if you seek, you will find. It took me years to find it. Maybe you will need to do the same at some point. If you are what I know you are, your life will not be easy, and there will be much that you have to answer to. But for now, you relax and see this place. See the street that leads to it. See the front door. And there is so much inside.

The floors are a mosaic that you can stare at for hours and think about the world. See the palm tree that grows through the center of the house? There is a clear roof that protects the opening from water when it rains. Come this way to the library. It smells of sandalwood all the time, and the walls are covered with amulets. The acoustics here bring any kind of music to life just as strongly as the words in these books bring ideas and stories to life. To learn is to live.

When the Nsibidi let her go, she was looking blankly at the bottom of the page. She could still smell sandalwood. *What a beautiful place that was,* she thought, lying back. "I want a place just like that when I grow up," she whispered. "Just like that." But what did it all mean? Why would her grandmother write a page of Nsibidi about this place? She hadn't even told Sunny where it was and whose place it was.

Maybe it's something she wants me to read when I'm under stress, Sunny thought. The fatigue that resulted from "reading" the powerful Nsibidi was tugging at her eyelids. She put the page away and closed the box. Then she lay in her bed. So relaxed. For several minutes, she thought about the house that sat in the strange city. *Maybe Grandma was a fiction writer,* Sunny thought with a chuckle. *Fiction written in Nsibidi, it would be better than a motion picture.* She chuckled some more. It was well past three A.M. As her eyes drifted shut, she hoped she'd dream about the beautiful house.

But she didn't.

Within minutes, she was dreaming . . .

She was in soft, warm water. Not choppy and rushing like when she was in the river during her initiation. No, this place was calm and blue, but she could feel its weight as she moved through it. And she could breathe here. She sped up. Her body seemed to know where it was going even if her mind did not. Faster and faster until the blue of the water became the blue of the sky.

She was flying. The rush of the cool air against her face took her breath away. She was high above a great forest, a rain forest. Mist moved through the trees like clouds that were too lazy to float. Then in the distance she saw it. A city of smoke. Burning so hot the buildings looked otherworldly. "Noooo!" she

screamed, trying to stop herself. But she couldn't stop. She just kept hurtling toward it. She was going to burn, too . . .

She was falling. She was jarred awake by her body hitting the floor, again. "Oof!" She blinked in the dark, her eyes adjusting. She looked around her room and sat up. A bed, a dresser, a closet. There was a rolled-up newspaper on the floor. She felt a moment of panic. She couldn't remember her own name. "Who am I?" she whispered, frowning.

She could not remember. The room was nice, comfortable, and pleasing to her eye, but it was foreign. *Where am I? What is all this?* She got up, fighting panic. The bed had yellow-and-rose-colored sheets that she'd pulled half off when she'd fallen out. She looked down at her legs and frowned. Her skin was so pale. There was a flat-screen computer monitor on the desk and a small computer box on the floor beside it. Schoolbooks were also on the floor. Yes, those were schoolbooks.

As she looked around the room, unsure of who or where she was, she began to remember other things. The wilderness. Like an impossible wonderful jungle full of . . . everybody . . . but the living. Mostly green, but every other color and kind dwelled there, too. The wilderness made the physical world seem flat, dead, and quiet. "Ekwensu," she whispered. And when she spoke the name of the powerful terrifying masquerade who'd nearly killed her and her friends a year ago, she felt

a deep anger rise in her. She hated no one; she didn't have the propensity for hatred. Nevertheless, the one who held that name was one she wanted to send to the darkest corner of the universe.

Her eye fell on the top of the wooden cabinet beside her window. She blinked. Then she burst out laughing. She sat down on her bed, her eyes still glued to the top of her dresser, and she laughed even harder. As she laughed, it was as if her spirit flew into her and filled her up; everything returned— her memories, her destiny, her self. She was Sunny Nwazue and she was Anyanwu. She was the daughter of Kingsley and Ugwu Nwazue and granddaughter of Ozoemena of the Nimm Warrior Clan. She was a Leopard society free agent, initiated over a year ago and witness to the suicide of the ritual killer Black Hat Otokoto and the banishment of the evil Ekwensu. And she was a most excellent soccer player.

Sunny was laughing because Della her wasp artist had created a brand-new sculpture out of some of the Oreo cookies in her backpack, a perfect replica of a stern-looking . . . Batman. As she watched and laughed some more, Della used a skinny leg to add one last flourish—a realistic sneer to Batman's lips probably made from the Oreo's cream.

Her belly cramped as she tried to stifle her giggles. She knew exactly where the large blue wasp had gotten its inspiration. She'd been reading her brother's copy of *Batman: Death by Design*, which their uncle had sent him from the

UK. There it was on the floor beside her schoolbooks.

"You are amazing, Della!" she said. "I love it!" She laughed again.

Della buzzed proudly and hovered beside it as Sunny snapped a picture with her cell phone. The wasp had grown to be about an inch and a half in length, its skills evolving beyond anything Sunny had ever imagined. Wasp artists that were happy were known to live as long as the human being they bonded to and develop skills that rivaled and even surpassed the greatest human workers of the arts. This Batman not only looked as if it would walk away at any time, but it resembled the dark, gritty Batman found in the recent films Ugonna had come to love so much.

Della buzzed happily and flew a gleeful loop the loop into the tiny mud nest it had built in the ceiling corner. Sunny sat on her bed. It was nearly dawn. She got dressed. Today was another day.

8

PEPPER BUGS

The next day was another day, too. A normal day. So was the next, and the next. For two months, things settled for Sunny. Well, it settled as much as it could for a free agent whose mentor was the Head Librarian of Leopard Knocks.

Sunny saw no more octopus-monster-propelled lakes, Mami Wata kept her distance, and reading Nsibidi was feeling more and more natural, though no less sublime. She didn't speak a word to anyone about her hardening body, and that made things easier, too. Better to just roll with it than try to explain it to anyone.

On the midnight of every Wednesday, she went with Chichi, Sasha, and Orlu for classes with Anatov. Half of

these times were spent in his hut reviewing readings, learning and practicing new jujus, and being lectured on Leopard
etiquette and history. Chichi and Sasha had recently passed
to the *Mbawkwa* level, and Anatov taught them and had
them practice higher-level jujus. Orlu and Sunny could only
sit and listen. They weren't even allowed to ask questions
during these portions of the lessons.

The other half of their Anatov nights were spent "learning by experience." Leopard education did not have any vacations or breaks aside from certain religious ones like Eid
Al-Fitr, Eid Al-Adha, Christmas, and Easter. For Eid Al-Fitr,
while Lamb school was on break, Anatov had all four of
them volunteer at a local Muslim orphanage and then work
later that night filling potholes along one of the smaller village roads. They'd used a dirt moving and packing juju that
Anatov had taught them that very night. For days, Sunny
was digging muck from beneath her nails and sweeping dirt
from her bedroom.

For tonight's "learning by experience," Anatov was sending them into Night Runner Forest to capture four pepper
bugs.

"What's a pepper bug?" Chichi asked, frowning.

Anatov smirked and pointed a long finger at her. "See,
you and Sasha consume all the juju, Leopard history, and
Leopard culture books, but yet you neglect the field guides.
And, Sunny, you haven't had time to learn about the crea-

tures of the Leopard world, except for those things you encounter personally, like ghost hoppers or the lake and river
beasts. Knowledge gaps are no good."

"I know *tungwas* and bush souls, too," she added. "And
wasp artists, and all those . . ."

Anatov waved a hand at her. "You know nothing of the
millions of magical creatures of the world. And I have yet
to assign you any field guides to read. For instance, you see
tungwas all the time, but who can tell me what *tungwas* actually are?"

Sunny looked at the others, barely able to contain her
delight. Even Orlu was silent, an annoyed frown on his face.
Being new to the Leopard world, Sunny had been deeply disturbed by the basketball-sized skin covered balls that exploded
into a shower of teeth, bones, giblets of meat, and tufts of
hair. To calm her mind, she'd done a bit of research on them.

"Even in the Obi Library, there was no concrete information about them," Sunny announced, smugly looking at Orlu,
Sasha, and Chichi. "One: no one really cares to know. Two:
some things in the world are just beyond logic and the *tungwa*
is one of them." She grinned and then added, "All this is according to Sugar Cream. I have to admit, I'm quite satisfied
with both of these answers."

Everyone stared at Sunny, and she stared back at them,
her grin fading.

"Well, *that* was surprising," Anatov said, after a moment.

"Anyway, for now, this exercise will do." He turned to Orlu. "I trust you know exactly what a pepper bug is."

Orlu nodded. "And I knew you'd ask us to go and find some."

"Why's that?" Anatov asked.

"For a few reasons," Orlu said. "The cost of tainted peppers just went up in the market. You like your food really hot. And the patch of peppers in your garden out back looks like something just came and ate it all."

Anatov grunted, irritably. "Yes, there is a small grasscutter that lives around my hut that has a taste for spicy food. Damn things are the woodchucks of Nigeria. They even look like them." He smiled at Orlu. "You are observant. Explain to them along the way."

Anatov gave Orlu a large metal pot, four spatulas, and oven mitts and then quickly ushered them out the IN door. "Good luck," he said. "And remember, the entrance to Night Runner Forest closes at dawn. Bring the bugs here before you go home."

Only Orlu was excited about the assignment. All of them remembered what Night Runner Forest was like as it had nearly killed them last year. But they'd all learned a lot since then. They knew how not to get killed or too badly hurt. Of course, that didn't make traipsing around in it at one A.M. any more tolerable.

"They shouldn't be that hard to find," Orlu said as Sasha

drew the tree symbol on the dirt not far from the Leopard Knocks bridge. Of all of them, Sasha was most used to entering Night Runner Forest because it was where his mentor Kehinde lived. "They are red and have long legs and square-shaped flat bodies that are kind of ridged, sort of like a leaf," Orlu said. "They look like tiny slabs of really lean beef or salmon."

"Disgusting," Chichi said.

Orlu ignored her. "They're about two inches in diameter, and they glow red in the dark."

"I'll bet they sting," Sunny said, as they stepped onto the path that opened up before them. "Things like that always sting."

"No, they don't," Orlu said. "They burn."

"Close enough," Sunny said.

According to Orlu, pepper bugs loved peppers. They would find a wild pepper plant and eat exactly one of the hottest peppers and then start to glow. This glow would nourish the plant and create a bond between the bug and plant. The bug would then inject the plant with a serum that would fortify the plant's health. So not only did the plant grow large, it grew healthier, too. Then the insect would defecate at the base of the plant and within one night another pepper plant would grow. Then another and another until there was an entire wildly growing pepper patch of at least ten plants. Then the pepper bug would do a glowing shaking dance that would

attract a mate and this patch would become their home. Pepper bugs were happy to share peppers with human beings if the human watered the patch regularly and didn't pick too many peppers.

"Anatov wants to regrow his patch," Orlu said. "Then he'll taint the peppers himself so they will grow super hot just the way he likes it."

Note to self, Sunny thought. *Never eat Anatov's pepper soup.*

"Why can't he do this himself, then?" Sasha asked.

"He's our teacher, "Chichi snapped. "Students shop for their teachers all the time. Go to the market and everything. Don't you?"

"Not in America," Sasha said. "That's called ass-kissing."

They trudged through Night Runner Forest, trying hard not to disrupt, step on, bump into, or disturb anything. Of course, this was next to impossible. "I hate this place," Chichi hissed. She was blinking hard, her eye watering. An evil weevil, a long-snouted foul-tempered insect with the ability to hurl small objects, had thrown a small seed directly into Chichi's eye. Orlu grunted, scratching at a round orange-red patch on his arm where a Mars fly had bitten him.

"Yeah, there are days I want to just nuke this place," Sasha said, throwing yet another stick into the forest. He blew some powder and muttered some words, and the stick got up and stiffly began to smack at the patch of jungle to their left.

Something large ran off. "Too bad no one's written a juju that could do that."

"Time might take care of it," Sunny muttered.

They were all silent for a moment. A glint in the forest caught Sunny's eye. "Hey," she said, pointing. It was red, like a bunch of Christmas lights in the thick grass.

"Good eye, Sunny," Orlu said. They all ran up to the peppers. The stems reached past Sunny's waist, and the peppers on them were plump and plentiful. Up close they looked exactly like those chili pepper lights Sunny would see in Mexican restaurants back in the United States. The pepper bugs were easy to spot as they lumbered contently up and down the stems, batting and pressing on the peppers with their thick antennae.

"Damn, never seen these before," Sasha said.

"That's because you probably only take a path to Kehinde's," Orlu said. "Pepper bugs live off the beaten path."

Sasha rolled his eyes. "Ugh, whatever."

"So how do we get them?" Sunny asked. "If we were asked to do this, I assume it's not going to be easy."

"We have to get them in this pot," Orlu said. "They're hot, so they'd melt through a plastic jar."

"Are they fast?" Chichi asked, looking at them with disgust.

"No." He handed them each a metal spatula with a rubber handle. "Get them to walk onto it, put them in the pot, and put the lid on."

Sunny crept up to one and almost immediately started sneezing. Not from juju powder, but from the strong peppery fumes that suddenly emitted from the insect. "Ugh," she said, sneezing again.

"Jesus!" she heard Sasha exclaim a few feet away.

"Oh, sorry," Orlu said. "I forgot to add that when they feel threatened, they 'pepper up.'"

"Then how are we supposed to get them?" Chichi asked.

"Like this," Orlu said, creeping up to one. "Slowly. Move smoothly." He gently coaxed the glowing insect onto his spatula. It put a leg onto the flat metal and then took it off. Orlu nudged it a bit more and eventually the insect stepped on. Slowly, Orlu placed it in the pot, where it stepped off. He put the lid on. "There." The pot began to grow red with heat. "That's why Anatov gave me the oven mitts. When they realize they've been captured, they get really angry and heat up."

Once she stopped sneezing, Sunny was able to catch her bug pretty easily. With much cursing and sneezing, Sasha managed to get his, too. Chichi, however, kept getting hit with fumes. By this time, the entire colony of pepper bugs was on to them. When she was blasted with fumes a fourth time after taking five minutes to creep up on one bug, she shouted, "I HATE ALL OF YOU STUPID BEASTS! GO AND DIE!"

Orlu took her hand. "Sorry, o," he said, as she blew her

nose into the tissue Sunny had given her. "Let me try some-thing."

He held up his hands and did that thing he naturally did that undid any negative juju. His hands bent, contorted, and twisted as he undid whatever juju the bugs had apparently worked. Then he said, "We mean no harm. We are just taking some of you to another place nearby to start a fresh pepper patch. I know you can fly. You can visit and cross-pollinate. If one of you wishes to be adventurous, come."

"Come on, dude, no insect is ever so reasonable." Sasha laughed.

But one of them was, for a pepper bug slowly walked up to Chichi. She looked at Orlu, who nodded. She bent down and let it walk voluntarily onto her spatula. When she put it in the pot, after about ten seconds, the pot's hot redness faded.

"It's cool," Orlu said when he touched the side of his pot tentatively. "That last bug must have told the others what I said." He picked up the pot using the oven mitts, regardless. "Most insects have a tricky side."

When they brought the bugs back to Anatov, they watched as he let them loose in his dying pepper patch. The four insects congregated in a square in the center of the dead and dying peppers and brought their legs and hands together, closing the square.

"You all did well," Anatov said, as they watched the in-

sects perform their healing ceremony. "They'll be at this all night. By morning there will be fresh new shoots. You can go home now."

Sunny's lessons with Sugar Cream were even more challenging. Unlike Anatov, Sugar Cream didn't have Sunny go out and buy books. She was the Head Librarian; they had all the books they needed right there in the building. They always met in her office on the third floor of the Obi Library. Usually, they met Saturdays. But this weekend, they met on a Sunday evening because Sugar Cream had had an important meeting Saturday afternoon. Sunny couldn't help but suspect that Sugar Cream also wanted Sunny to journey to Leopard Knocks at night, forcing her to deal with the river beast and her fear of the lake beast. Thankfully, Sunny's journey to Leopard Knocks that evening had been uneventful and she'd arrived at Sugar Cream's office promptly at nine P.M.

Sugar Cream was leaning against the doorway when Sunny reached the top of the stairs. "There you are," Sugar Cream said, smirking. "Come in. Let's get started."

Sugar Cream's focus for the first two weeks had been on the rules and regulations of being a Leopard Person. She had Sunny not only read the thin and annoyingly prejudiced book *Fast Facts for Free Agents* two more times, but she also had Sunny write a research paper pointing out and deconstruct-

ing the book's bias. Sunny had never had to write such a difficult paper in her life. It forced her to not only look at the *way*
she was given information but also at the background of the
author Isong Abong Effiong Isong. It turned out that Isong
was not only educated in the West but had fled from Nigeria
after a terrible experience with armed robbers. For this reason, Isong had developed a fear and hatred of all things Nigerian. Though the research paper was tough to write, Sunny
was glad she'd been forced to write it. Now she understood
not only the rules the book taught but how to read those
rules. Several small silver *chittim* had fallen during the writing of that paper.

Sugar Cream had also brought Sunny to several Library
Council meetings where Sunny had to dress up and sit quietly behind Sugar Cream. Her mentor met with elders from
all over the country and once with elders from all over the
world. In this way, Sunny learned that the Leopard People
were an organized group who kept many of the world's ills
from being worse than they were. Who'd have thought that
so much of Nigeria's corruption was stopped by the organized
jujus of Leopard elders from a variety of Nigeria's states? Certainly not Sunny. The idea that things in Nigeria could have
been a lot worse scared her deeply.

Sunny had also met some of Sugar Cream's important col-
leagues outside of meetings. Only two weeks ago, Sunny had
entered Sugar Cream's office and nearly run into the chest

of a tall Arab man. He'd worn white flowing garments and a white turban and smelled of sweet incense. Sunny had remembered him from a year ago during the meeting she and the others had with a group of Africa's greatest elders not long before they were sent to deal with Black Hat. From what she recalled, at least part of this man's name was Ali and he could shape-shift into a colorful toucan.

Sunny had stepped back. "I'm sorry, *Oga* Ali," she'd said in Igbo. Most library elders spoke many languages and at the meeting he'd expressed a serious dislike of Americans. Best to not speak her American-accented English.

He had surprised her with a smile. "Sunny Nwazue," he'd said. "You look well. Being mentored by Sugar Cream is good for you."

Sunny wasn't sure if this was a compliment or an insult. She'd smiled and said, "Thank you."

He had turned to her mentor, who had a frown on her face. "We will talk later, my dear."

Sugar Cream had nodded. "Go well."

"Inshallah," he'd said, closing the door behind him.

Sugar Cream fed Sunny books on African Leopard history and Leopard politics from around the world; she even gave Sunny a few novels by local Leopard authors. Sunny didn't think any of these were very good; Sugar Cream had laughed and agreed with her.

Nevertheless, it was the lessons in gliding that rocked

Sunny's world the most, and tonight, this was the focus. "Sit, Sunny. Sit," Sugar Cream told her. She set down her bunch of books on the floor, looked around for red spiders, and, when she saw none nearby, sat down. Sugar Cream settled at her desk, an agitated look on her face. She suddenly looked at Sunny. "I was going to test you on your Leopard history readings, but I have changed my mind. Watch closely."

As Sunny observed, she felt like screaming. Never had Sugar Cream changed before her. She'd only *spoken* of her natural talent. Sugar Cream could change into a snake, and then she could slip through time. Sunny had never been fond of snakes, so she wasn't eager to see her mentor do it. And now Sunny knew she'd been right to not ask.

Sugar Cream was a frail old woman of medium height. She had rich brown skin and a face that reminded Sunny of her grandmother on her father's side. She had no idea if her mentor was Igbo, Hausa, Yoruba, Efik, Ijaw, Fulani, or any other ethnicity. Sugar Cream didn't know either, really, since she'd been abandoned in the jungle when she was very young. If Sunny had to guess, she'd have said Yoruba. But all this began to melt. Her clothes billowed as they were emptied. The wrinkly skin on Sugar Cream's face began to shrink. Her entire body shriveled in on itself. Sunny felt nau-seated and couldn't hide the look of complete disgust on her face. Her stomach lurched, and she hunched forward just as Sugar Cream's now lumpy flesh of a body collapsed forward

on her desk with a soft thump. The same brown as her skin, it writhed and rolled.

Sunny gasped, shutting her eyes tightly. *Count to ten*, a papery and dry voice whispered within Sunny's head. *Then see me.*

Sunny slowly counted to ten. When she opened her eyes, she was looking into the green-yellow gaze of a large bright green snake. *To speak while in alternate form*, Sugar Cream said in her head, *must be learned. But to change, once you have mastered it, is not difficult.*

She did not move, her body still mostly in her clothes. When Sugar Cream changed back, Sunny understood why she'd stayed in place. She filled her clothes with the ease of an expert. "To see me change back does not have the nauseating effect," Sugar Cream said. "It's only the first time that throws one off. You will not experience that again when you see me change. Also, your gift is different from mine. When you change into mist and glide, you can bring your clothes."

They started first with breathing, for part of gliding between the wilderness and the physical world was understanding that you typically had to *stop* breathing to do it for any extended period of time. "You can glide across the bridge or through a keyhole. That is easy," Sugar Cream said. "But can you glide from here to your house?"

Gliding between the wilderness and the physical world was one thing, but Sunny knew what Sugar Cream was

slowly working her toward. Dropping completely into the wilderness. To do so meant she'd have to die, really truly die. But she was born with this ability, so she would be able to always come back . . . if she did it correctly. She wasn't in any hurry to try, and Sugar Cream wasn't in a rush to have her try, either. "Not this year," Sugar Cream said. "But maybe next year or the year after that."

Sugar Cream worked her hard. After the gliding exercises, they worked on Night Frames, various states of being that you achieved only during the night. Night Frames required a combination of juju knife flourishes, humming deep in the throat, and a blue juju powder that left her skin oily. Night Frames were primary phases of slipping wholly into the wilderness.

"You don't want to enter the wilderness and not be able to come out," Sugar Cream firmly said. "That is death, of course. So you practice slipping in and then out, bit by bit. The night is when the barrier between the physical and spirit worlds is thinnest."

One had to die in order to go into the wilderness, so one had to birth her- or himself back. And one had to be strong to give birth. Though Sunny was born with the natural ability to do both, even she knew that talent and ability was best honed. Sunny had solemnly nodded and then the work began. They practiced two frames, which Sunny achieved easily enough but found she had to work to hold. Over and

over, the humming, the blowing of the powder, the sneezing, then the colors that began to bleed into everything. By the time Sugar Cream sent her home, she felt as if her world was vibrating.

Sugar Cream's lessons; Anatov's teachings; Lamb school; hanging out with Chichi, Orlu, and Sasha; her strangely changing body—Sunny was overwhelmed, yet learning and absorbing so much. As she sat in her seat on the near-empty funky train home, she'd curled her body toward the window and shut her eyes. She took a deep breath, truly relaxing for the first time in hours, and this was when she felt that sensation of being pulled into two. Her eyes shot open and as she stared out the window, she began to quietly weep.

"Anyanwu?" she whispered. And then she heard herself respond in a deep voice, "Sleep, Sunny, I am here."

9

HOW FAR?

Sunny groaned as she opened the gate. The night sky hadn't begun to warm yet, but soon it would and the morning birds were already singing.

She'd slept the entire ride back on the funky train. Thankfully, the driver, a tall old woman named Magnificent, who saw her often at this late hour, knew Sunny's stop. Magnificent shouted, "Sunny! You're home! Go and sleep!" Sunny jumped to her feet and dragged herself from the juju-powered vehicle before she knew what was happening. The funky train silently glided off, leaving only a puff of rose-scented air and her in the dark standing before the gate to her house.

Her chin to her chest, she quietly unlocked and pushed

the gate open just enough to slip through. She trudged toward the front door. The house alarm wouldn't be on, nor would her father or mother be waiting up for her, though she suspected they were anxiously listening for her return. They didn't ask questions anymore. Good. That was one stress gone. Her skin still felt oily from the enhancement powder, and her sensitive nose was stuffed with snot. She'd need a good shower before going to bed and that would rob her of fifteen minutes out of the four hours of sleep she could snatch before she had to leave for school.

She stuck her key into the hole. She could pass through the keyhole, but there was always the chance that her brother or parents would be right there. Then she'd find herself sentenced to a caning by the Library Council for exposing the Leopard People's ways. Would they wipe or alter the memories of her family? Who knew what they did. Now that she didn't have to sneak around, it definitely wasn't worth the risk.

Creak!

She froze. Someone was opening the gate behind her. It was several yards away; she could throw the door open and lock it behind her. Or she could just risk it and pass through the keyhole. *Ekwensu,* she thought. *What if it's Ekwensu? But why would the physical world's greatest adversary have to push open a gate?* Armed robbers, then? But the gate was locked. Did they have a key? Was juju used to get in? Was the lock picked?

She whirled around, dropping her backpack and bringing out her juju knife. *What am I doing?* she thought, horrified.

The gate opened. Adrenaline flooded her system, caus-ing a ringing in her ears and cold sweat to break from her skin. She crept closer. A shadow peeked around the gate. He looked right at her.

"Sunny?" he gasped.

"Chukwu?" She quickly put her knife into her pocket.

"What are you doing here?"

"Why aren't you at school?" Sunny blurted.

They stared at each other. Her brother was dark-skinned and standing in the shadows, so she couldn't quite see the expression on his face.

"I . . . I just got home," she said, stepping closer.

"From wherever it is you go?" he asked. He moved away from her, holding on to the gate.

"Where's your Jeep?" she asked.

"Parked it on the street," he said. "Don't . . ." He stepped away from her some more and, in doing so, moved into the dim moonlight.

Sunny clapped her hands over her mouth and gasped. "What happened?!"

Her brother had gotten quite muscular in the last year. He'd not only discovered weight-lifting, he'd discovered that he really, truly, madly loved it. Sunny knew that aside from kicking a soccer ball around, there was nothing he loved more

than to be in the gym lifting until his muscles vibrated. Now Sunny could see that he'd gotten even bigger since leaving for school weeks ago. Still, at this moment, he looked like a pummeled, scared teenager. His left eye was swollen shut, and his mouth looked like it carried two golf balls. He held on to the gate with a big hand.

Sunny stepped up to him and touched his face. He looked away. "Chukwu, what . . ."

"Mummy and Daddy can't know that I'm here," he said.

"Why?"

"I need to get the money I have in my room. Then I'll leave." He looked into her eyes. "I don't want to put anyone here in danger." His face twitched and he frowned, one tear falling down his cheek.

Sunny felt her eyes sting, too. This was her brother Chukwu, whose name meant "Supreme Being," because he was "God's gift to women," or so he liked to brag. This was her oldest brother, who had tormented her since she was a baby, and protected her, too, in his own rough way.

"C-Come on," she said, her voice shaking. She wrapped her arm around his. "Lean on me. I'll get you inside."

They moved fast, heading straight to Sunny's room. Sunny banked on the fact that her parents would assume it was just her entering the house and not their oldest son who'd run away from the university they were paying so much for him to attend. She locked the door as he sat on her bed. In the

light, she saw that he looked far worse than she'd thought. She took a deep breath and steadied herself; this was not a time to cry.

"Where is the money?" she asked. "I'll get it for you."

He frowned. "What? No, no, it's in a secret spot. It'll be . . ."

"In your room?"

"Yes," he said.

"What if Ugonna sees you?"

"He'll be sleeping."

"Not if you wake him up. And what if Mom or Dad comes out of their room? I know they heard us come in. Sometimes Mom checks on me. She'll come and listen at the door. She doesn't think I know, but I do."

"Shit," he hissed. "Well, what do you want me to do? I need that money."

"I'll get it."

He considered it for a moment. "What will you say if Ugonna wakes?"

"He won't. You know I'm better at sneaking than you ever will be."

Chukwu nodded. "True. Okay . . . There's a loose floorboard near the window. The front right leg of my bed is on top of it. The money is inside."

"Okay," she said. "I'll be right back." She paused. "Shut your eyes and close your ears."

"Why?"

"Just do it."

He frowned at her, but then did as she said. She ran to the door, made sure it was locked, glanced back quickly, and then passed through the keyhole before he opened his eyes and asked her why she was asking him to do something so weird. The feeling was one of compression and coolness. It wasn't the same as when she'd done it that first time, back when she thought she was working the first juju of her life but was really using her natural talent. Since then she'd done this many times and it was easier and easier. However, the feeling was sharper, too. More deliberate.

She came out on the other side of the door and then ran toward the room Chukwu and Ugonna used to share that was now just Ugonna's. She checked to make sure the door was locked. It was. She passed through the keyhole. Ugonna was sprawled out on his bed, sleeping noisily. He preferred to study on the floor, so this was where his schoolbooks and sheets of paper were scattered. His large-screen TV's screen saver flashed images of shiny sports cars into the darkness of his room. *Good*, she thought. She could see. Soft jazz music played. Even better, background noise, though she shouldn't need it. She ran to Chukwu's bed and waited.

She was still insubstantial, gravity affecting her but not as much as it would if she were all there. If Ugonna awoke and looked right at her, he'd see nothing, but he might sense

her presence, even if he was a Lamb. Especially knowing how attuned he'd been lately. All the more reason to move faster.

She felt herself warm up and the smell of Ugonna's room slam into her. Sweat, cologne, and there might have been an orange rotting behind something somewhere in the room. She looked at Ugonna as he shifted positions. He was sensitive, all right. He was asleep but he *knew* she was there, that's how Anatov described this kind of thing. She didn't have much time.

Gently but firmly, she pushed the bed and touched the exposed floorboard. She felt around the edges and located the notch and lifted it up. There was the money. Rolls and rolls of American dollar bills and naira, held together tightly with rubber bands. She grabbed them and quickly began rubbing them on her arm. She rubbed and rubbed, watching her brother. He shifted in his bed again but then came to rest and didn't move.

She breathed on the wads of cash and then got up. He was now tossing and turning, trying to thrash himself awake. Unsure of what to do, she took the chance. If she failed and he saw her, she'd certainly be caned this time. Having Sugar Cream as a mentor, the very person who would decide on punishment, wouldn't ensure her of any sympathy. As a matter of fact, it would probably get her the harshest punishment. Sugar Cream was the best teacher she could have hoped for and one of Sunny's favorite people, but she was also a hard,

hard woman. There was a reason she was the Head Librarian.

Sunny ran toward the door, bringing forth her spirit face. She leaped over Ugonna's piles of books. Then she dove through the keyhole just as her brother sat up. Once on the other side, she ran off. She had seconds where she would not be heard. When she made it to her room, she waited quietly until she became substantial. Then she quickly grabbed the Mami Wata comb in her hair and used one of the teeth to pick the lock. She opened the door and went in.

"Did you get it?" Chukwu asked.

She looked down at her hands. Along with her comb, she was carrying the wads of cash. It had worked. She smiled, hearing a *chink* outside her door as a *chittim* fell in the hallway. She'd never carried anything with her before when she glided between the wilderness and the physical world like this.

She threw the money on Chukwu's lap. He grinned. "Thank you!"

She sat beside him on her bed. "You're not leaving until you tell me everything."

"No."

"Why?"

He looked at Sunny with eyes so ablaze that she nearly jumped off the bed and ran out of the room. "Why?" she asked again, grasping the rim of the bed to keep her steady. "What happened? Armed robbers? What . . ."

"Sunny. . . if I tell you, I'm putting you in danger. Even

seeing me here tonight isn't good," he said, looking away. "The less you know, the better it will be if they come looking for me here."

She touched his hard muscular shoulder and he winced. "Don't," he whispered.

"Is anything broken?" she quietly asked.

"I don't know," he said. "Maybe one or two of my ribs."

"Will you see a doctor?"

"Yes. When I can. I promise."

"Please, Chukwu, what happened?"

The pained look crossed his face again. And he thought for a long time. He glanced at the door. And then he started talking. And the very thing that Sunny suspected and had feared from the moment he left for school turned out to have happened.

10
BROTHERLY LOVE

Okay, Sunny. I'll tell you . . . but only you. You . . . you have a lot of secrets, but you know how to keep them, too.

I understand why Daddy wanted me to live in the government hostel, instead of the privately owned one. I'm not a fool. If you don't live life, you will be nothing. And to live life, you have to live with people. Real people. Yeah, I wanted to live with the high and mighty, the wealthy, the comfortable. Who wouldn't? Have you seen the satellite hostels, Sunny? They're self-contained. They've got laundry, a restaurant where they will make whatever you ask for, new furniture, you get your own room . . . or something like that. Of course, I wanted to live there. But it's expensive. It's a waste of money.

When Daddy said I had to live in the government hostel, I said fine. Whatever. It's all good. I knew he was trying to teach me a lesson. He thought I was soft after all those early years in America. I was just happy to get the hell out of the house and be on my own. My hostel room's hot and ugly. The beds are hard. You share the room with five guys, some are second and third year. They'll bring girls in there at night. I'm not even going to give you the details of that. You're too young.

Anyway, you know how I like to work out. There was a place in the basement of one of the off-campus hostels. They've got all sorts of free weights in there and a lot of the heavier weights where they'd use cement blocks and sand bags. Really serious stuff.

Adebayo and I started going there in the evenings after class, maybe three or four times a week. We both liked to pull heavyweight, so we had the same routine. You know Adebayo, right? We've been in the same class since we were little, and we played a lot of soccer together. Remember when I left for university? He was the one who went with me. Yes, him.

He and I, whenever there were parties we'd be the man show, you know, bodyguards, because we are so big and people are so afraid of us. And I was the head of the soccer team, so no one wanted to mess with me anyway. Adebayo and I, we were brothers from another mother. We thrived in that gym, like weeds. It was so hot in there, even though it was underground. It was just a bunch of guys, pulling weight like gorillas. Raw

power. There were no women, so sometimes we'd be pulling in our underpants while these big fans would be blowing on us. It stank of sweat and the walls were real grimy. Sunny, you'd hate that place. But I loved it. My classes were tough; I'd go there to relax my head. Life was good . . . at first.

It all changed last week. Adebayo and I went there that early evening. It was Friday, so I was in a good mood. Later, we were going to meet up with some ladies; there was a party, too. We were working out. Pulling 10/10. We had just started at about 160 pounds. Then we'd load more, gradually. I remember, we were on our fifth round when Adebayo excused himself. He said he had to go to the bathroom. I just kept working out. I was at seven reps, pulling really hard, straining, screaming. I wanted to get that burn, you know? When you bench, it's no pain, no gain.

Not only had Adebayo left, but now I saw two guys come in. Not as swollen as me, but they were big enough and obviously a bit older. Taller. They started applauding me. I kept pushing up on the bar, putting on a show. I was the only one in the gym, but it was just two guys, Sunny. You don't know me; I can defend myself really good. I know boxing as well as I play soccer. You and Ugonna never knew about the places where the matches took place, but I used to win lots of money boxing. How do you think I got that money I put in the floor? You all just thought my bruises were from soccer. Who no know, no go know, right? So I wasn't afraid. But then another two guys

came in. One of them was Adebayo, and he seemed to know the other three guys.

They all approached me. The three strangers were dressed for the street, so they must have come from outside. They were smiling and seemed nice enough.

"Well done," Adebayo said. But he didn't tell me the names of these guys.

"You are a strong man," the tallest one said, looking down at me as I struggled to put the bar and weights back on the bar rest. They didn't help me. "We are proud of you."

I smiled and sat up. I was wearing nothing but my boxer shorts and my muscles were bouncing. "Thank you," I said.

"We have something to tell you and it's very important." The other ones just stood behind him. "You need to know the rules and regulations of campus."

I immediately relaxed. This was all it was about, campus stuff. And I wanted to do well in school. These guys were here to help me. Great. Good. Since I'd gotten there, I hadn't had a mentor or any older student offer to show me how things were done and what was best. So this was a relief.

Right after that, we all went to a local cafeteria that we called the Cholera Joint. It was just down the road. The place is nothing special. They serve things like rice, beans, bread, and eba. Good, cheap food. You bring your plate to the stand and tell them what to put on it. Then you sit at one of the plastic tables and chairs and eat. It's mainly for us local students, but

you get kabu kabu *and* okada *drivers who come there often, too.*

So there the five of us were. I saw all of them as my friends because Adebayo was my friend and they were his friends. I remember what everyone ordered. All of them chose rice, plantain, and beef. I chose my favorite, rice and beans. They make them nice at the Cholera Joint. I paid for all the food. It was a lot of money for me, but I had it. You know me, if I have it, then I spend it and when I don't have it, I don't miss it. Plus, I was in a good mood. These guys wanted to help me fold smoothly into university life. I don't know why I didn't put two and two together at the time. I do not know. Maybe I was blinded by hope.

Anyway, by the time we finished, it was almost eight o'clock and getting dark. We walked down the street about a half mile. The area was mainly occupied by the other two-story satellite hostels, the occasional tree. It is not a busy street. As a matter of fact, the street was so empty that we only met a few people along the way and there were no cars. It was a warm night, so because I'd recently worked out and then eaten, I was sweating. Eventually, they stopped under a low shaded mango tree. By this time it was completely dark and under that tree, no one could see us. Still, I wasn't scared. Adebayo was with me, and I just knew I could handle the other three if I needed to . . . if they turned out to not be so friendly.

One of them flicked on a torch and flashed it into the leaves above.

"Look, we've been watching you," the tall one said. "We have something important to tell you." At this point I glanced at Adebayo, and in the dim light that reflected from the flashlight, I saw him look away. "You're a strong guy, physically. Smart, get good grades, you were near the top of your high school class, the ladies like you . . ." He paused. "And we hear your little sister is albeeno, maybe even one of those child witches you hear about."

"What?" I exclaimed. "She's not . . ."

"No, no, relax. It's good. A child witch is power. We like what we see when we see you," he said, holding a hand up for me to stop talking. "We want only your success. And you will have all the advantages in school if you join us."

"Huh? How . . . Where? Be clear, I'm not understanding," I stammered. My mouth suddenly felt dry. Sunny, it was only at this time that I realized what was really going on, and it was something I heard was very common, but I never imagined would happen to me.

"We are the Great Red Sharks," he said.

Shit, shit, shit, I thought. You've probably even heard of them. "Fine . . . good," I said, still not sure what to say or think.

"Do you understand? The Red Sharks is one of the strongest confraternities in Nigeria."

He'd confirmed it. Now I was scared. Dad warned me about all this confraternity nonsense before I left. You and Ugonna have heard the stories of students going missing or getting killed

in fights. It's scarier and more common than all that Black Hat stuff from last year. Dad said they'd approach me and that I was to always say no. But it's not the same when you are right there looking into their eyes and they are looking into yours and they know who you are. My best friend, Adebayo, was in the Red Sharks. And that meant they knew everything about me already, because he did. How had he kept this kind of secret from me for so many weeks?! I didn't even notice any change in his behavior. I saw him often enough that I didn't know he snuck off anywhere else. But then again, it's a known fact that all confraternity meetings happen in the night.

I almost ran. I considered it with every part of my being. I must have tensed up because Adebayo grabbed my arm and held it tightly. "Calm down," he said. "It's not what you think. You'll have a chance to get any grade you want. You'll get to be a lecturer! No one can harm you. You want money? Many of the Red Shark members are from filthy-rich families. They'll happily blow their wealth on you if you join."

I admit, I was a little dazzled. Especially by the idea of being a lecturer. I could already see the pride on Daddy's face when I told him about it. You know how he is. "I'll think about it," I said.

"You have three days," the tall one said.

For three days, I thought about it. I went out that night, met up with the girls, and partied. I studied hard the entire weekend. I worked out at the gym with Adebayo, and we acted

like nothing was happening. Come Monday morning, they showed up at my room. Adebayo wasn't there. It was the tall one and one of the others.

"What is your response?" the tall one asked.

I asked them to explain exactly what they wanted again, and he didn't hesitate or get irritated. The tall one pulled me into the hallway and quietly told me that this was an invitation to join the Red Sharks. Then he and the other guy waited.

I laughed and nodded. "Okay."

They both smiled and we all shook hands, snapping fingers at the end. I began to relax again. Maybe Adebayo is right, I thought. Maybe it isn't so bad.

"We'll come back tonight," the tall one said.

At one thirty A.M.*, the tall one pounded on my door. The noise woke and angered my roommates; they got even angrier when they learned that it was for me. I quickly dressed and left with the tall guy. When I got outside, it was dark because the power had gone out. But there were three sets of eyes in the dark, and they belonged to three big guys. "You must agree to join the others," the tall guy said.*

I nodded. They blindfolded me with a red handkerchief and tied my hands. At this point, so much was going through my head. I was thinking I'd made a terrible mistake. Sunny, I kept seeing you, Mummy, Daddy, Ugonna, everyone. I kept wishing I were with you all and not where I was. I started wondering if I'd ever see any of you again!

We must have walked about three miles. It felt like it. It was a long way. When they took the blindfold off me, we were in the bush. One that I didn't recognize. They untied my hands. I looked around. Someone had a lamp, and I could see faces now. There were ten guys. Three of them were my professors, two of them were classmates, Adebayo was one of them, too.

They were all wearing red shirts, black trousers, black caps, and red armbands. One of them was singing some native song, and some were dancing and clapping to it. They were all older than me, except for Adebayo, but none was swollen like me and I was sure none of them knew how to box. If I had to fight, I would.

"What is your name?" a stocky guy of about nineteen asked me. He was light-skinned, probably Igbo, and had several keloids on his chin nestled in his slight beard.

"Chukwu," I said.

The man turned to the others. "His name is Chukwu."

They all stepped closer and grunted that they'd heard him. I tried to make eye contact with Adebayo, but he wouldn't look at my face. Neither would my professors and friends. It was like they were pretending not to know me.

"I am the leader, the Capo," the man with the keloids said.

"Okay," I said.

"Lie down," Capo said.

"Why?" I asked, surprised.

Before I knew it Adebayo, my best friend, stepped up to

*me and slapped me hard across the face. I didn't even think;
I hit him right back with a powerful uppercut blow. He fell to
the ground. I know how to take a man out. Adebayo is my best
friend, but I was terrified and angry as hell. No one slaps me!*

They all jumped on me then. All ten of them, kicking,
punching, stomping. I curled myself into a ball, trying to protect my body as much as I could. I remember being horrified
but also very, very angry. I kept thinking, I'm going to get out
of here. When I do, I'll beat them down one after the other.
Just need to get out from under them. *But I couldn't, Sunny!
When ten people attack you . . . you have no chance. The strikes,
the weight, the pain, you* CAN'T BREATHE!

They beat you like that so that you will have no mercy in
the future. What I later learned is that in the bush, if an initiate died from the beating, he was buried right then and there.
That place was full of bones. It's haunted. How many dead
students were watching me, wondering if I would join them
in the spirit world that night? When you hear about students
disappearing, this is one of the places where many of them go.

*Those guys beat me until I was barely able to gasp for air.
Everything was silver blue red, but somehow I didn't lose consciousness. I felt that if I did fall into the darkness that was
calling me, I'd never return. I thought of you all. If I died, I'd
be putting you in danger because Mummy and Daddy would
come looking for me, asking questions. Who knows what the
Red Sharks would do to them if they got too close to the truth?*

So I stayed awake. I watched them start walking away, one after the other. Capo was the first to leave. "Let the devil that led you here guide you," he whispered into my ear. He firmly took Adebayo by the arm, dragging him away. Then the others left one by one. No one did a thing to help me.

I lay there, wheezing, painfully coughing, feeling the blood and sweat seep from me, mosquitoes coming in droves to bite me and drink my draining blood. I couldn't believe what had happened to me. It's one thing to take a few hits in a boxing match or a hard kick on the soccer field, it's another to be beaten down by ten big men. No mercy. No care for vital or sensitive organs. No rescue. I didn't know where I was and I was in the dark. In the bush. I was alone, Sunny. So alone.

I don't know how long I lay there. Maybe about a half hour. Sometimes things were very dim; other times, I was wide awake with terrible throbbing pain. Then I heard rustling and footsteps. Someone was beside me. That someone put his hands beneath my body and helped me stand up. I groaned and whimpered. I must have sounded like a dying old man. But at that time, I didn't care. I was barely conscious. The world was swimming, and I didn't know up from down. My chest was a knot of pain. My legs were numb. I felt wet all over. I could smell myself . . . I may have . . . there was more than the reek of sweat and blood on me. Slowly, we started walking.

"Never let anyone know I helped you," he said. I started weeping. He helped me get to my hostel. It was almost four A.M.

"That was the first phase of initiation," Adebayo said, looking at me gravely. "The next will be tomorrow night. It will go up to seven days."

"Oh my God," I whispered.

"Remember when I said I was robbed by those guys that first week we were here?"

When I realized, I gasped. "You were all bloody."

He nodded.

"And cut up. Your arms were . . . That was them?"

"If I can survive it," he said, "you can."

"No," I said. We stood outside my room whispering like devils in the night. Inside, my hostel mates were all asleep.

"There's nothing you can do to stop it now," he said. "You either make it through or you die. Now you know everyone's face. You can betray us." He gave me a first-aid kit and quickly left. That was the first initiation.

I cleaned myself up as best I could. I was aching all over, bleeding, cut. My hostel mates looked at me with fear, but none of them asked me a thing. I went to class that next day. No one was going to keep me down, I decided. I limped into class and stared my professor in the face as he lectured about mathematics. He acted like he was just my professor and I was just his student. He pretended that he was not one of the Red Shark members who'd tried to kill me the night before. Adebayo and I went to the Cholera Joint together for lunch. He, too, acted like nothing happened. He said nothing about my limping, but he did slow his walk for me.

Night fell. It had rained during the day, so it was cooler. My skin was itchy from mosquito bites and from scabbing skin. I felt inflamed all over. Again, I nearly ran. I wanted to jump in my Jeep and just drive. But . . . I don't know. I stayed. What could be worse than last night? *I thought.* I wasn't going to run from anybody.

They came at three A.M. *They didn't blindfold me or tie my hands. I knew where the place was, anyway. And I hadn't run, so to them I had resigned myself to my fate. I wasn't afraid. They brought me to the haunted bush where everyone was wait-ing for me. More than ten guys this time. Probably closer to thirty. All in red and black.*

They introduced me to "the family" from Capo to me; my new name was Yung C. Then Capo asked me to step up. When I did, Capo grabbed my shoulders. I immediately tensed up, a thousand different flares of still-raw pain went through me. But I stayed calm. Some guys came up behind and beside me and held my arms.

One of the members stepped up beside Capo with something in his hand. Another member shined a flashlight on my other hand. Those guys holding me began to push me down. "Don't fight," one of them said, straining as I resisted. Another guy joined them, and they eventually wrestled me to the ground and . . . and Capo brought these clamps out of his pocket. They were holding me down, and two more guys came and held my head down. One of them squeezed my cheeks hard and said, "Open! Open your mouth!" After a while, the pain was so much that I did.

Capo knelt over me with those clamps, and I understood exactly what was about to happen. I started bucking and trying to free myself. But there were so many guys, I was trapped.

"One of a Red Shark's teeth must be taken to signify he is one with the Sharks."

"You bite him and we kill you," the one squeezing my mouth open growled. The guy was serious. And he looked like he was hoping to have to do it.

"We take one of the ones near the back," Capo said. He was grinning, enjoying himself. How many times had he done this? I think he wanted me to give him a reason to bash my face with those clamps before pulling my tooth, anyway. I could see it in his eyes. So I stopped struggling. He took the one on the bottom right in the back. See the hole? I nearly blacked out. He pulled and pulled. Then I heard it rip. I whimpered with pain, saliva and blood filling my mouth.

"There it goes. Got it," he said. He didn't even wipe it off as he jiggled it about in his hand, laughing almost hysterically. Then he brought something out of his pocket and added it to my tooth in his hand. He shook them and together they made a clinking sound. Then he blew hard into his hand. When he shook it, there was no clinking sound. And when he opened his hand, my tooth was replaced with a larger, pointier yellow tooth—a shark tooth.

Several of the members gasped at his cheap magic trick. They all let go of me and I just lay there, feeling the mosquitoes

biting me—my own bite one tooth less. I glared at Capo as he grinned down at me. That Capo. He is an evil man. Him, in particular.

I was exhausted, but there was more to come. They sat me up.

"You see this?" Capo said, kneeling before me, holding the shark tooth to my face. "This was your tooth. You have become a Red Shark like the rest of us now." The smile dropped from his face. "Hold out your hand."

The shark tooth looked sharp as hell. They had to grab me again and force my hand open. They cut me deeply on my hand. I didn't scream, but I stamped my foot really hard and fought not to struggle. If I did, the guys holding me would hold me tighter and I didn't want that. I breathed through my nostrils and tears bled from my eyes as a clay pot was held beneath my bleeding hand. My blood mixed with the blood of the other confraternity members who'd all done the same thing for their initiation.

"This is a symbol of our love for one another," Capo said. "Blood is blood."

The pact was sealed. Afterward, there was no beating. They sang traditional songs and gave speeches of welcome. I heard none of it. I only had one thing in my head at this point.

The Capo was always the first to leave. Then it was in order of rank. With Adebayo and I leaving together last. He told me that the next night, I'd be given three tasks to complete.

But, Sunny, there was no way in hell that I was going to stick around for any of it. I was sure one of those tasks was going to be that I hurt or kill someone! They are looking for me right now. Probably turning my entire hostel room upside down. I feel sorry for my roommates. I took all my things, though. I didn't tell Adebayo. How could I trust him? He's the one who told them about me. You see this? A medical student friend of mine gave me these stitches just before I left. I was lucky he helped me. Otherwise, my hand would probably be infected. I've been staying with lady friends, one night here, another night there, since Thursday.

So there it is, Sunny, I . . . I am a member of a secret society of the most dangerous kind and I've just gone AWOL, I've deserted, run off. They will want to kill me. But if I stay . . .

Sunny just gazed at her brother as he looked away, shaking his head. "If I stay, they'll turn me into a monster," he said.

She needed a moment to get her mind around it. Her old-est brother, Chukwu, was in a secret society . . . just as she was. He'd been through an initiation as she had been. But it wasn't the same. She loved her society; he was running from his. He could speak about it, but she could not. She blinked away tears as she felt something hard and hot in her chest. Rage. Her brother had been one of the banes of her existence for most of her childhood, though since she'd become a Leop-

ard Person, their relationship had improved. Nonetheless, she could not ever, ever, ever bear anyone harming him. This realization surprised her as much as the intensity of her rage did.

"I have to go," he suddenly said.

"Where?" she asked, grabbing his arm.

Her brother frowned, looking at her hand gripping the flesh of his upper arm. "I have a lady friend in Aba who I can stay with for a few days. Then . . . I don't know."

Sunny's mind was so awash with anger and the pain of his story that she was finding it hard to focus. His face was so battered that he barely looked like her brother. Every motion he made was hindered by pain. On top of this, those idiots were robbing him of his future by scaring him away from school.

Her brother got up. Slowly.

"Wait," she said, running to her underwear drawer. She took out the plastic box where she kept the little naira she had and twenty American dollars from when they'd moved back from New York years ago. "Here," she said, shoving it in his hands. "Take this."

"I can't . . ."

"Yes, you can," she said. The wheels in her head had begun to turn. She wouldn't tell her parents. Not yet. "You have your phone?"

"Yes," he said.

"Okay . . . stay with your friend for now," she said. "But you're going to go back to school soon."

"Didn't you hear all I told you, Sunny? They'll kill me if I go back. They may even come here looking for me! I can't . . ."

"Have faith," Sunny said. "Have faith."

She gave him a gentle hug and then helped him quietly leave the house. She watched him slowly climb into his orange Jeep.

"Keep your phone close," she said. "Rest, eat, and . . . Chukwu, it's going to be okay."

He paused, looking into her eyes. "What makes you so sure?"

"Just trust me."

He smiled for the first time since he saw her. "Sunny, what's happened to you?"

She only smiled back.

"Whatever it is, it's good. It's good." He started the car.

"Keep your phone close," she repeated. Then she quickly added, "I'll call you in a day or so."

He nodded. "Not a word to Mummy, Daddy, or Ugonna."

She nodded.

Then he was gone. She went back inside and slept for three solid hours. She needed her rest. She had much more than school to handle come morning.

11
WAYS

As soon as Orlu climbed on the *okada* to go see his crazy auntie Uju, Sunny took off toward home. She leaped over the open gutter, leaving school grounds, and quickly jogged along the dirt path beside the road. She ran around students on their way home and avoided *okada* who drove dangerously close to the path as they sped and wove between cars and trucks.

She passed the usual shops and then the half-finished house that had been in construction for over five years. The run-down office building beside it looked even worse now that the house was almost complete. When she reached her neighborhood, she absentmindedly ran a hand over the smooth

trunk of the palm tree growing on the corner of the street. She slowed down now, bringing out a handkerchief and dabbing her brow. She shut her eyes and took a deep breath. Getting through the school day had been hard. Not telling Orlu had been even harder. Sunny knew he'd disagree with what she planned to do. He'd push her to tell her parents.

Her eyes stung now. Then they grew moist. All day, she'd avoided thinking about her brother's story and his face, oh, his face, as best she could. But now that she was out of school and away from Orlu, she just wanted to sit in the road and cry her eyes out. She walked faster. Her parents wouldn't be home yet, but if Ugonna was home and she saw him, she'd break down and tell him everything.

When she arrived at Chichi's hut and saw her sitting on a chair outside, she knew she'd done the right thing. Her eyes filled with tears as she approached the one person she thought could help her. Chichi was reading a thick book and when she looked up at Sunny, she grinned. "You've gotta see this book! It's a novel set entirely in the *wilderness*! Of all people, you'll . . ." The smile dropped from her face. She closed the book and got to her feet. She placed the book on the chair. "Sunny! What's wrong?"

Sunny let her backpack drop to the dirt path that ran up to Chichi's hut, now unable to control her tears. "I . . . I . . . I . . ." she sobbed.

"What happened?" Chichi said, running up and taking

both of Sunny's hands. Chichi was already short and she hadn't grown any in the last year, whereas Sunny was pushing five foot nine and had gained several pounds of lean muscle. Still, Chichi managed to hold Sunny up and help her into the hut. Sunny sat down hard in one of the cushioned chairs inside the hut, tears still draining from her eyes. Chichi knelt before her and looked into her face.

"Sunny," she softly said. "Did someone . . ."

"It's my brother!" she managed to wail. "He's in *terrible* trouble! They'll kill him!"

Sunny told Chichi everything. Recounting Chukwu's story between tears, foot stamping, and cursing, something Sunny rarely ever did. Retelling the story to Chichi seemed to bring it alive that much more for Sunny. It was like stepping into Chukwu's shoes. There were three reasons Sunny went to Chichi. The first was that she knew Chichi had always liked Chukwu. Chichi thought he was pretty and liking him had always been a source of argument between her and Sasha. The second reason she went to Chichi was because Chichi could keep secrets, even from Orlu and Sasha. And the third was that Chichi would be willing to break the rules and risk punishment to help Chukwu because trouble-making and daring were in her blood.

"Did you know that these damn societies were originally formed to make sure there was always academic freedom and to cure society's problems?" Chichi shouted as she paced the

floor. "People like Professor Wole Soyinka and Aig-Imokhuede started them!" She was as angry as Sunny. "Now these young people who know nothing are crippling the highest place of Lamb education?! The university is all the Lambs have! Without the university, they'd be intolerable. They have no other urge to learn. I didn't know it was full of . . . of social disease."

"It is," Sunny said. "You can't really be a top student there without having to join or at least deal with them."

They were quiet now. Chichi stood in the middle of the hut frowning. Sunny sat in the chair looking at her sandaled feet. There was no breeze outside and it was easily close to ninety degrees, yet inside the hut it was cool as a clam. The floor of the hut was dirt, the bed Chichi and her mother shared to the right and many stacks of books to the left. They had so little, yet Chichi and her mother combined were a force powerful enough to be of great importance to the Leopard Knocks elders.

"So what do you want to do?" Chichi quietly asked.

Sunny didn't look up. There was a storm rolling in her mind. She couldn't get the image of her brother's battered face out of her head. This was his life at stake and his future. "What happens if juju is performed against a Lamb?"

"You already know that," she said. "Remember what happened when you showed Jibaku your spirit face? You only got off easy because you were a new free agent."

"No, I don't mean minor stuff. Serious juju."

Chichi looked closely at Sunny, and Sunny didn't look away. "I don't know," Chichi said. She cocked her head. "Why?"

"I want to make them suffer," Sunny said, clenching her fists. It felt good to speak her thoughts to Chichi. "Not just his so-called friend Adebayo, or their Capo leader. I want to make *all* of them suffer."

They were quiet, staring into each other's eyes. Chichi looked away first.

"Even if you will suffer for making them suffer?" Chichi asked, looking at her feet.

"Yes," Sunny firmly said. "It will be worth the sacrifice. My brother will at least be able to go back to school. Just help me with what I have to do and then step back. I don't want you to . . ."

"Oh, I'm not going to let you take the fall alone," Chichi said, looking up.

"No . . . no, Chichi, if it's just me, maybe . . ."

"You came to me for a reason, right?" Chichi said. Now she was smiling that smile she only flashed when she was up to something. "You know I know . . . ways."

Sunny said nothing. She had never been a good liar.

"You waited until Orlu had to go see his auntie. You knew Sasha would be with Kehinde today. You wanted to speak to me alone," she said. "You're smart, Sunny. And when you need to use them, you have claws. Listen, I may know a way

around the rules. We will get caught but not for the worst of it, if we do this right."

"Do what?"

"Well, they think his sister is a witch, right?"

"Yeah, but not a Leopard Person, just one of those child witches," Sunny said.

"Well, be what they say you are, then," she said. "The Red Sharks always meet at night. So, let's meet them in the night."

Sunny reported back to her mother to tell her where she was and that she'd be home in a half hour while Chichi made some tea. As soon as Sunny got off the phone, Chichi said, "Come sit down."

She's set up two mismatched and chipped porcelain cups and filled them with tea, making Sunny's just as she liked it, Lipton with just a hint of sugar. "Let's relax for a second before we do this," Chichi said, pulling up a stool and picking up a cup.

The tea was nice and Sunny allowed herself to settle down for the first time since before seeing her brother. Her tea was bitter and hot. It warmed her throat. She took a deep breath and slumped back into her seat, pushing away all the questions that tried to crowd her mind. All the while, Chichi leaned forward and watched her intensely as she, too, sipped her tea.

"You feel better now?" Chichi asked.

"Actually, yes, I do."

"Okay, let's call him," Chichi said.

"What? Now?"

"Yes, now. If we don't act soon, those crazies are going to show up at your house. We need to get fast and clear information."

"About what?"

"The Red Sharks," she said. "The members. Especially this Capo guy and Chukwu's friend Adebayo."

"Why? Why them?"

"You want to make them leave your brother alone, right?"

"Yeah."

"Then we need information."

Sunny frowned, squeezing her cup. She brought out her cell phone and brought up Chukwu's number and gave it to Chichi.

"What do I do?" she asked, looking at the screen.

"Just touch your finger to his picture," Sunny said.

"Right on it?"

"Yes."

Chichi fiddled with it and frowned. "Now there's a picture of some guy with dada hair kicking a football. What's Arsenal FC?"

"What'd you do? That's my background picture," Sunny said, taking the phone from her. She brought up her brother's

number again. Not only did Chichi not have a cell phone, but she didn't even know how to use them. Sunny touched Chukwu's photo in her favorites list and handed it back to Chichi. "Just talk when he . . . Wait, give it to me."

Chichi gave it back, and Sunny listened to it ring. He picked up on the second ring. "Sunny?"

"Hello? Chukwu, how are you?"

"I'm . . . fine."

"You're at your friend's?"

"Yes. I'm at Ejike's apartment."

"Okay . . . um, hang on, Chichi wants to talk to you," she quickly said.

"What?" he said. "Didn't I . . ."

She quickly handed the phone to Chichi.

"Chuks," Chichi said. "How you body dey?"

Sunny got up and started pacing the room, bracing herself to hear Chichi say "Hello? Hello??" repeatedly because her brother had hung up the phone. But instead Chichi started laughing. Then she said, "Relax, *sha*. She didn't tell anyone else. But I know everything, yes." She paused. "About you and your cultist *wahala*. Look, we want to help you, but we need some information." She motioned to Sunny to relax as she slowly ambled out of the hut. "Names, descriptions, where they live, stuff like that . . ."

Sunny sat back and sipped her tea. But she couldn't relax. When Chichi came back, she was smiling, the phone

pressed to her ear. "I don't have a cell phone, but you can always come to where I live and pick me up. Don't take me to any restaurant. I like roadside food only." She listened and then laughed hard. "That works. But give us three days. You will see. Nothing is more powerful than Mami Wata. Okay, o. Here is your sister." She handed the phone to Sunny. "We've got what we need."

"Hello?" Sunny said.

"What are you two going to do?" he asked.

"I don't really know yet. But . . . don't worry."

"Sunny," he said. "Can I ask you a question and will you answer it?"

"If I can." She glanced at Chichi, who was busy scribbling things down in a notebook.

"So you've joined Owumiri?"

"Huh?"

"Those Mami Wata women," he said. "Don't lie. Chichi told me so. I've heard a lot about them, and now I know why you've been sneaking around and acting funny."

Sunny frowned, utterly thrown off. She knew of Owumiri, too. They gathered at the river and the seaside and sang and danced and scared men. "I . . ."

"Look, I get it, Sunny," he said. "You need protection because . . . of your albino-ness."

"What?!" Sunny screeched.

"I understand," he said, ignoring her. "I haven't been the

best brother. Should have protected you more from all the bullshit."

"Chukwu . . . it's not . . ."

"Listen, Sunny, okay? Don't get close to these Red Shark guys. Work whatever it is you want to work from far away. The Red Sharks will kill you. They've killed before. You saw what they did to me, and that was just to become part of them! And don't expect me to go back to see if whatever you've done worked. Put it behind you."

"Just . . . sit tight," Sunny said.

"I plan to. And why'd you have to tell Chichi?! You want her to think I'm some sort of weakling? Look, call me in a few days, all right? By then I'll know more about my plans."

When he hung up, Sunny looked for Chichi and realized she was no longer in the hut. She went out the back door and found Chichi sitting on a mat reading outside. "I think I know what we should do." She laughed. "If we do it right, the worst punishment we'll get is a warning."

"What do you have in mind?"

"We'll set Murks on them," Chichi said. "Sasha and I have had to read up on these as second levelers. Anatov didn't spend much time on them, but it doesn't take much for Sasha and me." She grinned. Chichi's and Sasha's photographic memories were exactly what got them into so much trouble.

"What are Murks? Are they dangerous?"

"Of course they are. What do you think we *need* for

these guys? Fluffy pink talking bunnies? Murks look like tiny bats and dwell in pools of darkness—under a fallen tree in a lake, beneath houses, under beds, whatever. They are physical world–dwelling spirits so they can't be crushed and suffocated. Normally if you leave them alone, they will leave you alone, but what makes Leopard People interested in Murks is that they can be weaponized."

"What, you pack them in a gun or something?"

Chichi giggled. "No, no. You get them in the right mood, and they will do whatever mischief you ask them to do, especially when it comes to harming others. Murks have 'murky souls,' that's how they got their name. Give me a day or so to read up a bit more on them. Just follow my lead. I know exactly what to do."

12

MURKED

Sunny and Chichi lay on their bellies peeking through a bush beside a palm tree. They wore black pants and black sweat-shirts with hoods they'd bought from Leopard Knocks.

It had taken one day to find them. Chichi had merely used Adebayo's full name in a dowsing charm she'd read about in a German book of juju. It took fifteen minutes for the funky train to get them to campus one night later, when the Red Sharks were set to meet and discuss what to do about Chukwu. Then Sunny and Chichi simply followed them into the bush. Once in, it had been easy enough to creep up on them, for they were singing and clapping. Sunny couldn't un-derstand the words to the song, but Chichi could.

"What the hell?" Chichi whispered, looking disgusted.

"What?"

"They're calling to the devil in Yoruba," Chichi said.

Sunny shivered.

Two of the guys started building a fire, another two set down a cooler and one other set down a chair. A light-brown-skinned guy with keloids on his chin sat in the chair. This had to be Capo, the leader. The one who after having her brother beaten by ten guys had pulled out Chukwu's tooth, cut him with a shark tooth, enjoyed all of it, and then left him to live or die. In the firelight, Sunny memorized his silhouette. Looking straight at the firelight made it hard for Sunny to see his face. She wasn't wearing her glasses and in the night; they would not have helped anyway. But she could make him out well enough. Sunny felt her own fire, which had been burning in her chest since seeing her brother's battered face.

After a few minutes, they stopped singing and all the members sat on the ground before Capo. One big beefy guy, whose muscles looked ready to burst out of his red shirt, stood behind Capo with his meaty arms across his chest. Then Capo was speaking, but he spoke in a low tone, and neither Sunny nor Chichi could hear. Sunny and Chichi weren't concerned about what was being said; they were just waiting for the right time. It came about a half hour later, when it must have been well past three A.M. They'd opened the cooler and had been drinking and drinking. Then Capo grabbed a bottle

of Guinness beer, drank it all at once, and started singing the devil song. Soon everyone joined him. As the minutes passed, their singing grew more drunken and frenzied.

"Okay," Chichi said. "I didn't plan for this, but it's *perfect*. We call the Murks on them, and they'll think it's the devil attacking them, not two Leopard girls hiding in the bushes. No council people can arrest us for that because we won't have broken the rules of exposure. I don't even think they'll have reason to give us a warning!"

Sunny grinned. "That's brilliant!" Her smile decreased a bit. "But what will the Murks do? Will it be enough? If we don't show ourselves, how will they know to leave us alone?"

"Just watch," Chichi said, bringing out her juju knife and a sack. "There's juju powder in here. Do *not* sneeze, no matter what."

The guys were singing crazily now. Sunny didn't think they'd notice if she sneezed her brains out.

"Bring your cell phone," Chichi whispered. "Remember, don't turn it on. The screen has to be dark."

Sunny brought it out and handed it to her. "I turned the contrast and brightness all the way down."

"Okay. And you set the timer, right?"

"Yes," she said. "It's ticking down now. Should have about thirty minutes before it stops."

"It won't ring or vibrate?"

"Right. It'll just stop timing."

"Okay. Here, touch the surface," Chichi said. "Run your fingertips over it."

After Sunny did this, Chichi took some powder between her fingertips. It looked like soot in the dim firelight. She blew it toward the men, and it traveled easily in a dark mist for several yards, mingling with and dimming the firelight. Chichi brought up her juju knife and spoke some rapid words in Efik, then she stabbed her knife into the soil and twisted it.

"Is that it?" Sunny asked, when nothing happened.

"Shhh," she said.

Sip! Something black flitted in front of them. Then it was gone. Then it came again and hovered before them. Even there in the dark, mere feet from the men who'd nearly killed her brother, Sunny found herself smiling. It was just so . . . *cute!* The small batlike creature was covered in downy black fur, its wings batting like those of a hummingbird. It hovered perfectly still so she could see its big black eyes, tiny snout, and pointy fox-like ears. It smelled strongly of perfumed oil.

"Who are you?" Chichi asked it.

It rapidly cheeped three times, and then said in a low voice that sounded like that of a very tall big man, "*Od'aro.*"

Every hair went up on Sunny's body as she went from delighted to terrified.

"It calls itself 'goodnight' in Yoruba," Chichi said. "Typical." Then she spoke to it in either Yoruba or Efik. It did a quick turn and then zipped off. Sunny heard it cheep, and

there were more responses from the treetops, which had started to shed leaves and shudder. The Red Shark members stopped singing, listening. One of them pointed at the fire, wobbling on his feet. But the fire was quickly dying, and soon they were all in darkness. Silence.

"Stupid boys think they are above reproach because they hurt and kill," Chichi whispered. "Let them learn."

"What are they going to do?"

"Watch."

The darkness that had fallen suddenly grew heavy and thick. The cheeping in the trees stopped, and the silence was as pure and weighted as the darkness. Sunny grabbed Chichi. She opened her mouth wide, to make sure there was still air and she could breathe it. She could. Then the screaming began.

"What is happening?" Sunny asked.

"Murks like to slap," Chichi said. "Their wings feel like hot steel."

Sunny and Chichi stood behind the bushes listening to the screams, yelps, and moans. *Let them hurt and remember my brother's face and his pain with every slap and scratch*, she thought. The sound of them running in all directions made Sunny freeze. For the amount of time Sunny had set the timer on her phone, the Murks would follow them to their homes, bringing their darkness and remaining quiet as air. And then when the members went to sleep, the Murks would bring the

nightmares. Nightmares that would call up her brother's face and name and warn the members to leave him alone forever or suffer more consequences. Chichi's plan was flawless. But it wasn't enough. Not for Sunny.

The darkness was lifting as the Murks broke away from one another and chose which member to harass. The fire exploded with light and for a moment, Sunny had a clear view. She saw the backs of several members' red shirts as they fled into the bush, some toward the way they'd come, others in opposite or adjacent directions. One member ran right into a tree, falling onto his back, a Murk scratching and slapping at his head. And there was Capo on the ground. He'd fallen over his own chair and was too drunk to get up with any speed. Beside Sunny, Chichi was quietly laughing her head off.

Sunny jumped up.

Chichi hiccupped as she fought to speak. "What the hell are . . ."

Stop, Sunny thought. At the same time, she dug within and touched but did not bring forth her spirit face. She didn't touch her juju knife. This was hers. Natural. Her temples ached and her skin cooled, just as Sugar Cream had said it would be. She didn't hesitate. She held out her hands and pushed as one would push water. She'd stopped the rush of time. Silence. Complete and total silence. And stillness. She didn't look at Chichi. Nor the suspended Murk that was

flying after one of the suspended members. There was Ade-
bayo, looking over his shoulder, a Murk right above his head.
Sunny didn't bother with him, either. She walked to where
Adebayo was looking. Toward Capo.

As soon as she saw him up close, she didn't doubt what
she'd done. The ground beneath him glowed a dull red, in the
shape of curled and sprawled skeletons. She could see them all
over, just beneath the ground. And Capo himself glowed with
the same dull light, especially his hands and mouth. This guy
was a Lamb version of Black Hat in the making. He'd killed
with his hands and mouth. Cannibal. Ritual killer. Sunny felt
her belly roll with nausea. How did her brother manage to fall
in with these guys? This man? Chukwu was lucky to manage
to fall out alive.

Capo was the only thing that was moving. He rolled onto
his back, clasping his throat. He wheezed loudly, his watering
eyes bulging. Sunny felt light-headed but otherwise perfectly
fine. She looked down on him with disgust and pushed back
her black hood. Capo's eyes grew wider.

"Do you know who I am?" she asked.

Still wheezing for air, slowly he nodded.

"You will die in less than a minute," she said. "You aren't
albino, so you can't move outside of time." She paused, utterly enjoying the look of pure terror and approaching death
on his face. And she enjoyed the fact that she was lying to
him. This was far more than a mere medical condition; it

was her being a Leopard Person born with a specific talent that she was practicing every day and . . . night. And it was her being *her*. "I'm Chukwu's child witch of a sister," she said. "You see me clearly. My name is Sunny Nwazue." His eyes were starting to close. "My brother will return to university. If any of you people lay a finger on him, I will bring a painful death to every one of your relatives and then you, especially you—I know what you've done. Do you understand?"

Capo nodded weakly as his eyes closed. Sunny quickly moved back to Chichi. Then she let go. Letting go was easier than getting ahold of time. She sank to her knees beside Chichi. She'd been standing on the other side of Chichi, and Chichi was still looking where she'd been. Now she turned to Sunny and did a double take. She looked where Sunny had been and then back to where Sunny now stood. "Sunny, what did you do?"

Sunny only shook her head, watching Capo yards away. All the others were gone. Capo wasn't moving.

"Did . . . did you kill him?" Chichi whispered. "Why didn't you just leave him?"

"You didn't see my brother," Sunny coldly said.

Capo twitched and suddenly jumped to his feet. He looked around drunkenly, and Sunny and Chichi ducked down. When he saw that he was alone, he started walking away. Then he turned back, dumped the water from the

cooler on the fire, and then stumbled back the way they'd all come.

Chichi and Sunny stayed down for a while in the dark. When it was clear that everyone was gone, they stood up. "What did you do?" Chichi asked again.

"What needed to be done."

Chichi looked hard at Sunny. "You were beside me and then you weren't. And I didn't see you near Capo," she said. "But . . . I saw him slump after you disappeared." She frowned as she thought hard. "Did you hold? Hold time? Is that what you and Sugar Cream have been working on?"

"Some, but that was the first time I tried it."

"He saw your face?"

She nodded.

"Shit," Chichi said.

"It's okay."

"No, it's not."

They walked back to the main road. It took them a half hour in the darkness even with a torch. When they reached the main road it wasn't five minutes before the black council car drove up to them and demanded that Sunny get into it. Sunny did so without a word of protest.

"Let my mom know that I'm okay," she told Chichi.

"Okay," Chichi said. She paused. "Give me your phone. If you don't, they will take it from you."

Sunny handed Chichi her phone. They looked at each

other for a moment. Then Sunny said, "I'll . . . I'll be okay."
For now, she thought. She didn't know about later. Still, as
the car drove soundlessly down the dark empty road, past
the satellite hostels where the university students who were
not up to satanic mischief slept soundly, Sunny felt it was
worth it.

13
DEBASEMENT

The ceremonial masks stared at Sunny. There were fifty-two of them. Over her months as Sugar Cream's student, she'd had plenty of time to count. The first time she was here, she'd thought there were only twenty, but then again, she'd been distracted by the fact that she was there at risk of being caned for showing her spirit face to Jibaku.

The masks didn't stay in the same spot, either. Every few days, some of them moved—sometimes across the wall, sometimes switching with the mask beside them. And some would change the expression on their faces. Sunny had learned early on not to touch them or mutter anything in anger near them. They would sometimes lick, smooch, try to bite or spit on her

hand, and they'd tell Sugar Cream anything she said.

Now all the masks looked either angry or deeply interested. Sugar Cream was scowling at Sunny. Sunny gazed right back. It was five A.M. and she'd walked up the Obi Library stairs alone, since she knew the way to Sugar Cream's office and she knew the consequences would probably be greater if she fled. She found Sugar Cream in her office sitting at her desk wearing a cream-colored nightgown, a cup of warm milky coffee in her hand.

"What happened?" Sugar Cream icily asked.

Sunny told Sugar Cream everything. She'd stood with her back straight and chin up. She'd fought keep her eyes dry and won, though when she described her brother's ordeal, her voice cracked twice and she felt light-headed. When she told of holding time, only then did Sugar Cream's eyebrows rise. But only the tiniest bit. Otherwise, her face remained like stone. This early morning, Sunny's mentor looked ancient. This morning, Sunny knew that she'd be caned.

"Chichi was right," Sugar Cream said when Sunny finished talking. "Do you see her here?" She paused. "Huh?" she suddenly snapped, making Sunny jump. "DO YOU SEE CHICHI HERE TO BE PUNISHED?"

"No, ma'am," Sunny quickly said.

"No, you don't. And it's not only because she made sure you two remained hidden and that those foul young men thought it was the devil attacking them and not you two.

Those men rock the foundation of learning in this country. We Leopard People have been working for *years* to eliminate these confraternities at their root. You two were given a pass for what you did. But then *you* crossed the line. You let your rage get the best of you."

Sunny looked down, frowning. *I don't care*, she thought. She knew if she had it all to do again, she'd do the same thing. She had to protect her brother. Sugar Cream knew this, too.

"With great power comes great responsibility, Sunny," Sugar Cream said. "You're young. You're a free agent who knows very little, but who is bursting with potential and passion. You're not the best or smartest of your age mates, but you are . . . interesting. This is why I took you on. But you need to learn control." She took a sip of her coffee. "And you need to learn the consequences."

After explaining to Sunny what would happen to her, Sugar Cream called two older students in the building. They were not to speak to Sunny. They weren't even to look at her. All they were to do was walk in front of and behind her. They led Sunny down the hallway to a gray door, and one of the students opened it. It led to a stairway. Sunny followed him in, the other student following behind Sunny. The walls here were made of a gray stone that looked like it had been carved bit by bit with an ice pick.

The steps were also made of the same roughly chiseled stone. As they descended, Sunny couldn't help the tears that

fell from her eyes. She counted thirty steps and still they kept going. It was like traveling into an underground cave. The air grew cooler and cooler until Sunny was shivering. She was glad that she still wore her jeans and the black hooded sweat-shirt over her T-shirt.

Down, down, down they went. To the Obi Library's infamous basement. Sugar Cream had ordered Sunny to stay here for three days as punishment for pulling a Lamb outside of time, a severe violation of Leopard doctrine, even for some-one of greater experience and age. Because Sunny was un-der twenty-five, her punishment was milder than if she were an adult. "If you were twenty-six," Sugar Cream had said, "you'd be caned and then sent down there for three months."

"Go in," one of the students now said. "And don't try to come up."

They left her. They didn't lock the door because there *was* no door, just an opening in the stone wall with the dimly lit stone stairway that led back up. Sunny turned around and took in her prison. The basement was large, smelled of dirt and mildew, and was filled with moldering bookshelves of moldering books. Books that had been replicated and brought down here to be disposed of in due time. The bookshelves had rotted, buckled, and fallen into decay. Obviously, some of the books had been forgotten. In the center of the basement was a dusty wooden platform with an old bronze statue of a squat toad with overly bulbous eyes. Sunny touched its large

head with her hand and sat on it as she watched the students leave.

Each day, they would bring her a meal and a large pitcher of water. She was given a bucket as her toilet, which would also be taken and emptied daily. Other than that, she would be alone down there. No blanket, no bathing, no light other than the dim one high on the ceiling.

As the sound of their footsteps receded, the fear set in. She'd heard terrible things about the basement. She sunk to the floor, leaning her head against the toad's head. "I did the right thing," she whispered. "I don't care what anyone says."

There were red spiders all over the place, especially on the ceiling. As she stared up at it, she noticed a large patch of churning red in the far left corner over one of the few bookcases that still stood. Slowly, Sunny walked across the dusty floor, her sandals grinding on the white marble. It wasn't just covered with dust, there was sand, too. From where, who knew? She stopped feet from the ceiling corner above, her mouth curling with disgust. Hundreds, maybe thousands of nasty, mewling red spiders churned in the corner. She squinted and shuddered. They were all milling around one enormous red spider the size of a dinner plate.

"Oh . . . God," she whispered, stepping away slowly. She was sure the thing was watching her, watching closely with its many eyes. She stumbled back to the large bronze toad,

the only thing in the room that felt . . . okay. She rested her back against it and wrapped her arms around her knees. The metal was comfortingly warm and immediately fatigue fell on her. It had to be nearing sunrise.

She'd snuck out of the house, journeyed to campus with Chichi, located and terrorized one of the most powerful confraternities in the area, and now here she was. This was the longest night of her life. Her eyes grew heavy. But there was no rest for the weary. The basement had no windows. She was deep beneath the ground; the place was like a tomb. And the one light bulb, which just *had* to be near the spiders, was greasy and dim, shining down on the older, used up, and discarded books. There were corners and crevices between fallen shelves, and the room was full of shadows and hiding places. All this made the scraping sound that much more terrifying.

The sound seemed to bear down on the marble floor. Then it dragged. Slow and steady. Then it stopped. Then it dragged and then stopped. It came from right behind one of the bookcases to Sunny's left. And she could see a bit of a shadow through two fallen shelves. But nothing more. Sunny had nothing with her. Nothing to throw. Nothing to clutch with fear.

"Oh," she whispered, trying to stay still. Willing herself to be invisible. She could become invisible. But not for very long. And to do so, she had to travel, to move. Would whatever it was come at her? *What* was it?

Scraaaaape. Pause. *Scraaaape.* Pause. It stopped just before it came into view. Sunny waited for what felt like fifteen
minutes, but the thing didn't show itself. Instead, quiet as
smoke, a flame burst from behind the books. A smokeless one.
No smell. No burning. Just the light and shadow of a flame.
Sunny, helpless and exhausted, leaned against the neck of the
bronze toad, staring at that which she could not see. Soon her
eyes went out of focus, and then slowly they shut.

Scraaaaape.

Sunny's eyes shot open and she jumped up. Her legs wobbled and buckled, and she fell against the toad, banging her
hip. A rotten-egg smell of sulfur stung her nose. She winced,
turning toward the sound and the stench. What she spotted
beside the bookcase made every hair in her body stand up.
Even from feet away, she could tell that they were human
bones, and not only because the one piled at the top was
a clearly human skull. One near the bottom was heavy and
long. A femur. And there was a hand sticking out of the center. The pile looked about the size of one human being, the
bones a dirty, rusty gray red.

Sunny didn't move. She couldn't move. Her eyes stared
and stared. Then they started to water.

Tap, tap, tap. She gasped and looked toward the staircase.
Someone was coming down. She looked back at the bones.
They were gone.

It was Samya, one of Sugar Cream's closest assistants. She was one of the few third levelers under the age of thirty that Leopard Knocks had. To pass *Ndibu*, one had to attend a meeting of masquerades *and* get a masquerade's consent to be a third leveler. To attend such a meeting, one had to slip into the wilderness, which meant the person had to die and come back. Only third levelers and up knew how this was done when one was not born with the natural ability. To reach the third level of *Ndibu* was like earning a PhD, and it was rare for one to be under the age of thirty-five. Samya was twenty-four.

She was a bookish woman who wore red plastic glasses and a long red dress, and had reddish-brown skin like Chichi and Chichi's mother. She'd piled her long braids atop her head as she carried the small tray. "Oh, Sunny, are you all right?" she asked. The worried look on her face cracked Sunny's wall of strength like a sheet of thin ice.

Her body grew warm and tingly, and her eyes stung with tears. "No," she whispered as Samya quickly came to her. She put the tray of food on the floor beside Sunny and gathered her in her arms.

"Why did you do it?"

"I had to!" Sunny sobbed. "I *had* to! It was my brother! You didn't see what they . . ." She couldn't breathe.

"Shhh, shhh," Samya said, holding her back. "Relax. Get ahold of yourself."

But Sunny's entire body was shuddering. Images of her

brother's battered face, eyes swollen, mouth swollen. His pain. Capo's terrified face as he gasped for air. Lying in wait in the bushes. Darkness. Screams.

"Sunny," Samya said shaking her. "You need to *calm down*." She paused. "There is something down here that can't know you are weak."

Sunny felt her nerves zing. There *was* something down here. She felt faint as she pushed her body to calm down. "What is it?"

"I can't say, and I can't come back," Samya said. "When someone is sent to the basement, a different student must bring down food on each day. I think Sugar Cream sent me first because she knew you'd need me. Don't expect the others that come to be helpful. They will . . . follow the rules."

"What rules?"

"Never mind," she quickly said. "Some things are worth it. Now listen, Sunny, and listen closely if you want to come out of here sane and alive. These books are old. They are used. They have been replaced, then cast aside. They will be dealt with eventually, but for now they are down here. Every book has a soul, every book . . . carries and attracts. There are sterilization and soothing jujus all over this room, but this is the earth. Something will always come and live here. In this case it is a djinn. It guards and hides in the books."

"Does it make fire that doesn't burn?"

Samya nodded and frowned. "So you've already seen it."

"Yes . . . its bones. I fell asleep and I woke up and it was right over there." She pointed to mere feet away.

"Oh my God, so soon?" Samya said, circling her head and snapping her finger. Then she looked at Sunny and gave the most pathetic reassuring smile Sunny had ever seen. "Listen, Sunny. It will try you."

"Try what?"

"*You*. It knows . . . Sunny, you aren't learned yet. You are just a free agent, but you were . . . are someone who did something in the wilderness. It was a good thing, I think. Otherwise, why would Ekwensu fear you? The thing down here is a djinn, and it'll read your past life as you being powerful in your present one, some sort of chosen one. So it will try you. It will want to see what you've got." She frowned. "Damn, Sunny, why did you have to get yourself thrown down here?"

"What do I do?"

Samya got up. "I don't really know." She looked at the staircase as if someone were calling her. Then she looked at Sunny. "Don't let it take you." She paused. "And . . . don't believe the silly Lamb stereotypes about djinni. They don't grant wishes and what they show you can be an illusion, but more times than not, it is real. They *can* harm you. Okay . . . I have to go." She pointed to the tray. "Eat all of it," she said. She looked Sunny in the eye. "*All* of it. You need your strength."

"Wait, wait," Sunny said as Samya moved quickly to the

staircase. "My parents! My family. Will someone . . ."

"Good luck, Sunny," she said over her shoulder. "Stay strong. Stay alive." Then she rushed up the stairs.

Sunny watched her go, listening as her steps grew fainter and fainter and then were gone. She sat against the bronze toad and stared at her tray of food. A bowl of dry-looking jollof rice with one chunk of tough-looking goat meat in the middle of it, an orange, and a bottle of water. She ate it all quickly, her eyes darting around like a scared rabbit. She didn't taste a bite of it. The scraping sound had begun again.

There was water somewhere in the basement. But she couldn't see it. *Drip, drip, drip.* Then stop. Then *drip, drip, drip.* Then stop. As if there was some machine turning it off and on. Trying to drive her mad. That would make two things with the same intention. A machine and a djinn. Sunny giggled to herself. Quietly. She had to stay quiet. The thing that was clumping and scraping about the room didn't seem to really see her. As the hours passed, she began to believe it was because of the bronze toad. Maybe there was something in it that kept the djinn at bay. For since that first time, it had not shown its bones to her. *Maybe I didn't really see the bones at all*, she thought. She giggled again. *If I don't move, then I'll be safe.*

The scraping was on the other side of the large room, its

noise echoing about the high ceiling. From where she was, she had a clear view of the red spiders, too. The big one was still in its spot. That was good. Yes, that was good. Her head pounded. How long had it been since Samya left? Three hours? Nine? All she had was the hanging dim light near the spiders.

"Chukwu, you better thank me when I get out of here," she whispered to herself. It was good to hear her voice, even if she couldn't raise it. "*If* I get out of here." She hugged herself closer to the bronze toad's warm body, pressing her head to it. Her comb clicked against the metal. She took it out and examined it, glad to have something else to focus on. She held it to her nose and smelled it. It smelled briny like the sea, but there was also a hint of flowers. The smell was pleasant. It smelled of outside. She smiled and whispered "Thank you" to the lady of the sea who'd saved her and then given her a gift that she could admire during a dark time.

"Whooooo oh whoooooo is Sunny Nwazuuuue?" she heard an ancient male voice suddenly sing. *Scraaaaape.* "Whoooo oh whooooo is Sunny Nwazuuuue?" the voice said again. Then another *scraaaaape.*

It had seen her. It had known she was there all along. The bronze toad was just a bronze toad. A decoration. An ornament in a room that was more a giant trash container than anything else. Sunny knew this. She'd just needed something to grasp because they'd given her nothing. They'd thrown

her down here, and they hadn't even given her a gun, a protective stone, a hard stick, nothing. She had her juju knife,
but she didn't know any protective charms against djinni or
ghosts.

She glanced up at the ceiling. The giant red spider was
still there and even from where she was, she felt more positive than ever that it was watching her. But the other smaller
ones had dissipated. Maybe they were all over the basement
now . . . including on the floor. She looked down and wasn't
surprised to see one scurrying across the sandy marble.

Suddenly, the entire room reeked so strongly of sulfur that
it hurt to breathe. Sunny jumped up and took off toward the
stairway that led out of the library basement, coughing. She
hadn't moved much in hours and her muscles were stiff, but
she ran up the stairway like a champion. Her sandals slapped
the concrete. She didn't dare glance back. Thus, she couldn't
have been more shocked when she found herself stumbling
right back into the Obi Library basement. Her sense of direction and gravity reeled for several moments as she came to
understand what had happened.

"What?!" she screeched.

"Whooo oh whooo is Sunny Nwazuuuue?" The voice
vibrated, coming from every direction and within Sunny's
head. She pressed her hands over her ears as she frantically
looked for a place to hide. There! A small space between two
fallen bookcases. Maybe she could hole up in that space for

two days, a day and a half, whatever amount of time she had left here. About to run for it, she shivered and looked to her left. This time she did scream. Because she'd been about to run, her leg muscles were like a tightly wound spring. She tried to change directions by a few degrees and her legs tangled. As she went down, she didn't take her eyes off the pile of bones. The skull had its jaw broken. There was a foot at the top. A hand tumbled down and landed facing upward like a dead white spider.

Phoom! The dried old bones suddenly burst into quiet smokeless flames.

Sunny hit the ground, and her hip was an explosion of pain. Still, she managed to roll to her side and pull her juju knife from her pocket. She did a quick flourish and caught the cool invisible pouch in her hand as she lay on her side. Then she drew a square in the air while muttering into the pouch the words Chichi had taught her. The only difference was that she spoke them in her native tongue of English instead of Chichi's native tongue of Efik. "Bring a thick barrier. Hold strong, too. From the very air I breathe. It must hold true!"

When the tumbled hand rolled toward her and then perched on its fingertips so that it could tap on the barrier, Sunny shivered.

"Free agent weak frightened magic," the voice said. "Shatters like glass." With these words, there was the sound of

glass breaking and falling to the marble floor. "What more do you have?"

Sunny had been practicing on her own and incorporating lessons Sugar Cream had taught her over the months. She calmed, forcing herself to look at the ancient pile of human bones that were engulfed in flames but not burning at all.

"Your entire body must relax, feel it drop. Then imagine your spirit dropping," Sugar Cream had said. "Think of Any-anwu. You are her and she is you. Remember your initiation? When you were pulled into the ground? Feel that. But feel it as if Anyanwu is pulling from your body." Before Sunny gave it a try, Sugar Cream had reminded her to make sure she was lying down.

Now Sunny was already on the floor. She rested her head back, keeping an eye on the bones. *Relax, relax, relax,* she thought. *Breathe.* She flared her nostrils, inhaling deeply through her nose. It took all she had, but she calmed herself. She would be okay. She might not have had too many real moments of terror in her thirteen years, but in her past life, she had. She couldn't remember them clearly, but she could feel those memories. Right on the tip of her mind. And she'd still gone on. Even if she died in this basement, she would go on in spirit. She relaxed more with the comfort of this remote knowledge. She relaxed. She dropped. She felt it physically, but it was much more than that.

"Oh, now it gets interesting," the voice said. "Welcome."

The marble floor was cool. It was a pure stone. An old, old stone. Maybe it had been in the earth longer than the Obi Library had existed. Maybe the basement was carved from what was already in the ground. It was so solid. Sunny got up. She flew, passing through the bookcases as if they were clouds. She was nothing but yellow mist. She knew there would be other things here, and she hoped she didn't run into them. But she couldn't afford to look around. She had to get away. And she couldn't stay partially in the wilderness for long. Not yet. Before she knew what she was doing or how quickly she'd traveled across the large room, she smashed into a wall.

They were made of the same marble. She could not pass through them, even if she dropped into the wilderness. How was this possible? *What kind of stone is this?* she wondered as she crumpled to the ground. *Scraaaape.* One by one, the bones dragged and tumbled toward her.

"Do you think this place is only *your* world?" the voice said. "It is physical and wilderness. It is a *full* place. You can't escape."

"What do you want?" she muttered. Not far from her on the floor were five red spiders. Two of them just stood there, seeming to watch her. The other three were running for cover.

"I want what you have," the voice said.

"Why?"

"They throw stupid Leopard People down here often. Timid, angry, weak-minded careless men and women who have nothing for me to take but a piece of their sanity, or some of a family member's future, meager gifts. But you . . . you have a soul that could release me from this place."

"Sunny?" someone called. "Sunny Nwazue?"

Sunny got to her feet, wobbly for a moment. Then steady. She'd hit the wall as something other than a physical body. She was shaken but okay.

"Sunny?" she heard the man call again. A human man. From near the staircase. Her second meal was here. She'd made it through the second day. But was it breakfast, lunch, or dinner?

"I'm here," she called, peeking around one of the book-shelves. He was a tall man of about her mother's age. He wore jeans and a black T-shirt and gym shoes. Not clothes she'd seen any of the Obi Library students wear during the day.

"Here is your dinner," he said, holding it out to her. If she had to guess, judging from his accent, this guy was from Lagos. He held the tray out to her. It was the same meal of jollof rice, goat meat, and water.

"Thank you," she said. "So, it's night, then? Do you know what time it is?"

The man didn't answer. He wouldn't even look her in the eye. He turned and started walking away.

"Sir? . . . *Oga?* Did you hear me?" Sunny asked, following

him as he walked toward the staircase. He moved quicker. Sunny put her tray on the ground, suddenly feeling panicky and invisible.

"Hey!" she shouted.

"I can't speak or look at you," he said stiffly, his back still to her. "The punishment is caning."

Sunny froze. Samya. She pressed her hand to her chest, shocked. "Oh," she breathed. "Oh no." She stepped away from the staircase, listening to the sound of the man's foot-steps grow fainter and fainter. *Stay strong,* Sunny thought, tears in her eyes. *I have to survive this. Otherwise, Samya will have been caned in vain.*

She whirled around when she heard a crunch. Her plate of rice looked as if a stone as heavy as a car had fallen on it. A red spider had been crushed beside it, too. The bottled water rolled and came to rest beside a bookcase. She heard the djinn chuckle from the other side of the room.

"That's really funny," she said, trying to keep her voice steady. Her mother had once told her that if she ever found herself facing a wild animal, never ever show fear. The djinn wasn't an animal. Well, not one of the physical world at least, but it was certainly wild. Up to now, Sunny had worn her fear on her sleeve. She couldn't help it; she was *scared.* However, her mother also liked to say that it was never too late.

Her legs tingled and shuddered as she slowly walked to-ward her water bottle. She bent and picked it up, unscrewed

the top, and took a deep, deep pull. The water washed into her parched body like rain on dry cracked earth. During the gliding lessons with Sugar Cream, she and Sunny never moved fully into the wilderness. Sunny was far from ready for that and to go in unready meant a quiet peaceful swift death to your physical body. However, Sugar Cream took Sunny "in and out," where she was in both the wilderness and the physical world, and instead of seeing one place, she saw two layered over each other. Sugar Cream described it as similar to looking at the world through an aquarium.

Learning how to go "in and out" or between was not so hard. Sunny had gone between naturally on her own when she'd first snuck out of the house through the keyhole thinking she'd worked her first juju. It was going into the wilderness completely that was extremely difficult. Whenever Sugar Cream had her do preparatory exercises for going into the wilderness, Sunny always found herself desperate for water afterward. "That's because water is life," Sugar Cream had said. "The body doesn't like for its soul to even *consider* entering the wilderness."

Sunny took another gulp and felt a little better. "You've forgotten what it's like to be human," she called out. "You should have crushed the water bottle. Humans need water more than food." Despite her fear, she smiled at her own words.

"I was never human," the djinn said.

As she drank, she looked around. More red spiders on the books feet away. The djinn's voice was still coming from the other side of the room but that didn't mean anything. Her eye went to one of the books in the fallen case in front of her. She pulled it from between two dusty hardcovers. Alex Haley's *Autobiography of Malcolm X*. A Lamb book. "What's that doing here?" she muttered. Beside it were several volumes on Leopard medicine and even more on Leopard world alliance law.

"Sunny!" She jumped. The voice was right behind her. "Eep!"

She was yanked back. There was a bright flash in her mind and a metallic sting so intense that she couldn't tell where she felt it. Then she was plunging into cool water. There was a splash. It was like her initiation when she burst into the river and was pulled along, except this felt like she was being pulled down, down, down instead of horizontally. She felt her body struggling for breath. She couldn't breathe! The cool water pressed in on her as she descended into the deep blue. She could see the dull basement light above her, slowly pulling itself away as she sank.

She thrashed and clutched her neck. Her lungs burned. Water rushed into her mouth, down her throat, into her chest. Even then she fought, but she was growing weak. She was dying. The djinn was drowning her.

The water was cool. She was cooling.

She let go of her neck. She let go.

Then the sensation of falling without falling. She hit some-thing hard. Colors zoomed around her. Mostly green. But she was vaguely aware of the library; she was in the library. Her chest felt heavy, full. She coughed sharply and grabbed for the bookcase. There was a red spider right beside her hand, but she didn't care. "No," the djinn said in her ear. "There is no escape. Come. Come completely." She could feel the bookcase melting in her hands, dissolving, as something yanked at her shoulders, pulling her back. She felt it in her chest, a warm sharp tearing sensation. Then she felt her spirit face rush forward.

"Oh," she heard the djinn say. Then it chuckled and drawled, "Who are you, Sunny Nwazue?"

She still felt the pain, but all over now, and she felt . . . dim, somehow muted. She'd held on to the case, trying to will herself out of the wilderness. But then she was holding on to nothing. Then the bookcase became a mass of bushes. But the spider on it didn't disappear; it sat there on the bush. She gasped. It was one of those creatures that existed in both worlds. It was still red but now the size of a basketball with fluorescent blue rings on its legs. The creature waved a leg at her and scurried away.

Sunny held on to the bush, realizing she wasn't breath-ing. She wore her spirit face. She was Anyanwu.

Her body. She was no body. She was yellow. The color of the sun. Light. In a sea of mostly green.

Green blobs undulated past. Pink and green insects with

green lines for wings. The wilderness looked like a jungle. There was sound, and it was thick and moist and fertile. Alive. She was afraid to speak.

"I see you," the djinn said. Its dusty voice was strong here. *It* was strong here.

All she could think of was death. How many seconds had passed? Would they find her body? Then the djinn was on her like a vampire. They went tumbling into some bushes as she fought to keep it from tearing off her mask. Was it a mask in the wilderness? Could it come *off*? She vaguely remembered what her father had said about masquerades: "Never unmask a masquerade. That is an abomination!" What happened if one's spirit face was torn off? Could the djinn then eat her soul like the meat of a cracked clam?

The djinn pinned her down in those bushes. It was stronger. It wasn't human. It wasn't dying. It knew this place. She was done for.

There was a large spider on its shoulder. It was red. With blue rings on it. Blue rings. Blue rings. Blue rings. The glimmer of sudden recognition was like a burning focal point of light in her brain, it was brilliant and it seared. She knew blue rings. She . . . *remembered.*

"I know you," she blurted, straining to hold the djinn off her.

"Yes, we've spent some time together," the djinn said, flashing a deeper red. "But don't worry. Soon, you won't know much else."

She wasn't talking to the djinn. As she desperately stared at the spider, she gasped, "I know you *all*."

The djinn's strength decreased as it tried to figure out what its prey was talking about and whom she was talking to. Then it noticed the spider on its shoulder. It released Anyanwu and scrambled back.

The spider leaped off the djinn and ran up to her and before she could say more, it turned its glowing backside to her and thrust its stinger into her yellow mist.

She was flying again. Backward, this time, across the marble floor. The sand beneath her bottom. Her skin was cool because she was soaking wet. She came to a stop just in front of the bronze toad. She opened her mouth and inhaled for what felt like forever. *Chink, chink, chink, chink!* Several tiny copper *chittim* fell beside her.

For several moments, her vision was distorted. She rubbed her eyes and tried to see. She was seeing too *much*! The green of the wilderness, the basement, through two sets of eyes, two minds, Sunny and Anyanwu. It was as if she was broken and her selves were sitting beside each other as opposed to being unified within. The sensation was horrifying. She heard her selves screaming. And just when she was sure she'd go mad, she came back together and her world snapped into focus.

She shivered and shuddered and then jumped up to find it. She ran to the bookshelf, looking at the ground. Where

was it, where was it? There. She grabbed it and downed the rest of her water. She was soaking wet, yet she felt horribly dehydrated. She grabbed her shirt and began to suck the wa-ter from it, too.

"Gah!" she groaned, stumbling back. She'd been able to suck up quite a lot of water. She was that soaked. Her body began to calm, but her mind was popping and crackling, memories exploding like popcorn. "I . . . What is this? I . . . I remember them," she muttered, confused as her mind crowded. She whirled around. "I remember you all!" There, by the toad. Hundreds of them. She was lucky she hadn't crushed them. But then again, they could probably move much faster than she thought. They were not just spiders. Where was the big one?

The back of her neck prickled. She looked up. The thick-legged spider the size of a dinner plate was perched on the wall right above her head. Sunny addressed it in Igbo because she knew this was its preferred language. She knew so *much*. "Ogwu," she said. "Descendant of Udide the Great Spider of all Great Spiders, I remember you. I remember you and all of your children."

The spider's entire body scrunched up with surprise. *Good*, Sunny thought. Then it began to descend on a thick thread of webbing. Sunny knew she didn't have much time, so she spoke fast. "Do you remember me? My name is Anyanwu but here, my name is Sunny Nwazue. I am the granddaughter

of Ozoemena Nimm. So . . ." She fought to remember what her grandmother had written in the letter she'd left for Sunny. She'd read it so many times, but she'd just died and come back to life. "So that makes me of the warrior folk of the Nimm clan, descendant . . . of Mgbafo of the warrior Efuru Nimm and Odili of the ghost people. I am thirteen years old, of Igbo ancestry and American birth, New York City. I am a free agent who only learned this fact a year and a half ago. So you have to know that I can't fight this djinn."

Its voice made her feel like a tuning fork was being held close to her flesh. The vibration made her want to stick her pinky in her ear. It was vaguely female. "I know you, Anyanwu," she said. She hung before Sunny's eyes. Even with her life being in danger, her fear of spiders made her tense up.

"I know what you all tried and failed at so long ago," Sunny said.

The spider clenched her legs to her body. Sunny suppressed a disgusted shudder.

"You were on the plane," Sunny said. "The *Enola Gay*. I know. You were on the bomb, and you tried to weave the storytelling juju your people are most known for. You wove a thick thread that was supposed to cause the bomb not to work when they dropped it on Hiroshima. But when you attached it, you misspoke one of the binding words, and it

snapped when the bomb was released. You failed and no one has seen you since. So, this basement is where you came with all your descendants to hide from the world."

"No, this basement is where Udide cursed us to stay until I have completed my task," she said. "Which is impossible because I have already failed."

The lights flickered. And Sunny heard a scraping sound from across the room. The djinn had located its nerve. *Such things never give up so quickly*, she knew.

"Wait, please," Sunny said. "Help me."

"We will not," Ogwu said. "We can't help anyone. I am useless and my children are useless. The djinn takes from those sent down here for punishment, but we have only seen it kill one person punished down here. And that was forty years ago. A young man whose bones were so strong they could not break. Let it take from you, some blood, some years from your life, some of your life's good luck. Then leave this place and never do anything stupid enough to cause your return. Or . . . maybe yes, it will kill you, Anyanwu. I will see you in the wilderness." Ogwu started to ascend on her web, and Sunny began to panic. The djinn feared the spider. As soon as she was far enough from Sunny, it would have nothing to fear.

"Sunny Nwazuuuuue," the djinn sang. "I'm coming for youuuuu!"

"I know how you can break your curse," Sunny quickly said. Ogwu stopped. She waited.

"I need to do what you all tried to do but on a larger scale." She was making it up on the spot. Sunny had no clue why she'd been shown the vision in the candle and was having the strange dreams. But this wasn't a time to worry about flat-out lying. "I've seen the end. And this time it's not just a city in flames, it's the entire world. I've seen it in a candle. That's what caused me to discover I was a free agent Leopard Person. And I've been seeing it over and over in my dreams for the last few months! So maybe it's supposed to happen soon! Oh, saving the world will require more than just me, but I am *needed*. Please. Help me. If you do, you'll be doing what you should have done back in 1945! And this time, it'll be on a grander scale! You won't just be saving a city, you'll be saving the earth! Fear of failure leads to more failure! And you won't fail this time! You will be able to leave this place, trust me. Remember sunlight? You'll see it again, if you help!! I am . . . I am ignorant. I can't defeat a djinn!"

"You're Anyanwu; we knew each other well. You can crush this djinn like a pepper seed."

"I don't remember how!"

"Then you have no idea who you are!"

Sunny pressed her lips together but didn't argue.

Ogwu paused and then quickly ascended up her web. Sunny's stomach dropped. When she looked at the bronze toad, all of Ogwu's children were gone, too. Hiding wherever they liked to hide. Probably poised to watch the djinn

take her life. Sunny would be like the guy from forty years ago. How could Sugar Cream throw her down here knowing *that* had happened? How could they send *anyone* down here knowing about it?! The Leopard People could be a callous people, especially when it came to adhering to certain rules. The damn rules.

Sunny brought out her juju knife. There were the bones. Right beside her. And the smell of sulfur. She ran through the handful of jujus she'd learned so far. How to bring music, how to keep mosquitoes away, healing minor injuries, staying dry in the rain, making a cup of polluted fresh water drink-able, testing if something was cursed or poisoned, how to push back a heavy aggressor, creating a barrier. She paused. The barrier, she was good at that one.

She held up her hand and opened her palm. Then she brought up her juju knife and made a circular flourish. She caught the pouch with the same hand while keeping the other one up. The invisible packet was cool and wet in her palm. "Stay back," she firmly said. Before she could speak the acti-vating words the wilderness descended on her, layering her world. A black shadow flew from the pile of bones. Eyes wide, Sunny stood her ground. She opened her mouth to speak, but it was on her too quickly. Something sank into her arm like fifty needles. She screamed and her entire world, both physi-cal and wilderness, flashed bright. She felt the djinn sucking as she tried to shake it off. But there was nothing to shake

off. It had no body. Not even bones. There was nothing but a thick oily brown shade.

Suddenly, it froze. Then it let go. Sunny rolled away, avoiding her arm. She got to her feet and ran for the nearest bookcase. Only when she got around it did she chance a look back. It was disgusting. Hundreds of red spiders had pinned the djinn to the floor like a sheet of brown-red solid smoke. Sunny had to blink to fully understand what she was seeing. On one plane, the djinn was a pile of dry bones and the spiders were the size of American quarters, Ogwu the size of a dinner plate. On the other, the djinn was a large blob of brownish smoke and the spiders were large as basketballs, Ogwu the size of a small child. On both planes they were tearing the djinn apart.

She could hear the dry bones snapping, crunching, and crumbling. And she could hear the wet smacking as the large spiderlike creatures tore off tiny pieces of the djinn with their sharp legs and ate them. All the writhing legs and bodies made her stomach turn. The djinn didn't make a sound. It accepted its sudden defeat like an old man giving up on life.

As they ate, the hanging light bulb at the ceiling brightened, flooding the basement. It was like sunshine in its purity and warmth. Sunny shaded her eyes.

"Udide has seen us!" she heard Ogwu shout. "Udide has seen us!!"

The spiders left the mess that was the djinn and went

running to the wall, Ogwu leading the way. Up the wall they crept. Then they scrambled to the ceiling. Toward the hanging light. Ogwu stopped above it and pointed a leg at the light. "Go, my children, go! We're free! I will show you the world!"

Group by group they lowered themselves on their webs into the light, which flashed blue whenever a spider entered it.

"Anyanwu," Ogwu said. "Sunny Nwazue, good luck! We've saved you here, but all of our lives depend on what you and the others do. Stop Ekwensu."

"How do you know it's her?" Sunny asked. She hadn't mentioned Ekwensu. "You've been down here all . . ."

"I've been down here, but you know my children and I are not just of this place. We dwell in the wilderness also. We know the news there."

The basement flashed and flashed as if it contained its own lightning. Sunny looked back at the remains of the djinn. She was firmly in the physical world now and there was nothing but dust left of it. "Is it dead?" she asked Ogwu.

"It was never alive."

"Will it rise again?"

"Not for a while. Eventually. But we will not be here when it does."

Sunny smiled. She had one more night to spend here and she'd spend it alone. Thank goodness.

"Sunny Anyanwu, Anyanwu Sunny," Ogwu said. Her children were all gone, and she was finally lowering herself toward the light. "Thank you for giving me this chance to finally act, to play a role. The Great Spider Udide blesses you. If you ever meet her, send her my greetings and love." Then she was gone in a flash of blue light.

Silence. A good kind of silence. Sunny was safe. She held up her arm to look at where the djinn had bitten her and saw that her bicep was swollen and red. What did a bite from a djinn do? She had at least half a day left down here.

"The medical books!" she said, remembering. There were volumes of them in the case near the bronze toad. Her muscles felt sore and her head ached. But she felt good. She felt strong. The memory of Ogwu's failure and curse was vivid in her head. As Anyanwu, she had been part of the group that sent Ogwu to stop the atomic bomb from dropping. She'd been a part of a group trying to prevent one of the worst human-caused disasters of all time, back in 1945. Wow.

It didn't take Sunny long to find information in the medical books about the bite of a djinn. Apparently, they were common in the Sahara and all over the Middle East. They could kill you and take your soul if they held you in the wilderness long enough, which was probably what it had done to the man with the hard bones forty years ago and planned to do to Sunny. However, their bites only caused a low-grade

fever and dryness in the mouth. Sunny would have to suffer until her final meal and release came.

Thankfully, the suffering was short-lived. Minutes after reading the djinni information, she sat beside the bronze toad and fell into a deep undisturbed exhausted sleep.

14

RELEASE

Pepper soup. Strong. With fish. She opened her eyes. Her stomach clenched with hunger. The light bulb was still shining brightly and Sugar Cream was glowing like Jesus Christ. The fact that she was wearing a long cream-colored dress and matching cream-colored veil added to the effect. Sunny's mouth and throat were so parched she couldn't speak. She was lying curled up on the sandy marble floor, her hoodie over her head, her sleeves pulled over her hands.

"Can you sit up?" Sugar Cream softly asked. She'd placed the tray of pepper soup and a large bottle of water beside Sunny.

She nodded, allowing Sugar Cream to help her sit up. She

scooted to Sugar Cream's desk, leaned against it, and gave her mentor a hard look. Her arm ached and itched, but she was alive. But she'd *almost* been killed.

"Oh, don't look at me like that," Sugar Cream snapped. "You suffer the consequences of *your* actions. Let that be your greatest lesson here. You make your bed, so you shall lie on it."

"It tried to kill me," Sunny whispered.

Sugar Cream stiffened for a moment, meeting Sunny's eyes. Then she picked up the bottle of water and handed it to Sunny. "Drink."

Cool, soothing, goodness. *Water is life; water is life; water is life*, she thought. She drank and drank, pulling in as much as she could. She finished more than half of the large bottle before bringing it down and sighing. "It bit me," she said.

"And what did you do about it?" Sugar Cream asked, handing her the bowl of soup. It was warm in her hands. A tainted pepper floated in the middle of the clear brown soup with large chunks of seasoned fish, tripe, and shrimp. It caused the soup to softly bubble. Sugar Cream handed Sunny a spoon, and she took it.

"I got the help of friends," she coldly said.

Sugar Cream grunted and smiled. "Ogwu and her children," she said. "Is that why the bulb burns as a portal?"

Sunny shrugged as she spooned the soup into her mouth. Her belly warmed and the rest of her body followed. For

once it was good to eat hot, hot, hot tainted pepper soup. When she finished, Sugar Cream helped her up, inspected the bite on Sunny's arm, and then, after deeming it not serious, helped Sunny up the many flights of stairs. Sunny's punishment was complete.

The walk up and through the library was like a dream. She'd come to know the first three floors of this place well over the last year. But now, though she recognized everything, it felt slightly unfamiliar. There was a strange distancing effect, as if she hadn't been here in five years as opposed to three days. She'd changed down there. And she was exhausted.

By the time they reached ground level and stepped into the lobby, Sunny felt stronger. She no longer had to lean on Sugar Cream and her headache was gone. The bite was itchy, but she could at least move her arm. Sugar Cream said it was past midnight, yet there were several older students browsing the bookcases here as if all was normal. They glanced at Sunny and some of them smiled at her, patted her on the shoulder, and said "You look good" and "Handled like a soldier."

Samya slowly came up to her, and Sunny hugged her tightly. She felt Samya cringe, and she quickly let go. "I'm sorry," Sunny said, looking into Samya's brown eyes.

Samya smiled tiredly. "Don't be." She hugged Sunny

again and kissed her on the cheek. "I'm glad you are okay."

"They really caned you?" Sunny asked, her eyes tearing up.

"Don't cry. You walk out of here with dry eyes, okay? I'm fine. As you know, some punishments are worth it." Sunny nodded, working hard to fight her tears. Samya squeezed her hand. "Go," she said, gently pushing Sunny along.

"You've become a bit of a hero," Sugar Cream said drily, after they'd moved on toward the door.

If Sunny weren't so tired, she'd have been deeply confused. How did one come out of three days' punishment a hero? When she stepped out of the Obi Library, the air felt so sweet.

"Sunny!" Chichi screamed, running up and throwing her arms around her, nearly knocking her to the ground. Orlu and Sasha stood behind her. "They told us to wait out here. That you had to complete your punishment by walking unaided out of the Obi Library. Unaided!" She held Sunny back and looked her over. "You look terrible!"

"I feel worse," Sunny said, pressing her arm.

"Chichi . . ." Sasha paused, an angry look crossing his face, but then he looked at Sunny and smiled. "She told us everything. I'd have done the same thing, no matter the consequences. That's family, yo. Always gotta protect the fam."

Sunny only nodded. Not even Sasha would understand

the consequences. When he'd used juju to switch the minds of two police officers back in the United States, he'd been caned. She, on the other hand, had nearly lost her soul. But both he and Samya were right; it was worth it.

Her eyes met Orlu's and again she nearly melted into tears. It was as if he could see right through her, witness all that she'd been through. His hands were at his sides, clench-ing and unclenching. She stepped up to him and Orlu gath-ered her into a quiet hug. "It's all right," he said. "You're with us now."

Sugar Cream went back into the library as soon as Sunny was in the hands of her friends. She said that Sunny was to return for her lessons in a week. The four of them stopped at Mama Put's Putting Place on the way back when Sunny said that she was hungry.

"Don't worry," Orlu said, pulling out a white plastic chair for Sunny. "I'm paying. Order whatever you want."

Sunny's pockets were full of the gold *chittim* that had fallen in the basement, but she didn't argue with him. She'd been gone three days and all her friends could do was worry. They needed to feel as if they could do something. Especially Orlu.

"It's late," Sunny said. "My parents, my brother . . . maybe it's best if . . ."

"Don't worry about them," Chichi said. "I've been going over there. They know you are at least okay."

"What?! What have you been telling them?" she asked.

"Nothing," she said. "I can't. They already know you are part of . . . something. They're beginning to understand. So all I've said is that you're fine and will be back tonight. The first day, your father looked like he wanted to kill me." She laughed. "Honestly, Sunny, your father doesn't know if he is coming or going when it comes to you."

"Your mother came to see my mother yesterday, too," Orlu said. "My mother said she looked okay . . . just worried about the reason you were gone."

Sunny ordered a plate of stewed chicken. Mama Put said it came with jollof rice, but Sunny asked to replace it with more fried plantain. She didn't think she wanted to eat jollof rice for a while, or goat meat. She also ordered three bottles of water. When the food came, Sunny's entire body responded. As she ate and drank and ate and drank, Chichi told her some surprising things.

"I called your brother that next day," Chichi said. "Remember, you gave me your phone." She reached into her pocket and handed it to Sunny.

"Thanks," Sunny said. "What'd he say?"

"Nothing much," she said.

Sasha sucked his teeth loudly.

"Oh, stop," Chichi snapped.

Sasha muttered something under his breath, and Orlu's eyebrows went up.

"What did you say?" Chichi asked, frowning.

"My brother," Sunny interrupted. "My brother . . . is he okay?"

"He's back in school." Chichi grinned.

"What? Really?!"

"He didn't believe me at first when I said he could go back. But then later that day, he got a phone call. His friend Adebayo couldn't stop apologizing and telling him that it was safe to return. That the confraternity is disbanded. Chukwu didn't believe it until one of his other friends who was not in the confraternity and knew nothing about Chukwu's prob-lem called his cell phone laughing and telling him that two of his professors had left their positions to join some born-again Christian group. When Chukwu returned, he found that the capo of the group had also become born-again, though he didn't drop out."

Her brother only missed a few days of school. Her parents never even knew he was gone. The next time he'd be home would be for Christmas, which was weeks away. He'd heal up nicely by then. Sunny looked at her phone. What was she going to tell him when she finally talked to him? She'd cross that bridge once she got to it.

When she returned home, she made it into the kitchen before anyone knew she was there. Her father stood in the doorway

in his nightwear. "Sunny," he said in a low voice. "Where were you?"

Sunny's heart slammed in her chest and she felt her throat tighten. She couldn't tell him even if she wanted to. "Dad, I . . ."

He held up a hand. "Something has always been wrong with you," he muttered. "What kind of daughter has God given me?"

"I swear, Dad, I'm not . . ." She froze as it started to happen, her body filling with terror. But she couldn't help it, no matter how hard she willed. Her spirit face was coming forward! And as it began to happen, Sunny could feel Anyanwu's shock, too. She turned from her father.

"Don't swear," her father snapped. "Don't swear a *thing* to me. What are you . . . What is wrong with you?"

Sunny was afraid to speak. But as her spirit face retreated, she relaxed. She turned back to her father's angry face. Two years ago, he'd surely have beaten her when he was this angry . . . and this scared him. She could see it in his eyes. She was old enough now and had faced enough scary things herself to recognize it. "Are you all right?" he asked in a low voice.

She nodded.

"Did anyone hurt you?"

"I'm okay, Dad," she said. The djinni bite on her arm itched and ached. Was losing control of her spirit face a side effect?

He touched his forehead and closed his eyes, letting out a breath. He opened them. "Will this happen again, Sunny?"

She pressed her lips together, steadying herself. If her spirit face had slipped forward, would they have returned her right back to the basement? Or something even worse? Why did that even happen? And her father made her angry. She had always known he resented her for not being what he wanted. He was like so many other Igbo fathers. Sons, sons, sons, even when you had two. And if not a son, then a beautiful, polite, docile daughter. "No," she said, just wanting to escape to her room.

"I'll tell your mother that you're home," he said, making to leave. He turned back to Sunny. "We love you more than life itself." He paused, his own words seeming to take his breath away. Then his face became hard and angry as she'd known it most of her life when he looked at her, and he continued. "But you worry her like that again and I will disown you from this family and throw you out of this house."

Later on, her mother didn't come running to the kitchen or her room. But Sunny could hear her sobbing with relief in their bedroom. She heard Ugonna go to their room. Then he came to Sunny's room, peeked in, and without a word returned to his room. Sunny lay awake listening to her mother's

sobbing and her father's soft consoling murmurs. She wished she could go to her parents' room as she used to when she was younger, before she became part of something that was entirely separate from her family.

She closed her eyes, tears streaming from the sides onto her pillow. Those days were over.

15

WAHALA DEY

A few nights later, Sunny walked into Anatov's hut with Chichi, Orlu, and Sasha. It was just past midnight. When they walked in through the OUT door and greeted their teacher, Anatov told them he had a special lesson for them tonight. Then he'd pulled Sunny aside.

"Come with me for a minute so we can talk," he said. "Excuse us," he told the others. He'd tied his bushy dreadlocks on top of his head tonight. Sunny noted this. When Anatov tied up his dreadlocks, it always meant the lessons that night would be tough.

They walked through the waist-high wooden front door labeled IN. It was painted with black and white squares that

Sunny had since learned were part of a protective juju that wove through the hut and the mile radius of forest around it.

As soon as they were outside, Anatov reached into his pocket. When he brought his hand up, he blew green juju powder in Sunny's face. She immediately began to sneeze and sneeze. She stumbled back. "What . . ." Then she was overcome by another sneezing fit.

Without a word, he brought out his juju knife and made several quick flourishes. He put his knife on the ground at his feet and then snapped both of his fingers in Sunny's direction. As soon as he did this, Sunny felt a force shove her backward. She stared at what remained in the place she'd just stood.

She sneezed another five times as she watched the green mist shaped like herself float there, slowly dissipating into the air like thick smoke. It looked around, as if shocked by its existence.

"What is that?!" Sunny said. Her stuffed nose made her sound nasally.

"You traveled fully into the wilderness. When people with your ability do that and then return, they always bring something back with them," he said, staring at the green Sunny-shaped mist. It was almost gone now, but it was still looking around in shock. It made no sound, but Sunny could smell something. She couldn't find the words to describe it. "It's like swimming in the ocean. You come out wet and when you dry, you're salty. You need to bathe."

"So I'm clean now?"

He chuckled. "Is being covered in sea salt dirty?"

"Well . . ."

"If I didn't do that to you, you'd become . . . strange," he said. "I've seen it happen. I didn't think I'd have to teach you how to perform bush medicine on yourself. Not so soon. But I guess when it comes to you all, things happen sooner rather than later. How do you feel?"

"I need a tissue."

He chuckled. "Aside from your juju powder allergy."

"I feel . . . lighter. Like I just took off a heavy coat."

Anatov looked pleased.

"And I . . . I can smell something," she said. "Even with my stuffed nose. What is that? Why's it so strong?"

Anatov nodded. "Can't describe it, right?"

Sunny shook her head.

"That's the wilderness," he said.

They paused, Anatov looking pensively at Sunny. Sunny sniffed loudly. Then Anatov smiled and shook his head. "What in Allah's name were you thinking when you did that to the society's capo, Sunny? I hope you've learned your lesson. You could have *died* in that basement. We'd all have been torn up, but the world would have moved on, eventually, and you'd have been gone. Don't you understand yet?"

"My bro—"

"I know it was your brother," he said stepping closer. "I

know you love him and that guy hurt him . . . badly. Nearly killed him. But *you* are in a secret society. A real *true* one that is older than time. And we have *rules*, strict, real, deeply upheld rules. While you were in the basement, Sugar Cream came to me angry as hell. She couldn't believe you'd do something so stupid. Do you know that? I have *never* seen her even break a sweat. But this night, she was shaking with fear and anger."

"I'm sorry," Sunny whispered.

"Tell that to your mentor and never ever cross that line again. We can't protect you if you do."

Sunny's nose ran and now her eyes were tearing up, too.

"You essentially died; that's what traveling fully into the wilderness requires," Anatov said bluntly. "When it pulled you in, if you weren't Sunny Nwazue, if you were Sasha or Orlu or Chichi or any other kid without your specific ability, you'd have *stayed* dead. Do you understand this?"

Sunny took a deep breath as his words sunk in. "I get it," she breathed.

"Good." He looked down his nose at her. "You set Ogwu and her young free."

"They were never really in prison," Sunny muttered. "She was just ashamed."

"Hmm," he said, putting a long arm around her shoulder. When she looked up at him, his nose ring glinted in the moonlight. Anatov the Defender of Frogs and All Things

Natural couldn't defend her from everything. "Come," he said. "I assume you brought your usual box of tissues?"

Sunny laughed and smiled, wiping her tears with her hand. "Yeah."

He grasped her shoulder warmly, pulling her into a hug. He smelled of his favorite scented oil—Egyptian musk—and his caftan was scratchy. "Good," he said. "Good, Sunny."

The four of them sat on the floor of Anatov's hut. Sunny had blown the heck out of her nose, but it still ran happily and freely. She pulled out another tissue, lifted her glasses a bit, and blew. By now her nose probably looked red as a cherry.

"You okay?" Orlu asked.

"Get her some water, man," Sasha said, chuckling. "With all that snot, she's going to get dehydrated."

"Tonight," Anatov loudly said. He spoke in Igbo. He did this often to help Sasha practice. "In celebration of Sunny's return, I've decided to throw out the planned lesson and replace it with something I think you all need: masking jujus. Jujus you use when you want to perform juju on or around Lambs but do not wish them to see or know it."

Sunny sat up straighter, deeply interested. There was juju for that? Leopards were allowed to perform juju on Lambs? She looked at Chichi, who looked equally surprised.

"One can perform juju on Lambs and around them," he

said. "We know this happens, sure. We can't live around these people and not be able to do this. However, you must take precautions. And those precautions are not so easy. And people are lazy." He switched to English, speaking with his African American accent. "They don't like to cover they asses. And if you mess up . . . well, y'all know the consequences."

He sat in his mahogany throne-like chair with its plush red seat. "Lord knows that Lambs can be damn annoying, with their silly materialism, hatred of education, and love of remaining stupid. They're obsessed with getting things fast, fast, fast, with the least amount of work, books, no instruction. It's universal." He chuckled. "Who can blame Leopards for wanting to throw some juju at them once in a while."

He went on to show them several jujus they could do. Empty Hands required a bit of common all-purpose juju powder and allowed one to punch someone without looking like one had done anything. Grace was a juju that you could do with only your juju knife; it allowed one to slip out of a situation unnoticed. *Ujo* only required a juju knife, too. This bit of juju filled a Lamb person with irrational crippling fear. It could be thrown from a distance of several feet, allowing the thrower to remain undetected.

Both Sasha and Chichi were especially good at performing this one. "I'm glad no Lambs are around," Anatov said, after watching both of them. "You'll both have to learn how to perform *Ujo* in strength grades . . . unless you want the

Lambs you work it on to run off screaming and vomiting with hysterical fear every single time you use it on them."

"Use *Ujo* sparingly," Anatov stressed to all of them. "Even a weak version of it can eventually cause brain damage when used on the same person more than once."

Of all the things Anatov showed them this day, Sunny's favorite was *Wahala Dey*. This was another juju knife spell that caused small things to randomly go wrong. One's pants would fall down, one would slip or trip, make a wrong turn, drop one's plate of food, one's computer would suddenly crash. It only worked on Lambs, and it was an excellent way to slip out of a bad situation or just ruin someone's day.

All four of them picked up on the jujus with only mild difficulty, and Anatov was pleased. "I hope this will keep all of you from any further trips to the Obi Library basement or, in your case, Sunny, worse." She felt her cheeks grow red. "And, Sasha, if you had known some of these, I doubt you'd have been sent here to Nigeria by your parents for being such a fool."

"Nah, I'd still have switched those two cops' minds," he said. "Police require something serious, *Oga*."

Chichi smiled at Sasha, and he looked ready to burst with pride. Orlu only rolled his eyes.

Anatov sucked his teeth with loathing, but in a fond kind of way. Their group wasn't his only group, but even Sunny knew they were his favorite. Chichi was his one mentee, and

no elder took on a mentee unless he or she truly deeply loved and felt great, great confidence in that student. "Sasha, like me, you definitely have African America running through your veins—irrational rebelliousness straight out of Chicago. May the gods help you."

Sasha jumped up and did the Crip Walk.

"I said *Chicago*, not Compton," Anatov said.

"South Siiiide!" Sasha proclaimed, laughing.

Anatov's nostrils flared as he clearly stifled a laugh. "Anyway, so before you all return to the safety of your families, I'd like you to go to Leopard Knocks and pick up some of the all-purpose powder that we used for the jujus today."

"But we have plenty of that already," Chichi said.

"You have the yellow kind," he said. "Get the white kind. It's the purest and best and safest to use with Lambs. Just a tiny pound you can hide on your person or in your purse and keep it *only* for when you wish to deal with Lambs."

It was nearly one A.M. when they stepped up to the bridge to Leopard Knocks. Finding the white juju powder wouldn't be easy. Anatov said it wasn't a big seller, since it was juju powder that was exclusively for "use on Lambs." Sunny just hoped they could find it quickly so she could get a few hours of sleep before school tomorrow.

She was exhausted and could barely hear herself think as she looked at the tree bridge. The noise of the crashing river

always seemed louder at night. She stepped up to the large smooth black stone and laid her hand on it. It was warm as she rubbed. The others were waiting behind her.

She was so, so tired, more tired than anyone understood. She yawned as she stepped up and faced the narrow slippery bridge. She relaxed herself and brought forth her spirit face. She was going to shift into mist and blow across the bridge, but she was just too tired. So instead, she felt her limber body stretch and she regally began to walk across the bridge.

Feeling tall and stately, she pointed her sandaled toes as she walked across. She was like a ballerina gracing the stage. Back straight, neck stiff, one foot in front of the other. She smiled softly as she looked down into the rushing water. The water gushed and coiled and thrashed as it tumbled downstream. What was it about this section of river that caused it to grow so turbulent? On each side, there were tangles of hanging trees, vines, and bushes both up- and downriver. How the trees grew at the river's edges was beyond her. The current should have carried them away.

"Hello," she whispered when she saw its great, round face just below the wild waters. The river beast. It was the size of a house and who knew what its full shape was. She'd never asked her friends, her teacher, or her mentor. She'd never wanted to show them that she was too curious about it. Their little game was between it and her, Anyanwu.

Every single time she crossed the bridge to Leopard

Knocks, even when she crossed as mist, it came up to watch her. Closely. Not casually. Not nicely. Initially, she had been afraid. The first time she'd crossed the bridge, it had nearly tricked her into falling into the river, and Sasha had saved her by grabbing her necklace. Lately, she was defiant, often stopping to look right back at the glaring monster who never broke the surface to show its certainly hideous face. Since her encounter with its cousin the lake beast, she was downright audacious when she crossed the bridge.

"Why do you wait?" Sunny said as Anyanwu. Her voice was deep and buttery, the voice of a sultry female radio DJ who played smooth jazz and midnight love songs. "I am right here. What is it you seek from me?"

It was hulking below her. She could see the girth of it now. She chuckled.

"Sunny?" Chichi called behind her. Her voice traveled through the mist as if from somewhere else. And technically it was, for the bridge linked the mundane world to the magical oasis that Leopard Knocks sat upon, which existed on no Lamb map.

"What is it you want?" Sunny asked, kneeling down to look the river beast in its submerged face. This beast's cousin had dragged her into its water. The djinn had dragged her into a sort of water that led to the wilderness. And now here was this damn thing, constantly threatening her with the same fate.

"Do you know who I am?" she said. She knocked her knuckles to her wooden spirit face. "I am Anyanwu." Sunny could only watch this other side of her taunt and heckle the river beast. Inside she shook and cowered. Normally, she felt right in line with her spirit self. Anyanwu was strong and old, and Sunny *loved* how she taunted the river beast. Anyanwu was Sunny. But, right now, Sunny was exhausted. She had no fight left in her. Not right now. And Anyanwu was picking another fight.

She rose up on her toes and then pointed her juju knife at the creature. The bridge shook, and Sunny felt like her heart would explode because not only was it shaking, something was cracking. Anyanwu gracefully crouched, her juju knife held firmly in her hand. There was something thick, green, and wet wrapped around the narrow bridge to her right. It looked like a mossy rope, a vine thicker than three fire hoses . . . no, a tentacle!

Oh come on, not again, Sunny thought. But Anyanwu laughed as the river beast finally surfaced. It was indeed the size of a house, as its shadow indicated. Craggy and pocked with calcium deposits and barnacle-like crustaceans, its horrible cranium was also covered with something like green-purple seaweed. The thing looked like a hideous sea garden. Its giant toothy maw was downturned and closed as it glared up at her with its dinner-plate-sized silvery eyes. She could smell it, too, like sea flowers if sea flowers had a scent. Sweet, briny, and oily.

It grunted and huffed and puffed out water at her, nearly blowing her from the bridge. The briny flower smell invaded her nostrils.

"Sunny!" she heard Orlu call. "Are you all right?"

"Yeah," she called back, still looking it in the eye.

None of them could come and get her. Only one person could be on the bridge at a time. Sunny was alone here. But she'd asked for this. Anyanwu had. A green seaweed-covered tentacle reached for her, and she danced back.

"You missed," she said. Then, without a thought, she leaped. This was Anyanwu's impulsiveness, but it felt great to Sunny. She wasn't a super-fast thinker like Sasha and Chichi, but there was a joy she experienced when she acted impulsively, and she felt it now. In mid-leap over the tentacle, she glanced down at the raging river below. She remembered how cold its waters had been when she'd moved through it during her initiation. With its wild, churning gray-white currents, no one would hear if she fell in and they would certainly spirit her away within seconds.

She landed gracefully on the side of the narrow bridge where she'd entered, the river beast's tentacle on the wood behind her; she was steps away from where Orlu, Chichi, and Sasha stood waiting to cross. She looked back and laughed, her voice Anyanwu's deep baritone that made her sound like an arrogant middle-aged chain-smoking woman. The river beast grunted wetly. Then it shivered with surprise and the crescent-shaped pupils of its silver eyes widened. Sunny

stopped and nearly fell to her knees. The images that burst into her mind stung sharply like angry attacking bees behind her eyes. Then she could have sworn she heard the river beast laughing, or maybe it was shrieking because it, too, was experiencing the vision that moved through it to reach Sunny.

It flooded in like river water. There was haunted music. The flute and the talking drum filled Sunny's mind. Even the water below vibrated to the beat of the masquerade's tune. Then she was looking at Ekwensu, the terrifying spirit she'd faced here last year. She grabbed the sides of her head and shook it; she shut her eyes. "No, no, no, no." She was already so weak. The vision kept coming, though. Ekwensu looked the same; a house-sized mound of packed palm fronds standing in a place of green grass. The only difference was that she seemed to be constantly spilling out red beads from between her dry fronds, some tiny as ants, some big as horseflies. And she was rising from the grass now. Two of the red beads seemed to fly at Sunny, and she flinched, snapping from her vision.

One of the bigger beads hit Sunny square between the eyes, and for a moment there was a strange sensation of her drifting to the side when she wasn't. The bead bounced on the bridge's wood and rolled into the river. The second bead flew into the water, plunging in feet away from the river beast. This seemed to wake it and when it did, it fled back into the deep. Sunny stared at where the river beast had

been, where the bead had flown, because the bead was real, a physical thing. Then she turned and ran off the bridge. Chichi screamed with relief as Sunny emerged from the bridge. "What happened?!" Chichi shouted. "We thought the river beast took you!"

"It tried," Sunny tiredly said.

Sasha and then Orlu came running. Sasha only touched Sunny's wet hair and hugged her head to his hip. Sunny leaned against him as Orlu knelt before her and took her hands. "What happened?" Orlu asked. His eyes were red and twitchy.

"Ekwensu," Sunny whispered. "She's back. She threw a bead and it was real and . . ."

Chichi used a drying juju on Sunny. She had to perform the spell twice because the first one left Sunny still damp and mildew-smelling. The second one left her dry, perfumed, and warm. "Thanks, Chichi," Sunny said. Chichi only looked at Sunny with stunned, puffy eyes. They hugged and didn't let go of each other for several minutes.

"Wait," Sunny finally said, pulling away from her friend. "I have to do something."

She stood up and brought out her juju knife and did the flourishes. When Anatov had shown her, she'd noticed that the shape he'd drawn in the air reminded her of Nsibidi. It was a skeleton of lines that was then dressed up with loops and swirls. When she finished, a strong force blew through

her flesh, leaving a green mist in the shape of herself facing her. She stepped away from it, feeling her nose tingle.

"What is that?" Chichi asked.

"Residue from the wilderness," Sunny said. She blew and the green lost its shape and began to separate and mix into the air.

"You were in the wilderness?" Orlu asked.

"Partially, I think. Maybe that's how I saw Ekwensu. It was like she pulled me in."

"Like turning someone's head to look," Chichi said.

Sasha nodded. "She waited to catch Sunny when she was weak. It wasn't you she wanted to see; it was Anyanwu."

"I think the river beast was also a diversion," Chichi added. "So Sunny could be too weak and distracted to stop Ekwensu from tearing into the physical world."

The four of them were quiet for a moment.

Chichi turned to Orlu. "So what happens if you don't get rid of the residue?"

"She'll get sick," Orlu said. "Physically."

Sunny sneezed and rubbed between her eyes.

"Bless you," Orlu said.

"Let's cross and get you something to eat," Chichi said, helping Sunny up. "Then I want to hear all the details." She glanced at the river and then leaned closer to Sunny and whispered, "It's time to deal with the river beast."

Sunny nodded. "It's such a sellout, siding with Ekwensu like that."

"Do you think you can cross?" Chichi said. "I mean, you don't have to . . ."

"I'll cross," Sunny said. "This time I'll glide so it's fast." The soccer field and Leopard Knocks were the two places she felt she belonged. She was not about to let the river beast rob her of one of those. She rubbed the black stone and stepped up to the bridge. But she knew as soon as she raised her head and looked at the narrow bridge that even if she wanted to, her foot would not move. She felt pain at the tips of her sandaled feet, as if she'd knocked them against a wall. She stumbled back, her eyes wide.

"Wha—" She looked at her friends, tears filling her eyes.

"Sunny, what is it?" Chichi screeched, grabbing her hands. "Are you all right?"

"She's . . . she's not there," Sunny said. "I can't bring her forth. My spirit face . . . I can't . . . What's happening? Anyanwu, where are you?" Her toes ached and she felt the world swim around her; the spot between her eyes where the bead had hit her felt warm and itchy.

"Here," Orlu said, putting an arm around her waist. "Lean on me."

"You can't call your spirit face?" Sasha asked. "How can that be?" He looked at Chichi and blinked. "Oh, I can't even imagine that."

Chichi nodded but frowned for him to shut up, and this made Sunny panic even more. She couldn't cross the bridge without Anyanwu. Who was she without Anyanwu? Where had Anyanwu gone?

"She has to be with you somehow," Chichi said. "Your spirit face isn't just a face. It's *you*, your spirit memory, you spirit future, your chi. You'd be dead if she weren't there. You're probably just in shock. You need some jollof rice and stew and Fanta. Come on, we don't have to go to Leopard Knocks today. I know a nice Lamb restaurant where we can get some good food."

Uzoma's Chinese Restaurant was small and almost full to capacity. They managed to get a table near the back of the restaurant.

"Sasha and I come here all the time," Chichi said, trying to sound cheerful. "Though the food is terrible."

"I ordered the egg rolls here once, and they were just a boiled egg stuffed in a hard roll," Sasha said, putting an arm around Chichi.

Sunny attempted and failed a smile.

"You all right?" Orlu asked.

"No," she muttered. She felt dehydrated and ready to fall asleep right there at the table.

The four of them looked at one another with wide eyes and solemn faces. None of the people in the busy open-air restaurant could have imagined what they'd recently been through.

"I feel like an alien," Sunny said. "I don't belong

anywhere." She was dry, warm, and smelled good, thanks to Chichi. She was wearing her favorite jeans and a white T-shirt, and they were dry. Unlike those of all the other Africans in the restaurant, her thick, bushy Afro was blonde with a comb given to her by Mami Wata herself. Her skin was pale yellow pink, and her eyes were hazel. She'd just seen Ekwensu succeed in coming into the physical world, and she couldn't find Anyanwu.

"You belong with us," Orlu said. "You're a Leopard Person."

"Ekwensu is back," she whispered. "She will kill everything. But first she'll kill me. You sure you want me with you?"

"You don't know for sure what you saw," Orlu said. "You can do things with time, sometimes. You don't know if that was the future or . . . what."

They were all silent for a moment, the happy chatter of everyone else swelling around them. They ordered puff puffs, one of the only Nigerian dishes on the menu. In America, Nigerians explained to non-Nigerians that they were "Nigerian doughnuts," a description that Sunny always found annoying. It was verbal shorthand that sold puff puffs short. They were sweet, soft, perfectly round pastries that were simply what they were. Sunny also ordered a large bottle of water. When the waiter brought the puff puffs and water, she drank it all and ate five large puff puffs, feeling more like herself

with each yummy bite. The others quietly watched her as she drank and ate.

Finally, Sunny took a deep breath and leaned forward. The others did so, too. "Do your spirit faces ever talk to you?" she asked. When they looked at her with perplexed eyes, she sat back and gazed at them for a long time. She bit her lip, frowned, and then just spilled it all; she told them how Anyanwu was her and she was Anyanwu, but Anyanwu spoke to her and she spoke back. Why not? Who else would she tell? Who else had her back? And now Anyanwu was gone. Sunny was glad for the noisy atmosphere; it covered up the cracking and wavering in her voice as she spoke. Then she told them about her dreams of the end of the world. When she finished, she wiped the tired confused tears from her eyes and ate the last puff puff.

"Who are you, Sunny Nwazue?" Chichi asked, imitating the djinn from the basement as she took Sunny's hand.

Orlu was staring at Sunny.

"I'm two people, and one of me is missing," Sunny said.

"Maybe you just need rest."

"Yeah. And you're a free agent, so your spirit face is new to you," Sasha said. "Maybe that's why it feels like a completely separate person. And yours is old, that's a lot of memory."

"And not just old, *busy*," Chichi added. "We're all old. Orlu and I have been to see the seer Bola, and we know

things about our past lives. We just don't talk much about it. Sasha, too."

"Yeah, I saw a Gullah seer in North Carolina," he said. "She told me I'd done all sorts of crazy shit over the centuries. Slave rebellions of all kinds and some other *wahala* in the wilderness. On some level I'm aware of it. It's all good."

Sunny smiled, feeling a little better.

"I used to talk to my spirit face when I was little," Orlu said.

"Me too!" Chichi said.

"But Ekwensu," Orlu said. "What is it between you and one of the most powerful, scariest beings around?"

"Anyanwu is powerful, so she will have powerful enemies . . . and friends," Chichi said proudly, squeezing Sunny's hands.

"Word," Sasha said. "What you did to those confraternity guys, Sunny, that was you, not Anyanwu."

"I was just protecting my brother," Sunny quietly said.

"No, that Capo guy got so spooked that not only did he become born-again, but his hair has gone gray! I was at Chukwu's hostel yesterday," Chichi said. "He said—" She froze, then her eyes cut to Sasha.

Orlu dropped his face in his hands and shook his head. "Oh God."

"What?!" Sasha screeched, his voice cracking.

"Oh, come on," Chichi said, her voice shaking. "It was just . . ."

"Just *what*? Girl, tell another lie! All you *do* is lie! You're a pack of lies, and you think no one notices." Sasha glared at her with pure disgust and rage. "*Anuofia!*"

"*Kai!*" Orlu screeched. "Sasha!"

"We're sitting here asking Sunny who she is; we should be asking *you*, Chichi!" Sasha snapped, ignoring him. He stood up. Chichi stood up, too.

"Who do you think you are?" Chichi said, pointing in his face. "You don't own me!" She turned and thrust her backside rudely at Sasha.

Sasha's eyes grew wide, his nostrils flaring. He looked ready to explode.

"Come on," Orlu said, pushing the fuming Sasha along. "Let's take a walk." Sunny was beyond relieved when Sasha allowed himself to be shoved along. "I'll get him on an *okada* back home. Chichi, can you get Sunny home?"

"Yes, yes," Chichi snapped.

"Sunny, we go to Bola's on Saturday, okay?" he added. "I think it's time."

"I meet with Sugar Cream on Saturdays, and you meet with Taiwo."

"Yeah. We'll go in the morning," Orlu said. "It'll just be one long day."

Sunny slowly nodded. Chichi kept her back turned as she muttered, "Nonsense."

"You haven't seen nonsense yet," Sasha shouted over his shoulder.

"*Biko*, please, just stop, o!" Orlu said, pushing him along.

"What the hell did I do?" Sasha asked Orlu.

"Just be quiet until . . ."

Their voices lowered and faded as they left the restaurant. Only then could Sunny relax. She hated seeing Sasha and Chichi fighting, although it was more than inevitable. She'd seen Chichi getting into Chukwu's Jeep at least twice in the last two days. If her father had any idea his son was visiting home without stopping by to say hello to them, he'd be appalled. Chukwu was supposed to be immersed in his studies. He was, but he was also falling in love with Chichi.

At the same time, Chichi treated Sasha with the same affinity. And though just about every teenage Leopard girl younger and older in the area was infatuated with Sasha and his American bad boy ways, it was only Chichi whom Sasha gave his real time to.

"So, Chichi, what are *you* going to do?"

"About what?" Chichi asked as she applied some fresh lip gloss. Even from where she stood, Sunny could smell its fruity aroma.

"You know what." Sunny rolled her eyes and Chichi smirked.

"Maybe I'll let them fight it out Zuma wrestling style," she said. "To the death. I'll be like you and have my own guardian angel."

"You seem to keep forgetting that you are talking about my brother and my good friend," Sunny snapped. "These aren't just two random boys."

"I know, I know." She paused and then said, "I don't know."

"You don't know what you're going to do?"

"No," Chichi said, growing serious. "I like them *both*. Wish I had it easy like you. You and Orlu are made for each other."

"I don't know about that," Sunny said quietly.

Chichi smiled and shook her head.

"So you've been to see Mr. Mohammed's wife," Sunny said.

"Call him Alhaji Mohammed; he made his pilgrimage a few weeks ago," Chichi said.

"Oh," Sunny said. "*That's* why that other guy was managing the bookstore for so long."

"I happened to be there the Sunday he returned," Chichi said. "It was crazy. He was actually giving discounts on books . . . Well, for a few hours."

They both laughed. Alhaji Mohammed was a businessman to the bone, hajj or not.

"But yes, I've been to see Bola," Chichi said. "With my mother once, some years ago."

"What for?"

"We can talk about that some other time." She looked

at Sunny unsmilingly. Then Chichi's smile came back. "Bola Yusuf. They call her 'the woman with the breasts down to here.'" She gestured with her hands to mid-waist level. "She is an Owumiri initiate."

Sunny gasped and stopped. "A Mami Wata worshipper! Is she a Leopard Person, too?"

"Yeah."

This was the water worshipping group that Chichi had let Chukwu think Sunny was a part of. Sunny touched the comb she wore in her hair. "Should I take this out when I go?"

"Oh no!" Chichi said. "That'll get you much, much respect. She'll love you for that. And she'll love that the lake and river beasts can't seem to get enough of you, even if it's because they are Ekwensu's minions."

Sunny waited until right before bed to try it. She locked her bedroom door and, on shaky legs, walked to her window. She usually raised the screen just a crack so that her wasp artist could come and go as it pleased. Now she pushed the screen to the top of the windowsill and waited. It didn't take long. She watched the mosquitos slowly fly in, pushed by their own ambition and the night's breeze. When she counted five, she shut the screen and brought out her juju knife and worked a Carry Go, a juju that drove away insects with the intent to bite.

She felt the cool invisible juju sack drop into her upheld hand after she did the flourish with her knife, and she sighed with relief. She spoke the words as she watched two of the mosquitos land near the top of her white bedroom wall. She frowned as she watched one of the mosquitos migrate to her and then land on her arm. She smashed it with a hard slap.

Then she stepped to her bedroom mirror and looked at her face. She ignored her flushed cheeks and the tears rolling down them. She looked into her wet eyes and with her mind, she called Anyanwu. She dug deep within herself, and then she tried to bring her forth. Nothing. Sunny sat on her bed as the sobs wracked her body. Images of the river and the menacing Ekwensu flashed through her mind.

She crept under her covers and curled herself as tightly as she could. She still wore her sandals, and she didn't care. And when she got up in the morning and found an itchy mosquito bite on her arm and two on her left leg, she knew for sure Anyanwu was gone. Who was she now?

16

HEAD OF THE HOUSEHOLD

When she saw her father that evening, she went to him.

It had been a while since they had watched the local news together, but today Sunny needed his company. Anyanwu was still gone, and Sunny felt lost. She'd seen him settling down in his favorite chair to watch the news, a cold bottle of Guinness on the side table, a bowl of groundnuts on his lap. She sat down on the floor beside his chair, and he'd patted her on the shoulder, pointed at the TV, and said, "You heard about this oil spill in the Niger Delta?"

"No," she said. "I've been studying."

"These idiots are . . . Just watch, here it is. Turn it up," her father said. She grabbed the remote control and clicked up the volume on the large flat-screen TV.

A thin old man looked deep into the camera, a micro-phone held to his face. His voice was reedy, his expression perplexed. "I came here when there was no crude, no spillage, everything was so fine. People were enjoying back then," he said. "It's a strange thing to us. How could this occur? Are these oil companies stupid? Ah-ah, don't they know what true wealth is? How could they? These people aren't from here."

As he spoke, oil-drenched riverways, creeks, mangroves, and grassy vegetation were shown. The story cut to a jour-nalist walking through the mucky forest in yellow hip boots as he spoke with a short young intense man, also in hip boots, named Murphy Bassey, head of the local watchdog group Friends of the Delta Organization. As they walked, they both pinched their noses.

"What's that smell?" the journalist asked in a nasally voice.

Murphy stepped over a fallen tree and stopped at a large black puddle in the soaked vegetation. "You see this here? It's not water." He brought a piece of yellow paper from his pocket, rolled it up, and stuck the end into the black liquid. Then he brought out a box of matches. When he used one to light the wet part of the paper, it burst into violent flames. "Whoo!" he exclaimed, dropping it on a dry patch of vegeta-tion and quickly stamping it out. "See that?" he said as he stamped. "What is that? This place is already mutilated by oil pipelines; now the forest and waters are poisoned."

"So all it would probably take to set this whole forest and the towns near it on fire is dropping a match in the wrong place," the journalist said, looking very worried.

"Correct," Murphy said with a bitter chuckle. "We won't do that, though."

"I should hope not. I don't even think you should have lit that paper just now."

Murphy nodded, a bit out of breath. "I needed you to see, though. Give it a few days and the very *air* will be flammable. We have more than one oil spill every day here. In an area that's already polluted," Murphy said. "These oil companies are so sloppy in their mining of crude oil. They don't care. It's not *their* home. This new spill happened last night! It is not as big as the Exxon Valdez spill, but it is very, very bad. You see for yourself, do you see anyone here? No one is doing anything about it."

Sunny sighed as she watched, trying not to think of her own problems. As Anatov said, the world was bigger than her. In some parts, the world was literally dying. Her father held his bowl of groundnuts down for her and she took a few. As she shelled one of them, he offered his bottle of beer. "Need a sip?" he asked.

When she looked up and met his eyes, they both burst out laughing. He took a gulp and put the bottle back on the side table, and Sunny popped a groundnut into her mouth.

The only woman interviewed spoke in Pidgin English

and had a shell-shocked look about her. But her words made Sunny's skin prickle and her head feel light. "I come to see the water las' night. Wetin my eye see na one big thing wey be like animal as it dey descend into the water from air. Like some masquerade tin'. Ah-ah, mek these people stop wetin dem dey do, o . . . Because it don begin to attract evil, o!"

The woman's words hit Sunny hard. She opened her mouth and took a deep breath. A "masquerade thing" descending into the crude oil-soaked water? Was this Ekwensu? Did that Lamb woman just tell all of Nigeria that she'd seen Ekwensu? Sunny remembered when she'd encountered Ekwensu last year at the shrine beside the gas station, the oily, greasy smell, like car exhaust. Sunny could imagine Ekwensu tearing open a tanker and then bathing in the freshly spilled crude oil, a substance toxic to the flesh of the earth. If Ekwensu had just forced her way into the mundane world, such a "bath" would probably strengthen her.

Sunny moved closer to her father. He took another deep gulp of his beer and belched loudly. "This is not normal," he said. "Everything in that creek will be dead by tomorrow, the people are getting poisoned, the whole place could go up in flames. It's not even on international news."

Sunny slowly got up, her legs feeling like jelly. "I should finish studying," she said. Her father grunted, his eyes still on the TV where they were now talking about a murder in Lagos.

˅ ˅ ˅ ˅

The next morning, when she received her daily Leopard newspaper, she didn't find one mention of the oil spill in the entire paper. Her father was right; this wasn't normal at all.

17

BOLA YUSUF

"Thank goodness it's this way," Sunny said, rubbing a hand over her drying Afro. She absentmindedly took out the Mami Wata comb and used it to pick her hair out a bit. They were walking down a dirt path that ran through the forest that they usually took to get to Anatov's place.

Orlu sucked his teeth. "If it were back in Leopard Knocks, we'd find a way to get there."

"Tired of having to 'find a way,'" she muttered. "Just want to be normal, like everyone else."

"It's not far now," Orlu said.

They were walking side by side, shaded by the thickening trees. Sunny suddenly felt glad that it was the middle

of the day. Who knew what was lurking in the bush. She giggled nervously to herself.

"What?" Orlu asked.

"I . . . I was just thinking, what could be worse than the river beast?"

"Sunny, there are crazy dangerous beasts like that in these forests, too."

Sunny quickly reached into her pocket for her juju knife. She fretfully babbled, "What . . . what kind of beasts? Are they big? Hidden like the lake beast? Do you think the lake beast would . . ."

"Put that away," Orlu said, chuckling. "The worst things around here and in Night Runner Forest come out at night, just after dusk. Relax."

When she still wouldn't put her knife away, he took her hand, and every hair on Sunny's arms and neck stood up. They walked in shy silence for the next five minutes, watching the trees or their feet. Then they came to a clearing in the trees. A large black solid steel gate stood here, with an image painted on each of the two doors. On the left was a painting of Mami Wata herself. She was more the Uhamiri version that Sunny didn't see very often. Instead of the long straight hair and Indian features of the more popular image of Mami Wata, the traditional Uhamiri version had skin black like a beetle's wings and long bushy dreadlocks that floated behind her like powerful-looking brown vines. She was grin-

ning with white teeth and holding her long fin against her human torso.

On the other door of the gate was the contrasting image of a brown-skinned man with thick matted hair wearing chains around his ankles and wrists. Sunny frowned. The man had to be *onye ara*, a person suffering from madness.

"Bola's a Mami Wata priestess," Orlu said, seeming to read the question in Sunny's mind. "So she's a healer."

"Of what? Like malaria or . . ."

"No, stuff Lamb doctors can't address. You know, people suffering from being *ogbanjes* and women who can't have children no matter what the doctors do . . . and"—he pointed at the gate—"madness. A lot of Leopard People are struck with it. Maybe from some juju misfiring or someone being bitten by something in our forests, whatever. But Bola's also a really strong oracle. Her predictions and visions are never wrong, when she has them."

She can do all that and she married a bookstore owner? Sunny wondered. But then again, these were Leopard People. A bookstore owner was probably like marrying a brain surgeon.

Orlu knocked on the gate, and a minute later a tall woman wearing a long blue skirt and a white blouse peeked out. "Good afternoon," she said. She looked right at Sunny with such intense eyes that Sunny took a step back. Orlu nudged Sunny with his elbow.

"Good afternoon," Sunny said. "We're . . . I'm here to . . ."

"I know. She's expecting you," the woman said. "Remove your shoes and come in."

Sunny slipped off her sandals and, upon stepping past the gate, she felt it. First in the ground beneath her feet that went from warm to cool and almost damp. Then there was the rush of humidity; it was almost as if her skin's pores opened up and began to drink. She'd stepped onto sacred ground . . . or something. She opened her mouth and inhaled. When she looked at Orlu, he was frowning and picking his shirt from his skin.

In the center of the compound was a moderately sized white house. The ground around the house was neatly packed red dirt, tall wild bushes growing against the compound's wall. They were led around to the back where they entered a room with wooden benches. It must have been some sort of waiting area, for several women and men, some young, some old, sat on the wooden rickety benches in various states of anxiety and misery. One woman wearing a dirty orange-yellow wrapper and matching top was crying into the shoulder of another woman dressed in a yellow blouse and jeans. A man in a sweat suit jumped up and then sat down when they walked in. Another man dressed like a rapper was talking to himself, pulling at his skinny jeans and biting his nails.

One man even bore a striking resemblance to the madman in the painting on the entrance gate's door. He sat on

the floor in the middle of the room, his long, unruly, matted hair flopped over his shoulder. He wore nothing but raggedy brown pants and a torn, dirty black T-shirt. He even had shackles on his wrists and bare feet.

"She will call you," the woman who'd led them in said. "Sit." Then she left.

Orlu and Sunny took a spot on the bench, squeezing between the crying woman and the mumbling man dressed like a rapper. After a few moments, Sunny realized he was actually speaking Arabic to himself.

"Glad I called and told my mom I'd be home late," Sunny said.

"Yeah, but we could be here all night," he said. "I've heard of . . ."

The door opened. "Anyanwu!" the little girl standing in the doorway called. "Who is Anyanwu?"

Sunny froze. She stood up and the little girl turned to her. The girl was about six years old, but she stood as if she belonged there and it was normal for her to order adults around. She even carried a clipboard. "Are you she?"

"Well, I'm Sunny, but my . . ."

"Yes or no?" the girl asked, holding up a pen.

"Y-yes."

"Come this way, then."

Sunny looked back at Orlu, who hadn't gotten up. "Come on," she whispered. "I'm *not* going by myself."

He got up and the little girl didn't stop him from following. She showed them down a narrow hallway with ocean-blue walls, and Sunny felt her eyes begin to water. She brought out the handkerchief in her pocket just in time to catch her sneeze.

"Sorry," the little girl said. "There's Catch 'Em in the walls. Eze Bola has had a few problems with imposters. People who are allergic always get sneezy here."

She wanted to ask the girl what constituted an "imposter" because maybe she was one now, but instead she asked, "What does Catch 'Em do to imposters?" She blew her nose.

The little girl giggled mischievously. "You don't want to know."

The girl led them to a large room with graceful high ceilings, white walls, wooden floors, and nothing in it but five white wooden chairs. They were arranged in a circle with blue cushions on the backs and seats. Bola Yusuf sat in one of the chairs, one leg crossed over the other.

Upon seeing her, Orlu stopped.

The little girl professionally grasped her clipboard. "Come on," she said, walking in. She motioned toward the chairs. "Have a seat, please."

Sunny followed her halfway across the room and then turned back to Orlu. "Come *on*," she whispered.

Orlu shook his head. He looked scared, sweat beading on his forehead.

Sunny bit her lip and frowned. "Geez, how old are you?! They're only boobs!"

It seemed to take all his effort to put one foot in front of the next. When he reached Sunny, she grabbed his hand and dragged him with her to Bola.

Bola was a thin middle-aged woman with long brown braids, three dark lines engraved on each cheek, and a large white oval painted across her forehead. She sat calmly in her chair wearing nothing but a flowing white skirt that reached her ankles. Her long skinny breasts did indeed hang well below her waist, touching her lap. She wore several blue and white bead necklaces that rested on her chest.

"You all look like students, and students can be stupid," she said in a hard voice. "So no photographs while you are in my compound. The last time someone did this, they angered Mami Wata and died in an accident upon leaving."

"We . . . we're students, but we're not here to study you," Sunny said.

"Good. Temitope, leave us now."

"Yes, ma," the little girl said, then she walked out.

"What is wrong with you?" Bola suddenly asked Orlu. He was sitting stiff as a piece of wood and looking at anything but Bola. "Haven't you ever seen a woman's breasts before? Weren't you ever a baby?" She lifted and swung them from side to side. Orlu looked as if he was going to pass out, and Bola laughed a loud raucous laugh. Before Sunny could

control herself, she burst out laughing, too. She clapped her hands over her mouth and looked apologetically at Orlu. Then another giggle wracked her body, and her eyes began to water from the strain of holding it in.

"Look, boy, I am the servant of Mami Wata, goddess of the water, and as black Americans like to say, this is how we roll," she said. She looked at Sunny. "Did I say that right? You'd know better than me." She winked.

"Yeah," Sunny said.

"Relax, Orlu. Okay?"

Orlu only nodded, looking at the ground.

"I'm glad you brought him with." She paused, narrowing her eyes at Sunny. "My husband has spoken of you. Can you read the Nsibidi book he sold you yet?"

Sunny nodded.

"I like your hair comb," she said, grinning.

"Thanks."

"Now, you know I can't do a divination reading for you without you having something to give, right?"

"Oh," Sunny said. She reached into her pocket. "Of course. I don't have much but . . ."

"No, no, no, not *chittim*, not even your Lamb money," she said. "I want a story . . . one from Anyanwu."

"Huh?"

"I have heard of Anyanwu, that she may not be a good teller of stories, but she has good stories to tell."

"I . . ." Sunny looked at Orlu and then at Bola.

Bola gasped and said, "Oh. I see it now."

Sunny nodded. "Something happened to me." She felt her face flush hot, her eyes filling with tears. "I feel lost."

"You are," Bola said, growing very solemn. "How long have you been like . . . this?"

"Two days," Sunny said, her vision blurring from the tears. When she blinked, she saw that Bola was staring hard at her.

"But . . . it should have killed you," Bola said, her eyes wide.

"What are you talking about?" Orlu asked.

"My spirit face," Sunny said. "She's gone. I can't call her up! That's why I couldn't cross into Leopard Knocks on Thursday. That night, I tried working even a small juju and couldn't! And Anyanwu is gone and . . ."

The shock on Orlu's face was so much that Sunny stopped talking.

"All this time?" Orlu asked. "Since Thursday? You haven't had a spirit face?"

"Tell me what caused it," Bola said.

When Sunny told her all about the river beast, what she'd seen, and the bead hitting her in the face, Bola said, "This explains the oil spills in the delta."

Sunny nodded. "Ekwensu."

"We all sensed Mami Wata's fury yesterday morning,"

Bola said. "Yeeee, there is work to do, o." She sighed deeply and shook her head, looking troubled, and then looked up at Sunny. "Keep talking. Spit it all out." Sunny told her the details about her battle with the djinn in the basement and her previous encounter with the lake beast.

"*Kai!*" Bola exclaimed, clapping her hands to enunciate her outrage, when Sunny finished. She got up and paced back and forth. "This is something new. This is something new, o." She started speaking in rapid Yoruba to herself.

Sunny felt Orlu's gaze burning a hole into the side of her face, but she refused to meet his gaze. She wished she'd had him stay in the waiting room.

"Okay, okay, o," Bola said, sitting back before Sunny. "Focus," she whispered to herself. "There is so much." She took a deep breath as she gazed at Sunny. Then she exhaled, pointed at Sunny, and said, "Okay. You. Sunny Nwazue. I know of this problem you have. Never witnessed a victim of it who still carried life, but I know the condition. It's called doubling. It sounds like a misnomer because you have lost a part of yourself, but your spirit face is just not here. So in a sense, you've been doubled. Ekwensu did it to you.

"She threw one of her beads at you. The moment it hit you—" Bola snapped her fingers loudly enough to make Sunny jump. "Anyanwu was cut from you." Bola narrowed her eyes and tapped at her head. "Ekwensu is smart. It was

the only way to distract Anyanwu enough so Ekwensu could push out of the wilderness without having to deal with Anyanwu while she was weak. But Ekwensu took a great risk, too. If you had caught that bead, you and Anyanwu could have destroyed Ekwensu right then and there. That bead was one of her *iyi-uwa*, her power.

"Anyway, it's done. She's in the world and you have been doubled, the connection between you and Anyanwu has been ripped apart . . . but somehow you both live. Your Anyanwu is out there. I don't know where she is."

Sunny felt ill. "Will she come back to me?" Sunny asked. Then she asked the question that had been nagging her since she realized Anyanwu was gone. "Even if the bond is broken, why would she leave me?" Tears welled up in her eyes again, and Orlu took her hand. "She's gone. I don't even feel her near. If this could kill me, why would she leave? Why . . ."

"Anyanwu is old," Bola said. "I know of her. All the elders, priestesses, priests, know her, Sunny. The ancient will travel; it is not for us to question. Especially with Ekwensu now probably able to occupy the mundane world *and* the wilderness, too."

"But . . ."

"Usually, I require payment for my services," she said. "My payment today is that you've shown me something I have never seen before: a living Leopard Person with no spirit face. I'd have said this was an abomination an hour ago, but

you have taught me otherwise. Debt paid. Plus, I want to see what the cowries tell me about you."

She stood up and stretched her back. Then she brought out some cowries from her skirt pocket and moved to an open space in the room.

"So what is it that you especially want to know, Sunny? Aside from how to find your spirit face?"

Sunny paused for a moment, thinking. Since Anyanwu had disappeared, she hadn't thought about much else. What did anything else really matter? Then she remembered. "I've been having dreams of the . . . end," she said. "Before I discovered I was a free agent, I was shown the world's end in the flame of a candle. Sugar Cream says that some of my spirit friends or enemies from the wilderness showed all of that to me. I don't know why. But in a lot of ways, it led me to Leopard society. But these new dreams . . . they're different." *They leave me asking myself who I am*, she wanted to say. But she'd never admit something so pathetic in front of Orlu. "I just want to know . . . what the dreams mean. Do they mean that soon . . ."

"Yes, yes, yes," Bola said, dismissively waving her hand at Sunny. "Shut up now. I've got it."

Sunny was glad to shut up. Once she started talking, it was as if she had diarrhea of the mouth. *Words gushing forth like . . . water*, she thought, getting up. Orlu was already standing to Bola's left, his hands deep in his pockets, something he

only did when he felt perfectly safe, which wasn't often at all. Bola's home must have really been protected.

"This can't be anything *but* interesting," Bola said as she knelt on the floor. "Let's see what the cowry catcher will show us today. Mouth open or mouth closed, only the cowry catcher knows." She blew on her handful of cowries. "I know some, but soon I'll know more."

"I hope it's good news," Orlu muttered.

"Whatever it is, at least I'll know what's going on," Sunny replied.

Bola brought the handful of shells to her lips and whispered something. Then she pointed and looked upward and said, "Inshallah. Chukwu is not concerned and only Allah can make it so." Then she threw the cowries. As they fell and tumbled to the hardwood floor, Sunny's right ear began to ring. She pressed her hand to it, and Bola looked at her and nodded. "That's the sound you hear when someone is talking about you. They are discussing your past, present, or future. I would tell you to whistle into your fist and say 'Let it be good,' but you cannot control those who inhabit the wilderness. Not when you are more than halfway there yourself."

Sunny pressed her ear harder as she watched the cowries settle. They took longer than was normal. Some of them tumbled in a circle over and over. Others hopped and bounced like popcorn kernels on a skillet. Some came to rest and then flipped back over. And several of them clicked together three

times before going into a feverish dance on their sides. But finally, after nearly a minute, they all came to rest.

The room was silent as the three of them looked hard at the shells—Bola with the gaze of an excited, intrigued expert, and Sunny and Orlu with confusion. Ten minutes passed and Bola still hadn't moved. It almost looked as if she were in suspended animation.

"Is she breathing?" Sunny whispered.

But Orlu was looking around, his hands out of his pockets. "Did you hear something?"

Sunny frowned, suddenly on edge. "No."

"Shhh," Orlu said. "Someone's here."

Sunny scanned the entire room. No one. The sun shone through the large wall of windows and the room was pleasantly warm. But . . . she smelled something. She flared her nostrils. "What is that?" she whispered. It wasn't sour, pungent, sweet, oily, or foul. It wasn't stinky, delicious, stinging, perfumy, or dirty. She couldn't describe it. But it was strong and it was permeating the room. She and Orlu moved closer to one another.

Suddenly, Bola turned to Sunny. Her eyes were twitchy, her face blank of emotion. She stiffly stood up and came closer. Sunny grabbed Orlu's arm, but she stood her ground, facing Bola . . . or whoever it was possessing Bola's body.

"Sunny Nwazuuuue, who are youuuuuu?" she sang. She chuckled drily.

Sunny shuddered, pressing closer to Orlu.

"I see you."

Bola stopped, squinting her eyes at Sunny. "Yes, the free agent lucky enough to twin with Anyanwu and unlucky enough to be untwinned from her twin." She looked Sunny up and down. "So young and you've lost one so old." She stepped closer. "But you still live. I can speak to you. It is you who is having the dreams and asked what they are about."

"Yes," Sunny squeaked. "I want to know . . ."

"If the end of the world will come tomorrow. You wake up quietly afraid every morning that the sun will rise only to burn everything to ash and you'll have nowhere to hide but back on the other side where you were such a powerful guide. Warrior Sunny Nwazue of Nimm by way of Ozoemena of Nimm. But who are you really, anymore?"

Sunny felt her face growing hot, tears behind her eyes. The words of the one possessing Bola were like the slash of knives.

"Yes, words can cut deep," the one who was not Bola said. "They are clearer than images, more exact. Especially the magical kind, like the Nsibidi. Keep learning Nsibidi, you will need it; the answers are within it, and so much more. Your dreams, you have misinterpreted. Think, think hard. What you saw. It was not like what the wilderling forced upon you. This was something else and you know it. This was you using what you have. Shape-shifter, who can step into our wilderness when

she learns that she can. Time folder, who can stop it when she hates someone enough." She crept closer to Sunny and cocked her head. "Smoking city or city of smoke?"

Orlu gasped. "Oh my God!"

"What?" Sunny asked.

"Ah, finally it dawns on you. See what happens when you only assume the negative?" Bola said, focusing for the first time on Orlu. "It's not always the worst."

"What? WHAT?!" Sunny asked him.

"Your man understands, that's what," she said. "The vision was just nudging toward where you must go to do what the world needs."

"But Osisi isn't . . . We can't *get* there," Orlu said.

"Yes, you can," Bola said. "Find Udide beneath the city of Lagos and have her weave you a flying grasscutter. Those can fly to Osisi easy. It will take you, if you can convince it."

"Lagos?" Sunny said. "How are we supposed to get to Lagos?! That's hours away! And what's Osisi?"

"Udide, she will be there? In Lagos?" Orlu asked.

"Yes."

"Through the market, as it says in the beast books?" he asked.

"Yes, for now."

"Flying grasscutters are obnoxious," he said, pinching his chin as he thought. "It'll get us all caned, or worse."

"Ekwensu has made it here. Time has run out and now

it'll be more difficult. A flying grasscutter is the fastest way to get to Osisi," Bola stressed. "If Ekwensu comes, a caning is the least of your worries."

Bola's face squeezed with pain and she stumbled back. She rubbed her eyes, opened her mouth, and hacked loudly. "Sunny," she gasped. "Both Leopards and Lambs in this world have jobs to do. It is not just you, but you have a job. You four, really. Ekwensu is getting her rest. She will strike soon. Gather yourselves. Sunny, you need Anyanwu. That old one is like an *ogbanje*. Tempt her back to you with love." She hacked again and sat down hard. Sunny then saw it, a periwinkle haze rising delicately from Bola's mouth and then dissipating into the air.

Slowly Bola stood up, straightening her skirt. She cleared her throat. "Temitope!" she gasped. She coughed and this time shouted, "Temitope!" The little girl came walking in with her professional walk.

"Yes, ma," she said in her tiny voice.

"We're done here," Bola said. "Send in the next client."

Once Sunny and Orlu were outside the gate, it was like stepping into another world. One that was not so full of water.

They walked in silence for several minutes. Then Orlu finally asked, "She's just . . . gone?"

Sunny nodded.

Silence for several more minutes.

"I'm sorry," Orlu finally said. "I can't even . . ."

"I'll get her back," Sunny said. Though she had no idea how. As she walked, she clenched and unclenched her fists. Doing so made her feel a little stronger. She kicked a large stone down the dirt road with her sandal and watched it sail far ahead. "I know her best."

"Yeah," Orlu said. But he sounded doubtful and . . . disturbed. As if Sunny had an unsightly gash in her cheek.

"What's Osisi?" Sunny immediately asked.

"You know how the living world and the wilderness are two places but they coexist?"

Sunny nodded. "Wait," she said, remembering. "I've read about full places. In Sugar Cream's Nsibidi book, she talks about how she and the baboons who raised her lived in a patch of forest that was full. Lambs were terrified of it because they saw it as a bit of forest they'd just never come out of."

Orlu nodded. "That can happen, yes. Osisi isn't just a patch of land, though. It's big. It's a town that is miles wide and long. It's somewhere between Igboland and Yorubaland and Hausaland . . . No one really knows exactly where but . . . wherever it is, you need to go there."

"Why?"

"Your dreams apparently are telling you to . . . probably yourself, somehow. Sunny, Osisi looks like a city made of

smoke." He shook his head. "I don't know how Sasha, Chi-chi, and I didn't put two and two together. I guess we all just assumed . . ."

"The worst," Sunny said. So she wasn't dreaming of the world's end this time. She was seeing a world that was full.

"Yeah," Orlu said. "The only way to get there, for *us* to get there—you're not going alone—is by having a beast called a flying grasscutter take us. I've studied these before because they're fascinating. There was one living in Night Runner Forest some decades ago, and there's information about it in the book I have." He shook his head. "You'll have to just see it to understand it. Fact is, we have to get to Lagos somehow."

Sunny just held up a hand. Enough. Enough. Enough. "I'm going to Sugar Cream's. I'll see you later."

18
CLOUDY SKIES

The next morning was a Sunday and Sunny was glad. She hadn't slept at all. Every time she started to drift off, she remembered that her spirit face was missing and she'd wake up. "Sleep is the cousin of death," she'd once heard, and the saying came back to her now. She didn't want to meet death without Anyanwu.

So, all night, she stared at her ceiling. Thinking and thinking. Where could Anyanwu be? What if she met Ekwensu? Where did one's spirit face go? Did it actually "go" places like a thing with a physical body? Did it return to the wilderness, where it could lose itself in the ebb and flow of spirit? Or did it just wink out of existence like a puff of smoke? All of these

possibilities made her feel ill with worry and self-pity.

She'd only been a Leopard Person for a little less than two years. Prior to that, she'd had no such relationship with the spiritual existence that was her spirit face. It shouldn't have been so devastating to return to the oneness of Lambdom. Nevertheless, if there was any evidence that she'd become a full-fledged Leopard girl, it was the fact that this was not the case. She felt the absence of Anyanwu so profoundly that she experienced moments of complete and total despair.

She lay in bed staring at the window watching the sun come up. She saw her wasp artist zoom out of its nest and out through the part of the screen she'd left open. She heard the morning activity of nearby neighbors. And she heard all this alone, as less than herself. While staring out the window, she had an idea. It made complete sense.

She rolled out of bed, glancing at the *Leopard Knocks Daily* newspaper on it. She considered reading through it for any possible news about Ekwensu or even more oil spills in the Niger Delta. Instead, she let it fall to the floor and went to her desktop computer. She put on her headphones and clicked on one of her favorite links, titled Six Hours of Mozart, and turned up the volume. The music washed over her and she closed her eyes, conjuring up an image in her mind of a ballerina she especially liked named Michaela DePrince.

She imagined her in a grassy field wearing jean shorts, a white T-shirt, and black pointe shoes. As the music danced,

so did Michaela, leaping, stretching, and swaying. Sunny smiled as she sat back in her chair, feeling more relaxed than she'd felt since before the lake beast incident. She called Anyanwu to come and enjoy. She called and called. And then she opened her eyes, her joy gone. She slumped in her chair. She pulled off her headphones. She crawled back into her bed and got under the sheets. She didn't sleep.

She spent the day hanging around her mother, who was cooking her favorite red stew. She helped slice onions, ginger, and garlic, and blended tomatoes and bell peppers while her mother chopped and baked chicken and smoked turkey. As the stew boiled, she sat at the table and stared into space while her mother watched a Nollywood movie.

Sunny was glad her mother didn't ask why she wasn't out with Chichi, Orlu, and Sasha. She was glad her mother didn't ask her much of anything. It was nice. Just being around her, working with their hands, cooking. Then later on, it was nice just sitting at the dinner table with her father eating rice and stew. He read the newspaper and she read her current book, a graphic novel called *Aya: Love in Yop City*.

All this soothed her, but by the time night came, it all sat right back on her shoulders, weighty as bags of sand. It was an overcast night and thunder rumbled in the clouds above. She'd slept poorly, as she had for the last two nights. She hadn't spoken to Chichi, Orlu, or Sasha, she hadn't worked one small juju, no Leopard Knocks, which meant no Sugar

Cream. She'd have said that this was her life before realizing her Leopardom, but it wasn't. Before, she'd had a group of other friends, and she'd never known of that other side of her that was now gone, and Sunny knew she could never ever go back. It was like being left on an island. Her Saturday meetings with Sugar Cream and Wednesdays with Anatov and the others. Even Lamb school would be a problem. How would she face Orlu?

No going forward, no going backward. "It's like being dead," she whispered. The thunder rumbled some more and she suddenly jumped up and strode to her closet. She threw on some shorts and a T-shirt, sandals, grabbed her soccer ball, and was out the back door. Her parents might wonder where she'd gone, Ugonna, too. *Let them*, she thought, tears streaming down her face.

The field where they played soccer wasn't far. Especially when she walked with purpose. Her long, strong legs got her there in no time, and when she stepped onto the empty, slightly overgrown fields, she dropped the ball and kicked it hard. She jogged after the ball into the center of the field and stopped it with her foot. She looked up into the churning gray sky. There was a flash of lightning and then several seconds later, the rumble of thunder.

She knew the juju to prevent being struck by lightning, a variation of the rain-deflecting juju one used when caught in a downpour. Sunny chuckled bitterly to herself and kicked

her soccer ball. "Let it strike," she muttered as she worked the ball with her fast feet. Back, to the side, tapping it in the air and catching it with the bottom of her foot behind her back, kick it lightly forward, behind, around. She smiled as she moved and dribbled the ball. She did a turn and kicked it back toward the other goal.

She ran across the field and shot it into the goal, the soft whisper of net against ball making her heart leap with a familiar joy. She grabbed the ball with her feet and worked it across the field to the other side and did it again. And then she did it again. All alone under the churning sunless sky, she enjoyed her own footwork, imagining that she was playing a one-on-one game against herself. The air rushed in and out of her lungs. She threw off her sandals so she could feel the hard, uneven ground with her tough feet.

She imagined she was trying to move the ball around herself, and this made her feet move faster. She did a bump and run, shoving herself out of the way and then taking off with the ball across the field. She laughed, because it had almost felt like she'd shoved someone. She'd shot the ball directly at the goal when she realized it. And her realization was immediately verified when the ball didn't go in. Instead, it was deflected by a seemingly invisible force.

Then the force became visible, and Sunny thought for a moment lightning had struck the field. She stood before the goal as the ball rolled to her feet. She rested a bare foot on

it and wiped sweat from her brow. All the movement had cleared her mind, eased her muscles, and filled her with joy. Nevertheless, it was almost as if the clarity made it so that the anger could flow through her blood more easily. It flooded her system so hot and full that the world around her seemed to swell.

"Why'd you leave?" she shouted.

Then she blasted the soccer ball right toward the blurred but bright yellow figure standing in the goal. The ball sailed through it, and then the blur dissolved to nothing. Sunny stood there staring with wide eyes. Raindrops began to fall.

"I had to attend a meeting."

Sunny felt fury and surprise flip her belly as the rain came down harder. "A meeting?" she shouted. "You . . . you left me to go to a *meeting*?" Hot tears squeezed from her eyes and mixed with the cool rain.

"Rain Shelf yourself," Anyanwu said.

"I can't!" Sunny snapped. But maybe she could, now that Anyanwu was near. She decided to try, bringing out her juju knife. She blinked away tears as she worked the simple Rain Shelf juju and immediately the rain stopped falling on her, as if she held an umbrella.

"You're foolish," Anyanwu said. "And needy. And insecure."

Now the tears came harder for Sunny, and she plopped down on the grass. The squelchy wetness of the grass felt

as awful as she felt. When she looked up, she found herself facing a figure of soft, glowing yellow light. They stared at each other for what felt like minutes. Around them, heavy rain splashed down, lightning flashed and thunder responded. They sat in the middle of the soccer field, and for the moment, to Sunny there was no one else on earth.

"Shut up," Sunny muttered. A flash of lightning nearby made her jump. She looked at Anyanwu. "You did that!"

"I didn't do anything," Anyanwu said.

Sunny didn't believe her. "You . . . you have always known who you are. You're old, you know everything." She had to stop to catch her breath, tears in her eyes again. "How am I supposed to believe in what I am when no one even knew this could happen? Even Orlu looked at me like I was an alien!"

"Yes. You are insecure."

Sunny grabbed a handful of wet grass and threw it at Anyanwu. She blinked when the clump hit the soft glow and fell to the ground. She threw more. Then Anyanwu grabbed an even bigger clump and flung it at Sunny, hitting her right in the face. Some of it got in her mouth, and she spit it out.

"Do you think I make you a Leopard Person?" Anyanwu asked.

"Yes!"

Anyanwu laughed. "I'm your spirit memory, I'm you outside of time, I'm your spirit face, I am *you*. You are me.

Our Leopardom is within all that makes us."

"Then why couldn't I go to Leopard Knocks that day?"

"Because, as I said, you're insecure."

Sunny pressed her lips together and frowned.

"Our bond's been broken," Anyanwu continued. "That trauma . . . few will ever know it. We've gone through it twice; it took two traumas to tear it completely. When that djinn pulled us in and when Ekwensu took advantage and finished the job."

Sunny nodded as they both felt a ghost of the sharp pains that had reverberated through their entire being. Twice.

"The second time, did you feel when we drifted?" Anyanwu asked.

"Yes."

"That was when we should have died. We'd have lost this connected duality and returned to the wilderness as one again. But we lived, because we are Sunny and Anyanwu." Sunny felt Anyanwu's confident pleasure at this fact. "Sunny, you can work whatever juju you please, whether I am there or not. That's why I say you're insecure. You couldn't get into Leopard Knocks because you didn't believe you were a Leopard Person without me."

"But . . ."

"Work a little harder and be more confident. Our bond is broken; some compensation is required. It's like loving and cherishing someone without needing the bonds of marriage

to enforce it," Anyanwu said. "By sinister means, you and I are free."

Sunny sat with Anyanwu's words, staring into the pouring rain. The lightning and thunder were fading. But even if they didn't, she wasn't afraid of being struck anymore. Sunny took a deep breath and then asked, "What was the meeting?"

She could feel Anyanwu smile. "None of your business."

Sunny stared at Anyanwu for a moment and then burst out laughing. She got up and grabbed her soccer ball. It flew out of her hands as Anyanwu took off with it across the field. Sunny had to run fast to catch up with her. And the two played like that until the rain stopped.

On the way back, she came upon Sasha walking up the road, his hands shoved in the pockets of his jeans. By this time, the air had taken on so much humidity that breathing it was almost like drinking water.

"What are you doing in the rain?" Sunny asked, slapping and grasping hands with him.

"Looking for you."

"I was playing soccer," she said, tossing her wet ball up and catching it.

"With the lightning and thunder?"

"You could say that."

"You've been avoiding us all weekend."

Sunny shrugged. They began to walk.

"How come Orlu didn't come?"

Sasha shrugged again. "Said you probably needed some time to yourself. Me, I don't mess around. I came to see what's up. So, you good?"

"Yeah, I'm fine," she said.

"Even after . . . after what happened with . . ."

"Yeah. We can go to Leopard Knocks today, if you all want." She hesitated and then said, "The river beast won't stop me." She could feel Anyanwu within her as she said it. And she could feel that her presence was different. Not so locked. And this was verified when she realized she suddenly didn't feel Anyanwu within her. Anyanwu had gone off again, to wherever she went off to.

Sasha looked at her, narrowing his eyes. "You're different somehow."

"Yeah," she said. Then she laughed, tossing her soccer ball in the air and catching it with her feet. She passed it to Sasha, who caught it and then tapped it back to Sunny. She caught it, brought out her juju knife, and worked a quick juju that rubbed off the mud. It hadn't been difficult, but she noticed that she did have to concentrate a little harder on mentally aligning her words with her juju knife flourish.

"Jollof rice and goat meat at Mama Put's Putting Place?" Sasha asked.

Sunny smiled. "Definitely. My treat."

19
TRUST, *SHA*

"My clothes were ruined, but I knew that would happen," Orlu said, grinning wider than Sunny had ever seen him grin. "Nancy took me over the ocean!" His jeans were filthy with bright red palm oil and splashes of mud, as were his T-shirt and red Chuck Taylor gym shoes.

He'd been working closely with his mentor Taiwo's Miri Bird for the past two weeks, and he'd had a particularly interesting weekend. The bird, whose name was Nancy, regularly flew him up to Taiwo's palm tree hut, and the two had cultivated a friendship. Orlu had since taken it upon himself to study Nancy's species and ancestral bloodline. Flattered by his interest, the bird had agreed to take him for an extended

ride to visit its mother forty miles east in the Cross River Forest.

"You're crazy to let that big chicken fly you that far, man," Sasha said.

Orlu only rolled his eyes. His general philosophy when it came to Sasha's smart mouth was, Do not engage. Sunny thought it worked every time.

Chichi, who sat in the doorway, loudly sucked her teeth and looked away. Sasha glared at her, and Sunny could practically feel the temperature rise a few degrees.

It was a rare Sunday where they'd all finished their chores, homework, and assignments, and none of them had any relatives or family friends to visit with their parents. It was Chichi's idea to meet in her hut. Her mother was at Leopard Knocks giving a lecture to some other third-level students. Thus, Chichi sat in the doorway, the cloth curtain piled on her back, a Banga brand herbal cigarette in her left hand. She took a puff and Sunny squeezed her face and looked away. Bangas were healthier than tobacco cigarettes and smelled nicer, but Sunny agreed with Orlu: a cigarette was a cigarette. And cigarettes were filthy.

"If you've got something to say, don't bother saying it," Sasha snapped. "Nothing comes from your mouth but lies."

"Come on, you guys," Sunny whined. "Can't you just . . ."

"Just what?!" Sasha screeched. "She's been cheating on me with your brother! She doesn't deny it!" He looked at Chichi. "Deny it."

Chichi slowly blew out smoke. "How old are we? We're not attached at the hip."

"Why am I even here?!" Sasha shouted. He started to walk away, but Orlu caught his shoulder.

"Because I asked you to come," he said. "Please. We're an *Oha* coven, remember? We can't . . ."

"Black Hat is dead," Sasha snapped. "Nigga killed himself. We all saw it. Our coven is *dissolved*."

"It's not over," Sunny said. "Ekwensu is here now! We . . ."

"If we are a coven, then there should be trust," Sasha insisted as he looked at Chichi.

"You think I don't know about Ronke? *Months*, you and her," Chichi spat. Sunny and Orlu looked at Sasha with raised eyebrows. Sasha's mouth hung open with shock.

"Trust, *sha*. It goes both ways," Chichi quietly said.

"Who is Ronke?" Sunny asked.

But Sasha's and Chichi's eyes were locked. They stayed like this for several moments. Chichi was the first to look away. She looked at Orlu. "There is a reason I asked you to have us meet here," she said. She momentarily looked at Sasha. "*All* of us. I have been thinking about it all. Black Hat, Ekwensu, Sunny, your dreams, that first vision you had in the candle. I've been thinking most about your . . . condition."

"You mean being doubled?" Sunny said. "Sheesh, it's not like Voldemort's name, you can say it aloud."

"Sorry," Chichi said, wrinkling her nose as if she smelled something bad. "It's just so . . . ugh."

"I know, right?" Sasha said. "I don't even know how you deal with it. It's like a guy waking up one day, looking down, and finding his . . ."

"Shut up, Sasha," Orlu groaned. "Chichi, what were you saying?"

"It's not your fault, Sunny," Chichi said. "Plus, I think you will change. Soon."

"What are you talking about?" Sunny asked, frowning. She'd told the three of them about being torn from Anyanwu, but not the full extent of it. Her relationship with Anyanwu who came and went as she pleased was as much her own business as the sight of her spirit face. But was there something else she needed to know about all this?

Sasha stepped closer. "It's obvious. Chichi has an idea," he said flatly. "What is it?"

Again, Chichi and Sasha looked at each other for a long time. Sunny looked from one to the other. She hated when they did this. Even when they were fighting, they shared some weird telepathy-like communication. It had something to do with their natural ability, that lightning-fast photographic thinking they both possessed. Orlu put his hands in his pockets, waiting. He was also used to it.

"Okay, so, Sunny, you . . . *we* have to get to Lagos to find Udide, according to Bola, right?" Chichi said. "You can't do this alone and it only makes sense for all of us to go."

"Well, yeah," Sunny said, biting her lip. "But how are we supposed to . . ."

"Your brother can take us," Chichi blurted.

Sasha cursed loudly and walked away.

"What?" Sunny said. "But Orlu and I are in school. It's not . . ."

Sasha had turned back and was looking at Chichi again, his face still angry. But not *as* angry. Chichi nodded at him. "This is messed up," he blurted.

Chichi shrugged. "But you know it's a good idea."

"Can you two please tell us your plan," Orlu said, sounding irritated, "since Sunny and I are too slow to follow your mind-reading?"

"I've asked Chukwu already," Chichi said. "Sunny, he knows he owes you. After making the greatest, most dangerous mistake of his life, he's back in school and alive because of *you*. He knows it was you, even if he doesn't know exactly *what* you did. He's got friends in Lagos and he's got his Jeep. We can go after Christmas, during your break."

"A road trip?" Sunny said. "We *drive*?!"

"Yes," Sasha said.

"But Aba Road is not friendly," Sunny darkly said. "It's . . ."

"I can't afford a plane ticket," Chichi said. "And I will never get on one of those filthy things, anyway. When I reach third level, I'll teach myself how to glide so I can travel distances in a more sophisticated *sanitary* way."

"Well, maybe my parents could . . ."

"Sunny, you know they'd ask too many questions," Chichi said.

"How about a funky train, then?" she asked. "There must be some that travel to Lagos."

"How will you explain going away for so many days, this time?" Chichi said. "You can convince your parents more easily if you go with Chukwu."

"What of Anatov and all our mentors?" Sunny asked. She hadn't told Sugar Cream about Bola's words or her doubling, nor Anatov. She wanted to, but she just didn't know *how*. Or maybe she wasn't ready.

"It's a road trip," Sasha said. "They'd all love for us to do that kind of thing."

"Well, it'll take forever, if we live," Sunny said. "I made that drive once with my father and brothers years ago. It was crazy."

"We can work some protection jujus," Orlu said. "It's doable."

"We're Leopard People and we've faced worse things," Chichi said.

Sunny couldn't argue with that.

Orlu turned to Sasha. "If we go, will you come?"

He paused. Then he said, "Yes. For Sunny. If Sunny goes."

Orlu smiled and so did Sunny.

"But my parents will never allow it," Sunny said. "That's, like, a ten-hour drive! And it's dangerous and . . ."

"Leave that to your brother," Chichi said. "He'll get them to say yes."

Chichi was right. Chukwu, God's Gift to Women, the Apple of Her Father's Eye, He Who Was Named After the Supreme Deity of Igbo Cosmology, could do no wrong. Ever since they were young children, her father had given Chukwu the freedom to do basically whatever he wanted. When Chukwu insisted on it, there wasn't a problem.

"And remember, he has friends in Lagos, too," Chichi added. "He can say he's going to see them and we're just going along for fun."

"Chichi," Sasha said.

"Fine," she said, getting up.

Neither Sunny nor Orlu said a word as Chichi and Sasha walked up the road, several feet between them, backs stiff, talking softly.

Orlu took Sunny's hand and Sunny smiled. He squeezed it.

"Do you really want to do this?"

"Do I have a choice?" Sunny asked. It wasn't a good time to do this, either. The doubling made working juju more difficult, and the effects of it still left her feeling . . . beside herself. And even if they made it to this full place, what effect would being there have on someone who'd been doubled?

"Yes," Orlu said.

Sunny chuckled. "If my parents allow it, I do. Will you come?"

"You need to ask me?"

"For this, I think I do."

He nodded. "I'll come."

"I'm not sure if I like the idea of being in a Jeep with Sasha and Chichi with Chukwu driving."

"Sasha will sit in the passenger seat," Orlu said. "That'll calm his ego. Chichi will sit behind him. You will sit in the middle and I will sit behind Chukwu. There will be less trouble that way and you'll be in the most protected position."

"You think I need to be . . ."

"Yes," he said. "Sunny, I don't think you fully understand your position in this."

"I do," she said.

"No, you don't."

They were quiet. Sunny thought of the last thing the possessed Bola had said just before the friendly wilderness spirit possessing her left her body: "Ekwensu is getting her rest. She will strike soon. Gather yourselves." Ekwensu would strike at her, Sunny, first.

"Maybe," Sunny said. "But Ekwensu hates me *and* I've seen what was in the candle, Orlu. I know better than anyone what's coming." She paused. "If I can help stop it, I'm ready to do what I need to do." She sighed. "Sometimes ignorance is bliss."

"Can't argue with you there."

20
ROAD TRIP

It was days before Christmas, and Chukwu had come home from university. Sunny was in the kitchen cooking rice and stew when she heard him drive into the compound blasting Nas. Sasha would have been impressed. Nas was Sasha's favorite rapper of all time.

Chukwu was with his best friend who'd nearly gotten him killed, Adebayo. Sunny eyed him as she added the last of the chicken wings to the stew and set it on low heat. She knew Adebayo but not that well. When he came by, he'd disappear into her brothers' room with Chukwu to play video games. As they grew older, they'd immediately be off to play soccer or join those boxing matches Chukwu had never told her about or whatever they did.

The Adebayo whom Sunny knew was from that fateful night with the Red Sharks. He hadn't seen her, but she'd seen him. All she could think now as she approached him and her brother, both of whom were bobbing their heads to the loud music, was that this idiot had slapped Chukwu across the face. How were they still friends? And from the swollen looks of the muscles bursting from their designer T-shirts, they'd continued working out in that dank sweaty basement of a gym.

"Welcome," Sunny said, smiling at Chukwu as she walked up to the car. "How na dey?"

"I dey kanpe," he said, giving her a hug. "I'm fine."

She looked at Adebayo and felt a cool satisfaction when even with his muscles he seemed to shrink in her presence. "Good afternoon," she said to him.

He grunted, "Hello."

Sunny waited for Chukwu to greet their parents with Adebayo, drop Adebayo off at his home, and come back. She cornered him in the kitchen when she knew Ugonna was in his room submerged in a video conversation on his computer and their parents were watching a Nollywood film in the living room. Chukwu was microwaving some jollof rice and two large pieces of goat meat.

"Is that supposed to be a snack?" she asked.

"Yes," he said, moving past her to sit at the table. He flexed his arms as he put the plate down. "Gotta feed these."

Sunny rolled her eyes and grabbed two plantain. "Want some?"

"Of course."

She brought out a knife and sliced the first one down the skin. She removed the thick peel and put the plantain on a plate and did the same with the next. "So how have things been?" she ventured. "At school." Her back was to him but she didn't have to look to see that he'd stiffened.

"Very well," he said.

"Good."

"Next semester, my biology professor wants me to be his assistant lecturer."

This time Sunny stiffened. To be a student lecturer was a highly respected position that students fought tooth and nail to get. It gave you valued teaching experience and broadcast to everyone that you were a top student. In addition, it showed that you had clout. It was one of the biggest reasons people joined confraternities.

"Really?" she said.

She turned around to find her brother looking straight at her. His face serious. "Yeah," he said. "Everyone is afraid of me." His face cracked into a smile. "They think I have strong juju, so they don't want to mess with me."

Sunny sat down across from him.

"What did you and Chichi do?" he asked.

"Can't tell you."

"So you did something?"

"Can't say."

He laughed. "That's what Chichi says. She gets all tricky and mysterious and tight-lipped. You want to know what Adebayo thinks?"

"What does he think?"

"He had terrible nightmares about me when I was gone," he said. "About me being sliced up and my parts given to some ritual killer. He said he woke up with his heart slamming in his chest. He thought he was having a heart attack. He thinks God sent witches to take his life. Capo, I have seen him, but he won't even look at me. He gets all shaky, starts muttering about Jesus, and practically runs in the opposite direction. All the teachers, I don't know what people are telling them. They smile a lot at me and ask me if I need any help with studying. My math professor offered to give me answers to the exam. I said no."

"Take no help," Sunny snapped with disgust. "What would be the point if it was all just . . ."

"I know," he said. "We both love soccer. What would be the point if we didn't have to play well to win, right? Same thing with school. I believe in *learning* . . . just like you."

Sunny nodded.

He smirked. "That's what I like about Chichi. Well, and because na dey beautiful, o."

Sunny rolled her eyes. *Does he even know about Sasha?!*

she wondered. She considered asking, then decided it wasn't her business.

"Chukwu," she said. "I've got a favor to ask you." She got up to finish slicing the plantain.

"What is it?"

She sliced for a bit before speaking. If he said no, she had no idea how they'd get to Lagos. Maybe they'd find a funky train that drove out there. But how would she get the time away . . . without their father disowning her? No, she had to do this very, very carefully.

"We need to go to Lagos for something," she blurted, turning to him. "Can you take us? It's important."

She quickly turned to her plantain, horrified with herself. She'd never been good at subtlety. That was Orlu's strength. This was her brother who used to punch her hard in the arm and call her Clorox as a way of showing sibling love. How could she be subtle or careful with *him*?

"What's so important there?" he asked.

"Don't tell Mom or Dad," she said. "I . . ."

"You aren't involved in some dangerous cult thing, right?" he asked.

"No," she said. "Nothing like that. I just need to . . . meet with someone. Please, I can't say more. You just have to trust me. Even if you won't take . . ."

"I'll take you," he said.

"Huh?"

"I'll take you."

"Really?"

"Yes. I owe you."

Sunny shook her head. "No, you don't."

"You did something that got me out of a bad situation."

"You'd do the same for me. You're my brother."

They stood looking at each other for a long time. Sunny's heart beat fast with emotion as she remembered how he'd looked that night. She couldn't keep the tears from welling up in her eyes.

"Okay," he said softly. "I don't owe you."

"So why help me?"

He shrugged. "I want to make sure you're safe."

"Okay," Sunny said, her throat tight. She turned back to her plantain, grabbing a pan and pouring vegetable oil into it. She added a bit of palm oil for flavor, just as her mother had taught her, and then turned on the heat.

"Plus, Adebayo will be there. He's spending the break at the house of his rich uncle and auntie. They're traveling to London, and they needed someone to watch their house." He laughed. "He'll have a huge mansion on Victoria Island all to himself. Living there like a king. Let me call him. When do you want to go?"

"Just after Christmas. We can spend New Year's there, maybe."

"So you and Chichi? And those other two, too?"

"Yes, me, Chichi, Orlu, and S-Sasha." Her face grew hot.

"Who is this Sasha? The American, right?" Chukwu asked.

Sunny bit her lip. "Yeah, he's . . ."

"Oh, I know about him," Chukwu said. He said no more and Sunny was relieved.

"You think Ugonna will want to come?" Sunny quickly asked.

"And not be here with his sweetheart to ring in the New Year? Doubtful."

Sunny scrunched her nose. "You mean Dolapo?" She'd met the girl once and was deeply annoyed by the way she looked Sunny up and down and then giggled. Since, Sunny hadn't spoken a word to her when Ugonna brought her around.

"The one and only."

"I'll ask anyway," Sunny said.

But Chukwu was right. Ugonna wasn't interested in Lagos, unless he could bring Dolapo. Plus, there wasn't enough room in the Jeep.

With Chukwu doing the asking, convincing their parents was even easier. "I guess you could use the break," her father said. He didn't say a thing about Sunny and her friends tagging along. He didn't even look at her. With the proud way he clapped Chukwu on the back, Sunny knew they'd be assured plenty of gas money and her father would entrust Chukwu with a nice amount of spending money, too. Good. She was going to Lagos to meet a giant spider.

21

BOOK OF SHADOWS

Today, it's raining in the forest. But by now you know that the water will not drench you. Not that badly. The Idiok have taken shelter, however. They don't like the mud, and the sound of the rain hitting the tree leaves is good for sleep. Those with young babies will be blessed with much-needed rest.

We are walking in my favorite part of the forest. I was attracted to this place, and that was how the Idiok knew to teach me Nsibidi. Look around you. Do you see that tree to your left with the smooth, narrow trunk and the tiny oval-shaped leaves? Yes, look all the way up and see that it stretches so high that it disappears into the rainclouds. It goes much higher than any normal tree. Imagine the things that crawl up and down that tree, into and out of the forest.

Do you see the vines that wind around it? Yes, you are see-ing correctly. They have light green delicate leaves that look deli-cious enough to eat. I have eaten them; they taste fresh like let-tuce. And see their white-pink flowers? See how they open and close, not slowly, not quickly? Like they are one great winding beast that is breathing? And see the ghost hopper perched on the tree trunk beside it? This part of my forest was full—a place that was both wilderness and physical world.

Lambs of the area avoided this place, deeming it long ago a forbidden forest. The patch of forest was small, no more than twenty square meters and easy to avoid, so for centuries, maybe even millennia, it had simply been left alone. For me, being a Leopard Person, it was seeing two layers of reality at once—the magical and the physical. I loved this place as the Idiok did.

By now, you may have come to understand. This book isn't about learning Nsibidi or my life or how to shape-shift. These are all things that I used to pull you off the ground. If you've gotten this far, you are strong in mind and body now. You know how to eat to live, you know how to plan, you know when you need rest, and you love Nsibidi. You are not my equal but you have my respect, for you are one of my kind. Good.

Right now, this book is about the city of smoke, a huge swath of land in this country that is full. Osisi. I pray that you will not have to see it, for it's not a place for any person who values his life, but if you have, if you have dreamed it, then you currently are the purpose of this book. There will be more than one of you, but only a handful. You . . .

Sunny had to fight her way out of the Nsibidi's grasp. This was one thing wholly unaffected by the doubling: her ability to read Nsibidi. She shook her head, flaring her nostrils and frowning, pressing Sugar Cream's book to her chest. As soon as she could see the light of her reading lamp and she could move her hands, she threw the book across the room. Tomorrow would be hard enough. Now this. All the threads of her life seemed to be winding into a tight bizarre rope that the universe expected her to walk across. Her brother, her questions, Sugar Cream's book . . . yes, *Trickster* was a damn good name for it. A perfect name for it. *Nsibidi: The Magical Language of the Spirits* literally shape-shifted, and not only in appearance (the symbols on the cover moved around like bugs) but in reasons for existing, in voice, in narrative. Was it even the same book for every reader?

And why did she have to get to this part on the morning they were leaving? "This is *wahala*," she whispered, lying back in her bed. She felt the usual reading fatigue that came with reading the book, and her head still ached from her fresh braids. Last night her mother had cornrowed her bushy yellow hair. The braids were long enough to touch her shoulders. Her hair was really growing. It was nearly the length it had been back when she'd burned it off while gazing into the candle. Two years ago. She'd pressed her Mami Wata comb into one of the side rows. It looked a little asymmetrically

strange, but she'd come to see the comb as good luck. She wasn't about to stop wearing it when they were going where they were going to do what they were going to do.

Bzzz!

She smiled and got up to turn on her bedroom light. It was about five A.M. and still dark outside, and she'd been using her reading light. When she turned her light on, Della buzzed its wings louder. Sunny's eyebrows went up, and she slowly walked to her cabinet for a better look. Then she just stood there, her mouth open. Staring.

It was a head. She could not tell what Della had used to create it. Maybe the petals of some sort of yellow flower or maybe yellow paper or some kind of yellow paste that it had found in the market. There was gold, too. The face was ringed with pointy gold rays, like a sun. The nose was wide-nostriled and flat like her father's. The yellow lips were smiling. The eyes were hazel, as if "God had run out of the right color." They were her eyes. This was her. Della had sculpted a perfect blend of her human and spirit face, Sunny and Anyanwu. *How does one hug an insect?* she wondered. "Della," she whispered. "I . . ."

The insect quickly flew circles around her head and then hovered in front of her eyes. Sunny smiled. This was its way of saying, *No need for words.*

"Do you understand that I will be gone for a few days?"

The insect buzzed.

"You've been in here when Chichi and I were talking," she said. "So you know what is going on."

It buzzed again.

"Should I be afraid?"

It flew to its art, stood on top of it, and buzzed its wings.

Sunny chuckled. Her wasp artist seemed to know who she was more than she did. And it thought rather highly of her. Della flew up to her and touched her forehead with its long, limp legs and then zipped into its nest on the ceiling.

There was a knock on her door. It was Chukwu.

"Good morning," she said. "I'm going to get dressed in a little bit. I . . ."

"I need to know something," he quietly said, coming in.

Sunny shut the door behind him. "Okay," she said.

"You still can't talk about it, can you?"

She shook her head. If she spoke, her words would feel heavy and slow the way they always did when she skirted too close to speaking directly about being Leopard.

"Is . . . whatever you all are doing in Lagos dangerous?" he asked.

Sunny thought about it. "We can handle it," she said.

"It doesn't involve any of these ritual people? Because they're murderers and . . ."

"I've never ever been involved with those people," she firmly said.

"Lagos is a big crazy place for you," he added.

"No more than it is for you. Plus, Orlu and Chichi know it well," she said. "And Sasha has . . . international street smarts."

Chukwu scoffed. "Sasha? No comment."

"We'll be fine," she said. "And I'll have my cell phone." But if all went as planned, there would be a few days where he wouldn't be able to reach her. She'd cross that bridge when she got to it.

What Sunny was more worried about was Sasha and Chukwu being in the same space for so many hours. As far as Sunny knew, Chichi refused to make a choice between the two, and both refused to cut things off with Chichi, so the love triangle was very much intact. How was this even going to go?

There was another knock on the door.

"What are you talking about in here?" Ugonna said, coming in.

"Just the trip," Chukwu said. "Why are you up?"

"Are you planning something?" he asked, ignoring Chukwu's question. He was looking at Sunny.

"No . . ."

"Because I don't see why you and your friends are going," he continued.

"If you want to go," Sunny said, "you could squeeze in. We talked about this."

"I'm not going," he said. "I just want to know why *you*

are." He put his arms across his chest. "I got a weird feeling about it."

Sunny was about to say he was just imagining things. She was about to laugh and say he sounded like their superstitious aunt Udobi. But she couldn't do it. For months her brother had been sensing things about her, drawing and drawing pictures that she now realized were of Osisi. He was worried about her in a way that only a brother could worry about his sister. "It's something I have to do," Sunny said, taking his hands and looking right into his eyes.

He looked back into hers. He let go and said, "Okay."

Sunny breathed a sigh of relief. She couldn't have said more if she wanted to.

"Text me," Ugonna said. "Not Mom, not Dad, *me*. Both of you."

"We will," Sunny said.

There was an awkward pause among the three siblings. The air was so heavy with secrets that Sunny could practically feel them pressing down on her shoulders. But at the same time, never in her entire life had she felt so close to her brothers. And that's why she did something she'd never done: she reached out to both of them and pulled them to her in a tight hug. For a moment, they resisted, but then they gave in.

"Sunny, I will whoop the hell out of you myself if anything happens to you," Chukwu said into her neck.

"Okay," Sunny whispered.

When they let go, her brothers quickly left the room. "We leave in an hour and a half," Chukwu said as he closed the door behind him.

Sunny climbed back into bed. She was tired from reading her Nsibidi book. A good half hour would do. Plenty of time.

Orlu arrived within the hour, early as usual. Chichi and Sasha arrived together minutes later. Sunny stood in the kitchen watching as Sasha and Chukwu were introduced to each other by Chichi. She quickly took off her glasses, wiped the lenses, and put them back on. She wanted to see this clearly. Sasha and her brother were nearly the same height, Sasha being tall for his age and standing not far from Chukwu's six feet. But where Chukwu was made of bulky muscle, Sasha was lean, springy muscle. Chukwu seemed to flex his biceps more as he held out his hand to shake Sasha's. Sunny wished she could have been outside to hear them greet each other.

Sasha quickly used the excuse of packing his bag in the Jeep to walk away from Chukwu. Chichi came into the kitchen all grins.

"That is so wrong," Sunny said.

"What?"

Sunny just shook her head. "You brought *Udide's Book of Shadows*, right?"

"Right here," she said, putting her backpack down. She

brought forth the satchel slung over her right shoulder and took out a large brownish-black book. The pages were thick and yellowed with age and dirt. It carried the smell of burned paper that Sunny could smell from where she stood. The cover was etched with hundreds of slightly raised lines, like it was wrapped in the thin long legs of spiders. Sunny felt skittish just looking at it. She kept imagining the lines lifting from the cover, unfolding, and the book standing up. She shuddered.

"You want to see?" Chichi asked. "The writing is so neat, but really small. It's like a computer wrote it!"

Sunny held up her hands and shook her head. "No, that's okay."

Chichi giggled and put it back in the satchel. "Sasha finding it . . . He really has a good eye, *sha*. I hear that it can only be seen when it wants to be seen. It's got a mind of its own like that ring in Lord of the Rings. The book isn't all evil, but it's not all good, either. Sasha and I were studying it last night. Udide likes to speak in stories. The spell for how to find her is in there, but she tells it in third person as an adventure story about some stupid guy who doesn't know how to mind his own business. He was some teenage Yoruba guy from a long line of wealthy kings near Lagos who thought he was entitled to know everything."

Sunny chuckled. "I know a guy like that."

"We all do," Chichi said. "And he's not always a Yoruba guy."

"Yeah, but it's always a guy," Sunny said, grinning.

They both had a good laugh. "So anyway," Chichi continued. "Udide hears most things and she especially hears all things that involve her."

Sunny frowned at this. "So most likely, she knows we're coming."

Chichi nodded.

"I don't like that," Sunny said.

"Doesn't matter what you like. It is what it is. So this guy's nerve in trying to find Udide annoyed the hell out of Udide. Udide has always made it known that she has to allow people to find her. You cannot just decide to find her and find her."

"So we have to ask her?" Sunny interrupted. "Do we make some offering or . . ."

"Just listen," Chichi snapped. "Because of the guy's arrogance, Udide decided to give him what he wanted. She showed him the way in a dream. Of course, him being an arrogant *mumu*, he thought the dream was all him. He immediately jumped out of bed and ran to his little brother's room. He needed three blue marbles, and his little brother just happened to have plenty. Imagine that. He did as the dream instructed and sure enough, he found Udide in a cave beneath Lagos. But when he found her, the sheer *sight* of her . . ."

"He turned to stone?" Sunny screeched. "Oh my God, is

she like Medusa in Greek mythology?! We're doomed! How are we going . . . we need a mirror then. Or . . ."

"Sunny, shut UP!!" Chichi shouted. "Geez, did you drink coffee this morning, *sha*? Or some of your dad's *ogogoro*?"

"My dad doesn't drink that. He drinks Guinness."

"Just listen! When he saw her, she was such a horrifying sight to him that part of his hair turned white. Remember he was only about sixteen. So he looked very strange. He ran off and never looked for Udide again. She ended this story with this line, 'Without knowing a way through at daytime, never attempt to pass through at night.' Udide has a dark sense of humor."

"I guess," Sunny said. "But if she does, well, is it smart to use this same way to find her? And what if it's just a story?"

Chichi shook her head. "Udide's stories are *never* just stories. And I think it was more about the intent that got that guy messed up. We are looking for her for a *good* reason, Sunny. These dreams you're having about Osisi are serious. Something bad is going to happen, Ekwensu is on the loose and you are involved. There is something you need in Osisi and the only way to get there is by something only *she* can create. We're not seeking her out to prove how powerful we are."

Sunny hoped Chichi was right. Her hair was already yellow. She didn't need white streaks from terror to make it even lighter.

vvvv

The five of them stood in front of the Jeep as Sunny smoothed out the map on the car. Chukwu put his finger on the city of Aba. "Okay, so we're near here. We should take the Port Harcourt–Aba Expressway to . . ."

"I know the way," Chichi said. "I studied a local map I bought at the market." She tapped her forehead. "Got it all up here."

"Me too," Sasha said. "Plus, I checked out Google Earth and Mapquest. Nothing much there, unless you're looking at Lagos itself. But this map is more accurate than a GPS or anything online. Anyway, it's not the way that'll be difficult. It's not getting robbed or driving the car down a pothole that'll be the real test. I ain't from here, but I been here a minute now."

"We can stop in Benin City and stay with my uncle," Chichi added.

"Oh no, hon," Chukwu said with a chuckle. "If we leave soon, we'll get there by sundown, trust me. We'll be at my friend's aunt and uncle's house in no time."

Chichi paused. Then she smiled sweetly and said, "Okay, o."

Orlu laughed to himself.

Within fifteen minutes, they were all piled into the Jeep. Chukwu grasped the wheel, trying not to look at Sasha. Sasha plugged his phone into the Jeep's stereo system and

was looking for just the right music so that he wouldn't have to talk to Chukwu. Chichi was behind Sasha, a Banga cigarette in hand that she planned to light as soon as they were past the sight of Sunny's parents. Orlu was behind Chukwu looking worried. And Sunny was in the middle waving at Ugonna.

"Call in a few hours," their father told Chukwu.

"And don't drive too fast," their mother said.

Sasha clicked PLAY and as soon as the song he'd chosen started, Chukwu's eyes lit up and he grinned. "Nas!"

Sasha looked surprised and then nodded appreciatively. And together they said, "*Illmatic*."

They hit the road, the Jeep bouncing on a cloud of hip-hop beats.

Within a half hour, Sunny had a raging headache. Chukwu was speeding down a good stretch on the freeway. Sasha had the stereo bumping nearly as loud as it would go. At some point, Chukwu had installed a new, more powerful sound system, and this one was like the ones Sunny remembered from the streets of New York. She even suspected that Chukwu's system could do that thing where it set off car alarms if it was turned up to the highest volume.

As they sped, they bumped Nas's *Illmatic* so loudly that Sunny felt as if her head would explode. She could feel the bass vibrate through her entire body. The only time she'd ever felt anything remotely similar was when Ekwensu's drums were booming when she'd tried to break into the physical world

last year. But this time, with each body-shaking beat, Sunny laughed and Sasha and Chukwu rapped "It Ain't Hard to Tell" along with Nas.

Sunny looked at Chichi; she looked annoyed. Sunny giggled. She couldn't have expected the two to bond over Nas. Orlu had fallen asleep, his head resting against the window. When he'd arrived, Sunny had noticed he looked tired.

"I'll be fine," he said when she asked him if he'd slept that night. "Stayed up late beading protective spells onto Chukwu's Jeep."

"Shit," Chukwu suddenly hissed. He slammed on the brakes.

"Whoa, whoa, whoa!" Sasha said.

Sunny, the only one who insisted on wearing a seat belt, was thrown against it, her glasses flying off. Sasha held on to his seat. Orlu quickly woke and threw a hand forward just in time to keep himself from mashing his head into the front seat. Chukwu managed to slow down and swerve, narrowly avoiding an enormous pothole.

"Didn't you see that coming?!" Orlu said.

"No!" Sasha said, shaking his head. He turned around. "Everyone okay?"

"Barely," Chichi said, picking up her book, which she'd dropped on the floor.

"Two words," Sunny said, putting her glasses on. "Seat belt."

Chukwu sucked his teeth and waved a dismissive hand at her.

"Weak American," Sasha said, grinning. "Don't you know we in Nigeria?"

Sunny shook her head, disgusted. Sasha had bragged from the moment he'd come to Nigeria about his hatred of "confining" seat belts and how he never wore them even when in the States and neither had his dad.

"The roads are going to get bad," Orlu said. "We should slow down from here on."

"I know how to drive," Chukwu snapped.

"And that's why we all just nearly died?" Orlu asked. "I'm not saying you're a bad driver, though. I'm just giving you sound advice."

Sunny smiled. Orlu was four years younger than Chukwu and far less beefy, but he'd always had a way of talking to Chukwu that Chukwu couldn't dominate. Even now Chukwu only looked at Orlu in the rearview mirror and said nothing. He slowed down, too.

Orlu glanced at Sunny and slipped an arm around her waist. Sunny felt tingles from her shoulders to her cheeks. For a moment, she even managed to pry her mind from Lagos and what they had to do there. She did not call Orlu her boyfriend and he didn't call her his girlfriend. The only kisses they'd exchanged were the one he'd given her on the cheek last year and the one she'd planted on his ear when he'd nearly

killed himself bringing the two toddlers back from wherever Black Hat's cruel juju had taken them. Nevertheless, Chichi liked to joke that she and Orlu were "betrothed," and Sasha was always telling them to stop "beating around the bush." Chichi and Sasha were always so sure of and forward with everything. What Sunny knew was that she liked being near Orlu and they held hands often. Also, once in a while, he put his arm around her. He was her friend who was always on her mind.

Chukwu slowed the car down to nearly a full stop as they came upon a crater swallowing more than half the road. The sunken crust of asphalt quickly gave way to thick red dirt. There was a car stuck in the crater. Two young men stood on the raised asphalt staring at their car. They had their hands in their pockets and looked hopeless. An SUV crept around the stranded car by driving mostly in the dirt and plants on the roadside. When it was Chukwu's turn, he slowly drove past the car. Sasha opened the window.

"Do you . . . need help?" He added an Igbo accent to his speech to mask his Americanness. It was flawless. He switched to Pidgin English. "Wetin na want maka do fo' na? Na need any help?"

One of the men looked annoyed. "Anytin' wa u fit do to help, *sha.* Come lift am with bare hand." He sucked his teeth irritably and looked away and muttered, "Nonsense."

Sasha looked back at Orlu. Sunny looked from Orlu to

Sasha and back. Orlu looked at Chichi. Chichi was looking at Chukwu and then Sasha. Chukwu was looking at Orlu, Sunny, and Chichi in his rearview mirror and ignoring Sasha beside him.

"Chukwu," Sasha said. "Wait."

When Chukwu slowed down, Sasha got out. Chichi opened her door, too. "No, Chichi," Sasha firmly said. "Just Orlu." He paused. "We don't know these guys, *sha*." He was still speaking in his accent.

Sunny wanted to ask what was going on, but Chukwu was there. So she said nothing. Orlu got out on the other side of the Jeep and stepped into the tall grass. He walked up to Chukwu's window. "Drive all the way up," he said. "We'll meet you there."

"No," Chukwu said, putting the Jeep in park. "I'll help. I'm stronger than you both. And you don't know who these guys are, either. They won't mess with me."

"It'll be fine," Orlu said. "You need to stay in the car with Sunny and Chichi." He paused. "Don't worry."

Chukwu started to open the door. "Let me just . . ."

"No, none of us can drive," Orlu insisted. "What if another car comes and wants to get by?" He pushed Chukwu's door shut. "We'll be back in a second."

Sunny turned to look back as Chukwu reluctantly drove the Jeep a bit down the road. She could see Sasha talking to the guys, but Orlu was still watching them go.

"Keep going," Chichi said when Chukwu slowed to a stop about an eighth of a mile away. They rolled along a few more yards to where the road curved and they could no longer see Sasha, Orlu, and the guys.

"Okay," Chichi said. "That's good."

Chukwu frowned deeply as he put the Jeep in park. He didn't turn it off. "What are they doing?"

"Helping them, I guess," Chichi said vaguely.

"How the hell can they help those guys? That car needed a tow truck to pull it out. A powerful one."

Chichi shrugged.

"I should go and help," he said, turning the Jeep off and making to get out. "You two stay here."

"No!" both Chichi and Sunny said.

"Why? I'm the strongest and oldest. This makes no sense!"

Chichi quickly got out of the car and got into the passenger seat.

"They'll be back," she said. "No shaking." She smirked coyly and leaned closer to him. Chukwu's frown immediately began to melt.

Chichi was wearing one of her long, old-looking skirts and a T-shirt. She'd taken off her sandals and left them on the floor in the back. She was so small that she could easily and cutely curl herself into the passenger seat, pulling her long skirt demurely over her short legs.

"So how are you doing?" she asked, batting her eyes at Chukwu.

"Oh my God," Sunny muttered, looking at the trees outside the window.

Ten minutes later, Sunny heard a car zooming up the road. Chichi was sitting on Chukwu's lap telling him for the millionth time how amazing his muscles were and Sunny was outside the Jeep, leaning against her door. It was the car that had been stuck in the ditch, all right. But Sunny only recognized it from its color and shape. It zoomed past them at probably over ninety miles per hour. She barely caught a glimpse of the guys in the car, but she saw them, especially the driver. He looked terrified.

When she looked up the road she saw Orlu and Sasha coming, keeping to the side. She ran to them. A few cars passed, but otherwise the road was quiet. She was sweating by the time she met them. The day was growing humid.

"What'd you do?" she asked as they walked to the Jeep.

"A little bit of this and a little bit of that," Sasha said.

"Hardest part was getting them to turn away," Orlu said. "They started thinking we were armed robbers. But if we didn't get them to turn around and they saw what we were doing, we'd be in a Library Council car on our way to the Obi Library's basement like you."

"We had to use *Ujo* on them," Orlu muttered. "So they were too scared to look at what we were doing."

Sunny's eyebrows went up. That was the juju that Ana-tov had taught them that caused Lambs to feel a deep irratio-nal crippling fear. So *that* was why they went speeding away.

Sasha suddenly picked up his pace, leaving Sunny and Orlu to walk together. "So you won't be taken to the council? I know you used juju on that car."

He shook his head. "Remember, part of being a good Leopard Person is doing your duty for your fellow human beings. When we saw those guys, if we could help, we would help."

"You've got to be kidding me," Sasha shouted. He was standing at the passenger window staring into the Jeep. "Oh, so this is how it is? This is what you are?"

"Oh no," Orlu said. They both ran to the Jeep.

Chichi climbed out from the driver's side. Then Chukwu came out, also from the driver's side.

"What the hell is wrong with you?!" Sasha shouted at Chichi.

"Lower your voice," Chukwu said, his voice booming.

"*You* don't speak to me," Sasha said, pointing a finger at Chukwu.

Chukwu laughed hard. "Or you'll what?"

Sasha's eyes grew very big, and he looked as if he was go-ing to say something. Then he glanced at Sunny and seemed to change his mind. "I don't give a shit how big you are," Sasha said. He moved toward Chukwu.

"Come on, then," Chukwu growled.

"Okay," Orlu said, immediately putting himself between Sasha and Chukwu. "Okay, o. Okay, o."

"Keep your hands off her," Sasha said, pointing at Chukwu over Orlu's shoulder.

"Sure, but I can't help it if she can't keep her hands off *me*," Chukwu said, laughing.

Sasha turned to the side and spat. "We will see."

Sunny went and stood beside Chichi. "What were you thinking?" Sunny snapped.

"I wasn't exactly thinking," Chichi whispered, but Sunny caught the hint of the smile on her lips.

"Let's all just get back in the Jeep," Orlu said. "We have a long way ahead of us."

Sasha was looking at Chichi, who was looking right back at Sasha. Chukwu angrily got in the driver's seat, slamming his door. Sunny and Orlu got in. Then Chichi. Sasha was the last to get into the passenger seat. He glared at Chukwu, but Chukwu just started the Jeep, ignoring Sasha. Minutes later, Sasha put Nas back on, moving on to the next album, *It Was Written*. But the vibration of the beats wasn't nearly as delicious as before.

22

FRESH, FRESH, FINE *EWUJU*!

It was as if the roads were trying to kill them.

There were potholes and craters everywhere. In one place the road seemed to have sloughed off completely, and they'd had to bumble their way across the jagged remains. Somehow the tires did not flatten, but the poor roads made the going slow and dangerous. A few times they passed parts of the road that were so uneven from erosion that they nearly tipped over. Thankfully it was dry season; otherwise the roads would have been muddy impassable gullies.

Then there were the go-slows, traffic that robbed their trip of precious time. Two hours after suffering the pothole- and crater-riddled road, they'd sat on the expressway for a

whole hour and a half without moving. On the sides of the road were occasional shanties and stretches of trees, and from both of these came an assortment of beggars and hawkers. One of the beggars was a young man in scruffy clothes with knotted hair and a mad look in his eyes. He reminded Sunny of the man they'd seen in Bola's waiting room. He leaned against Chichi's window staring at her. No matter how many times Sasha told him to go away, he wouldn't budge until Sasha had actually gotten out of the car and chased the man off.

The hawkers sold all sorts of things, from raw corn, pure water, and bread to skewers of beef *suya*, plantain chips, and roasted bush meat. One man had even held up a whole bush rat to Orlu's window. "Fresh, fresh, fine *ewuju!*" he proclaimed. He'd asked for six hundred naira and even offered to skin it while they waited. The bush rat looked as if it had been killed minutes ago, still dripping blood.

Orlu had simply waved him off.

When the go-slow finally let up, they began encountering the checkpoints where Chukwu was forced to "do Christmas" for the police in order to get by without being delayed. The blatant demand for bribes especially irritated Sasha, who held a particular hatred for police officers. Chichi had to grab his hand as Chukwu dealt with the road police so that Sasha would keep his mouth shut. When they were stopped by a third police checkpoint within two hours, Sasha was ready to jump from his seat and "slap the man across the face." This

was when Orlu said they should stop and find a hotel.

They were in Benin City, only halfway there, and already the sun was going down. Thankfully, Chichi had planned ahead. "Chukwu, pull over. Sunny, give me your phone, let me call my uncle."

Chukwu pulled into the parking lot of a roadside market. Chichi dialed the number. "I told him we'd be coming," she said as she waited for him to pick up.

"You sure it'll be all right?" Sunny asked.

"Of course. They have a big house and they love me," Chichi said. "This is my aunt, my mother's sister . . ." She held up a hand. "Hello? Hello? Uncle Uyobong? Good evening." She grinned and laughed and then began to speak in rapid Efik.

"I'm not sure if I like the idea of being on the road New Year's Eve," Orlu said as Chichi talked to her uncle.

"I know," Sunny said. "But if we keep driving, trust me, we will be robbed . . . or have to fight robbers."

Chichi was laughing very hard as she cupped the phone to her ear.

"Do you know Chichi's uncle?" Sunny asked.

"I've heard of him but never met him."

"Good things?" Sunny asked.

"Yeah," Orlu said, smiling. "He likes flowers." He lowered his voice so Chukwu wouldn't hear. "They're both Leopard People, and her aunt's a third leveler like Chichi's mother."

"Okay, everyone," Chichi announced, handing Sunny her phone. "They have dinner waiting for us. Let's go."

"Which way?" Chukwu asked.

Ten minutes later, they pulled through the gates of a small but beautifully designed compound. The house was painted blue, and the compound was made pretty with tall palm trees and colorful flowers that seemed to glow even in the near darkness. The small parking lot in front of the house was black and smooth, as if it had been freshly tarred.

"Nice," Sasha said.

"I'm going to warn you all one more time, treat my uncle's flowers like little human beings," Chichi said. "And God help you if you step on one."

"What kind of man loves flowers that much?" Chukwu said with a laugh as he got out of the car. "What is he, some kind of wizard?"

They all froze, avoiding eye contact with one another.

"He's a botanist; he studied at the University of California in the States," Chichi said.

"Oh . . . okay," Chukwu said.

Sunny let out a breath.

A pathway led to the front door and along the sides were all sorts of plants: tiger lilies, sunflowers, a bush with red flowers, and there was even a tall cactus on the right side of the path's beginning. "Don't touch any of his flowers," Chichi stressed again.

"Ah!" Chukwu hissed. "Damn it!" He was ahead of Sunny, and Sunny had seen precisely what happened. The cactus had leaned forward and swiped at his arm with a thorn! Thankfully, Chukwu hadn't seen it do this. He'd only felt it. "I didn't touch it," he said. He looked at his arm with irritation. "It touched me or something. I wasn't even . . ."

"Who is that?" a deep voice said from inside. The door unlocked and a man peeked out, frowning. He had a smooth, bald head and a handlebar mustache and bushy beard that reminded Sunny of the man on the Internet years ago who was always complaining about the rent being "too damn high."

"Who is touching my plants?"

"Uncle Uyobong," Chichi sang. "It's us!"

He frowned and then his face broke into a smile when he saw Chichi. "*Ah-ah!* Chichi," he said, hugging her tightly. A woman with a bushy gray Afro and large gold earrings came to the doorway, and Chichi hugged her tightly, too. "Auntie," Chichi said.

"And this must be Sunny," her uncle said.

Sunny stepped forward. "Good evening."

She was quickly scooped into hugs from them both. "We've heard all about you," Chichi's auntie said. Sunny glanced at Chichi and she quickly shook her head. *She better not have told them*, Sunny thought. No one else needed to know of her doubling besides the four of them.

Sasha, Orlu, and Chukwu all received tight hugs, too.

"Chukwu," Chichi's uncle said, cocking his head. "You are at the University of Port Harcourt?"

"Yes."

Her aunt took his head in her hands and looked from one side to the other. "You heal up well," she said, hugging him.

Chukwu frowned at Chichi, who only shrugged. "Thank you, ma," Chukwu politely said.

"Come in," she said. "All of you. We've been waiting."

As soon as they stepped in, her uncle put his arm around Sasha's shoulder and said, "Come, you and I need to talk." Then they walked into another room.

Sunny was too busy taking in the spectacle that was the inside of their home to ask where Chichi's uncle and Sasha were going. The house . . . could she call this a house? A greenhouse maybe. It was nice and cool inside, yes, but there were plants . . . all over the place. They hung from the giant chandelier on the ceiling. Vines wrapped themselves around the banister of the stairs. There were potted trees flourishing against the walls.

"Wow," Chukwu said. "The house looks a lot bigger on the inside."

"It's the glass ceiling," Chichi's aunt said. They all looked up, and indeed in the large front room, the ceiling was made entirely of glass.

"This is my partner's home," Chichi's auntie said. "I own nothing."

"She and my uncle, they aren't married," Chichi said, moving closer to Sunny, so Chukwu wouldn't hear. "Remember, we are Nimm, and Nimm women can't marry."

"Oh," Sunny said. "Right." She'd been wondering this very thing. The house was lovely, but it looked extravagant. Chichi's mother lived in a hut and was proud of that. Still, even if she didn't own it, it seemed odd for a Nimm priestess to live so lavishly.

"My uncle built it for her but more for himself," Chichi said. "Did I tell you he loves flowers?"

"I don't think I've ever seen a place like this," Chukwu was saying to Chichi's auntie.

"Well, I'm glad to broaden your mind," she said. "Come, I'll show you where you'll be sleeping, and then you can eat dinner."

Sasha, Orlu, and Chukwu were to stay in a large room downstairs where every wall was taken up by a bookshelf. There was a large plush couch that curved into a horseshoe big enough for two of them to sleep on and a cot set up behind the horseshoe couch, which Chukwu quickly claimed.

"Why don't you boys get settled down?" Chichi's auntie said. "We'll be right back." She took Chichi and Sunny to a smaller bedroom upstairs. "You're fine sharing a bed, right?"

"Of course, Auntie," Chichi said.

Sunny nodded. "It's a lovely room."

And it was, with its large leafy plants winding up a pole

beside the curtains, creeping out through the cracked door over the balcony.

"Have you been good with your brother, Sunny?" her auntie asked.

"What do you mean?"

"You know what I mean, honey. Are things okay with his school? We don't need you dragged off to the library basement again."

Chichi snorted with laughter.

"I'm still here," Sunny said, embarrassed.

"Good," Chichi's auntie said, patting her on the back. "I know it's hard for free agents. You know the Lamb world better than us, and Leopard People can be assholes, so your kind can be short-tempered. For good reason. It's not easy living on the border of such different worlds."

A black cat smoothly skulked from beneath the bed and stood in front of Sunny and looked up at her. Waiting. Sunny ignored it as Chichi's auntie spoke.

"But you'll get used to it," she continued. "And you better do it fast, because I think something big is expected of you."

"I guess," Sunny said, glancing at the cat. It was still sitting there.

"Pick her up," her auntie said. "What do you think she's waiting for?"

Sunny bent down and slowly picked it up. She wasn't too familiar with cats, so she held it like a baby. It turned and

twisted into a comfortable position in her arms. She petted it, and it began to purr.

"That's Paja," Chichi said, taking one of the cat's front paws in her hand. "See her paws? Cool, right?"

The cat had six digits on its paw.

"Is it . . . what if Chukwu sees it?"

"So?" Chichi said. "These aren't magical. Well, all cats are of the Leopard People, but Lambs have these cats, too. They're called polydactyl cats. It's a natural mutation. They're really smart, too."

The cat purred and rested its head against Sunny's chest, and Sunny nearly melted with delight. She sat on the bed with the cat in her arms and she stroked its soft black fur.

"I've contacted your mother," Chichi's auntie told Sunny. "She's glad you made it."

"Thank you," Sunny said. She'd also send Ugonna a text. He'd probably heard from her parents that they were okay, but she'd told him she'd keep in personal contact with him.

"Are you sure about this trip?" Chichi's auntie asked.

Sunny nodded.

"Okay," she said. "No more talk of it. Let's go have dinner."

Sunny brought the cat with her.

The dining room was in the back and also completely made of glass, various types of plants and potted trees stationed in

the corners of the room. The table in the center was large and made of thick wood, as were the chairs. And the chairs were grooved with intricate designs, their edges smooth with age. Sunny found them extremely comfortable. The wood even felt warm.

Dinner was already set on the table in a large bowl and several smaller ones. The large white porcelain bowl was filled with *edikaikong* soup, and in each of the smaller bowls were fried plantain, puff puffs, and sliced mango. On a plate were fist-sized balls of gray *garri*. The soup was heavy with periwinkle snails, beef, and stockfish, and it was light in palm oil. The perfect balance. Sunny's mother didn't make this particular vegetable soup. *Edikaikong* soup was an Ibibio dish, not an Igbo one. However, since Chichi's mother was Efik, a subgroup of the Ibibios, Sunny had had it plenty of times at Chichi's house, so many times that she'd grown a taste for it. When she finished eating, she sat back, satisfied and exhausted. Her eyes were drooping when a sliver of the conversation happening around her floated into her ears.

"Sure, I'll go with you."

"Great," Sasha said, perking up. He'd eaten more than Sunny, but it seemed to have the opposite effect on him.

"I'm going with!" Chichi said. "You never take me out when *I* visit."

"Ah, but these three are men," Chichi's uncle said. "It's not the same."

"Go where?" Sunny asked.

"To taste the local nightlife," Sasha said. "It's almost New Year's Eve. Everyone's off work and partying already. We're in a new place, let's go see what it's like!"

Sunny looked at Chukwu, who wasn't saying anything. He clearly wanted to go, just not with Sasha. Orlu even looked interested. "Um, okay," Sunny reluctantly said. "I'll go if everyone else is going." And everyone else was. She groaned, but too quietly for anyone to hear. She'd rather climb into bed, read for a little bit, and then go to sleep. It had been a long, long day and tomorrow was probably going to be longer.

So this was how Sunny found herself at her first night-club. Orlu had his arm tightly around her waist, and she was glad because the place was dark and packed with the undulating and wiggling bodies of people dancing, talking, and shouting. Not far away, she could see Sasha getting down on the dance floor, surrounded by five women who were close to twice his age. Chukwu was dancing with Chichi several feet away, but Chichi kept looking at Sasha. And who could forget Chichi's uncle and aunt who were out there dancing like maniacs, too? Chichi's uncle had a bottle of Guinness in his hand and was somehow not spilling it.

Sunny yawned, leaning on Orlu. Suddenly, he let go of her and started pushing his way farther in. "What are you doing?" Sunny asked.

Then the crowd surged forward, as people moved to get a better look. She was pushed along with it, and then she saw where Orlu was going. Two guys who looked to be in their twenties were swinging at Sasha. He ducked and one guy missed, but the other managed to punch him in the gut. Then there was Chukwu jumping on that guy, turning him around and socking him in the face. The guy stumbled back as two more of his friends joined him. They paused as they looked at Chukwu, who shouted over the music, "Come on, then!" He held up his fists. The guys weren't as dumb as they looked because none of them took Chukwu up on his invita-tion to fight. Orlu grabbed Sasha, and Chukwu pushed them both along.

Chichi's uncle joined them, shouting for the guys to stay back. Chichi's aunt was behind him looking angry and ready to fight, too. Sunny moved after them as they all exited the club. Once outside, Sunny was shocked to see that Sasha, Chukwu, and Chichi's uncle were all laughing. Even Orlu looked mildly amused.

"Damn," Sasha said, holding his aching belly. "Chukwu, I don't think I have *ever* seen four grown men afraid of one younger man. I don't even care, you get some dap for that. No doubt. Respect, respect." He grasped Chukwu's hand, slap-ping his other hand over it.

"I saw them coming at you," Chukwu said. "You had all their ladies, and you don't even look twenty."

"It's my American swag," Sasha said with a lopsided grin. He coughed and held his side.

"Are you all right?" Chichi's uncle asked.

"Yeah," Sasha said. "I managed to flex at the last minute. It's nothing a night's sleep won't cure."

They quickly got into the car in case the guys Sasha had angered came out for more. Sunny was just glad to leave that place earlier than they would have. Exactly an hour later, after the short drive back, showering in lukewarm water, brushing her teeth, and climbing into bed, Sunny closed her eyes. Chichi was already fast asleep, having taken an even shorter shower before Sunny. Ten minutes later, Sunny heard someone riffling through her and Chichi's bags not far from her head.

For a moment, Sunny just lay there in the darkness, reluctant to get up and switch on the light. She was exhausted and comfortable. *Maybe I'm just hearing things*, she thought. There was an air conditioner in the room that clanked and loudly dripped water. But the more she lay there, the clearer the sound came. *Crinkle, crinkle, rummage, rummage.*

Her juju knife was in the pocket of her night clothes and slowly, she reached for it. The light suddenly switched on. And what Sunny saw on her backpack shocked her, but only for a moment. It was a large black bat. And it was clutching her wallet, her glasses in their hard green case, and *Udide's Book of Shadows* in its strong sharp claws.

Without thinking, Sunny did the swift juju Sugar Cream had taught her for getting rid of those large wall spiders Sunny hated so much. She missed and the bat scrambled up the windowsill. "Oh no!" she breathed. She nearly dropped her juju knife but managed to grasp it and work the juju again. She caught the pouch in her hand and threw it at the bat as she said, "Stay there!" The bat dropped the book on the sill and her glasses and wallet fell to the floor. The bat was flattened right on the windowsill.

"Good thinking, Sunny!" Chichi said, looking impressed. She was standing at the light switch.

"You heard it?" Sunny asked, pressing her forehand. She'd had to focus her mind to a point to rework the juju correctly because of the doubling, and the effort was rewarding her with a throbbing headache.

"Yeah, after you woke me up by moving around. I was going to shred whatever it was to pieces. Your way is more humane."

They stepped up to the flattened bat. It was soft with black fur on its body and reddish fur on its head and had the delicately elegant face of a fox. It looked up at them with blank eyes.

"You think it was sent?" Sunny asked. *It was*, she heard Anyanwu whisper. Immediately, Sunny's headache went away.

"Of course."

"By who?"

"You *know* who."

"Udide?"

"No, *Ekwensu*," Chichi said.

Sunny gasped.

"It's a stupid thing to do," Chichi said, kneeling down to look at the bat. "She's toying with you. She just wants to scare you by letting you know that she knows. If she really wanted the book or your money, she'd have just made them disappear."

So Ekwensu knew she was going to Lagos in order to get to Osisi. Sunny shut her eyes. The thought of something powerful, terrible, and violent taking interest in her made her ill. Suddenly, she wanted to go home.

"What are we going to do with it?"

There was a soft meow at the door, and they looked at each other.

"No," Sunny said when Chichi went to open the door.

"Why not?" Chichi asked.

"What if it . . ."

Chichi opened the door and Paja skulked in. She trotted toward the immobile bat and looked at it. She meowed again. Then she arched her back and hissed, bringing her face right up to the bat, and the bat began to struggle against the charm Sunny had put on it. Then Paja appeared to gnaw at the air around the bat, and soon the bat flew out the window. Sunny

shut it and smiled. "Paja," she said, picking up the black cat. "I'm glad you don't believe in capital punishment, either." The cat purred, rubbing its soft face against Sunny's.

Chichi rolled her eyes. "What kind of cat are you? You're *both* hopeless."

23
IBAFO

The next morning, after three hours of driving, they reached the town of Ibafo, about fifteen miles from Lagos. Almost there. The problem was that they were again caught in a go-slow, and not just any go-slow, a colossal go-slow. It was the wrong time to be there. Sunny could just barely see the source of their woes about a mile up the Lagos–Ibadan Expressway. There was a cluster of cream-colored buildings, and the parking lot around the largest of the buildings was packed. It was the Redemption Church Camp.

Being the early afternoon of New Year's Eve, people were just arriving. And those who could not find parking in the lot were parking right on the road. The go-slow was so thick that

traffic wasn't moving at all. Some people even parked where they were stuck, left their car, and went on to the church.

"Are you kidding?" Sasha shouted out the window at some people in front of them who'd just left their car. They ignored him as they stepped into the grass and kept right on going, wearing their Sunday best, although it was Wednesday.

"Can you get around their car?" Orlu asked.

"I'll try," Chukwu said, driving onto the red dirt pathway near the center of the road. There was already a line of cars stuck there and Chukwu opened his window. "Excuse me, sir. Will you . . ."

The man in the passenger seat pinched his face and said, "Na no see way we dey hook here like person wey dey inside rat cage?"

The driver ducked down to see Chukwu. "You think I am fool?" he snapped. The man was old enough to be their father. "I let you in and the whole world will be squeezing."

"The people in the car in front of me have left it," Chukwu said. "Just let . . ."

The driver closed his window.

"What is wrong with the people here?" Orlu asked, disgusted.

"It's not them," Sunny said. "Chukwu, remember when we all came through here?"

Chukwu nodded.

"It wasn't this bad, but it was bad," Sunny told Orlu. "People know that, so they are mean. It's faster when you don't let anyone else in."

In front of them a large truck carrying about fifty people and a great pile of oranges belched out exhaust, and the people in the back coughed and waved at the polluted air. The exhaust soon reached them, and they coughed as Chukwu turned the Jeep on and closed the windows. When the air cleared, he opened them again. Best to save gas by not using the air conditioner.

"If this were a funky train, we wouldn't be here," Chichi whispered.

"Yeah, we wouldn't be here," Sunny said in a low voice so Chukwu wouldn't hear. "We'd still be at home because my parents wouldn't let me travel for so many days without Chukwu."

Chichi sucked her teeth and opened the door to stretch her legs. Sasha got out and leaned against the car with her.

It was hot and humid, and the shanties that housed a small market were booming with business, selling pure water, plantain chips, and cell phone car chargers. Sunny was looking at the cloudy sky, glad that a few of the puffier clouds were covering the sun, when the idea popped into her head. She had asked Sugar Cream about this very possibility, so she knew a little about it.

"Can Leopard People control the weather?" she'd ques-

tioned Sugar Cream one horribly hot day. The entire library had felt as if it would melt back into the earth from which it came. "Or even just temperature? I'd have thought there'd be some juju to at least cool it down in here."

Sugar Cream had laughed and said, "Can you imagine the world we would live in if we *could* do that? The entire Earth would be in chaos."

"Oh," Sunny'd said, leaning back on her elbows. As usual, she had been sitting on the floor of Sugar Cream's office. She'd tried her best to ignore the red spider scuttling across the floor a few feet away.

"The weather is the business of Chukwu," Sugar Cream had said.

For once, Sunny hadn't needed an explanation. Chukwu was her brother's name, but he was named after someone much greater. First and foremost, Chukwu was the name the Igbo people used for the Supreme Being. The great deity known as Chukwu was so inaccessible to human beings that one didn't even pray to it. If Chukwu gave you audience, you probably would have no idea why and you'd be in such awe, it wouldn't really matter.

"But," Sugar Cream had said, raising an index finger. "If the weather is already moving in a direction, we can sort of push it along. For example, if it's breezy, with some effort and consequence, a skilled Leopard Person can make it windy."

"What kind of consequence?"

Sugar Cream had laughed loudly. "Nothing worth discussing. There's a reason not many Leopard People play around with changing the weather."

Now, as Sunny looked up at the cloudy sky, she wondered. She climbed out of the Jeep and walked around to the other side where Sasha and Chichi stood smoking cigarettes.

"I don't want to hear it," Chichi said, rolling her eyes. "We're outside and there's a breeze."

Sasha blew out some smoke as he scrutinized Sunny. Then he said, "She's not here to whine. She's got an idea."

Sunny nodded. "I do," she said. "Well, it'll only work if one of you guys can do it. I know I can't." She glanced at Chukwu, who was fiddling with the stereo. Orlu was behind him reading the *Book of Shadows*, his brow furrowed with concentration.

Sunny nodded her head toward the sky. "It's supposed to rain later today. Can you make it rain now? Either of you?"

They were silent as they considered. It didn't take long. "If it rains, people will return to get their cars," Sasha said.

Sunny nodded.

"But only if it rains hard. A deluge that covers the roads," Chichi said.

"Exactly," Sunny said. "Can you . . ."

"Of course, we can," Sasha said. "But it's the consequences that bother me."

"What'll happen?" Sunny asked. "It can't kill you, right?"

"No, no," Chichi said. "Water no get enemy."

"Water is life," Sasha added. "*Aman iman.*"

Chichi was quoting Fela, Sasha was quoting old proverbs and speaking in some Arabic type language; Sunny was completely lost.

"Sunny, get in the car," Sasha said, bringing out his juju knife. He lowered his voice. "Talk to your brother and Orlu for a while. We'll be right back."

Chichi poked her head in the Jeep window. "Chukwu, we're going into the market to find something real to eat. Do you want anything?"

Chukwu shook his head. "Just want to get the hell out of here."

"Orlu?"

"Nothing," he muttered, his eyes still on the book.

Sasha and Chichi quickly walked away, without a glance back. Sunny climbed into the car and sat beside Orlu. She wanted to explain to him what was going on, but Chukwu was right there. Orlu seemed too preoccupied with the book, anyway.

"Daddy warned me not to take this way today," Chukwu moaned. "I completely forgot. With all that craziness last night, I was distracted. We should have been there by now."

"Don't worry," Sunny said. "We'll get there."

"So close yet so far."

❤ ❤ ❤ ❤

A half hour had passed, and they'd only moved up about twenty feet thanks to two cars that were pushed off the road because they'd run out of gas. Drops of rain started falling just when Sasha and Chichi returned carrying bags of *chin chin*.

"That's all you got?" Chukwu asked as Chichi got in. "What took so long?"

"There wasn't much to eat," Chichi quickly said.

Sasha slowly climbed into the passenger seat. He looked ill, his face sweaty. Sunny frowned as he sat with his legs pressed together. He smiled weakly at her. Chukwu looked at him, frowned, and asked, "What is wrong with you?"

"Just gotta pee," he said.

"Then go do . . ."

The rain started hitting the car in large droplets. Then it began coming down like a waterfall.

Orlu looked up for the first time from the book. He looked at Sasha and then Sunny, and Sunny nodded.

"Turn the car on," Chichi shouted.

As soon as Chukwu did, she closed her window. They all followed suit as the car was pounded with rain. Sasha groaned and jumped out of the car. "Can't hold it!" he screeched. Sunny turned away as he stood in the rain right there beside the Jeep and relieved himself.

When he finished, he got back in the car, still looking strained. He pressed his legs together. Whatever he had done,

it had only been him who did it. She couldn't imagine Chi-chi suffering the same problem. That would have been more complicated.

"What kind of rain is this?" Chukwu asked, leaning forward. Outside, they could see people running for shelter and to their cars. All around them, vehicles were starting and the paved double road ran with sludgy red mud. For several minutes, it was chaos. Women in their best church clothes took off their heels to hop into cars or beneath canopies. Men in church-appropriate suits and caftans jumped into driver's seats. The cloudburst above was like nothing Sunny had ever seen. And poor Sasha kept having to pee and pee. He was soaked from jumping outside to urinate and then getting back into the Jeep. Needless to say, Chukwu was perplexed and deeply annoyed by Sasha's problem.

"Did you eat some bad mango?" he asked, reaching beneath the seat and pulling out a blue battered towel. He threw it on Sasha's seat.

Thankfully, within minutes the go-slow began to move. Within a half hour, they'd outrun the strange weather and were cruising down the road. Sasha's peeing fit continued but decreased the farther they got from the Redemption Church Camp and soon, exhausted from the agony to his bladder, he fell into a deep sleep.

A half hour after that, they entered Africa's biggest megacity, Lagos.

24
THIS IS LAGOS

So many people. All in a rush.

In Lagos, people were perpetually on alert because anything could happen at any time. The roads were narrow,
overcrowded, and littered with street traders and beggars of
all kinds. There were so many rickety golden-yellow *danfo*
packed with people. Even the air quality was different. At
times it smelled like burning cedar wood, rotten medicine,
garbage, exhaust. It was noxious. Was it even air? Sunny felt
like she was breathing fumes, better yet, juju powder.

By the time they reached Victoria Island, her nose was
running like crazy and she'd gone through half her box of
Kleenex. Maybe Lagos really *was* dusted with juju powder. It

was a crazy idea, but she had to wonder. She'd been to Lagos with her family many times before her initiation into Leopardom and never had this problem. She'd never had any type of allergy . . . other than being allergic to the sun.

When they entered the gated community where Adebayo's aunt and uncle lived, it was like driving into yet another world. A world of super wealthy people. Sunny had been to this part of Victoria Island before when the family had visited one of her father's friends. She'd felt displaced in the same way back then, and she didn't exactly come from poverty, either. Coming here after the crazy drive through Nigeria's many worlds of poverty, wealth, rural and city, trees to concrete jungle was even more unsettling. It was as if they'd left Nigeria and entered the cushiest part of the United States. The houses here were huge and gluttonous in the way that they were in the wealthiest suburbs of New York.

The streets were paved and pothole-free, clean and lined with flowers. A white woman walked a tiny white dog. A man in a jogging suit walked fast, sweating like crazy as he shouted into his cell phone in Yoruba.

"Okay, we're going left," Chukwu said into his phone. Adebayo was guiding him. "Oh . . . okay, I see it. White with the yellow Hummer in front." He laughed hard. "You can drive that? *Ah-ah.*"

"Ugh," Chichi said, disgusted. "I'll bet half these people work for the government and oil companies."

"What's wrong with that?" Chukwu asked, holding the phone aside.

Sasha laughed hard and shook his head.

Chichi only looked salty.

"Okay," Chukwu said into his phone. He laughed loudly, playfully dropping into Pidgin English. "I dey road now, I dey come to your big, big house. I dey yahn you so that na go dey ready for me, o!" He listened for a moment and then laughed hard. "Okay, o!" Still chuckling, he ended the call. "Adebayo is ready for us."

Sunny didn't feel elated at arriving. The closer they got to the house, the closer they got to their destination. Tomorrow was New Year's Day. What did the New Year have in store for her?

Adebayo was waiting for them in front of the house as they drove onto the large curved driveway. He was wearing costly jeans and a brand-name T-shirt. Sunny rolled her eyes; he didn't normally dress so flashily. And the neighborhood must be incredibly safe. Sunny couldn't remember seeing this type of home that was *not* surrounded by a concrete gate.

Adebayo and Chukwu hugged and slapped hands. Then Chukwu introduced his friend to Sasha and Orlu. When he came to Chichi and Sunny, the smile on Adebayo's face wavered. His whole demeanor was false. How much did Adebayo understand about Sunny and Chichi's involvement in the destruction of his confraternity? Was that understanding

conscious or subconscious? Judging by the way he quickly turned his back on them both, he recalled *something*. Sunny was glad. It would be a long time before she forgave him for introducing her brother to the Red Sharks and slapping him in the face that night, if she ever did.

"Welcome. Come in," Adebayo said, putting his arm around Chukwu's shoulder. "Let me show you everything."

The house was enormous. There were two kitchens, one for the mistress and master of the house and one for the house girls. Both had fully stocked and functioning refrigerators, cabinets, and cupboards, and both were used mainly by the house help, all of whom had traveled home to visit relatives until January second.

"And even then," Adebayo said as he gave them the full tour, "my aunt and uncle won't be back from London until the sixth."

The mansion had ten bedrooms, so they all had their pick of rooms. Sunny chose one on the third floor with a small balcony. It had a thick sliding glass door and a heavy-duty lock that she tested before choosing the room. It was a bit dusty and smelled as if it hadn't been occupied in some time, despite the gorgeous satin sheets, dreamlike bed with a canopy, and soft luxurious deep-blue rug. This wasn't surprising since only Adebayo's aunt and uncle lived here. Their children were at university overseas and the house help stayed in the small house out back.

"So wasteful, isn't it?" Chichi asked, coming in.

Sunny had put her things on the small plush lavender couch beside her bed and plopped onto the cool sheets. She sighed and grinned at Chichi, who rolled her eyes and sat on the floor. "I am so hungry."

"Me too," Chichi said. "I'll bet there's a whole market in all five of the refrigerators in the house."

"There are only two fridges."

"Same thing."

There was a knock on her door. "Come in," Sunny said.

Orlu had taken his shoes off and put on a fresh T-shirt. "I'm in the room across the hall," he said. "After your bat incident, it's probably best if I stay close."

"She can take care of herself," Chichi said. "And she's got me. I'm next door."

Orlu grunted, sitting on the couch.

Chichi smirked and pointed at the door. "Ten, nine, eight, seven, six, five, four, three, two . . ."

The door opened. "Sunny, you in here?" Sasha asked.

"Aren't you supposed to knock?" Chichi asked.

Sasha cut his eyes at her as he leaned against the wall, shutting the door behind him. He was carrying *Udide's Book of Shadows.* "I'm in the room downstairs near the front door," Sasha said. "Someone's got to stand guard, right? Especially with your . . . condition."

Sunny rolled her eyes.

"I put up a perimeter, too," Sasha added.

"Good idea," Orlu said. "Hopefully no one notices all the lizards that'll be on the outside walls."

"Yeah, it's not the most discreet juju, but it's powerful. Nothing will come in without me knowing. Like last night." Sasha looked at the door, locked it, and moved inside. He sat beside Chichi, and Orlu got up and sat beside Sunny on her bed. Sunny scooted up. They were all face-to-face, and for several moments, they didn't speak.

"We go tomorrow," Sunny said.

"Yeah," Orlu said.

"The market in J. City," Chichi said. "It's the biggest in Lagos. We can take a *kabu kabu*."

Sunny frowned. "But Ajegunle is . . ."

"Relax, I know how to deal with 'one chance' robbers and any other kind of stupidity," Chichi said, holding up a hand.

Ajegunle District, nicknamed "The Jungle" or "J. City," was the worst part of Lagos. Sunny's father described it as a slum, saying that it was full of garbage, poisonous water, filthy shantytowns built on muddy land and in some places islands of garbage. It was a place of rough, rough commerce.

"One chance" robbers were all over Lagos, but they thrived in Ajegunle and with vehicles that were heading to Ajegunle. "One chance" robbers were guys who drove *kabu kabu* or *danfo*. Their vehicles would be nearly full, so the driv-

ers would advertise that they were giving people "one more chance" to get in at a reduced price. When the victim got in, he or she would be set upon by a bunch of thieves. Sunny had heard all kind of Lagos horror stories. And of course, there was the added danger of her being albino, and thus the target for ritual killers.

"Can't Adebayo just drop us off?" Sunny asked. Even as she spoke, she knew it was a stupid request.

"And bring all that attention to us with that hideous Hummer?" Chichi asked.

"And like your brother, Adebayo can't know where we are going, either," Orlu added.

"They can't," Sasha said, shaking his head. "Not even a little."

They were quiet again.

"It's New Year's Day, the markets will be empty," Sunny said, her throat tight. "It'll be easier for strangers to notice us, too."

"Some will," Chichi said. "But they aren't Chukwu and Adebayo."

"Fine," Sunny said. "We take a *kabu kabu* or *danfo*." She sat up straighter. "I have the marbles."

"Blue?" Sasha asked, looking pleased.

Sunny nodded. The juju required blue marbles to work.

"You've read it well," Sasha said. "I'm impressed."

"In the morning?" Orlu asked.

"People will be too tired from celebrating to notice us," Sunny said. "We leave at seven A.M." She paused, looking at all of them. "Sound right?"

They all agreed.

"Does anyone need to read more of this?" Sasha asked, holding up the book.

Orlu frowned. "That book is dangerous."

Sasha laughed. "I know. It's awesome."

Orlu sucked his teeth and shook his head in disgust.

"And if I'd never bought it, where would we be in all this?" Sasha said.

"You should give it to Sunny," Orlu said.

Sasha shrugged and handed it over. "I've read it three times, anyway. Plus, it feels like holding a million scratchy spiders." He tapped on the side of his head. "Got it all up here."

"Me too," Chichi added. They slapped and shook hands, snapping each other's fingers.

"I wouldn't keep it too close when you go to bed," Sasha said.

Sunny took the book and asked, "Why?" She shivered at its roughness and immediately glanced around her room, searching for spiders hiding in the corners. She'd seen a large wall spider in the room downstairs. She was reminded of one of the first lines in *Udide's Book of Shadows*: "Even in palaces, there are spiders."

"Just trust me," Sasha said.

"Oookay," Sunny said, putting the book on one of her cabinets. "So, what do we tell my brother?"

"I'll handle that," Chichi said.

Sasha groaned and got up. "On that note, I'm out of here. I'm going to explore around this edifice of excessive extravagance. If my boys from the States saw this place, their eyes would pop out. I had a friend ask me just before I came here if Africans have schools! He was a Lamb, sure, but he was a black dude, like me. Black folks be so *ignorant* sometimes."

"Overconsumption is a universal human trait," Orlu pointed out. "And so is ignorance."

"Yeah, but you've got to admit, black Americans, no, *blacks of the world* are into self-hate more than any other group of people. I know what I had to deal with when I was in the Chi. If it weren't for me being a Leopard, I'd have grown up as ignorant as anyone else. Leopard People read books by everybody and everything. We look outside *and* inside. But you have to be secure with yourself to do either . . ." He shook his head. "It's too hard to explain. Sunny, you know some of what I mean."

Sunny nodded. But her mind was not on the problems of the black African diaspora. She was thinking about what it was going to be like to meet with a giant sentient spider who was thousands, maybe millions, of years old while she was impaired by doubling.

Chukwu and Adebayo went out to the clubs to celebrate

the New Year. The four of them opted to stay in. Sunny and Chichi cooked up an elaborate meal of fried plantain, jollof rice, *egusi* soup and *garri*, fried chicken, and pepper soup heavy with fish (there were no tainted peppers, which was a shame). There was so much food in the house that what they'd cooked up would probably not even be missed. The business of cooking took Sunny's mind off what lay ahead, and she found herself laughing and joking with Chichi. When they finished, exhausted from cooking and wanting privacy, Chichi and Sunny sat down to eat before presenting the food to the others.

"Damn, this is good," Chichi said, savoring a spoonful of pepper soup.

Sunny took a bite out of a long slice of fried plantain. "Best dinner ever."

They ate for a while, Sunny's words lingering between them. Sunny knew they were both thinking the same thing, neither daring to speak those thoughts aloud: *Last supper.*

"I can't imagine this thing that's happened to you," Chichi suddenly said.

Sunny stopped eating. "You don't have to."

Chichi took a gulp from her glass of orange Fanta. "I mean, no, I don't mean it like that." She shook her head. "You're just full of surprises, Sunny."

"You're telling me," she muttered.

"You know you should be dead, right?"

Sunny slammed her fork down and looked at her friend. "What are . . ."

Chichi put both of her hands up, a grin on her face. "*Ah-ah, biko-nu*, don't kill me, o. I'm telling you, you are so *strong* and amazing, Sunny. And you don't even know it." She laughed, clapping Sunny on the back. "Eat your plantain and keep on surprising everyone."

Sunny bit into her plantain and as she did, she could feel Anyanwu's presence. Not like the stirring of herself, as Chichi would have felt her spirit face, but as the shifting of someone outside herself, yet who was herself. And for a moment, she saw through two sets of eyes. This had happened once before, about a week ago when she'd woken up after a good sleep. She'd lain in her bed staring at her room. And this had gotten her thinking about her cultural halves, American and Nigerian, how she'd always felt like two people in one. Then she'd wondered how Anyanwu felt about the American part of her. And then she knew for a moment because she was Anyanwu, but with the broken bond, it felt like Anyanwu was separate from her.

Now it wasn't so consuming because both she and Anyanwu were angry at Chichi for the same reason.

Chichi was watching her closely, and now Chichi laughed. "I see you! That's because of the doubling. Wow. I look in your eyes and see you *both*." She chuckled some more, picked a piece of fish from her soup, and ate it. "Full of surprises."

When the countdown began, Sunny was so stuffed with food that all she wanted to do was sleep.

But Chichi had found a bottle of wine and wine glasses, and before Sunny knew it, she was carrying her first glass of wine. They all screamed "Happy New Year" and clinked glasses when the time came. Chichi and Sasha shared a prolonged, nearly obscene, kiss.

"Happy New Year," Orlu said to Sunny, giving her a tight hug and planting a third kiss directly on her lips. It tasted like red wine.

"Happy New Year, Orlu," Sunny said, looking into his eyes. There was a hint of fear in them, and she wondered if, like Chichi, he saw Anyanwu in her eyes. However, she ignored this as she took another sip of wine. It tasted both awful and wonderful.

"Here's to saving the world," Sasha said. They all clinked their glasses again and sipped.

And surviving tomorrow, Sunny thought. She sipped again.

Sasha put on some rap music that Sunny wasn't familiar with. It was in the Ghanaian language of Twi. Both Sasha and Chichi started getting down, and even Orlu smiled and laughed, doing a few moves himself.

"Ah-ah, look at Orlu," Chichi shouted. "That's nice!" She imitated his steps and soon all three of them were doing Orlu's dance. Sunny felt a little dizzy from her wine, so

she sat down, enjoying the moment with her closest friends. With her peripheral vision she saw a hint of a yellow figure sitting close beside her. "Happy New Year, Anyanwu," she whispered. The yellow intensified for a moment and then was gone. *But always there*, Sunny thought, taking another gulp of wine.

Later, after a brief phone call to her relieved parents and a ten-minute-long text message exchange with Ugonna, she stepped out onto her balcony. "Wow," she whispered, grasping the doorway. The railing was peopled with over thirty green and orange lizards. They looked at her, but not one ran away. She sat on the balcony floor and flipped through the *Book of Shadows* for a few minutes, but she was too tired to read.

When she went to bed, she placed the book on the other side of the room near her backpack. She must not have put the book far enough away because her dreams were full of scuttling and cartwheeling spiders. She stood, a glowing yellow figure, in a jungle that rippled and heaved with them—red ones, black ones, green ones, small ones, and an enormous one that waited for her in the deepest leafy darkness.

25

THE JUNGLE

When the rickety dented red *kabu kabu* stopped, the four of them piled in. Within seconds, five other guys tried to get in, too.

"Hey, no room!" Sasha said, kicking at a guy who tried to squeeze in. He shoved him out and slammed the door just in time. The car chugged off. "Damn, where are those guys going at this hour?"

"Home," the driver said, laughing.

"Oh," Sasha said. "Right."

"Where na wan' go?" the driver asked them.

"Ajegunle Market, please," Sunny said.

"Shey you know e close now," he said.

"It's okay," she said. "We're just meeting someone around there."

The drive took a half hour because of traffic. And by the time they got there, Sunny felt light-headed from the exhaust that wafted in through the car's floor. It was so old and rusted that you could even see the road through large holes.

"I'll pay," Orlu said when they arrived at the market. Judging from the grin and number of thank-yous the driver gave, Orlu had tipped him well.

"You didn't need to do that," Sasha said. "I've got plenty of cash."

"It's New Year's Day," Orlu said. "Plus, today is important. Don't worry about it."

The large market was a series of wooden dividers, shacks, benches, and stalls. All were vacant. It was like a ghost town. "Let's walk in a bit," Orlu said.

"*Na wao*," Chichi said, running a hand over a bench as they passed it. "I have never seen this place empty."

"I'll bet this is when the ghosts come to do business," Sasha said.

"I think the ghosts do business all the time," Chichi said. "They're not afraid of the living. Our world is nothing but a lesser version of this Osisi place we are trying to get to."

"True that," Sasha said. "Back in the States, I've got an uncle in Atlanta who says there's a place near a local farmers' market where once a year at midnight a spirit market opens

and the only people who can go are old folks. If you're not old and you go, you come back all mentally messed up or mute or something."

"They have those here, too," Orlu said. "There's one in Ikare that my great-grandfather has been to twice."

"What does he buy there?" Sasha asked.

Sunny tuned out their chatter. She felt ill. The marbles were cool in her sweaty hand, but this didn't help. She didn't like spiders, for one thing. But that wasn't the worst of it. What if they succeeded in convincing Udide to weave them this flying grasscutter creature? What if the grasscutter took them to Osisi? What was waiting for her there?

Everyone agreed that it was a wilderling that had shown her the vision in the candle. But everyone also agreed that there was no way to tell if that wilderling was friend or foe. The wilderling's intentions in showing her the future were unclear. Was this the same with the dreams? What if this was all a trap?!

Her slick hands fumbled with the marbles. "What am I doing here?" she whispered. "Why am I doing this? I could just go home."

But she continued to lead the way, looking side to side as they walked through the empty market. She felt Anyanwu close and intimate, and this was comforting. They came to a large group of stalls covered by sheets of corrugated tin to make one big roof. It was cool in the shade. They stopped,

quiet. The breeze blew and a small bird flew by cheeping. It flew through a ray of light, leaving a wake of dust. Sunny sneezed hard.

"There's . . ." Orlu stepped forward and held up his hands.

"Is there something to undo?" Chichi asked him.

"No," he said. "But . . . this part of the market . . . Leopard People sell here."

Sunny nodded, rubbing her nose. "Juju powder, I'll bet."

They walked on for another few minutes beneath the tin roof. "This place just goes on and on," Sunny said, her voice nasally from her stuffed nose. "It didn't look this big from the outside."

Sasha chuckled and shook his head. "Of course it didn't. This is a dark market. They can't be seen from the outside."

"Dark market?"

"Leopard market," he said. "They're common. The ones in the U.S. are actual buildings that move to a different place every month. They're nothing like the ones here. The prices are set and things are just . . . sterile."

"Dark markets are like the market in Leopard Knocks but nestled on Lamb grounds," Chichi added. "This one doesn't move around, but some other ones in Nigeria do. This one blends with the normal market, but you can only walk into it if you are Leopard."

"Well, once in a while a Lamb will walk in," Orlu said. "Usually sensitive Lambs. Those people are never the same

afterward." He just shook his head. "Nothing is perfect or absolute."

"Yeah, except Library Council rules," Sunny said.

As they walked, she could feel the hairs on her arm stand up. Only the rays of light that crept between the roof's tin sheets lit their way. Nothing looked any different, not to her eyes. However, Sunny was sure there were . . . things around them. Small shadows in the corners kept moving right outside of her peripheral vision.

"Can we at least *get* somewhere?" Chichi impatiently said after another five minutes of walking.

Sunny looked back and indeed she could see the way they'd come in, just barely.

"Did you see the size of that ghost hopper?" Sasha asked.

"The one standing in that sun beam?" Orlu asked.

"Had to be over a foot long," Sasha said.

"Wonder what it sounds like when it sings," Orlu said.

"It probably sounds like a factory," Sasha said. "The bigger they are, the worse . . ."

"Oh, screw it." Sunny dropped to her knees. "I can't take it anymore. Let's just try it here." She rolled the marbles like small bowling balls, and they tumbled smoothly over the dirt ground. "Come on," Sunny said, jogging after them. They followed the marbles, which had begun to dimly—then strongly—glow light blue.

They ran and ran. Passing wooden booths, tables, medi-

ans, and stands. All empty. The marbles rolled straight ahead, maintaining their speed. Soon the corrugated roof ended, and they were in bright sunshine. They passed more empty tables, but there weren't as many. There was a lot more space with even trees growing between the tables. Then there were no tables and only a dirt path that ran through a back alley. Sunny could hear the hustle and bustle of the Lagos streets not far away.

When the dirt path began to slope downward, the marbles rolled slower. They decelerated to a fast walk. Then a slow walk. Then the marbles stopped completely. Sunny bent down and picked them up, and they continued to glow brightly in her hand.

They were about eight and a half feet below ground level, red dirt overrun with green creeping plants on each side. Above and to the left was the side of a tall office building and to the right was a busy expressway with people walking along the sides. Sunny could make out people in the office building. A man looked out the window but he didn't look down at them. And on the expressway, people walked on the narrow sidewalk without so much as a glance below.

This was yet another Leopard space hidden in plain sight. Sunny blew her nose and then inhaled through a somewhat unclogged nose. If direct juju was involved, it wasn't with the use of powder, at least not according to her nose.

"Oh God," she whispered.

The path descended at a steadier, sharper decline a few feet ahead. And this led right down into what could only be Udide's lair. The cave looked like the yawning cavernous mouth of a great beast of black jagged rock. And it fit so perfectly into the ground that Sunny could only accept the fact that the cave had probably been there before Udide made it one of her many homes. Maybe it had always been there. *Yet only a small part of the city's population can even see it,* Sunny thought. According to Sugar Cream, only .05 percent of humanity was Leopard People.

"Might as well keep going now," Chichi said. "She certainly knows we're coming."

She's known for a long time, Sunny heard Anyanwu say in her head. Sunny felt a shiver go up her spine as she remembered her dream. Of all things, why a spider? Why, why, why? She imagined Udide scrambling out of the cave lightning fast, right at them, her movements like thunder. Udide wasn't just a spider; she was one of the Great Ones. She was an ultimate storyteller. She was a weaver. And she was a really excellent writer. Sunny had read more of *Udide's Book of Shadows* than its numerous spells that Sasha and Chichi were obsessed with. Udide wrote short stories, too. Sunny had been most fond of those. There was one in particular about an alien invasion in Lagos that she especially enjoyed. It was set in the past, a few years back, and it was funny like a Nollywood comedy . . . with aliens.

Yes, Udide was not just some irrational arachnid that ate flies and looked horrifying. The thought that she was a crea-ture that could be spoken to and possibly negotiated with set Sunny at ease a bit. At least she could beg for her life, if it came to that. She felt Anyanwu nearby bristle at the thought.

The closer they got to the cave the more strongly Sunny could smell it. Smoky, acrid, chemical. Sunny frowned. "Like burning houses," she whispered. She'd seen a house go up in flames once in New York not far from their townhouse. Sunny had only been five years old when she'd stood in the crowd a block away holding her mother's hand. However, she would never forget the smell. She shivered at the memory. "Why does it smell like burning houses?"

"What else is a giant spider going to smell like?" Sasha asked. He tried to smile, but it was clear that even he was afraid.

When they got to the opening of the cave, the smell was almost like inhaling smoke itself. The marbles in Sunny's hands lit everything up. The edges of the cave were covered with thick webbing and when Sunny looked closely she could see that the webbing was peopled with tiny black spiders and dead insects wrapped in more white webbing. This was going to be much worse than sitting on the floor of Sugar Cream's office.

"You think those are her children?" Chichi said, looking closely at the cave's wall.

"Either that or her minions," Sasha said.

"I wouldn't get too close to the walls if I were you," Orlu said as they entered the cave.

The ground was free of webbing but not of spiders. There were tiny and not so tiny spiders all over the place. For a while, Sunny looked down as she held up the marbles and tried not to step on them. But eventually she realized that these spiders weren't stupid and were not about to allow themselves to be crushed. With relief, she stopped looking down.

The cave was cool and damp, the burning house smell stronger than ever. The wide path led even deeper beneath the city. Then it opened wide and high as it came to an end. When Sunny laid her eyes on Udide the Ultimate Artist, the Great Hairy Spider, she screamed.

Udide not only smelled like burning houses, she was the size of a house. She was black with a gray sheen in the marble-light, and her many eyes glowed a rich brown, like truck-tire-sized jewels. She was covered with stiff hairs. Her abdomen was bulbous, the better to weave with, and tipped with a great black stinger. She was on her back, the spiked tips of her eight powerful legs pressed to the cave's ceiling. And Sunny saw her through both her and Anyanwu's point of view, which meant she saw Udide on both the spiritual and

physical planes. Orlu clapped his hand over his mouth. Sasha started hyperventilating. Chichi just stood there staring, slack-jawed.

Sunny's eyes were watering as the great spider wriggled slowly, twisting and turning her body so that her legs were on the ground. Then she stood looking down at them. Sunny had watched this process through blurred twitching eyes. Her heart felt as if it was trying to beat itself to death against her rib cage. Of all the things she'd seen since entering Leop-ard society—ghost hoppers, bush souls, the river beast, the lake beast, the infamous Ekwensu—this creature was the one who threatened to break her grasp of reality.

Udide crouched down, bending her legs to get a closer look at them. Seeing the great spider move again filled Sunny with a strange warmth. The world around her began to swim.

"Do *not* faint," she heard Orlu say into her ear as he held her up. He spoke firmly and slowly. "Get a hold of yourself, or we're all dead."

His words touched her and she fought her fear with everything she had. Her body wanted to curl up and shut down into a defensive sleep. *No, no, no, no, no,* she thought. She reached for Anyanwu but couldn't grasp her. Where had she gone? Sunny wished she could go back in time, be-fore any of this. When she was a different person in a differ-ent world. When she wore her hair longer because it looked nice and not because Mami Wata preferred it long. When

she wasn't doubled and had no idea that she *could* be doubled.

Then she felt the sting on her leg, and she screamed again. There was a large spider on her pant leg working its fangs through the cloth deeper into her flesh. She shuddered and swiped at it, dropping the marbles. She felt Anyanwu start with surprise, and when she looked at the cave wall to her right, she saw a dim golden glow spread over the surface. She screeched again, stumbling into Orlu. Her leg felt like a rod of heat. Orlu began frantically looking at the ground, as he held her. "Are there more?" he babbled. "Sunny, you okay?"

"No!" Sunny screeched.

Udide used a leg to grip her webbing, and then Sunny saw her throw the web at Chichi. It hit Chichi in the chest and she screeched, too, pulling at the thick gray sticky rope in the dim marble light. Sasha grabbed Chichi from behind, but Udide yanked her right out of his grasp and then proceeded to wildly wrap Chichi around and around in webbing.

"Nimm princess," Udide said. Her deep booming female voice shook the cave so hard that dirt and pebbles tumbled from the ceiling and the walls. The spider's every hair vibrated at the sound, and all the spiders in the area ran in circles at the sound of her voice. "Trouble. *Wahala. Kata kata.* Tricky strong women and strong sneaky men. You have taken something from me."

"Taken what?" Sunny screamed as she strained with pain. "We just got here! We . . ."

"The beginning is never the beginning," Udide said. Chichi was wrapped now from feet to neck and struggling uselessly.

Sasha pulled out his juju knife and threw juju at Udide. Whatever it was, it didn't even move one of Udide's many hairs. He tried throwing another juju and received the same non-result. He picked up a rock and threw it. It bounced off Udide like a pebble.

"There is no juju that can kill a spider," Udide said. "We are sacred."

"Sasha, stop it!" Orlu said, his voice calm. But his eyes were watering with tears.

"She's going to kill her!" Sasha screamed, his voice cracking. He looked around and spotted a spider. He stamped on it.

Udide angrily puffed out a great stench of burning houses.

"You don't like that?!" Sasha screamed. He grabbed his backpack and brought out a can of Raid. "You think you're smart? I'm smarter!" Before he could fumble the cap off, Orlu let go of Sunny to grab Sasha. The can of Raid dropped to the ground. The two tussled, but Orlu was stronger. He held Sasha's wrists. "Stop!" Orlu said, straining, as Sasha looked around wildly.

"Please!" Chichi said. "I don't know what you're talking about!"

"But your name does, DNA does, your molecules do,"

Udide said. "I should kill you myself instead of letting my people feast on you."

Sunny had fallen to the ground, her heart beating dangerously faster than ever. She stared at the glow pressed to the wall feet away; she could hear Anyanwu in her mind, though she sounded so far away that Sunny couldn't understand what she was saying. When Sunny spoke to the great spider, she could barely catch her breath and her mouth felt slow and gummy. "Udide . . . Ma . . . *Oga* Udide, we came a long way . . . We need to . . ." She felt another sting, this time on her neck. She could feel the scratchy spider scramble to her cheek. She groaned.

"Nimm warrior," Udide said. "Something is wrong with you, and that is interesting to me. You are two, but you both are one. They will take you next. Thieves. All of you. I let you live out there only because you people make for good stories, and you have the nerve to come down here and face me."

She wrapped Chichi some more and more, thicker and thicker. Chichi wriggled and wriggled to no avail.

"*Oga* Udide," Orlu said, moving forward with Sasha. He pressed his hand to Sasha's mouth, and Sunny heard him whisper, "Not a word." He stood up straight and spoke loudly. "My friend Sasha here is from Chicago, in the United States. He grew up on the South Side, in a place called Hyde Park. His grandparents are from Mississippi and participated fully in the civil rights movement, though they were more on the

Malcolm X side than the Martin Luther King Jr. side. They passed that down to Sasha, too. He's a fighter, born and bred through the racist fire that still burns in the United States of America." He paused. "He . . . he was sent here to Nigeria to stay with my family and me because his parents wanted to keep him out of trouble. He's too smart and rebellious.

"He is the one who found your *Book of Shadows*. And Chichi, there, Chichi is the Nimm princess you are wrap-ping up and preparing to kill. But she is Sasha's girlfriend, and she, too, is obsessed with your words and ideas. Both of them used one of your jujus to call an Aku masquerade at a party almost a year ago. Your teachings are good and effec-tive, though dangerous to the reckless.

"Me, I have read parts of your *Book of Shadows*, but it is not your spells and stories that I am interested in. It is *you*, Udide. I've read a book called *The Book of High Beasts*. In it, you are cited as the true creator of destiny. You are one of the few who answers only to Chukwu, the Supreme One. There is a Great Crab who lives deep in the Atlantic Ocean whom you love and see once every millennium. The hairs on your body can change the passage of time. You and Mami Wata have inspired human rebellions on every continent."

"You know much," Udide said.

Orlu nodded frantically. "And . . . and this girl here, Sunny Nwazue. That is her name. I love her very much." He glanced at Sunny. She could feel saliva running from the

side of her mouth. "Sunny recently met and freed the spider named Ogwu and her children."

"She did *not* free Ogwu," Udide said. "Ogwu freed herself. Ogwu saved your Sunny from a djinn."

"Sorry, Ma Udide," Orlu said respectfully. "You are right. But Sunny helped Ogwu free herself, and Ogwu sends her greetings to you from a place of freedom." He paused, taking a breath. "Please, Chichi is like my sister. Please. We have come here for a good reason. I know your kind can sting venom *and* the antidote to the venom into a person. Please do this for the girl I love and my . . . my sister. Don't let them die. Please." He calmly nodded his head and again said, "Please."

There was a long, long pause. Then Udide hummed deep, sending out a vibration.

Sunny heard them first. More spiders. Then she saw them. These ones were tarantula-like with hairy abdomens and wiggling tails on those abdomens. They scuttled up to her. Then she also heard the sound of their fangs puncturing the skin on both her hands. She gritted her teeth against the pain. Immediately, even that pain began to fade and she started to feel better. Her muscles loosened and Orlu quickly helped her up. "Okay?" he asked.

"Weak . . ."

"Fake it," he whispered. "She doesn't respect weakness."

When she straightened in Orlu's arms and looked up, she

was positive that the great spider was looking directly at her. Into her. With her many, many eyes. *Fffffff!* The smell burst from the spider in a soft powerful warm blast. The whole cave could have been filled with a thousand burning houses. Sunny fought not to cough and fought even harder not to sneeze. Udide dumped Chichi on the ground, and Sasha ran to drag the wound-up Chichi away from the giant spider. When he got to Orlu and Sunny, he tore at the webbing. Chichi quickly wriggled out like a caterpillar. "Goddamn insane bug," Chichi muttered, rubbing her arm. "I think one of those spiders left a fang in me."

"Shut up," Orlu hissed.

"Sunny Nwazue," Udide said.

Sunny felt as if her head would explode from the sheer vibratory force of Udide's voice. She held her head and as she did, she felt Anyanwu come to her. Then she did the only thing that she could do, even with her friends there. She brought forth her spirit face.

"Greetings, *Oga* Udide," she said, her voice low and sultry. She stood up straighter. She could stand on her toes. Udide would see her as poised and graceful.

The great spider gave off her stench again, and Sunny stumbled back. "Anyanwu," Udide said.

"Yes."

Udide stared at her. "I know you."

"I know you, as well."

"In this life, you've been doubled and you live. You're strong in many ways."

"It's a strange life, this one."

"I want to speak to Sunny Nwazue. Because she wants to speak to me."

The others stood behind her as she let Anyanwu retreat into her.

"We're here, Sunny," Orlu whispered.

"Yes," Udide said. "But what difference does that make?"

"We're her friends," Chichi said, stepping up beside her. She leaned heavily on Orlu, trying to look tough. "We'll suffer whatever she suffers. She's not alone."

"And we don't suffer without making others suffer," Sasha added.

"Sasha from America," Udide said. "My *Book of Shadows* found you, and it will kill you. That will make a great story."

"Don't worry. I know how to use it," Sasha said with obviously false bravado.

"That's not how your story goes," Udide said. "You will die by that book."

"No, he won't," Chichi screeched. "We've both used it! We're . . ."

"I only have business with this incomplete, damaged one," Udide said. "Sunny Nwazue, why have you come?"

"I . . . I need something from you. A flying grasscutter."

"What will you give me in return?"

Sunny thought about it for a moment. Then she said what she'd planned to say, especially after Orlu had just saved all of them by doing the same thing. "A story," she said. Udide's hairs rippled with what Sunny could only guess was delight.

"You know me well," she said. "But you must remember, I am storyteller. I am old. I've dwelled for years at a time beneath this city over many decades. Since its birth. I lie on my back and I put my legs to the ceiling of this cave and I listen to the vibration of Lagos. I listen to its millions of stories. And I weave just as many. Lagos breathes stories. It is life and death; it is many worlds in one. And I have done the same in many cities of the world. New York, Cairo, Tokyo, Hong Kong, Dubai, Rio. Tell me a story I have not heard."

The spider got down low in front of Sunny. She came very close, within a foot. Sunny felt her bladder try to let go. She squeezed and stayed where she stood. Her friends were behind her, but as Udide stared deep into Sunny's eyes with her door-sized eyes, Sunny was alone. Alone with a giant storytelling, probably immortal, hyper-intelligent, merciless spider.

"No," Sunny said. She felt Anyanwu inside her, part of her. "I can't tell you a story you have not heard. But I can tell you my own particular story. It's mine. Only mine. There is only one me in this world. So in a way, maybe yes, this is the only story of its kind." She took a deep breath and then began to talk.

"I lived the first nine years of my life in New York City." Her legs were shaking, and something in her said she should sit down. Her experience with Sugar Cream's office told her that there would be spiders on the floor, but these spiders were smart and she doubted they'd climb on her. Even the ones in Sugar Cream's office knew not to do this . . . unless they meant to. So she sat before Udide in the dirt of the cave. She turned to her friends and nodded. They, too, sat. Then, miraculously, Udide also settled. She did not sit, be-cause spiders do not sit. However, she rested her legs a bit and puffed out her fumes and made a contented hum that seemed to come from deep in her abdomen.

Sunny shut her eyes for a moment and calmed herself. *Anyanwu*, she said in her mind. *Give me strength. Help me tell this well.* Once Sunny started talking, she found that it wasn't as hard as she thought to tell a giant spider and her best friends about the most painful day of her childhood.

I went to a Catholic school in Manhattan. My classmates were all kinds. You had Africans; African Americans; American whites; all kinds of Caribbeans; some Asians, mostly from India and Pakistan; multiracial; Muslims, Jews, Christians, Hindus. I should have fit right in. Mostly, I did. I had a lot of friends. But though we were all mixed up there, the other kids really didn't mix, you know? Kids stayed with their own kinds, especially black and white. The African people kept to them-

selves in my school. The African Americans acted like they were kings. And queens.

I sort of moved from group to group. I didn't fit in any-where. I was African, but not really African. I was born in America, but not really African American. Half the time, I didn't understand African American slang. I had a bit of a Nigerian accent that I'd picked up from my parents, which was strange since I was born in America. I loved the Caribbeans, but we all knew I wasn't one of them, either. I was light-skinned like the whites, but my puffy hair and the way I look, I could never fool anyone.

This one day when I was in third grade was bad. Those older African American girls, I don't know why they hated me so much. They truly truly hated me. I think if I had been hit by a car and was dying in the street, they'd point and laugh and watch my slow death. Anyway, this day, I went to the bath-room during my lunch, and they followed me in there. They must have followed me. You had to ask permission to go to the bathroom, and there were four of them. No teacher would have let them all go at the same time like that. They snuck out. To follow me. It wasn't a coincidence.

I knew they were in there with me while I was in my stall. So I waited and waited. But I could see their feet. They weren't going anywhere. They were waiting, too. For me to come out. Anytime a girl would come in, they'd bark at her to go use another bathroom. Eventually, I knew I had to come out. I

couldn't stay in there all day and miss my classes. So I flushed the toilet and came out.

These were sixth graders. Big ones. The leader was this overweight, very angry girl named Faye Jackson. She was always getting into fights with other girls in her grade. She'd only spit cruel names at me; we'd never fought. I don't know why they came after me this day.

I moved quickly to the faucet to wash my hands. They stood at the sink near the door, blocking any quick exit I could make. So I was forced to go to the sink farthest away from them, near the foggy window on the far side of the bathroom, farthest from the door. Bad move. As soon as I did this, they closed in.

"Why you so ugly?" Faye asked as they stood over me.

"She so nasty," one of the other girls said. Her name was Shanika, and she was never mean to me except when she was with Faye. "Shouldn't you be at the retard school?"

"At least away from us," Yinka said. Yinka was Nigerian, but you wouldn't know it the way she tried to hide it. She was very dark-skinned, too, except for her face, which she was always slathering with skin-bleaching cream. And when she wasn't, her mother was. You'd see her mother do it to her every morning when she dropped her off at school. "Wouldn't want any disease that would eat all my color like that," Yinka added.

I could feel myself getting mad. I needed to get back to class, and I didn't know why they were trying to scare me. They were standing very close, towering over me. I was only eight, and I

wasn't very tall for eight. I've grown a lot in the last three years. And in the last year, I've gotten really strong and muscular, but back then, I was small, and they were all tall and big.

"It's not contagious," I muttered, my hands wet as I turned off the faucet. And that's when Faye slapped me on the side of my head. I stumbled as the world got really bright and I saw stars. She'd hit me really hard. For no reason. Without me even speaking directly to her.

I was angry as hell now. I'd been harassed before and it upset me, but never had I grown angry like this. I was in there alone. I hadn't done a thing to them. They'd pressured me to move into the far part of the bathroom while one of them stood watch at the door. I was like prey to them. Because what? I don't know.

"Dirty African booty scratcher," Faye spat. "Filthy diseased Shaka Zulu bitch. Yo' mama probably got AIDS and yo' daddy got syphilis, that's why you came out looking like that."

Yinka cackled hysterically. I couldn't believe it. What was wrong with that girl? Who was diseased?! Even at eight years old I knew when something was completely twisted. Shanika looked a little worried, but she didn't do anything to shut her friend up. The one at the door, whose name I didn't know, was peeking back into the hallway. The bell rang. Lunch was over. I felt more rage boil in me.

Faye was about to hit me again when I looked her right in the face. I was sweating and shaking, and that's when I saw it.

Right there on Faye's white pants. A large circle of red. Blood. My mom had explained periods to me earlier that year. So I knew exactly what I was seeing and why Faye was probably so angry. I knew many things in that moment. So I went for the kill.

"I'm filthy?" I growled. "You, YOU'RE the one who is filthy! Look at your pants. You're bleeding all over them. Phew! Stinking! Filthy akata! Who are you?"

The word was something my mother sometimes called African Americans when she was talking to her friends. Some told me the word meant "cotton picker," others claimed it meant "bush animal." Whatever anyone thinks it means, it is a nasty word. At the time, the way those girls were behaving, I was glad to call them "akata." I'd have loved to see the pain in their faces if they then learned what the word meant. But a word like that, you don't really need to know what it means. The meaning is all in the way it's said, the sound of it. It's ugly. It's an insult. It's like a dagger that is a word. She was bleeding, and I'd just drawn more blood.

She looked down and saw the blood on her pants, and a look of horror passed over her face. She was so embarrassed. The other girls looked embarrassed, too, and a disgusted look passed over Yinka's face. Yinka was just a mean, foul person, turning on everyone in two seconds. In all the years I'd known her, she was always the same. Mean, and loyal to only herself. Faye's embarrassed face changed then to that look girls get when they are going to destroy something.

I tried to run, but there was nowhere to go. They descended upon me. Slapping me in the face, pulling my hair, shoving me against the wall. Then Faye dragged me to the coat hooks. She was so big that picking me up was easy. I struggled, but the other girls helped, too. They hung me there by my sweater. I couldn't get down, no matter how hard I tried. They laughed at me, and then they left me there.

I was bruised and achy. My face felt like it was on fire, and my nose was bleeding onto my white sweater. My cheeks were wet and itchy with tears. I was so mad, but I was also ashamed and scared . . . scared of myself. Even back then I knew what I'd said was evil. I was American, too. And their history was connected to mine, even if it was not exactly the same. Faye's ancestors had made America what it was, built it with their own blood, sweat, and tears, by force. They'd suffered and persevered. She was the product of survival. I knew this better than my mother, who wasn't born there. And I shouldn't have made fun of that girl's shame, either. I knew what it was like to be made fun of and hated because of the way I looked.

But they hurt me. Just because I was African and had a defect. They, too, called me dirty. Why do we people from Africa always call each other dirty? Even I did. And why did they hate me so much? Why? I know why I confuse people. When people are confused, sometimes they get mean and violent. I wonder if this has anything to do with what I saw in the candle. Confusion.

"That's my story," Sunny concluded. She let out a long breath, not wanting to look up at the spider or at her friends who now knew something about her that even her mother didn't know. "You may have heard it before, or not. But this version is mine."

When she heard nothing for several moments, she looked up. Udide seemed to be staring at her, her fuzzy black mandibles working in and out and her many hairs rippled. She felt a hand touch her shoulder and then squeeze, but she didn't look back to see whose it was.

When Udide finally spoke, her voice was deep and booming but less harsh. "Yours is part of a long story of humanity," she said. "Always a treat to my sensitive hairs." She blew out the burned house smell and stood up and turned around. "Home, one's house, dwellings doused. In flames, sad games, you'll all be ashamed. It'll be the greatest story ever told and only those like me will see it unfold."

Sunny ventured a look at Orlu, Chichi, and Sasha. It was Sasha's hand that was on her shoulder.

"Sorry," she said to him.

"For what?"

"That word."

He shrugged. "If I'd been in your shoes, I'd have said a lot worse."

"Step back," Udide said. She'd moved to the far side of the cave. "To weave one, I'll need space."

"The flying grasscutter?" Sunny asked.

"Step back," Udide repeated.

She held up a leg and pulled webbing to the tip of this leg with another leg. Then she moved both legs away, and the piece of webbing hovered softly in the air. She brought another thread of webbing to that one and then something stranger began to happen. All of the hairs on her body rippled in such a fluid motion that it looked as if she were encased in water. Sunny shuddered and again felt her bladder contract. She could even smell a hint of salt water over the smell of burning houses. Another smell accompanied these two conflicting smells of fire and water. She could not describe it but she knew its origin. The strange smell and the presence of water—Udide was calling on the wilderness.

"Three of you, move away, unless you want to abandon your bodies and cross over," Udide said. Her voice rumbled and vibrated; rocks fell from the cave's ceiling this time. "Sunny-Anyanwu, you may stay or move with your friends."

Sunny stayed. She wanted to see this. She could feel it rising around her now. It was like standing on the rising surf of a large beach. It was rising all around her, gradually. Sunny blinked as her perspective doubled with Anyanwu's, but her attention was on Udide and what she was weaving. Udide was still black and hairy, but she was also turning red and growing larger. And Sunny could see another version

of Udide juxtaposed with the other two; this version of her looked as if she were made of shiny metal.

Udide worked fast, wrapping more webbing around the suspended strand. It took the shape of a white sticky-looking sphere about the size of a tennis ball. Then Udide raised a leg and started spinning. It whirled, slowly at first and then quickly. Then the great spider really began to work. She attached and wove and shaped so quickly now that Sunny's eye couldn't follow it. And as Udide worked, Sunny saw some of the spirits around her stop to watch. One looked like the shape of a man, only he was nothing but oily blue light. He stood beside Udide, a hand on a hip. Then he raised his other hand, brought it to his chin, and seemed to blow. His breath was blue, and it wafted right into the thing Udide was weaving.

Another wilderness creature came and did the same thing. And as they each added these ethereal ingredients, Udide's creature began to shift and take on different colors. It went from being spherical to a blob with many appendages on the sides, top, and bottom. It also began to grow. From tennis-ball sized to the size of a horse and then to the size of a van.

Sunny had since moved back to join her friends, who were all gawking.

One of what Sunny had begun to call colored-spirit people came and blew at the large still-growing mass Udide was weaving, and Udide seemed to get annoyed and shoved

it away. For some reason, this made Sunny's belly cramp with
hysterics.

"What is wrong with you?" Chichi whispered, frowning
at her. "Are you all right?"

Sunny only shook her head. "Maybe the leftover spider
poison is making me giddy, I don't know." Her body certainly
still ached. But this didn't stop the laughs that kept bubbling
up from within her. When she looked up, she saw Anyanwu's
dimly luminescent form perched upside down on the cave's
ceiling, surrounded by spiders as she watched Udide weave.

"What is so funny?" Sasha asked. When she looked at
him, he was smirking.

"This . . . everything," she whispered.

And that got Sasha snickering, too. Orlu tried his best,
but he, too, was clearly tired and overwhelmed and terrified.
Soon, his eyes were watering from trying not to laugh. Only
Chichi sulked, her arms across her chest.

Sunny was laughing so hard that when the large hovering
mass that Udide was weaving plopped to the floor, she wasn't
afraid. She took a deep breath and tried not to think about
the fact that she was deep in a cave beneath the city of Lagos
with a spider the size of a house who was weaving some mass
of webbing that was starting to wriggle.

She turned away from everything and looked down the
dark cave. That helped quell her giggles. The marbles she'd
dropped lit the cavernous cave well enough, but their light

didn't reach down the tunnel for even a few yards. It was as if the light bent toward Udide. Sunny inhaled and then exhaled and inhaled again. She could feel each place where the spiders had bitten her to inject venom and then the antidote. Those spots felt itchy and were probably red and swollen. But she was otherwise okay.

"What a life I have," she whispered.

To her left, she could see about thirty large spiders on the cave wall scrambling into the darkness. To where, she had no idea and didn't care one way or another.

All four of them bounced as Udide lifted the great web-wrapped mass and then let it fall to the ground again. They coughed and scrambled together, grabbing each other as the cloud of dust rushed over them. Everything was light blue as the blue marbles that sat on the ground between them, and Udide and her creation glowed brighter in the settling dust.

"Oh my God, it's exactly how I imagined," Orlu said. "*Thryonomys volante*, wow."

"You *imagined* this?" Sasha asked, pointing at it.

"Disgusting," Chichi said.

The mass was undulating. The blue marble light only lit part of it. There was something inside. *Unt, unt, unt,* the thing inside grunted. It sounded like a giant pig. Udide scurried around the mass three times, laying three of her legs on it after each rotation. Then she plucked a hair from her back and stuck it into the mass like a pin, using two of her legs.

The mass calmed, and Udide let out a great billow of her smoky stench, which made Sunny's eyes water. Then Udide stepped back and waited.

"One of us has to release it," Orlu said after several moments.

They all looked at Sunny. She shook her head. "I . . ."

"Because we'll all die if we get close to it," Chichi said. "We can't survive the wilderness."

"It is safe now," Udide said. "Just like Osisi is safe for you all; I have pulled down the veil of the wilderness. The creature is mortal and alive."

"Then you go," Sunny said to Orlu. "You're the one who likes animals so much."

"Yeah," Sasha agreed. "Which one of us knew its scientific name?"

"Okay," Orlu said.

"We can't all go?" Chichi asked.

"No, only one at first," Orlu said. He crept forward and slowly walked across the great cave. It took him nearly five minutes to get halfway across. He stopped, his hands clenching and unclenching. Then he started moving them quickly in the air.

"What is that?" Sunny shouted.

"It's . . ." He worked his hands some more. "Never mind. I'm okay."

"He's undoing jujus," Chichi said.

"It's protected itself," Orlu shouted. "And . . . well, I think it's joking with me. But not in a good way. If any of you had been in my shoes, you'd be on the floor itching and screaming right now from the stings of Seven Stinger Mosquitoes."

"Damn!" Sasha said. "I used that juju once in the Leopard Library of Chicago because this guy shoved me aside to get a book we both wanted. The man hollered like crazy."

"It's not even out of its cocoon, and it's already showing it's got a sick sense of humor," Orlu shouted. "This is why it's best for only one person to approach it." When he reached the cocoon, he paused and stared at Udide. "I know exactly what he's feeling," Sunny muttered. There was nothing like having Udide's undivided attention.

Orlu was too far for them to hear anything, but he was clearly speaking to Udide. Then he stepped up to the cocoon and brought out his juju knife. Sunny could hear the cutting from where she was, sort of an unzipping sound.

"Oh my God," Sunny whispered when she saw the shiny gray-brown head pop out of and then rip through the cut Orlu had made. Its big head was round, it had round fluffy-furred ears and large round blue eyes. It had some sort of black markings on its forehead, but she couldn't see them from where she was. It didn't look much like the grasscutters she was familiar with, large groundhoglike rodents related to porcupines. It sniffed around with its great nose. It sniffed Orlu, who stood very still. Then it looked

at Udide, started, and retreated back into its cocoon.

Udide brought a leg up and kicked the back of the cocoon, and the flying grasscutter grunted loudly like a pig and shot out. It came running right at Sunny, Chichi, and Sasha; its huge blue eyes wide with fear and shock. They all turned to run. Then Sunny heard Orlu's voice right beside her ear. "Get down!" And because she was so used to trusting her friends, Sunny dropped to the ground, landing on top of Chichi. Sasha dropped right beside them.

Foooo! The flying grasscutter lived right up to its name as it took off low enough over their heads that they could feel and hear its wake. Sunny looked up just in time to see it whip and snap its long furry tail as it zoomed toward the cave ceiling and then disappeared.

"Just wait," Orlu's voice said. When she looked back, he was standing there, his juju knife to his neck. He was using voice-throwing juju and specifying it to just the three of them.

"There!" Sasha said, pointing at the entrance to the cave that led into darkness.

The flying grasscutter stood with its backside pressed to the wall as it looked into the cave.

"It wants to run, but it's too scared," Chichi said. She laughed.

From afar, the great creature looked forlorn and kind of cute as it grunted and pressed itself to the wall. It was basi-

cally a newborn. What a place to wake up to—a giant spider
and a dark cave full of smaller spiders. "I'd be scared, too,"
Sunny muttered.

"Don't let it flee," Orlu's voice said. He was walking to
them. "If it flies into the cave, it'll escape and we won't be
able to catch it, trust me. They are intelligent. It's made by
Udide, so it'll understand any language. Talk to it or . . . something . . . *softly.* But hurry."

They walked over to the grasscutter. It stared at them,
its nostrils flaring widely. The marble light was dim here,
but it reflected its eyes and in that moment, Sunny knew she
could gaze into them for hours. They were like jewels and
they were kind, too. But there was something else about the
creature's face as a whole that made her want to slow down.
It wasn't just cute, it was sneaky and sly. This was verified
when she felt the ground pulled from beneath her feet. She
fell awkwardly.

Chichi also tripped and fell as a tree root came up from
the ground right in front of her foot. She cursed in Efik as
she stumbled. Sasha looked at them, then he chuckled. "Just
go," Chichi said. "If you haven't fallen, then maybe the damn
animal likes you." She tried to get up, but the root wrapped
more tightly around her foot. Sunny knew not to bother and
just sat there.

"'Sup," Sasha said to it. "I think I've got wha'chu need,
dude." He brought his backpack around. He looked back.

"Orlu," he said, as Orlu came up beside Chichi and Sunny. Sasha motioned him to come. "See if it lets you."

"Are you guys okay?" Orlu asked Chichi and Sunny.

"Yeah," Sunny said. "I think it just likes Sasha."

Orlu looked and then took a few steps forward. When nothing happened, he kept going and was soon standing beside Sasha. The flying grasscutter looked at them both with narrowed eyes. It took a tentative step back, but that was all. Sasha opened his backpack and Orlu looked inside. When Orlu laughed, the flying grasscutter didn't flee as Sunny had been sure it would. Instead, it moved forward to see what was in the backpack.

"Sasha, you're a genius." Orlu said.

"It dawned on me this morning," he said.

When he brought out the first handful of grass, the flying grasscutter lapped it from his hands with a giant blue tongue. It chewed and as it experienced its first taste of "foodular" pleasure, its entire body shivered with joy. Sasha fed it some more grass.

"Come," Orlu said to Sunny and Chichi. Slowly they got up and came toward the beast. It eyed them suspiciously but inflicted no more juju on them. Sasha handed the backpack to Sunny. "Give it some grass."

It didn't hesitate to take the handfuls she offered it. She watched as it ate, noticing that it wasn't just gray brown. When Anyanwu appeared beside her, so dim that Sunny sus-

pected only she saw her, the grasscutter paused in its chewing. It sniffed at Anyanwu and then humphed and continued
chewing. Its brown fur was tipped with white filaments that
looked like thick spiderwebbing. Sunny frowned and took a
chance and stepped closer. It watched her as she reached forth
and touched its furry cheek. She'd been wondering what it
felt like. Was it sticky like spiderwebbing? No. It was soft. So
very soft.

When Chichi fed it, the creature left slobber all over her
hand. Orlu shook his head at her, and she swallowed what
was surely an exclamation of disgust. Sunny could have sworn
she saw the grasscutter's eyes twinkle. Chichi quickly moved
behind Orlu and Sasha, fighting the urge not to rub her wet
hand on her clothes.

"My name is Orlu and I am a human being," he said.
"This is Sasha. This is Sunny. And this is Chichi. We are on
Earth, a planet. We will show you. Can you read?"

Sunny thought Orlu had lost his mind, but then the
grasscutter grunted, shoving its tongue into the backpack
and taking more than half the grass.

"Good," Orlu said, smiling. "What is your name?"

Sunny gasped as the image burst in her mind. A huge
field of green, green grass under a lovely sun in the sky. *Chop!
Chop! Chop!* an enormous pair of flat teeth cut at the grass
like a lawnmower.

"Grasscutter?" Orlu said. "That's your name?"

It grunted. Another image burst into their heads. They saw *Udide's Book of Shadows* suspended in midair. The pages opened up and flipped this way and that way until they found one of Udide's many stories. An image of an old man and a grasscutter in deep discussion rose from the pages. The old Efik man had a strong accent. His yam farm was constantly raided by a grasscutter and he'd had to travel into one of its burrows to negotiate with it. In the story the grasscutter had liked how the man said its name.

Orlu pronounced it the way the old man did. "Grashcoa-tah? That's how you want us to say your name?"

It affirmed a happy assent by blowing air through its nose.

Sasha laughed. "Oh my God."

"Well, would you like another name?"

The grasscutter grunted an obvious no.

"Okay, Grashcoatah," Orlu said. "We understand."

"Ow!" Chichi screeched. "Who pinched me?!" She looked at Grashcoatah. "You did!"

Grashcoatah grunted gleefully and whipped and snapped its ten-foot-long narrow black tail.

"Well, most of us understand," Orlu said. "Will you come with us?"

It took more grass from the backpack.

"We can show you more than more of this grass," Sasha said. "We can show you a place where the grass is different colors!"

Grashcoatah purred deep in its belly, its eyes lidded with pleasure.

"Don't lie to it," Orlu said.

"I'm not," Sasha said. "I heard that there are all kinds of weird grasses in Osisi."

The ground vibrated as Udide approached them. "This is what you wanted?" she asked.

Grashcoatah suddenly disappeared down the cave behind them. But Sunny could hear its soft grunting. The creature was still there.

"Yes," Sunny said.

"You will treat it well?" she asked. Sunny could sense the threat behind Udide's question. Saying yes was only a small part of Udide's request. If anything happened to Grashcoatah, they would suffer.

"Yes," Sunny said.

"Then go," Udide said. "But there is one thing." She pointed a great leg at Chichi and then at Sunny. "The venom of my people is in both of you now. It will never leave you. It has decoded and bonded to your DNA. I can find you anywhere. I will know where you are at all times."

Sunny shivered. In all the excitement, the ache of the bites had retreated to the back of her mind. Now she felt their heated ache again.

Chichi gasped.

"Yes, you know what I am talking about, Chichi. You

know more than you let on. You are not ignorant. Not completely. You have heard rumor. You have heard myth. You have heard gossip. You know who to ask. When you finish this quest, bring me what is mine. Go to your people and bring it back. This one, Sunny, she is of the warrior clan of your people. She will be your 'woman show,' your bodyguard. If you don't bring it back, I know where to find you."

Chichi nodded, her eyes wide with terror.

"Smart child," Udide said. She walked back to where she'd been when they first arrived. She turned onto her back and pressed her thick hairy legs to the ceiling. "Leave me. It's a new year. Lagos is the tangled web I weave."

The marbles rolled back to Sunny, and she picked them up. As they left the cave, escorted by a parade of the nastiest spiders Sunny had ever seen, Orlu explained to Grashcoatah that it had the power to make itself invisible. Then Orlu explained *why* it had to keep itself invisible. Grashcoatah, who glided above them, only grunted that it understood. Whether it would cooperate or not was something they'd have to learn when they exited the cave.

26

FLYING GRASSCUTTER

When they emerged from Udide's cave into the harsh sun, Grashcoatah took its first look at the world outside. It grunted and then hummed deep in its belly. It did a slow turn in the sunshine, its large feet stomping on the dusty dirt ground. Then it shook out its furry brownish-white coat.

In the sunshine, Sunny could more clearly see its strange brown and white-tipped fur. The white parts were light and feathery and almost floated as if there was a breeze when there was none. She could also see that its eyes weren't quite blue but a soft periwinkle color, like that of an alien ocean. Its eyes were lovelier than she'd initially suspected.

When it turned those mysterious eyes to her, she sighed.

Its gaze was disarming. Yes, mysterious ocean was the perfect description; when Grashcoatah looked at her, she felt the flow of the ocean. The wilderness. Sunny wondered if the others felt the same watery sensation when it looked at them.

"Do you like the outside?" she asked.

It purred louder in affirmation.

Sunny smiled and said, "Well, you haven't seen anything yet. But . . ." She glanced at Orlu and he nodded. "But . . . so that we can show you things and so that no one will harm you, you need to stay hidden."

Grashcoatah suddenly disappeared right before her eyes. Sunny felt her entire body grow alarmed. This strange van-sized rodent with strange hair had been standing before her, and then, without one movement, it was gone. No matter how much magic she saw as a Leopard Person, she couldn't seem to stop having moments like this. Moments where she felt her brain would break; her entire foundation of what is right and what is wrong, what is normal and what is not, what is possible and what is not seemed constantly on the verge of a complete meltdown.

Grashcoatah reappeared and then began to snort as it watched her. It was laughing. It knew precisely the effect its disappearance had on her, and it found this very funny.

"That is just wrong," Chichi said, but she was smiling.

"Sunny, you should see the look on your face," Sasha said. When she frowned at him, he stepped back, holding his

hands before him, as he grinned. "I'm just saying, your reac-tions are so extreme. I can see why it'd want to scare the hell out of you. It couldn't resist."

Before she said anything, the beast stopped laughing and looked her square in the eyes. It stepped forward, and then it bowed slowly. The gesture was so charming, especially com-ing from a giant rodent, that Sunny forgot her anger. Grash-coatah nodded and then disappeared.

"See, no shaking," Chichi said. "It's going to cooperate."

Mmmph, the invisible creature said. It was right beside Sunny, judging from the blast of warm beast breath Sunny felt on the side of her face, blowing between her cornrows. Its breath smelled like the sweet incense her auntie in America liked to burn when she was stressed out.

"Thank goodness," Sunny said. She turned toward where Grashcoatah probably was. "Thank you so much! We . . ."

"Not yet," Orlu quickly said.

"Oh," she said. "Oh . . . we, um, we really, really truly appreciate your understanding." She frowned at Orlu. Grash-coatah only thought it was going with them to Osisi. If they didn't ask it now about *carrying* them there, then when? When they needed to leave? No one, not even a smart beast, liked to be asked such things right before the favor had to be done. But for the moment, she was relieved. At least they would manage to get back to her brother's friend's place more easily. How long had they been gone? A few hours? He'd be really worried.

"One thing at a time," Orlu said.

She nodded. At least one phase of their journey was behind them now; they were done with Udide. And now Grashcoatah was going to stay invisible and thus avert the chaos and disaster of a bunch of Lambs seeing what they'd only deem a monster.

Getting the flying grasscutter back to Adebayo's aunt and uncle's house was a nightmare.

It was such a ridiculous disaster that Sunny couldn't stop laughing and saying, "There is a haunted basement with all of our names on it waiting for us at the bottom of the Obi Library!" Then she'd laughed harder as the driver of the *kabu kabu* carrying her, Chichi, Sasha, and Orlu whimpered and whined as he stared into the rearview mirror and pressed down on the accelerator. Grashcoatah had a sick sense of humor and he (Sunny had just seen Grashcoatah fly overhead and, yes, Grashcoatah was *definitely* a he) had zero intention of staying hidden to the world.

At first things were okay. Strange, but okay. When they'd arrived at the back entrance to the market, about a fifth of a mile from the entrance to Udide's cave, they found the market booming. It was packed with people as if it were the middle of any non-holiday week.

On top of this, as soon as they stepped past the first couple of booths, Sunny's cell phone began to buzz like crazy as it received text message after text message.

"Are you kidding?" Sunny whined as she shoved past a group of women waiting in front of a woman selling large tomatoes.

Orlu grabbed her hand when she got through, pulling her closer. She felt her phone buzz again, this time indicating that she had voicemails, too. "No, I'm not," he said. "What do your eyes tell you?"

Her eyes told her what she knew was the truth. At least a day had passed since they'd entered Udide's cave. The New Year was well on its way.

"Udide loves a good story," Orlu said. "So why not thicken our own plot by throwing us off a few days?"

Sunny felt ill. She knew exactly what all her messages were about. She just didn't know how severe. Were they from her brother or her parents?

"Hurry up," Chichi said over her shoulder. Sunny and Orlu hurried after them. Chichi was right. Grashcoatah had told them he would meet them on the outside of the market. It was best not to keep him waiting.

The chaos began long before they made it out of the market. It started with nervous whispering and people losing interest in buying. Sunny caught snippets of conversation.

"Need to get out of here . . ."

". . . . the other way."

"Something near the . . ."

". . . if they're armed robbers, I have my cutlass . . ."

The four of them kept moving, and soon they found themselves fighting against a tide of increasingly terrified people. Sunny and Orlu grabbed a wooden pole as the deluge of people increased, sweeping past them. Some were screaming, all were rapidly fleeing. When the tide of people slackened, Sunny saw that Sasha and Chichi were clinging to another pole. They silently looked at one another and then broke into a run. When they emerged from the market, the normally packed entrance was deserted. The last few people were fleeing in cars, *okada*, and on foot. There was a great cloud of dust rising in the open area in front of the market, and Sunny's stomach dropped.

"You didn't!" Sasha shouted at the settling dust.

"Don't!" Orlu said. "Don't acknowledge him."

Sasha immediately understood, closing his mouth. He stopped running and walked back between an abandoned cassava-and-melon stand and a booth selling bunches of bushy green *ugwu* and water leaves. Sunny stepped up behind him. "Why would he do that?"

Sasha laughed. "He thinks this is all funny."

"I'll bet he landed in the middle of everyone and appeared for a second and then disappeared," Chichi said. "Just long enough to make people think they saw something and not be sure of what they saw. There are Leopard rules for beasts like Grashcoatah, too. If he causes too much trouble, the Library Council would come and put him down."

Sasha nodded. "Yeah, appear for a millisecond and let Ni-gerians do the rest. Y'all already superstitious as hell. An owl landing in a tree will cause a riot. It doesn't take much."

"We have to get him out of here," Orlu said. "Before people come back, out of curiosity."

"I have an idea!" Sunny said. She felt giddy, pleased with herself. "Sasha, Chichi, throw out two *Ujo*. Strong ones. That way all Lambs will be too irrationally scared of this place to come near. And since both of you can produce strong *Ujo*, we'll have a large perimeter around the grasscutter." She pointed at the *ugwu* and water leaves beside them. "It's not grass, but maybe we can get his attention with it. He's cer-tainly never tasted it before. Orlu, you're good with animals, you approach him. I'll stand behind you with more leaves."

They all paused, looking at Sunny. Then Sasha grinned. "Nice one."

Chichi brought out her juju knife and worked an *Ujo*. Sa-sha did the same, throwing his in the opposite direction. Orlu grabbed a bunch of leaves. Sunny reached into her pocket and brought out some naira and placed it in the money box beneath one of the largest bunches. Then she grabbed some *ugwu* leaves and followed Orlu.

As soon as they stepped out into the open, Sunny heard Grashcoatah *humph* deep in his throat. Then he made a wheezing laughing sound. "I hope you've had your fun," Orlu said firmly.

Grashcoatah laughed some more, appearing slowly before them. He eyed the leaves they carried, his nostrils flaring as he sniffed toward them. He took a step forward, and Orlu and Sunny stopped.

"Just as you know how to read," Orlu said, "you know what will happen to you if you show yourself again. Here, this is for you."

"Pff!" Grashcoatah said, defiant. He rushed forward, and Orlu and Sunny jumped back as Orlu told Grashcoatah, "No, no, no! Not like that."

Grashcoatah stopped, eyeing them with his large beautiful eyes.

"You want this? I know you can take it. But we know this world and you do not. You carry Udide's knowledge, but you don't have access to it all. I know. I've read about your kind. We'll explain our world to you, we can show you books to read, we can tell you about foods you'd love to eat." He held up his leaves. "These are *ugwu* leaves and we Igbo people use them in *ogbono* and *egusi* soup. They have a nice taste and . . ." He looked at Sunny. "Hold them up!"

Sunny held up her bunch of leaves. "Those," Orlu said, turning back to the listening creature, "are water leaves. They . . ." He turned to Sunny with a frown. "Do you know what they're used in? I'm not a cook. I barely know *ugwu*!"

Sunny shook her head.

"It's used in *edikaikong* soup. That's an Efik dish." Chi-

chi said from behind Grashcoatah. As Grashcoatah turned to look at her, she pointed at her chest. "I'm half Efik and half Igbo."

"Sunny and I are Igbo people," Orlu added. "These are human . . . ethnic groups. Do you know the word 'ethnic'? Tribes?"

Grashcoatah grunted and stomped his foot. Then he looked at Sasha who was standing by his side.

"I'm . . . I'm American," he said. He grinned. "African American. I have no tribe. Not one that I know of at least." When the Grashcoatah just looked at him, waiting, Sasha quickly went on to tell Grashcoatah the story of the stolen Africans, the thieving Europeans who stole them, the Native American peoples who got wrapped up in it all, and how he was a descendant of "all that bullshit."

Grashcoatah listened with complete interest and attention. Clearly, he loved stories just like his mother, Udide the Spider. Then Grashcoatah ate the *ugwu* and water leaves ravenously; he liked the water leaves much more and went on to eat every leaf in the abandoned booth. The four of them had to pool several naira together to pay for the creature's meal.

Sunny was relieved when they finally got the grasscutter to consent to fly with them back to Adebayo's house on Victoria Island. Grashcoatah agreed to fly above them while they caught a *kabu kabu*. As soon as Grashcoatah disappeared, they got moving. Who knew how long it would be before the

creature had another urge to scare the hell out of the citizens of Lagos.

They'd had to walk about a quarter of a mile before they found a *kabu kabu* who would stop. Chichi and Sasha's *Ujo* spell was indeed strong and far-reaching. Up to that point, if there was even a person nearby, he or she would have such a look of terror on his or her face that none of them even wanted to speak to the person. There were several *okada* that had been abandoned by their terrified drivers as well. Sunny was relieved that none of them had crashed. And people driving cars kept coming and then making a U-turn and screeching off.

"Make na come in!" the driver shouted at them. He was a young man with a shiny bald head, a neat goatee, and a wild nervous look in his eye. "Heard there was something happening around here and where things are happening, there are people who need rides. But the closer I get to the market, the more I feel like I SHOULDN'T BE HERE!"

They jumped in the car and Sunny was pulling the door shut as he sped into a wild U-turn and drove them off, shouting something frantic in Yoruba and then whooping with fear. The farther they got from the market, the more the man calmed, and soon he was back to being rational. As he drove, he apologized over and over. "I've had a long day," he said. "I get you where you need to go, no shaking, no shaking."

As they drove, Sunny looked into the air. Just as she did, she saw Grashcoatah do it again. Just for a split second, he

showed himself. A man on an *okada* must have looked up in time to see him. So had a driver driving a loaded truck full of oranges. It all happened in slow motion, every moment drawn out.

"Oh no!" Sunny said, turning to Orlu. "He did it a—"

The truck full of oranges was in front of them, and it swerved across the dirt median of the road into oncoming traffic. Two cars and an SUV dodged the truck as the truck's driver panicked and tried to dodge the two cars and SUV and, in doing so, lost control. Tires burning rubber, it whipped sideways and capsized, spilling oranges all over the road.

As soon as the truck lost control, the *kabu kabu* driver took them right off the road and screeched to a stop. It was in this way that they also witnessed the *okada* and its driver fly into the ditch on their side of the road and tumble into the tall grass. He jumped up and looked at the sky with his mouth agape. Then he looked at them.

"Did you . . . I saw . . ." He looked toward the chaos in the street and forgot the rest of his words.

Sunny was sure she heard the grasscutter's sneaky laughter from nearby. She even thought she saw some of the spilled oranges disappear. "That is so wrong," she muttered.

"At least no one is dead," Chichi said.

They all got back into the *kabu kabu* and were quiet for the rest of the ten-minute drive, and as soon as they got out of the car, the driver sped off without even demanding his pay.

27

QUICK CHOICES

Sunny breathed a great sigh of relief. For one thing, no council car appeared. This meant that Grashcoatah's indiscretions hadn't been severe enough to warrant punishment. Secondly, Adebayo's car wasn't there. Her brother and Adebayo were out. They hadn't seen Chukwu and Adebayo since the two had left to party on New Year's Eve. But what of the house help? What day was it? The stress settled on her shoulders again. What would happen if Lambs saw the grasscutter? *Really* saw him? For more than a millisecond? Once inside Adebayo's compound they stood there. Waiting. Then the dust in the large parking lot puffed up as Grashcoatah softly landed.

"What'd you have to go and do all that for?" Sasha shouted at him. "People could have died!"

More grasscutter laughter.

"Please," Orlu softly said, stepping in front of Sunny. "Have some rest, Grashcoatah. You've just come into being. I know you're tired."

Sunny heard the grasscutter grunt.

"Take a nap," Orlu said. "No one will harm you here. You are safe and it's nice."

A soft wind picked up and the dust wafted up on the side of the compound close to the house. Grashcoatah purred softly. Sunny could see the weeds growing there flatten as the grasscutter settled down. When he made no more sound, the four of them congregated quietly in the doorway.

"Grasscutters turn invisible when they sleep," Orlu said. "It's a protective mechanism. They sleep for about five, six hours after birth, so at least we'll have until nightfall. I think we should get out of here by then. Otherwise someone's going to see him. He can't resist the temptation to scare humans. He's smart enough to keep it short. But sooner or later he'll slip and we'll all end up in the Obi Library basement and he'll be plant food."

Sunny knocked on the door. If days had passed, the house girl who lived in the servant house might be inside cleaning the house or cooking a meal. When no one answered, they all sat on the staircase in front of the house. Sunny brought out

her phone. Without bothering to read all the messages, she called Chukwu. It rang once before he answered.

"Chukwu," Sunny said. "Hi! I . . ."

"Sunny? SUNNY?!"

She held the phone away from her ear, his shout was so loud. "Yes, it's me."

"WHERE ARE YOU? Are you all right? Where have you been?"

"I . . ."

"Are you all right?!"

"I'm fine," she said. "We are at the house."

"Oh, thank God! Thank God, o!! I thought ritual killers had taken you! I thought you were dead! I thought . . ."

"I told you, we have nothing to do with any of that."

"What the hell are you are involved in, then?" he snapped. "You disappeared for two days! Is this even you?"

"Yes!" Sunny shouted.

"I don't believe you, o," he said. But he sounded calmer. "Why should I?"

Sunny's eyebrows went up. Two days. That was bad but not too bad. She slapped her forehead. Why hadn't she thought to check her cell phone's date?! Days of being so close to Chichi, Orlu, and Sasha were rubbing off on her. She was losing her reliance on technology by the second. "Did you call Mom and Dad?"

He paused for several moments. "No," he finally said.

Sunny's legs wobbled with relief as she leaned against the door. "Thank goodness," she whispered.

"I wasn't sure," her brother said. "I should have but . . ."

"I'm glad you didn't! I'm fine. We . . . we did what we needed to do but, Chukwu, there's more. We have to stay here longer."

"What? How long? School starts in a few days. I have to go."

"Then . . . then go. I can . . ."

"No. I go home when you do. Where have you been?"

"I can't say."

"Then where are you going?"

"I can't say that, either."

There was a long pause.

"I'll be there in five minutes. I'm with Adebayo. Since you all disappeared, we've been searching for you all over." He was silent again for a moment. He was not telling her something. She didn't ask.

"Okay," she said. "See you soon." She clicked END and turned to the others. "He's on his way."

"As long as they don't try to park the car on that side of the compound," Orlu said, pointing to where Grashcoatah was sleeping, "we should be fine."

Adebayo wouldn't stop giving Sunny strange looks. Sunny's brother had hugged her tightly, and she even thought she saw

tears in his eyes. "I'm okay," she told him. "Really."

Chukwu only grumbled something and pushed past her to scoop Chichi into his arms. Chichi giggled as he hugged her, and Sasha looked ready to burst.

"I gave the house girls a few more days off," Adebayo said, unlocking the door. "Your brother . . . he owes me. We've been eating trash for two days."

After taking long showers, Chichi and Sunny cooked up a meal of *edikaikong* soup and fried plantain. They all ate and then watched a Nollywood movie on the wide-screen TV. Then the sun was going down. Adebayo was engulfed in video games on the huge TV, and he'd put on bulky headphones to experience maximum sound. Chichi and Chukwu sat on the couch too close to each other, chatting quietly. At some point, Sasha had left the room. Orlu took Sunny aside.

"We need to leave tonight," he said.

Sunny rubbed her forehead and sighed. "This is all moving too fast; I can barely catch my breath."

Orlu nodded, patting her on the shoulder.

"Maybe we can convince the grasscutter to take us when it's dark," Sunny said.

Orlu nodded. "But what if he refuses?"

"And what if he makes too much noise? What if my brother comes out to see what is going on? What if . . . Orlu, I can't go in that basement again," she said. She shivered, suddenly feeling tears come to her eyes. She hardened herself,

thinking of the damage that had happened there. "I won't."

"Don't worry," he said, taking her hand.

While Chichi kept Chukwu preoccupied with her batting eyes and idle conversation and Adebayo played his game,
Sunny and Orlu went to the kitchen and packed some of the
food into their backpacks. They filled plastic containers with
frozen jollof rice and goat meat they found in the front of the
fridge, and Sunny fried more plantain. They also found pack-
ets of biscuits and bottles of water in the cabinet. Her brother
and Adebayo had cleared out most every other cooked item
in the fridge.

"That should be enough for a day or two," Sunny said.
"Hopefully, it won't take longer than that. Sugar Cream says
time is different in Osisi. You know how days passed when
we were in Udide's cave for an hour? It's the opposite in
Osisi. If we can get there quickly, we won't have to worry
about it so much. When the timeless wilderness mixes with
our world, time dilutes, I guess."

"Can you hold that?" he asked as she tested out her full
backpack on her back.

"It's heavy but . . ." She hoisted it up higher. "I think I'll
be okay."

"Remember, if this goes right, you'll be hanging on to fur,
hundreds of feet in the air, *and* holding that backpack."

"I can do it," Sunny insisted.

Orlu laughed and shrugged. "Okay."

They both looked at the window. It was dark outside. Time to go. In the living room, Sunny saw Sasha walk past Chichi and Chukwu on the couch. He gave them a dirty look and came straight to the kitchen. Chichi turned to watch him pass. The ends of Sasha's cornrowed braids were undone, his shirt was rumpled, and he weaved slightly as he walked. And the grin on his face was enormous and almost scary. He was carrying his MP3 player and ear buds in his shaking hands.

"Go outside!" Sasha mouthed to Sunny and Orlu. He didn't want Chukwu to hear. Sunny nodded and Orlu pretended to look somewhere else.

"There isn't much to eat," Orlu said, his voice, too loud.

"Just need a drink," Sasha said, grabbing one of the smaller bottles of water. He took a big gulp as Sunny and Orlu watched him.

"Are you okay?" Sunny quietly asked.

"Come with me outside," Sasha said in a low voice.

Grashcoatah was outside. What had he done? She hadn't heard any crashes or crunches. Had he eaten the trees? Was he visible? When Sasha left the kitchen, they both quickly followed.

"We'll be right back," Sunny said to Chichi, looking her full in the eye.

"Okay," she said, returning Sunny's look.

"Everything okay?" Chukwu asked.

"I don't think so," Sunny said over her shoulder.

Adebayo cursed loudly, and they all jumped and looked at him. But Adebayo didn't notice. He couldn't even hear them with his headphones. His eyes were locked on the military game he was playing with several people online. The guy was in another world. Sunny rolled her eyes and followed Sasha to the front door.

Outside, Grashcoatah stood in the spot where he'd slept. In full view. His head peeked over the concrete wall that surrounded the compound. His haunches were tense, his lovely eyes were wide, his strange brown-white fur was puffed up, and his nostrils were flared. If a giant rodent could smile, this one was smiling. Sasha walked right up to the grasscutter and put a hand on his fur. The grasscutter nudged him with his head and Sasha laughed.

"He just flew me high over Lagos!" Sasha said. "He . . ." Then he again laughed. "He and I have something *very* important in common." He fiddled with his MP3 player, and it began to play Nas's album *Hip Hop Is Dead* out loud. The grasscutter's eyes grew wider and his fur tensed, and then he started doing something that caused both Sunny's and Orlu's mouths to fall open. Grashcoatah was dancing, swaying side to side, rippling his fur and undulating his body in a sort of wavelike motion. All to the beat of the music.

"He's a hip-hop head!" Sasha proclaimed. "I came out here and put in my ear buds and was listening to my music and next thing you know, he's breathing over my shoulder. I put the ear

buds to his ear, and he just came *alive!*" Sasha laughed again. "You should have seen it. It was like seeing a baby hearing music for the first time. I played jazz, blues, some metal, country; he liked them all but nothing got him moving like hip-hop."

Grashcoatah did a slow turn as he made his fur ripple like tiny waves on water. It was almost hypnotic.

"So I figured, he was digging my music and in a good mood and all, so I asked him what we needed to ask him."

Sunny held her breath.

"You . . . you asked if . . ."

"Yeah, I told him we needed to not only get there, but we needed a dang ride. He's cool with it. He took me up to show me how it would be. Better than any roller coaster! Whoo!! Was awesome."

Sunny needed to sit down, and she sat right there on the ground. Grashcoatah bobbed his head to the beat, resembling anyone enjoying the beats of Nas. "What am I seeing?" Sunny whispered. "This is . . . this is so weird."

"Eeeeeeeeeee!" The girlish-sounding screech came from the doorway right behind her.

"Don't!" she heard Chichi shout. "Just listen to me!"

When Sunny turned around she saw her brother's bulky form walking toward the open doorway, dragging Chichi along as she tried to pull him back inside.

"He wouldn't listen!" she shouted. "He wanted to see and he wouldn't listen!"

"What the hell is that?!" Chukwu screeched. "What is THAT?!"

The grasscutter roared with shock and disappeared. But Chukwu had gotten a nice five-second view of him.

"What was that?!" Chukwu screamed again. His eyes were red and wide, sweat beading on his face. "It's still here! I can smell it! It smells like incense! WHAT WAS THAT?!"

They all stood there in silence. Then Sasha said, "We have to leave!"

"Right now," Orlu added.

"WHAT WAS THAT?" Chukwu shouted again.

Soon curious neighbors would look out their windows or come out of their doors.

"Grashcoatah!" Sasha shouted. "Reappear!"

A few seconds passed and nothing happened. "Please," Sasha insisted. "He's seen you. It's too late. All we can do is go. But we can't go unless we can see you."

More seconds passed and then slowly, gradually, the grasscutter showed itself.

"Chineke!" Chukwu screamed. He grabbed Sunny and tried to shove her behind him. "WHAT IS THAT?!"

Sunny fought him, trying to get in front of him, but he was too strong. "It's not going to hurt you," she said, trying to move past him. He shoved her back.

"It's a monster! It's a spirit! *Mmuo!* This is witchcraft!"

Spit flew from his mouth as he spoke, and his red eyes were glistening with shock.

The bottle of water in her backpack and the containers of food sloshed and shifted as she tried to push past him.

"Get on," Sasha said. "The council will be here any minute now!"

He climbed onto the beast's back. Chichi hesitated for a moment. "Don't worry," Sasha said. "His fur is really, really strong. I don't even think it's completely fur. You can yank it and he doesn't feel it. Come on!"

Chichi grabbed the grasscutter's fur and climbed up. Orlu looked at Chukwu. "We . . . I'll keep her safe. We have to go or worse things will happen, trust me. You've seen what you shouldn't and we'll suffer the consequences. Not you."

"I'm not letting my little sister on that thing! Where are you even going?! WHAT IS THAT THING?!"

"It's a . . . grasscutter," Orlu said. He looked as if he were trying to say more but could not.

"Grasscutters are the size of cats! That's HUGE!" His eyes bulged and twitched as he held on to Sunny.

"I know," Orlu said.

"Shit!" Chukwu screeched. "Look at the head!! *Kai!*"

"Please, we have to go."

"I'm not . . . I'm coming with," he said, still grasping Sunny's arm and walking toward the grasscutter.

Orlu stepped in front of him. "You can't! You don't under-

stand where we are going. I . . . I don't know if you'll survive."

"I'm not letting my sister go somewhere like that without me!"

"Of all people," Orlu said, "*she* will be fine."

Chukwu looked at Sunny, sweat pouring down his face. She pleaded to him with her eyes. He turned back to Orlu. "If . . . if you can tell me where you are going, then I will stay."

When Orlu could not, Chukwu let go of Sunny and pushed forward, about to grasp Grashcoatah's fur. Lightning fast, Sunny made a decision and she felt Anyanwu come, settling just below her flesh. Sunny felt strong and aligned. She grabbed her juju knife and worked as fast as she could. She caught the juju bag in her shaking hand. She could hear a vehicle pull up to the compound gate outside. The council had arrived. She threw the *Ujo* at Chukwu. She hated to do it, but it was better than seeing him harmed. A Lamb would surely go mad or die in Osisi . . . or worse.

The terror that bloomed on her brother's face made her want to weep. Hadn't he been through enough in the last few weeks? His wounds from his beating weren't even fully healed. The patch of healing skin from where they'd cut his face twitched as he backed away from Sunny.

"I'll be fine," she said, tears falling from her eyes. "Remember that. Tell Mom and Dad that I'm fine! And I'll be back."

But her brother wasn't seeing her. She didn't know what he was seeing. But whatever it was must have been horrifying for he opened his mouth and hollered loudly, turned, and ran wildly into the house. She just stood there. Then she felt someone grab the collar of her shirt. "Sunny, get on!" Chichi said, leaning almost upside down to grab Sunny.

But Sunny couldn't get her feet to move. All she could see was her brother's face. How it had broken into terror and how he'd run off like a madman. Had her *Ujo* been too strong? Had she just driven her own brother insane? Suddenly, her vision blossomed and she felt herself pulled physically backward. Then it was like she was a passenger in her own body watching herself climb onto Grashcoatah. As soon as she was on, Anyanwu mentally shoved her forward and Sunny gasped, looking wildly around.

Sasha was seated at Grashcoatah's neck, Chichi clasping Sasha's waist, and both staring at her with open mouths. She felt Orlu's arm grab her tightly as they took off. Instinctively, Sunny grasped handfuls of the creature's hair, her mind still trying to hold too many things at once. Grashcoatah's body was hard; it reminded her of the thick hide of a pig or an elephant. But its strong hairs were soft to the touch.

When the grasscutter flew into the air, Sunny felt no exhilaration. As they zoomed high over the house, away from the council car that was sitting at the gate as the council police pushed the gate open, Sunny cried and cried. All she

could see in her mind was the look of terror on her brother's face. It was a look that said he was seeing a monster. *I am a monster*, she thought.

Yes, it was juju, but he was her older brother trying to protect her from danger. And make no mistake, she was heading to a very dangerous place. And she'd forced him to flee like a terrified child. If that wasn't something only a monster would do, she didn't know what it was.

28

THE YAM FARM

They were on the run. There was no getting out of this without being arrested. They could not return home without facing harsh punishment. No matter what they discovered in Osisi.

For the first half hour, Sunny could think of nothing but this fact and the look on her brother's face. Then, maybe it was the feel of the wind blowing in her face, or maybe it was the smooth motion of Grashcoatah's flight, or maybe it was the sound of Orlu's rare delighted laughter. Whatever it was, it caused the veil of sadness and doom to lift from her shoulders. And soon she, too, was in awe of the whole experience.

Grashcoatah flew high in the sky where it was cool and

382 ☼ *Nnedi Okorafor*

silent. His body was remarkably warm, so none of them was uncomfortable. And he flew so smoothly. It was not like an airplane slicing through the air. It was as if his very presence caused the air to part and give way. There was no loud wind, though they flew fast. They were heading northeast.

Grashcoatah communicated in his own way that he instinctively knew the way to Osisi. According to Orlu, who was best at understanding the beast, Grashcoatah could smell the way. They were invisible to the world around them. When Grashcoatah made himself invisible, they also disappeared as long as they held on to his hairs. Sunny could even feel it, a warm sensation that traveled up from his body. At first, Sunny welcomed this visual nothingness. She was just wind passing through the air, similar to when she glided.

Once they were out of the city, they all agreed that it was okay for Grashcoatah to make himself visible. The night was dark and they were over mostly trees and small unlit villages. Sunny looked at her cell phone. It said NO SERVICE AVAILABLE. Grashcoatah was quiet as they flew. Sunny wondered if he was worried about what the council would do when they caught him. In Nigeria, intelligent beasts who broke protocol by showing themselves to Lambs would face execution.

"Even if we make it to Osisi without getting caught, I don't know what I'm looking for," Sunny said.

"Well, at least you'll arrive there in the same way that you arrived in your dream," Orlu said. "By air. Maybe you'll

remember the rest of the dream when we get to that same point."

"*If* we do," Sunny said.

Hip-hop music began to play. Sasha was holding his MP3 player near Grashcoatah's ear. Grashcoatah purred, gleefully flying in a wavelike motion.

"Haha, yeah," Sasha said. "That's more like it. Cheer up!" He turned to Sunny and Orlu, Chichi holding on to his waist. "All of you, cheer up. We're going to a full place! How many of our peers will be able to say that? And we're doing it while on the run from the law. This is stuff that books are made of, man. Live in the moment. Don't know about y'all, but I'm going to make the most of this. I want to see this Osisi place."

"Me too," Chichi said. "The council won't be able to find us there anyway. Not even the best tracking juju can find anyone in a place that is blended with the wilderness. Worst they can do is catch us when we try to go home."

Sunny frowned. This didn't make her feel that much better.

"One thing at a time," Orlu grunted.

"Correct, my man," Sasha said. "One thing at a time." He turned his music all the way up.

They decided to stop at a small rural village after flying for hours. The sun was coming up and it was beautiful. Sunny

couldn't help thinking about the last time she'd been out at dawn—when she'd been released from the Obi Library basement. She shivered, thinking yet again, *I can't go back there.*

She couldn't use the GPS on her phone; that rarely worked even during normal times. At the moment, the time on her cell wasn't even working. Maybe it was something about the grasscutter or maybe it was where they were. Whatever the case, she was left to guess their location. They'd been traveling northeast from Lagos. Maybe they were in Ondo State or even Kogi State. Grashcoatah was flying so fast, and without the sense of wind they could have traveled much farther than she thought. Whatever the case, the village below was quiet, cassava and yam farms stretching beyond the small cluster of houses.

They were invisible as they landed beside a large pond. "Shhh," Orlu said as they looked around. "Anyone see anyone?"

"There," Sasha whispered. "In that yam farm." They all looked. About a half mile from the pond, past lush blooming farmland, an old man with a machete was bending over and inspecting the vines and tubers of his farm. Aside from this man, the place was quiet. The pond looked clean and peaceful, several of the farm plants growing right at its edge to sip the water. It was the kind of place that women used to wash clothes or bathe. This village was lucky to have such a healthy pond.

"He probably won't even notice us," Sunny said.

"Maybe," Orlu said.

"*Ah-ah*, come on," Chichi said. She appeared as she let go of the grasscutter's fur and began to climb down. "I will die if I don't get off this thing for a bit." Once on the ground, she stretched her back and looked around.

The others followed suit, though Grashcoatah stayed invisible. When Sunny got to the ground, her thigh muscles cramped up. "Argh!" she said, stumbling.

"Riding a flying grasscutter is good exercise," Chichi laughed.

"I'm going to be sore for the rest of my life," Sunny said, gritting her teeth as she pounded on her thighs to loosen the lean muscles. "I feel like I've been playing ten hours of soccer. I need to eat two bananas, at *least*."

"Grashcoatah, there are plenty of plants," Orlu said. "I see wild grass, weeds, and things. Don't eat the man's crops, please!"

Grashcoatah grunted in a way that sounded sullen to Sunny.

They sat in a dry patch of dirt near the pond and ate a nice breakfast of plantain, bread, and groundnuts. It was communal eating, and they were all so hungry that no one cared about the dirt. The best they could do was wash their hands in the pond before eating.

When they finished, Sunny walked to the pond. She

dipped her hands in its clear water, marveling at the tiny brown fish darting away. One came back to eat the dollop of *egusi* soup that had washed off Sunny's hand. She strolled along the edge of the pond, in the opposite direction of the farmer, watching the tall grasses closely for snakes. She'd never imagined she'd ever be in a place like this, at this moment, for this reason.

She looked out at the still waters. The pond was so calm. And so . . . big. *We should get out of here*, she thought. Otherwise someone would see them. There were bound to be people using it this early morning. She brought out her phone. The battery was charged all the way up but still no service. She considered reading the text messages from her brother and parents that had been sent when she was in Udide's cave. She shook her head. *No, I'm keeping all that out of my mind until I finish this.*

She was putting the phone in her pocket when she noticed the red snake inches from her feet. *No!* she thought, her body filling with adrenaline. *That's not a snake!* As soon as this registered, the tentacle wrapped tightly around her ankle and pulled. She fell back, dropping her phone as she banged her elbow onto a rock. A second, bigger tentacle wrapped itself firmly around her waist and squeezed. Before she knew it, she was underwater.

Not a pond. A lake. One that wasn't normally there. The old

farmer hadn't looked beyond his precious yams. They must have been in Igboland. Only an Igbo farmer would be so focused on his yams that he didn't notice that an entire lake had arrived with the morning sun, sitting a half mile away.

All this spun around in Sunny's frantic mind as she fought with water, the tentacle, and for air. As she ran out of air, she felt her spirit face pulled from her. Just like that. As if they were being whipped about in a tornado and could no longer hold on to each other.

Anyanwu! she screamed in her mind. No response.

Pain burst in her chest as she was pulled deeper. Bubbles escaped her lips. The light retreated from the surface. Water entered her mouth, her eyes, her ears. Something yanked her by the neck. Pulling her backward. *Plash!* She landed in living grass, flopping onto her back like a fish out of water. She opened her mouth wide. She had a mouth, but she still felt herself fading. And then she felt Anyanwu jump into her. She breathed; death had not found her yet.

"Where?" She quickly sat up, her body aching. She touched her face; instead of flesh, she felt wood. Her spirit face. But her voice was not the low voice of Anyanwu. She heard a flute play a haunted tune, and she moaned.

Ekwensu spoke with the low voice of an earthquake, gravelly like tumbling stone. It made all the hairs on Sunny's arms stand up, for she'd somehow carried her body into the wilderness. "When crocodiles walk on waters, the ripples are

obvious," Ekwensu rumbled. "I am deep in the water, so you cannot see my open mouth.

"Meet Death, my close friend and ally," Ekwensu said. "It is good that I've brought you fully here. He would like to acquaint himself with *all* of you."

He appeared behind Sunny. She could smell him, like de-caying carrion. She could feel him, cool and damp. She could sense him, for his presence absorbed all the sound around him—it was as if a black hole stood behind her.

"Face me, child," he said in the voice of her father. "I've been waiting to meet you properly. The wilderness is not a place I normally come to, for there is no life here. But you are a special occasion. *Face me.*"

"Why?" she asked. She didn't dare turn around. "What do you want?"

"You make me feel powerless," he said with a chuckle. "You die and return, and your body is still alive. You come and go, come and go. You are unbound, but you still live. Why does your body not die *here* after so many seconds? Who are you?"

Have to get out of here, she thought. "I don't know," she said, gritting her teeth.

"Turn around," Death commanded.

Don't turn around, Anyanwu said in her mind. Sunny took several deep breaths. She hummed as she exhaled.

"It won't be painful," he said soothingly, sounding like

her father. She missed him so much. "Turn around. Both of you."

She shut her eyes, touching her wooden face and picturing the ocean, vast and full. Just beneath the water, schools of fish and larger beasts swam, the water protecting them from the sun's harsher rays. The waves rippled, never still, never at rest because water was life. Sunny would break the surface and Anyanwu would cause more waves, more ripples—because she was alive.

"Surface," she whispered. Death was at her back, but she had to focus her mind to a needle-sharp point, just as Sugar Cream had taught her. Never had she brought her physical body to the wilderness. Who would purposely *do* that? Even when she glided, Sugar Cream said that the essence that was her physical body became light and invisible and stayed in the physical world. Now, the lake beast had pulled her completely through, or maybe Ekwensu had used the creature to do it.

Nevertheless, the process of getting her body out had to be the same as coming here as spirit. She called her name in her mind, *Anyanwu Sunny Nwazue*. She grasped her shoulders, giving herself a hug, and she glowed a strong sunny yellow.

She took a deep breath, one last one, then slowly she turned to Death. Just before she faced Death, she shut her eyes. And just as she did, she kicked herself back as if she were in water.

She heard the angry growl of Death as her body shot

away. Her momentum slowed and she felt herself falling to the ground. *Oh no!* she thought. Then she plunged into water. She flailed, shocked by its wetness and weight. Her body was glowing like the sun, piercing the aqueous darkness. She turned and came face-to-face with the surprised eye of the lake beast. She looked right into it. Then she grinned. Her body was still glowing a yellow white, blinding the great water beast.

She kicked with both her legs, swam at the lake beast's eye, and buried her fist in it. She felt something burst, and the lake beast roared and began to thrash in pain. It spun, slapping around with its tentacles. Then it twisted, pulling all parts of its body into a huge tight ball, and then shot off into the depths.

Sunny flailed in the water. Still glowing, though the glow was fading. She felt pressure in her chest. She needed air. She swam to the surface until her head broke it. She threw her mouth open and inhaled deeply. Then she sputtered. The closest bank was at least forty meters away.

"Sunny!" she heard Orlu shout.

Sasha leaped wildly into the water. Sunny had always been a strong swimmer, but she was tired and overwhelmed. So she did what she always did when she got tired in the water; she floated on her back. She looked at the morning sky. So clear. So alive. She blinked and coughed a tired laugh. There was Grashcoatah, hovering in the treetops near the lake.

"Are you okay?" Sasha asked when he reached her.

"Yeah."

He was swimming with one of the large empty water bottles in his arms. Keeping the bottle between them, he linked his arms through hers from behind and began to swim with her backward toward the bank. "I took some lifeguard lessons two years ago," he said as they swam. "Just relax your body. I'm not tired at all, so I can carry you."

Sunny was glad to do so, and in no time, he had her out of the water. Orlu helped her to dry land. "What happened?" he asked.

Sunny was about to speak, but then she noticed the old farmer standing beside Chichi. She looked at Orlu.

"That lake beast knew you were coming," the farmer said in Igbo. "Seen it here before, but now I know what it was waiting for."

Sunny's mouth fell open.

"He helped us fight it on land," Orlu said. "*Oga* Udechukwu is a third leveler. We'd be dead if he weren't."

Only then did Sunny notice the tentacles lying in the cassava garden beside the water. There were three of them, thicker than fire hoses and frozen solid, white mist rising from them.

"It pulled me into the wilderness! It was trying to kill you guys at the same time? Was there more than one?"

"The lake beast has three brains," the farmer said. "I stud-

ied it, its cousin the river beast, and several of their other kin extensively when I was a youth. Fascinating beasts. But they have a habit of aligning themselves with negative or evil people or forces." He sucked his teeth, looking at the lake. "I knew that lake beast was up to something. *Kai!* I can't wait to tell my wife. She was sure that it was just passing through."

The old man took them to his small hut of a home and introduced them to his wife, who gave them each cups of hot tea, since they'd already eaten. She also took Sunny's clothes and dried them using a combination of the sun and a hot iron. "No use in using juju when nature has a better method," she said. She gave Sunny a long colorful caftan to wear in the meantime. The farmer and his wife were Leopard People who'd decided when they were young that after years as Obi Library students, they wanted to live like their forefathers and foremothers. "There is more knowledge to be gained from reading Earth's books than any book in the library," his wife said. She was a rail-thin old woman with strong arms and crinkly gray hair.

Chichi sniffed and shook her head. Sasha kicked her to shut up.

"We're on our way to Osisi," Orlu said. "Do you know of it?"

"Osisi?" he turned to his wife. "You see, Nwadike? Look at how they dress. They must be from Lagos. All the way

out here hours from the border? Where else would they be going?"

His wife sucked her teeth. "Kids today are always trying to make their lives so complicated," she muttered, getting up and collecting their empty cups. "Cell phones, gadgets, silly juju, and always running to Osisi."

The farmer turned back to them. "Why?" he asked. "Why do you want to go to that dreadful place?"

"We have to find something there," Orlu said. "It's not for enjoyment or anything like that."

"We've never been," Sunny added. "We just . . ."

"You *shouldn't* go," the farmer said. "It's not a place for human beings; I don't care if it's full. Why can't you four just live a simple wholesome life? Study your books, then find husbands and wives, have children. Stay out of trouble. Be positive forces to the world."

"*Oga*," Sunny said. "This journey is important. Did you see our flying grasscutter? We even went to Udide to . . ."

"Grasscutter?" the farmer said, jumping up. "You brought a grasscutter here?!" He ran out of the hut, looking around, his skinny knees knocking together. "Where is it?! My farmland, my farmland! It'll be the end of me. I know what those things do. Some stupid kids flew one here ten years ago trying to get to Osisi the fast way. They couldn't control it and it ate *everything*!"

"We told it not to eat anything, sir," Sasha said.

"Oh, those things never listen," the old man said. "You all have to go. Now, now, now, *biko!*" He gently but firmly ushered them all out. When his wife found out about the grasscutter, she, too, went into a panic and brought Sunny's clothes all folded and fresh. "Take the caftan, it's yours. Just get your beast and go, please!"

"Grashcoatah!" Orlu called. Grashcoatah flew down, landing in the same place he'd landed before, beside the pond that became a lake.

They all climbed on. "Sorry," Sunny said. "But if it helps, you see that he did not destroy your garden."

The farmer nodded. "For the moment. Grasscutters are known liars and equally known for their trickiness. Trust me when I say that you can trust a flying grasscutter as far as you can throw it. Be careful!"

Grashcoatah humphed, offended.

"And please consider our advice about living a simple life," his wife added.

"We will," Sunny said. "Will you be okay with that?" she asked, pointing a thumb at the lake.

"Oh, sure," the farmer said. "It'll move on now that it's done what it came to do."

"And since you punched it in the face," his wife added. They all laughed.

They flew off, leaving the farmlands. As they climbed into the sky, Sunny looked back at the farm just in time to

notice the sleek black BMW pulling up to the hut on the narrow dirt road. Even out in the middle of nowhere, the council had found them. They'd escaped completely by chance.

"We just have to make it to Osisi," Orlu said. "If that farmer was right, we won't have to make more stops."

The grasscutter grunted with relief, and Orlu patted him on his side. "Don't worry. We won't let them harm you."

"We forgot to ask them where we were," Sunny said, minutes later.

"Does it really matter?" Sasha asked. "As far as I'm concerned, that was very much the middle of nowhere."

For hours, they all were quiet as Grashcoatah flew on. Sunny didn't know what the others thought about as they stared into the clouds ahead, behind, or to the side, but she was glad for the silence. A chill had fallen over her flesh, a headache at her temples, and in her ears she heard a high-pitched screaming. And in the back of her mind, like the powerful afterimage left if one happened to see lightning strike, she saw the image of Death. She hadn't looked right at him, but she'd seen him with her peripheral vision as she pushed back.

And she was still seeing it—a blaring whiteness that could swallow anything if you faced it. She'd been so close. She shut her eyes, stifling a sob that came from deep within. Ekwensu had been there, Death had been there . . . and she was falling apart. *And if I had looked at Death, what makes*

me Sunny would have died. And I'd just be Anyanwu. Which means I wouldn't really be . . . She felt Anyanwu hiss protest at her thought, and Sunny sat up straighter.

But it took hours for the image of Death to fade and even when it did, it didn't fade completely. Sunny didn't think it ever would.

29

FULL PLACE

Sunny didn't know exactly when they crossed the border into lands that were full. There was no obvious line. But within four hours things had shifted . . . drastically. Below them were miles and miles of the lushest green rain forest Sunny had ever seen. A massive, thick blanket of treetops. From above, it looked like the top of bunches of broccoli. She was sure they had to be somewhere near the Cross River Forest. What other part of the country could look like this? But that wouldn't have made sense with the northeast direction they were going. She'd tracked this by the location and movement of the sun.

Then, at first she thought Grashcoatah had decided to fly

lower. However, upon several minutes of closer inspection, she saw that it wasn't that they were lower; it was that the trees were higher, much higher, and bigger. Monstrously gargantuan trees of a type she'd never laid eyes on. They were over a thousand feet in the air, and Grashcoatah now had to weave around several of them.

Grashcoatah stopped making himself invisible. "What are you doing?" Orlu asked. "Someone will . . ."

"See him?" Sunny asked. They both laughed uncomfortably. There were far stranger things in the air and on the ground and in the trees. She'd seen some sort of insectile creature as big as Grashcoatah flying in the distance.

"Look!" Orlu said as they slowly passed the highest mahogany tree Sunny had ever seen. Its rough trunk was wide as a house, and within its top leaves were red furry creatures that looked like something right out of the Muppets. They had long swinging arms, and the fur on their bodies was so thick that they looked like giant red puff balls. They were picking and gathering the softball-shaped light green mahogany fruits and putting them into cloth sacks.

Sunny blinked and looked again. The sight was all types of abnormal. As they passed, mere yards away, Sunny saw that their eyes glowed orange yellow like setting suns. One of them raised its hand and let out an ear-splitting howl as the grasscutter flew by, and all the others waved with their big humanoid hands. They had no fur on their palms. Sunny,

Orlu, Chichi, and Sasha waved back. From that point on, it was strange creature after strange creature.

There was the flock of hummingbirds and praying mantises, all matching bright green, that flew with them for ten minutes. Some hitched a ride on Grashcoatah's tail, much to Grashcoatah's annoyance. They made cheeping sounds and seemed overly curious about Orlu's hands, flying around them and landing on them when he held them up. Then they let a draft of wind carry them off.

There was the shadowy thing that peeked up from a dead part of the jungle below, merely a set of staring huge eyes. This thing reminded Sunny of the river beast. She was willing to bet that it was another cousin of the river and lake beasts and that the farmer had probably studied this beast when he was a student. She was glad when the thing did not leap up and try to snatch them.

They saw what could only have been a small masquerade sitting at the center of a palm tree top. Then a patch of jungle that was all slowly undulating giant blades of grass. A pine tree with white ants the size of small children running up and down its trunk. And a hill-sized pile of what looked like dumped garbage and smelled like it, too. They passed over the first town that looked like smoke and, even without Grashcoatah's indifference, she knew this was not the place they were looking for.

"You're sure?" Orlu asked as they passed over the cluster

of modern-looking houses that wavered in the breeze. Smoky, wraithlike people walked on the very definite paved roads. There were no cars.

"Yeah," she said. "What I saw in my dream was much, much bigger. It was like New York."

Soon the trees gathered again, and they were back over dense jungle. Sasha and Chichi were near Grashcoatah's head quietly having an argument. Judging from the way they were snapping at each other, Sunny knew exactly what the argument was about. The state of their relationship was the last thing she was going to think about when they were so close to Osisi, so she ignored them.

Orlu sighed. "How come there are no *people*?"

Sunny hadn't thought of that. She shivered. What if Osisi was just full of spirits, even though it was technically a place where one was in both the physical world and the wilderness? "We're in the air," she said, hoping she sounded convincing. "People would mostly be on the ground, right?"

They saw Osisi an hour later. From afar, it seemed to be a burning city enveloped in smoke. Sunny had lost track of time but judging from the setting sun, evening was approaching. The effect of the orange sky and the orange city wreathed in black-gray smoke was overwhelming. It was just as it had looked in her dream, and she experienced a moment of vertigo as dream and real world, physical world and wilderness, meshed together.

She shut her eyes and when she opened them, they were right at the moment of her dream where she woke up. She gasped. Osisi *did* look like the apocalyptic place in her dreams. Her belly dropped. They were flying right to it.

"Grashcoatah," she screamed. "What are you doing?"

Sasha was cursing and shouting at Grashcoatah, and Chichi was looking everywhere for a way to get off the flying beast.

"Everyone, just get down," Orlu said. "Cover your heads!"

"But, but, but . . ." Sunny babbled. She was sitting straight up, unable to tear her eyes from the burning city. Orlu grabbed her and pulled her close to Grashcoatah's fur.

"He's not suicidal," Orlu said.

Grashcoatah grunted annoyed agreement.

Then they flew through the first of the flames. It felt like being slapped with a bucket of water, except it didn't leave them or Grashcoatah wet at all. "Oh," Sunny whispered as she peeked through Grashcoatah's warm fur. The flames dissolved the closer they got to the city, revealing a skyline more spectacular than New York's. Osisi was surrounded by a large ring of green. Sunny frowned. There were boats moving in it; was it bright green water?

"'When you walk through the fire, you shall not be burned; neither shall the flame scorch you.'" Sasha recited. "The book of Isaiah, chapter forty-three, verse two."

Grashcoatah flew low, playfully touching the surface with his forepaws. No, not green water, water covered with bright green algae. Once they'd passed the first wall of flames and smoke, the sky grew clear and blue. Osisi was a giant megacity of glittering glassy skyscrapers, large colorful stone buildings, and bulky wide leafy trees that looked older than time. It was simultaneously ancient and modern West African. And even from a third of a mile away, Sunny could see that it was full of spirits.

The first building they flew over was a large stone hut flanked by two skinny, impossibly tall palm trees. The hut sat so close to the water that it looked as if it would fall into it. At the very edge, Sunny could see the bottom of the building where the land was crumbling away to reveal roots . . . roots from the *building*, not the tree. There was also a large greasy shadow looming over the building's shingled roof that actually shrank away as Grashcoatah flew by.

Above the buildings, Sunny could see several large winged, floating, gliding, swooping creatures. Some were landing on buildings, others just passing through. A large batlike creature clambered its way up the side of a tall skyscraper, tearing at the building's façade with its claw-tipped wings as it climbed. They even passed another flying grasscutter, and this delighted Grashcoatah so much that he nearly flew into a building.

"Where should we land?" Orlu asked.

"Where the tallest buildings cluster," Chichi said. "That should be the downtown area where the action is."

"But we're not looking for action," Orlu said. "Not really." He turned and looked to Sunny. "Do you have any feeling about anything?"

She shook her head. "I know this is Osisi. It's the place where I was going in my dream. We were in the exact spot from my dream, somewhere back there. I don't know what to do next."

"Let's get on the ground," Sasha said. "This place is awesome. I'm dying to see more. Did you see that tree covered with spiders?"

Sunny hugged herself. "This place seems like a good place to get killed."

Chichi laughed. "Something tells me that dying here is not the same as dying back home."

"I mean, do people, like, work here? Do they pay rent and have mortgages?" Sasha asked. "What the hell? Did you see that building that disappeared and reappeared a block to the left? It created a new space!"

Sunny rubbed her forehead. "Let's just get on the ground."

Orlu leaned close to Grashcoatah's ear. "You all right?"

Grashcoatah grunted.

"Do you like this place?"

Grashcoatah grunted again and happily rippled his fur. Orlu smiled. "But it's not all great, right?"

An image flowered open in Sunny's mind. Judging by the looks on the faces of her friends, Grashcoatah was showing them all the same thing. There was a man standing beneath a tree. A coconut fell on his head and before he hit the ground, the tree had bent down, caught the man, opened a mouth full of sharp leaves, and chomped the man's head off. Blood spurted from the opening in his neck as the body fell and twitched.

Sunny shut her eyes, but the vision was in her mind. She felt her body seize up, ready to vomit what she'd eaten three hours ago. "Argh!" she shrieked. "Why'd you have to show us that?" Her eyes watered as she tried to hold back tears.

Sasha was shaking his head, as if trying to dislodge and discard the nasty image.

Orlu was frowning very, very deeply.

"I get it," Chichi solemnly said. "That's a warning."

Grashcoatah grunted.

"Best to know how dangerous the place is," Chichi continued. "It doesn't look so scary from up here."

"Speak for yourself," Sunny whispered.

"Take us down," Orlu said to Grashcoatah. "And . . . thanks for the warning."

An image of Udide flashed into their heads. Grashcoatah knew what he knew because of his mother.

Grashcoatah descended slowly between two large houses onto a wide quiet road. They climbed down and looked around. The building they'd landed in front of that looked

so much like a house appeared to be a small library, a sign with a large open black book sitting in front of it, flanked by green bushes heavy with black berries. There was not a soul walking up or down the roads, nor was there anyone coming out of any of the buildings, at least as far as Sunny could see.

"So quiet," Chichi whispered.

"Shhh," Sasha said. "Looks can be deceiving. Can't you feel it? Someone's around."

Orlu's hands came up and he held them before his face. Sunny felt her heart flip. Orlu's natural gift was instinctively undoing harmful juju. His hands were like a radar, raising and preparing to dismantle before the bad juju attacked. Something was at work here.

Sunny looked at the road. It was packed red dirt. A strange contrast to the modern buildings that loomed all around her. She frowned as a memory tried to burrow its way up in her mind. She absentmindedly followed the others as they walked up the road. A warm breeze blasted as they passed a building made entirely of glass. Inside the building, what looked like human beings in traditional Hausa attire bustled about carrying papers and sitting in cubicles that housed computers and desks. The breeze materialized into one of these Hausa-looking people at the front door, but the man didn't open the door; he simply slipped into the wall.

The wackiness of Osisi made Leopard Knocks look mundanely normal. Osisi was the Lagos of Leopardom in Nigeria.

Sunny wanted to climb back on Grashcoatah and close her eyes, but she couldn't. She was on the verge of something. It was the road. "There are no paved roads here," she said to herself.

"Yes, I noticed that from above," Orlu said.

She pointed at an enormous stocky tree with a bouquet of leaves at the top, biting her lip as whatever she tried to remember moved right to the tip of her tongue. "And that's a baobab tree."

Orlu nodded, saying nothing. Grashcoatah was beside her, looking closely at her face. Chichi and Sasha were in front of them giggling about something. Sunny didn't want to speak. She didn't want to move. She didn't want to breathe. It was right there. Something. Something . . .

The wind suddenly blew, warm and damp. When it stopped, they were in the same place but a different place. At least to Sunny. She was seeing as both Sunny and Anyanwu again. They were standing in the empty dirt road where office buildings, houses, and a giant fat tree jostled for space, and people within the buildings looked and acted like . . . people. At the exact same time, Sunny was surrounded by a busy market that went for about a block.

Yards away, there was a woman who was not a woman selling fruits that were not fruits. When a man stepped up to her and picked up one of the applelike non-fruits, it disappeared. There were old women perched atop two of the

booths, hungrily looking down at customers. One of them pointed at a young man, and they all grinned and nodded. A man walking by chatting on a cell phone stopped and then quietly slipped into a tear in reality. Sunny's mouth hung open. She inhaled loudly. "Can . . . can you all see this?" she asked. Again, she felt ill. This place felt heavy, packed, it felt . . . full.

"See what?" Orlu asked. A spirit of blue light passed right through him to step up to a booth run by a woman who looked barely there. She was selling small bags of popcorn.

"It feels a little cooler," Chichi said. "That's all."

Grashcoatah was looking around frantically, trying not to step on things from two different places. So he saw the wilderness, too.

"I see . . . There's . . ." Then she remembered. A red dirt road. Down one of these roads flanked by tall buildings and trees and bushes. Modern and old. A sunflower-yellow stone house. Her grandmother had shown her the place in the message she'd left Sunny. The sheet of Nsibidi. Her grandmother knew Osisi. And the house, Sunny knew what it looked like. And now that she was here, she knew where it was. When she looked up, it all snapped into place. She'd been here before. When she read her grandmother's Nsibidi note. *The house!* she thought.

"I know where to go," she said. She stared at Orlu as it all flooded her brain. "I . . . I know where to go!" She stumbled

to Grashcoatah and grasped his fur. He bent his head toward
her. "You see it, too?" she asked. Grashcoatah nodded, moving closer to her.

"Where?" Orlu asked.

"See what?" Sasha asked.

Chichi wrapped her arms around herself, shivering.

"There's a house," Sunny said, trying to stay focused.
The wilderness market was all around her. If she and Grashcoatah stayed where they were, "people" willingly moved
around them. "It's not far from here. Grashcoatah, we will
climb on you, then fly straight up."

They all got back on, and Grashcoatah flew straight
up as quickly as he could. Below, the empty road of the
physical world and the busy market of the wilderness mingled in a profound act of coexisting. Staring at it made her
eyes and temples throb harder than they had since entering Osisi, but she looked anyway. The market stretched
along the road for about a half mile. So, though it was in
the wilderness, it still acknowledged the road in the physical world, for the booths were set up along its edges. Yet
the spirits walked right through people who could not see
them, like Sasha, Orlu, and Chichi. And why did they
make Chichi cold?

"Okay, hold on," Sunny said to Grashcoatah. He seemed
relieved to hover in the air far above things for the moment.
In the distance a large green glowing centipedelike creature

spiraled between two skyscrapers. Sunny wondered if the others could see it.

"What was happening down there?" Orlu asked. "I didn't see anything. Just empty road and quiet buildings."

"Me neither," Sasha said.

"I dunno," Sunny said, rubbing her aching temples. She was tired in the same way that she was when she read Nsi-bidi. *Anyanwu*, she called in her mind. *What is happening?* Though she continued to see in the double vision, Anyanwu didn't respond. Where had she gone? Tears fell from Sunny's eyes, her nose ran, and her heart began to beat fast. She sniffled and shut her eyes tightly. She took a deep breath. Some-one took her hands. "Inhale," Chichi said. Sunny inhaled. "Exhale." Sunny exhaled. "Do it again, Sunny. Breathe. We need you to be strong now," Chichi softly said.

Sunny inhaled and then exhaled, and each time she re-peated this, Chichi squeezed her hands reassuringly. She opened her eyes and blinked away her tears.

"She's gone again," Sunny whispered.

"What?" Chichi asked.

I'm incomplete, she thought. *Can't you tell?* However, she didn't say this aloud. Sunny only shook her head. "Why are we even here? I had a vision I *thought* was the apocalypse, and then some crazy lady who refuses to wear a shirt told me to come here. What is that?"

"Anatov says the universe guides us all," Chichi said.

"It's up to us to listen. The universe is pushing you here. You know it. Stop being a coward. You're a Leopard girl, you should know better."

"The world is much bigger than me, right?" Sunny said.

"Right," Chichi said with a smile.

Oddly enough, the phrase she'd been told over and over by her Leopard teachers and mentors, the phrase that had always seemed so callous, made her feel better in that moment. The universe may have wanted to make use of her, but its purpose was not to specifically harm her.

Chichi brought out her juju knife and held it up. Sasha did the same, then Orlu. Sunny brought hers from her pocket. When they touched them together, as friends touch wine glasses together in a toast, there was a large periwinkle spark and a jolt. One felt through the tip of one's juju knife as if that tip was part of his or her body. However, when they touched their knives together, it was like feeling with four knives.

Also, for a moment, Sunny saw through four pairs of eyes at once. She saw herself, Orlu, Sasha, and Chichi in ways that she didn't normally see them. She saw herself as yellow-skinned and yellow-haired, but different. She was herself, but she was beautiful. Was this how Orlu saw her? She saw Sasha as lighter-skinned with sharper features and a warm red aura wafting from him; this was Sunny seeing through Chichi's eyes. She saw herself again, her yellow features glowing like

the sun, her spirit face not visible but looking ready to burst forth at any moment. This was how Sasha saw her?

The periwinkle spark hovered in the air as they pulled their juju knives away. They watched it as it rose a few inches. Then it burst into white light, startling Grashcoatah. He roared with surprise and rose higher. Chichi exclaimed something in Efik as Sasha grabbed her arm so that she wouldn't tumble off.

"It's okay," Sunny said, patting Grashcoatah's side. "It's okay."

He slowed his ascent and grunted. Sasha climbed to his ear and put some music on. "Here, vibe to some Jill Scott, classic," he said, playing a song called "A Long Walk."

Grashcoatah's ears perked up and turned toward the soothing funky beat. Sasha leaned on the ear, a grin on his face as he held up his MP3 player.

"There's a house," Sunny pushed herself to say. She scanned the area. "Oh!" She pointed. "There! I see it! That yellow house! Grashcoatah, do you see it? Go there!" She paused. That was the one, all right. "That's the house my grandmother told me about."

As they flew, she told them about the piece of paper her grandmother had left her. It was hard to explain how one "read" Nsibidi. "It's something that you kind of have to *do* to understand it." But the fact that she could describe the smell of flowers that lingered around the yellow stone house and

its thick clear front door that was round like a hobbit's door convinced them quickly to just go with it.

In front of the house was a lawn of tall thick overgrown blades of grass. In her grandmother's Nsibidi note, the lawn had been short and kept. This one was like a large wild field between two large stone librarylike buildings. No one had been here for a long, long while. Before they could climb off Grashcoatah, he went to work and started eating the grass like crazy. *Chop, chop, chop!* He was like the happiest lawn-mower on earth. He didn't notice when they all tumbled off him and ran to the side.

"Jesus, look at him go," Orlu said as they watched the grasscutter do what his name said he would do . . . cut grass.

"Check out his flat teeth," Sasha said. "Reminds me of Barney."

Sunny laughed.

"Who the hell is Barney?" Chichi asked.

"Big annoying purple dinosaur for kids on TV," he said. "It's got this super fake, constant grin of flat white mono-teeth on the top and bottom."

Grashcoatah grunted with pleasure as he went at the grass. But Sunny was more interested in the house. Even the overgrown lawn. She shaded her eyes in the sun.

"Why is . . ." Chichi tapered off.

"I don't know," Sunny said. "It didn't look this big in the Nsibidi." She called Anyanwu yet again. No response.

The overgrown area surrounding the house was like its own prairie, as opposed to a lawn. The yellow stone house itself was significantly bigger than the librarylike buildings beside it. From where she stood, she could see a palm tree with a very bushy top growing out of the center of the house. It, too, was wide and expansive. But in the Nsibidi the leaves had been green and alive. Now they were tan and dried up. Had the tree died since her grandmother had been here? They crossed the wild grass.

"So *that* door is made from some see-through beetle's wing?" Sasha asked as they walked up to it. "The beetle must have been as big as an SUV!"

The door stood over twenty feet high.

"Bigger than that," Orlu said, craning his neck to look up at it.

"*And* it's impossible to destroy," Sunny said. "Or so my grandmother said." *But why didn't she tell me that the house belonged to a giant?* Sunny wondered. *Hmm, so one can lie or omit facts in Nsibidi.* A tiny gold *chittim* fell to her feet. She wouldn't have noticed it if she hadn't been looking down at her feet thinking and trying to piece it all together. She bent down, picked it up, and placed it in her pocket.

"What was that for?" Chichi asked.

Sunny just shrugged. The simple two-story house took up the space of four houses. It was flanked by two normal-sized living palm trees and a large angry-looking bush growing in

the back. Sunny stood there, looking up at the place. None of it made any sense. She'd thought that her grandmother had given her the Nsibidi because she found this house beautiful, a peaceful image to show Sunny. Or maybe it was a place that she wanted Sunny to eventually visit. But what could *live* here?

A group of four women carrying large jugs of water on their heads walked by on the dirt road that passed in front of the expansive patch of wild plants. They waved at the four of them as they passed and Sunny, Sasha, Orlu, and Chichi waved back. One of the women cupped her hands and shouted something in Yoruba.

Sasha and Chichi laughed. Grashcoatah grunted loudly and did a slow turn and then stretched a leg, rippling its fur. Sasha stepped forward, answering back. *When did Sasha learn to speak Yoruba?* Sunny wondered.

"What are they saying?" Sunny asked him.

"They're admiring Grashcoatah," he said. "And they are impressed that we met Udide in person."

Chichi ran over to the women and spoke with them for a bit. Sunny turned to the door and touched it. It was smooth and domed out toward them like a thick unpoppable bubble.

"Whose home is this?" Orlu asked.

"I don't know," she said. "I can't figure out why my grandmother took so much time to tell me all about it. I know what's inside, where everything is. But how come she didn't tell me that the house itself is gigantic?"

"Maybe she didn't want you to know," Orlu said.

Sunny frowned at him.

"There's no juju keeping it closed," he said, nodding toward the house.

"The door?"

"Yeah. I don't sense a thing. What if someone's in there?" Orlu asked. "We can't just . . ."

"No one is in there," Chichi said, coming up behind them. "Those women said this place is abandoned. They don't know who lives in it or owns the property, but most people stay away. They said some of the local elders will know."

"Did your grandmother say anything about how to get in?" Sasha asked.

"No," she said. "The door just opened or something. I dunno."

Chichi brought out her knife and blew on the tip, made a circular flourish, and tapped softly on the door. Her eyes grew wide. "Ouch!" she screeched, jumping back.

"Heh, I had a feeling a simple door-opening juju was not going to work," Sasha said.

"Felt like it *bit* me!" Chichi said, rubbing her right hand as she held her knife.

"I thought you said there's no juju protecting it," Sunny said to Orlu.

"It's not juju," Orlu said.

"Ancestral land, then," Sasha said.

"Exactly," Orlu said. "Whoever's ancestral land this is is not human."

"Let me see your hand, Chichi," Sasha said, taking it.

"See the red mark?" Chichi said, her voice softening as Sasha stepped closer to her.

"I see," he said. "Want me to kiss it?"

Sunny rolled her eyes and Orlu looked away, uncomfortable. "*Na wao*," Orlu muttered.

They stood there looking at the door for a moment. "Well, if your grandmother liked Nsibidi so much, maybe she used it to open the door," Chichi offered. "Do you know the Nsibidi for 'open'?"

Sunny was about to say that she only knew how to read Nsibidi. But then an image bubbled up in her mind. She saw the door opening when she'd read her grandmother's Nsibidi note. Slowly it swung open like a thick dome of glass. She was playing the image again in her head when she realized there was a flash of something. "Wait," she whispered. "Wait." She replayed the image in her mind; there it was again. She held up a hand, closing her eyes. "Wait. Nobody talk."

She replayed it again, this time slowing it way down. Again, but even slower. And that's when she saw the symbol. Clearly. It was more than "open." It was stronger. It was tricky demand and force. Her grandmother had broken into this house when she'd come here. A heavy bronze *chittim* fell. She heard it clink against the door and felt it land on her

sandal. She opened her eyes, slowly bent down, and picked it up. She looked up and smiled at her friends. "Did you know that the images Nsibidi creates when read can be separated from the symbols?"

Always swift with understanding, Sasha and Chichi made her job so simple. "So . . . if you remember the image, you can call back the symbols?" Chichi asked.

Sunny nodded, putting the *chittim* in her backpack.

"Oh, I get it. You were remembering the image of the door opening," Sasha said, nodding. "And in that image is the Nsibidi symbol. Clever."

"Nsibidi, de tin' dey cool," Chichi said, impressed.

"I don't get it," Orlu said. "But if you can open the door, open it, *sha*."

Sunny put a hand on the door's cool surface. She brought out her juju knife. She paused. The blade of her knife was nearly identical to the substance of the door. Was her knife made from the wing of a beetle from some distant land? She'd consider this later. With her knife, she drew the symbol she'd seen in her grandmother's Nsibidi on the surface of the round door. She worked slowly, carefully, holding the image in her mind as she tried her best to duplicate it. Gradually, the surface of the door pulled her knife to it like a magnet pulled steel. *Pop!* The four of them jumped back. Then there was a deep hissing sound as the enormous door unsecured itself. A few budding plants and roots growing over and inside the

door ripped and fell, and dust and dirt rained down. The strange clear door opened like a reluctant mouth.

Hands up, Orlu led the way in, then Sunny, Chichi, and Sasha. Once they were inside, the door softly shut behind them. However, only Sunny vaguely noticed. They were too busy looking ahead.

30
ABOMINATION

They slowly entered the high-ceilinged main room. It was like entering a palace. The sound of their footsteps echoed off the intricately mosaicked walls. A closer look at the walls revealed that the fractal patterns were made from the tiny wings of black, red, green, and blue beetles. As she walked toward the center of the tennis court–sized room, Sunny felt the temperature increase with each step. Orlu came up beside her, his hands raised and ready to undo the juju that came at them. He lowered them. "It stopped," he said.

"What did?" Sunny asked.

"Something was about to happen," Orlu said. "And then it didn't."

"I'll bet it's because of Sunny," Sasha said.

Sunny looked down at the floor. It was smooth and glossy, as if it had been polished an hour ago. And it was tiled with millions of flat circles that could have been glass, plastic, or something else. They were arranged in a fractal pattern that made Sunny woozy when she looked at it for too long. She couldn't say what color it was because it used every color she could imagine. It was like a constantly blooming flower. At the center of the room stood the trunk of the fat dead palm tree that reached through the wide circular hole in the ceiling. The top of the palm tree probably kept the rain out, if it did rain here.

Hung on the walls were large ceremonial masks, intricate and expressive. It reminded Sunny of Sugar Cream's office, if her office were magnified by ten and the masks were creepier. There was one that hung on the wall that looked made of solid gold. It was as tall as Sunny and as wide as the expanse of her arms. Its face was thick-lipped, wide-eyed, and bulbous-nosed. Its lips were pursed and puckered as if it was ready to spit a lot of something. Sunny moved out of its range.

She moved on to the one that appeared full of water, the wall visible through it. It had the expressive round face of a smirking woman with Yoruba tribal markings on her cheeks. Sunny couldn't resist; slowly she reached out to touch it. She hesitated. If this place were booby trapped with juju, maybe she shouldn't. But she'd always been this way with

gelatin, bubbles, and any liquid substance that took a shape. She couldn't help just one poke. Her finger sank right into it. "It's water," she said to herself. Yet here it defied gravity and hung on the wall.

There were four others. One made of wood, but it sprouted roots that created a mane around the roaring face. It also hung from roots that burrowed into the wall. The next mask was made of bronze. It was the head of a wall-sized dragon creature. One was a small boulder of stone with rudimentary openings that made two eyes and a tiny hole for a mouth. And one was made out of pressed garbage, plastic bottles, tin cans, crumpled paper, dried orange and banana peels, cassette tapes, and more. This mask took up the entire wall on the far side of the room. It was grinning.

Sunny wondered if the masks could call out to Anyanwu. "Where are you?" Sunny whispered, trying to calm her nerves. Anyanwu had said they were always one, but why wasn't she answering? Where *was* she? Sunny did *not* like the feeling of being in this scary house with these scary powerful masks without her. There were doorways on the left, the right, and the center that led to other parts of the house. All of the doorways were enormous like the front door. Everything was huge. *Whose house is this?* Sunny wondered yet again.

They entered every single room in the house and indeed, all were rigged with some sort of juju. And each time Sunny walked into the room, the juju disarmed itself. Had her grand-

mother embedded something else in her Nsibidi note? Sunny wanted to stop and figure it out, but the longer they were in this place, the more nervous she felt. Whatever she needed to find here, she needed to find it soon. Even if there *was* something protecting her, the fact was this place was full of jujus that were meant to harm all of them.

For an hour they explored. Sasha and Chichi investigated a library upstairs where they had to work together to bring down and open even the smallest books. Sunny remembered this place from her grandmother's Nsibidi tour; she could even smell the sandalwood.

"Oh man, these books are soooo forbidden," Sasha excitedly said. "Not even fourth levelers are allowed to see these!" He and Chichi had dragged a book the size of a suitcase from the lower part of one of the bookcases and when they threw open the cover, it was like a universe slowly swirled within the pages—a billion blue, yellow, red, and white stars rotated in the giant swirl that occupied both pages. Sunny backed out of the room as they knelt down to further inspect the strange book.

"Is that safe?" Sunny asked from the doorway.

"Doubtful," Sasha said as he read some words that were appearing in the page's edges.

Chichi had brought out her notebook and pen and started writing things down. Sunny looked for Orlu and found that he'd managed to get the giant front door open again.

Apparently what had closed it was simple juju that he'd easily undone. He was outside with Grashcoatah showing him a book from the house.

"Come and help me get Sasha and Chichi out of that library," Sunny called out the door. "They're looking at some weird books in there!"

"They're not going to stop no matter what I say," he said, holding the book for Grashcoatah. Grashcoatah grunted and Orlu turned the page. He looked at Sunny. "We'll give them a few minutes."

Sunny nodded and decided to look around a bit more. Upstairs she found a spacious room with shiny marble floors. It was completely empty except for the trunk of the palm tree that grew through the center. There was a corner near a gigantic window where sunshine streamed in. She sat here and let her body grow quiet. She didn't like this house at all, despite its artistic walls, library, and masks. Since entering the place, she'd had a bad feeling. But then again, she suspected she'd have a bad feeling upon entering any house that looked like the house of the giant in Jack and the Beanstalk, especially without Anyanwu. All she could think was, *What about when the one who lives here comes back?*

But this *had* to be the place she was meant to find. All things pointed here. The Nsibidi note her grandmother had left, her tricky Nsibidi book, the lake and river beasts, Ekwensu's passive-aggressive attacks, Bola, her dreams. "So

now what?" she muttered. She sighed and, despite it all, found herself relaxed by the warm sunshine and the quiet solitude of the grand room. She tilted her face toward the sun and shut her eyes. Everything glowed red behind her eyelids. She heard soft buzzing. When she opened her eyes, a red wasp was hovering right before her face. She stayed still as it lazily flew into the room, its limp legs hanging down.

Sunny slowly got up, as another wasp came through the open window. Then another. They didn't pay her any mind as they flew toward the palm tree. Where were they coming from? *Maybe there's a hive on the side of the house*, she thought. Something buzzed and landed on the edge of her ear, and her body tensed. She twitched and slapped the side of her head hard enough to cause her ear to ring. When she brought her hand away, she saw that she'd crushed a large flying ant or termite. "Ugh!" she said, wiping the crushed insect on the wall.

She made for the stairs, her heart pounding. Something wasn't right. "Chichi? Sasha?" she called as she jumped down the stairs. "We should get out of here! I . . ." They weren't in the library.

"We're down here," Sasha called. They were standing near the front door. The ceiling and walls were swarming with termites, and Sunny spotted more wasps and a few mosquitoes flying around, too. Chichi looked particularly horrified.

"What's going on?!" Sunny asked, running to them.

"Wait," Sasha said, frowning deeply as he held up a finger.

Suddenly, Chichi screeched, turned tail, and ran through the open door, out of the house.

"Chichi," Sunny called. "Where are you . . ."

Outside, Grashcoatah suddenly roared viciously. Sunny and Sasha looked at each other and ran to see what was happening. They stepped out just in time to see the great swarm of termites wrap around the screaming Chichi and whisk her into the air. The grass looked like an undulating black sea. It was writhing with black ants.

"Ow, shit!" Sasha said, slapping his arm.

Sunny felt a sting on her calf. Her leg involuntarily buckled from the pain, and she grabbed Sasha's arm. "Are you all right?" Sasha said, his face squeezed from the pain of his own sting.

"I . . ." she said. "Are you?" She looked down and saw a bee still wiggling its stinger into the leg of her pants. She brushed it off and nearly screamed from the pain.

"No," Sasha said, looking at his arm. "My arm's numb!"

Over the sea of ants, the swarm of stinging insects whirled into a chunky shape, swallowing Chichi's screaming form. There was a shimmery blue cloth that appeared at the base of the roiling form, and gradually the cloth ascended over the hovering mass of termite bodies. It looked like it was made of silk and was the deep blue of the ocean on a clear day.

"Okay, that's the Mmuo Aku Chichi called up last year,"

Sasha said. The one that had nearly killed them all at the so-cial during the Zuma Festival. Oh yes, Sunny remembered it clearly. Death by stinging. Orlu had sent it back but before it left, it had whispered something to Chichi in Efik that even weeks later, Chichi refused to tell Sunny, insisting that what the Mmuo Aku said to her was "private business." Chichi liked being secretive, and this annoyed Sunny so she eventu-ally just stopped asking. Now that very same Mmuo Aku had shown up in Osisi, found them, and swallowed Chichi, taking her to goodness knew where. Sunny made a key deci-sion at the same time as Sasha.

"What are you doing?" they said to each other.

"Stay here," they both responded.

They stared at each other.

"Don't go near the Mmuo Aku! But get out of there!" Orlu shouted from the back of Grashcoatah, who hovered above.

THOOM! THOOM! THOOM! Sunny's ears itched and her teeth chattered from the sound. The deep beat continued as the crisp tune of a flute laced itself around it. The tune was like a sweet-throated bird serving as the harbinger of death and destruction. Ekwensu was here. Ekwensu was here. Ekwensu was here.

Sunny and Sasha looked at each other. Then Sasha ran one way and Sunny turned and ran in the other direction. Toward the trunk of the dead palm tree growing in the

center of the house. The palm tree trunk whose roots now bulged upward as a termite mound pushed through the soil. Sunny clenched her fists and felt her knuckles crack. And still, Anyanwu did not come. The world around her sparkled with shades of a thousand colors. The masks on the walls were looking at her. They had been watching her since she'd entered this place, she realized. She just hadn't really taken notice.

She hadn't noticed a lot of things. Like how the leaves of the palm tree that grew through the house were dry. *Maybe they were never green*, she realized. *Maybe the greenness in Grandmother's Nsibidi was another lie.* Sunny felt faint as she understood. Maybe her grandmother knew Sunny wouldn't come here if she knew this was the home of Ekwensu. *Not just home*, Sunny thought. *Ancestral land.* She thought of the ancestral land her father owned and how he and his brothers (such land was only passed through the men) fought over it like dogs. To build on one's ancestral land was to keep one's family name alive. It was immortality. One was most powerful on one's ancestral land. *But also most vulnerable*, Sunny thought. *Right, Grandma?*

Termites wiggled out of the rising bulge and flew about the large space. Something also started happening to the tree's trunk; it had begun to swell, water droplets forming and then dribbling down the smooth bark. The wood snapped and split in several places, but still the trunk continued to swell. The

space took on the acrid smell of oil and tar as it warmed.

She could hear commotion outside—Grashcoatah roaring, a squishy sound, buzzing, Sasha giving a warrior's cry.
Something large hit the front of the house where she and
Sasha had been standing moments before. A blast of frigid
air flew in, conflicting with the warm air inside. But Sunny's
focus was on the giant tree in the center of the house that
wasn't really a tree, not anymore. It had expanded by ten feet
in diameter, now twenty, thirty, bringing down the ceiling
above and then the roofing. Then bark fell away to reveal
tightly packed and layered dried palm leaves. There Ekwensu
stood. Again.

And now, for the first time, Sunny could see her face.
Faces. At the top of the great mound of tightly packed palm
fronds was a cloth hood of wooden masks. Sunny could see
three of the masks, one facing her and one on each side, and
there was probably one more she couldn't see. Like the Aku
masquerade Chichi had called last year, each mask had a different expression; the one facing her was smiling.

Water began trickling down through the open roof. It
was raining. With the deep rhythmic drum that was beating,
Sunny hadn't realized that a storm had come in, too. The rain
hitting the dried palm leaves of Ekwensu made the sound of
a large audience clapping.

Ekwensu began to dance. She rocked her huge body
of packed dried fronds back and forth to the musical flute,

bringing down more of the house. Chunks of stone fell; some landed right before Sunny. She was afraid, so afraid. But she didn't move. She stared at Ekwensu with dead eyes. Ekwensu began to spin.

Sunny heard the crash of lightning and Orlu screaming her name. Something meowed loudly like a giant cat. There were spirits lurking all around the room. She could see them clearly as she'd seen the market over the empty road. There were glowing blades of grass in the walkway that swayed to the rhythm of the flute music and large blobby white shapes pressing into the corners. Something green cartwheeled away from her on her left, leaping into the open mouth of the gold mask.

They feared Sunny. Even without Anyanwu. What did that mean? But they were not her concern. Sunny stretched her neck as she watched Ekwensu preparing to strike. That's how she'd always operated, Sunny remembered. Sunny flexed her legs and rolled her shoulders, the way she'd always seen Chukwu do just before running onto the soccer field for a game. She touched the juju knife in her pocket and focused on Ekwensu's spinning body, squinting as she tried to see individual leaves. If she waited any longer, Ekwensu would be spinning too fast. Sunny held her breath and ran forward. *If I die now, I die*, she briefly thought. And she meant it.

There!

She grabbed on to the first frond her eye caught. It

crumbled in her hand, and she quickly grabbed another, reaching as close to the root of the leaf as possible. The velocity took her, and soon she was spinning. For several moments, Ekwensu didn't notice and Sunny took advantage of this, using her strong, strong arms to pull in her body and then haul herself up as the great masquerade spun. She saw a red bead like the one that had hit her between the eyes tumble from between the fronds and drop to the floor. Then another. She gasped, looking frantically for more. Hadn't Sugar Cream said if Sunny caught one of those beads she could end Ekwensu?

She saw another bead, but it was too far to grab. "Damn it," Sunny hissed, out of breath. "Can't get it!" Ekwensu was spinning faster now, and the beads were flinging this way and that. Sunny decided to ignore them and keep climbing.

Ekwensu had always been arrogant, Sunny knew. She had expected and assumed Sunny, naked and so young without Anyanwu, would run *away* from her, not *to* her. Ekwensu's dried-up leaves were wet, making them easier to climb. And they were tightly packed, so as long as Sunny grabbed the right leaf, she found purchase and hauled herself higher. Sunny felt all her muscles flex. She was made for this. She was like an Idiok baboon in a forbidden forest. She focused on the wet leaves to avoid dizziness. She was almost there. She had to move faster!

Suddenly, Ekwensu stopped spinning, red beads clicking and clacking as they hit the walls and floor. Sunny held on

with all her strength and managed not to go flying. When she looked up, one of Ekwensu's faces was looking right at her. The smiling one. Its angry smile widened as the blank wooden eyes glared at her.

Ekwensu roared and Sunny felt the powerful masquerade's warm body flex in a way that nothing made of dried leaves ever should flex. For a moment, Sunny nearly lost all her faculties. How could wet dried leaves not only be warm but *feel* like some kind of . . . flesh? The contradiction made her woozy, but she held on. A black substance began to ooze from between the leaves in millions of hairlike filaments. Wherever they touched Sunny's body, they stung.

Sunny couldn't hold on much longer. And she could feel it; Ekwensu was about to fly off. Sunny glanced below. If she let go and landed just right, maybe she would live to face Ekwensu another day? This thought gave her little comfort. And then a swarm of dragonflies was whipping around Sunny's head. No, not dragonflies. One of them slowed down right before her eyes and she gasped. Nsibidi. Loops, coils, swirls, lines of living yellow script. One of them stopped right before her eyes, and she grasped its meaning: *Remember, I never leave you. Read this*, it said.

"Anyanwu?" she whispered. "Is this from you?"

Ekwensu's body swayed and then slowly, she began to spin again. Sunny grunted and hung on tighter, as she fought to focus on the Nsibidi symbols floating before her. They

moved with her, and the combination of trying to read them while Ekwensu rotated made her stomach violently lurch. She gagged as she read, then saw, heard, smelled . . .

Forest, silt, craggy waters, all drenched with greasy black ooze. Sunny knew this place. She'd seen it on the news. *The bitter smell of dead rotted trees, sulfurous like a thousand farts. The place is silent because everything is dead. Then I saw Ekwensu bubble up from a great pool of black-brown mud surrounded by a ring of dying trees. Mud bubbling and blurping as she rose. Then she began to spin and one of her faces spat out an orange-yellow spark. It arced into the pool of blackened mud and the whole place went up in flames. I pulled back far enough to see the forest burn, then the nearby town, and another town, all as Ekwensu danced in the burning forest.*

Sunny stopped reading the moment she understood. The Nsibidi disappeared. Setting the recently oil-soaked part of the Niger Delta on fire was only Ekwensu at play. It was only the first thing that would happen if Sunny didn't succeed right *now.* Once Ekwensu really got started, she would turn the world into the apocalyptic place Sunny had seen in the candle's flame. Her eyes were watering, not from tears but from Ekwensu's fumes and the pain of the stings as Ekwensu spun faster and faster. Sunny continued to climb. Everything depended on it.

The deep drumbeats grew rapid and the flute crescendoed into a shrill screech as the weakening Sunny climbed

up the side of the masquerade, her body threatening to give out under the searing pain of the masquerade's stings. She was between the smiling and frowning face. Both of them twisted down and tried to bite her. She leaned out of reach. She knew what she was looking for and moments later, she saw it: a small space between the packed leaves and the faces, the bottom of the mask.

With all the brute strength she had left, she grabbed the edge of the masquerade's mask and yanked. It didn't give. It didn't budge. She'd gotten so close, yet now she would die. Sunny had fought Ekwensu once long ago in a past life, in the wilderness. She'd used her juju knife because it was a knife like the one she had now—one that could travel with her into both worlds. She'd been of both worlds back then, as she was now. And back then, she'd defeated Ekwensu and sent her away. Then, a year ago, Sunny had defeated Ekwensu with magical words she'd remembered from when she was only Anyanwu. She'd used juju again.

And now here they were, a third time. And this time, Sunny had turned things on their head and fought Ekwensu in a way that Ekwensu had not expected. Not with juju knives and magic, but with hand-to-hand combat, physical strength. And Sunny had almost won again. Almost. But Ekwensu's mask would not come off.

Sunny pulled and pulled. Deep and guttural, Ekwensu began to laugh an awful ugly sound that forced nauseous im-

ages of smoke, fire, death, and blood into Sunny's mind. She felt her gorge rise. Then she saw the very image that she'd seen in the candle two years ago. It wasn't a small sight in the flame of a candle this time. It bloomed before her with a certainty that spoke to her soul and the memories of her ancestors and the dreams of her future offspring. She shrieked and pulled again. And pulled. And puuuuuuuulllllled!

It gave.

Like her last baby tooth that had hung by a thread for a week. The mask had been coming off all this time, it was just that neither she nor Ekwensu had realized it. Ekwensu's mask finally slipped off. And so did Sunny. As she fell, she could see her arms. They were dotted with red marks from being bitten all over. The lean muscles on her arms bulged. When had she grown so strong? Her veined hands were clutching the enormous mask that was bigger than her entire body.

She fell and fell. It felt as if she fell for days. Maybe time in a full place was not only different from time in the physical world but had a way of stopping and starting and slowing at certain moments. Maybe. Maybe this was the case now because Sunny saw everything around her clearly. Hundreds of red beads and several large bronze *chittim* fell with her. She could see Ekwensu's body, the black filaments breaking off now, stiffening like threads of pencil lead, the wet dried leaves beginning to fall apart and crumble on their own. She

heard Ekwensu's spirit music falling out of rhythm one beat at a time, one note at a time.

"Eeeeeeeeee!" The screams of Ekwensu made Sunny's eardrums vibrate, but even worse, the noise was physical. Like a thousand pins poking into her skin. And the mask that fell with Sunny was looking right at her. Only one of the faces faced her. The surprised face. Its eyes burrowed into hers. Its black O-shaped mouth was impossibly wide with shock. And the knob on its head glowed an angry red as it let out white smoke. Then Sunny hit the floor and her glasses flew off. She was pelted with red beads as the mask landed on top of her, and both air and sense were knocked from her body.

Sunny's father belonged to the local secret masquerade society. She'd never thought twice about this until now. At certain times of the year, her father would go meet with "his people" and come back late at night. And during celebrations like the New Yam Festival, he'd be gone, too. Usually, his disappearance coincided with when the masquerades would parade down the road. "None of your business," her father had snapped when she was five years old and had asked him about what it was like to dress up as a masquerade.

"Well, maybe next time I see one, I will snatch its mask off," she'd said defiantly.

Her father had looked at her with the most serious expression she'd ever seen him make and said, "Never unmask

a masquerade. You hear me? That is an abomination!"

So Sunny had learned this long before she knew a thing about Leopard society. The fact that unmasking a masquerade was forbidden was common lore among Nigerians. So after all that she'd become and all the deep African juju she'd learned while spiritually crippled, she'd defeated Ekwensu with brute physical strength and local knowledge she'd possessed since she was a little girl. She smiled, a laugh on her lips.

There was no house, no mask, and no crumbling masquerade around her. She lay on her back in a field. A field of grass. "Grass." It was a fresh light green, and it wriggled playfully beneath her. The sky above was no longer broken open and dropping angry rain. Instead, the sun shone. She sat up, a hand pressed on the soft but firm squishy blades of "spirit grass." And in the bright light, she could see everything clearly despite the fact that she wasn't wearing her glasses.

When she looked down, she saw that she had hands and a body and her skin glowed a brilliant yellow. She was wearing a scratchy raffia dress that went to her knees. It was nearly identical to the one she'd found herself wearing when she was initiated. Was this some sort of second initiation? Or maybe she had died and this was the attire of the wilderness.

"Whatever," she grunted as she stood up, her bare feet pressing down on the worm-like grass. "It is what it is." She was relieved when the grass didn't bite her. She looked ahead,

then to her left and right. Nothing but miles and miles of wriggling grass. She sighed and the sound of it carried as if she were in a large room. She exhaled and her breath was a soft yellow. She didn't want to speak; to speak would disturb the peace of this strange place. The back of her neck prickled, and the backs of her bare legs felt warm, as if she stood beside a space heater.

Slowly, she turned around. Then she pressed her hand to her chest and fought to stay on her feet. Now she *did* feel as if she was dying. She had seen masquerades before. She had just faced, climbed, and unmasked one of the most powerful ones. Now she felt this way because she understood that the being she was looking at was just projecting itself as a masquerade, because it was far more than one. She knew who it was but the very idea was impossible. It was impossible. So she let her eyes tell her what she saw. She was seeing one far more magnificent, infinitely more powerful and encompassing than Ekwensu could ever be.

The Unapproachable Supreme Creator of All Things. Chukwu!

And sitting beside it was a figure made of softly glowing yellow. Anyanwu.

The yellow aura wafting from Sunny's skin grew brighter. She was trembling, her throat was dry, and her voice cracked when she spoke. "I greet you, Great *Oga*."

Chukwu was the size of a large elephant. It looked like

a haystack made of layers of blue, yellow, red, and green soft cloth and it had multicolored mist bubbling from the top of its head which was a four-sided ebony mask. And on each side was a curious-looking face. It didn't look cruel or kind, and each face carried the same inquisitive expression as it scrutinized Sunny. Where it stood, dark green vines burst from the ground, stretched several feet, went limp, dried, and crumbled to dust. Yam vines swelled with large tubers that deflated, grew moldy, and finally melted back into the wriggling grass. Plants sprouted, bloomed with white flowers, dropped the flowers, fruited, and died. As Sunny stared up at the creature, her eyes dried and began to burn. She blinked and blinked, tears rolling down her cheeks. Terrified as she was, Sunny also felt fascination. She was drawn to the creature. No. Not creature. So much more.

"Sit," she heard it say. The voice was neither male nor female. Had it even spoken? She took her juju knife from her pocket and placed it on her lap as she sat beside Anyanwu. Before her, it seemed to sink ever so slightly into the wriggling ground, more plants blooming, fruiting, and dying around it. It was "sitting." She caught a whiff of its scent—soil, fruit, decay, and rain. It was a good smell.

Silence. Sunny stared at it and it stared at her. A white plate appeared between them. When the kola nut materialized on it, Sunny almost burst out laughing, and, beside her, Anyanwu actually did laugh. It wasn't enough that Chukwu

had turned its eye toward her, but now it was going to break kola with her? She stifled her urge to giggle.

"Kola has come," Sunny and Anyanwu recited.

Chukwu's face did not change, but Sunny felt that it was pleased. The kola nut sat on its tip and then fell into seven lobes. From within the haystack of cloth came a long, thick arm of raffia and beads. When Chukwu touched the plate, two raffia stalks wrapped around a piece of kola. Several blue and red beads spilled onto the plate. Chukwu placed the piece of kola into the mouth of the face in front of Sunny. *Crunch, crunch, crunch, crunch.* The crunching was so loud that Sunny thought her head would pop. She was so mesmerized by the noise that she nearly forgot her role in the ritual.

Both she and her spirit self reached forward and took a piece of kola. Chukwu took another piece and for several minutes, Sunny, Anyanwu, and the Supreme Being watched one another and crunched away on kola nut. The kola had a nice flavor.

After what felt like an hour, Chukwu's head began to turn and each face took a look at Sunny and Anyanwu. First one face, then the next, then the next, and then the fourth. This one squinted at Sunny and then opened its eyes wide. Anyanwu slowly disappeared, and Sunny felt her settle comfortably within her, more comfortably than she'd felt since they'd been doubled. *Chukwu invited me here. All I could do was push you to fight; you had to fight Ekwensu alone,*

Anyanwu said. And Sunny understood. One did not decline an invitation to meet with the Supreme Being. Not ever.

"When did you learn to write in Nsibidi?" Sunny asked.

"I don't know," Anyanwu said. "But I suspect being close to God can cause . . . revelations."

Chukwu motioned at her with its strange arm. It seemed to be pointing at her head.

"What?" Sunny asked, touching her face. "Here?" When it kept motioning, she touched the comb on her head. She pulled it out, and the face on Chukwu smiled. "This was a gift," Sunny said. "From Mami Wata." She held it out and Chukwu took it. In Chukwu's hands the comb broke, and the iridescent part of it fell to the grass as three large iridescent shells. Then the shells started moving, ghostlike snails with long, bulbous antennae pushing out and dragging the shells.

"Oh," Sunny said, watching the snails munch their way through the grass. Chukwu reached forward. As the arm came toward her face, there were two things she could do, flee or stay still. One didn't run from God. She held very still. When Chukwu's arm was inches from her face, she saw that it was tipped with what looked like a sharp needle. Sunny shut her eyes and gave in to her fate. Chukwu touched her forehead and the world exploded.

When the world came back together again, Sunny was in a coconut grove. She was standing, wearing the raffia dress,

her juju knife in hand. The air here was light and when she inhaled, she felt it fill her chest and then leave through her nose. She was breathing. She was back in Osisi. She touched her face and found that she was wearing her glasses. And she was glad because in *this* sunshine, it was hard to see clearly.

She touched her forehead. There was a slightly sore spot in the center, but otherwise she felt fine. She frowned. When she tried to remember that part of her that was from over a lifetime ago, she couldn't grasp anything—not even the depth of her hatred and fury with Ekwensu. All she could recall was that they'd once fought in the wilderness and she'd used her juju knife.

The coconut grove was a few blocks wide and long. Like all the coconut trees she'd seen in Osisi, these ones were heavy with coconuts. Behind her was a tall skyscraper that looked as if it was made of blue marble. There was no sign on the building, nor did any of the windows have glass. Inside, the building looked empty, except for the occasional shadow that passed by. To her right were more trees. And to her left, past the coconut grove, was a librarylike stone building that she recognized. *Oh thank goodness*, she thought. *The house is just on the other side.* She felt blood rush down from her head and leaned against one of the slim trunks. There was a great crashing sound and a cloud of dust or smoke rose from the other side of the building.

Sunny froze as things grew quiet again. A coconut fell

from one of the trees beside her. Then another from another. Then another. She looked up just in time to see another coconut fall. Her body was so sore and slow that she couldn't react quickly enough. Just before the coconut smashed into her head, a large brown hand appeared and caught it.

Over ten feet tall, the being was humanoid with skin fibrous and rough like the husk of a coconut. Its long head's face was a mere imprint with no definition, as if its face were covered with a layer of coconut skin. It had long arms and long legs, and its shape seemed vaguely male. Gracefully, it handed the coconut to Sunny.

"Thank you," Sunny said, putting her juju knife in the large pocket at the front of her dress and taking the coconut in both hands. She'd been offered kola by Chukwu and now was offered a coconut by a coconut masquerade. What next? The masquerade stepped into a coconut tree's trunk and was gone. She put her coconut down and then did the cleansing flourish with her knife. The green wilderness residue that she left when she stepped to the side was so thick that it was like standing beside a solid green shadow of herself. She stared at it as it turned to her and seemed to stare back. Then it began to dissipate in the gentle breeze. When it was gone, she picked up her coconut and walked past the trees onto the street toward Ekwensu's land.

As she walked, others joined her, heading toward the noise. There were people who looked as if they'd come from

her town, some who were dressed more fashionably like they were from Lagos, some who didn't seem quite human, and some who looked as if they were in the wilderness. Sunny was part of a crowd by the time she arrived at the house . . . or at least where the house used to be. It had crumbled into dust, leaving nothing but a tall lonely palm tree. The dust glowed like embers in a fire and was slowly disappearing back into the wilderness.

"Orlu!" Sunny shouted, pushing past the various people in the crowd. She decided to glide through them, feeling her body cool and separate in that strange way she was still getting used to. She flew through misty blobs and felt them question where she was going. *They're my friends*, she thought to them as she passed.

When she reappeared in front of Orlu, a silver *chittim* dropped and she caught it in her hand absentmindedly as she stared into Orlu's wet eyes. He was covered in the strange dust, and it glowed orange yellow on his skin like jewels. He twitched as his eyes met Sunny's, then his eyes grew wide. "Sunny?" he whispered.

Sunny grinned.

Orlu removed her glasses, placed both hands on her cheeks, and pulled her face to his. His lips were warm and the glowing dust on them made Sunny's lips tingle. Then he pulled her into a tight hug. "You were dead. We were sure you were dead," he said into her ear.

Over his shoulder, Sunny saw Grashcoatah standing to the far side of where the house had been. Sasha and Chichi were using their juju knives to cut long, long hairs that hung from his back and sides. At Grashcoatah's feet was a big pile of bronze *chittim*. He was nudging some of them with an inquisitive foot. Sunny frowned and let go of Orlu.

"I . . . No, I didn't die. But . . ." What was she going to say? That she'd broken kola with Chukwu the Supreme Being? What would that *sound* like? Would Orlu even believe her? She touched her forehead and for a moment, the world brightened and deepened. She took her hand quickly away from the spot. "I pulled off Ekwensu's mask."

Orlu held her away from him, put her glasses back on her face, and really looked at her. He touched her arm, rubbing a finger over the red marks from Ekwensu's stings. He brought up his hand and was about to touch the center of her forehead. She caught his hand. "What happened? Did something hit you there?" he asked.

Sunny shook her head.

"Then what is . . ."

"Sunny!" Chichi screamed, running over. Orlu stepped back, his eyes still on Sunny's forehead. When Chichi got closer, Sunny noticed that there was blood on her shirt and that her arms were covered with raised welts. Then Chichi was hugging her. She smelled of sweat and something sour.

"That Aku masquerade wanted to settle a score," Chichi

said. "It thought that it had a better chance of getting me when Ekwensu attacked you. But it hadn't counted on dealing with Sasha, the world's best bug killer." She laughed and slapped hands with Sasha. Sasha flashed a look at Sunny, his smile faltering the slightest bit. She glanced at Orlu and he looked away.

"Are you all right?" Sunny asked Chichi. "Where . . . The blood, where'd it come from?"

Chichi pressed her lips together in a smile and then shook her head. "I'm fine. Alive."

The various people who'd gathered began rummaging through what was left of Ekwensu's home. Some were actively eating the disappearing sparkling dust, others were scooping it into their pockets, bags, and even shirts. They cautiously kept a distance from Sunny and her friends, though some boys were standing around Grashcoatah. They were helping him gather the *chittim* he didn't seem to want and offering him handfuls of grass. Grashcoatah happily accepted the grass.

Orlu related the story of what had happened as they watched the people of Osisi collect the dust. The Aku masquerade had tried to pull Chichi into the wilderness so that Chichi could die while it watched. The masquerade saw Chichi's conjuring it at the Zuma Festival as an attempt to enslave it, and it hadn't forgotten the insult of such an attempt. It had probably been tracking Chichi from the moment they entered Osisi. Waiting for the right time to strike.

Only Sasha's quick desperate thinking saved Chichi as the masquerade swallowed her and prepared to cross over with her. Sasha had enhanced the common mosquito-repelling juju, wrapped himself with it, and dove into the swarm. Insects burst around him as he swam deep, deep, deep into the swarm of stinging biting ants, termites, bees, and wasps that were the physical body of the masquerade until he found Chichi. Horrified and defeated, the masquerade vomited them out and fled, but not before inflicting a painful wound on Chichi's chest. Chichi only felt it after Sasha had dragged her away.

"Turn around," Chichi said to Orlu and Sasha.

"Why should I?" Sasha said, looking annoyed. "I saved your life. And it's not like it's anything I haven't seen already . . ." He grinned. "More than once."

"Stop it," Chichi said, growing serious. "Just turn around."

Sasha and Orlu both turned away. Chichi stepped closer to Sunny as she looked around to make sure people were still more occupied with collecting the strange dust than watching her. Then she undid a few buttons on her shirt and opened the top. Sunny leaned forward to look. She gasped and stepped back.

"Sasha used some of the ants from the Mmuo Aku to close it up," Chichi said.

"Is that what those stitches are?" Sunny asked, through her hands covering her mouth. Her eyes watered.

"Yeah, they have big and strong biting pincers," she said. "You get them to bite down, then clip the body off with your nail."

"That's nasty," Sunny said, disgusted.

Chichi only shrugged. "Better than dying. I remembered Orlu talking a few years ago about ants used for sutures."

Chichi's swift photographic memory had saved her yet again. As she lay there with the large wound on her chest bleeding and bleeding, she'd remembered what Orlu had told her. Then she told Sasha to find the ants. He'd turned around and found a large group of them at his feet, almost waiting for him. "They *were* waiting," Chichi said. "I made them come and wait as soon as I could see them clearly in my head." Sasha and Chichi's natural gifts were always unclear to Sunny. But every so often, like now, she was in awe of their power.

When Sasha had rescued Chichi, swimming up through an avalanche of exploding insects, the opening to the wilderness just behind him, one of the Aku masquerade's insects had struck. Chichi said that she felt it crawl into her shirt and that it was large. But she was so focused on getting out that she couldn't do anything about it. It was big and it tried to cut out her heart. If Chichi hadn't fallen on her chest just as they emerged and crushed it, she would have been dead. It turned out to be a giant brown sticklike insect with razorsharp front legs. It had cut a gash beside Chichi's heart that was two inches long. It wasn't too deep, so it didn't get to

her sternum; the nasty bug was just getting started.

"And there was more," Orlu said. Ekwensu had planned to deal with Sunny without any interference. Thus, when Orlu and Grashcoatah tried to get into the house, several of Ekwensu's minions had attacked. They were shadowy and brilliantly colored spirits that could somehow affect the physical world, and they started with knocking Orlu off Grashcoatah's back. Then they tried to push Grashcoatah to the ground as well. Orlu had hit the ground hard and lost consciousness for at least thirty seconds. When he came to, there was insanity happening right above him.

"Grashcoatah was like Spider-Man," Orlu said. "He was hovering over me to protect me, and there were spiderwebs shooting from his fur! They'd wrap and wind around the spirits, and the spirits would fall wriggling to the ground and then dissolve, I guess, back into the wilderness." He shook his head. "Sunny, you might have been able to see where they went because you can see both places. Grashcoatah was amazing."

When the fight was over, Grashcoatah had many ropes of webbing hanging from his fur, but there was no time to pull or cut it off. There was a great flash from within Ekwensu's house, and everything went dead silent. "I'll bet people all over Osisi felt it!" Chichi said. Then Ekwensu's house began to crumble. With Sunny seemingly inside it, it crumbled to dust. To nothing. Nothing but a palm tree.

Sunny told her friends everything . . . Everything except the part about meeting Chukwu. That was hers. None of them asked where her Mami Wata comb was, and she was thankful. Let them assume that it had been knocked off when she fell from Ekwensu. Or something like that. It was better this way.

"So are you still . . . doubled?" Chichi asked.

Sunny nodded. "But I'm . . . we're okay with it."

The three of them looked at her skeptically.

As they flew out of Osisi minutes later, glad to leave the place behind, Sunny used her knife to crack open the coconut the masquerade had handed to her. She gave it to Chichi. "Drink," Sunny said. Chichi happily obliged and said it was delicious. Moments later, the wound on her chest grew warm and itchy. When it began to flake off along with the ant stiches, revealing new skin underneath, Chichi wept. "It hurt a lot more than I said it did," she whispered, wiping her tears. "I wasn't sure if I could take the pain much longer." Sunny broke the coconut fully open, and they shared the sweet, buttery meat. Even Grashcoatah ate a piece, though he preferred to eat the crunchy shell.

31

AND SO IT WAS DECIDED

As soon as Lagos came into sight, Sunny checked her phone. It was evening and in the darkness the screen of her phone glowed like a star. It had one bar of energy left. When she saw the date and the time, she laughed. She leaned back, her hand pressed to her chest. She shut her eyes. Only a few hours had passed since they'd flown away from her irrationally terrified brother.

Her relief only lasted a few seconds. She sat up. "If no one else is going to ask, I will," she said. "What are we going to do?"

"Let them whoop our asses and throw us in one of the other library basements where you haven't killed whatever is lurking in there," Sasha said.

Sunny gasped, whispering, "Oh God, we're all going to die."

Sasha shrugged. "What else can we do? Go on the run? I ain't. I've got an education to obtain. I'd rather just face the music . . . whatever it is."

"But what about Grashcoatah?" Sunny said. "Maybe he should have stayed in Osisi. There are more of his kind there, anyway."

"I thought about that," Orlu said. "But he'd never really be safe. They'll still eventually find him." He patted Grash-coatah's back, and Grashcoatah grunted. "We've already talked it over."

"You and Grashcoatah?" Chichi asked.

"Yes," Orlu said. "I wanted him to stay in Osisi, but he convinced me that it was better if he took the chance and tried to clear his name. He doesn't believe he did anything wrong; it was an accident. Really, there are moments of breach between the Lamb and Leopard worlds all the time. Someone sees, hears, or walks into something. And usually Lambs don't believe or understand what they see. No one gets punished for those because they're *accidents*. Well, this was an accident, too."

"True," Sasha said.

"It's still risky, though," Chichi said. "The council's rigid as hell."

"We have to state our case well," Orlu said. "Really well. Grashcoatah could lose his life."

"So could we, if they put us with something like that djinn," Sunny said. But she understood the difference. For Grashcoatah, death could be guaranteed.

"Sunny just defeated Ekwensu," Orlu said. "She sent her back into the wilderness, and now she can't cause the *apocalypse*. I think the council will take well to the idea that Grashcoatah helped make that happen. We need to explain things. Sunny's brother *had* to be with us, or Sunny wouldn't have been allowed to come to Lagos to meet Udide who wove Grashcoatah who took us to Osisi. You see?"

They all did. And so it was decided.

Invisible, Grashcoatah softly landed in the compound. They all climbed off, making sure to hang on to his fur. Adebayo's Hummer and Chukwu's Jeep were parked and the house was quiet except for the sound of the TV in a room on the second floor. It was close to midnight.

"Okay," Orlu whispered. "One, two, three!"

They all let go of Grashcoatah's fur at the same time. The warm breeze met Sunny's face. They were visible now. She could hear Grashcoatah quietly move to the side of the house. "Goodnight," she whispered. Part of one of the bushes disappeared and she could hear Grashcoatah chewing.

They rang the doorbell, Sunny standing in the front. She took a deep breath, holding on to the doorway to steady her-

self. Was her brother even *here?* Maybe they had taken him. Maybe he'd run off into the street and been killed by oncoming traffic. The door opened. He took one look at her. His eyes grew wide and his nostrils flared. Then he grabbed her into a hug. "Thank God," he said.

When he let her go, he looked at the others and they looked at him. He clearly wanted to say something. Then his mouth pressed shut. "Have . . . have you had dinner yet?" he finally asked.

They all said no.

"You and Chichi can go make it, then," he said with a laugh. "Adebayo and I haven't eaten, either."

They all went inside. Before following them in, Chukwu looked outside at the parked cars and the rest of the compound. Sunny stayed back and caught his shoulder. "Are you all right?" she asked.

He opened his mouth to say something. Then instead paused for a very long time, an uncomfortable look on his face, again. "I . . . I am now, Sunny," he said. "You should call Mummy and Daddy."

She nodded, bringing out her cell phone. She watched Chukwu join the others in the kitchen. From his behavior, it was clear. The council had performed a trust knot on him, yet they hadn't altered his memory. How much did he know? And why was he *allowed* to know? She called her parents.

32

REALIGNED

The drive back to Aba was different from the drive to Lagos. Chukwu gritted his teeth as he looked ahead at the road and mashed down on the accelerator. They were speeding down the expressway at eighty miles per hour.

"You might want to slow down," Sunny said. She was sitting in the passenger seat this time, and her seat belt felt like a flimsy piece of toilet paper over her chest. Chukwu's favorite album of all time was playing yet again, but in this moment, it was *not* helping matters at all. Track four of *Who Is Jill Scott?*, "Gettin' in the Way," belted out of the speakers. It added another layer of attitude to the foul one that Chukwu was cultivating.

"I know how to drive," he muttered, looking straight ahead.

Behind him, Chichi sat snuggled close to Sasha, his arm over her shoulder. They were looking at one of Sasha's books, whispering to each other, oblivious to Chukwu's growing rage. They'd been this way since Sasha had saved Chichi from the Aku masquerade. Chichi hinted to Sunny that there was something amazing Sasha had done while in the maelstrom of biting insects that had cleared her mind and reminded her of why Sasha was her "truest love." Of course Chichi didn't bother to explain even the most mundane aspects of this to Chukwu. That wasn't Chichi's style.

Sunny looked back at her, giving her a dirty look. "Stop it!" she mouthed when Chichi glanced up at her.

"What?" Chichi asked.

Sasha smirked, pulling Chichi closer as he looked Chukwu in the eye through the rearview mirror.

Sunny turned back to the front as Chukwu pushed the car to drive faster.

"You're not going to be able to get away from them by doing that," Sunny muttered.

"Yeah, but we'll get home faster," he said.

Behind Sunny, Orlu was fast asleep. He hadn't told her all that he'd been through with Grashcoatah, but it must have been something. He and the grasscutter had spent most of last night in quiet conversation, Orlu taking a mat and sitting

beside the invisible creature, quietly speaking to him, and Grashcoatah grunting and sharing mental images with Orlu. Sunny had left them alone and gone to bed. Come morning, when she looked out the window, she saw Orlu lying on the mat, assumedly beside the still-invisible grasscutter.

To cover for his behavior, Chichi rather convincingly explained to Chukwu and Adebayo that Orlu was from some remote Christian sect where they liked to pray for hours outside and then sleep where they prayed. Nigeria was full of so many different types of Christians that neither Sunny's brother nor Adebayo thought anything of it. Sunny wondered what Orlu and Grashcoatah had spoken about as she watched Orlu sleep so deeply that he didn't notice the shenanigans among Sasha and Chichi and Chukwu.

Grashcoatah flew above the Jeep, invisible to the world. Sunny would have rather been up in the sky with Grashcoatah, even if it was drizzling. Anyanwu was up there, sitting on Grashcoatah's back, feeling free as a bird.

33

GRASSCUTTER STEW

An hour later, about halfway through the drive back, they stopped at a raggedy-looking shack on the side of the road. It looked as if the next rainy season would wash it away. The walls were made of worn-out wood, the roof made of tin. Behind and beside it were tangles of trees, bushes, and plants. There were no buildings to its left or right. The shack had no sign. Yet there were cars parked all along the roadside.

"What are we doing here?" Chichi snapped.

"Lunch," Chukwu said, putting the car in park.

"They serve food in *there*?" Chichi asked. "And you want to go in and eat it? *Kai!* Do you want to die of dysentery?"

Sasha snickered.

"Why not just wait until we see a better place?" Sunny asked.

"Don't let the look of the place fool you," Chukwu said. "I'm not just stopping here randomly. Adebayo told me about this place. He said it serves some of the best grasscutter stew he's ever tasted. He said the meat is so sweet you'd think they fed the thing chocolate for a year before they slaughtered it."

"Let's do it!" Sasha said, getting out of the Jeep. "My father had grasscutter meat the first time he came to Nigeria and hasn't stopped talking about it since. I want to try it."

Chichi got out, too. "I know good grasscutter stew. Let's see if Adebayo knows what he is talking about."

Orlu was still in the car, frowning. Sunny got out and opened his door. He didn't have to say anything; she knew what he was thinking and why he was frowning. She took his hand. "Come on. They are not going to be serving the meat of *flying* grasscutters. Just the regular kind. And you can eat something else. If it makes you feel better, I will, too. I've never liked eating grasscutter, even before we made friends with a giant flying one."

Orlu sighed and got out of the Jeep. They both heard a soft grunt directly above them. An image of lush bush bloomed in Sunny's mind. Grashcoatah was going into the bush behind the building to see what he could find to eat.

"Okay," Orlu said.

"How will he know when we leave?" Sunny quietly asked

Orlu, as they followed Chukwu, Sasha, and Chichi.

Orlu smiled mysteriously. "I'll tell him."

The grasscutter stew was indeed the best on Earth, at least according to Chichi. Sasha ate three bowls, Chukwu four. By the time they were all done, he and Chukwu were in such high spirits that they were talking and laughing at each other's jokes.

"It's like they are drunk on stew," Sunny told Chichi, as they walked out the front door. The owner of the restaurant had told them the restrooms were in the back. Sunny wasn't too confident about what she thought they'd find. If worse came to worst, she was content with going in the bushes.

"Well, it *was* good stew," Chichi said, picking at her teeth with a pinky finger.

"They make good *ogbono* soup, too," Sunny said. "With chicken."

"They just need to do some remodeling," Chichi said. "At *least* a sign for the place. Word of mouth can only go so far."

The sun was setting, but the heat of the day seemed intent on staying. The pepper soup Sunny had eaten was extra spicy. Not tainted-pepper spicy that left her tongue and mouth tingly while enhancing the flavor of everything else she ate, just a normal type of spicy that warmed every part of her and cleared out her sinuses. This warmth mixed with the heat of outside made her feel a little dizzy.

As soon as they walked to the side of the shack, the chat-

ter from the filled dining room receded. The grass here was tall and unkempt, a narrow path through it roughly hacked. When they got to the back, the grass was shorter. Sunny expected to see Grashcoatah at work here making the grass even shorter, but he was nowhere in sight.

On the back of the shack was a large door with garbage bags on both sides of it. The door was ajar, and Sunny heard the clink and splash of cutlery, cups, and dishes being washed. There was a small clearing of dirt directly behind the shack where a large thick wooden table sat. Behind the table were three red outhouses with tin roofs. And behind the outhouses, more trees and bushes grew.

"Disgusting," Chichi said, stepping up to the large table. It was slick with congealing and dried blood, bits of meat (there was even a chopped-off paw), and milling flies. "I hope this isn't where they cut the meat they use in the restaurant."

"It probably is," Sunny said, the food in her belly rolling.

Chichi picked up the grasscutter paw and held it up.

"Ugh!" Sunny said "How can you touch th—"

Click. Click, clack, click.

Chichi looked past Sunny and her eyes grew wide. "Oh my God."

Sunny stared at the source of the clicking. Then she quickly slapped the grasscutter paw out of Chichi's hand. But really it was a useless gesture. If the oily-looking black vultures with wingspans wider than her height standing on

top of the outhouses had wanted the paw, they'd have taken it long ago. There were five in all. The click-clacking sound was their talons on the tin roofs of the outhouses as they moved around.

"They're probably here for the meat when they are chopping it up," Sunny said. "Disgusting, lazy birds. I'll bet they live here, scavenging off of whatever the restaurant people throw away." She shook her head and started to step away. "I'm going to go pee in the bushes. I'm not going near those vultures, let alone those nasty outhouses. I can smell them from . . ."

"Sunny," Chichi said. And that's when Sunny noticed that Chichi wasn't even looking at the vultures. She was looking toward the trees. As Sunny turned her eyes in that direction, she felt every hair on her body stand up. There was a ringing in her ears and pressure on her face. Sunny's nostrils flared. She smelled smoke. A very specific type of smoke.

"Shhh," Chichi said, still staring toward the trees. "Don't speak."

Sunny had to resist the urge to scream. If she screamed, someone from the kitchen might hear and come to investigate. Then he or she would see the glorious giant bristly spider with legs powerful enough to part trees standing in the shadows. Would seeing Udide be a breach of the Leopard rules? Udide was more than a magical beast. Udide was one of Chukwu's deputies . . . a deity.

Udide blasted a thick puff of breath at them. Burned houses, that was the specific smoky smell. Sunny and Chichi clutched each other, the soon-to-set sun beating against their backs.

"Didn't I tell you that I can find you anywhere?" Udide asked, her voice vibrating in Sunny's head like a passing train. By the look on Chichi's face, the same was happening to her, too. "The venom of my people is bound to your very DNA."

"I know what you want," Chichi said, straining. A line of red tumbled from her nose to her lip. Sunny touched her nose and found that hers was bleeding, as well. "Please!"

"You have heard rumor," Udide said. "You have heard myth. You have heard gossip. You know what I ask."

Sunny shook her head. "We don't . . ."

"We can't go in there," Chichi said. She paused. Sunny was shocked to see that Chichi looked absolutely horrid, tears streaming down her face. "The last time my mother was there, they nearly killed her!" She took a deep breath. "Because of *me*. They . . . they nearly killed her."

"It is a story," the spider said. "*My* story. Written as a ghazal on a tablet-shaped Möbius band made of the same material as your juju knife, albino girl of Nimm, so you will recognize it. It will call to you. It cannot be broken. It is mine. One of my greatest masterpieces. It belongs to me. Go there, get it, and bring it back to me. My venom is in your blood. The doubled albino girl is a Nimm warrior; this story has made that clear. She will be your woman show."

Sunny frowned, rolling the idea in her mind. Woman show? Her brother had worked as a "man show" during wrestling matches when he wasn't wrestling. A bodyguard. She would be Chichi's bodyguard.

"You are a Nimm warrior, Sunny. Like your grandmother," Udide said, retreating into the trees. Her voice was fading now. "My venom is adhered to your DNA." Then she was gone. Chichi stood there, silent, tears flowing from her eyes.

"Let's go," Sunny said, putting an arm around Chichi. Never had she felt so much taller than her best friend. So much bigger. Physically so much stronger. Chichi looked up at her with trembling eyes and pressed lips.

"What is it?" Sunny asked. "Why are you looking like that?"

Chichi only shook her head and tiredly looked away.

"Let's just get home," Sunny said. "We'll deal with all this later."

34

JUDGMENT DAY

The council came three hours before daybreak.

Chukwu was able to drop off Chichi at her hut. Then he dropped Orlu and Sasha at Orlu's house, Grashcoatah following Orlu and landing in his compound safely hidden behind the house's surrounding wall. At home, Sunny had time to greet her parents, peek into Ugonna's room where he just grunted a hello and went back to sleep, take a shower, and unpack her things. It was just as she lay down to get a few hours of sleep that she felt her toes tingle. Then she felt the tingle travel up her body all the way to the top of her head. And it was in the center of her head that she felt the tug.

"Oh no," she whispered as she was pulled through her

bedsheets and window. Then there she was, standing barefoot in her nightgown in front of the council car.

"Get in," the driver said in American-accented Igbo. She was a small woman with long straight black hair, lots of makeup, and large earrings that clinked when she turned her head. Sunny got in.

On the front lawn of the library, Grashcoatah was chained, shackled, and muzzled. He lay there, looking forlornly at Sunny as she passed. He would flicker into invisibility and then reappear, groaning in despair and biting at his chains.

"Hang in there," Sunny said as she was ushered inside. "We'll get you free!" She hoped. She hoped.

"Move," Sunny's escort said, shoving her along. "Worry about yourself."

Sunny would never forget the black classroom in the Obi Library. Even the leather seats and table were black. Sitting in the plush chairs were Library Council members or officials or executioners, Sunny didn't know or care. They all looked like they could be her angry mean aunt or unforgiving uncle. The only one Sunny recognized was Sugar Cream. Sunny went and stood with the others before the table of adults, feeling irrational with fatigue and anger. She fought back tears of rage.

"Pull yourself together," Orlu whispered to her. "Grashcoatah's life depends on it."

Anyanwu, she said in her mind.

I'm here, Anyanwu responded.

She felt her muscles flex as she stood up straight and faced the stern, mostly unfamiliar council members. Some were her mother's age; most of them were much older. But Sunny didn't care. She was in a sort of zone.

"Again, here you are, Sunny Nwazue," an old woman said to her in Igbo. She wore her hair in thin white-gray braids and she looked more ancient than Sugar Cream. "Your third offense. You'd think nearly dying at the hands of a djinn would teach you to follow the rules. Yet here you are, and you've dragged your *Oha* coven and a grasscutter into the trouble with you."

Orlu stepped forward. Sunny put her hand on his shoulder. "I've got this," she told him. She was shaking, but it wasn't from fear; she felt she would burst if she didn't say what she desperately wanted to say. She told them everything, from the beginning to the current moment. She spoke about her brother being in the secret society, how she ended up thrown into the Obi Library basement, the djinn, the dreams, being doubled, meeting with Bola, Lagos, Udide, almost facing Death, and then Osisi and their great battle with Ekwensu, the Aku masquerade, and Ekwensu's minions. But again, she kept her encounter with Chukwu to herself.

When she finished talking, the council officials just stared at the four of them. For several minutes, it was like this. They did not discuss among themselves. They did not write things

down. They did not ask questions. They didn't even move. They just stared.

"To be doubled is very sad," Sugar Cream finally said. "Death is always close by, but for you, he will always stand behind you."

Recalling the image of Death in her peripheral vision, Sunny felt the shiver run up her spine and an uncontrollable urge to burst into tears. Almost. She remained stoic, mostly due to Anyanwu holding her steady.

"Your brother," a tiny dark-skinned man about her mother's age said. "We didn't alter his memory. We gave him the choice of forgetting or entering a trust knot. We told him that to enter the trust knot was the hazardous choice. He was still under the *Ujo*, screaming with terror every few moments. And even then, he chose not to forget. Instead he chose to remember and suffer because he can never share the memory. We don't normally allow this with Lambs, because with the wrong people this can cause madness. But for your brother, due to the circumstances and his passion to protect you, we allowed it. What will you do with him now?"

"Protect him," Sunny said, before she'd fully thought her answer through.

Again the silence.

Not long after that, the four of them were told that they could go. Outside, Grashcoatah was released. And quickly, calmly, steadily, they all walked away from the Obi Library. It didn't matter that it was nearly morning and they weren't

sure how they'd get home. Best to leave before the shock the council members were in wore off. Best to not run in order to maintain the look of innocence. Once they reached the Leopard Knocks shops, they climbed on Grashcoatah and off they flew.

35
HOME, AGAIN

Sunny arrived back at home around eleven A.M.

It was Saturday and her parents weren't home. Ugonna was at his girlfriend's house. But Chukwu was there sitting on the doorstep as if he'd known she was coming. He had his cell phone in his hands and it buzzed as Sunny walked up to him.

"You all right?" he asked, glancing at the text message he'd just received. He put the phone in his pocket and looked up at Sunny. He was wearing sweatpants, Adidas slippers, and a T-shirt. All clothes their aunt had sent from America, clothes that Chukwu only wore when he was trying to passive-aggressively impress.

"Yeah," she said.

There was a long pause. Neither of them could speak their thoughts to the other and the cause for this was juju, not reluctance.

"Why are you home?" Sunny asked.

"Came to see Akunna. She's coming over," he said. "Of all the girls, she's the coolest. Otherwise, I'd just ask her to come to the university to see *me*."

Sunny smiled, sitting beside him. "Such a gentleman."

They sat like that for a while. Shoulder to shoulder. Full of questions. But relieved. Relieved to be alive and well and home. When Akunna arrived, Sunny waved at her and got up and went inside.

In her room, Sunny threw her purse on the floor, shut and locked the door, and lay on her bed. She savored the quiet. The stillness. Her brothers were visiting with girlfriends. Her parents were at work or food shopping. They were okay. Everything was okay. But she couldn't quite smile. She looked at her barely used computer, her dresser and cabinets, her pile of books, the early edition of the Leopard Knocks newspaper on her bed, and the window. Then she hugged herself. She looked around her room again. The effect remained. Her room didn't feel the same. This place felt cramped, useless. It felt like it belonged to someone else.

She frowned, trying to hold the tears in. She'd gone out to find herself and in the process lost her home . . . and in a way, herself. How had that happened? At the same time, she

and Chukwu were closer than ever, she and Ugonna, too. And though her parents felt more distant, a sort of understanding had developed between her and them. They had not stayed home and waited for her to return. But maybe they'd gone out because they couldn't stand the waiting. So much had changed in the last two years.

Something buzzed beside her ear. "Oh," she said, sitting up. "Della!!" In all the adventure and trouble, she'd forgotten about her wasp artist! Her entire body tensed up. Wasp artists were known to be overly emotional, especially when neglected. Their response to neglect was stinging their owner/audience with a paralysis-inducing compound. The paralyzed victim was then forced to watch the wasp artist dramatically commit suicide. Sunny had been gone for over a week and when she'd returned last night, she hadn't had time to check on Della. She frantically looked around the room.

There was a loud buzzing coming from her closet. She crept up to it and paused before sliding it open. If Della was in there, maybe it was better to keep it trapped. But it clearly could get out, since it had just been right beside her ear. She threw open the closet door. For a moment, Sunny wasn't sure what she was looking at. Then she wondered if she was seeing correctly. Could wasp artists create things like this? Della had indeed been improving in its artistic skill but . . . "Is this . . ." She knelt down and picked it up. "For me?" she whispered. "Is it mine?"

Della buzzed loudly, now hovering above her head, watching Sunny's reaction closely.

"I was gone for so long," she said, holding the hair comb. "You knew I was coming back?"

It buzzed again. How did it know that she no longer had the hair comb Mami Wata had given her? *Only Chukwu knows,* she thought, as she pressed the comb into the side of one of her cornrows. She went to admire herself in the mirror. The comb looked like it was made of tiny shiny multicolored glass beads, even the teeth. Yet it had a way of sparkling yellow orange when she turned her head just so. She took it out and held it to her eyes. When she looked closely, she saw only shiny sparkling pin-sized dots of light. "What is this made of?" she asked.

Della flew circles around her head until she let her question go and laughed. "Yes," she said. "I love it. I love it so much. It's the most beautiful thing I've ever seen!"

More loop-the-loops, and then Della zoomed into its mud hive on her ceiling and was quiet. "Wow," Sunny said, admiring the piece of wasp art. She lay back on her bed, smiling as she tucked it into her hair. There was a flash of red on her dresser. A ghost hopper was walking down the side. As it walked, it slowly disappeared.

Now her room felt more like her room.

36
THE ZUMA ROCK FESTIVAL

The Zuma Rock Festival came a month later. All of them went, except Orlu. He and Grashcoatah had gone instead with Taiwo and Nancy the Miri Bird to witness the mass spawning of some sort of butterfly in the Cross River Forest. Sunny missed him, but Orlu's excitement about going delighted her more than his absence depressed her.

Despite all that she'd been through, she was still able to experience the festival with fresh eyes. The three of them went to the art fair, and Sunny bought a new wrapper and matching top. Chichi bought a bookmark made of shed Eji Onu masquerade raffia. When placed between the pages of a book while reading the book, it made the images one

imagined that much more alive. Sasha didn't buy anything because he was saving all his money for the book fair near the end of the festival.

A jewelry maker was awed by the hair comb Della had made for Sunny. He offered to pay her an insane amount of *chittim* AND naira for it. He said that it was made of zyzzyx glass, a serum that wasp artists secrete when they reach their first artistic peak. Few wasp artists willingly gave away their zyzzyx glass artwork; it was too beautiful to merely be worn as a "bauble by some young girl." Insulted and intrigued, needless to say, Sunny refused to sell her zyzzyx glass hair comb.

They moved on to the book fair. It was enormous. They hadn't been to this last year, and Sunny was kind of glad. The festival had been so overwhelming back then that she'd nearly gone catatonic. If she'd been to the book fair, she would have screamed to go home and never had her amazing experience of playing soccer in the Zuma Cup.

The book fair consisted of row after row of books packed on the field that would later be used for the Zuma Cup soccer match. Here, people argued and sometimes fought over books, and some of the books argued with and fought people. Sasha got into a disturbing altercation with a dark-skinned man wearing a Tuareg-style indigo face veil. All Sasha had done to spark it was reach for a thick, brand-new-looking book with *The Great Book* burned into the spine in Arabic. To Sunny's

shock, the man had slapped Sasha's hands and then slapped him hard across the face as he shouted something in Arabic.

Sasha had shouted right back at the man in Arabic. The man simply ignored him, turning his attention to the book as he grabbed and opened it. Sasha was too angry to notice and Chichi was too busy trying to pull him away. However, Sunny saw the inside of this book. It wasn't really a book at all. Its inside looked more like the touch screen of a tablet.

Then she was helping Chichi shove Sasha away from the man. After looking at other books, Sasha settled on a book that was the size of his hand. It was sticky with old honey and had print so small that even a child with 20/20 vision would need a magnifying glass to read it. It also had several pages torn out of it. "But it's a book of practical joke jujus written by an Abatwa!" Sasha said. He purchased it for a whole bronze *chittim*, managing to haggle a discount due to the missing pages. He refused to talk about *The Great Book*.

They skipped the wrestling match and from what they heard it was again a bloody match, though neither of the champions was killed like last year. Nevertheless, Sunny found herself watching the sky and the constant milling festival crowd around her, looking for the fallen champion turned guardian angel Miknikstic. She even snuck to the spot where she'd first met him last year in front of the soccer field. Sasha and Chichi were at the table where they'd all just eaten lunch. They were debating the recent election of the gover-

nor of some state, and their discussion was so heated that
they hadn't even noticed her slip away.

Now she stood in the very spot looking at the field. It was
here where Sunny had felt so out of place, so overwhelmed . . .
by everything. Not this time. The festival now felt almost un-
derwhelming, even with the intriguing and fascinating parts
like the book and art fairs, even the wrestling match.

She turned around and looked at the Leopard People going about their business. They laughed, talked, explored, did
their juju. They were so comfortable. Like her parents and all
the Lambs she knew. When did she wind up on the outside
again? She'd met Miknikstic here, as well, a man who less
than an hour later would transform into so much more. She
crossed her arms over her chest, squeezing the muscles of her
strong ropy biceps with her hands. With her right foot she
sketched a series of loops and swirls into the dirt—the Nsibidi symbol for "I am here." She paused for a moment, looking
for any sign of movement in the symbols. As if she were good
enough at it yet. She chuckled and returned to her friends.

An hour later, she stood center on the field holding the soccer
ball. The field had been cleared of the stacks and cases and
shelves of books. Now there was nothing but uneven grass
and the white lines of the field, bold and perfect. She felt good
in her white uniform, and this time she wore brand-new soccer cleats that she'd bought with some of her *chittim* in Leop-

ard Knocks, months ago. Sasha was behind her to her left.

She looked at Godwin, the green team's leader. He was playing goalie. He gave a nod of confidence.

"I'm going to wipe the field with you, ghost girl," Ibou said. Sunny grinned at him, setting the ball down. "No," she said. "You're not." Ibou had grown about three inches and his shoulders were even broader. But Sunny had grown taller and become more muscular, too. The ref blew his whistle, and Sunny took the ball with her dancing feet. She felt Anyanwu reveling in the art of motion and grace. She kicked the ball to Ibou's left as he came at her. She did a turn, moved behind him, and caught the ball with her feet. She laughed, spotting her teammate Agaja to her right. He was open. As she passed the ball to him, she could already see Agaja blasting it into the goal.

Goooooooooal!

ACKNOWLEDGMENTS

First and foremost, a gracious thanks to the Universe for bringing this novel together on its own time.

I'd like to thank my former Penguin editor Sharyn November for helping me strengthen the continuation of Sunny's story. Thanks to my current editor Regina Hayes for jumping in and making this novel really shine. Thanks to my Nigerian editor Bibi Bakare-Yusuf for helping me smooth away so many of the Americanisms I couldn't help putting in the novel. Thanks to producer Mark Ceryak and filmmaker Barry Jenkins for those days years ago working on that film treatment that ended up helping me generate some of the ideas in this novel. Thanks so so much to Success T for letting me weave the nonfiction of his own experiences with confraternities into this novel; that chapter was practically word for word. Thanks to illustrator Greg Ruth for the two stunning renderings of Sunny Nwazue that are the covers of *Akata Witch* and *Akata Warrior*. Thanks to Jim Hoover, who designed this book's beautiful jacket, for his meticulous eye for detail and zing. And thank you to my mother, my father, my daughter Anyaugo, Ifeoma, Ngozi, Emezie, Dika, Obioma, Chinedu, and the rest of my family in Nigeria and scattered about the Diaspora, because family na family, o.

The masquerades dance and the ancestors smile,
And these in themselves make it all worthwhile.

TURN THE PAGE FOR A PREVIEW OF SUNNY'S EXCITING BEGINNING!

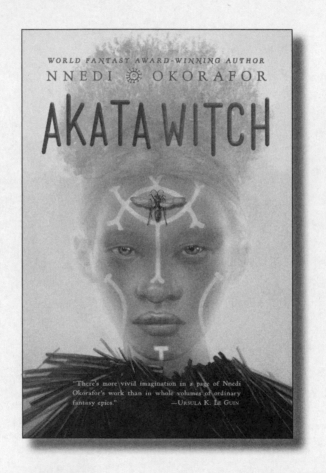

"Jam-packed with mythological wonders."

—Rick Riordan, #1 *New York Times* bestselling author of the Percy Jackson and the Olympians series

PROLOGUE
The Candle

I've always been fascinated by candles. Looking into the flame calms me down. Here in Nigeria, PHC is always taking the lights, so I keep candles in my room just in case.

PHC stands for "Power Holding Company of Nigeria," but people like to say it really stands for "Please Hold Candles in Nigeria." Back in Chicago we had National Grid, and the electricity was always working. Not here, though. Not yet. Maybe in the future.

One night, after the power went out, I lit a candle as usual. Then, also as usual, I got down on the floor and just gazed at its flame.

My candle was white and thick, like the ones in church.

I lay on my belly and just stared and stared into it. So orange, like the abdomen of a firefly. It was nice and soothing until . . . it started flickering.

Then, I thought I saw something. Something serious and big and scary. I moved closer.

The candle just flickered like any other flame. I moved even closer, until the flame was an inch from my eyes. I could see something. I moved closer still. I was almost there. I was just starting to understand what I saw when the flame kissed something above my head. Then the smell hit me and the room was suddenly bright yellow orange! My hair was on fire!

I screamed and smacked my head as hard as I could. My burning hair singed my hand. Next thing I knew, my mother was there. She tore off her *rapa* and threw it over my head.

The electricity suddenly came back on. My brothers ran in, then my father. The room smelled awful. My hair was half gone and my hands were tender.

That night, my mother cut my hair. Seventy percent of my lovely long hair, gone. But it was what I saw in that candle that stayed with me most. I'd seen the end of the world in its flame. Raging fires, boiling oceans, toppled sky-scrapers, ruptured land, dead and dying people. It was horrible. And it was coming.

❧ ❧ ❧ ❧

My name is Sunny Nwazue and I confuse people.

I have two older brothers. Like my parents, my brothers were both born here in Nigeria. Then my family moved to America, where I was born in the city of New York. When I was nine, we returned to Nigeria, near the town of Aba. My parents felt it would be a better place to raise my brothers and me, at least that's what my mom says. We're Igbo—that's an ethnic group from Nigeria—so I'm American and Igbo, I guess.

You see why I confuse people? I'm Nigerian by blood, American by birth, and Nigerian again because I live here. I have West African features, like my mother, but while the rest of my family is dark brown, I've got light yellow hair, skin the color of "sour milk" (or so stupid people like to tell me), and hazel eyes that look like God ran out of the right color. I'm albino.

Being albino made the sun my enemy; my skin burned so easily that I felt nearly flammable. That's why, though I was really good at soccer, I couldn't join the boys when they played after school. Although they wouldn't have let me anyway, me being a girl. Very narrow-minded. I had to play at night, with my brothers, when they felt like it.

Of course, this was all before that afternoon with Chichi and Orlu, when everything changed.

I look back now and see that there were signs of what was to come.

When I was two, during a brief visit to Nigeria with my
family, I contracted malaria. It was a bad case and I almost
died from it when I got back to the States. I remember. My
brothers used to tell me that I was a freak because I could
remember so far back.

I was really hot, absolutely burning up with fever. My
mother stood over my bed, crying. I don't remember my
father being there much. My brothers would come in once in
a while and pat my forehead or kiss my cheeks.

I was like that for days. Then a light came to me, like a
tiny yellow flame or sun. It was laughing and warm—but a
nice kind of warm, like bathwater that has been sitting for
a few minutes. Maybe this is why I like candles so much. It
floated just above me for a long time. I think it was watching over me. Sometimes mosquitoes would fly into it and get
vaporized.

It must have decided that I wasn't going to die, because
eventually it went away and I got better. So it's not as if
strange things haven't happened to me before.

I knew I looked like a ghost. All pale-skinned. And I was
good at being ghost-quiet. When I was younger, if my father
was in the main room drinking his beer and reading his paper,
I'd sneak in. I could move like a mosquito when I wanted.
Not the American ones that buzz in your ear—the Nigerian
ones that are silent like the dead.

I'd creep up on my father, stand right beside him, and wait. It was amazing how he wouldn't see me. I'd just stand there grinning and waiting. Then he'd glance to the side and see me and nearly jump to the ceiling.

"Stupid, stupid girl!" he'd hiss, because I'd really scared him—and because he wanted to hurt me because he knew that I knew he was scared. Sometimes I hated my father. Sometimes I felt he hated me, too. I couldn't help that I wasn't the son he wanted or the pretty daughter he'd have accepted instead. But I couldn't not see what I saw in that candle. And I couldn't help what I eventually became.

What Is a Leopard Person?

A Leopard Person goes by many names around
the world. The term "Leopard Person" is a West
African coinage, derived from the Efik term
"ekpe," "leopard." All people of mystical true
ability are Leopard People. And as humankind
has evolved, so have Leopard folk around the
world organized. Two thousand years ago
there was a great massacre of Leopard People
worldwide. It was first sparked in the Middle
East after the murder of Jesus Christ (this is
dealt with in Chapter Seven: A Brief Ancient
Historical Account). The killing rippled out all
over the world. Nowhere was safe. The massacre
is known as the Great Attempt. However, we
are invincible, I tell you, and so we have since
revived. Obviously, juju was used to cover up
the fact of the Great Attempt, very strong juju.
By whom? There are many speculations, but
nothing solid (again, see Chapter Seven).

from *Fast Facts for Free Agents*
by Isong Abong Effiong Isong

1

Orlu

The moment Sunny walked into the school yard, people started pointing. Girls started snickering, too, including the girls
she usually hung with, her so-called friends. *Idiots*, Sunny
thought. Nevertheless, could she really blame any of them?
Her woolly blonde hair, whose length so many had envied,
was gone. Now she had a puffy medium-length Afro. She cut
her eyes at her friends and sucked her teeth loudly. She felt
like punching them each in the mouth.

"What happened?" Chelu asked. She didn't even have the
courtesy to keep the stupid grin off her face.

"I needed a change," Sunny said, and walked away. Behind her, she still heard them laughing.

"Now she's *really* ugly," she heard Chelu say.

"She should wear some bigger earrings or *something*," Buchi added. Sunny's ex-friends laughed even harder. *If you only knew that your days were numbered*, she thought. She shivered, pushing away the images of what she'd seen in the candle.

Her day grew even worse when her literature and writing teacher handed back the latest class assignment. The instructions were to write an essay about a relative. Sunny had written about her arrogant oldest brother, Chukwu, who believed he was God's gift to women, though he wasn't. Of course, it didn't help that his name meant "Supreme Being."

"Sunny's essay received the highest mark," Miss Tate announced, ignoring the class's sneers and scoffs. "Not only was it nicely written, but it was engaging and humorous."

Sunny bit the inside of her cheek and gave a feeble smile. She hadn't meant the essay to be funny at all. She'd been *serious*. Her brother was truly an arrogant *nyash*. To make things worse, her classmates had all scored terribly. Out of ten points, most received threes and fours.

"It's a waste of time trying to teach you all proper English," Miss Tate shouted. She snatched a boy's essay and read it aloud: "'My sista always beg though she make good money. She likes to have but not give. She no go change.'" Miss Tate slammed the essay back onto the boy's desk. "Do you come

here just to stare into space? *Eh?* And you were all so timid in what you wrote. Who wants to hear 'My mother is very nice' or 'My auntie is poor'? And in rotten English, at that! This is why I had you write about a *relative*. It was supposed to be *easy!*"

As she spoke, she stomped and clomped about the classroom, her face growing redder and redder. She stepped in front of Sunny's desk. "Stand, please."

Sunny looked around at her classmates. Everyone just stared back at her, with slack faces and angry eyes. Slowly, she stood up and straightened her navy blue uniform skirt.

Miss Tate left her standing as she went to her desk in front of the class. She opened a drawer and brought out her yellow wooden switch. Sunny's mouth dropped open. *Ah-ah, I'm about to be flogged,* she thought. *What did I do?* She wondered if it was because she was twelve, the youngest in the class.

"Come," Miss Tate said.

"But—"

"Now," she said more firmly.

Sunny slowly walked to the front of the class, aware of her classmates' eyes boring into her back. She let out a shallow breath as she stood before her teacher.

"Hold out your hand." Miss Tate, already bloated with anger, had the switch ready. Sunny shut her eyes and braced

herself for the stinging pain. But no sting came. Instead, she felt the switch placed in her hand. She quickly opened her eyes.

Miss Tate looked to the class. "Each of you will come up and Sunny will give you three strikes on the left hand." She smiled wryly. "Maybe *she* can beat some of her sense into you."

Sunny's stomach sank as her classmates lined up before her. They all looked so angry. And not the red kind of anger that burns out quickly—but the black kind, the kind that is carried outside of class.

Orlu was the first in line. He was the closest to her age, just a year older. They'd never spoken much, but he seemed nice. He liked to build things. She'd seen him during lunch hour—his friends would be blabbing away and he'd be to the side making towers and what looked like little people out of Coca-Cola and Fanta caps and candy wrappers. She certainly didn't want to bruise up his hands.

He stood there just looking at her, waiting. He didn't seem angry, like everyone else, but he looked nervous. If he had spoken, Miss Tate would have boxed his head.

By this time, Sunny was crying. She felt a flare of hatred for Miss Tate, who up to this day had been her favorite teacher. *The woman's lost her mind*, she thought miserably. *Maybe I should smack her instead.*

Sunny stood there carrying on the way she knew her mother hated her to do. It was pathetic and childish. She knew her pale face was flushed red. She sobbed hard and then threw the switch on the floor. This made Miss Tate even angrier. She pushed Sunny aside. "Sit," Miss Tate shouted.

Sunny covered her face with her hands, but she cringed with each *slap* of the switch. And then the person would hiss or squeak or gasp or whatever suited his or her pain. She could hear the desks around her filling up as people were punished and then sat down. Someone behind her kicked her chair and hissed, "You stupid pale-faced *akata* witch! Your hours are numbered!"

Sunny shut her eyes tight and gulped down a sob. She hated the word "*akata*." It meant "bush animal" and was used to refer to black Americans or foreign-born blacks. A very, very rude word. Plus, Sunny knew the girl's voice.

After school, Sunny tried to escape the school yard. She made it just far enough for no teachers to see her get jumped. Jibaku, the girl who'd threatened her, led the mob. Right there on the far side of the school yard, three girls and four of the boys beat Sunny as they shouted taunts and insults. She wanted to fight back, but she knew better. There were too many of them.

It was a school-yard thrashing and not one of her ex-friends came to her rescue. They just stood and watched.

Even if they wanted to, they were no match for Jibaku, the richest, tallest, toughest, and most popular girl in school.

It was Orlu who finally put an end to it. He'd been yelling for everyone to stop since it started. "Why don't we let her speak?" Orlu shouted.

Maybe it was because they needed to catch their breath or maybe they truly were curious, but they all paused. Sunny was dirty and bruised, but what could she say? Jibaku spoke up instead—Jibaku, who had slapped Sunny in the face hard enough to make her lip bleed. Sunny glared at her.

"Why did you let Miss Tate beat us?" The sun bore down on Sunny, making her sensitive skin itch. All she wanted to do was get in the shade. "Why didn't *you* just do it?" Jibaku shouted. "You're a scrawny thing, it wouldn't have hurt much! You could have pretended to be weak as you hit us. Or did you *like* seeing that white woman beat us like that? Does it make you happy because you're white, too?"

"I'm not white!" Sunny shouted back, finding her voice again.

"My eyes tell me different," a plump boy named Periwinkle said. He was called this because he liked the soup with the periwinkle snails in it.

Sunny wiped blood from her lip and said, "Shut up, you snail-sucker! I'm *albino!*"

"'Albino' is a synonym for 'ugly,'" he retorted.

"Oooh, big words now. Maybe you should have used some of those on your stupid essay! Ignorant idiot!" She added bass to her voice and enunciated the word "idiot" with her most Nigerian accent, making it sound like *eeedee-ut*. Some of the others laughed. Sunny could always make them laugh, even when she herself felt like crying. "You think I can go around hitting my own classmates?" she said, snatching up her black umbrella. She held it over herself and instantly felt better. "You wouldn't have done it, either." She humphed. "Or maybe *you* would have, Jibaku."

She watched them grumble to each other. Some of them even turned and started walking home. "What is it you want from me? What would I apologize for?"

There was a long pause. Jibaku sucked her teeth loudly, looking Sunny up and down with disgust. "Stupid *oyibo akata* witch," she spat. She motioned to the others. "Let's go."

Sunny and Orlu watched them leave. Their eyes met, and Sunny quickly looked away. When she turned back, Orlu was still watching her. She forced herself to keep her eyes on him, to really see him. He had slanted, almost catlike eyes and high cheekbones. He was kind of pretty, even if he didn't talk much. She bent down to pick up her books.

"Are . . . are you all right?" he asked, as he helped.

She frowned. "I'm fine. No thanks to you."

"Your face looks all red and, well, punched."

"Who cares?" she said, putting the last book in her satchel.

"Your mother will," he said.

"Then why didn't you *stop* them?" she screamed. She slung the satchel over her shoulder and walked away. Orlu followed.

"I tried."

"Whatever."

"I did. You didn't see Periwinkle and Calculus do this?" He turned his head so she could see his swollen cheek.

"Oh," she said, instantly ashamed. "I'm sorry."

By the time they got to the intersection where their paths home diverged, she felt a little better. It seemed she and Orlu had a lot in common. He agreed Miss Tate's actions were way out of line, he liked reading books for fun, and he, too, noticed the weaver birds that lived in the tree beside the school.

"I live just a little that way," Orlu said.

"I know," she said, looking up the paved road. Like hers, his house was white with a modest fence surrounding it. Her eye settled on the mud hut with the water-damaged walls next door.

"Do you know the lady who lives there?" she asked.

There was smoke coming from the back. *Probably from a cooking fire*, she thought. She had only once seen the woman who lived in it, some years ago. She'd had smooth brown skin

tinted slightly red from the palm oil she rubbed into it. Most of the people in the area believed she was some sort of witch and left her alone.

"That's Nimm's house. She lives there with her daughter," Orlu said.

"Daughter?" she asked. She'd assumed the woman lived alone.

"Hey!" someone yelled from behind them. "Orlu! Who's the *onyocha*?"

"Good Lord," Orlu groaned. "Will the drama never end?"

Sunny whirled around. "Don't call me that," she said before she got a good look at the girl. "I *hate* when people call me that. Do I look like a European? You don't even know me!"

"Seen you around," the girl said. She was fine-boned, dark brown, and elfin, but her voice was loud and strong and arrogant. So was her smile. She wore an old-looking red, yellow, and blue dress and no shoes. She swaggered over to Sunny and they stood there, sizing each other up.

"Who are you?" Sunny finally asked.

"Who are *you*?" the girl retorted. "Did someone run you over?"

Orlu sighed loudly, rolling his eyes. "Sunny, *this* is Chichi, my neighbor. Chichi, this is Sunny, my classmate."

"How come I've never seen you at school?" Sunny asked, still irritated. She dusted off her hopelessly dirty clothes.

"You look around our age, even if you are kind of . . . small."

"I've never needed your stupid school." Before Chichi could say any more, she and Orlu exchanged a look. "And I'll never tell you my age. I could be older or younger than you. You'll never know, even if you *are* half ghost and half human." She smirked, looking Sunny up and down, obviously itching for a fight. "Even when you speak Igbo you don't quite *sound* Igbo."

"That's my accent. I'm American," Sunny said through gritted teeth. "I spent most of my life there. I can't *help* the way I speak."

Chichi put her hand up in mock defense. "Oh, did I hit a sore spot? I am *so* sorry." She laughed.

Sunny could have slapped her. At this point, another fight wouldn't have made much difference.

"Well," Orlu quickly said, stepping between them, "this isn't going very well."

"You live there?" Sunny asked, leaning around Orlu and motioning toward the hut.

"Yeah," Chichi asked. "My mother and I don't need much."

"Why?" she asked.

Orlu stepped back, looking perplexed.

"I'll never tell you," Chichi said with a sly grin. "There's more to the world than big houses." She chuckled, turning

away. "Have a nice evening, Orlu. See you around, Sunny."

"Yeah, if I don't step on you first," Sunny said.

"Yeah, and if I can even *see* you coming, ghost girl," Chi-chi shot back over her shoulder.

Orlu only shook his head.

COMING SOON...

Look for the third installment of Sunny's adventures, in which Sunny and her friends have some unfinished business with a giant god-like spider, and that spider so magnificent it would strike fear into Anansi.